the
house
book

A comprehensive guide to
making a home

the
house
book

p

This is a Parragon Publishing Book
This edition published in 2003

Parragon Publishing
Queen Street House
4 Queen Street
Bath BA1 1HE
United Kingdom

Copyright © Parragon 2002

Created and produced by The Bridgewater
Book Company Ltd, Lewes, East Sussex

Creative Art Director Stephen Knowlden
Art Directors Colin Fielder, Sarah Howerd,
Michael Whitehead, Johnny Pau
Editorial Director Fiona Biggs
Editorial Mark Truman, Sarah Yelling, Sarah Doughty
Photographers Steve Gorton, Alistair Hughes,
Steve Tanner

ISBN: 0-75259-054-5

Printed in China

Contents

COLOR IN YOUR HOME

DESIGNING NEW ROOM

MAKING SOFT FURNISHINGS

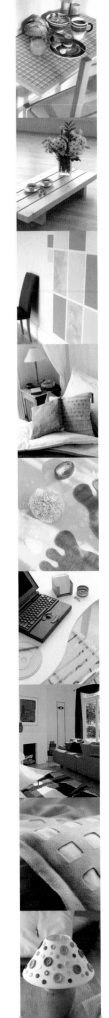

The house book

The House Book has four sections. Beginning with Home Decorating, the first section will show you how to transform your home. Color In Your Home then guides you through the world of color schemes available for you and your home. Designing New Rooms gives you inspiration for transforming every room in your house. Finally, the section on Making Soft Furnishings will help you to add comfort and style to your home.

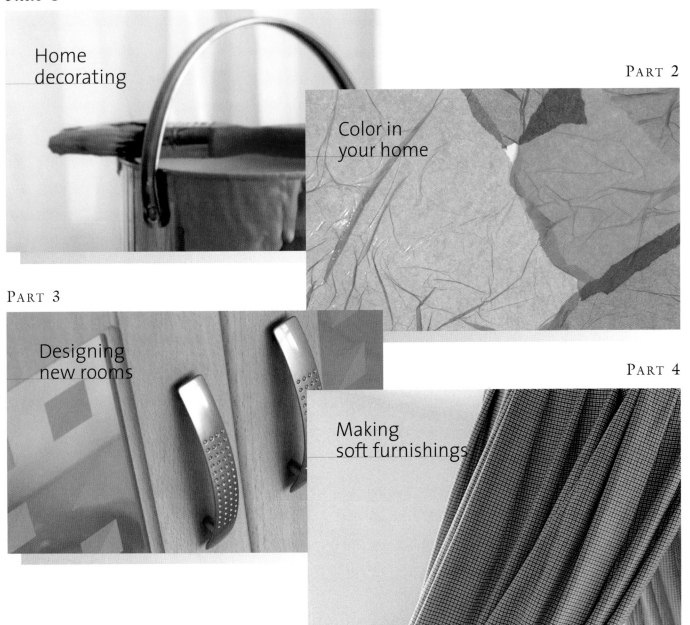

PART 1

Home decorating

PART 2

Color in your home

PART 3

Designing new rooms

PART 4

Making soft furnishings

The house book

Introduction

Whether you are an expert looking for bright ideas to give your home a fresh new look, or a complete beginner requiring basic information on decorating, The House Book is the book for you.

The walls in this sitting room have been painted porcelain blue with a white glaze swirled in.

Part 1: Home Decorating

This section will enable you to make a professional job of all your decorating tasks. There are tips to help you to plan the job properly and work out your budget. You'll need to decide on color schemes and the kind of paint to use—guidance is given to help you choose from the countless varieties now available on the market.

Painting techniques are described in detail and you'll find suggestions for interesting effects to give your rooms a special look. These methods include sponging, colorwashing, and textured paint. However, if you decide to hang wallpaper instead, you'll find it's not as difficult as you might think, as long as you plan the work carefully and accurately.

Perhaps you hope to make a radical change to the look and feel of your home by removing plaster to reveal the original brickwork, laying handmade tiles, or creating your own wood paneling. Everything you need to know is covered here, from the basics about wood and bricks to decorative effects using mosaics and mirrors.

Flooring is a vital part of your home makeover. Here you will find practical advice on choosing materials wisely, depending on your budget and the uses of each room. A section is dedicated to woodwork, which includes basic painting skills along with special effects such as crackleglazing, and instructions for french polishing.

Once the decorating is completed, look up the clever storage tips and ideas for livening up your accessories and making the best use of the space available.

Part 2: Color In Your Home

This section is full of inspiring ideas to make your home more attractive. The information on color theory explains why some colors blend comfortably together while other colors clash, creating visual friction. With this in mind, you'll be able to use your instinctive color preferences in a sensible combination and have the satisfaction of creating a home using your preferred color schemes.

The chapter on the influence of color demonstrates how the colors you choose can have a significant effect on your state of mind. Aqua and turquoise can be calming, while pale pink has a soothing effect.

If you're brave you may go for a strong color, such as orange, a great favorite with professional interior designers. Yellow is an inviting, sociable color that suits a contemporary style of decor.

Paint effects are making a comeback, so let your imagination run wild. There are ideas on how to create simple, fun effects, such as stenciling, and produce clever 3-D effects with color. Applied textures are also fashionable—why not consider lining your walls with a natural material such as cane or bamboo?

Perhaps you want to renew your home in a particular style. Think about which theme fits best with your lifestyle: a country feel, with soft, muted colors; or maybe the rich, earthy colors of a Tuscan farmhouse. Maybe you are a more of an urban minimalist, preferring a limited color palette and a clutter-free environment. Or go farther afield for inspiration, looking to Morocco or India for rich, intense colors to liven up your rooms.

Use of a bold color on nearly every surface may not appeal to everyone as a decorating option. If the color is applied with confidence, however, the results can be stunning, and certainly make a strong statement, often reflecting the personality of a room's occupant.

Part 3: Designing New Rooms

This section takes you through the process of revamping your home, room by room. Decide whether to go for the traditional or the contemporary look, and take it from there. Don't despair if you can't afford to rip out that old kitchen and start from scratch. There are many ways of ringing the changes in an economical way. Try fixing new doors on your kitchen units or even simply replacing the handles.

By simply removing cupboard doors from a plain base unit and using willow baskets on the shelves as pull-out drawers, you can give a room a completely new country look.

The sitting room is the public face of your home, so show off your personal style. You could go for a traditional look, with heavy bookshelves and comfortable sofas, or an uncluttered minimalist look. If you have a sitting-dining room, try defining the dining area with low walls or screens to reinforce the fact that the room serves two different purposes. Or if you're lucky enough to have a separate dining room, look up the imaginative ideas for flooring, lighting, and furniture that will make the most of it.

The bedroom, the least public room of the home, is the perfect place to express yourself but don't spoil the effect with clutter; keep it at bay with some sensible storage methods. When you decorate the kids' bedrooms, take into account their basic needs for study, play, and relaxation in a safe, comfortable environment and make sure you involve them in your decision-making!

The chapter on bathrooms helps you to create a practical design in a traditional or contemporary style, with ideas for shower rooms and en suite showers. Then consideration is given to creating a perfect home-office environment, neatly designed to take up minimum space yet with comfort in mind.

Part 4: Making Soft Furnishings

This section is full of ideas for using fabric to enhance your living space. There are projects for both the novice and the experienced needleworker. Fabrics and trimmings are described, along with explanations of equipment and haberdashery.

Ready-made curtains are expensive, so why not make your own? Go for a modern style, such as tab-top curtains, or the traditional swag and tails. If you're a beginner, start with a simple unlined pair. Instructions for making all the accessories and for creating your own blinds are included too. Think twice before buying new furniture—it's easy to revitalize your chairs and sofas by changing the fabric. Ensure you have enough seating for all your visitors by making your own cushions or bean-bag chairs or give a deckchair a new lease of life for outdoors. At mealtimes, impress your guests with hand-made table linen and napkins, a simple but very effective soft-furnishing project that anyone with even the most basic needleworking skills can attempt with confidence.

A colorful border can make an ordinary sheet into a special item of bed linen.

Storage is always a problem especially in small flats or town houses. Consider making beautiful fabric bags, lined baskets, and clothes covers to remove clutter from your bedroom. Improve your bedroom further by making your own bedding. It's not as hard you might think. Not only is it economical, you can use exactly the color and fabric that you desire and personalize it by hand-embroidering your own decorative motifs. Go to town with piles of cushions in luxurious fabrics, bordered sheets, or for a special change, make a dramatic bedspread that becomes a centerpiece of your bedroom.

Finally, there are ideas for decorative touches—the braid, trimmings, bows or rosettes that make your soft-furnishing project really special.

Home decorating

Introduction

As the world enters a new millennium, people's lives have never been more stressful, their workstyles more fractious and time specific, or their complex lifestyles more fragmented.

Carefully chosen calm and soothing colors will ensure that your bedroom is a relaxing place in which to spend your time.

Consequently, relaxation at the end of a difficult day has become more of a basic requirement than ever before, and to be able to wind down in comfort and style in esthetically pleasing decorative surroundings is not so much a bonus as a necessity.

Relaxing in familiar surroundings usually involves personal input to the area in question; favorite colors and textures, controllable lighting systems, displays and pictures and mementoes all act as a "welcome home." Whether the "home" is owned, mortgaged or rented or whether it is a house, cottage, or apartment, the decorative personal touch is essential if home is to be where the heart is.

Employing third parties to do decorating work is expensive, and it is indeed time-consuming finding the right people for the job. The work that is done for you still requires a lot of personal input and it carries no real guarantees of workmanship. So instead, why not channel the energies of personal attention into the task itself?

There are important points to bear in mind, however. You will always need to be aware of the possible complexity of the task, whether it is merely deciding on color schemes for walls or whether it involves a complete makeover, in line with those shown so regularly on television.

In order to retain viewer interest, home improvement programs edit down technical job sequences from hours to seconds. This could lead the unwary or naive into the erroneous belief that a decorating job can be done in the time it takes on television.

The most important function of this book is to bring a sense of reality to the initial discussions and scheduling, allowing decorating decisions to reflect a proper timescale, and to take into account the available skill levels and budget for the project.

Throughout these pages a proper professional approach is encouraged, from the drawing up of a detailed plan to the application of top quality materials and power tools in a safe and

responsible manner. The tools required are discussed at the start of each chapter, and step-by-step sequences show each job in progression, and can be easily followed and understood.

Whether these pages help with a simple painted frame or a complex zonal plan, hopefully, after it is completed, you will experience much greater satisfaction in having done a quality job in the home, rather than paying to have one done.

Choosing and fitting your own wallpaper is not a complicated job, as long as you follow some simple guidelines and do the preparation work correctly.

Planning

In today's highly competitive consumer-orientated marketplace, modern businesses must have carefully considered strategies and working schedules to ensure their survival and growth. You are probably aware of this requirement in your own daily working life and the same is no less true of planning home improvements. Most households already have some kind of general strategy for running the home smoothly, varying from a basic task "duty roster" on a kitchen notice board to a complex time-specific system that includes family members and budgets, all logged onto a home computer. Forward planning is an essential part of running a home and is equally vital when it comes to making improvements, whether major or minor.

Practical considerations

No matter how small the job appears to be, forward planning is needed when you are considering refurbishing or decorating your home. Inspiration gained from a magazine or television "makeover" needs to be turned into a plan of action if home improvement is to be successful. Here are some tips on what to think about before you start.

Clear brief

Imagine you have an independent builder taking on the job. What he would expect from his client is a clear brief, detailing all that is required from the finished work, which materials are going to be used, and which color scheme is required. Just because you intend to tackle the project yourself, don't skimp on the details when devising the plan of action. And beware: "making it up as you go along" is liable to end in unsatisfactory results.

Questions to consider

Whether you live alone or with others, it is worth considering the following questions:

• Is the planned change suitable for the particular room that you have in mind?

• Is it practical?
• Will everyone in the house benefit?
• How long will it take?
• How much upheaval will there be?
• Can you live with it in the long term?

Budget

If the household members like the ideas and are happy to live with the works in progress, then you need to consider:

• How much will it cost?
• Is it affordable?

The job budget involves the adding of prices from builders' and decorators' lists, the cost of any new tools required and delivery charges for materials and/or garbage clearance.

When planning a refurbishment, seek inspiration from a variety of sources, including magazines. Measure the room, draw a plan, and collect color cards, paint testers and material swatches.

Skills and time

Presuming a reasonable skill level with a basic tool kit (the skills and tools required for each job are discussed throughout this book), try to devise a logical order of work, bearing in mind the following factors:

- The amount of work needed each day will depend on the size of the project, but don't take on too much in one go. Popular decorating programs on television may give the impression that a room can be completely transformed in a mere 25 minutes, including a commercial break, but this is far from being the truth.
- Be realistic in assessing how long you think each part of the project will take.
- Cutting corners on any part of a job may lead to difficulties later on and may ultimately add to the time the job takes.

Implications of refurbishment

The eventual resale value of your property is not the only thing to bear in mind when assessing standards of workmanship. Removing period features from a room for "modernization" generally does not meet with approval today, so consider all the implications before you start. Sympathetic decorating and subtle changes can sometimes be more beneficial than wholesale refurbishment.

In years to come, you may tire of the changes you have made and seek to reinstate an earlier look, but if you have disposed of vital features, you may encounter considerable difficulty in replacing them. Give yourself time to come to terms with your plans; put them away for a while, then come back to them and reconsider what you have thought about. Don't be afraid to change your mind or tone down some of the more ambitious aspects of the project.

BEFORE

Ugly view

Somber wall color

Dark cabinets

Obtrusive dresser

Stark display cabinet

Same-color edging

Mat floor

Disjointed appearance

AFTER

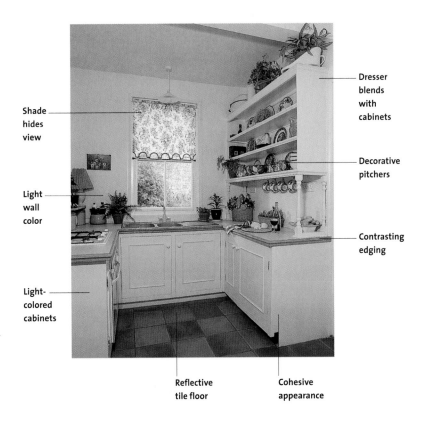

Shade hides view

Light wall color

Light-colored cabinets

Dresser blends with cabinets

Decorative pitchers

Contrasting edging

Reflective tile floor

Cohesive appearance

Assessing room functions

If your work is not confined to one room and a complete makeover of the house is needed, then your plans must be more elaborate. Maybe you've just moved in or your family circumstances have changed dramatically. Whatever the reason, the first step is to assess the basic areas—living, working, and sleeping—plus the role of the kitchen and bathroom.

Living areas

The living room must cater for all members of the household, who will use it for different reasons. Its main function is to provide a seating arrangement for family and friends where privacy is not possible. Several activities may take place in this room simultaneously—for example, reading, listening to music or watching television, family discussions, and hobby pursuits, such as playing computer games. Decide whether an open-plan style is in keeping with this lack of privacy, or whether a breakdown of the living room into two separate functional areas is possible. In a period house, the downstairs living areas would usually have been arranged as a day room, near the cooking area for convenience, with easily cleaned flooring, and a separate evening area, with more luxurious fixtures and fittings, suitable for entertaining.

Living areas often benefit from being divided into separate areas for different functions.

Working areas

What constitutes work, and what doesn't, may present an ever-changing issue in the contemporary household. Computers are used for schoolwork, business, and family leisure activities. Digital interactive cables have transformed the television into a potential shopping mall and banking service. As certain areas become multi-functional, a study or home office may be a welcome retreat. This is a real necessity if you work from home full time; otherwise, professional commitments can easily spill over into everyday family life.

Sleeping areas

The younger members of a household often consider their bedroom space to be out of bounds to anyone not specifically invited. These areas are already catering for several activities, and must be furnished accordingly. The bedroom

used solely for its intended purpose is usually the parents' room, traditionally the largest. Consider the benefits of young children sharing this room instead. It will double as a nursery or play area, possibly freeing up a room elsewhere in the house. A good night's rest, however, relies on peace and quiet, so the location of bedrooms away from sources of noise is very important.

The kitchen

Generally the working hub of the home, the kitchen is frequently in use for food preparation, cooking, dish washing and general cleaning. Home to many major labor-saving devices, such as the washing machine, dishwasher, and food processor, it may need to accommodate several family members at the same time and to double as a breakfast or snack room. Easy access to other eating areas, such as a dining room, may be needed, so that cooked food reaches the table quickly. A large serving hatch between the kitchen and dining room may be the ideal solution, providing a practical and visual link.

The bathroom

In a large household, a second bathroom is a modern necessity, and builders' merchants stock all types of space-saving units with this in mind. If your main bathroom is fitted out traditionally (i.e. with a bath tub), a shower room would be a good idea, along with a second lavatory, possibly incorporated in a downstairs cloakroom. If space precludes all these options, another possibility would be to divide the lavatory off from the rest of the bathroom.

Interconnecting spaces

In an ideal world the home you inhabit would grow and change with you and your family. This is possible if the house layout is flexible. Corridors that have a decorative scheme encouraging adjacent areas to interact, rather than divorcing one from another, are a particularly good start.

The decor in any area becomes more interesting if flexible design lets the occupants see through to another, different space.

Linking rooms does not necessarily have to mean sacrificing privacy, either. Decorative screens can be used to temporarily isolate parts of the open space as and when you wish.

If you have the room to create open spaces in this way, however, you should try to avoid overcompensating by adding too much furniture—an understandable temptation.

Minimalism will not be an option for a family unit, of course, but too much clutter will rapidly reduce or destroy any feeling of spaciousness that you endeavour to create.

Opposite ideas often work well together. For example, a small apartment will appear larger if it is visually sparse. By contrast, a large loft apartment benefits from an aggressive color scheme that is used to reduce the overwhelming impact of the space.

LEFT: This bedroom in the loft area of the house lends itself to several purposes at once: a sleeping area, with storage in the foreground, a sewing area, and, at the back of the room, a shower area.

The space on this floor has been utilized to make a home office on a separate balcony, which divides up the living and working areas.

Accommodating the new

Period housing has many features that can live happily alongside modern innovations in this technological age, and it is worth assessing how modernization will work in your home without removing original features. In addition, you will need to consider how the requirements of the household members will be met by your refurbishment choices.

RIGHT: **A small space can be successfully multifunctional, as a bedroom, washing area, and work unit, if it is well planned and the various components form an integral whole that is pleasing to the eye.**

A hall area ideally needs to be reasonably spacious, to have a floor surface that is easily cleaned, and plenty of room for hanging up coats and storing umbrellas, boots, and shoes.

Original features and new technology

Technology can work in any surroundings, and stylish period features don't have to make way for contemporary interiors to accommodate innovations. Original fireplaces, baseboards, cornices, and decorative moldings can all be updated by adventurous color scheming, irrespective of their Georgian, Regency, Victorian, or Edwardian origin.

Water and electricity supplies in older properties must meet modern standards and regulations, but they can be largely hidden away, and the growing reproduction marketplace supplies period-style radiators and switch surrounds. Brand-name paint manufacturers offer a range of period colors, and architectural salvage

yards are full of interesting period pieces suitable for the bargain-hunter.

Opposites can work very well together. A digital sound system can look and sound superb in an elaborate Victorian Sunday room. If you are considering a large-scale refurbishment program, keep your mind and your options open to the possibilities for accommodating new technology in a traditional setting.

Unique family needs

Along with considering room function, period styles and linked color schemes, you also need to assess requirements that are unique to your family. Every person who lives in the property should be allowed an input because any form of alteration or decoration is a family affair.

Needs alter as the years pass. Children who once shared a room will want to move apart,

eventually to leave altogether. Elderly relatives may join the household. Flexibility is crucial. It may be difficult and time-consuming to adapt a house to fit the occupants, but equally it may be difficult to change the habits of a lifetime to suit the layout of a property.

Here are some points to consider:

- Is there adequate provision in the entrance hall or lobby for wet outdoor clothes, boots, and/or sporting equipment?
- Can this area be cleaned easily?
- Is there space in this area to put down shopping items temporarily, while a cab is being paid off or a vehicle is being unloaded?
- Can late-night arrivals get to their rooms directly without disturbing the rest of the household?
- Do all the sleeping areas have easy access to both the bathroom and the lavatory?
- Can a meal cooked in the kitchen be served in the dining area easily and quickly?
- Does the kitchen have a back door, to let deliveries arrive and garbage be removed easily? Is this access protected from the weather?
- Can you view the rest of the property, and any garden where the children may be playing, from the kitchen?
- Is there enough storage space and hobby space?
- Can a bedroom double up as a study area or home office during the daytime?
- If a workshop with power tools, such as a garage area, is open to everyone in the house, is it safe?
- Are all potentially dangerous tools locked away?
- If you have a pet, is it catered for in all weathers?

Nobody knows more about your family circumstances than you do, so adapt the questionnaire to your own situation. Put your requirements in writing. They will provide invaluable guidance when you come to make final decisions.

ORIGINAL FITTINGS

Period fireplaces have an innate charm, and an old fireplace surround can often be adapted to take modern fittings and painted in either traditional or modern colors. In the summer, grates can be filled with pine cones and massed with greenery, so that they do not look redundant at this time of year.

Old radiators still have a certain appeal, and can often be bought at architectural salvage yards and brought back to life. Alternatively, you can purchase a reproduction radiator and enjoy all the benefits of modern technology with the esthetic values of another era.

Major or minor changes?

If your decision involves changing the function of a particular area, consider how major those changes will be. A bedroom to be used as a study, for example, will require largely cosmetic changes, such as new shelving, a worktop for a computer, and decor to be approved by the new inhabitant. However, enlarging a kitchen by, say, connecting it directly to a utility room may involve leveling one of the floors for retiling, removing doors, and matching paneled interiors. Any major kitchen or bathroom work will involve water facilities and the services of a plumber, so consult a local tradesperson before final redesign decisions are made. Electrics are another consideration. Are there enough outlets, and are they in the right place? Is the lighting good enough, especially if the house is old? Unless you have experience in this field, seek the advice of a professional electrician. Major disruptive work needs to be completed before any cosmetic details can be started.

Making plans

Whether your plan is complex or simple at this stage, whether you intend to divide up a room space or merely paint a floor, you will find a detailed plan on paper makes life a lot easier. It doesn't have to be a work of art, but it does need to be accurate. If you have a computer with suitable software, you can draw up your plans and alter them using a grid system. You might even be able to put together a three-dimensional drawing.

necessary, and note down the sizes of the chimney breast, all built-in closets, window areas, and doors, marking on your plan which way the doors open.

You will find it easier to write down initial measurements on a rough sketch. You can also add items that cannot be easily changed, such as radiator positions and pipe runs, electric outlets and light fittings to this first drawing, even if they are not relevant to the final scheme.

ABOVE: **The essential tools required for measuring a room are graph paper, some colored pencils, a notepad and pen, a clear plastic rule, a pair of scissors, a retractable steel measure, and a calculator.**

RIGHT: **Mark on the plan the room's basic dimensions, noting in particular any unusual shapes that distort the room's appearance, and all the doors, windows, and other features such as closets.**

Measuring up a room

To measure up a room, use a retractable steel measure of at least 16½ft./5m total length, with a lever to lock the tape at any given distance. Adding distances together from shorter tape measures, or using cloth tapes that are prone to sag, leads to inaccurate figures.

Measure the basic dimensions of the room first—the wall height and length. Measure the room from corner to corner to confirm that it is square, or at least square enough for your purposes. Add on any bay window and alcove areas, where

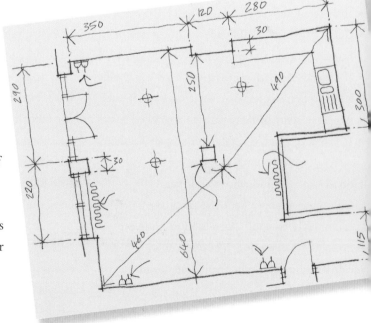

Transferring to graph paper

Using a pencil transfer your plan from rough sketch to graph paper and scale the area to size using the squares. Include only the items that you consider relevant from your comprehensive measurements. Simplify the plan as much as possible to reduce the risk of errors. If your room is furnished, or if you know what items of furniture will eventually be included, then represent these objects with small pieces of card cut to scale. You will be able to rearrange items of furniture at will, to establish their best position and to make maximum use of the available space.

Draw in shelving systems or new cabinets to go in alcoves, change access doors, and so on, until you are happy that the plan is complete.

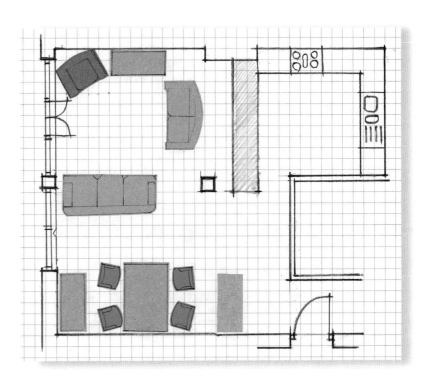

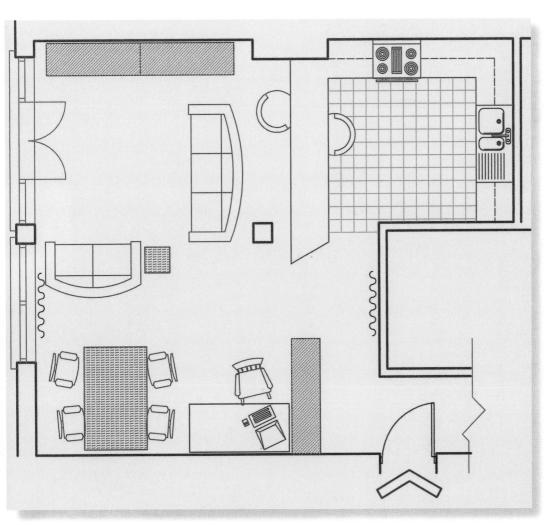

ABOVE: **A plan comes to life when the items of furniture are colored in and you can see how they relate to one another and how they fill the space. Try moving them around to ascertain the ideal configuration.**

LEFT: **Because of the positions of doors, windows, and chimney breasts, there are only so many combinations that will work in any given space. With trial and error you should finally arrive at the perfect solution.**

Color

Choosing the correct color scheme for your home is vital
to your sense of comfort and well-being. Individual tastes in color are,
of course, highly subjective, but there are also several important
objective factors involved in the selection of color schemes. In this
chapter we look at the color wheel, which will help in choosing
contrasting and complementary color schemes, and also discuss the
importance of natural light, the psychological effects of particular
colors, and the visual tricks that can be achieved through careful color
scheming. Successful use of color has the potential to transform
rooms in an exciting and gratifying way, and in many instances
involves no great expense to you, so it is well worth
taking your time considering all the choices available.

Designer's notes

When making notes, the designer always considers the features that are inherent in the original design of the room, and their current status and condition. Whether these features are emphasized or visually disguised by the new color scheme will be a decision for the room's occupants, influenced by some basic color rules.

FAR RIGHT: **Stripping paint away to reveal whatever lies beneath is just one part of the decorating process and can have intriguing results.**

BELOW: **Using a similar light color on the walls and furnishings opens up the space and creates a feeling of airiness. This scheme is cheerful and uplifting, and enhances whatever light there is in the room.**

Designer's questions

Before you make plans for redecorating, imagine that you are an independent interior designer looking at your home for the first time and ask yourself the following questions:

- What is the aspect of the room (i.e. in which direction does it face)?
- How much natural light comes into the room?
- Is there an original feature in the room. If so, is it to be retained?
- Will the room need joinery additions, such as built-in storage and shelving in an alcove, which will alter its basic shape?
- Can paint schemes be applied to existing features such as doors and windows?

- Will these items have to be replaced (for example, to restore a period feel)?
- Can the desired effect be achieved simply by cosmetic changes or is major work necessary?

Color for emphasis

You may feel that an old, ugly tiled fireplace is at odds with your twenty-first century ideal and want to remove it. On the other hand, you may have an older property suffering from 1970s "modernization" that needs the fireplace reinstated. Either possibility will involve a great deal of mess, in the form of soot, so obviously works of this nature have to be tackled first.

If you are in a position to undertake purely cosmetic changes, then you need to

LEFT: **A bedroom decorated in the three primary colors of red, yellow, and blue is bold and invigorating, although some might find it too vibrant to sleep in.**

Bear in mind, however, that stripping a wall may involve you in a considerable amount of making good before it is suitable to be left exposed. The original mortar may be in poor condition and need repointing. Don't assume that every wall will be suitable for such treatment; in some cases, the underlying brickwork will have been laid carelessly and will never be attractive to look at. Be prepared to carry out some exploratory stripping of the plasterwork to ascertain what lies behind.

Other surfaces can also be stripped, such as floors. Here, the beauty of the grain of wooden boards can be brought out by careful sanding and varnishing. But again, repairs may be necessary. Always be prepared to amend your plans if it turns out that you can't achieve exactly what you desire.

Paint can be used to good effect to enhance original features, such as this attractive wooden door.

examine the features in the room even more closely. Working with what you have is always a good principle in home redecoration. This lets you emphasize the best features of a room using color. An old built-in closet, for instance, when it has been relieved of its multiple layers of paint, may reveal fine, sympathetically crafted woodwork. Using subtle dyes to enhance the grain can make a real feature of the joiner's art. A pale color on the surrounding walls will emphasize the beauty of the wood and will not compete with it.

Decorating is usually seen as an additive process, which involves bringing paint, paper or some type of paneling/joinery to a room or replacing the existing scheme. However it can also be a subtractive process—for example, stripping paint off joinery. So, when you consider your intended wall scheme, you might think about removing wallpaper entirely in order to paint a wall a flat color, or even hacking off the plaster to reveal the traditional brickwork that lies underneath.

The color wheel

The color wheel is a vital tool in the visualizing and selection of color schemes. It shows how all the colors of the spectrum act in relation to each other, and helps you to decide on contrasting or complementary schemes. The more advanced wheel shows how tints and shades of complementary colors can work together.

How color works

When a white light source, typically the sun, consisting of different wavelengths passes through a prism, it splits to reveal the visible spectrum. It is often portrayed as a rainbow effect. The visible part of the spectrum runs from violet through to red. Ultraviolet and infrared, either side of the visible spectrum, cannot be seen by the naked eye (e.g. we cannot see radio waves or Xrays). When the walls of a room receive this white light source, they absorb all the wavelengths except those of their own color, which they reflect. The human eye responds to

RIGHT: **The walls of this room receive a source of white light and absorb all the wavelengths except that of blue, which is reflected.**

these reflected wavelengths and identifies them as color. So, a wall absorbing all wavelengths except blue, which it reflects into the room, appears to the human eye as a blue wall.

The wheel

The color wheel is a circle based on the color spectrum. The primary colors, red, yellow, and blue, are opposite the secondary colors, green, violet, and orange. Selecting colors that are opposite each other on the wheel, such as red and green, results in optimum color contrast because you are using complementary colors.

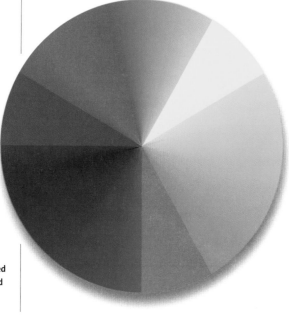

Complementary colors in the color spectrum include red and green, blue and orange, and yellow and violet.

Selecting colors next to each other on the wheel—say, blue and green—results in a more harmonious scheme because they blend into each other in the spectrum. Blending adjacent colors together creates a third set. The wheel is divided up into twelve segments that can be used to plan all your color combinations.

Complementary colors

Complementary colors provide optimum contrast if used together in a room. They can make uneasy companions, however, if used in their purest form. All colors can be lightened by adding white to make tints or darkened by adding black to make shades of those colors. A more complex color wheel shows not only the colors at their most intense, but also the tints and shades in a gradation. This is useful because it shows how the color contrast is increased further if one of the colors is a tint or a shade.

A good example of this is provided by the use of red and green together in a room. Large expanses of these colors in their purest form

cause problems for the eye, because they have a similar tonal value, meaning that they reflect similar amounts of light. If you imagine these two colors side by side in black and white for a moment, then they would appear as almost identical shades of gray—neither color would advance or recede. Consequently the eye and the brain become confused. All colors from opposite sides of the wheel have a similar effect if they are of the same tonal value. However, using a tint or a shade of one of them can solve this problem. If you look at the second color wheel, you will notice how dark green will effectively partner red or a tint of red. Conversely, dark red combines well with a tint of green.

LEFT: **Being complementary colors, red and green work better in tint and shade combinations than in pure forms. But just looking at nature should be enough to convince us how well they can harmonize: think of pink wild flowers amid a meadow or of red berries against green foliage.**

Using a darker shade with a lighter tint of its complementary color avoids the visual problems caused when similar tonal values reflect similar amounts of light. FAR LEFT: **Red and green in pure form confuse the eye (neither advances or recedes).** LEFT: **The pale green recedes; the darker red appears dominant.**

Light, color, and mood

Light and color both play an important role in the way we feel—you have only to think of how much easier it is to get up on bright sunny days than it is when the skies are gray and overcast. So it is important to take into account both the direction that your room faces and the amount of light it receives when deciding what colors to use there.

Natural light

The amount of light reflected by a color, and thus the intensity of that color, depends on the light level that the color receives from the sun. As available light recedes at the end of the day, colors will appear less and less bright, until finally they have no color at all. With this in mind, consider carefully the amount of natural light that enters the room during the day, and what effect it will have. All the walls in the room will work in unison, reflecting the available light received. Lighter colored walls will reflect more light than dark ones, and will project it farther. For example, a bright blue reflected into an otherwise white room will engender a cold blue tint, whereas a bright red will project a warm rose-like tint. When selecting colors, bear in mind that walls reflecting the same color back and forth will intensify that color considerably—otherwise you may end up with a much more powerful scheme than you envisaged.

The availability of natural light depends on the season. An important point to consider when choosing a color scheme is the light level the room receives throughout the year. The more northerly the property location, the more extreme the difference between summer and winter, so a color scheme reflecting warm summer days also needs to work during long winters under artificial light.

Aspect

Consider the aspect of all the rooms in your intended scheme. Light enters through windows or glass doors, so which direction do they face?

Yellow walls will enliven a hallway that faces north and can be rather dark for much of the day.

Northern aspect

A room facing north is usually cold, benefiting from direct sunlight only during the height of summer. A warm color scheme will be essential in this room. Red, yellow, and orange will brighten the winter days and reflect what little light there is. Cold blues and greens should be avoided.

Southern aspect

A room facing south is warm and sunny, with lots of natural light. You will not need to add to the light levels, so use darker colors, particularly green. When these are combined with lighter tints of brown, blue, and green a summery feel can be created even during the winter months.

Eastern aspect

The powerful early light of sunrise becomes less potent as midday approaches, with no sunlight shining into the room in the afternoon and evening. A mix of color works well here. Both cool blues and warm oranges together will offset the midday change in lighting conditions.

Western aspect

This room will receive afternoon and evening sun, a sunset if conditions are favorable and dull light in the morning. Bright colors such as reds and yellows will overemphasize the warmth of

the afternoon; a more neutral scheme involving greens and grays will work better.

Color and mood

The psychological effect of certain colors in certain situations should also play a part in your color scheme selection. Bright colors such as reds excite and invigorate. Cool blues and greens are much more relaxing. Make allowances for this in certain rooms, particularly in a child's bedroom, where colors that stimulate the mind will not be conducive to sleep.

There is a place in the home for earth tones such as brown and beige, and for neutral grays, especially in a work area such as a home office. Here concentration is needed and bright colors will be distracting.

A basement or garage workshop containing potentially dangerous equipment is another area where attention should be on the task in hand and not on the decor.

Likes and dislikes of color effects are ultimately subjective. People who share the room space will have individual tastes and preferences, so canvas the thoughts of all the occupants before making a decision on a color scheme.

LEFT: **In east-facing rooms, such as a nursery that receives light in the early morning, a blue scheme looks good and is also restful on the eye, lulling the child to sleep.**

Work areas need to promote concentration, so neutral tones are often chosen in preference to vibrant primary colors.

Choosing color schemes

There are various examples of colors and finishes to help you select the right combinations in your color schemes, from color paint cards to sample pots of paint. There are also certain visual tricks that it is worth being aware of, as they can help you make the most of your available space and maximize its potential.

After choosing a color from the card, buy a sample pot. This lets you evaluate a sizeable color area on the wall you plan to decorate.

Color cards and sample pots

One of your first steps in selecting colors for your home decorating will be to consult a brand manufacturer's color chart or card—but this may not be the best way to choose paint. The colored rectangles on the card, while being as accurate as possible, may not be exact. They are very small and are positioned on a white background, which gives a slightly false impression of brightness. Remember, too, that the light reflected and absorbed by a tiny square or rectangle of color will differ immeasurably from that reflected or absorbed by an entire wall of that color. Yellows, for example, will seem much more powerful, because they reflect more light. Blues will appear darker because they absorb more light.

In response, paint-makers have introduced small sample pots of their colors. These provide an ideal way to experiment with your chosen scheme on the wall itself. Small pots of paint, swatches of curtain or furniture fabrics, carpet samples, wood off-cuts, and wallcovering samples can all be used together to give a first impression of what the finished room will look like.

Visual trick color schemes

Combining wall colors of different reflective qualities will allow you to play visual tricks with the size and proportions of the rooms and their interconnecting areas. Paint one wall red, for example, in an otherwise white room and that wall will appear to advance toward you, shortening the room. Conversely, painting one wall in a cool blue in an otherwise darker room will result in that wall receding visually and appearing to lengthen the room. If the ceiling is too high, paint it in a darker color. You can lower it farther still by painting the top part of the wall (above the picture rail, if there is one) the same color as the ceiling. The opposite effect is achieved by painting a ceiling white to heighten it.

Walls can be made to appear higher if you paint the baseboards the same color as the walls. When all the walls and the ceiling are the same light color, as in monochromatic schemes, the natural angles of the room are much less noticeable. This gives a feeling of increased space, almost as if the room were open plan.

If your rooms are linked by narrow corridors, as in many older properties, light colors will appear to increase the width. A darker color at the end of a corridor will make it seem shorter. The most dramatic change in small or narrow linking areas occurs when the floorcovering is dark and the ceiling is painted in an advancing color, which compresses the space vertically. To expand the horizontals, paint the walls white or use a receding color. Using the same technique in all interlinking areas has a unifying effect throughout the property and will make your color schemes appear more effective.

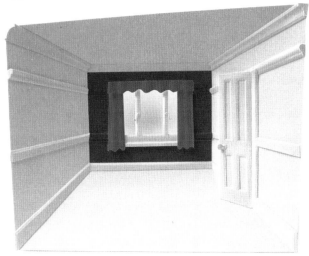

Red is the dominant color in both these locations.

LEFT: **The end wall advances, making a long corridor appear shorter.**

RIGHT: **The tint and shade of red act together, appearing to the eye to change the shape of the room.**

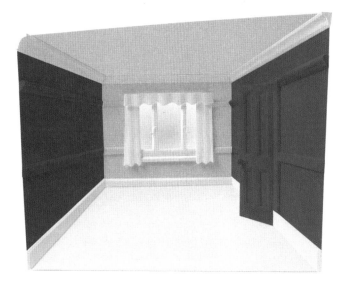

Receding colors are used visually to create a more spacious feeling.

LEFT: **Subtle pale combinations make a corridor appear larger without appearing to alter any of the dimensions.**

RIGHT: **However, a receding tint of blue on the far wall appears to lengthen an otherwise darker room.**

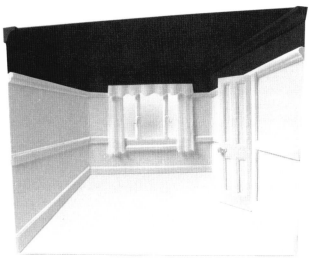

Compressing space vertically can be achieved by using color.

LEFT: **In a neutrally colored corridor, dominant red and orange appear to lift the floor and lower the ceiling, thereby expanding the horizontals.**

RIGHT: **A ceiling is lowered visually by use of an advancing color.**

Monochromatic schemes

If you are considering a monochromatic scheme, that is, one color only, then the color you choose must form a strong relationship with the fabrics and soft furnishings, the woodwork and the flooring that surrounds it. Neutral grays, soft beiges, off-whites, and creams are frequently chosen because they offset and therefore enhance patterned fabrics, and look good with natural wood finishes.

The term "monochromatic" is a misnomer, because patterns on floorcoverings and soft furnishings, wood varnishes, and general household pieces have their own color content.

An easy introduction to such a scheme is to visualize the room and its contents in black and white for a moment. A rough sketch of the room with everything white will let you position colored fabric and carpet swatches, and color in areas clad in wood, such as the fireplace. Adding a touch of harmonious color to the previously white scheme is then straightforward.

Schemes using contrasting colors, shades, and tints are just as easy to approach in this way.

A white room with one black wall, or a white-walled room with black baseboards, cornices, and picture rails, shows the most extreme contrast achievable. Then, simply substitute your colors. Black may become dark green or mid-blue, and white can be softened into cream or pale yellow. The contrast is retained, but your choice of colors will define how dramatic that contrast is.

TOP: **A beige and cream color scheme works well in many rooms, complementing natural wood and giving an uncluttered look.**

RIGHT: **Color scheming—sketch your room and its contents in black and white, then make color substitutions from the chart.**

Black and white sketch	
Color substitutions	

Schemes using a combination of colors side by side on the wheel would be represented in a black and white sketch by mid-gray. Color contrast is not an issue because these are harmonious colors. There is no dividing line between the gray areas, so any two adjacent colors such as red and orange or blue and green can be substituted.

Swatch watch

When working on a room, designers will make up a swatch or sample board, consisting of colors, materials, fabrics, wallpapers, and wood off-cuts stuck down onto a card to assist the decision-making process. All colors envisaged in the scheme are side by side on the board, and can be held in front of any of the walls for a suitability match. It is easy to put one together by collecting samples from shops. Use the material or paint you are considering, however. Never substitute a cut-out from a magazine because this involves a different printing process and will not be accurate.

When your board is complete, use it to compare differing available light levels, and note down the changes in color in bright sunshine, dull, overcast or shadowy conditions, and under artificial light. The artificial light should ideally be the lighting system that is going to be used in the room. If it is going to be different, then find the closest match you can.

The great divide

A house is divided into many areas, and you may or may not have a preference for a color linking system, that is to say linking all rooms on one floor by using the same door frame and baseboard color. You may wish to keep these natural divisions and, indeed, emphasize them by using different color schemes. However, one-room dwellings, spaces for both living and working, or popular city loft-style apartments are not compartmentalized. Therefore the same contrasting scheme or linking system is advisable throughout. Variations will work, such as substituting a cream finish for white on one wall with the same frame or trim color, but they must not compromise the integrity of the overall scheme. Attempting too many color divisions in an area designated as one space works against the original design concept and is doomed to failure. At best the end result looks fragmented, at worst it offends the eye.

BOTTOM LEFT: **To assist in planning your room scheme, make up a swatch board of sample colors and materials.**

BELOW: **This loft apartment has a pleasing cohesive look and is visually united by its wooden flooring and units, and by the consistent use of black as an accent color: on the sofa cushions, piano, and dining chairs.**

Painting

Of the hundreds of weekend tasks that home improvement enthusiasts take on in their homes, the most common is the simple paint job. A vast selection of paints and finishes is now available for all surfaces, and recent additions to paint-makers' ranges have increased the options considerably. This chapter guides you through the selection of paint, offers advice on paint schemes, and shows you how to tackle your first paint job.

Designer's notes

To anyone approaching a makeover for the first time, the vast array of paints must be confusing. The latest paint technology has led to boasts that a professional finish can be attained by a novice. However, it is important to assess modern paints in terms of what they will do, and relate them to older-style paints that may have been used in the house.

Doors and their surrounds have traditionally been painted using oil-based finishes because they are harder-wearing. Special paint is available for decorating outdoors.

Paint types

The paint in your can will be either water- or solvent-based. Both types are made up of pigment, which provides the color, and a binder that holds the pigment particles together. This combination in water is generally called latex. In a spirit-based solvent it is known as oil-based enamel or low luster. Decorators have traditionally used water-based latex paints for interior walls and oil-based finishes for woodwork, such as doors and surrounds, because they are harder-wearing. Today's technology lets the manufacturer offer the choice of water-based enamel or satin paints for woodwork. These

reduce the drying time considerably. Traditional descriptions are altering, too. Silk vinyl latex paints are often labeled "washable" or "wipeable." Mat latex is referred to as "non-reflective"—also "nonwipeable." Water-based enamel may be "nondrip, no undercoat needed" or "one coat only." Often oil-based enamel is offered as "liquid enamel," or, implying use by professionals, as "trade" enamel. Don't be misled by the "trade" label into thinking that this paint is superior in some way; it isn't.

As you contemplate your choice of finish, consider only the durability of water-based versus oil-based paints. Oil-based paints are tougher,

Traditionally, water-based paints have been applied to interior walls, while oil-based enamel paint has been used on woodwork, but conventions are changing as new materials and finishes are now becoming available.

onger-lasting, and easier to clean. Water-based paints are easier to use, environmentally friendly, and the job is done in a quarter of the time. You will, however, need to repaint much sooner if you use water-based paints.

Choosing appropriate paints

On walls and ceilings, which are particularly large areas to paint, don't consider oil-based finishes unless you intend to apply a special effect such as ragging, in which case low luster is ideal. Large areas of oil-based paint are unpleasant to apply, environmentally unfriendly, and time-consuming to change. Latex paints are designed for the job, but make sure your wall surfaces are suitable first.

Once you have a color scheme in mind, examine the room. What is the current state of finish? If it is a painted scheme on plaster, liner paper, or wallcovering that can be painted, and you are merely altering the colors, your task is straightforward because paint is the major decorating factor. Perhaps the current finish incorporates wood paneling, tiles, or even a powerful wallpaper pattern that is to be retained on some of the walls. Your paint scheme must take into account what the room inherits from its previous life, and combine with existing materials to achieve a matching or contrasting effect.

Old and new together

Retaining parts of someone else's room scheme may seem unappealing at first, but don't dismiss it out of hand. If the room has a particular feature that dominates it, then it may provide a better visual result if you work with it, not against it. If you like a particular characteristic, it makes no sense to remove or disguise it, and it can become the axis for the new scheme.

In any combined scheme, remember that decorating can be done wall by wall, slowly building up a new look. It doesn't necessarily

have to be drastically altered all at the same time. In the same way that you must consider what effect the floorcovering, carpet, or wood floor will have on painted walls, you have to view the walls themselves in relation to each other.

You may want to offset a feature, such as a fireplace surround, by painting it in one finish against a wall of a different finish.

TYPES OF PAINT

Primers/Undercoats	Finishes/Top coats
Stain-blocking primer	Vinyl mat latex
Wood primer	Vinyl silk latex
Aluminum wood primer	Enamel latex
Alkali-resisting primer	Enamel
Penetrating stabilizing primer	Low luster
Red oxide primer	Low luster emulsion
Acrylic primer/Undercoat	Smooth masonry paint
Oil/Resin undercoat	Floor/Tile paint
	Ceiling paint
For detailed notes on paint types	Textured paint
see pages 256–257.	Radiator enamel

Adding to a scheme at any time has never been easier. Original paintings, prints, or tapestries can be hung, small areas painted as a special effect, or rugs used on the floor. This slightly alters the overall appearance, and the way that the walls interact with it, particularly if the scheme is monochromatic and the main color theme is continued in the pictures.

RIGHT: **Kitchen walls need to be washable and will probably be subject to much wear and tear.**

BELOW: **Geometric paintings provide an eye-catching focal point in this neutral scheme.**

As a final thought, you should consider carefully the condition of the walls when you are making your decisions. If you find wood paneling or very heavyweight wallcoverings in the room, stop and ask yourself why they are there. What are they covering up? Many enthusiastic decorators have ripped off tongue-and-groove paneling only to find that the wall underneath needs to be taken back to the brick, damp-proofed, sealed, and replastered.

Practicalities

It is important to take into account the function of the room area when choosing paint for a particular scheme. Entrance hallways, for example, may have hooks for wet hats and coats, and a place where people remove muddy boots and leave umbrellas. Don't consider a paint scheme that is not washable. Any wood here will need a tough finish, such as oil-based enamel, or, if it is varnished, an exterior sailboat varnish, to cope with everyday knocks. A wood paneling on the lower, more vulnerable, half of the wall may work to your advantage here.

The walls of the bathroom and kitchen should be washable, but the bathroom is a room that needs to be a warm and friendly place, so you will want to offset the sometimes cold or austere feel of tiles and glass.

Rooms used by everyone in the home need to be both decorative and functional. These are the truly multi-purpose areas. The philosophy of "change a little at a time" is practical here.

Children's rooms and play areas need paints that are washable and tough to withstand heavy use. Two topcoats are a good idea, so that surface scratches do not reveal a different color underneath. Avoid mat latex paints in children's rooms, as these will become shiny where inevitable smudges and fingerprints have to be cleaned off. Go for paints with a silk or semisheen finish.

Bedrooms have to be more robust these days because often they double as teenage living space. However, bedrooms are more personal areas, and schemes can be the choice of the individual. The paint job can be bold and imaginative, whereas communal areas sometimes call for compromise. A scheme in the main living area, for example, of bold, pure, vivid colors, may

ABOVE: **A deep sea-green is a restful color for a bathroom, offset here by the white units and upper walls. The paint you select to decorate your bathroom should be washable, warm, and friendly.**

LEFT: **Instead of the traditional white, paintwork can be given a darker or contrasting color to the paint chosen for use on the walls.**

have seemed spectacular when you were doing it, but even after a short while may become rather irritating to the eye.

Basic skills: guide to paint

There is more to painting than simply choosing your ideal color. Sound preparation of the surface to be painted is a must otherwise you risk having to redo it in the not-too-distant future and ending up with a patchy appearance. You also need to know how best to store your paint and use the tools that are vital to the process.

ABOVE: **Wooden furniture must be properly prepared before it is painted. It must be sanded or washed down first, and will then require a coat of primer, undercoat, and finally a topcoat in your chosen color.**

ABOVE RIGHT: **To avoid your paint soaking straight into the wall, you will need to use either a sealer or a primer before you apply any latex. This will stop the paint from being absorbed by the wall.**

RIGHT: **Brushes, rollers, and paint: the essential components of painting.**

Before using the "Paint: Types and Uses" table on pages 256–257 as a guide to paint finishes, consider your surface and what type of preparation, sealing and priming it may require. Latex paint on bare walls needs a sealer to prevent it from disappearing into the wall altogether. On old walls you should use a stabilizing primer or a diluted mix of PVA. New plaster needs a plaster primer, although a stabilizer

will do, but you must ensure that the new plaster is properly dry or you will be sealing in damp.

Before applying your chosen paint to wood paneling, coat the knots in the woodgrain to stop them from seeping resin, which will show through the paint finish. Use stain-blocking primer for this, followed by a primer, an undercoat, and lastly a topcoat. Traditionally, primer was an oil-based paint, but acrylic primer and combined primer/undercoat have now gained in popularity due to their ease and speed of use, and also because they are environmentally friendly. The latest technology offers gloss or satin finishes in a "nondrip" form that requires no undercoat, just a primer.

Paint pots

However good your paint job, accidental chips and scratches can occur, and a supply of retouching paint is always a good idea. A small amount of paint left in a can is best decanted into a suitable jar, with a lid, for storage. The more paint there is in the jar, the less air there is, and less chance of a skin forming on the top. Avoid getting paint around the rim of the jar or inside its lid; otherwise opening it some time later will be tricky. And don't forget to label the jar.

Color paint charts are useful, but sample pots will be more accurate.

BOTTOM: **Tongue-and-groove paneling might be hiding a wealth of problems in the walls behind, and it may be better to leave it in place and repaint it, rather than rip it off and have to sort out the underlying problem.**

A large volume of paint can remain in the original can. Many tradespeople then store this upside down. If you do so, make sure that the lid is hammered down securely or the paint may leak out. You may prefer simply to invert the can for a few minutes in order to let the contents run around the lid seal, and then to store it the correct way up.

Tools and equipment

As with all tools of the trade, investing in cheap, badly made decorating equipment is a recipe for failure. There is nothing quite as expensive as trying to save money. An inferior tool can ruin a job or a finish by underperforming at a crucial stage, so invest wisely. Here is a selection to start off your essential tool kit for painting.

Left to right: palette knife, putty knife, scraper

Tools and equipment

For walls and ceilings you will need a set of tools to take off the existing finish, and another set to put on the new scheme. Before you begin, always remember to protect the floor and furniture by covering them with large drop cloths.

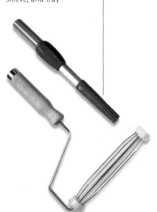

Painter's masking tape

Sugar soap and glasspaper

If you are repainting a papered wall, you only need to ensure that it is clean; household liquid soap applied with a soft cloth will remove grease. Make sure the wall is dry before you start painting. Repainting a masonry or plaster wall with latex is easier if the wall surface is "keyed" to receive the paint, so lightly abrade the surface with medium, followed by fine sandpaper. Before painting over a gloss, satin, or mat oil-based surface, with either oil- or water-based paint, use flexible wet-and-dry paper to remove the surface "sheen." Soak medium and fine-grade sandpaper in a bucket of hot water with sugar soap, an all-purpose cleaner. Abrade the surface as before, using lots of water. Rinse the surface and dry it.

Brushes, pads and rollers

Good-quality paint brushes will apply paint evenly, and will not shed bristles all over the wall, although cheaper versions probably will.

Above: Mini-roller, spare sleeve, and tray

Textured roller

Four sizes of paintbrush, long-handled fitch, small retouching brush, and bridge-handled stippling brush

Flogger (dragging brush)

Graining roller

Roller handle, extension, foam, and pile rollers

Paint tray and paint pad

Left: Heat gun with various attachments

Butane gas torches

Four sizes of brush are available—½ in./1.2 cm, 1 in./2.5 cm, 1½ in./3.8 cm and 2 in./5 cm. This choice should suffice for any standard painting job. Larger sizes of brushes, up to 6 in./ 15 cm are available for working with, but they may make your hand and arm ache. For painting larger areas, it is better to use a paint pad or roller. When painting always decant the paint into a kettle or bucket. Never paint straight from the can. The pad and roller will have their own loading containers, and as an option solid emulsion has its own tray.

The roller may be foam or fiber. Fiber rollers are available with different pile lengths. The more uneven the surface, the longer the pile you will need. For large areas use rollers, and to reach small awkward places use radiator rollers.

Other equipment

You can reach high ceilings by using an extension pole; however, high corners will have to be done with a brush. Always use a stable stepladder that has an integral top platform for placing your brush and paint kettle. Masking tape and paint masks can be used to protect adjacent areas of color. If you do overrun, use a soft, damp cloth.

Maintenance

Always clean the brushes, rollers, and containers. Oil-based paints can be removed with mineral spirits, turpentine substitute, or a brand-name brush cleaner and restorer. Water-based paint can be cleaned off in hot water and soap. After brushing out excess paint on old newspaper, work the cleaning solution well into the brush. Remove partly dried paint with an old comb. Rinse and partly dry the brush with a soft cloth.

Never leave your brushes to soak overnight; they will end up with a "permanent wave" that will make accurate cutting-in of colors impossible. To remove excess paint from rollers and pads, wash them out in their respective trays. Squeeze the rollers and hang them up to dry.

TOP TIP

As your brush dries, protect the bristles in plastic wrap and use an elastic band around the end to keep the tips square with the handle. This will ensure that it always keeps its shape. Avoid leaving brushes soaking in a jar of brush cleaner too long, because the bristles will splay out.

Mineral spirits

Drop cloth

Bucket, soft cloth, and sponge

Paint shield

Soft cloths

Paint remover, brush, and wire wool

Shave hooks

Assorted solutions and fillers

Sanding block and papers

Paint strainer

Paint

General preparation

The finished job is only as good as your preparation. Walls and ceilings need very careful assessment before you reach for the roller and prise open the paint pot. They may need to have cracks repaired, and will need to be washed down (and possibly "keyed") before you can apply latex or oil-based paint.

The qualities of paint

A thick coat of paint cannot be used to disguise a bad wall. Paint contains a binder, and the binder's job is to ensure that the colored particles (pigment) dry together on the wall as a continuous protective film, on top of, but not hiding, any bumps, cracks, or imperfections. Even thickening agents used in nondrip paints will not cause jelly-like applications to dry out any other way than flat on the wall. It is usually accepted that darker, glossier, more reflective colors show up imperfections more than pale, subtle tones, but this is not a recommended selection criterion. All flat areas of color will emphasize wall damage, and the only proper course of action is to eradicate the problem during preparation.

Repairing damaged walls

Don't be unduly worried, however, if your walls are not in pristine condition. Cracks and crevices in plaster are commonplace.

New plaster frequently develops hairline cracks as it dries out, often where large areas meet at an angle, such as a wall and ceiling.

A slight settling of the building on its foundations, or a small amount of subsidence, will result in fairly obvious cracks appearing in the plasterwork on the walls and ceilings. Check all around the room thoroughly if this is the case. You may find other evidence of settling, where baseboards meet the walls, and around door frame moldings.

All these cracks can be easily made good, using a decorator's pack of all-purpose joint compound, which comes in white powder form to be mixed with water. Cracks caused by movement that is likely to recur, where the baseboard skirting joins the wall in the stairwell, for instance, should be repaired with a spacking compound. These compounds are available premixed in cartridges, are usually applied by means of a simple-to-use cartridge gun, and have a nozzle that can be cut to fill a specific width.

Overpainting

Overpainting wall areas with latex, whether in the same color or not, is a common task in the home. Provided your walls are sound, you only need to ensure that they are clean and free from contamination by dust, dirt, and grease. Usually, household liquid soap, hot water, and a sponge will do the job. However, if a wall or ceiling has

Holding the cartridge gun at an angle to the wall, squeeze the filler into the crack, before smoothing it out with your finger or a putty knife. Once dried, the filler can be sanded down flush with the wall.

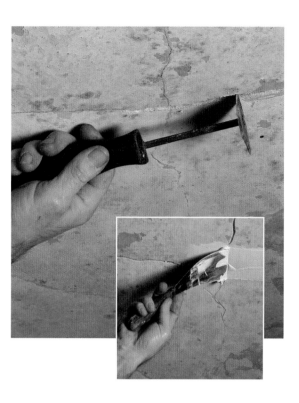

an unsightly stain caused by a leaking roof or upstairs appliance, you must seal it or it will quickly show through the new paint finish. The easiest way is to paint over the stain with oil-based enamel or low luster in an appropriate color, let it dry, and then apply the emulsion. Alternatively, stain sealers are available in spraycan form.

If the walls have an oil-based paint finish, low luster or flat oil, then in addition to washing them down, you will need to provide a "key" for the new paint finish to adhere to. Lightly abrade the surface using abrasive paper wrapped around a sanding block.

Use medium paper for enamel and fine paper for low luster. Alternatively, you can combine both operations by keying the surface while it is wet, using flexible wet-and-dry paper. Soak the paper in a bucket of soap and hot water for at least five minutes, while prewashing the wall using a sponge. Using plenty of water, lightly abrade the wall surface to remove the sheen. Finally, wash down the wall with clean water.

Preparing paint

It is important to read the manufacturer's directions and familiarize yourself with the information on the side of the can at the start of the job. Make sure the top of the paint can is clean before you open it. If you are not careful, any dirt there may fall into the paint once opened. Insert a screwdriver blade horizontally under the lip of the can and turn it slowly until it is vertical, repeating farther around the rim to prise off the lid. This minimizes damage to the lip, and it will make resealing easier. If the can is already half-empty, carefully remove any top skin and stir the paint. Any remaining tiny pieces of skin or debris must then be removed by straining the paint. This can be done by decanting the paint into a paint kettle or a bucket through a piece of stretched stocking.

LEFT: Use a shave hook to rake out any loose material and dirt in the crack, and to undercut it slightly to give the filler a good grip. Then press the filler firmly into the crack using a putty knife.

BELOW: Sand an oil-based surface lightly with abrasive paper to provide a "key" for the paint to adhere to.

BOTTOM: Remove the lid of the can using a screwdriver. Old paint may need to be strained into a kettle or bucket.

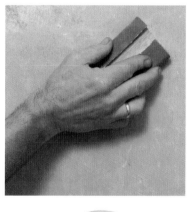

Abrasives

The generic term "sanding down," referring to surface abrading, is a vitally important part of decorating preparation and is still in common use, even though "sandpaper" as such has not been commercially produced for many years. The modern equivalent and all other suitable abrasives are available at your local home improvement store and are outlined here.

Never cut abrasive paper with blade or scissors. Fold a sheet into quarters and tear it along the edge of the table.

Preparing the ground

Quality preparation is the key to a quality result, and a smooth surface is essential for a paint or varnish finish. This means rubbing down with the correct abrasive; using the right materials speeds up the task and gives the best result. Some surfaces must be rubbed down dry (bare woods, surfaces containing water-based fillers), some wet (enamel paint that is being recoated), and some, such as floorboards, are suitable for both applications. Common sense will play a part in your decision. Wet abrading of water-soluble materials, including fillers, often leads to little more than a paste-like mess; dry rubbing of dirty, greasy surfaces will clog the abrasive in no time, and be ineffective and expensive because the paper cannot be reused.

Wet or dry?

Traditionally, rubbing down was a dry process, starting with coarser grades and finishing with finer ones, the finest grade of all often being referred to as "flour" paper. With the legislation of the Lead Paint Act (1926) in England as a spur, the dry abrading of lead-based paint was made illegal, so manufacturers introduced a waterproof paper so that a lubricant could be used with the abrasive. Initially not a popular choice, because of its cost, it was used in coach finishing and other high-quality work, and general decorating workers continued to dry rub. Today, silicon carbide used with a lubricant is recognized as a real alternative to dry papers. It is faster and more efficient because of its cutting action, lasts longer, doesn't clog easily, and can

Green aluminum oxide is generally suitable for heavy-duty and machine use.

LEFT: Cloth sanding belts are available for all belt sanding machines, basic and heavy-duty machines alike. The abrasive is aluminum oxide; the belt is full resin cloth, flush joined at a 45-degree angle to give maximum life.

RIGHT: Yellow aluminum oxide sheets (here torn from a standard 6in./15cm roll) are suitable for hand and block use. You can clearly see the difference in grit sizes.

ABRASIVE SHEETS

LEFT: **Conventional sandpaper: coarse, medium, and fine grades in standard sized sheets.**

RIGHT: **Waterproof, latex-backed synthetic silicon carbide is commonly called wet-and-dry paper.**

be rinsed clean in a bucket on site. This offsets its higher cost (it is four times the price of sandpaper).

Today's cutting edge

The home decorator is able to make the same choices in buying and using as the working professional:

Conventional sandpaper

This is used dry, available in sheets 1⅛ in. x ⅞ in./ 2.8 cm x 2.3 cm, graded 3 (coarse) to 00 (very fine) or simply labeled coarse, medium, and fine, depending on the manufacturer. It is suitable for hand or machine use. It's cheap but clogs very easily and selection of inappropriate grades can result in scratching of the workpiece.

Aluminum oxide

This is used dry, available in sheets, 1⅛in x ⅞ in./ 2.8 cm x 2.3 cm, or in rolls 4½ in./11.5 cm wide and sold by the roll or in metre lengths cut from a roll or in precut sizes ready-made for machine sanders. Graded in grit sizes, 40 grit (coarse) to 240 (very fine). Electrobonded, with a grit size giving a more controlled cut, it is frequently used instead of sandpaper because of its longer life.

Silicon carbide (wet-and-dry paper)

This can be used dry or lubricated; if regularly rinsed in the wet application it is long lasting. Available in sheets 1⅛ in. x ⅞ in./2.8 cm x 2.3 cm, graded 100 (coarse) to 1200 (very fine), but frequently found in home improvement stores as a "decorator's pack" containing a couple of sheets of coarse, medium, and fine flexible papers. Tough, flexible and long-lasting when lubricated, it should be a first choice for painted surfaces.

Steel wool

This can be used dry or lubricated, available as boxed rolls about 2¾ in./7 cm wide, or as pads. Graded from 5 (coarse) to 0000 (very fine), often packed as a kit with coarse, medium, and fine pads. Can be used as a cleaner or degreaser on flooring to scour wood following the use of water-washable paint remover, or to apply waxes to prepared surfaces. Always wear gloves to use it.

Use an abrasive with a sanding block to maintain an edge on the corners of the work. Always sand in the direction of the grain, particularly if you intend to apply a varnished finish, because cross-grain scratching will show up badly.

A roll of steel wool. Always wear gloves when you handle this product and, as with other abrasives, wear a dust mask.

RIGHT AND BELOW: **Rubbing blocks.**

How to paint

It might appear that painting is a perfectly straightforward procedure, but there are numerous tips—on the selection of your brush, roller, pad, or aerosol—that can make the task much easier. If you know how to apply the paint properly and what sort of stroke to use, the result will be much more pleasing.

Using a brush

Always select a brush of a suitable size for the job and make sure that it is clean. Ensure that the bristles are in good condition by working the brush up and down on a dry surface. This will make any dust and defective or loose bristles fall out.

For very small wall areas, for blending in, and for finished detail work on roller-painted walls, use a small brush, 1 ½ in./3.8 cm or 2 in./5 cm size. Hold it between your thumb and fingers on the metal casing, or ferrule, which encases the bristles.

Larger brushes, although quicker initially, will soon become tiring and difficult to control, and are no substitute for a roller. However, if you decide the large 6 in./15 cm brush is for you, then you will find it easier if you hold it by the handle.

For maximum control of a small or medium-sized brush, hold it by the ferrule, or metal casing, dip it into the paint to one-third of the bristle depth, and, use long, sweeping strokes to apply the paint.

If latex surfaces, the easiest to paint, do not dry out uniformly flat, simply apply a second coat. Oil-based finishes must not dry out at the edges before the entire surface is finished, or the brush strokes will be obvious, so blend in the wet edges continuously as you move from side to side across the surface. Frequent changing of the direction of the brush stroke will result in a more even distribution of paint.

Using a roller

A paint roller is the most time-efficient way of applying a water-based finish to a large area. The only shortcoming is that you cannot butt up to other color surfaces or into corners, and you will need a small brush to complete the job. Oil-based paints are equally easy to apply, but they will retain some of the texture of the roller in the finish, whereas latex paints all dry flat. If an absolutely dead flat finish is needed in an oil base, use a brush.

• Select a suitable roller sleeve for your wall, remembering that the smoother the surface, the shorter the pile required.

• Pour the paint of your choice into the reservoir of the paint tray, level with the ribbed rolling area.

• Immerse the roller sleeve in the reservoir, then roll it out gently on the ribbed area to ensure an even distribution of paint.

- Apply the roller to the wall using even pressure throughout, in vertical overlapping strokes.
- Finish off by changing to horizontal strokes, which will ensure an even coverage.
- Don't try to cover too big an area each time you load the roller. You may find it helpful if you visualize your wall broken down into imaginary squares and then fill one at a time.

If paint spatters onto adjacent surfaces as you roll out the paint, it's because you are driving it too fast. This is always a temptation, particularly when using an extension pole to paint a ceiling. So slow down, and remember that paint splashes from above you can land on your head. Always wear eye protection.

Using paint pads

Paint pads come in a variety of sizes and the larger ones can be used with an extension pole to reach ceilings. Edging pads are available to cut into corners and angles. Pads come with their own paint tray and special loading roller.

TOP TIP

Using your second finger as a pressure guide on either the handle or ferrule of a brush can quickly result in a blister, particularly if you have soft hands. An astutely positioned sticking plaster, or even a length of painter's tape wound around the finger, will protect against rubbing.

Try to keep the brush handle and ferrule free of sticky, semidry paint or varnish at all times, because this exacerbates the problem.

LEFT: **Paint pads are useful for getting a smooth, even surface, without any brush marks, but cannot be used for oil-based paint.**

LEFT: **Roll out excess paint on the ribbed area of the paint tray before applying a roller to a wall.**

ABOVE: **Sprayguns and aerosols are best kept for concentrated detail where the area to be painted is masked off with tape.**

Pour in your paint, and load the pad by running it back and forth across the ribbed cylindrical loader. Paint in vertical overlapping strokes to achieve a smooth even coat. While paint pads are simple to use, bear in mind that they carry less paint per loading than a brush or a roller, so you are likely to need an extra coat.

Aerosols and sprayguns

Universally available in solvent or water-based form, aerosols are very useful for spraying small areas as special-effect patterns on a plain painted wall. Yet they are expensive, and require accurate and detailed masking. They are not suitable for spray painting an entire room. For this you would need to rent an electric airless spraygun with a changeable paint reservoir. These guns have a viscosity measuring cup to ensure that the paint for the reservoir has been thinned down correctly. Useful accessories include a flexible extension nozzle, for spraying a ceiling, and more powerful models have a fine adjustment control for flexibility of spray volume. However, unless you are experienced in the use of guns, you are advised to choose another application method.

ABOVE: **A roller on an extension pole is ideal for painting ceilings, although you will need to use a brush to fill in corners.**

PROJECT
Special effects: textured paint

Textured finishes were once kept almost exclusively for ceilings but are becoming increasingly popular on walls—or perhaps just one feature wall in a room—to create a particular look. They also have the advantages of helping to cover uneven surfaces, being simple to apply and being adaptable to your own designs.

Textured paint

Recently built properties frequently have textured paints on ceilings. These appear as fairly uniform overlapping swirls, or single twists in a geometric pattern, usually with very basic light fittings and plain walls with no surround. The advantage here is that water-based paint with added thickeners is used, so the finish is flexible and can disguise cracks and movement in the original surface. The addition of a joint compound will give the paint a smooth finish, which is easily manipulated by a texturing comb. Blending in sand will result in a much rougher appearance. You can decide which finish is right for you. One factor to consider when using textured finishes, however, is their ability to attract and trap dirt and dust. They are therefore best avoided in the kitchen, bathroom, or the workshop.

Application

Apply the textured paint with a roller or brush, taking a manageable area at a time—about 3½ft./1m^2 should be ideal. Apply the paint as evenly as you can over the surface area. Make sure that the depth of finish will obliterate any defects that are apparent. Then simply apply the texturing decoration of your choice, using the comb supplied, a sponge, scrapers, or a piece of plastic that has been cut to size. You can also buy patterned roller sleeves in order to create special effects, such as repeating geometric patterns.

Although intended primarily for ceilings, these easy-to-use finishes have become increasingly popular elsewhere—for example, on feature walls giving an impression of Spanish or Mexican styling. It's well worth experimenting on a square yard/meter of hardboard first to see what the effect looks like.

Most of these latex paints are white, but you can add any water-based color of your choice for a Mediterranean-style scheme. Simply treat the textured paint as sealed plaster. The principle of overpainting in various colors can be explored

A Mediterranean look can be created using textured finishes on the walls.

MAKING A PATTERN IN PAINT

STEP 1 You can apply textured paint with a roller or paint brush. Work on a manageable area at a time, making sure that you spread an even thickness. That way, the results won't be patchy.

STEP 2 A sponge dabbed onto the textured base will create a simple pattern. This is the look often chosen to reflect a rustic style and, when combined with basic furnishings, can be very effective.

further by using a special texturing base and color waxes, which are available in kit form.

Spread the base onto the feature wall with a trowel or something similar, and then create a relief pattern of your own design. This can be as complex as you like; the base is reworkable for up to an hour, giving you plenty of time to produce a pattern you like. When you are satisfied with the base texture, brush on one or two coats of your chosen color wax. This will be absorbed into the textured base at different rates, and will dry out to an irregular toned finish, giving the impression of sun-kissed walls.

Textured finishes can be very effective in minimalist surroundings. Like all specialist decorative techniques, the best thing is to

give them plenty of space in which to work their magic. This means the less clutter, the better. Try offsetting a texture against bare unvarnished floorboards, or you might want to make a relief feature of one wall and leave the others plain.

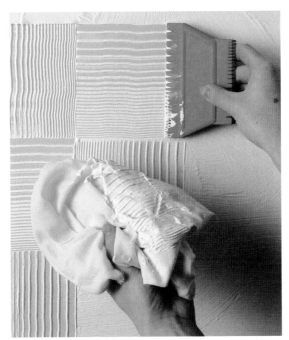

STEP 3 Apply the textured base to your surface, spreading it out well over a small area.

STEP 4 Brush on the water-based color or wax of your choice when the textured surface is dry.

STEP 5 Use a comb or piece of plastic cut to size to create a pattern. This might be geometric, swirling spirals, or simply an abstract design. You can rework the textured base for up to one hour.

PROJECT
Special effects: glazes

Glazes are semi-transparent paints that let the underlying base color show through. They have become increasingly popular because they can be used to create a whole range of different effects and are relatively easy to use. With a little practice, you will find that you are able to emulate the look that a professional painter can achieve.

Decorative finishes for walls, from simple rag-rolling to more complex crackle glazing, can be undertaken successfully on correctly prepared wall surfaces. It is always a good idea to experiment on a spare piece of board first. It will prove a lot easier to throw out a scrap piece of board if you don't like the color or the effect, than to redo an entire wall or room.

Preparation

Whether your intended finish is based on oil or water, a correctly prepared surface is essential. Since several popular effects are common to both oil and water bases, you do have a choice. However, oils are easier to work with because they dry more slowly and are much more resilient. Water bases dry quickly, which is helpful only if you are attempting a multilayered build-up of colors. For durability, a water-based surface requires several coats of varnish.

Rectify any wall defects, cracks, crevices, and holes, as you would for a straight latex roller job. For an oil-based finish on bare plaster, prime the surface with all-purpose oil-based primer-sealer. For water-based finishes you can use water-based primers or PVA thinned with water. Sand the surface of previously painted plaster walls to provide the necessary "key," using a medium-grit abrasive paper. Now apply the underlying coats that will partly show through your glaze. One or two coats of oil-based low luster will suffice for oil finishes; one or two coats of water-based undercoat or latex for water-based finishes. If you want a second coat, you can lightly abrade the surface of the first coat using fine-grade abrasive paper.

The walls in this sitting room have been painted porcelain blue wih a white glaze swirled in.

APPLYING GLAZE

STEP 1 Apply your base coat to the wall in the usual manner, using long sweeping strokes.

STEP 2 Abrade the surface of the wall between coats with fine grade sandpaper.

STEP 3 Blend a little color with turpentine and mix it into the glaze, avoiding lumps of color.

YOU WILL NEED:
- PAINT FOR BASE COAT
- BRUSHES
- ABRASIVE FINE GRADE PAPER
- WATER OR OIL-BASED GLAZE
- DILUTE (LINSEED OIL AND MINERAL SPIRITS OR TURPENTINE)
- OIL-BASED COLOR

Choosing and making glazes

Most finishes require oil-based glazes. A slow drying time lets you handle the medium easily, even when you are attempting more ambitious effects. Water-based glazes are thinner and dry very quickly. Colorwashing and sponging techniques aside, water-based glazes are unsuitable for most finishes. Water-based glazes are simply made up from colored acrylics thinned with water, or a water-based latex glaze, often with the addition of white latex to tint the color. However, oil-based glazes consist of scumble glaze, available from good paint retailers, which can be diluted with a mixture of linseed oil and mineral spirits, or it can be diluted using turpentine. In both cases more scumble in the mix slows down the drying process, and gives more time for playing with the effects.

You need to start with a basic ratio of 50:50 if you are mixing scumble glaze with turpentine, adding more turpentine to thin down the mix, and the finished glaze, if preferred. If you decide to use linseed oil and mineral spirits instead of turpentine, you will find that more mineral spirits will thin the glaze and shorten the drying time. Increasing the amount of linseed oil will result in a smoother, oilier finish. The exact proportions are a matter of personal preference, and you may need to experiment a little before starting the job.

If you are happy with the consistency of the glaze, add the color of your choice, making sure you add just a little at a time. Any oil-based color can be used, but remember to mix specialist artists' oil paints carefully with a small amount of glaze to start with.

This will show you whether the color is what you expect, and it will also prevent the problem of the mix becoming lumpy.

A selection of oil-based glazes showing the mixed-up version and the combed-out glaze.

TOP TIP

Photographs in magazines and books may appear to show exactly the effect that you want, but you should bear in mind that these are reproduced by a four-color process that is not necessarily an exact color match, particularly where metallics are concerned.

YOU WILL NEED:

SPONGING:

• COLORED LATEX

• TRAY OR KETTLE

• SPONGES

COLORWASHING:

• LATEX FOR SEALING
  WALL

• WATERED-DOWN
  GLAZE

• DRY BRUSH

PROJECT
Sponging and colorwashing

Two of the simplest, and most widely used, paint effects are sponging and colorwashing. Both of these broken-color effects work over the underlying base coat that has been applied to the wall, although sponging involves dabbing on additional color, whereas colorwashing creates effects and texture in a colored glaze. Experiment to find an effect that pleases you.

Sponging

Sponging is a very simple paint finish and the variations open to you with this technique are endless. Applied on a plaster, lined, or papered wall, it should be water-based, but if you try sponging on a wood-paneled wall use an oil base, such as low luster, because it will last longer. You will need natural or marine sponges for this technique. Select a large one that is easy to hold, and a smaller example in another shape to put on a second color or add patches of different color intensity. Pour your colored latex into a small tray or kettle, and partially immerse the sponge. Dab it onto a sheet of paper to remove any excess and to check the effect. If you are completely satisfied, dab the sponge onto the wall base color. Vary the angle and try to avoid making it look too uniform. When it is dry add a second color with the other sponge.

Colorwashing

Colorwashing can be used to create a rustic effect, with subtle color on a roughened surface. The wall must first be sealed with two coats of latex as a base. Then the watered-down colors are brushed over the base, before being worked into the wall with a dry brush. Aging and distressing techniques can be applied if desired, using watery white to achieve a dusty, chalky feel. While similar colors are used on textured walls, contrasting colors used on smooth, flat surfaces give an entirely different result with almost the same technique. For this, latex the wall as before, brush on the colored glaze, and then use a very wide, dry brush to create long, sweeping strokes in a haphazard manner. The base coat underneath will show through.

SPONGING

STEP 1 Apply the larger sponge lightly to the wall, without making the pattern look too regular.

STEP 2 Reload the sponge as necessary, changing its position and adding more color in some areas.

STEP 3 When the first color is dry, dab on the second color with a smaller sponge until it is complete.

COLORWASHING

STEP 1 Apply a base coat to the wall in the standard manner, using long, sweeping brush strokes.

STEP 2 Add a liberal coat of colored glaze. The best effects will be created by using a contrasting color.

STEP 3 Using a dry, wide softening brush, work over the glaze in a random direction, using long strokes.

PROJECT
Stippling and rag-rolling

Two additional techniques are stippling and rag-rolling. Stippling with a brush is a one-off finish, which creates a pleasingly mottled appearance on a wall. Rag-rolling, which is also known simply as "ragging" can be built up in layers, provided that each layer is left to dry completely before the next one is added.

Two-color finishes

Both of these techniques produce a two-color finish and are best used with oil-based glazes. Both require similar wall surfaces and give a pleasingly subtle result. Two coats of low luster are required as a base color in both cases.

Stippling

To achieve the best finish, stippling needs an even glaze on the base coat, because the aim is to remove all brushmarks from the surface. A special stippling brush is best purchased specifically for this task, although you can experiment with any large, reasonably stiff brush.

The object of stippling is to hit the painted wall surface with the end of the bristles. The bristles must be reasonably dry, however, or you will simply put glaze back onto the surface, so unload your brush regularly by stippling onto a clean rag.

Stippling gives a rich, powerful finish. It is ideal for emphasizing bright, strong colors, so choose your combinations bearing this in mind. It needs to be done quite quickly, so it is best to have someone else help you.

Rag-rolling

Ragging involves dabbing a dry, crumpled-up ball of cloth onto a glaze coat, to remove parts of it before it dries. As you roll the rag across the glazed surface, irregular patterns will be created. A design can be created using a variety of contrasting materials. Softer or harsher patterns can be made, resulting in quite different visual effects, depending on the fibers in the cloth.

Often the techniques of stippling and ragging are combined, with a surface that has been earmarked for ragging being stippled first in order to remove all the brushmarks.

Make sure you have plenty of rags and keep turning each rag to expose a clean surface as you work. When a rag becomes clogged with glaze, replace it with a clean one. Work on small areas at a time, otherwise the glaze may become too dry.

STIPPLING

STEP 1 Brush the glaze onto the underlying base coat. The stippling action will remove any brush marks that show.

STEP 2 Hold the stippling brush at right angles to the wall and stab briskly at the surface.

RAG-ROLLING

STEP 1 Brush the glaze over the base coat in a random way, so that some of the base shows through.

STEP 2 Using a crumpled cloth, dab at the wall to remove some of the glaze while it is still wet.

STEP 3 Vary the direction and change the rag as necessary, so that you end up with an irregular pattern.

YOU WILL NEED:
WOODGRAINING:

- **LOW LUSTER BASE
  COLOR**
- **BRUSH**
- **DRY BRUSH**
- **OIL-BASED GLAZE MIX**
- **GRAINING COMB**

DRAGGING:

- **PALE BASE COLOR**
- **CONTRASTING COLOR
  OR GLAZE**
- **BRUSHES**
- **DRY LONG-HAIRED
  FLOGGER**

A woodgrained blue wall with stenciling applied to the beams is offset by the simple table and ceiling in this dining room.

PROJECT
Woodgraining and dragging

These techniques are variations on the same theme; woodgraining is merely an extension and amplification of dragging. However, dragging will show up any imperfections in the wall, so it is best kept for surfaces that are perfectly smooth. Woodgraining effects can look stunning in the right situation and will add interest to an otherwise plain interior.

Both of these techniques involve pulling or dragging a dry brush through an oil-based glaze to create irregular linear patterns. Skilled decorators can achieve imitation wood finishes in this way, by raking long, narrow strokes with special straight-haired brushes called floggers.

You can use any dry brush, however, and many irregular patterns and line widths can be achieved, depending on the condition and age of your brush. Dragging through a wall glaze using a fine, soft brush results in a subtle fine-line finish. Adding a graining-comb finish to distort and offset these lines can give the appearance of exotic wood. This technique works well on furniture and wood panels.

Woodgraining

Using the woodgraining technique, you can make your surface look like the raised grain on planed lumber. Select your low luster base coat carefully, for example, using a mid-yellow base showing through an orange glaze to imitate pine. Other combinations will give an appearance similar to other types of wood. Use a 50:50 mix in your chosen oil-based glaze and brush it on evenly. Any brushmarks that are left visible must run in the final direction of the grain. When you are satisfied with the even

WOODGRAINING

STEP 1 To woodgrain, apply glaze generously over the base coat, working parallel to the grain on wooden surfaces.

STEP 2 Using a dry flogger, drag a series of parallel lines in the glaze to create the pattern of the grain.

STEP 3 Use a graining comb to manipulate the parallel lines and make interesting patterns.

easier if you drag the second half of the wall upward from the floor, meeting in the middle. Lessen the pressure as you move through the join, and don't meet in exactly the same place as you move along the wall. Try to vary this by 1 ft./30 cm or so.

Other effects

A variety of effects involving oil-glaze graining and dragging can be achieved using manufacturers' paint-effect kits, consisting of base coat, top coat, and effect applicators. For example, you can create your own blue-jeans wall finish in this way. A denim-blue top coat is rollered over a dry, very pale blue base, and then dragged with a long-haired flogger brush, which can be used to create a denim jeans-effect, from ceiling and floor to the middle of the wall. Follow the kit instructions because a protective final coat may be needed.

On modern, smooth walls, a floor-to-ceiling denim effect adds a cool, unusual feel. Alternatively, if you prefer, the traditional blues can be replaced by other color combinations.

FAR LEFT: **To drag a surface, once you have applied the base coat, draw a dry flogger over it, working from the top to about halfway down.**

NEAR LEFT: **Then drag the brush upward from the floor, meeting at different points along the wall. Don't worry if the lines are not perfectly straight.**

color, drag a dry brush through the glaze, leaving veins of base color exposed. The width of the grain effect will depend on the age and condition of the brush. Rubber rockers and graining combs can be used to imitate the peculiarities of a natural wood surface, such as the fibers, grain spirals, bands of paler tissue, and so on.

Dragging

Dragging is, in reality, the first part of woodgraining, but if you select an entire wall for this effect, only drag half the wall at a time otherwise the brush will overload because it picks up too much glaze from the surface. Always keep the brush as dry as possible—you may find this

DRAGGING

STEP 1 To create a denim effect, first paint the wall surface with a very pale blue base coat.

STEP 2 Paint the surface with a denim blue, which should contrast well with the underlying color.

STEP 3 Drag a long-haired flogger over the wall from top to middle and bottom to middle.

PROJECT
Spattering

Spatter effects, sometimes called speckling, are achieved professionally by using a spraygun fitted with a special decorators' spray head at very low pressure. The color is not atomized and hits the wall as a series of tiny splashes. You can imitate this finish by flicking single colors onto a surface with a brush, slowly building up the overall color.

Making a splash

For spattering you can use water- or oil-based paint. Oil will last longer, but a sealer can always be applied to latexed surfaces. Whichever you use, you need to carefully mask and protect the adjoining surfaces. By applying small splashes of red, yellow, and bright blue from separate cans in a dense pattern, you can make a wall look dark brown; only close inspection will reveal the secret.

Method

The technique consists of sharply tapping a paint-laden brush against an offcut of wood, directly in front of the wall. The size of the splashes will vary, depending on how near you are to the wall, and the quantity of paint on the brush. You can experiment on a large piece of scrap card to get a feel for the technique. Flick bright yellow paint onto a white base, carefully building up an intense pattern of irregular splashes.

Clean the brush and repeat with bright red, and then bright blue. Although the paint on the wall is in reality a kaleidoscope of colored dots of varying shapes and sizes, viewed from the other side of the room it will appear to be dark brown. This build-up of color is similar to that in a

SPATTERING TECHNIQUE

STEP 1 Begin spattering by tapping the brush against a piece of wood to flick the paint onto the wall.

STEP 2 Start adding the second color, in this case red, in the same manner, building up an even coverage.

STEP 3 Finish off with a spattering of blue. When viewed from a distance, the finish will appear as a brown.

printing process, and you will probably want to try out different combinations.

Spatter blue on a yellow base to make green. Try a black and white scheme using black and gray splashes to achieve a dull finish, and then liven it by adding white. If the combined effect is deemed unsatisfactory, you always have the option of adding another color. You can do this without waiting for the others to dry, so it should not become too time-consuming.

This technique is somewhat haphazard, the size and shape of the spatter effect being difficult to control. Experimentation with scrap board or card is essential. If you find it very difficult, try dragging an old blunt knife along the bristle tips of a large wall brush. Hold the brush bristles down and run the knife toward you. As the bristles spring back, paint is flicked onto the near surface.

Do not confuse this technique with multicolor finishes. These are special trade paints that achieve a spattered effect in one coat. Such industrial paints have pigment particles that remain permanently in suspension. They don't bind in the usual way, and as a result must be sprayed conventionally. Airless and hot sprays are unsuitable methods of application; neither are brush and roller an option. This a special purpose finish which is best left in the hands of professional decorators.

You can create a soft focus effect in your home by using the spattering technique. Depending on the color scheme you select, the effect can be cool or, as shown here, warm.

YOU WILL NEED:
- **OIL-BASED LOW LUSTER PAINT**
- **TURPENTINE AND SCUMBLE GLAZE WITH OIL COLOR**
- **COLOR GLAZES**
- **BRUSHES**
- **CLOTH**
- **ARTISTS' BRUSH**
- **CLEAR OIL-BASED VARNISH**

RIGHT: **You can copy the veins and colors of marble in paint.**

BELOW: **Marbling is ideal for bathrooms, giving a feeling of opulence, but don't overdo it, as the effect can be overpowering.**

PROJECT
Marble finishes

Marbled paint effects are time-consuming and complicated to apply. However, careful consideration of the chosen surface, a suitable piece of marble, or picture, that can be used as reference, attention to detail, and sympathetic use of color in the rest of the room can transform any area in an attractive fashion.

Bathrooms and shower areas

Bathrooms and shower areas will benefit from a marble makeover, but be selective and don't overdo this effect. Smaller wall areas, bath panels, shower sides, and other places where tiles might be found are all suitable targets for experimentation. If you attempt to recreate the ultimate Roman bathing room, however, you may find the overall scheme a little intimidating.

Method

To begin, find a piece of marble to copy. A tile, for instance, in the appropriate colors, makes an excellent starting point. If you intend to marble a bathroom wall, first ensure it is completely flat and that it is in prime condition.

Make good any defects, and coat the wall with oil-based low luster. Now brush on a contrasting glaze, using equal portions of scumble and turpentine mixed with the artists' oil color that matches your scheme. Put on a thin coat, then add more or a different artists' color to the glaze. Apply this to selected parts of the wall, creating random areas of different color strengths. Blend these areas together by dabbing lightly with a soft cloth or natural sponge, or by stippling the surface. This removes the glaze, creating lighter tones in parts.

To create the marble veins in contrasting color glazes, use a small artists' brush and vary the width, sharpness, and direction of the veins across the wall. Complete the wall by adding more oil glaze to some of the veins, stipple more color onto selected areas, and lighten others until you are happy with the result. Leave the wall to dry completely, then apply at least two coats of clear oil-based varnish in satin or low luster, depending on whether you prefer a polished appearance or not.

MARBLE FINISH

STEP 1 Begin by painting the wall with an oil-based low luster paint and leave it to dry.

STEP 2 Working on a manageable area at a time, brush on the colored turpentine and scumble glaze.

STEP 3 After adding a third color, dab a cloth into the glaze to blend the colors together.

STEP 4 Paint in the veins with a small brush. Vary their thickness and direction as in real marble.

Alternatives

As an alternative to an overall varnished finish, if you find a paneled pattern that suits the room, it is relatively simple to transfer the design to your finished marble effect wall using painter's tape to define the panel shapes. Adding different color tints to the satin or enamel varnish will alter or enhance the colors of panels making up a geometric shape. Several coats of tinted varnishes can be applied to the same areas, building up the depth of the design. Leave your geometric panel design to dry and finish as before with two coats of clear varnish. As an alternative to enamel, satin coat can be polished to achieve a sheened finish.

STEP 5 Add more glaze until you are happy with the the result. When dry, add a clear varnish.

BOTTOM LEFT: **Varnished finishes have been popular throughout history, as evidenced by this beautiful lacquered cabinet from China.**

VARNISH OVER PAINT

Building up a depth of finish, using several layers of varnish to give a "coach" finish on top of the color-tinted glazes and varnishes, protecting the geometric patterns created, is a technique not confined to marbling. Any wall finish can be overvarnished. The wall must be in good condition.

- Prime the surface, roller on a flat color of your choice and leave it to dry. Divide your wall into geometric areas, stripes, or hoops of horizontal stripes, or be more adventurous with squares or different sizes of interconnecting rectangles. Brush on clear gloss varnish over the shapes you want to define.

- Use one coat for some, and two or three for others so that you build up a pattern of definition. Special paint finishes can work well if they are accentuated in this way.

- You could try using a metallic paint, such as copper, but remember to stir the paint throughout the operation. Varnish on top adds either a slight sheen or a spectacular mirror effect, depending on the number of coats you apply.

YOU WILL NEED:

STAMPING:

- FOAM RUBBER OR
  A CORK TILE
- SNAP-BLADE KNIFE
- PAINTER'S TAPE
- PENCIL
- CARD
- ROLLER OR BRUSH
- LATEX PAINTS
- BRUSHES

STENCILING:

- STENCIL MATERIAL
- TRACING PAPER
- PENCIL/
  WATERPROOF
  MARKER
- STRAIGHTEDGE
- SNAP-BLADE KNIFE
- STENCIL PAINTS
- STENCILING BRUSH
- PAINTER'S TAPE

PROJECT
Stamping and stenciling

Both these techniques are perfect for adding a unique character to your decorative scheme, an individual touch that defines the room as yours and yours alone. Symbols, simple cut-outs, silhouettes, abstract shapes, and caricatures can all be stamped or stenciled as a painted finish, in a continuation of the color scheme or as a complete contrast.

Stamping

Stamping involves rolling color onto an individual raised surface, a stamp, then offsetting the color onto a wall, forming a deliberate pattern or random marks. This technique is best suited to decorative borders and for framing larger areas of color.

Ready-made stamps, in a variety of designs, are widely available from artists suppliers and decorating stores, and generally come in kit form with a selection of paints and a small applicator roller. You can, of course, make your own stamp, drawing a design or image onto cork. Or you can use a foam rubber about 2 in./5 cm thick, and cut around the external shape. The internal details can then be cut out and

You can buy ready-made stamps for creating decorative patterns.

Stenciling is a very effective method of adding decorative borders and paint features to a room. Either buy stencils ready-cut from a home center, or buy the raw materials and make your own.

removed to a depth of 1 in./2.5 cm with a snap-blade knife. Try using your design to form a two-color creative border; use strips of tape to mask the edge of a wall stripe, and paint the stripe in a complementary color to the rest of the wall. Remove the painter's tape when the paint is dry. Roll the second color of your choice onto your stamp, and gently press it onto the wall stripe at regular and equal intervals, starting in the middle.

Latex is the best paint for stamping. Remember to roll color onto your stamp evenly, and try a test-pressing first to remove excess paint. Never dip the stamp directly into the paint.

Stenciling

Stencils, like stamps, are usually associated with edgings and borders, such as chair rail, or smaller decorative panels, but you could use this versatile technique over an entire wall.

You can stencil by brush or sponge, applying paints or crayons onto a surface, through shaped areas cut into a mask that removes areas of background, onto sections defined by painter's tape, or through holes in paper and card. Anything that partially masks your working surface can be referred to as a stencil.

Commercial stencils are available from artists' suppliers, either in a transparent plastic film or flexible waxed card. Waxed card is easier to cut and cheaper. Card is opaque, so consider film if your design is complex, because you can see through it. Trace your design onto the stencils, making a different stencil for each color. To copy from an original, size it by using a photocopier, and either use it as a mask or trace it down, using carbon paper or tracing paper from an artists' shop. To ensure that the colors all fit together in the finished design, you will need to use a

STAMPING

STEP 1 To form a two-color border, begin by masking off a stripe on the wall and paint it a contrasting color.

STEP 2 Complete the stripe with a darker shade to create a sunset effect and then remove the painter's tape.

In this sunny yellow room, stenciling has been used to good effect to enliven the plain colored walls and outline the doorway. It is ideal for decorative framing and for use as a border.

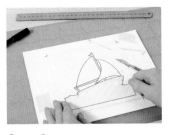

STEP 3 Draw the stamp design on card, cut it out, and use it as a template for cutting out of a cork tile.

STEP 4 Brush or roll the desired color of paint onto the stamp, making sure that it is evenly coated.

STEP 5 Press the stamp onto the colored stripe to create the pattern, recoating with paint as necessary.

STENCILING

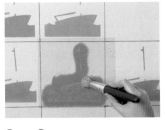

STEP 1 Trace your selected design onto the stencil material, making a separate stencil for each color.

STEP 2 If you want to create a tiled effect, set out a grid with a waterproof marker and straightedge.

STEP 3 Apply the first color, taping the stencil in place and adding the color with a stippling action.

STEP 4 When the first color has dried, add the second in the same way, aligning the stencil very carefully.

registration system to place the stencils one on top of the other on the wall. Either cut an "x" through all the layers when they are correctly positioned, one on each side, or cut notches in the sides. If you are using transparent film, you have the option of lining up the stencils visually.

Stencils can be used to decorate entire walls; for example, a patterned tile effect for a bathroom. The finished area is sealed with an exterior quality varnish to waterproof it. Decide on your tile design and size, draw it onto acetate stencils, one for each color, and mark the tile size as a black outline. Draw the tile size in grid form on the wall using a waterproof marker. Stencil the design onto the tile grid, completing the wall in one color before starting the next. For a large wall a stenciling brush and quick-drying stencil paint is fastest. Redraw over the tile grid with a waterproof marker, using a matching color, to indicate lines of grouting. If required, a border can be added using painter's tape to stencil straight horizontal lines.

YOU WILL NEED:

MURAL:

- **REFERENCE PICTURE**
- **TRACING PAPER**
- **PEN/PENCIL**
- **RULER**
- **PAINT AND BRUSH**

COLLAGE/MONTAGE:

- **IMAGES OF SPORTING STARS**
- **SCISSORS**
- **GLUE**
- **PAINTS/STENCILING MATERIALS**
- **BRUSHES**
- **PAINTER'S TAPE**
- **CLEAR VARNISH**

PROJECT
Murals and one-wall effects

You may find inspiration for the mural in a magazine or newspaper or want to use an old photograph as reference. To draw or paint your chosen design onto a wall you will need to "scale it up" first. Scaling up can be done by drawing a grid of squares over the picture you want to copy. Use a tracing-paper overlay if you don't want to mark the original. Now draw a similar grid of squares onto the wall at the increased size, and copy the design over square by square. You must be accurate when transferring the marks, paying attention to detail where lines leave and enter the squares. If this appears too complex, technology is at hand. Specialized stores that offer a photocopying service can produce an enlarged image over several sheets of paper that can be stuck together. A feeder tray loaded with heavyweight tracing paper will produce an image that you can see through, assisting the positioning. Photocopy specialists may have color machines that can reproduce an overhead visual on film from your image or design. This is then enlarged onto the

MURAL

Often used to decorate children's rooms, you can also consider murals as a way of decorating main living areas, too. By using a grid system to scale up the design, even large expanses of wall can be treated with great success.

STEP 1 To scale up a design for a mural, first of all lay a sheet of tracing paper over the picture that you want to copy.

STEP 2 Draw a grid of lines over the reference picture you have selected. Then draw the same number of squares on the wall to the desired size.

STEP 3 Copy the picture onto the wall square by square, paying attention to where lines leave and enter the squares. Finally, paint in the colors.

wall via an overhead projector, and traced. Any of these methods can help you build up a series of images into a wall mural.

Combination images

Projected images can be used in conjunction with other, simpler paint techniques. A garden mural, for instance, may incorporate trelliswork diagonally masked out by 1 in./2.5 cm tape. Stipple pale blue and white latex into a sky effect, combining your stencil and colorwashing skills, or create an illusion of depth by washing over backgrounds with a thinned-out white latex, so they disappear into the mist. Painting in stronger colors to the foreground base will emphasize this three-dimensional effect.

Collage and montage

More accurately a paper finish, images from posters can be stuck onto painted walls to create a unique mural. Try cutting out figure images of a favored sporting team and positioning them on a grass green wall in playing formation to liven up the decor of a hobby or work room. Tramlines marking out playing areas can be masked out with tape, or backgrounds of

Murals need not be confined to children's rooms; they can make very effective decorative effects in your home's main living areas too. In this case, the floor-to-ceiling garden scheme has even been extended to the window shutters with great success.

spectator enclosures stenciled in, all adding to the graphic effect.

This technique can be used to produce a wide range of interesting and decorative effects. When you have finished make sure that the edges of the images are firmly stuck down, then when the glue has dried, paint over them with one or two coats of varnish in order to seal and protect the work and provide a hard-wearing finish.

COLLAGE AND MONTAGE

STEP 1 Images of sports stars, cut from magazines or posters, can be used to liven up a sports-field mural.

STEP 2 Using red paint, add "mud patches" to your green football field after masking off tramlines with tape.

STEP 3 When the paint has dried, carefully remove the painter's tape to reveal the tramlines.

STEP 4 Paint in the figures of spectators to give the appearance of a football game in progress.

YOU WILL NEED:
- FOAM OR SPONGE
  ROLLER/S
- STRING
- SCISSORS
- BRUSHES/DRY BRUSH
- PAINTS

PROJECT

Geometric art with a roller

Optical art forms that rely on contrast between light and dark areas in a patterned format for their visual effect, or on the interaction of the colored areas themselves, frequently have a hard edge.

A more subtle approach is described here, with a vignetted or damaged edge allowing colors to bleed together, with a broken, less confrontational result.

Painted lines, squares, and rectangular shapes don't necessarily require a hard edge to form a geometric pattern. However, hard-edge paint effects can be achieved by masking the wall with tape into squares or diamond shapes, then stenciling, brushing, or rolling conventionally. The finished wall design may be harsh. If this is the case, a softer, more subtle broken edge is needed. For this you will need a foam or sponge roller sleeve used for creating patterned finishes, often with textured paints—a pile roller, for example, will not do here. Roller sleeves are available in 7 in./18 cm and 9 in./23 cm widths. The larger sleeve will roll out a slightly larger width, so check what you need before selecting.

To create an oval paint effect, try the following. Using a measure, locate and mark the centre point of the sleeve, then tie a length of string around the center, pulling it tight and cutting it close to the knot. Tie two more lengths of string around the sleeve, about ½ in./1.2 cm

VERTICAL AND HORIZONTAL STRIPES

STEP 1 Find the center of the roller sleeve and tie a piece of string tightly around it just at that point.

STEP 2 Tie more lengths of string around the sleeve at the center and ends to create two oval paint surfaces.

STEP 3 Roll a series of stripes onto the wall from floor to ceiling, carefully touching in the edges with a brush.

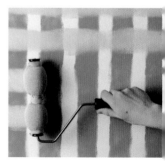

STEP 4 Now apply a different color to the roller. Then add a series of horizontal stripes to the wall.

each side of the center string, securing and trimming off as before. Tie some string around each end of the sleeve, and your roller now has two oval paint surfaces to offer to the wall. Using a conventional short-pile roller for latex, roller the base or background color onto the wall and leave it to dry.

Stripes

To create a stripe effect, run the roller onto the wall from the ceiling to the floor, keeping it upright and parallel with the edge. The stripes go on two at a time, so try to match the gap between them as you repeat the process. Don't overload the sleeve with paint; roll some off onto scrap paper, removing any excess. This will also give you a preview of the effect. To finish off the stripe neatly where it meets the ceiling, cornicing, chair rail, baseboards or floor, use a fairly dry brush to touch the paint in. But be careful—too much paint on the brush will ruin the continuity by making the ends of the stripe stand out.

Hoops

Hoops can be designed using horizontal stripes. Make sure the roller runs parallel to the ceiling or baseboard, however, or the floor will appear to slope. By simply combining stripes and hoops you will create a pattern of squares, but the squares will be quite small, being the gap in the

middle of the sleeve. If this design appeals to you, though, make sure the colors are applied in the right order. The small squares will be in the base or background color, and the dominant color will be the one with which you rollered the stripes and hoops.

Tiles and diamond patterns

Tiles and diamond patterns are created using smaller rollers, such as 4 in./10 cm long-handled radiator rollers with foam or sponge sleeves. Alternatively, you can use enamel paint mini-rollers. Roll out a sequence of 4 in./10 cm squares in level rows, lining up as accurately as you are able. Make sure that you leave a tiny gap all around to represent the colored grout. Slight distortions and the inevitable irregularities are intended to resemble hand-glazed and individually fired tiles.

Rolling on alternate individual squares along the wall diagonal, that is at 45 degrees to the wall edge, creates a diamond pattern on a base color. It will help if you mark the diagonal first, so that the line of the first set of squares is correct. Use a taut piece of string held in position by painter's tape for this.

Because all these paint effects are rollered onto a new or existing wall base color, careful choice of top coat can result in either a positive or negative pattern, since one of the colors will have a tendency to dominate the other.

LEFT: A diamond pattern can be applied to a wall with a small roller. The pattern becomes more interesting if two colors are applied over a base color that is allowed to show through in places.

FAR LEFT: The soft edges of the patterns painted onto this living room wall avoid the harsh effect that generally results from clearly defined geometric patterns used in decoration.

One possibility in geometric art is to use a roller to create a series of colored squares like tiles. By leaving gaps for the base color to show through, you can simulate grouted joints.

Paper finishes

The decorative styling and design features that are built into the modern dwelling differ in visual and practical ways from the basic amenities in the house that our grandparents lived in. A more time-conscious lifestyle, a greater reliance on electronics and labor-saving devices, the need for security, and an eye for fashion have all contributed to visual change in the home. One of the few things that has not altered, nor even updated, is the use of wallpapers as the prime means of decoration. The versatility of the wallcovering, from providing a cozy decorative feel to disguising poor surfaces, ensures its continued popularity.

Designer's notes

Selecting a suitable paper for a room surface, be it in a Victorian row house or a part-finished loft apartment, is an intimidating task. As multiples of choice do not usually simplify selection, it is a good idea to approach the pattern books with a clear concept, otherwise you will face a bewildering array of shapes, colors, patterns, and styles.

Wallpapers offer a wide range of decorative effects, from exuberant floral patterns (right) to subdued stripes (below right) and everything in between. Choose carefully to reflect the style of room you want.

The interior designer today is faced with a huge choice in wallcoverings. Hand-blocked, nineteenth-century designs can be bought, but most wallcoverings are descendants of machine paper runs begun in middle of that century. Factory production techniques, cost-effective paper runs and new color dyes opened up the Victorian marketplace for wallpaper.

Just as paint-makers have introduced period colors to modern paint systems to allow for environmentally friendly historical colors, wallcovering manufacturers have reintroduced popular papers of the past. You can find simple Georgian hand-blocked designs and Regency stripes, as well as the familiar large patterns and floral designs of Victorian taste and the subtle, pale color combinations of the Edwardians.

The Victorian love of wallcoverings often ran to two different papers on a single wall, separated by a chair rail or paper border. Visually breaking up the wall height in this way can be very effective, provided the patterns do not compete for attention. A thin stripe and a bold, heavy stripe together, or a standard small-patterned paper on top of a heavily embossed one can work well. Many embossed wallpapers are specifically

Wallpaper with vertical stripes can be used to create the illusion of greater wall height.

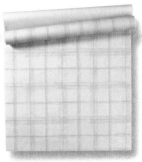

Choose a horizontally striped paper to make walls appear lower and wider.

made to be overpainted, and they are very hard-wearing on the bottom half of the wall. Consider, too, on a half-and-half wall, wood paneling on the bottom half. It does a similar visual job while protecting the wall from knocks, and is a useful asset in entrance halls and corridors. If this combination appeals, try paneling the base of the wall with vertical tongue-and-groove (TGV) woodstrips finished with a horizontal shelf or chair rail. Then paper the top half in a subtle stripe that suggests a repetition of the joins in the TGV paneling below it.

Visual tricks

Unlike wall areas of flat color, patterned wallcoverings use deliberate placement of designs and shapes to attract more, or less, attention. Visual illusion is caused by the arrangements on the surface area, not the area itself. Just as walls painted in different colors will advance or recede, papered surfaces use small patterns to create an illusion of space. Larger, more powerful designs can produce a highly dramatic impact. Place a sample of a delicate small repeat pattern next to a large colorful design, and you will see how this works in practice.

When choosing paper, ask yourself the same questions about room sizes that you would if you were painting the walls. If your ceiling is low, heighten it with a vertical stripe. A hoop or horizontal stripe will appear to lower the ceiling

Consider the design carefully: bold designs always work better on larger wall areas.

Papering the top half of the wall and adding wood paneling to the lower half can be effective.

Use paper to create visual illusions: a large pattern will make a room seem smaller.

If you want the appearance of greater space, choose a small repeat pattern.

and increase the width of the wall. A small patterned paper will increase the feeling of space in a small room. Using bold colorful motifs will make the wall area look smaller and nearer. Vigorous small designs that are good at hiding wall deficiencies are also easier to hang, because mistakes are disguised. A wall that is out of true unfortunately will be emphasized by symmetrical stripes. When hanging more than one paper in a room, consider which paper carries the dominant color, and use this color as a match or contrast for the woodwork paint scheme.

TOP LEFT:
Many wallpaper manufacturers offer ranges that duplicate Georgian, Regency, and Victorian patterns, letting you recreate the original look of rooms in a period property. Although more expensive than standard papers, they are worth considering.

Basic skills: choosing wallcoverings

Be aware of the job you are asking your wallpaper to do, and consider your requirements. Perhaps its purpose is to be purely decorative, or it might have to disguise a badly cracked wall. It might get accidentally wet, in a bathroom area for instance, and so need to be water-resistant, or it may get dirty and you might have to be able to wipe it clean.

BELOW RIGHT: **Lining paper provides a good surface for papering. Machine-printed papers (right) are the most common.**

BELOW:
Hand printing of wallpaper is an expensive process and is used for short runs only.

Certain paper types are intended for specific purposes. Your local decorating supplier or superstore will carry a range of all the popular paper types. But if you want something a little out of the ordinary there are speciality suppliers by offering proprietary papers with period designs, hand-made papers, and hand-blocked or screened untrimmed rolls. If you are in search of a unusual paper, start with the classified advertisements in the back of fashionable home interior magazines. If you are starting with pattern books, simplify the selection process by dividing the papers into two main categories: those that are made to be overpainted and those that are not. Wallcoverings for overpainting will usually have a relief design, with a textured finish like woodchip, or a raised surface pattern like molded or embossed papers. Wallcoverings that have a printed pattern that is not meant to be painted can be further divided, into washable (often ready-pasted) and nonwashable papers.

Liner paper

This is used to line the wall, providing a sound, uniform surface prior to hanging top-quality decorative or heavy-duty embossed papers. It is useful for improving uneven walls and disguising recently repaired surfaces. It comes in various weights and can be easily painted.

Machine-printed paper

Multicolored and available in different weights and qualities, this is the most common wallcovering. "Pulps" are cheap papers where the printing inks sit on the paper surface. "Grounds" are more expensive machine papers where inks sit on a prepared surface, coated with a "ground" of color. These are both produced in bulk and are therefore more economical to buy.

Hand-block printed papers are at the quality end of the market and often recreate historic designs.

Woodchip sandwiches wood shavings between layers of paper to make a cheap relief paper.

Hand-printed paper

Whether block-printed by hand or screen-printed through a frame, this is more expensive because of the labor cost. Large-scale designs and special colors can be incorporated on very short runs.

Woodchip paper

The cheapest of the relief papers, this has wood shavings sealed between two layers of paper. The rough textured finish works well on substandard surfaces, disguising cracks and imperfections, but it difficult to remove. It is sometimes called "oatmeal" paper.

Embossed papers have a raised pattern and they are often supplied white for overpainting.

Flocked paper has a raised pattern formed from velvety fibres bonded to a backing paper.

Embossed paper

This has a relief pattern pressed into it when damp. A pattern is produced by pressure from an embossing roller. Color can be added simultaneously, or the paper produced with a white finish for overpainting. Damp embossing, as opposed to dry, enables the relief to retain its shape better when receiving paste.

Washable papers are protected by a thin plastic film and are often ready-pasted for easy hanging.

Vinyl wallcoverings provide a tough, hard-wearing surface, but they require special adhesive.

Vinyl paper

Also available in heavy-duty, hard-wearing formats, vinyl paper consists of simple designs printed onto plastic or vinyl film with special inks, bonded onto a backing paper. It is tougher than washable paper, but more expensive. Some varieties need a heavy-duty wall adhesive.

This paper can be difficult to remove. If you can lift a corner, it may be possible to peel off the top layer to leave the backing paper behind, which must be stripped in the normal manner. Otherwise, they must be scored to let moisture reach the backing—a laborious task.

Flock paper

Originally an expensive hand-made paper where a blocked adhesive print had wool or silk fibers dusted onto it, it is now available as a more economical machine paper. The elaborate design has a velvety, raised pile on a backing paper, and synthetic fibers are used to produce vinyl papers with a flock pattern effect.

Washable paper

Machine-printed designs with a film of protective, transparent plastic on top, this wallcovering is often found in ready-pasted form.

Tools and equipment

Paperhanging equipment is not expensive or difficult to source, and many items serve other decorating purposes too. Only specialist brushes, a pair of paperhanger's scissors, single seam roller, plumb line, and paste table are unique to this job. The remaining multipurpose items will form a useful part of your household tool kit.

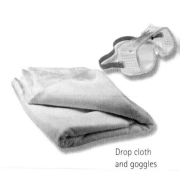

Drop cloth and goggles

If you are painting, a stepladder or extension arms will give you access to ceilings or high wall areas. Paperhanging is a more difficult task. You need to be able to reach the top of the wall safely while carrying the pasted paper roll. For ceiling work you need a platform giving 8 in./20 cm head clearance that allows you to hang an entire length without getting down.

A stable stepladder will suffice for the wall, but a sturdy platform is required for the ceiling. Use two scaffold planks tied together side by side across adjustable trestles, which you can rent. For stairwells, a combination of extension ladder, plank, and adjustable stair or multipurpose ladder will be needed. Cover the area with protective drop cloths, and use a retractable measure, spirit level, and pencil to mark starting points and horizontals. You will also need a plumb line to line up your first roll, a bucket for paste, a stick to stir the paste, and some string stretched across the top of the bucket to wipe off excess paste from

Safety stepladder

Combination or adjustable ladder

Paste table

Adjustable height trestles and scaffold planks

Metal ruler

Water trough for ready-pasted paper

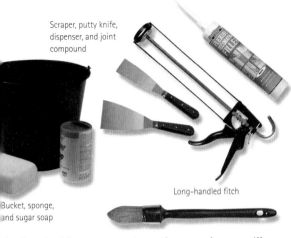

Scraper, putty knife, dispenser, and joint compound

Long-handled fitch

Bucket, sponge, and sugar soap

the brush. If your paper is ready-pasted, you will simply need a wallpaper trough filled with water.

Measuring up

There are several ways to count up the number of rolls you will need to paper a room or wall, and one or two extra factors to consider. Use a roll of paper to measure all around the baseboard, and count up the number of full lengths, ignoring short lengths under windows and above doors. Now measure the room height, to see how many full lengths can be cut from each roll, allowing for pattern wastage. Now divide the first figure by the second, the number of full lengths by the number cut from each roll, to give you the total of rolls required. Part of a roll must be reckoned to be a complete roll. Or you can work out the surface area in square feet (meters) and calculate one standard roll per 16½ft./5m square, or use the standard table for your wall height and length. The chart (see page 257) assumes the roll is 33ft./10.05 m long and 20½ in./52 cm wide. Hand-made papers vary, so check the total surface area of the paper you are using, and adjust as necessary.

The standard chart assumes an average door and window area per room. If you have large windows, reduce the quantity accordingly. Papers with a repeat pattern or design will produce more wastage as you line up, so add the pattern depth to the height of the room when calculating. Very large patterns will need an increase of one roll for every five.

When calculating the number of rolls for a ceiling, use the first method described above, measuring the length of the ceiling and working out how many of these lengths can be cut from a single roll. Using a roll of paper, count up how many lengths will be needed, and calculate the total number of rolls. When the mathematics are completed, buy your rolls at the same time and from the same batch—a batch number is included for this purpose. This is important because slight color variations are possible between batch numbers. Your retailer can also supply the manufacturer's recommended adhesive, which may be heavy duty.

Protective gloves

Wallpaper scissors, plumb line, chalk line, snap-blade knife, and seam roller

Above: Bucket and string, brush, mixing stick, sponge, and measuring pitcher

Stringed bucket, kettle, and hook (for use when working on a ladder) and paperhanging brush

Spirit level

Wallpaper stripper, misting handgun, and all-purpose joint compound

YOU WILL NEED:

- SCORER
- WALL STRIPPER
- HOT WATER
- BUCKET
- BRUSH
- BROAD-BLADED SCRAPER
- PROTECTIVE GOGGLES AND GLOVES

Preparation of surfaces

If your wall surface is not stripped plaster in good condition, you have a job or two to complete before papering. First, place drop cloths on the floor to collect debris and protect the carpet. You may need to strip off old paper, make good parts of the surface, wash down and key a painted surface, or simply seal and stabilize the plaster.

Previously papered finishes

Papered walls have to be taken back to the plaster. Leaving on old paper or vinyl backing leads to an unsatisfactory finish, because it may not bond well to the wall. Over-papering can cause it to lift away and form small air pockets. If the existing paper is vinyl or washable, it won't adhere properly.

Stripping printed wallpapers is time-consuming and messy, but is not difficult. In older properties you may find yourself removing several layers of paper at once, and a great deal of patience is needed. The greatest danger is that when the last layer comes off, it pulls off old plaster with it, so try to avoid digging the scraper into the wall. Be very careful at this point; it may save you a lot of time spent filling and sanding later.

Scrapers

Soaking or stripping with hot water

Hot water will penetrate and soak printed wallpapers, but to speed the job up, mix stripper, in powder or tablet form, with the correct amount of hot water in a bucket. To aid water penetration, run a spiker or scorer over the surface of the paper. Wearing eye protection and gloves, soak the wall, a little at a time or it will start to dry out before the scraper gets to it. Let the solution penetrate fully and then remove the paper gently with a broad-bladed scraper. On stubborn areas you will have to repeat the process. The scraper has a stiff blade, not to be confused with a flexible putty knife, so try not to scratch the wall surface. It's a good idea to clear up the mess as you work, otherwise the paper dries out where it falls and sticks to the drop cloth and your shoes.

SCORING AND SOAKING

STEP 1 To aid penetration of the stripping solution, go over the papered surface with a scorer.

STEP 2 Working on small areas at a time, brush the paper with the solution and allow it to soak in.

STEP 3 Use a scraper to remove the soaked paper from the wall, taking care not to gouge the plaster.

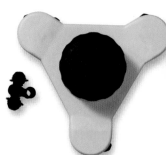

A scorer has sharp wheels that cut through the surface of the paper, improving penetration of water.

You can rent a steam stripper for major jobs.

Dry-stripping vinyls

The two layers making up the paper can be separated fairly easily by carefully lifting the top layer at the corner, and pulling up and away from the wall to free it from the backing paper. It is inadvisable to leave the backing paper on the wall. It doesn't double as lining paper, so you should ideally strip it off the wall using hot water.

Using a steamer

This speeds up the process. Steam penetrates the surface under the pad, lifting the paper away from the wall. You can rent a steam stripper fairly cheaply, but familiarize yourself with the machine before you start. Prime the reservoir with hot, not cold, water, switch it on, and wait for it to come to the boil. Wear protective gloves, a long-sleeved shirt, and glasses or goggles. Position the steam pad on your starting point. Hold it for about half a minute, then move along the wall to the next position while scraping off the steamed paper. The best results will be achieved by scraping with your writing hand and holding the steamer pad in your other hand.

Wall furniture

Permanent wall furniture, such as a radiator, is best removed, if possible. Isolate the radiator from the water supply at the valves, drain the water into a shallow bowl and lift it off the wall supports. If this is not possible, however, a long-handled radiator roller can be used to press the pasted paper into the problem area. Electric switches and outlets must be isolated from the supply before the faceplate screws are loosened, if this is necessary to strip away the paper behind. Curtain rails can be left in place, and pelmets need be removed only if they interfere with paperhanging around the window area.

A steam stripper provides an effective means of stripping wallpaper quickly. With practice, you can hold the pad to steam one area of the wall while scraping paper from a previously treated area. Remember that steam can scald you, so take care and wear protective clothing.

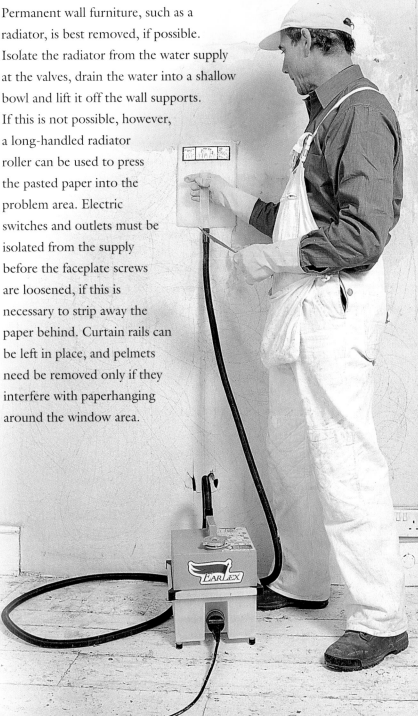

YOU WILL NEED:
REPAIRING CRACKS
AND HOLES:
- **WATERCOLOR FELT-
  TIP PEN**
- **SCRAPER**
- **SMALL PAINT BRUSH**
- **DUSTING BRUSH**
- **WATER**
- **JOINT COMPOUND
  AND PUTTY KNIFE**
- **ABRASIVE PAPER**
- **SANDING BLOCK**

A scraper, putty knife, a
brush, joint compound
and gloves

Safety goggles

Repairing walls

Once the wall is back to the plaster, inspect the surface. Look out for cracks, holes, and deep scratches in the plaster surface as a result of the stripping, or because removal of the paper has revealed previous damage. All these imperfections will have to be made good. Mark them all clearly as you find them using a watercolor fiber-tip pen. To prepare the crack for filling, carefully rake it out with a scraper blade, so that no loose debris remains, and clean the damaged area with a dusting brush. Using a small paintbrush, dampen the entire area with water so that your joint compound bonds with the wall plaster, and ensures that the wall does not draw too much water out of the filler too quickly, causing it to shrink and fall out.

Mix up your compound, using a proprietary "decorator's pack." Following the makers' directions, try to achieve a smooth, but firm, consistency. Don't mix up too much at once; the makers claim a workable time of one hour, but this is less on a hot day. Fill the damaged area using a flexible putty knife, overlapping the joint edges slightly and leaving the compound raised proud of the surface. This allows for shrinkage when drying, and for sanding back. Make sure the compound is

completely dry before you abrade the surface. Deep cracks will be dry on the surface long before they are dry all the way through. Sand with your choice of abrasive until the area is uniformly smooth and flush with the wall surface.

Decorator's packs and other general-purpose joint compounds are suitable for all peripheral wall damage. Deeper crevices can be filled if they are "layered." Apply a little at a time and leave each "layer" to dry. Don't attempt to save time and try to fill a deep crevice all in one go. The compound will be unable to bond properly, and will slide out, forming a bulge.

Larger cracks and holes are best filled with plaster. You can buy small amounts (11 lb./5 kg) of multifinish from your local builders' merchant. Don't assume plaster is like joint compound and apply it the same way. Plaster is stronger and must be applied with a trowel, not a putty knife. Plaster surfaces are not meant to be sanded, either, so a flush, smooth finish must be your aim. Old wall surfaces will be very dry. If you apply plaster without a sealer, the wall will draw all the water out of the mix and the plaster will fall out. Splash a solution of one part PVA diluted with three parts water liberally in and around the damaged area, and leave it to dry, preferably overnight. Repeat this just prior to

REPAIRING CRACKS AND HOLES

STEP 1 Go over the wall looking for cracks and other damage. Mark them all so that you don't miss any.

STEP 2 Use the blade of a scraper to rake out all the loose debris and undercut cracks slightly.

STEP 3 After raking out, use a brush to remove any remaining dust from the cracks.

STEP 4 Dampen with water to prevent the joint compound from drying too quickly.

STEP 5 Fill the cracks, applying the joint compound with a flexible-bladed putty knife. Press the compound well into the cracks and leave it slightly proud of the surrounding surface. Leave plenty of time for it to dry.

STEP 6 When the compound has dried, sand it flush with the surrounding surface using abrasive paper wrapped around a sanding block. You may need to add a little more compound here and there.

PLASTER FINISHES

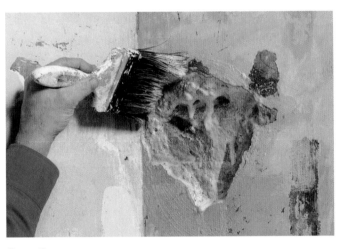

STEP 1 Large areas of damage are best repaired with plaster, and you can buy special packs for the purpose. First treat the area with a PVA solution to seal it and help provide a good bond with the new plaster.

STEP 2 Mix the plaster with water and trowel it into the hole. Use the trowel to strike it off flush with the surrounding surface, or leave it just below the surface and finish off with regular compound.

plastering. Now you have sealed the wall, the area is "keyed" and the plaster will bond better. Use a trowel to smooth the surface flush. If you are not confident you can do this, leave the plaster just shy of the top surface, and finish the job with joint compound, which you can sand back when dry.

Cracks caused by movement around doors, or where baseboards meet the wall, particularly on the stairs, should be filled with a joint compound. These are available in ready-mixed tubes and are applied with a dispensing gun.

Finally, as with all home decorating projects, it is important to consider the health and safety aspects. Remember that sanding filler will produce a lot of dust, so protect adjacent surfaces with drop cloths and wear old clothes. Wearing a dust mask and a pair of protective goggles is a good idea, too, in order to avoid irritating or damaging your eyes while you are working.

YOU WILL NEED:

PLASTER FINISHES:
- DILUTED PVA SOLUTION
- TROWEL
- PLASTER
- WATER
- JOINT COMPOUND OR SPACKLING COMPOUND
- DUST MASK AND PROTECTIVE GOGGLES

YOU WILL NEED:

WASHING/SEALING:

- **SUGAR SOAP SOLUTION**
- **SPONGE**
- **RUBBER GLOVES**
- **BRUSH**
- **BUCKET**
- **PVA SOLUTION**

APPLYING SIZE:

- **SIZE OR WALLPAPER PASTE**
- **WATER**
- **BRUSH**
- **BUCKET**

Washing, sealing, stabilizing, and sizing

The wall surface should be cleaned thoroughly, using a solution of sugar soap and hot water. Wearing gloves, sponge down the wall. Rinse it with clean water and let it dry overnight.

Old wall stains can eventually show through the wallpaper, so they need to be sealed with a coat of oil-based primer to stop them ruining your finish. If the stains are a result of an old (and cured) damp problem, oil-based primer or a damp sealant will prevent further stains from appearing. However, if the patch is still damp to the touch, or you suspect it is still active, investigate the cause of the trouble before proceeding. Don't attempt to seal over it, and don't ignore it. Consult a professional builder.

Stabilizing the surface results in an equal amount of suction on all parts of the wall, preventing problems caused by shrinkage due to patchy, uneven drying. Walls that are very dry, and therefore very porous, should have a thin coat of PVA adhesive diluted with water. Mix this up one part to five. When it has dried, run the palm of your hand over the surface. If white powder comes off onto your palm, the wall needs a second coat.

When the wall is ready, apply a size to the surface. A coating of size will let you manipulate the paper on the wall, enabling you to slide it carefully into position and line up the pattern. Without size, the paper will stick to the wall immediately, and moving it on the surface will be difficult, often resulting in a tear. If you are working on a lined wall, size the lining paper just as you would a bare wall, before you wallpaper over it. A coat of thinned-down wallpaper paste can be used instead of size.

Wall defects

While damp areas that are still active demand professional advice, areas of mold or fungus caused by moisture can be cleaned using a fungicidal wash. Investigate the cause of the moisture before proceeding. It is most likely to be poor or nonexistent ventilation. If mold containing live spores is present on the underside of the paper you are stripping, you must take precautions to stop the mold infecting the new finish. Wrap the old paper up and discard it immediately, or preferably, burn it.

Condensation encourages the growth of mold, particularly in older properties not built for today's central heating systems. Make sure you have adequate ventilation and air circulation. It is interesting that wall paints that "breathe," like distemper, are becoming popular again in

WASHING AND SEALING

STEP 1 Wash the wall thoroughly using a solution of sugar soap and hot water. Rinse it well and let it dry completely.

STEP 2 Treat the wall with a PVA solution to stabilize the surface and reduce the amount of suction, which could cause shrinkage problems.

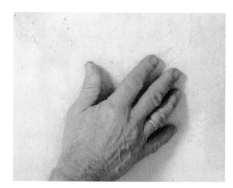

STEP 3 When dry, run the palm of your hand over the wall. If it becomes coated in white powder, a second stabilizing coat will be required.

older houses because they do not trap damp below the wall surface.

Fluffy white deposits on plastered walls are the result of soluble salts coming to the surface as the wall dries out. Called efflorescence, this surface problem can simply be brushed away, but it must be done with a dry brush. If you use water, the salt will dissolve, become reabsorbed into the wall and the problem will reappear later. If the wall suffers from flaking paint, either the finish cannot adhere to the surface because of under-preparation, or a damp area has been painted over. Once the cause of the damp has been determined, the wall area must be properly sealed.

Water penetration causes brown stains on ceilings and walls. They remain even when the cause of the problem has been dealt with.

They may show through paintwork and light-colored papers, so cover with an oil-based paint to seal them before papering.

APPLYING SIZE

STEP 1 Sizing the wall will make it easier to slide the paper into position. Mix the powder with water.

STEP 2 Brush the size onto the wall, making sure you cover it completely, and leave to dry.

Damp patches that remain active must be investigated and dealt with. Seek professional advice; don't try to cover up the problem, as this may make it worse.

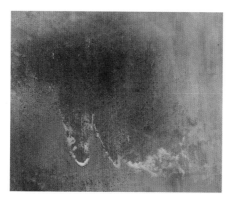

Efflorescence is caused by salts within the brickwork being carried to the surface as the wall dries. Dry brushing should remove it. Don't try to wash it off.

Flaking paint occurs because it has been applied over a dusty, damp, or incompatible surface. It should be scraped off and the surface sealed before proceeding.

Condensation produces damp patches on walls and encourages mold growth. Improved ventilation should provide a cure. Treat mold with fungicide.

Staining is caused by damp penetration and the cause must be found and cured before proceeding. Treat stains with an oil-based paint to prevent bleed-through.

Lining the walls

If the surface is still not ideal for hanging the patterned wallcovering directly onto it, you need to line the wall. Use a plain paper roll, about 1⅜ in./3.5 cm wider than the standard patterned roll. It is hung in the same way as the final paper.

Liner paper is available in several weights, either as an uncoated pulp or with a smooth finish. It helps to disguise wall imperfections, and some particularly rough areas can be lined twice. If you do this, make sure the seams are not in the same place, or hang the first paper vertically and the second horizontally. It is better to butt-join lengths at a room corner, rather than take a narrow strip the height of the room around the corner. If the walls are not square, there will be a slight, uneven gap where the vertical lengths don't quite meet. Disguise this by smoothing a length of spackling compound into the corner.

You will need to take a narrow strip around a chimney breast. The breast face should be lined in the opposite way to the walls; if the room is lined vertically, then line the breast face horizontally. The walls may not be square, so line horizontally first and wrap the paper around the corner each time. The next vertical length sits on top of these overlaps, and you need to cut the paper from ceiling to floor 1½ in./3.8 cm from the edge, parallel with the corner line. Use a snap-blade knife and a steel ruler for this. Remove the overlaps after peeling back along the length, so that you do not have a double weight

LINING WALLS

Lining a wall: Adding a liner paper to a wall before papering is a good way of improving the surface and is essential when hanging high-quality papers. It may be necessary to hang two layers of liner paper to disguise surface imperfections.

STEP 1 Hang liner paper horizontally so that the seams don't coincide with those of the wallpaper.

STEP 2 When doubling up layers, fold back the edges and tear them off later to prevent ridges.

STEP 3 Butt-join lengths of paper at internal corners. If they don't quite meet, add spackling compound.

Lining a chimney breast: Chimney breasts need treating slightly differently from the rest of the room because of the narrow reveals on each side. Horizontal lengths of paper should be hung on the face of the breast and wrapped around over the reveals and onto the adjacent walls.

STEP 1 Cut paper long enough to span the breast, cover the reveals and lap onto the adjacent walls.

STEP 2 Overlap the next vertical length and cut down through both layers of paper, removing the waste.

STEP 3 Brush the edges of the paper down and they will meet in a perfectly butted seam.

of paper, and smooth the vertical length back into position with the paperhanger's brush, to achieve a butt join. Cross-lining is not mandatory.

PREPARING TO HANG

If lining a wall horizontally, start at the top; the widths won't divide into the wall height exactly and pasting on specially cut widths is easier at the bottom.

STEP 1 With a steel tape measure and a waterproof pen mark the paste table in 12 in./30 cm increments. This will speed measuring the paper.

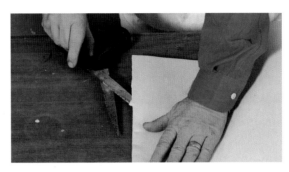

STEP 2 Allow for a slight overlap of paper on each length. Fold the paper and use the blade of your scissors to slice along the fold.

STEP 3 Lay the paper on the table and paste it, working out from the center. Overlap the edges of the table slightly to keep the table free of paste.

STEP 4 As you paste, gently fold the paper back on itself in concertina fashion to make the length manageable for hanging.

Using the paste table

- Set up your paste table in the center of the room.
- Paper lengths will be longer than the table, so make sure you have enough space at the ends.
- Keep your buckets of paste and water under the table where they can't be accidentally kicked over.
- The paste table will double as a measure if you mark it out along the edge. Use a waterproof pen so that you don't wash the measurements off. Mark in increments of 12 in./30 cm.
- Keep the paper square on the table. This reduces the risk of inaccurate cutting when using the edge measure.

- Cut the liner paper, leaving a small overlap at each end for final trimming on the wall.
- Apply the paste evenly, starting at the center of the paper and working outward.
- Keep the table clean. Wash it down with a warm wet sponge and dry it with a clean cloth after pasting each length.

YOU WILL NEED:
- LINER PAPER
- WALLPAPER
- PENCIL
- STRAIGHTEDGE
- SCISSORS
- PASTE TABLE
- PASTE AND BUCKET
- DAMP CLOTH/ SPONGE
- PLUMB LINE
- BRUSH
- MEASURING TAPE
- SEAM ROLLER
- SHARP KNIFE
- SCREWDRIVER
- VERTICAL SPIRIT LEVEL

PROJECT
Papering walls

The key to successful paperhanging involves preparation, so that the bare surface provides uniform suction and manipulation (the final positioning of the paper on the wall) is easier. Never skimp on the preparation, because ultimately it will affect the final result, and although you have an expensive wallpaper, you may not have an expensive-looking finish.

Cutting

First, check the uniform color of the rolls of paper as variations can occur within the same batch numbers. Then, using the measuring guide you marked on the table when lining, cut the lengths required. Add on a small amount top and bottom for trimming in position. Cutting a repeat pattern to length is more difficult, because you have to match up the patterned design. Mark your cutting lines in pencil on the face of the paper, using a long straightedge as a guide.

Pasting and folding

Paste should be mixed according to the maker's directions, but do ensure it is not too thin, otherwise, sliding the paper on the wall during precise positioning becomes very difficult. Line up the paper's edge with the paste table edge, and apply paste by brushing from the middle to the edges, which reduces the possibility of paste contaminating the face of the paper. If paste does accidentally meet the patterned face, wipe it off immediately with a damp cloth or sponge.

As you finish pasting an end, fold it over on itself as if you were starting a concertina, and carry on pasting the rest of the length. Fold the remainder to complete the concertina. Set the paper aside to let it absorb the paste before attempting to hang it. The manufacturer's data sheet will tell you how long the soaking time is for your paper, which is usually ten to fifteen minutes. It's a good idea to write down the length number and the hanging time, and leave this next to the concertina, ensuring it goes onto the wall at the right time and in the right order.

Hanging the paper

The most important length of paper is the first length you hang. It must be plumb vertical and in the correct place in the room. If the room has

WORKING WITH REPEAT PATTERNS

STEP 1 When working with a repeat pattern, cut one piece to length and match others to it.

STEP 2 Line up the lengths of paper on the table and check that the pattern will match.

STEP 3 Cut each length with the scissors, allowing the repeat pattern height at top and bottom.

STEP 4 Pasted paper should be folded concertina fashion, pasted face to pasted face.

a chimney breast, any repeat patterned paper must be centered on it, so you need to hang your first length here. If not, start by dropping a plumb line to one side of the main window and work away from the major source of light. Starting with the first length centered on the chimney breast requires accurate measuring to each side. Subtract the width of the paper from the width of the breast, and halve the figure. Measure in this amount from either edge, and mark by drawing along a vertical spirit level. Line up the first piece using this guide, and paper the entire breast first.

To start at the window, drop a plumb line from ceiling to floor. If the frame is plumb vertical, start at the frame. If it is not, drop a line just less than the width of the paper away from the frame, mark the line at several points with a pen, and join up the marks using a straightedge. You will need to paper three sides into the last corner, return to your starting point and paper in the other direction to finally join in the window corner. This corner will best disguise a non-matching join, as the wall contains the major source of light.

Check to see whether the pattern is designed to be hung in a specific direction. Some designs appear to be truly abstract, but an initial

A PLUMB VERTICAL LINE

STEP 1 Use a plumb line to establish a perfectly vertical guideline for hanging the first length of paper.

STEP 2 Carefully align the edge of the first length with the guideline. This is essential for a good job.

impression can sometimes be wrong. When such patterns are hung as a complete wall, you may discover there is a definite top, and bottom, to the image. Time taken getting the first length plumb vertical, the pattern centered satisfactorily over the wall depth and trimmed equally at both ends, will be well spent because the following lengths can be positioned more easily.

When hanging the paper, begin at the top of the wall, brushing it into place with the paperhanger's brush and gradually unfolding as you go. Make sure that the first drop is aligned perfectly with the guideline, as this will affect the position of all subsequent drops.

FITTING THE PAPER

STEP 3 Work down the wall, unfolding the paper and brushing it flat to remove air bubbles.

STEP 4 At the ceiling, crease the paper into the angle with the scissors, then cut along the crease.

STEP 5 Make cuts in the paper so that it can be fitted around, for example, crown moldings.

STEP 6 Use a seam roller to flatten any seams that have lifted, adding more paste if necessary.

AROUND A CROWN MOLDING

STEP 1 At the corner of a crown molding, make a diagonal release cut and paste the paper onto the wall around the frame.

STEP 2 Crease the paper with the scissors, pull it away slightly, and trim along the crease to fit. Finally, brush it into place.

Wall obstacles

Hanging lengths against a straight wall is simple, so long as your first length provides a good template. Papering around obstacles such as window or door crown moldings involves cutting a diagonal into the corner where the molding meets the wall. Now crease a cutting line along the frame edges with the scissor points. Be sure to take the weight of the excess paper when you do this or it will tear. Pull the paper away from the frame edge, and cut carefully along your crease line. Paperhanger's scissors are the best tool for this, but if you use a snap-blade knife, make sure the blade is sharp. You must keep it clean because paste drying on the blade will

blunt it, and the paper will consequently tear. The snap-blade knife is very useful for the intricate detail to either side of the mantelpiece, however. Drop the paper from the ceiling, and let it drape over the front of the fireplace. Using the paperhanger's brush, crease the paper into the right-angled join along the mantelpiece and trim to each corner. You will need to support the weight of the paper again, and smooth the side papers into position, making a series of cuts into the side molding details. Crease a cutting line around the moldings and the sides, and trim the sides with scissors. You may find the sharp knife is better for cutting around the edges of the detailed moldings.

Electrical fittings

To paper over a square surface fitting, indent the paper with a finger to mark the edges. Cut a hole in the center, cut diagonally toward all four corners, and bend back the paper to expose the fitting. Trim the paper sufficiently so that it will fit neatly under the faceplate, and isolate the fitting from the supply. Loosen the two screws and push the paper underneath. Or, you can trim the paper to fit flush with the edges of the fitting. This will be your preferred method if the faceplate is not flush. Wipe any excess paste off the electrical fitting with a dry cloth.

AROUND A MANTELPIECE

STEP 1 At a mantelpiece, crease the paper into the angle with the wall and cut it to size.

STEP 2 At the sides, make a release cut in the corner and brush the paper onto the wall.

STEP 3 Use the scissors to make a series of release cuts around the detail of the fireplace surround.

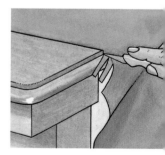

STEP 4 Brush the paper into place, removing the slivers of paper with a sharp knife.

AROUND A LIGHT SWITCH

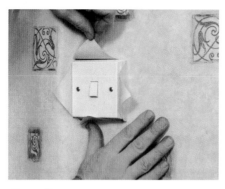

STEP 1 When you encounter a light switch, drape the paper over the top and make diagonal release cuts out from the center.

STEP 2 Fold back the paper flaps and brush the paper flat onto the wall around the switch. Turn off the power and remove the faceplate.

STEP 3 Slacken the mounting-box screws and pull the box out slightly. Trim the flaps and brush them under the box. Replace the unit.

Pasting the wall

Some papers are made to be hung dry, directly from the roll, onto a pasted wall surface. Mix up your paste, following the directions, and use a pasting brush to coat the wall. Paste an area slightly wider than the roll width, and smooth it out evenly. Hang the paper from the roll or, if you prefer, cut it to length and match the pattern in the usual way first. A fitch is useful to re-paste seams if you hang by this method.

Prepasted papers

Vinyl or wipeable papers normally come ready-pasted. There is a dried coating of paste already on the back of the paper. The manufacturer's recommended soaking time is given with the roll. A water trough, usually supplied with the rolls, is used to soak the paper, paste side out, which is then positioned on the wall. Many patterns can be hung directly from the trough if it is placed at the baseboard below the intended position, and moved around the room as hanging progresses. You still need the paste table, though, and when you are cutting and matching large designs, you may prefer to place the water trough at the side of the table. This lets you check the pliability of the soaked length before hanging by folding

inward in conventional concertina style on the table. When the paper is ready, carry it to the wall as normal.

It is fine to apply your own paste to ready-pasted papers, treating them as conventional machine-printed papers. Many decorators are of the opinion that self-pasting gives better control of the paper, especially during manipulation on the wall, and the data sheet supplied with the roll may acknowledge this.

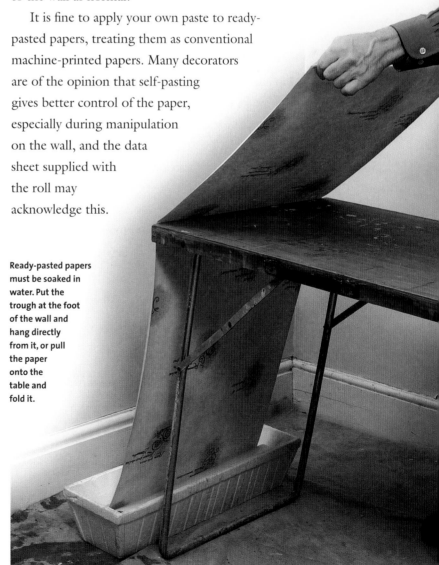

Ready-pasted papers must be soaked in water. Put the trough at the foot of the wall and hang directly from it, or pull the paper onto the table and fold it.

YOU WILL NEED:
PAPERING:
- **MATERIALS AS FOR PAPERING WALLS (PAGE 92)**
- **PLATFORM**
- **SCAFFOLD BOARDS**
- **ADJUSTABLE TRESTLES AND STOOLS**
- **CHALKED STRINGLINE**

AROUND ROSE:
- **SCREWDRIVER**
- **SCISSORS**
- **SHARP KNIFE**
- **CLOTH**

Papering a ceiling

Don't avoid this job just because it looks difficult; in many ways a ceiling presents fewer problems than a wall does, because there are no radiators, electrical outlets, or frames; a ceiling rose will probably be the only complication. Remember that a good working platform is essential and, if it's your first time, make sure you have a helper.

The pasting, folding, and carrying technique used to position and brush paper onto a ceiling is the same as that used when covering a wall. Make sure that you have safe access to the ceiling without having to stretch or to continually move ladders.

Decide which direction you are going to paper in. You may think it's easier to paper the shorter ceiling width, but if there are two of you, it will be quicker to start with the longer lengths. Professional decorators will paper parallel to the window wall, or if there is more than one window, parallel to the bigger light source. This means that they will start at the window wall and paper away from the light.

Starting the job

Set up your working height platform underneath the proposed first length. Never try to over-reach on a stepladder. The best arrangement is two scaffold boards tied into position across two adjustable trestles, with a step-up stool at each end. This arrangement gives access to the complete paper length as it is unfolded along the ceiling, and is stable and safe to use. The cornice or angle on the window wall will not give an accurate line for your first length, so measure out from each end of the wall 20 in./50 cm, and join these two points with a chalk line. This will give you your starting line, with a small overlap onto the window wall for trimming off. Position the pasted concertina at the starting point, allowing for a small wall overlap, tightly against the marked line so that each loop opens out as the length is pasted across the ceiling. Make sure each loop is brushed firmly into the correct place before releasing the next. A second pair of hands to hold the pasted concertina simplifies matters

PAPERING THE CEILING

STEP 1 Use a chalked stringline to snap a guideline onto the ceiling for hanging the first length.

STEP 2 Have your assistant hold the concertina of paper while you align its edge with the guideline.

STEP 3 Work across the ceiling, one of you opening out the paper while the other brushes it into place.

THE CEILING ROSE

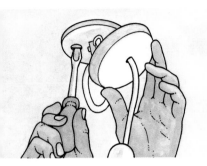

STEP 1 Before you begin papering, turn off the power, remove the light fitting cover, and release the baseplate from the ceiling.

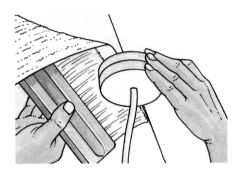

STEP 2 Let the light fitting hang on its cord and brush the paper onto the ceiling behind it. Then replace the light fitting.

STEP 3 If the fitting ends up in the middle of a length of paper, work up to it and make a small cut in the paper at the center of the fitting.

STEP 4 Carefully pull the cord and bulb holder through the hole. Brush the remainder of the length into place.

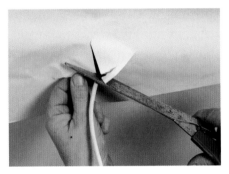

STEP 5 Make a series of release cuts out from the hole to the edge of the light fitting. Brush the paper tightly into the angle.

STEP 6 Finally, use a sharp knife to trim off the slivers of paper to leave a neat finish. Clean any paste off the fitting with a damp cloth.

considerably. If you are working alone, support the folds on an unopened roll of paper. Crease and trim the length and width to the cornice or wall angle. This first length will be a difficult, time-consuming job, but having completed it, a marker will have been established on the ceiling, and the remaining lengths will be easier.

The ceiling light fitting

By measuring out from the window wall to the center of the light fitting, you can arrange the paper lengths so that a seam join runs through the middle. A larger overlap on the window wall may result, but it will simplify things in the center of the room. Either make small cuts in the edge of the paper, starting from the center of the fitting, to allow a cutting line to be marked with the point

of the scissors and then trimmed off, or, if possible, remove the fitting. Switch off the power if you do this, unscrew the cover, and remove the retaining screws. The fitting can be left to hang from the wire for a few minutes while the papers are smoothed into position and the screw holes marked with a point. Replace the screws and put back the cover. Should you reach the fitting with the middle of a length, mark the position on the paper where the wire will drop, and cut a small hole, supporting the paper as you do it. Pull the wire through and brush the remainder of the length into position. Make a series of outward scissor cuts starting at the center of the fitting, to allow a cutting line to be marked at its circumference. Exchange your scissors for a snap-blade knife and trim. Wipe off any surplus paste.

Papering problem areas

Whether your problem area is a simple light switch or electrical outlet, or an intimidating stairwell where the drop is the height of the house, there is a technique to help you. Even difficult jobs are simplified if you approach them in the right way. However, safety must always be paramount when using platforms, so make sure they are quite safe.

Stairwells and landing areas

The biggest problem areas in your house will be the stairwell and landing, particularly in older properties where the stairwell drop is the entire depth of the house. There are no more difficulties here than you have already encountered elsewhere, apart from the length of drop. A second pair of hands is needed to support the pasted concertina, or it will tear under its own weight as you hang it from the top. The real problem is one of access to the walls at a convenient working height. However, small, interlocking scaffold towers that will fit a stairwell are available for rent. As an alternative you can combine ladder, stepladder, combination (multipurpose) steps, and trestles with scaffold planks to let you complete the job safely. Set up your platform, ensuring it is safe. Remove all stair carpets and underlays, and clear the area of obstacles. If the ladder feet rest on a stair tread, nail or screw a cleat support in place to prevent the feet from moving, and tie a soft cloth around both head ends where they contact the wall, to prevent marks. Double up scaffold boards to minimize sagging, and tie them to each other and to the supporting ladders or steps.

Survey the task ahead. Identify the edge of the longest length you have to hang and drop a vertical plumb line from the ceiling to the baseboard. Make a mark with a pen and a straightedge to make a guide for the first length.

RIGHT: **Make a dog-leg platform from two sets of boards supported on ladders and a suitable low platform. Tie everything securely.**

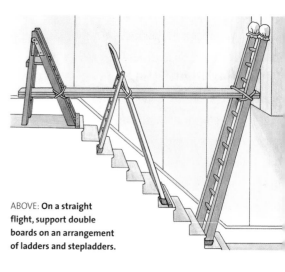

ABOVE: **On a straight flight, support double boards on an arrangement of ladders and stepladders.**

Begin by marking a vertical guideline on the wall with the aid of your plumbline.

Remember to allow for the fact that each drop will have a long edge and a short edge.

Make small triangular cuts in the paper to fit it neatly against a curved baseboard.

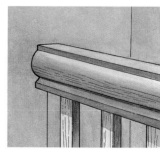

Make a vertical cut beneath a banister, shape the paper around the rail, and paste to the wall.

This length must be correctly positioned because it will be a template for what follows. When you calculate a drop onto stairs, remember that the paper has two edges of different lengths; measure the longer edge, or the paper will come up short. It is better to paper up the stairs, not down, as a mistake in calculation can be re-sized farther up the wall. It can even be the next length if you are not matching a pattern and the stair baseboard rises consistently.

There are some difficulties with stairwells. For example, the baseboard and the strings are likely to be shaped, and the banister rail on top of the balustrade may be joined to the wall on the landing. If your baseboard curves around at the top of the stairs, then the paper must curve as well. Make a series of triangular cuts butting up to the baseboard, and smooth the paper around the corner. If the banister does not butt to the wall at the edge of a paper length, cut from the bottom of the length parallel with the side so that the two strips can fit each side. Make a series of small cuts from your initial slit outward, shape the two pieces around the banister with the paperhanger's brush and trim with the scissors.

Arches

It is not really possible to match a pattern into an arch. Papering the inside of the arch is done in two sections, one from each end with a straight butt join at the arch center. The best approach is

When papering an arch, cut two strips of paper that will meet in the middle; otherwise the pattern will be upside-down on one side.

to take the patterned paper from the face wall around the corner into the arch, trimming to leave about 1 in./2.5 cm overlap. A sequence of small triangular cuts in the paper edge will let you wrap around the curve. Paper the inside of the curve with a one-piece heavyweight liner paper. Cut it flush to the facing wall. Paint the lining paper in a matching or opposite color.

Take a small margin of paper from the face wall onto the arch, then paper the arch itself.

YOU WILL NEED:
- TAPE MEASURE
- PENCIL
- SPIRIT LEVEL
- BORDER DESIGN
- PASTE (UNLESS SELF-ADHESIVE)
- BRUSH
- STEEL RULE
- SNAP-BLADE KNIFE

PROJECT
Special effects

Use a matching or contrasting (by color or pattern design) border strip, as a decorative dividing line between different papers, as a paper chair rail on a half-and-half wall, as an outline to emphasize a window recess or as a simple mitered frame around a serving hatch to add an attractive and rather stylish feature to your home.

Patterned borders

Borders can dramatically change the look of your newly refurbished room. Small patterned wallpapers with an overall base color can have the effect of that color emphasized or muted by a border. Small rooms that need plain, pale walls to make them appear larger can still have a decorative effect in miniature. Apart from the obvious color and decorative qualities, placing a border or frieze at the ceiling/wall junction will appear to lower the ceiling, and bordering a window will make it look larger.

To save expensive mistakes, try positioning the border with painter's tape first, so that you can study the effect. When you have determined your border position and height, use a spirit level and pencil to draw a line around the room.

Take care to maintain a dead level; nothing looks worse than a sloping border. If the ceiling or baseboard has a pronounced slope, don't add a border anywhere nearby, as this will emphasize the slope even more.

Wallpaper manufacturers produce some border designs to complement a range of their own papers, and you can select both at the same time. There are several widths available, and two application methods. One involves using backing paste like conventional wallpaper, and the other is self-adhesive. You simply peel off the backing paper to stick down the self-adhesive type. But once laid it is not designed to be repositioned.

Printed borders applied using wallpaper paste can be manipulated on the wall just as wallpapers can, but beware of paste getting onto a nonwipeable paper because it can stain the face. You can always wipe clean water-resistant coverings with ease, but you require a special adhesive, available from your decorating store, to stick the border onto vinyl or wipeable finishes. In all instances, if you use a seam or small roller to flatten the border onto the surface, protect both border and existing paper with a tear sheet of liner paper, and roll on top of that.

Patterned borders can enliven newly papered walls.

PATTERNED BORDER

STEP 1 Mark the position of the border, using a tape measure and pencil. Make light marks only.

STEP 2 Using a spirit level, mark out a continuous horizontal or vertical guideline for the border.

STEP 3 Apply paste to the border, folding it concertina fashion as for normal wallpaper.

STEP 4 Brush the border onto the papered surface, aligning it carefully with the pencil guideline.

MITERED CORNER

STEP 1 Paste on the horizontal and vertical borders so that they overlap at a right angle.

STEP 2 Using a steel rule and sharp knife, make a diagonal cut down through both border strips.

STEP 3 Pull back the ends and remove the offcuts. Finally, brush the ends back for a neat mitered seam.

Mitered corners

These are simple, provided your border angles are square. Even if the window you are outlining is slightly out of true, measure and draw a positioning line in pencil that has 90-degree corners; do not follow the window shape. Paste up the top horizontal border strip first, followed by either vertical, adding on 2 in./5 cm or so at each end. Overlap the lengths at 90 degrees, then draw a guide line from corner to corner, using the 45-degree angle of a set square. Cut through both strips together with a sharp snap-blade knife, and carefully peel away and discard the waste pieces.

Matching a bold, obvious pattern at each angled join will not be possible, so you could consider smaller, intricate or more abstract designs that will serve to camouflage rather than to emphasize any discrepancies.

Paper dividers

Some of these do the same job as a chair rail and can be used for a purely decorative effect, acting as a border to separate two different designs or styles of paper, or they can have an important function. Running a paper divider up the stairwell at the same height as the banister rail lets you replace the bottom section of paper (and the border), while leaving the top part intact. As

the bottom of the wall is more likely to suffer human traffic damage, and the top section is the one that causes all the difficulties, this can save much time and money. In a divided room, hang the two different papers together, completing the bottom paper run first, butting up to the guiding line around the room. Overlap the top paper by the exact width of the border. Now hang the border on top, using the paper join as a base guideline. However, if the lower part of the wall is to be covered by a vinyl paper, you will need to overlap this onto the upper paper, and use the join as a top guideline. The reason for this contradiction is that ordinary paste is not an effective adhesive on vinyl, and when running the border you must use border or overlap adhesive.

Patterned borders have many uses, but they can be particularly effective when used to create a chair rail effect. In this case, they match the height of the banister.

Wood, brick, and tile finishes

Repainting existing wood finishes and hanging a new paper on the walls of a room are cosmetic changes, and, although a facelift results, the area is not radically altered. Removing the plaster to reveal and emphasize original brickwork, using hand-made tiles or wood panels on complete or half-and-half walls, or building paneled shelving and storage into a recess, have a much more far-reaching effect. The nature and "feel" of the room are changed, as different materials have been brought together in exciting new combinations.

Designer's notes

Changing the feel of a room space by using new materials, building in a purpose-designed storage solution, or uncovering or paneling wall areas require you to accurately assess your constructional capabilities. As always, a scale drawing of the scheme is a good first step, before starting on any minor or major construction work.

Changing the color of your walls or repapering a surface to upgrade the appearance of an internal area are really cosmetic alterations. Cosmetic paint and paper alterations utilize the existing features in the room, and any decorative change they make is on the surface. If you decide to physically change an area of your home, then you must progress from decorative techniques to basic carpentry and building work. Spare a few minutes, initially, to consider space and how it is perceived in a room. Any form of clutter, particularly on the floor, will make a room look smaller. Simple steps such as racking magazines, putting books onto shelves, and tidying up generally may create the feeling of spaciousness you desire. Coordinated seating arrangements and plain flooring, rather than a mix of mismatched chairs and brightly colored rugs, can give an ordered, somewhat geometrical feel, which assists the impression of spaciousness. The issue of spaciousness becomes more important as property becomes increasingly expensive. Families are often forced to accept

smaller living areas and need to maximize the available area and yet create a spacious feel. Everyday clutter needs storage space in closets and shelves, so that the main room area can be free from obstruction. If you are able to create this space without altering your room dimensions, however, and thereby make good use of previously "wasted" areas like alcoves, you have the ideal solution.

Storage solutions

Do not think of a storage solution as several shelves, cabinets or closets in a room, think of

Coordinated seating and a plain floor will help to create the impression of space and order.

your solution as an integral part of your new scheme. Not only can you achieve a matching decor, but you can visually disguise the true function of any storage unit that matches and continues the line of the wall surface. Even a unit constructed from different materials will instil a sense of geometric order, provided it does not interrupt the wall line.

Other possibilities include half-wall units, preferably floor-standing, with the ceiling line recessed, letting the top half of the recess be paneled, tiled, or taken back to the brick. This is, visually speaking, little more than a practical chair development of half-wall finishes, where the chair rail divides two different decorative effects, or where the bottom half of the wall is paneled for protective purposes. Shelving utilizing the top half of the wall, with the floor line interrupted, is also possible, but somewhat self-defeating as anyone using the floor space is in danger of banging their head. For this reason the area underneath tends to become a more obvious and unsightly storage area itself, so you might as well

include it in the plan in the first place. As always, a sketch or drawing of the intended scheme is a good first step because it will let all interested parties voice an opinion on its viability. Measurements should, of course, be precise. A storage unit that does not house certain items because they are too big for it is no use at all.

Once you have worked out the kind of storage you need, consider whether you will buy it ready-made or build it yourself. There are many storage systems and items of furniture on the market, but to make the most of the available space, you may be better off constructing something that meets your needs exactly.

ABOVE:
Freestanding, half-wall-height cabinets can be used to good effect in alcoves.

LEFT: **In a kitchen, make the most of available space with built-in storage cabinets.**

Using color with different finishes

Which base color is most suitable to match a pine wood finish in a bathroom?
How can you emphasize the subtle colors of a local stone? Which wood finish
best complements hand-made tiles in earth colors? The answers—you will not be
surprised to discover—indicate that natural materials have their own color associations.

In sketching out your scheme for consultation,
consider the effect the raw materials could
have on the finished room decor. Woods,
whether solid planks or veneered man-made
boards, can be varnished or oiled to enhance as
well as protect their color characteristics. Wood
colors like dark reds, oranges, browns, and
yellows will look their best alongside green and
blue schemes. They are at their most familiar and
friendly too, because we associate trees with
green fields and blue skies. Any natural materials
that you use in your own environment will have
color associations that are dependent on their

source, and you should consider these, without
feeling restricted by them, when making color
decisions. An obvious example is to place pine
paneling on the bottom half of a yellow wall.
Because pine is predominantly yellow the colors
will match well, but the impact will be lost and
the cost of the raw materials wasted. Far better to
take the darker green of pine needles, or the mid-
brown of a pine cone as your contrasting color
for the top half of the wall, thus emphasizing the
yellow textures in the wood.

A color scheme that lets the lumber be the
focal point is essential if you decide to use sawn,

FAR LEFT: **Exposing rough-sawn ceiling joists by removing the plasterwork can produce an eye-catching ceiling. Team it with sturdy wooden furniture to create a harmonious decorative scheme.**

LEFT: **A chimney breast will often be the focal point of a room. You can emphasize it by stripping off the plaster to reveal the brickwork. Exposed wooden lintels can also make dramatic statements.**

unfinished lengths (i.e. not planed), for a rustic, more traditional look.

If you strip off the plaster to reveal a wall made of local stone, as opposed to brick, find out about the soil in the area. Is it red, sandy, or brown in color? A tint of the local color will be a natural partner for the stone, and the finished scheme will be pleasing to the eye. Back-to-the-brick finishes are focal points. Mixed yellows contain subtle colorings that will be wasted if they are juxtaposed with vivid or abrasive color. The scheme will be more successful if you use white as a base and mix this with just a hint of the brick coloring as it will let the brick finish tell its own story.

Using colors with wall tiles

The way that you consider colors when they are used with wall tiles must generally differ from considerations made for wood and stone because the clay of the tile is not in its natural state. Original tiles are available that use earth oxides, for example, or tiles that have a mat finish on pale blue clays, but these are hand-crafted exceptions. Commercial mass manufacture has introduced an extra process, a colored glaze fired onto the surface of the original clay. Colors created in this way can be matched or contrasted in the same way as painted walls, because nature's colors have been superseded. Blue and white may

have come to be regarded as the classic tile colors through the years, but they are not the original colors of the raw material. Consequently, unless you source a hand-made tile from a specialty limited-edition workshop, your color scheme will be man-made. This lets all kinds of decorative patterns and designs appear on a tile, more suitable, perhaps, for smaller wall areas.

Backsplashes above and behind basins and sinks, bath panels, and shower areas are ideal places for tiles. They are practical, being waterproof and easily cleaned, and in a confined space need not dominate the room. Pick a wall color to match a specific hue within the tile for a coordinated room scheme, or note the overall base color of the tile and pick its opposite on the color wheel for your wall.

BELOW: **A tiled backsplash behind a kitchen counter provides a wonderful opportunity to make a statement with color while taking care of the need for a hygienic, easily cleaned surface.**

Basic skills: wood

The strength to weight ratio of wood makes it the most versatile of constructional materials, as well as the most attractive. Your lumberyard holds wood stocks and manufactured boards in specific sizes, and before you start to draw up and price a project you need to find out what they are.

Measuring up

A sketch of your intended construction serves as more than just a discussion piece. When you add accurate dimensions, it becomes a working drawing, letting you calculate how much lumber you will need, and what sizes you should buy. This is not quite as straightforward as it seems because lumber is cut at the mill and the size given is the original sawn size. If you are buying sawn lengths, this is fine. If you require finished lumber, machine planed all round (PAR), however, then the nominal size still applies. Always remember that the finished size includes the discarded machined waste. Strange measurements have resulted from metrification, too, because wood sizes given in metric are conversions from traditional imperial sizes. For example 1.2 cm x 3.8 cm equals ½ in. x 1½ in. Calculating for machine waste adds another complication. Nominal size 2.5 cm x 10.1 cm, 1 in. x 4 in. imperial, actually arrives at your door as approximately ¾ in. x 3¾ in./1.9 cm x 9.5 cm. If you calculate a reduction of ⅛ in./4 mm on all sides, from the given or nominal size, then you won't be far wrong. In England, home improvement stores carry wood stocks in finished metric sizes, but specialized smaller woodyards may accept imperial, converting to metric at the till to conform with European trading standards. Don't mix the two systems, but use a retractable rule that has both markings, so you can convert.

Buying considerations

There are three categories of wood: hardwoods, softwoods, and boards. Hardwood, such as oak, beech, and birch, is cut from deciduous trees, is difficult to find and expensive. Good lumberyards usually stock mahogany, but again, prices may be prohibitive. Softwood is cheaper and is stocked by all lumberyards. Redwood, spruce, and yellow and white pine are all fairly common, but they are simply sold as "softwood," and not by individual name. Pine may be the exception, however, particularly parana pine.

Flush siding is machined from softwood with a tongue on one edge and a matching groove on the other, and is thus easily joined together for paneling. Sizes vary, but ½in. x 4in./1.2cm x 10.1cm is popular. Deal and cedar are good choices for

Man-made boards come in a variety of types and sizes. Always take a tape measure with you when buying lumber or boards.

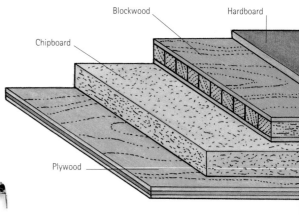

Chipboard
Blockwood
Hardboard
Plywood

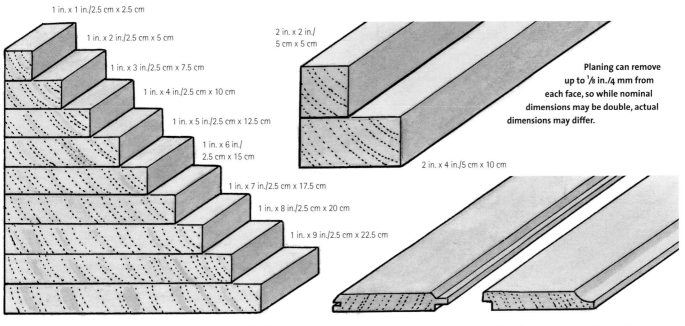

1 in. x 1 in./2.5 cm x 2.5 cm

1 in. x 2 in./2.5 cm x 5 cm

1 in. x 3 in./2.5 cm x 7.5 cm

1 in. x 4 in./2.5 cm x 10 cm

1 in. x 5 in./2.5 cm x 12.5 cm

1 in. x 6 in./
2.5 cm x 15 cm

1 in. x 7 in./2.5 cm x 17.5 cm

1 in. x 8 in./2.5 cm x 20 cm

1 in. x 9 in./2.5 cm x 22.5 cm

2 in. x 2 in./
5 cm x 5 cm

2 in. x 4 in./5 cm x 10 cm

Planing can remove up to 1/8 in./4 mm from each face, so while nominal dimensions may be double, actual dimensions may differ.

Softwood is sold in a range of standard sizes. However, the quoted size is the original sawn dimension, not the finished size.

Paneling boards may be tongued-and-grooved (left) or shiplap (right).

tongue-and-groove boards. Plywood boards are real wood veneers sandwiched together with glue so that the grains alternate at 90 degrees. Blockboards surfaced with a real wood veneer, but sandwiched inside are small irregular blocks of scrap wood. This can lead to different cutting resistances during the same sawcut, and this board is not as popular as plywood. Both are normally supplied in 8 ft. x 4 ft./2.44 m x 1.22 m external dimensions, and ¼, ⅜, ½ and ¾ in./6 mm, 9 mm, 1.2 cm and 1.8 cm in thickness. The top layer of veneer, or facing, varies. You can buy birch-, beech-, or oak-faced boards, usually one-sided, and the price varies according to quality. Other boards are available, such as chipboard (or particle board), which is used as a substitute for wooden floorboards, and hardboard, useful for subflooring.

Choosing and cutting

Lumberyards stock in sizes, depth x width. When you draw up a plan for the job, a knowledge of standard sizes will be invaluable. Select linear wood carefully; try to avoid knots—particularly

dead ones as they fall out—and look for lengths cut from the center of the log. (These have growth rings closer together.) Look down the length to see that it is not distorted, bent, warped, or twisted. The lumberyard will cut exact lengths if pressed, but it is to your advantage to pick pieces slightly longer than you need, which you can cut to the exact length on site. This lets you cut off ends damaged in transit, or suffering from shakes (splits along the grain, caused by uneven shrinkage) and splits in the end grain. When buying large boards, make sure the yard has a machining service. They may charge extra for this, but your boards will be professionally cut to the right size, saving you time and trouble. If you are starting a big job, or one that utilizes wood taken out of another room which involves lots of cutting, consider renting a dual-purpose "flip-over" saw. This machine cuts to length and miters on one side of its table, and, when rotated, cuts as a conventional table saw on the other side. Not only can this save on cutting charges at the lumberyard, but it will let you resize materials as you need them.

Tools and equipment 1

It may be true that "a bad workman blames his tools," but it is also true that first-class results cannot be attained with substandard and inaccurate equipment. Always buy the best tools that you can, maintain and look after them, because in most cases they are an investment that should last a lifetime.

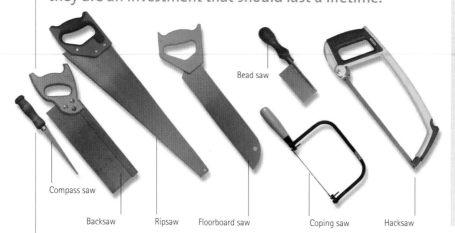

Bead saw

Compass saw

Backsaw   Ripsaw   Floorboard saw   Coping saw   Hacksaw

TOP TIP
If funds are limited, buy several hand tools rather than one powered tool. They will let you tackle a far wider range of jobs and will help you develop useful manual dexterity. Once you've assembled a good kit of hand tools, add powered examples.

Make sure you use the correct tool for the job. Ensure guidelines are level with a spirit level and mark them with a high-quality steel straightedge. Use a retractable steel tape to measure larger boards and linear lumber, and a steel rule for smaller dimensions. Square up with a try square or engineer's square, and mark miter cuts with a combination square. A good-quality combination square will include a detachable steel rule and a carpenter's level. Nonstandard angles can be measured and transferred using a sliding bevel. Cutting lines for boards should be made with a carpenter's pencil, but a marking knife must be used for small cuts and wood joints. Keep a conventional pencil and a general-purpose snap-blade knife in your kit as well. Saw wood across the grain with a crosscut saw; when sawing with the grain use a ripsaw. A panel saw is, in effect, a smaller crosscut saw, used for cutting boards. The more stable-bladed backsaw cuts large wood joints. Smaller or restricted-access cuts need a small backsaw.

You can cut holes in panels with a keyhole saw. Make right-angled cuts on the bench supported by a bench hook, and cut mitered angles in a miter box. Sink brads and molding pins with a ball-peen hammer; pull out pins using a curved claw hammer or pincers. Counterpunch pin heads below the surface with a nail set or punch. Use an awl to make starter holes for small screws, and a tee-handled gimlet for threaded pilot holes, remembering that the correct bladed screwdriver is needed to drive screws. Large woodscrews require a drilled pilot hole. To do this, use an awl and twist bits, or a self-starting

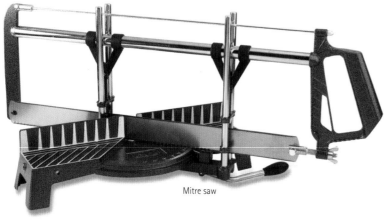

Mitre saw

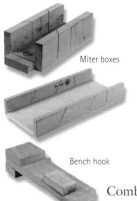

Miter boxes

Bench hook

auger bit in a hand drill or brace. A countersink will ensure the screwhead is below the wood surface, and a plug cutter will produce neatly chamfered plugs to fill screw holes.

Combination drill-drivers that are powered by mains lead or rechargeable battery can combine these jobs, particularly if fitted with a screwmate or combination screwsink. Any power driving into masonry will need a drill-driver with a hammer action, usually called a combi-drill.

Rebate waste wood can be removed with a mortise or firmer chisel, driven by a wooden mallet if necessary. Keep sharp chisel blades in their protective plastic casings; if they are blunt or chipped, sharpen them using an oilstone.

Always secure the workpiece with a C-clamp or bar clamp, and use a sash cramp to hold glued joints until dry. Small pieces of waste wood can be positioned to protect the workpiece from cramping indentations. Smooth edges using a jack file or smoothing file, and keep all edged blades sharply aligned. Chisels, drill bits, and files can be sharpened at your local hardware store.

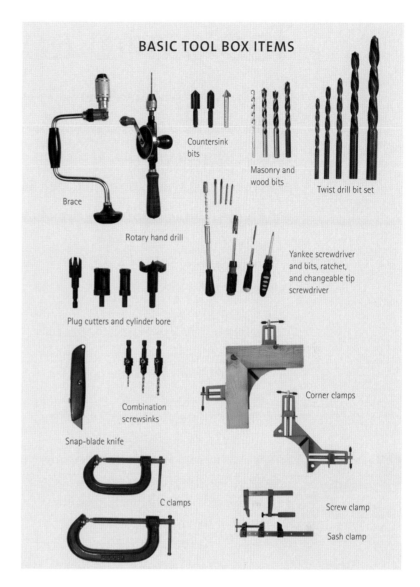

BASIC TOOL BOX ITEMS

Brace

Rotary hand drill

Countersink bits

Masonry and wood bits

Twist drill bit set

Yankee screwdriver and bits, ratchet, and changeable tip screwdriver

Plug cutters and cylinder bore

Combination screwsinks

Snap-blade knife

Corner clamps

C clamps

Screw clamp

Sash clamp

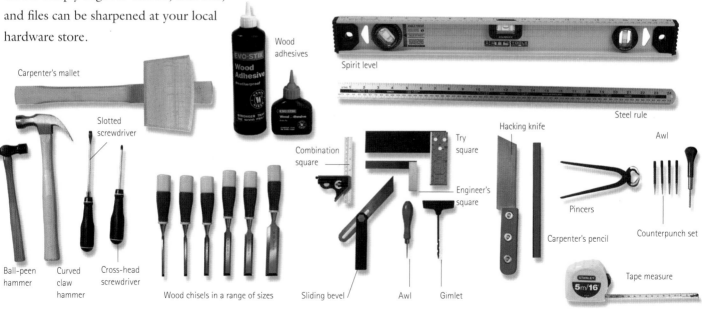

Carpenter's mallet

Wood adhesives

Spirit level

Steel rule

Ball-peen hammer

Curved claw hammer

Slotted screwdriver

Cross-head screwdriver

Wood chisels in a range of sizes

Combination square

Sliding bevel

Awl

Gimlet

Try square

Engineer's square

Hacking knife

Pincers

Carpenter's pencil

Awl

Counterpunch set

Tape measure

Tools and equipment 2

Power tools are "boy's toys" and cheap versions of drills and saws are on special offer in every home improvement superstore. But don't be tempted—remember that inaccurate, badly made power tools merely do a poor job even faster. Buy a brand name with a good reputation, and go for the top of the range. It will be worth it.

Mains-powered jigsaw

Power drills

Drills feature in the basic tool kit either as hand drills, or possibly as small cordless drill-drivers. These portable units have become very popular due to their ease of use and price. They will let you take on small jobs around the home, but will be found wanting if you attempt to tackle anything heavy-duty. Even the drill-drivers of a professional standard are intended to penetrate only wood, plastics, plasterboard, and block. Drilling into masonry is left to the hammer drill, which is basically a drill-driver with a hammer facility for driving into brickwork. Cordless drills are rated by the battery-pack voltage; drills for home use are often 9.6V or less, while professional hammer drills for high

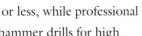

Cordless drill with battery pack

performance in concrete will be 24V. A good cordless hammer drill for the home kit would have a 14.4V battery pack, and have a drilling capacity of ½ in./1.2 cm in masonry and 1¼ in./3.2 cm in wood. The price is high, though, and a compromise may provide the answer. If you already have a drill-driver, you could extend your capability by adding a traditional, top-quality electric (non portable) hammer drill, which is powered by the mains, at considerably less cost.

Power saws

Two basic types of power saw are available: the jigsaw (or saber saw) and the circular saw. The jigsaw will cut curves and irregular shapes, while the circular saw cuts in a straight line. The jigsaw has easily interchangeable blades that are designed to cut different materials, and a tilting baseplate for bevel cutting. The saw cuts with a powerful reciprocating motion, and

BOSCH
PSB 750-2 RE

Mains-powered hammer drill

Cordless circular saw

TOP TIP

Always adopt a safety-first policy with powered equipment. Wind leads around handles when not in use and never let them trail across the floor. Store tools in their carry cases or in a locked cabinet, out of the reach of children.

Belt sander

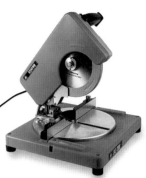
"Snip-off" miter saw

better models have an orbital-action blade. Variable speed control is a real advantage. Try to find one with a top knob handle so that you can use both hands. The circular saw also has changeable blades, but it is a more complicated tool, and a unit usually comes supplied with a tungsten-carbide-tipped blade for cutting both hard and soft materials. The depth of cut can be adjusted, and the baseplate tilts to make beveled cuts easy. A blade diameter of 7¼ in./18.5 cm is ideal. Make sure your saw comes with a guide fence. Miter saws are basically "pull-over" circular saws mounted on a swivel turntable on a mountable base. The saw cross-cuts and swivels up to 45 degrees to miter cut. Better models have soft start, a fence clamp, adjustable debris guard, and a dust collection bag.

Power sanders

Orbital sanders are sanders used for fine surface finishing. A rectangular base holds the abrasive paper, and is driven in an oscillating motion by a motor, thus "orbiting" the sanding surface, usually in a

Palm sander

Finishing sander

¼ in./6 mm/diameter. The abrasive paper can be changed quickly, from medium to very fine grades for the ultimate finish. All-purpose random orbit sanders come with a supply of quick-fit perforated sanding discs. A standard size is 5 in./12.5 cm, and a flexible dust skirt and dust extraction bag are also provided. Detail sanders that use circular disks and triangular bases allow access into tight corners and confined spaces. Belt sanders are used primarily for more heavy-duty abrasive work, such as leveling surfaces, rounding off corners, and reducing lumber widths. An interchangeable sanding belt moving at a continuous speed removes wood stock very quickly. A 3 in./7.5cm belt is a good width, and is available in coarse, medium, and fine grades. Better machines have variable speed control. If you intend to sand the surfaces of boards, invest in a sanding frame to ensure even removal.

Routers

An electronic plunging router will cut a rebate, channel a groove, or cut a mortise. The router bit is driven in a clockwise direction, plunged down into the wood through the hole in the center of the baseplate, and carefully guided from left to right, cutting into the workpiece. Slow-start and variable speed are real assets, giving more control. These tend to be features of only the more expensive machines, however.

Plunge-type

Electric planers

You can shape linear lumber to fit against uneven wall surfaces with an electric planer. It can be used to rebate, chamfer, bevel, and smooth. It is faster than a manual tool, so beware of removing too much wood! A blade width of 3¼ in./8.2 cm and cutting depth up to ⅛ in./3 mm is adequate for household projects. Make sure yours has a setting gauge and fence guide.

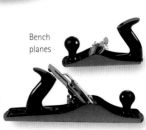
Electric plane

Bench planes

YOU WILL NEED:
• WOOD
• CARPENTER'S PENCIL
• CRAMPS
• SQUARE
• BENCH HOOK
• BACKSAW
• DRILL AND AUGER BIT
• RUBBER DEPTH STOP

Basic wood techniques

The basic requirement in cutting wood to fit is accuracy. Ensure that you measure, mark, and saw the wood carefully. You don't need excessive strength to use a saw, but you do need patience, a stable workpiece, and a sharp tool. Drilling also needs a secure workpiece, a marked starting point, and a sharp bit.

Measuring and marking

Remember the woodworker's basic rule: measure twice, cut once. Measure at right angles if you are measuring across a board, and parallel to the edge when measuring along its length. Don't let tapes sag or kink. Mark cuts to be made across boards with a carpenter's pencil, and cut on the waste side of the line. Blow away sawdust if it obscures the line as the saw moves through the piece. If you use a circular saw, remember to calculate for the width of the blade. Mark cuts across the grain with a marking knife, and cut on the waste side of the marked line. Wood joints are halved by accurately marking one half to use as a template to mark the other, so you only need to measure the one half. If you mark a miter, use a combination square at 45 degrees, then transfer the workpiece to a miter box or saw.

Cutting

The first rule of cutting is to have a stable workpiece. Any movement or slipping of the wood causes inaccuracy and is potentially dangerous. Secure your board with clamps when possible, supporting any overhang on a trestle or something similar. Adequate support is also needed for long sections of wood, but shorter pieces cut on the bench can be stabilized by using a bench hook.

When making cuts with a large hand saw, whether cutting across the grain (cross-cutting) or along the grain (ripping) of lumber stock or cutting manufactured board, hold the saw at an angle to the workpiece throughout the cut. Establish the cut with backstrokes first, and then cut using the entire blade length, with your index finger pointing along the top edge of the saw. This will help keep the saw straight and aligned with the cutting line. Keep the cut just to the waste side of the line; if you center the blade on the line, your finished piece will end up too short. You can always plane or sand the sawn piece back to the line. When cutting wood with a hand saw undue force should not be necessary.

MARKING FOR CUTTING

To cut at a right-angle to an edge, use a try square and pencil to mark the guideline.

Using a marking knife to mark cutting lines severs the surface grain, preventing splitting.

When marking out angled miter cuts at 45 degrees, use a combination square.

To make an accurate mitered cut, place the wood in a miter box, which has slots at 45 degrees.

USING A BACKSAW

STEP 1 Secure the wooden board with a clamp before you start to saw.

STEP 2 When cutting smaller pieces of wood with a backsaw, stabilize them on a bench hook.

STEP 3 Make a saw cut by holding the blade at an angle to the edge. Pull back a few times.

STEP 4 Cut with the backsaw blade horizontal, clamping the work to scrap wood to finish off.

Backsaws have a rigid back, so the blade is stable when you make a cut. Establish the cut as before, but as you progress gradually lower the blade until it is cutting horizontally through the workpiece. Don't cut all the way through the wood, as the grain will tear and splinter as the blade breaks through on the underside. Stop the cut just before completion and clamp the workpiece onto a scrap piece of wood. Now continue the cut through into the scrap to achieve a clean finished cut. Another way to stop the wood splitting is to turn the wood over when it has been partly cut and finish cutting through from the other side.

Drilling for screws and dowels

This is a simple technique for joining wood pieces. To insert a screw, first drill a small pilot hole (to guide the screw thread), then a hole the same diameter and depth as the screw shank (the shank clearance hole) and finally the countersink (to take the head below the wood surface). Some screw types do not have a shank, because the thread is continuous, so the shank clearance hole can be dispensed with. Always drill a pilot hole, however; otherwise the screw is unlikely to run straight and may bind so much when you insert it that it becomes impossible to turn. A finishing hole is essential for a countersunk screw; otherwise the head will end up slightly proud of the surface. Countersunk heads can be filled before painting so that the screwhead is hidden. Alternatively, use a combination screwsink that will drill a pilot, shank, and counterbored hole at the same time. Insert the screw and fill the hole with a plug of the same wood cut to the size of the hole with a plug cutter. Drilling holes to join wood pieces with dowels needs a self-starting auger bit with a rubber depth stop. Adjust the rubber ring to indicate the correct depth of hole if you are using fluted dowels, so you don't have to bore all the way through the wood. If you intend to drill completely through the wood, cramp it to a scrap piece of wood. Drill straight through to the scrap, minimizing damage as the auger bit leaves the hole; otherwise you risk splitting the grain. Be sure to use the correct sized auger bit. If you buy a pack of fluted dowels, however, the bit is usually supplied as part of the kit.

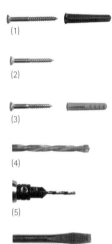

TOP TO BOTTOM: **Number 8 screw and wall anchor (1); a number 8 countersunk screw (2); a screw and wall anchor (3); a number 12 masonry drill bit (4); a number 8 combination drill and countersink (5); 7 mm slotted driver blade (6).**

USING THE DRILL BIT

Drill large holes with a self-starting auger bit. It has a sharp point to allow easy centering of the bit on the hole position.

A rubber depth stop can be attached to the bit and adjusted so that you can drill holes to an accurate depth.

Advanced wood techniques

Joining wood pieces together is an art form in itself. If you don't feel confident about tackling an open mortise-and-tenon, start with a simple halving joint. Accuracy is everything in producing good wood joints, so it makes sense to practice a little on an off-cut first.

Simple wood joints are not difficult, provided you measure and cut accurately with correctly set, sharp tools. Use a marking knife, not a pencil, and use one half of the joint as a template for the other to ensure a tight fit. Joints and housings that are identical, but cut from separate wood lengths, can be clamped together and marked for simultaneous cutting to ensure uniformity. Cut the wood precisely and assemble it "dry" to check the fit, remembering that a loose joint has no strength. Do not rely on excessive amounts of wood glue acting as a filler in a badly crafted, ill-fitting joint.

Use dowels to reinforce any of the following joints:

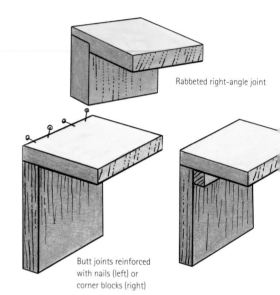

Rabbeted right-angle joint

Butt joints reinforced with nails (left) or corner blocks (right)

• butt joining, L-joints and block reinforced joints
• tongue-and-groove joint (for panels, bought premachined)
• halving joint
• rabbeted joint
• 45-degree miter joint
• bridle joint/open mortise-and-tenon.

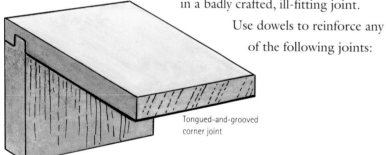

Tongued-and-grooved corner joint

L-shaped butt joint

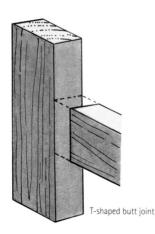

T-shaped butt joint

BRIDLE JOINT/OPEN MORTISE-AND-TENON

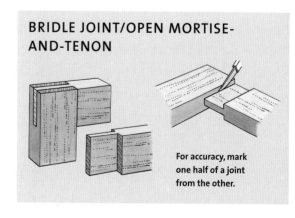

For accuracy, mark one half of a joint from the other.

JOINTS

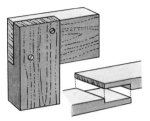

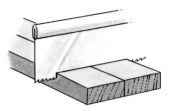

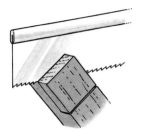

STEP 1 Halving or lap joints can make right-angled and inline connections.

STEP 2 For an exact fit, clamp the pieces together and cut them both at the same time.

STEP 3 Clamp each piece to the bench and begin cutting down the grain at an angle.

STEP 4 Finish the cut with the saw blade parallel to the cut across the grain. Check the fit.

TOP TIP

Removing waste wood from a cut housing is simplified by making several parallel cuts side by side to the housing depth with a small backsaw. You will find it much easier to remove slivers of waste wood one at a time with a ¼ in./6 mm chisel than to try to chisel out the housing in one piece with a larger blade.

REINFORCING JOINTS

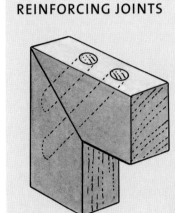

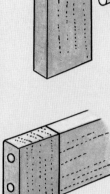

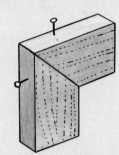

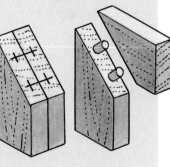

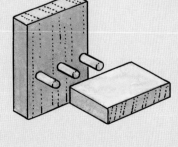

Boards sold for paneling have a simple machined joint system with a tongue on one edge and a groove in the other. When the boards are assembled, the tongue fits into the groove. They are secured by nails driven through the tongues.

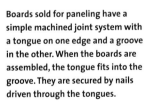

For strength, glued butt joints should be reinforced. One method is to drive nails through one piece into the other. However, wooden dowels are far better and can be concealed within the joint in blind holes. If visible, their ends should be trimmed flush with the wood. If hidden, careful marking out is necessary to ensure the dowel holes coincide exactly.

YOU WILL NEED:

WALL ANCHORS:
- **DRILL AND DRILL BIT**
- **WALL ANCHORS**
- **SCREWS**
- **SCREWDRIVER**

FRAME FIXERS:
- **DRILL AND DRILL BIT**
- **FIXER**
- **SCREWS**

Wall fixings and hardware

Wall fixings and hardware are now so widely available that your hardware store and even the local general store will have a selection on sale; there is no need to visit the home center. The difficult task is discovering the type of wall you are trying to fix into, and trial and error is just about the only way to find out.

To fix objects to a wall you need the appropriate wall fixing. This involves selecting an anchor to receive the screw, and the type of anchor will depend on the original construction of your wall, usually whether it is solid or cavity.

Solid walls

If your wall is solid all you need is a simple nylon or polypropylene wall anchor. This has grabbing lugs or pointed teeth to stop it turning in its hole as you insert the screw. You will need to predrill a

hole, and you must be very accurate in lining up and marking. Manufacturers have a color-coding system: yellow anchors for small to medium-sized screws; red anchors for medium to large; brown "heavy-duty" anchors for large.

The drill, anchor, and screw sizes are all related. Anchors sold in packs have the required drill size and recommended screw shank acceptance size pressed into the plastic center strip. Frame fixers are long-shanked screws in their own sleeves and do not need previously marked and drilled wall holes, letting you drill through the wood directly into the masonry. The anchor is fitted directly through the wood piece, and, as the screw is tightened, counter-rotation lugs open out to grab the wall. Some forms of frame fixer are designed to be hammered home. In this case a screwdriver may be needed for final tightening and to remove the screw to allow removal of the framework.

For very heavy-duty fixing in solid masonry, an expanding bolt should be chosen. It works on the same principle as a wall anchor, the segmented steel body of the fitting expanding in the hole as the bolt is turned with a spanner. Removing the bolt leaves the body of the fixing in place.

Cavity walls and wallboard

Anchors designed for these walls are to be pushed through a hole in the wall until the petals or arms reach the cavity and can open out to spread

WALL ANCHORS

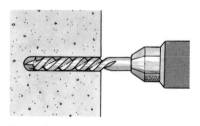

STEP 1 When using wall anchors, you need to drill a hole of the correct size and depth for the anchor in the wall.

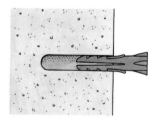

STEP 2 Push the anchor into the hole until it is flush with the surface. Do not hammer it, as this may distort it.

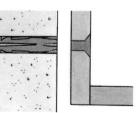

STEP 3 Hold up the fitting to the wall and align the screw hole with the wall anchor. You can then insert the selected screw.

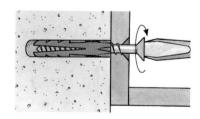

STEP 4 Tighten the screw. When the screw enters the anchor, the latter will expand, gripping the sides of the hole.

against the back of the wall as you turn the screw. They are simple to insert, but not very strong. Heavy-duty expanding fixings, which consist of a metal sleeve around a central bolt, will take more loading. The sleeve fits the hole precisely and expands outward when the bolt is tightened, gripping the sides and back of the hole. Spring toggle bolts have metal wings that are pushed through the hole into the cavity and spring open. Then, as the bolt is tightened, the wings grab the back of the wall. This fixing has a drawback in that the hole must be quite large, because the wings pass through it, but the open wings spread the load effectively. It is often recommended for walls of low structural strength. Self-drill wallboard fixings are anchors with a screw thread. You make a pilot hole and insert them with a screwdriver until they are flush with the wall surface. Then treat them like any wall anchor. A screw is supplied with the anchor, but longer ones of the same type will be needed for cleats.

Hinges and catches

Cabinet doors and shutters built in to your new room will need hinges. Butt hinges, which need to be recessed to fit flush, are the most common. Flush hinges are designed for lighter load-bearing duties. Their advantage is that they are designed to screw to the surface, and no cutting in is necessary. Small matching cabinet doors that are fiddly to align often utilize concealed adjustable hinges, adjustments being possible after the doors are hung. These hinges were primarily designed to let doors not inset into the frame open at right angles in confined spaces. Some concealed adjustable hinges are spring-loaded to keep the doors closed. For other hinge styles, you need to fit a catch. Magnetic door catches are easy to fit, usually being an enclosed magnet case screwed to the cabinet, which attracts a small metal plate fixed to the door. Harder to fit is the automatic latch. The mechanism is cased inside the cabinet unit, and the latch lever is lined up on the inside of the door. You press the outside of the closed door to unlatch it, and it swings open.

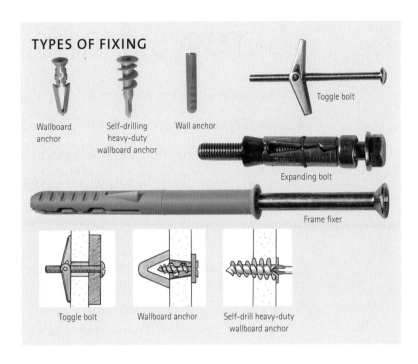

TYPES OF FIXING

Wallboard anchor

Self-drilling heavy-duty wallboard anchor

Wall anchor

Toggle bolt

Expanding bolt

Frame fixer

Toggle bolt

Wallboard anchor

Self-drill heavy-duty wallboard anchor

FRAME FIXERS

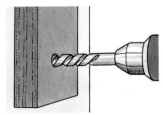

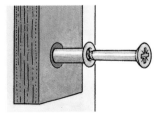

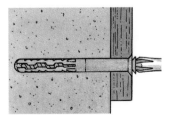

STEP 1 Frame fixers let you hold the wood framework in place and drill straight through into the wall.

STEP 2 The fixer comprises a long, heavy-gauge screw and long expanding plastic anchor.

STEP 3 Pass the fixer through the wood into the wall so the anchor end is flush with the frame's face.

STEP 4 Tighten the fixer's screw to expand the anchor and secure the frame to the wall.

Screws, nails, and adhesives

There is an amazing number of screws on the market in all types, sizes, and finishes, with slotted- or cross-heads in countersunk, raised, and round-head form. Nails, too, come in many different types and sizes for specific purposes, while there are plenty of glues to choose from to meet your home improvement needs.

Screws

Despite the confusing array of types, hold onto the basic principle that screws are used to draw together and join two previously separate items. This may be two pieces of wood for permanent fixing or it may be holding a cleat against a wall by gripping the inside of an anchor, or simply holding hardware, such as hinges, against a wooden surface.

Of the types you may find in your hardware store, slotted screws have been used in carpentry for many years, manually driven by a matching bladed screwdriver. Screws with cross-headed slots, like Phillips, require a matching cross-headed driver, and many users claim that this type of driver is less likely to jump out of the slot.

Cordless drill-driver users rely on cross-slotted screws, particularly Pozidrivs and Supadrivs, partly for this reason, and partly for speed. The length and "grab" of the thread varies. Conventional woodscrews have a shank, the diameter of which determines the size number (e.g. 6 or 8). Cross-heads have a continuous thread that can be quite pronounced with a high "grab," and are often similar in appearance to self-tappers. The head can be countersunk, intended to be driven below the work surface, unless a screw cover is used.

The other head shapes are domed (round), often used with washers and when the screw may be removed periodically, and raised, when the

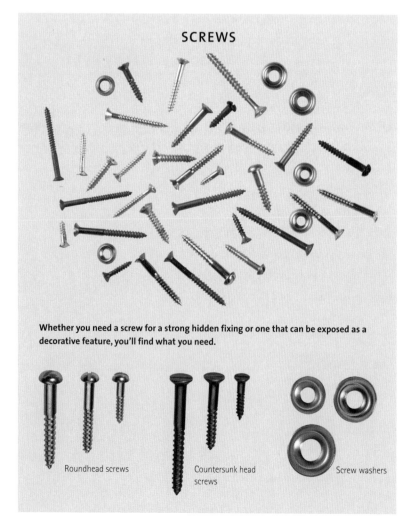

SCREWS

Whether you need a screw for a strong hidden fixing or one that can be exposed as a decorative feature, you'll find what you need.

Roundhead screws

Countersunk head screws

Screw washers

Use the correct blade size for the screw head. A blade too small for the head will damage the slot and jump out; a blade too wide will damage the workpiece as the screw is inserted.

MODERN NAILS AND PINS

manufacturers prefer to offer hundreds of different types and sizes of round nail.

Nails have different heads, lengths, and thicknesses (gauges), and you will find that the reference name usually describes the use. For general use about the house, a tool box could contain round lost-head or finishing nails, 1½ in. to 3 in./4 cm to 7.5 cm, oval brad or lost-head ovals 1 in. to 4 in./2.5 cm to 10 cm, and a selection of panel pins and molding pins. Hardboard nails, masonry nails, and wallboard nails, all self-descriptive, can be bought for more specific jobs.

Glues

Wood glues, particularly when used in conjunction with pins or screws, will give a very strong joint. Jointed surfaces must be supported, either by screws, C-clamps, sash clamps or similar, while the glue dries, usually overnight. Both waterproof and non waterproof glues are available in handy sizes, starting with mini-packs and 4-fl. oz./125-ml containers with easy-to-use applicators, up to 3-quart/5-liter professional packs. Moldings are sometimes glued to the wall surface with a rapid setting, fast-grab panel adhesive. This is a high-strength gap and filler adhesive. It is usually available in a tube, which comes with a dispenser similar to a skeleton gun.

Wood adhesives are available as waterproof and non-waterproof.

head is set in a cup for decorative effect. Screws can be steel or brass; brass may look better, but steel is stronger. Steel screws may be stainless, bright, galvanized, zinc-plated, or chrome-plated for protection against rust.

Nails, brads, pins, and tacks

Modern nails, brads, pins, and tacks are the distant relatives of hand-forged nails produced in the smithy; they had tapered, sharp-cornered bodies or shanks. These original fasteners held better than today's machined round nails, because the sharp shank cut through, as opposed to spreading, the wood grain. Buying cut floor or floorboard nails is as close as you are likely to get to a piece of history, however, as today's

Interchangeable driver bits

CUT FLOOR OR FLOORBOARD NAILS

Cut floor (floorboard) nails have sharp-cornered bodies designed to cut through the wood grain.

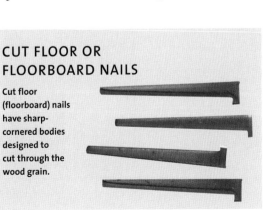

Wooden moldings

Wooden panel moldings and crown moldings provide a finishing flourish to offset a sometimes functional piece. For this reason, they have long been used as decorative features on built-in room units, doors, and cabinets. Moldings can line recessed panels, provide a decorative edging to shelves, and hide screwheads around fixed frames and room panelwork.

Softwood moldings

Most wood moldings are routed from softwood. Baseboards and picture and chair rails will all be familiar, as will door and window crown moldings, and they can be found in a multitude of shapes and designs. Period styles with ornate patterns or more austere, modern chamfered lengths are available to suit or match any room. A few basic examples are shown here. They vary in molding detail from supplier to supplier, so you need to buy from the same source.

The growth in the refurbishment market has led to some period designs being available "off the shelf," but you will need to find a specialist supplier for more unusual and imaginative designs. Some suppliers may be able to match your existing molding if you provide them with a sample. Panel moldings that give a finishing touch to plain surfaces and decorative pine strips for smaller areas like cabinet doors can be found at most home centers and good lumberyards.

Hardwood moldings

Hardwood moldings are for edging the outside of boards and the inside edges of cutaway panels, where the layered sides of the board would otherwise be visible. Boards with a hardwood veneer can thus be edged with a matching strip, and oiled or varnished. Small hardwood moldings in ramin or mahogany can be employed as decoration for cabinet doors, as contrasting finishing lengths on panelwork and frames, or as internal edging on right-angled corners.

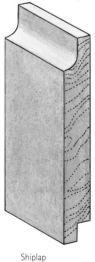

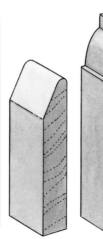

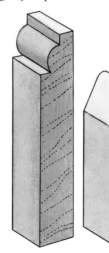

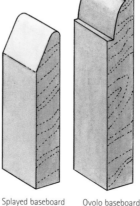

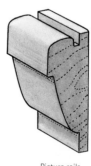

Picture rails

Tongue-and-groove   Shiplap   Torus baseboard   Splayed baseboard   Ovolo baseboard

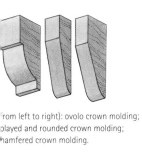

(from left to right): ovolo crown molding; splayed and rounded crown molding; chamfered crown molding.

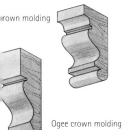

rown molding

Ogee crown molding

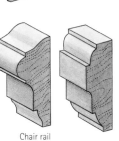

Chair rail

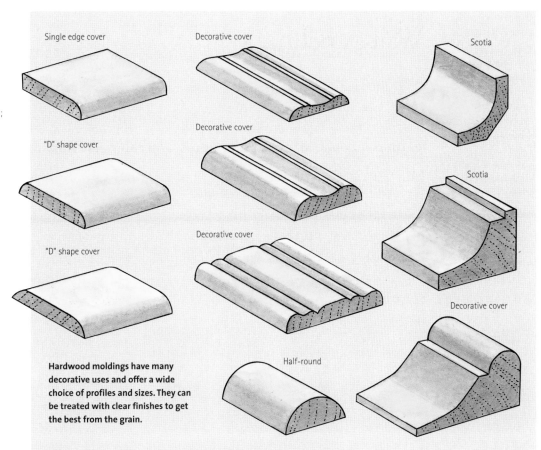

Single edge cover

Decorative cover

Scotia

"D" shape cover

Decorative cover

Scotia

"D" shape cover

Decorative cover

Decorative cover

Half-round

Hardwood moldings have many decorative uses and offer a wide choice of profiles and sizes. They can be treated with clear finishes to get the best from the grain.

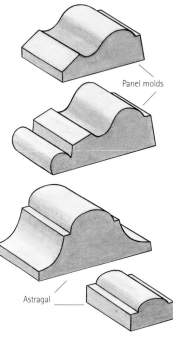

LEFT: **Chair rails tend to be chunky to withstand knocks from chair backs and other furniture.**

Panel molds

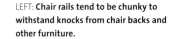

Astragal

YOU WILL NEED:
- **CLEATS**
- **NAILS (MASONRY)**
- **WOOD PANELING**
- **SAW**
- **DAMP PROOF MEMBRANE**
- **HAMMER AND PINS**
- **NAIL PUNCH**
- **ANCHORS AND SCREWS**
- **SCREWDRIVER**
- **PENCIL**
- **SET SQUARE**
- **TONGUE-AND-GROOVE BOARDS**
- **SPIRIT LEVEL**

PROJECT
Wall paneling

Wood has a unique way of altering the look and feel of a room. As a natural material, it has an aroma all its own and a visual elegance second to none. Whether you opt for vertical or horizontal paneling, pick an appropriate finish, not only to go with the room decor, but to enhance the natural beauty of the wood itself. Prepared lumber lengths for paneling a wall can be bought from home

30 cm units. Before buying specific lengths, be sure you know whether the paneling is to run horizontally or vertically. This way you will minimize wastage when cutting to size on site.

Wall surface

Before you start any planning, examine the wall that you plan to panel. If it is even very slightly damp, the paneling will exacerbate the problem and fungi will form on the reverse side of the wood. Simply fitting vents in the paneling will not solve the problem. You will need to cure the damp, and this will require professional advice. Whatever the state of the wall, a coat of wood preservative on the wood is recommended.

Wood paneling should be pinned to softwood cleats fixed to the wall. An ideal size for the cleats is 2 in. x 1in./5 cm x 2.5 cm. These must be horizontal for vertical paneling, and vertical for horizontal paneling. Fix the cleats to the wall, approximately 18 in./46 cm apart, using the same spacing for the fixing points. If you are driving into bare masonry, you can use masonry nails. Plastered surfaces, however, require anchors and screws; countersunk 2 in./5 cm number 8 are ideal. The framework of cleats must be in a true vertical plane. You can check this by placing a spirit level on the uprights and on a long straightedge held across the horizontal sections. If the wall is very uneven, pack out the wood with strips of cardboard or thin plywood.

HORIZONTAL CLADDING

STEP 1 On an external wall, trap a damp-proof membrane behind the cleats, then add the boards.

STEP 2 The ends of boards should reach halfway across the batten to ensure adequate support.

STEP 3 Tongue-and-groove boards should be "secret nailed" through their tongues, shiplap through the face.

centers, usually in shrink-wrapped bundles priced per yard/metre. Traditional paneling is intended for interior use only. Exterior siding, such as clapboard and shiplap can both be used outdoors. Alternatively, buy your wall paneling from your local lumberyard. Both tongue-and-groove and shiplap will be priced per foot run or

Baseboard

Whether you retain the baseboard or not is your choice. If the new paneling is intended to fit flush from ceiling to floor, then the existing baseboard merely becomes part of the cleating because it is the same depth. But if the baseboard is part of

RIGHT: **When paneling walls, boards can be run vertically and horizontally. The supporting cleats always run in the opposite direction.**

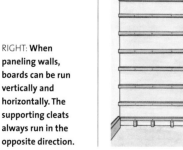

the new scheme, it must be carefully prised off. Position a cleat so that you can nail the baseboard back in position to complete the job.

Vertical paneling

Centering vertical lengths on your chosen wall requires precise mathematics. You need to measure the visible width of the wood first. A popular size is 3½ in./9 cm. Divide this figure into the wall length. If you are lucky, the paneling will fit exactly or fall very slightly short, allowing a slight opening of the fit between tongue and groove to take up the space. Otherwise an equal amount should be taken off each end, effectively centering the wood lengths on the wall. If this does not worry you, or the paneling is continuing around the corner, simply start at one end. With the exception of the first piece, which is pinned through the center of the face, TGV paneling should be invisibly pinned through the tongue, the groove in the next length hiding the fixing. This means that whichever end of the wall you start, the groove must butt to the wall.

Shiplap starts the same way round, but is fixed through the face of the wood, just before the lap. The pin needs to be punched below the surface and the hole filled. The first length must be plumb vertical. If the wall is not, plane the wood to fit. Build up the paneling with successive

VERTICAL PANELING

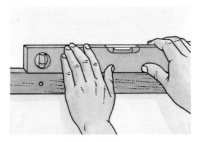

STEP 1 When attaching horizontal support cleats to the wall, check with a spirit level that they are accurate.

STEP 2 At switch and outlet positions, nail a framework of cleats to the wall around the mounting box.

STEP 3 When you reach the switch or outlet with the boards, mark them and cut them to fit around it.

STEP 4 Screw the faceplate to the mounting box so that it overlaps the cut edges of the boards.

lengths until you reach the end of the wall; the end piece may require planing to fit in the same way as the first piece. If the paneling fits flush, a decorative panel molding around three sides will complete the job. If it doesn't, nail the baseboard back into position on top of the paneling.

Horizontal paneling

Start with the groove against the ceiling line, using a spirit level to ensure it is straight. If not, and the ceiling is slightly bowed, plane the length to fit. Retaining the horizontal level line, pin the lengths down the wall to the floor. The final piece must be cut or planed lengthwise to fit flush, and panel moldings added to finish. Or you could stop just below the level of the baseboard. In this case, pin short offcuts onto the remainder of the cleating, down to floor level, and reposition the baseboard, nailing through the offcuts onto the cleats.

LEFT: **Wooden wall paneling is a versatile means of providing a room with a unique look. You can stain it or paint it to suit the style you want.**

YOU WILL NEED:

PANELING:

• CLEATS

• PENCIL

• TAPE MEASURE

• SCREWDRIVER

• SCREWS

• KEYHOLE SAW

• PINS

• GLUE

PROJECT
Plywood paneling

This kind of wallcovering gives you an opportunity to explore the concept of paneling further, either by matching the veneered surfaces and the woodstrips, using a stock such as beech, or by using a mix of different woods to make up the wall area and running different water-based stains into the grain.

Plywood ¼ in./6 mm thick can be found in various finishes, from fairly crude exterior grades to one-sided hardwood-veneered interior panels. You can buy sheets of 8 ft. x 4. ft/2.44 m x 1.22 m and have them machine cut to size, or you can purchase smaller panels of 6 ft. x 2 ft./182.7 cm x 60.7 cm or 4 ft. x 2 ft./122 cm x 60.7 cm. The smaller sizes are made for home improvement purposes and are consequently more expensive, but usually have a good veneered finish. The idea is to produce a wall that looks like old-fashioned paneling, but at a fraction of the cost. This style is effective in study rooms and home offices, giving your home-based business center the appearance of a traditional library.

Positioning and centering

Sheet paneling must be pinned into position on cleats, in the same manner as TGV lengths. This time, however, the cleats must form a horizontal and vertical grid, making an identical grid to the finished panel work. The reason is that when the finishing strips are pinned through the veneered sheet onto the wall cleats, all board joints will be hidden under the strips. The grid you choose can be to any dimensions that suit your purpose or the wall effect you desire, provided the cleats and finishing strips line up and the joints are neatly concealed by the finishing strips.

Cleating

Attach 2 in. x 1 in./5 cm x 2.5 cm cleats to the wall, using 2 in./5 cm number 8 screws and countersinking. Masonry nails can be used if the wall is bare brick. Vertical cleats must be positioned so that their centers coincide with the joints between boards: for example, a board machine cut 8 ft. x 2 ft./2.44 m x 60.7 cm wide requires a cleat centerpoint 2 ft./60.7 cm from the starting wall edge. The horizontal cleat centerpoints are the same, and the 8 ft./2.44 m edge will fall in the middle of one. You will need to decide whether your paneling design should be centered on one wall, or could turn one corner to partly cover the next. Whatever the dimension of the vertical cleat spacing, replicate it exactly when positioning the horizontals, so that the finishing strips which conceal the joints form a pattern of a square.

Finishing

When the cleat grid is complete, check the system for accuracy by holding up a board, making sure the joints will be covered. Mark the position of the grid on the face of the board with a carpentry pencil. Apply panel adhesive to the cleat grid, and pin the veneered sheet into position with ¾ in./1.8 cm panel pins, punching flush with the surface. Position the remaining boards. Following your marks on the surface, draw the grid again to act as a guide for the finishing strips to make up the squares. Glue and pin the strips into position using 1 in./2.5 cm molding pins. Some 2 in. x ½ in./5 cm x 1.2 cm vertical strips with butt joined horizontals will give a square, right-angled finish, but it is worth attempting a molded panel finish. Try a finishing strip size of 1 in. x ½ in./2.5 cm x 1.2 cm centered over the cleats, butt joined as before, forming squares. Select a small decorative panel molding, no larger than 1 in. x ½ in./2.5 cm x 1.2 cm, and cut and mitre to size to fit the inside angles of each individual square. Glue and pin at an angle into the cleat with ¾ in./1.8 cm molding pins.

Wall fixings

Wall switches and outlets that are not proud of the wall surface must be replaced with surface boxes. But first, remember to isolate electrical fittings from the supply before attempting to work on them. Fix cleats in a square around the box, and measure the position of the box relative to your panel and its dimensions. Mark this with a pencil, then drill a pilot hole in one corner. Cut out the shape with a keyhole saw, and secure the panel, ensuring that the cut hole fits neatly over the surface box. Fit the cover plate, so that it overlaps neatly.

Painted paneling offers a simple and effective means of concealing a lavatory tank.

FAR LEFT: **Although plywood is a very functional material, with a bit of imagination and effort, it can be transformed into stylish wall paneling.**

WALL SWITCHES

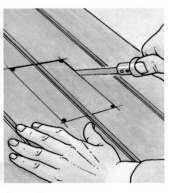

STEP 1 Make a cut-out for a switch by drilling a small hole at each corner and joining them with a keyhole saw.

STEP 2 Fit cleats around the switch mounting box and hold up the panel. Then pin the panel in place.

YOU WILL NEED:
- SUPPORT CLEATS
- WOOD PIECES AS SPECIFIED
- CLAMPS
- DRILL AND DRILL BITS
- NUMBER 8 COUNTERSUNK-HEAD BRASS SCREWS
- SCREW SEATS
- PINS
- SANDPAPER
- GLUE

PROJECT
Adjustable room-height shelving

You can customize your shelving to suit your individual household requirements with this entirely versatile scheme. Constructed simply from the same wood stock, it can form part of a paneling project, or be fixed directly to a decorated wall surface. Any varnished wood finish can be used to match a room scheme.

If planned and measured accurately, different cleat grids fixed to a wall can serve as a secure base for a variety of projects. Using this grid, a shelving system can run at right angles to the vertical paneling and can perform functional or decorative duties. An advantage is that all wood stock is the same size, 2 in. x 1 in./5 cm x 2.5 cm, so you can buy in bulk from a lumberyard. The system has been devised to support 5 in./12.7 cm

wide shelves, but, if this is too wide, it can easily be revised to accept 4 in./10 cm shelves that will still hold paperbacks and decorative objects. Simply cut the slot-in shelf supports to 4 in./10 cm rather than 5 in./12.7 cm. Any number of shelf uprights can be incorporated into this versatile scheme, depending on the length of the shelves that will complete the wall. Reckon on one support for every seven TGV uprights, if using 3½ in./9 cm paneling, which gives a support every 25 in./63 cm. Aim to space out and fix the wall cleats (see vertical paneling project, page 125). Anchor the wall even if you have bare brick, because of the weight the uprights might have to take. Use number 8 countersunk 2 in./5 cm steel screws, butting short horizontal lengths between the floor to the ceiling shelf-support cleats. All cleats should be 2 in. x 1 in./5 cm x 2.5 cm, which is the same size as the shelf-support pieces.

Shelving supports

This system employs two sizes of vertical support, screwed to the face of the wall support, creating a gap, into which the horizontal pieces that will support the shelf are slotted. For each upright you will need wood pieces cut from the same stock 5 in./12.7 cm long, positioned starting from flush top, leaving ¾ in./1.8 cm dividing gaps as you progress down the length. These pieces are secured by center drilling 1½ in./3.8 cm from the bottom edge, and screwing through to the upright using 1¼ in./3.2 cm number 8—raised—countersunk head brass screws and seatings. This gives a screw finish resembling a brass stud. A second layer of support pieces is needed only where the shelf supports are to be slotted in. 3 in./7.6 cm pieces

are thus screwed flush with the top of the designated 5 in./12.7 cm pieces by center drilling 1½ in./3.8 cm from the bottom edge in exactly the same way as before. Slot in the shelf support horizontals, which are also 5 in./12.7 cm pieces, to check the fit in the slot and to see if they hold a spirit-leveled shelf correctly. When you are happy with it, sand all the pieces lightly to remove sharp edges and any splinters. For added strength, glue as well as screw the pieces together.

Finishing the wall

Now that the shelving system is complete, invisibly pin the TGV uprights to the horizontal cleats. Seven should fit snugly between the uprights. You may need to file to fit wall edges. The join at the TGV can be expanded slightly to take up a minor shortfall. The paneling can then be varnished with the finish of your choice, as can the shelving uprights and support pieces, and a baseboard added if liked.

Finally, the shelf supports can be slotted into place. The shelves are intended to be cut from 5 in. x 1 in./12.7 cm x 2.5 cm wood, to the length of your wall. However, shorter cut lengths in groups or seemingly random positioning can prove to be equally pleasing to the eye in this versatile scheme.

MAKING SHELVES

STEP 1 Lay out the 5 in./12.7 cm long pieces of timber on the wall support cleat. It is advisable to space them with the shelf cleats in order to ensure a tight fit.

STEP 2 The next stage is to clamp and then screw the sections of wood to the support cleat. For this you should use countersunk-head brass screws and screw seats.

STEP 3 Attach the 3 in./7.6 cm/ lengths of cleat to the first lengths in the same manner, flush with the top edge. You should use countersunk-head brass screws and seats as before.

STEP 4 Finally, check the fit of the shelf support cleats in their slots. It is important that the fit is exact; if the shelf supports are loose, the shelf will not be stable.

FAR LEFT: **This versatile adjustable shelving system can be installed on its own or as part of a wall paneling system. It is constructed from simple 2 in. x 1 in./5 cm x 2.5 cm softwood cleats.**

Wooden ceilings

Wooden ceilings look wonderful, particularly in older houses, cottage-style properties and unusually shaped rooms. Converted lofts with roof windows as a natural light source and interestingly shaped shadow areas can show off quality lumber paneling to great advantage. And you can either paint the wood or use a natural finish to show the texture.

ABOVE: **Storage units can be incorporated to make the most of the space.**

ABOVE: **In this loft room TGV runs at right angles to the rafters.**

ABOVE RIGHT:
When teamed with exposed roof beams, a TGV ceiling provides an interesting decorative feature. Adequate support for the boards is essential, as their combined weight will be considerable.

Shiplap or TGV matchings can be used on ceilings in a similar way to walls. Cleating supports are used as before, and light fittings should present no difficulty. Varnished wooden ceilings can have a crown molding surround, similar to a cornice, and even a ceiling light fitting cut to a plain circle or a wavy-edged design with a coping saw. The ceiling will appear, and in fact be, lower. The wood finish will advance toward the eye, and physically it will be 1¼ in./3.2 cm closer, that measurement being the depth of the lumber.

Two difficulties you may encounter are locating the joists (hidden ceiling beams) to which you fix the cleats, and the fact that all the fixing work goes on over your head. To locate the joists, measure accurately from the floor above. If it is the loft, and the wood beams are exposed, your task is straightforward; otherwise you must lift a floorboard. Note the direction of run, measure the distance between joist centers, and draw the positions onto the ceiling. If you cannot reach the joists from above, the only solution is to tap the ceiling with a screwdriver handle and listen for the sound to change from a hollow ring to a solid tone. When you think you have found a joist, probe with an awl to check. Decide which way the TGV is to run, and hold up a first cleat length (cut to size) at right angles to that direction. Mark the drilling centers with

an awl, and drill the cleats on the bench to accept 3 in./7.6 cm countersunk number 8 screws. Mount the cleats on the ceiling, and invisibly pin the TGV through the tongues as described above. Isolate the light fitting from the electrical supply and remove it. Cut a hole in the wood and thread the wires through, reassembling and repositioning on the finished side of the wood length. Cornicing or crown molding, if desired, should be wall-mounted, butting up to the new ceiling.

Loft areas

Loft conversions must be left to a qualified builder but the decorative finishing is up to you.

Consider a wood finish for the inside of the loft. TGV fixed horizontally across the rafters not only strengthens the entire roof structure, but also gives a natural, relaxed feel to the area.

Have your builder tackle all structural work, leaving the roof area as a shell. The roof needs to be lined inside by ⅜ in./1 cm thick wallboard first. Use a board with metallized polyester on one side as an insulator, which should face the rafters. Mark their positions in pencil as you go.

Make a feature of the board fixings by using screws and screw washers rather than nails.

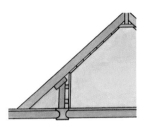

Boards can be fixed horizontally across the rafters and vertically to cleats attached to the studs.

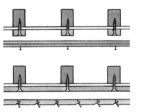

Establish the direction of ceiling joists before deciding on the method of cleat attachment.

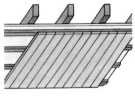

The support cleats must always be at right-angles to the boards.

Fix it in place with wallboard nails, using as few as you can get away with. With the insulation in place, line the roof area with TGV, starting at the apex and working down to the short vertical support studs tied into the rafters. Fix the wood with 1½ in./3.8 cm number 8 brass screws with screw washers. Screw them through the insulating wallboard to the marked rafters. These screws have the appearance of studs, creating an almost marine feel. Loft window recesses can be lined with wood, and chamfered or decorative crown molding can be used as an internal lining

border. The short vertical support studs hide the eaves storage space.

To provide access, a small door needs to be made up to fit, preferably in the same style as the TGV paneling work. TGV can be run horizontally each side of this access. If the insulation is continued on the inside of the rafters down to joist level, inside the eaves' space, then invisible pinning directly onto the studs is best. However, if the studs carry the insulation, then

you will need to screw the TGV into position as you did on the rafters.

Loft floor

If you intend opting for this type of wood finish, it is worth asking your builder to fit a chipboard floor. A natural fiber woven floorcovering is the perfect finishing touch, fitted so that the floor is not seen. This solves the problem of wood overkill, which would result if wood were used to floor the loft, and because chipboard is a great deal cheaper than wooden floorboards, this option is economical too. Make sure you have access to underfloor services, however.

Wood paneling is an excellent means of providing finished wall/ceiling surfaces in lofts and can make use of much of the roof support structure. It is also ideal for lightweight partitioning.

Basic skills: brick

An exposed brick finish on one wall, often the chimney breast, adds a new visual dimension to a room, and can complement natural wood paneling or a flagstone or tiled floor. It is worthwhile getting to know more about the bricks available and how finishes are achieved, even if you don't do the hard work yourself and have to call in the professionals.

You don't need a bricklayer's skills when decorating or refurbishing the rooms of a structurally sound property. However, a knowledge of brick types and their use, pointing, and the method of knocking up a mortar mix is useful. It will also help if you can recognize bondings and the different form of mortar joints available for decorative duties, should you decide to take a wall back to the brick. Although the same basic principles apply to walls constructed of local stone, the irregular stone formation of the wall requires only an examination of quality of construction, and the number of gaps and crevices that need filling.

Bricks

You may encounter three types of brick as you investigate what your house is made of.

Facing bricks

These are well made, often have a textured finish that allows their use as an exposed internal wall, and come in a variety of colors.

Common bricks

These have no special finish, and are intended to be covered up, usually by plaster or render. They can be identified by their mottled pinkish appearance.

Engineering brick

Facing brick

Common brick

Engineering bricks

These are super-smooth and are often used as damp-proof, nonabsorbent foundation courses due to their density and strength.

If you think an exposed brick wall will add to the character of your room, check the type of brick and bonding before starting work, because normally only an outside or load-bearing wall will be suitable. Carefully remove a small patch of plaster from your chosen wall, using a flooring chisel and mallet, to uncover the bricks.

If they are consistent with the rest of the house, the bond is uniformly well laid, and the mortar a regular depth, the wall is suitable. If you find pink common bricks that are badly laid and inconsistent with the house finish, stud walls where brick debris is laid between wooden uprights, or lightweight, aerated, or dense solid blocks, do not proceed. This wall was never meant to be seen. Your only option is to repair the hole in the plaster and rethink the plan.

Removing plaster

Assuming your wall is suitable, remove the plaster with a flooring chisel as before. This is a dirty, dusty process, so you should wear protective clothing, eye protection, and a dust mask.

At the top of the wall carry down lumps of plaster if you can, but don't drop them. Try to remove smaller pieces directly into a garbage bag. This will keep the amount of dust to a minimum. Remove the baseboard and clean up around the base of the wall. A cornice needs care; cut in with a flooring chisel directly underneath and proceed

very carefully; a stable molding (one that is not cracked) should remain in position as you remove the plaster below it, even though you will damage the bottom curve slightly.

Repair and smooth off the bottom edge of the molding as soon as possible. It will be ultra-absorbent, so a solution of water-diluted PVA should be applied, wetting the edge. Leave this to dry, repeat the process, and carefully smooth off with multifinish plaster. It is not a good idea to use joint compound in this instance, because it isn't strong enough.

Glass bricks can be used in external and internal walls as a means of letting light pass through, but without the clarity of a normal window. They are usually square in shape.

THE PARTS OF A STANDARD BRICK

The various faces of a brick have specific names. The stretcher face is the long side; the header face the end; the frog is the recessed upper face; and the bed face is the flat bottom. Bricks are laid frog-up, although in a garden wall, the top course may be laid frog-down to provide a flat finished surface.

Frog

Stretcher face

Header face

2½ in./6.5 cm

Bed face (underneath)

8½ in./21.5 cm

4 in./10.25 cm

Raking out with a plugging chisel.

Cleaning down

As the plaster repairing the cornice starts to dry, wash the wall down with warm water, beginning where the plaster ties the cornice into the brick, achieving a smooth line. Continue down the wall, washing away the surface dust to reveal the state of the brick pointing, and leave the wall to dry out. If the wall is absorbent, or the surface of the brickwork is flaky or floury, brush on a coat of masonry stabilizer. This solution has an unpleasant, sticky finish. Always wear gloves and protect your eyes from splashes.

Pointing the wall

Now you have revealed the bare brick face of a plastered wall. At best the mortar joints will be roughly and haphazardly finished, and probably recessed slightly. For this wall to become a "display" surface, it needs pointing and shaped, decorative mortar joints. Pointing compresses the original mortar and waterproofs the brick joints when used on an external wall. For an internal wall compression and angular decoration are the aims.

Preparation

Assuming you have washed down, and stabilized the surface if necessary, make room for the new pointing by raking out the old, crumbling mortar to a depth of 1 in./2.5 cm. You will need a cold chisel for this, preferably a plugging chisel with a slanted head, sometimes with a groove cut into it, to clear out the waste faster. You may find a

highly useful tool known as a seaming or chasing chisel or seam drill. If you use a chasing bit in a power drill for this task, particularly if it has hammer action, take care not to damage the brick corners because any damage done to the bricks now will spoil the effect of displaying the wall.

Mortar—proportions and mixing

Knocking up a mortar mix may seem simple, but accurate measuring is vital. Proportions are designated by volume, not by weight, so use a bucket. Don't be tempted to "measure" by using a spade as a yardstick because sand and cement will not "sit" on the spade the same way. Avoid the use of dishwashing liquid instead of a plasticizer. A liquid plasticizer is a liquid air entraining admixture that forms air bubbles in the final mix. These bubbles are spaces into

THE FOUR MAIN TYPES OF BOND

English bond: The courses of bricks alternate stretcher-on and header-on.

Flemish bond: Bricks in each course alternate header-on and stretcher-on.

Header bond: Bricks in every course are laid header-on, the wall being a full brick wide.

Stretcher bond: Bricks in every course are laid stretcher-on, the wall being half a brick wide.

POINTING

STEP 1 Measure out the correct amounts of sand and cement. Accuracy is essential.

STEP 2 Adding plasticizer to the mix will make it more workable and prevent cracking as it dries.

STEP 3 Turn the ingredients over dry until they are well mixed. Form a crater in the middle of the pile.

STEP 4 Gradually add water to the crater and mix well. Take care not to make it too sloppy.

which the water expands, stopping cracks appearing. Plasticizers are available from builders' merchants in multiples of 1 quart/1 liter. Add to your sand and cement mix in the quantity specified on the container. Use soft sand, also called builders' sand, and ordinary Portland cement in a mix of

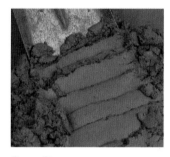

STEP 5 The mix is correct when it holds ridges formed by chopping the spade across it.

STEP 6 Fill the vertical joints first, using the tip of the pointing trowel to form a neat profile.

STEP 7 Finish off by pointing the horizontal joints, creating your preferred decorative profile.

5½ to 1, plus plasticizer, if you buy separate ingredients. Otherwise use a dry ready-mix and add plasticizer, or a dry masonry mix (containing plasticizer) and add sand. Measure the correct proportions, and blend the dry mix well, using a 10 in./25 cm bricklayer's trowel. You will need about the same amount of water as cement. Add the right amount of plasticizer, and pour half the water into a crater in the middle of the dry mix. Mix from the outside inward, slowly filling in the crater, adding more water as absorption takes place and turning the mixture several times. When you can chop firm, smooth fillets into the surface with the trowel, the mix is ready.

On the hawk

Use a small brush to dampen the recessed joints with water. It is important to attend to only a small area at a time; otherwise you will find that the joints will dry out. Put some mortar on a hawk, select a slither with the pointing trowel edge, and draw it into the vertical, then horizontal joint. Flush pointing is finished with the side of the trowel; vee or struck pointing is finished with a backward sliding action of the trowel point. Concave pointing is finished with the trowel handle or similar, and recessed pointing is finished by pressing a sized length of wood into the joint. For internal joints, concave pointing shows off the bricks to advantage, and flush pointing is a good idea if the brick edges and corners are damaged. Recessed pointing should only be attempted on brickwork that is in near-perfect condition, and weatherstruck finishes are, as the name implies, for use on external walls.

Top joint:
flush pointing
Bottom joint:
struck pointing

Top joint:
concave pointing
Bottom joint:
weatherstruck pointing

Top joint: vee pointing
Bottom joint: recessed pointing

Tools and equipment

Tools for brickwork and wall surfaces can be categorized as implements of either destruction or construction, in the form of breaking and shaping tools, such as brick chisels and masons' chisels, measuring and mixing tools, and application and finishing tools. A few may already be in your general tool kit, but most will have to be bought specifically for the job.

Plumb line

Wetting brush

Wall brush

Remove old plaster or render with a bolster or mason's chisel, driven by a mallet weighing at least 2½ lb./1 kg Lesser weights will cause vibrations, making the chisel difficult to control. A crowbar will be needed if a fireplace has to be taken out.

Chop out old mortar with a plugging chisel. Clean the wall with a large paint brush and wet the joint areas with a small paint brush. Measure out your materials in a bucket, or a small plastic container depending on the required amount, mix them with a bricklayer's trowel on a mixing or spot board, and carry smaller amounts to the job on a bat or hawk.

Ensure the wall is plumb and level with a spirit level and plumb bob. Use a pointing trowel to insert slivers of mortar and finish joints.

Render or plaster larger areas with a plasterer's trowel, use a straightedge for leveling the floating coat and obtain a flat finish by polishing the area with a wooden float. Damp down the wall and splash water on the trowel with a brush.

Buying materials

Buying in bulk is generally more economical than buying small amounts because storing items for future use reduces the unit price. Materials that degrade, however, become a liability. Cement bought in a 55-lb./25-kg pack is not economical if you have to throw three-quarters of it away, which will happen if it gets even slightly damp. A cement binder sets by water action, and must be completely dry when mixing starts.

Storing badly sealed, partly used packs on concrete floors, in cellars, or in outbuildings is pointless. A better proposition is available from home centers, in the form of dry ready-mixes, sand and cement prepacked in quantities of 11 lb./5 kg, and multiples thereof. Be sure to pick the correct premix.

Bricklayers' mortar mix contains the soft sand you need for pointing. A sand-and-cement mix for general use, like flooring screeds, will contain sharp sand, which is not suitable. Plasticizers to add to the mix come in powder and liquid form. Usually the liquid is easier to measure and use, and is available in quart/liter containers.

TOP TIP
Always consider your personal safety before starting building work. Bags of sand are extremely heavy and must be lifted correctly, the legs taking the weight, to reduce the chance of a back injury. Wear protective shoes or boots, safety glasses to keep flying debris and dust out of your eyes, a dust mask, gloves, and knee pads, which are invaluable if you are spending time scrabbling about on the floor knocking up mortar.

Cleat or ground (thickness guide)

Steel rul

BASIC TOOL KIT

Bricklayer's trowel

Plastic float

Pointing trowel

Mallet

Hawk

Steel float

Bucket

Spirit level

Brick chisel with hand protector

Mason's chisel with hand protector

Plugging chisel

Mason's chisel

Bat

YOU WILL NEED:
- HAMMER AND FLOORING CHISEL
- BRUSH
- WATER
- BUCKET
- PLASTER
- WOOD CLEATS
- NAILS
- HAWK
- SPOT BOARD
- TROWEL
- PROTECTIVE GLASSES
- DROP CLOTHS

PROJECT
Plastering

You may never need to plaster an entire wall in your property, but a knowledge of basic techniques is useful. Practice can improve your technique and make smaller "patching" jobs and improving parts of a wall surface easier.

Preparation and plaster types

Absorbent old brick walls draw water out of a plaster coat too quickly, resulting in severe cracking. Absorbency can be tested by brushing on water. If it disappears immediately, it is a high-suction surface. If it sits on the surface or partly runs off, it is a low-suction surface. For jobs around the house, coating the wall with water-diluted PVA will seal and stabilize the surface.

Walls should be damp prior to plastering, and smooth surfaces must be roughened or "keyed." Mixed plaster is applied to the wall surface in two consecutive coats. First, apply a thick backing or floating coat, known as bonding. Follow this within two hours by a thin skim coat, known as the finish. Don't confuse the finishing skim with thistle board finish, which is a single skim coat for use on wallboard partition walls.

Mixing

Mix equal amounts of water and plaster in a bucket. Crumble any lumpy bits, and wait while the plaster absorbs the water. Stir well. The backing coat should be stiff. The finish should be

PREPARING AND SPREADING

STEP 2 Test the suction of the wall by brushing on water. Choose a plaster to suit.

STEP 3 Nail wooden cleats, known as "grounds," to the wall to provide a guide to the depth of plaster.

STEP 1 Remove all old plaster by hacking it off with a hammer and flooring chisel. Wear eye protection to guard against flying particles. This is a very dirty and dusty process, so protect adjacent surfaces.

STEP 4 Mix the plaster with water in a bucket; a mixing attachment in an electric drill speeds the job.

STEP 5 Practice lifting plaster from the hawk until you are happy that you can do it well.

STEP 6 Hold the hawk close to the wall and scoop the plaster from it onto the wall with the trowel.

STEP 7 Spread the plaster up the wall, keeping the lower edge of the blade pressed in.

STEP 8 Look for any gaps, hollows and imperfections in the surface and fill with more plaster.

thinner, and easier to work. Empty the contents of the bucket onto your spot board and knead the mix into ridges with a plasterer's trowel. The bonding should hold the ridges, but the finish should be slightly too liquid to do so.

On the hawk

Position the hawk under the spot board, and push some plaster onto it with the trowel. Hold your trowel at right angles to the hawk, and push the plaster mound away from you, while tilting the hawk upright. Scrape the trowel up the surface and off, loading the plaster onto the trowel ready for application onto the wall.

On the wall

The required depth of plaster is usually marked out on the wall by wooden cleats, called grounds, stuck or nailed to the wall. Cleats should be about ½ in./1.2 cm thick, and spaced roughly a yard/metre apart. Plaster between them; when the bonding coat has partially set, remove a cleat and reposition it farther along the wall. Continue the plaster up to the cleat, repeating the process until the wall is covered. Start the plaster at the base of the wall, hold the hawk against the right-hand wooden ground and scoop the plaster onto the wall, with the bottom edge of the trowel on the cleat, tilting up. Push the trowel up the wall slowly to unload the plaster, spreading it evenly. Subsequent plaster loads can be spread parallel to the first, keeping to the same thickness throughout, until the whole area between the grounds is covered.

A straightedge resting on the two grounds will scrape off excess plaster. As the backing coat goes off, it needs to be keyed to accept the finish coat. Do this by scratching the surface lightly with two nails hammered through a wood off-cut.

Skimming

The finishing coat comprises thinner plaster. This is spread onto the wall in a thin coating. Work an area you can easily reach in one arm movement, troweling evenly. Return to the starting position and apply a second, thinner coat over the top. Cover the wall in this way. Dip the trowel blade in water, hold it at an angle to the surface, skim off any splashes, and leave it to harden. Polish the wall to a flat finish with the trowel surface.

Key the backing coat by scoring the plaster surface as it begins to go off. Spread on a thin finish coat (a thinner plaster), working from the bottom of the wall to the top.

Wall tiles

If you think wall tiles are suitable only for kitchens and bathrooms, think again. There is now a tile for every purpose and situation, be it decorative or protective. There is an amazingly diverse choice, and you can stick tiles on tables and cabinets, in alcoves, and on storage shelves.

Ceramic tiles have been used as wall decoration for centuries, as these classical designs show.

FAR RIGHT: **Tiles are perfect in a kitchen, providing a hard-wearing, hygienic surface for walls and counters. Use them on large areas such as walls or backsplashes behind basins and work surfaces.**

BELOW: **A backsplash behind a washbasin is the ideal first project in tiling. By combining tiles with different patterns and colors, you can create an eye-catching decorative feature that is practical too.**

Choosing wall tiles

The history of tiles can be traced farther back than the birth of Christ, to the eastern Mediterranean and beyond. Early techniques of ceramic decoration were carried from the shores of this sea to North Africa and Western Europe, where an important center was established in the Netherlands. Stone, marble, and glass, particularly in mosaic form, were features of Roman buildings, and many of their decorations are preserved on historical sites today.

An interest in this history has led many independent designers to experiment in limited editions of distinctive handmade tiles. Now tiles for wall decoration and protection can be chosen from an array of glazed and unglazed ceramic, glass, iridescent glass, mirrored glass, mosaic, stoneware, relief, metallic, and cork.

Small independent workshops have abandoned the familiar sizes too: just about any dimension and proportion can be found or ordered. For example, a tile range of 3 in. x 6 in./7.5 cm x 15 cm/is available, which was inspired by London subway stations. A happy compromise between the old imperial 4¼ in. and 6 in. square choices is found at 5 in. x 5 in./13 cm x 13 cm. It is a better idea to select tiles before working out areas, as handmade designs can differ in their dimensions.

Whatever tile size you favor, you will find that the border tile, glazed over two edges, and used at the edges or corners of the wall design, is no longer made. Today's universal tiles or square edge tiles have at least two edges finished and glazed, so that they can be placed either in the middle of a tile run, or at a corner. These tiles were often called field tiles in the past and were fitted with spacing lugs at each edge. Now, they have either a universal joining system based on beveled edges, which butt at the base, or are squared up and require separate spacers. In both cases the resultant surface gap is then filled with grout.

Practical and decorative uses

Kitchen areas, bathrooms, shower units, and backsplashes are traditional places for tiling. A vast range is available today to replace or upgrade your existing finish. Don't neglect other areas, though. Hand-crafted tile sets, complete with a choice of matching or contrasting border tiles and a ceramic chair rail, will give a traditional welcome to your visitors in the entrance hall.

Inside windowsills and surrounds that receive a lot of light will look better if you fix tiles that do not reflect it. Try a finish quality similar to stone, containing muted, subdued colors with an almost satin-like sheen. Stoneware tiles are also suitable for work surfaces in kitchens; they can often provide an attractive alternative to dreary mass-produced worktops. Their slightly uneven surface causes imperfection in color and variation, which breaks up large areas visually. In a food preparation area, however, you will need a waterproof adhesive and a special grout, for hygienic reasons.

Glass tiles

On smaller areas of wall, such as backsplashes, wafer-thin metal designs that are sandwiched between layers of glass give a particularly unusual light effect, with the colors in the metals appearing almost lost inside their tile. Glass is transparent, so the tile adhesive must be evenly applied on a good, flat surface. If you use a notched spreader, the ridges will show through.

For partitioning off small areas without reducing the light levels, try glass blocks. They can be bought as a kit, which includes spacers, reinforcing rods, and mortar. The last can be colored to appear as a grid.

It is important to remember, however, that glass blocks tend to be heavy and will therefore need to be positioned on a substantial foundation. They cannot be built onto a suspended wooden floor.

Cork tiles

Cork has been around a long time, mainly as thin floor tiles. However, it is unsuitable for flooring because it is easily damaged by heels and heavy furniture. It will serve well on a complete wall surface, though, or as part of a half-and-half wall. Thick cork tiles (about ½ in./1.2 cm thick) make a good studio or home office pinboard. You can apply them to form a square or make a shape out of the tiles, then edge them with mitred wooden cleats.

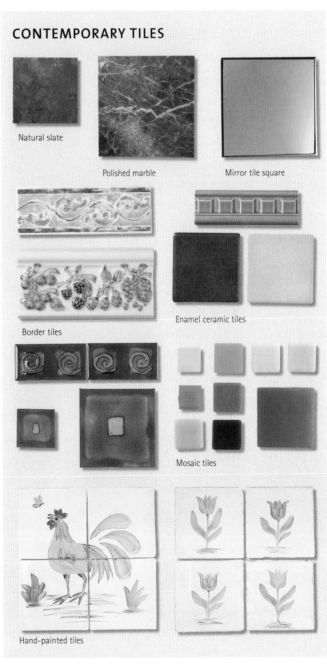

CONTEMPORARY TILES

Natural slate

Polished marble

Mirror tile square

Border tiles

Enamel ceramic tiles

Mosaic tiles

Hand-painted tiles

Tools and equipment

A number of items needed for tiling will be used for other jobs and so may be in your tool kit already. Some of them are "homemade," such as the tiling gauge or marker. Starter kits available from home centers may supply all you need for small tiling jobs and the more expensive items, like tile-cutting jigs, can be rented.

Tile scorer, pencil, and waterproof pen

Starter kits

If you are contemplating just a simple tiling job on a straight wall, it may only be necessary to buy a tiling starter kit, comprising:

• a tile snap cutter and nipper
• a tile edge sander
• adhesive spreader
• tile spacers
• a grout spreader and finisher.

More advanced kits are available; they include:

• tile-cutting machines that incorporate a measuring guide
• angle jig, which works with universal or square-edged tiles.

Ceramic tiles are cut by simple "pencil" scorers, fitted into a tile cutting guide if required, or by a heavy-duty cutter and nipper with a tungsten carbide wheel. In both cases the scored tile is snapped over a match or thin edging strip. Cutting machines with measuring guides and heavy-duty cutting machines capable of cutting tiles up to ¾ in./1.8 cm thick are ideal for large jobs. Tile files will keep the edges smooth, and a tile saw with a tungsten carbide blade will cut in any direction. This will prove essential when pipework must be tiled around. Tile nippers nibble out odd shapes and sizes. Space and plan using tile spacers, a tile gauge, and marker cleats, a spirit level, a retractable steel tape, a pencil (for the wall), waterproof pen (for the tile), and hammer and masonry nails to attach the cleats. Painter's tape will be useful for holding insert tiles (like soap dishes) in position while the adhesive sets. Adhesive and grout are supplied in ready-to-use plastic containers, often with the required spreader. Use water-resistant adhesive and grout where tiles may be splashed, but in shower cubicles and sunken bathtub surrounds a waterproof adhesive and grout are needed. Worktops need a special two-part epoxy resin grout if they are to be used for food preparation. If one is not provided with the adhesive, you will need a notched plastic spreader. For large areas, use a notched trowel. A grout remover, flexible spreader, and finisher will complete the job. Keep a supply of cloths for cleaning and polishing to hand at all times.

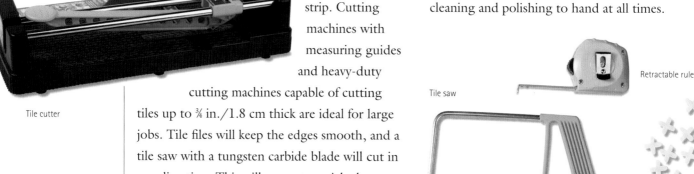

Tile cutter

Tile saw

Retractable rule

Tile spacers

Spirit level

Motorized tile cutter

Adhesives
and cloths

Cork tiles do not require
any special tools for cutting.
A sharp craft knife, steel
straightedge, and accurate
measuring are all that are needed
when using ½ in./1.2 cm cork. A special ready-
to-use water-based adhesive with a notched
applicator binds the tiles to the wall. Wooden
cleat frames used as a decorative border for these
tiles also protect the vulnerable outside edges
from damage. Finished lumber ½ in. x 1¾ in./
1.2 cm x 4.2 cm can be bought in packs, and will
fit the edge depth. You will need to miter the
corners to fit. Secure the cleats to the wall with
1¼ in./3.2 cm number 8 countersunk head
screws. You can easily disguise the heads by
overlaying the same lumber size ½ in./1.2 cm to
the inside, overlapping the cork edge, and
pinning or gluing it into position. If you are
using cork floor tiles on a wall for a decorative
effect, you can apply polyurethane varnish as a
sealing finish, or simply leave them unsealed.

Heavy-duty snips
and cutter

Notched
spreader

Bucket

Tile side nippers

Cloths

Sponge

Masonry nails

Curved claw hammer

Homemade
tiling gauge
and cleat

YOU WILL NEED:
- PENCIL
- PRIMER OR DILUTED PVA
- SPIRIT LEVEL AND PLUMB LINE
- CLEATS
- HAMMER
- MASONRY NAILS
- TILES
- SANDER (IF REQUIRED)

Basic skills: preparation

Grout lines between tiles form very obvious geometric patterns and are often emphasized by colored grouts for decorative purposes. For this reason you need to be sure that the patterning will fit square to the walls. Thus accurate measuring and marking out are vital, for nothing looks worse than sloping tiling.

Preparing surfaces

First, examine the surface carefully. It must be flat and sound, and clean and dry without being too absorbent. Bare plaster surfaces are ideal, but if they are porous, they will quickly draw moisture from the adhesive, and the tiles will become loose. Brush on a coat of stabilizing primer or a diluted PVA solution. If the plaster is unsound or cracked in part, it must be filled. Rake out all loose material and brush the surface down well. Coat the area with diluted PVA as before, to stabilize the cracked edges, before making good the damage. New plaster must completely dry out, and an entire wall should be left for six weeks before a stabilizing solution is brushed on.

Man-made boards present no problem, provided their surfaces are sealed and dirt, grease and fingermarks are cleaned off. Wallboard is likely to be found as a wall surface. If you are erecting your own, use the rougher side of the board as an outer surface because it will provide a better "key." Smooth, man-made worktops will need abrading by hand or with an orbital sander.

All sound, previously painted surfaces need is a "key" for the adhesive, but flaking paint must be removed. Never attempt to tile on top of wallpaper, no matter how well it appears to adhere. You must strip the surface and treat the bare plaster as described above.

Previously tiled surfaces are a good base for new tiles, but, as usual, the surface must be sound. Stick down any loose tiles, and clean the whole surface thoroughly. It is not necessary to fill small cracks or defects because the new adhesive will span any gaps. Bare brick and rough concrete walls will be uneven and need to be treated as you would floor surfaces. You need to level the surface using a cement render and then set the tiles in a thick bedding adhesive.

Estimating, marking, and setting out

The number of tiles needed to cover a wall area depends on their size. Manufacturers issue tables indicating tiles per square yard/square meter based on standard sizes. For example, 72 tiles of 4¼ in. x 4¼ in./10.8 cm x 10.8 cm are needed to

Tiled surfaces are traditional for bathrooms. In this instance oblong tiles have been laid with an overlapping bond much like brickwork, rather than the usual grid layout.

cover a square yard, 86 of them to fill a square meter. However, with the availability of limited edition and hand-made tiles of varying sizes, it is a much better idea to make your own calculation from a homemade measuring gauge.

Select your tile and two lengths of (straight) wooden cleating. Mark out the tile positions on the cleats with a pencil, including the grout lines for the horizontal and vertical rows. If your chosen tile is square, then one tiling gauge will suffice. Place the gauge against the wall and count the number of tiles in each direction, then multiply the horizontal number by the vertical number. Add a few extra tiles to guard against mishaps, such as breakages and cutting errors.

Now that you have worked out the numbers, consider your next move carefully. Tiling must

Now check the walls for square with a spirit level and plumb line. If the baseboard is a true level, it can be used as a starting point, otherwise nail on a support cleat so that it is level, its top edge just under a tile height from the baseboard, or from the floor if the baseboard is not part of your plan. You can accommodate any unevenness in the baseboard or floor by cutting tiles to fit the gap between it and the first row of whole tiles.

At the tile vertical line nearest to the corner, nail a vertical cleat; place a loose tile at the right-angled join to check accuracy. The cleats support the tiles while the adhesive sets. Use masonry nails to fix the cleats in place but don't knock them all the way in—you will need to pull them out later with a curved claw hammer and remove the cleats. Fill the remaining gaps with cut tiles.

PREPARING TO TILE

STEP 1 Mark a guide line for the horizontal support cleat a tile's height above the skirting.

STEP 2 Check the adjoining wall for plumb with a spirit level. If it is vertical, use it as a tiling guide.

STEP 3 Or, nail in a vertical cleat in line with the last whole tile position before the corner.

STEP 4 Check the baseboard with a spirit level; if truly horizontal you can use it as a tiling guide.

start in the correct position on the wall, and lines must be level and plumb, not necessarily following baseboards or crown moldings. Set out and mark the wall area using the tiling gauge to plan exactly where complete tiles will lie, and where you will need to cut to size. On a plain wall, start in the middle, but if the wall has a window or a door, it is a good idea to center the tile layout on the opening, so that the pattern formed by the tiles does not make the room seem unbalanced. Move the starting point if necessary.

STEP 5 Otherwise, nail a horizontal cleat to the wall as a support for the first row of tiles.

STEP 6 Check the two cleats meet at an exact right-angle by holding a tile in the corner.

YOU WILL NEED:
- CLEAT SUPPORT
- TILES
- ADHESIVE
- GROUT
- NOTCHED TROWEL
- CRUCIFORM SPACERS
  (IF REQUIRED)
- SPIRIT LEVEL

PROJECT
Basic tiling

Tiling is not a difficult skill to master, but if you've not done any before it's a good idea to start with a small, simple "squared-up" area, such as a wall backsplash behind a basin. When you are happy with an elementary project, you will have the confidence to move on to a more taxing job involving corners and cuts.

Basin backsplash

The easiest way to get used to tiling surfaces is to start with a basin backsplash. All you have to do is center the tile design over the basin, and make sure that it is level.

Measure up one tile height from where the basin joins the wall, and mark a level line with a pencil—don't assume the basin is square or level.

Use your tile gauge, resting on the pencil line, to find the center, and mark the tile grid on the wall. Then nail on a support cleat, with the top edge butting the pencil line. Cover the marked area with adhesive (a notched spreader is usually supplied with the tub), applying firm pressure against the wall. You need to make even, equal ridges over the tiling area, so that the tiles sit uniformly when positioned. Use a twisting action

of the wrist to press the tiles into place, separating them with small plastic spacers. Leave the adhesive to set for 24 hours.

Lever off the support cleat and complete the last row of tiles. You may need to adjust the tile size slightly with a tile file if the basin is not level. The final step is to apply the grout. Use the flexible spreader supplied to push the grout between the tiles, pulling the spreader firmly across the face of the tiles. Gently scrape off the grout left on the surface of the tiles. Run the grout finisher along the joints to smooth them off, achieving a consistent appearance. Clean the tiles with a damp sponge. Finally, polish with a soft cloth.

Tiling a wall

If you have completed a basic tiling job, the only difficulties you are likely to encounter with an entire wall involve accurate setting out and tile cutting. Measure, mark, and set out your grid on the wall in such a way that cut tiles appear at the end of the wall, not in the middle, under a window or over a door. Other obstructions, such as bathtub panels that are to be incorporated into

TILING A WALL

STEP 1 Working on a manageable area at a time, spread adhesive on the wall with a notched trowel.

STEP 2 Place a row of tiles along the cleat, then add the second row, pressing them firmly into place.

STEP 3 To ensure uniform grouting gaps, insert plastic cruciform spacers between the tiles.

STEP 4 Check periodically with your spirit level that the rows of tiles maintain a horizontal run.

the overall design, may designate a starting point of a different height; a complete row of tiles looks better at the top of the panel rather than at the bottom. If your wall has a recessed window ledge, a row of cut tiles will look better next to the window frame instead of butting the main wall surface.

When a basin or sink is positioned under a window, you must consider both. If the gap between basin and sill is not an exact number of tiles, the cut row butts the sill, not the basin. The first line of tiles on the sill is still a complete line, however. Don't be tempted to try to match two tile halves over a corner by starting the sill with the cut row, because the grout lines will become too fragmentary.

The rule is always to attempt a symmetrical layout around doors and windows. Narrow tile strips that have to be cut to fit one side of a frame only will stand out visually, the grout lines emphasizing an off-center arrangement. Center your layout over a door, using an imaginary vertical line drawn through the middle, and fix guide cleats around the frame, to let all complete rows be set in place first. Cut tiles can be positioned later, once the adhesive has set and the supports have been removed. Follow this procedure for a single window, but if you have a wall with two openings side by side, imagine a vertical line drawn halfway between the two, and center your whole tile layout on it.

If you have a wall with a number of features that must be tiled around, draw up a scale plan on tracing paper and lay this over a sheet of squared paper to represent the tiles. By moving the traced plan of the wall and its features around, you can determine the best starting point for the tiling.

The tiling technique is the same as that used for a backsplash: start at the cleated right-angled corner, and spread just enough adhesive onto the

wall to fix about a dozen tiles. Universal beveled-edge tiles will space themselves, but square-edge tiles need spacers at the corners. Work in level rows, using the cleat support, but checking at intervals with a spirit level, until the wall is covered with whole tiles. The adhesive must set for 24 hours before cleats are levered off and cut tiles placed into the gaps.

Ceramic tiles can be used to create a small decorative backsplash behind a handbasin in a bedroom or half-bathroom.

YOU WILL NEED:

- WATERPROOF PEN
- STEEL STRAIGHTEDGE
- SCRIBER AND NAILS
  (OR CUTTING
  MACHINE)
- NIPPERS
- TILE SAW
- TILE NIPPERS
- TILE FILE
- TILE ADHESIVE
- PAINTER'S TAPE
- GROUT
- CORNER TRIM
- DAMP CLOTH/SPONGE
- GROUT FINISHER OR
  DOWEL OFFCUT
- TRIM OR BORDER

PROJECT

Cutting, completing and finishing

Cutting tiles to fit is easy, but take care to measure each one accurately. Then either score, using a hand-held scriber, and snap over a couple of nails, or use a cutting machine just like the professionals. You can rent one from your specialty supplier very cheaply, and it makes the whole process simpler and speedier.

Cutting

Cutting tiles to fit into the gaps at the ends of whole rows, or to fit around door crown moldings and other obstructions, can be done simply with a "pencil" scriber, tile-cutting guide, and a couple of masonry nails. Hold the tile up to the wall, mark the area to be removed using a waterproof pen, and place the tile on a cutting surface. Score a line on the glazed face with the

scriber and guide. Then place a masonry nail under the scored mark at each end and snap the tile cleanly by applying downward pressure on each side. The guide is especially useful for the accurate cutting of narrow pieces, but for cutting thicker ceramics, a heavy-duty cutter with a tungsten carbide wheel is a better tool.

A cutting machine will save time on major jobs. Some heavy-duty versions have angled jigs as well as measuring guides, enabling you to cut tapers and angles by adjusting a side fence. Angled cut-outs and holes for fitting around pipes can be made by scoring the shape of the cut on the glazed surface, then breaking off the waste part of the tile using nippers or a small pair of pincers. Alternatively, make the cut-out with a tile saw fitted with a tungsten carbide rod saw

CUTTING TILES

STEP 1 Mark tiles for cutting with a waterproof pen, holding them in place over the last whole tile.

STEP 2 Hold a steel straightedge across the face of the tile and score the tile with a scriber.

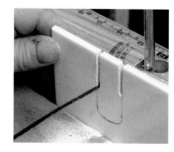

STEP 3 Place a nail under each end of the line and press down with your thumbs to snap the tile in two.

STEP 4 Use a cutting machine if you have a lot of tiles to cut. Set the tile in place and score it.

STEP 5 Use the integral nipper to cut the tile to size. Angled cuts are possible using some machines.

STEP 6 For small cut-outs, use tile nippers to gradually nibble away the waste area of tile.

STEP 7 A tile saw is useful for cutting intricate shapes, as its rod blade will cut in any direction.

STEP 8 Tile nippers have angled jaws that make it easier to break a tile in two than using your thumbs

LAYING AND GROUTING

STEP 1 Butt tiles together at an internal corner or use a plastic corner molding for a neat finish.

STEP 2 At an external corner apply adhesive and butt the tiles up to those on the adjacent wall.

STEP 3 If your tiles don't have rounded edges, use corner trim to finish off an external corner.

STEP 4 As you grout, wipe off the excess with a damp sponge. Don't let it dry on the tile face.

blade that you can angle in any direction. Any jagged edges can be removed with a tile file before the piece is held up to the wall.

Completing

If space is tight, such as in an internal corner where small strips of tile must be placed to complete a row, spread the adhesive directly onto the tile back, not the wall surface, and push the tile into position. Unless you are using plastic corner trim to finish off an internal corner, the tiles on one wall should fit up to the adjacent wall, then the tiles on that wall should be cut to leave a grouting gap at the corner.

Some cutting machines have a removable cutting gauge that can be used to measure the size of cut tile required and which makes an automatic allowance for the grouting gap. Since the tiling will always be centered on the wall, or some feature on it, it is unlikely that you will finish a row at an internal or external corner with a whole tile. If you have insert tiles as part of the layout, for example a bathroom-roll holder, leave the correct space on the wall when tiling. Its extra weight means the insert tile must be fixed when the remainder of the wall has set. Use strips of printer's tape to hold it in position while the adhesive sets. Grout the tiled surface and keep wiping the surface with a damp cloth. Run the

finisher from your tile kit, or a small offcut of dowel with the end rounded by abrasive paper firmly along the grout channels for a uniform grooved finish.

Finishing

Tile trims, beads and rails, slimline borders, and chair rails are often available to add a finishing touch. Workshops that make tiles by hand offer overall schemes with matching border and finishing tiles, and it is a good idea to investigate all the possibilities. You can also edge tiles with hardwood moldings that use the tile adhesive as a fixing. Try ramin quadrant or mahogany scotia as a top edging on a half wall, or use a hardwood angle molding pressed into an internal or external corner.

STEP 5 Give the grouted joints a neat profile with a grout finisher. Then polish the tiles clean.

You can buy a variety of narrow ceramic border tiles to finish off the edges of tiled areas.

TOP TIP

Most tile grouting is white, but sometimes a plain or very basic patterned tile can be given a new lease of life by using one of the colored grouts available. Existing white grout can also be transformed by treating with a contrasting colored dye, which will emphasize the grid lines and linear structure.

YOU WILL NEED:
- **MIRROR TILES**
- **DOUBLE-SIDED PADS**
  OR FIXERS
- **PENCIL**
- **HORIZONTAL AND**
  VERTICAL CLEATS
- **NUMBER 8 HEAD**
  SCREWS/
  WALL ANCHORS
- **SCREWDRIVER**
- **HARDWOOD**
  MOLDING STRIP

PROJECT
Mosaics and mirrors

If small paneled areas of mosaic in a room are purely decorative, then mirror tiles can perform a useful function. Iridescent glass mosaic in pewter or cobalt can be bordered with waxed woodstrip in a small display; mirror tiles in a cleat grid can reflect much-needed light patterns along a dull corridor.

The use of wood strips to outline or emphasize specific tiled areas on a wall is particularly apposite when bordering mosaics. This usually decorative technique combines small pieces of ceramic, stone, or glass, called tesserae, to make up a larger picture or abstract image. Areas of similarly colored tesserae that are visually broken up by lines of grout benefit greatly from an external definition in the form of a natural wood border. This border can form any shape around any display; it does not have to be square or rectangular, although floor-to-ceiling strips of mosaic can be very effective on otherwise plain walls.

Using mosaic squares

The easiest way of making up a panel is to buy sheets of mosaic squares, consisting of equally spaced tesserae held in place by a mesh cloth backing or, in some instances, a paper facing.

You will find a popular size is 30 cm x 30 cm, about a square foot, although other sizes are available. Specialist manufacturers offer many different color combinations, from strong greens and pinks to muted yellows, and with a suitable border these will add considerably to any scheme you choose. Being able to position complete sheets of ready spaced tesserae one after the other on the wall surface speeds up the whole process enormously.

Traditionally, the individual pieces would have been laid separately. All you need to do is stick and grout, as you would larger wall tiles. Mark out and prepare the wall as you would for any ceramic tiling job, then spread adhesive onto the surface. Some manufacturers recommend applying grout to the back of the mosaic sheet first, then bedding down on the wall with a homemade tamping block (a piece of plywood with a square of old carpet glued to it). Others ask you to follow tradition, which is to bed to the wall, leave it to set for 24 hours, remove any facing, and then apply the grout. The second method is faster, because you are able to grout the spaces between the tile sheets at the same time as the tesserae, as opposed to having to grout twice.

MIRROR TILES

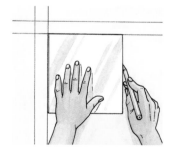

STEP 1 Use a tile to mark out a grid, allowing spaces for the horizontal and vertical battens.

STEP 2 Screw the framework of softwood cleats to the wall and finish them as required.

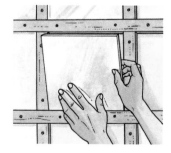

STEP 3 Attach double-sided pads to the backs of the mirror tiles and press them firmly into place.

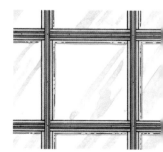

STEP 4 Pin lengths of hardwood molding to the centers of the cleats conceal the fixing screws.

Grids

The grid formed by strong grout lines can look striking. Dark grouts emphasizing pale mosaic squares make an interesting reverse image; the lines are almost more important than the squares. The grid theme can be taken further by using large tiles spaced by wooden cleats; in this case the wood strips form a grid.

Mirror tiles

Using mirror tiles inside the grid gives an interesting result. When placed on a wall that receives direct sunlight, the reflected light patterns adjacent walls and increases overall light levels. A short corridor can be lengthened visually in this way. Simply draw a grid of squares onto the appropriate wall using the mirror tiles and 2 in. x 1 in./5 cm x 2.5 cm planed wood as a dimensional guide. Fix the wood lengths to the wall following the grid. Screw 2 in./5 cm number 8 countersunk head screws into wall anchors, or use a contact adhesive. Position the mirror tiles in the squares formed by the cleats

TOP TIP

Mosaic artists make up their own grout mix because the grout is an important part of the design. Use soft sand (3 parts), cement (1 part), and a cement dye to color the mix before adding water. The color of the grout can contrast with or complement the tesserae. Current thinking is that white grout lines form a visually distracting grid pattern, as well as appearing to pull color away from such small pieces. If this is a problem on your wall, ready-mixed grouts are available, but color choice is limited. Any acrylic paint color can be added to a water-based mix. Color can also be added to the grout after it has set, but this would be a tedious job on a large area of mosaic. Similarly, attempting to shape the grout joints is not worthwhile, as the grout would dry before you had finished; simply sponge them flush.

and stick them securely with the double-sided fixers. Pin a ¾ in./1.8 cm hardwood molding strip on top of the cleats as both a decorative finish and to hide the screwheads.

TOP LEFT: **Use the mirror-tile grid idea to transform a narrow dark corridor. The tiles will reflect any available light onto the facing wall, giving the impression of greater space and airiness.**

TOP RIGHT: **Mosaics are a natural for bathrooms. They are supplied in panels, letting you tile large areas quite quickly. What's more, individual tiles can be removed from the panels for fitting around obstacles. If any do need cutting, this can be done with nippers.**

YOU WILL NEED:
FOR SHELVING:
- **SUPPORT CLEATS**
- **DRILL, HEAD SCREWS, AND WALL ANCHORS**
- **HAMMER AND PINS**
- **SPIRIT LEVEL**
- **SHELVES**
- **DECORATIVE MOLDING/BEADING**

PROJECT

Shelving: wood and tile effects

B uilding shelves into an alcove is easy—they sit on cleats screwed to the walls. You could also try something more adventurous like pinning TGV lengths to the cleats above and below the back and two sides of each shelf, thereby creating a stylish wood surround that also hides all the cleat fixings.

Built-in shelving

The need for shelving to hold frequently used items is not confined to kitchens and bathrooms. The modern home has books, tapes, disks, and other paraphernalia that must be to hand. These items may still be kept in traditional free-standing

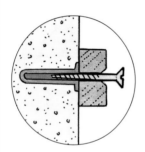 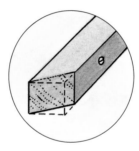

Shelves in alcoves can be supported by screwing cleats to the back and end walls. In a solid wall use wall anchors; in a hollow wall, screw to the studwork.

For neatness, miter the outer ends of the side cleats so that they become less obvious. Or hide them with a cleat beneath the front edge of the shelf.

bookcases, which were once essential items of room furniture. Their obvious advantage over built-in shelving is that they could be moved from room to room as needs altered. That advantage now seems outweighed by the amount of wall space needlessly taken up by such large pieces of furniture.

Built-in shelving solves storage problems while taking up previously unusable room space, such as small alcoves, chimney-breast recesses and dead-end corridors. When shelving is placed at head height, the shelf fixings are fairly obvious, and support cleats with exposed screwheads will need a smaller woodstrip pinned on top to hide them. The cleat arrangement must then be painted to match the wall. The shelves should be varnished or painted a different color, so that the eye picks them out first, and the supports appear to be part of the background wall.

Floor-to-ceiling shelving

Ideal for an alcove, this scheme maximizes the storage capacity of a small area while taking up the minimum of floor space. If sited next to a chimney breast, for example, the floor line should

BUILT-IN SHELVING

 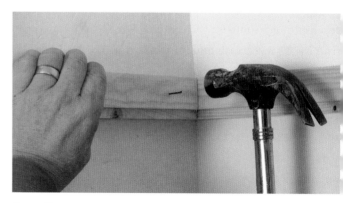

STEP 1 Cut the shelf support cleats to length, drill and anchor the wall, and screw the cleats to the back and end walls of the alcove. Make sure that they are truly horizontal by checking with a spirit level.

STEP 2 Countersink the fixing screws, then conceal them by pinning on thinner strips of wood or decorative molding. Make sure this is flush with the top edges of the cleats.

FLOOR-TO-CEILING SHELVING

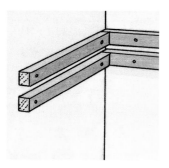

STEP 1 To line the alcove with paneling, fit cleats to the walls above and below each shelf position.

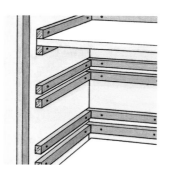

STEP 2 Slide the shelves into the correct position. Then fit a vertical cleat to each side of the alcove.

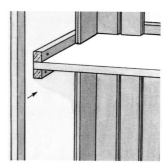

STEP 3 Pin paneling to the cleats above and below the shelves, finishing flush with the vertical cleats.

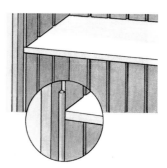

STEP 4 Conceal the leading edges of the paneling where it sits on the vertical cleats with beading.

continue the line of the breast face for the neatest finish. On no account should a previously recessed area be brought out farther into the room than the adjacent baseboard, because this will destroy the whole visual balance.

If you are considering a floor-to-ceiling scheme, support cleats can be disguised slightly by painting them to match the wall, but a more attractive solution is available. Cleats supporting shelving can perform another task: supporting wood paneling cut to fit between the shelves and giving the entire alcove a rich wood finish.

For this finish run two sets of cleats per shelf, instead of one, fix one below the shelf in its usual position, and one above so that the shelf slides in between the two. Position the shelves and fix two vertical lumber lengths to the right front and left front, butting the ends of the horizontal side cleats. TGV or shiplap boards fit snugly between the shelves, pinned to the cleats. Cut the sides level with the shelves, and finish off with a vertical length of beading or molding pinned to the side uprights and the front of the shelves.

Alternative shelving finishes

Combining different finishes in the same scheme always adds interest, both during the project and as a talking point when it is completed. Plain

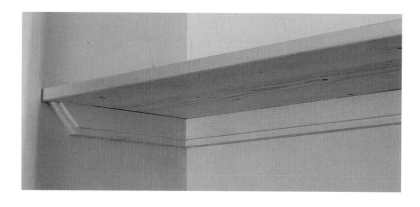

color wall tiles may look less than pleasing on a large wall area, but when added to a wood scheme they can act as a perfect partner for the complex grain structure in the lumber. Consider using 6 in./15 cm tiles as a shelf surface. You need to add 1⅛ in./2.9 cm to allow for the back cleat and paneling, plus ½ in./1.2 cm for a front beading, to the overall width. Allowing for grouting, you need to buy 8 in. x 1 in./20 cm x 2.5 cm PAR. Consider the colors with care; try a dark purple tile in a wood scheme where purple water-based dye has been run into the grain, sanded, and clear varnished. Contrasts work well too, such as royal blue with a yellow pine paneling, or a pale green colorwashed wood combined with dark red tiles. Smaller shelves can have mosaic tiles, visually complex areas that offset simple clear varnished woods.

This simple shelf is easy to install, but very effective and practical. When the support cleats are painted to match the walls, they become less obvious, as though part of the background wall.

YOU WILL NEED:

DOORS FOR
  SHELVES:
- PLYWOOD OR
  BLOCKBOARD
  SHEETS
- HARDWOOD STRIPS
- PINS AND HAMMER
- HALF-ROUND
  MOLDING
- MITERING TOOLS
- FLUSH HINGES
- SCREWS/
  SCREWDRIVER
- DOOR CATCHES

Combination storage

Floor-to-ceiling shelving in any recessed area gives economic storage space, but you can take the principle a stage further. Instead of having open shelves from top to bottom, which only collect dust and partly protect the contents, you can enclose them. You can hang doors on all or some of the shelves, creating a customized unit. Although paired doors can cover the entire front, and obviously give the best protection, most rooms benefit from a combination of base cabinet and face-level shelves.

Bulky storage can be accommodated at floor level, and smaller items, such as books and tapes, can be stored on the shelves. Being open, these shelves are also an ideal place to put flowering and trailing plants.

Creating cabinet space at the base of your unit is not very different from the floor-to-ceiling shelving project, because the top of the cabinet becomes, in practice, another shelf about 37 in./94 cm off the floor. You can construct the top of the unit as before (see page 152), using wood paneling between the shelves, and screwing vertical wooden supports to right and left. The last shelf, now the cabinet top, needs a support under the front edge and at both sides, at right angles to the vertical side pieces. For these supports, 3 in. x 1 in./7.5 cm x 2.5 cm PAR is an ideal size. A final front piece level with the cabinet top edge acts as a joining length, as the sides and horizontal support can be fixed to it by screwing through from the back. Screw a base cleat to the

floor to support the back of the side pieces, and consequently the hinges. You have now created the paired door opening. A parting bead, measuring ½ in. x 1 in./1.2 cm x 2.5 cm, pinned to the inside with the rounded side facing out is a good finishing touch and accepts a flush hinge.

Cabinet doors

Probably the most intimidating part of the job, doors must be equal in size, square cornered and fit the opening well. The simplest doors are cut from ¾in./1.8cm blockboard or plywood, and

RIGHT: **Floor-to-ceiling shelving can provide a lot of useful storage space. Putting doors in front of the shelves will not only conceal their contents but also protect them from dust and sunlight.**

FITTING DOORS TO SHELVES

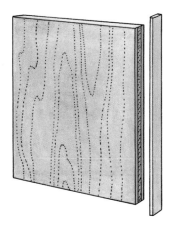

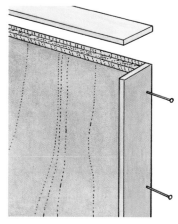

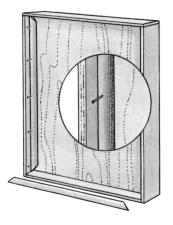

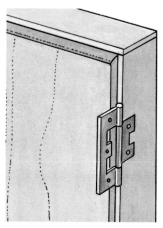

STEP 1 Shelves can be fitted with doors cut from plywood or blockboard sheets. Have them cut undersize and edge them with hardwood strips to provide a neat finish and protect the edge of the veneered face.

STEP 2 To make features of the doors, use edging strips that are wider than the doors' thickness. Pin these to the doors so that they are flush with the rear faces and project beyond the front faces.

STEP 3 Finish off the doors by pinning a half-round molding around the inside of the projecting edging strips. Miter the ends of the molding so that they fit together neatly in the corners.

STEP 4 Fit the doors with flush hinges top and bottom (add a third if the doors are floor-to-ceiling height) and screw these to the framework surrounding the shelves. Finally, add some suitable catches.

you can have them machined to size at the lumberyard. Measure the sizes needed to fit the opening, then deduct ⅛ in./3 mm from every side. This will let you pin a hardwood edging strip around the outside. This protects the outer veneer, and gives a professional finish. If you pin a 1 in./2.5 cm edging strip to a ¾ in./1.8 cm board door, flush with the back edge, overlapping at the front, a lip is created.

A ½ in./1.2 cm half-round molding, pinned on the board face abutting the lip and mitered at each corner, gives a simple, effective border, although many more decorative moldings are available.

If you have been tempted to tile the shelves used on the open part of the unit, you could try the same tile scheme on the door fronts, as a coordinating effect. The doors are cut as before, and edged with 1 in./2.5 cm hardwood strip, overlapping at the front edge. Seal the door surface if needed, and clean off any dirt or

grease. Apply tile adhesive and position the tiles centrally, so that any small pieces of tile cut to fit are equally spaced around the edge. Leave this to set for 24 hours, then grout in the usual way. Alternatively, center complete tiles only, and pin a suitable molding around them to form an inner border. The door lip can be used to form its own outer border with a half-round mitered molding as before.

Another way of constructing paired doors is to pin a simple mitered molding on a man-made board cut to size, imitating a paneled door. The board needs to be edged with a hardwood strip, and looks better painted instead of varnished. The technique used to make wooden shutters (see page 206) can be easily adapted to make smaller cabinet doors. If necessary, the paneling can be fixed to both sides of the frame, making the door extremely strong. Finally, because the cabinet opening can be made any size you like, second-hand doors can be used.

YOU WILL NEED:

CHIMNEY BREAST
INVESTIGATION:

• SCREWDRIVER

• CHISEL

• RUBBER GLOVES

• MATERIALS FOR
CLEANING UP

PROJECT
Customized fire surrounds

After a period of unpopularity following the advent of central heating, the fireplace as a decorative room feature is back in fashion. Whether you have a surround that you don't like, one that needs refurbishing, or merely a boarded-up hole, the focal point that a fire surround provides can be custom-built to fit or custom-decorated to match your decor.

Take it out...

Although they had been a functional part of room design for centuries, the fireplace and surround really came into their own as a decorative feature in Victorian times. They were a piece of built-in room furniture, a multifaceted talking point that contributed much more to the living space than just its primary function, the supply of heat. With the introduction of central heating (a cleaner, more efficient way of heating the home) came a new style of living where the fireplace was no longer the center of attention. Designers had created a more modern environment, and the fireplace became part of history. Cast iron, tiled, marble, slate, and wood surrounds alike were thrown away.

...and put it back

Recent interior design principles do not entirely hark back to Victorian thinking, but they have resulted in a revival and reinstatement of the fireplace. Contemporary design and period fixtures are no longer considered to be mutually exclusive. Original features can be updated with different color and paint finishes, giving them a new lease of life, and ensuring they coexist happily alongside modern schemes and furniture.

Replacing the fire surround is not a difficult task, but first you need to look at the chimney breast. The mantelpiece and surround may have been removed, but the opening and fireback left

BELOW: **A fireplace often provides a focal point in a room. This period bedroom would be lost without its fireplace, which gives a feeling of warmth despite the tall ceiling.**

RIGHT: **Simple tiled fire surrounds are common to many pre- and postwar houses. Although basic, they can look good when teamed with sympathetic decor.**

in place, cleated, covered with wallboard and skimmed with plaster. If this is the case, there ought to be a ventilation grille, but if there isn't, you need to investigate further by stripping back the wallcovering. Look for a join in the plasterwork, then chisel away to reveal the wood frame fixed

inside the opening. Then remove the cleats, wallboard, and the resultant mess. If you are unlucky, and the opening has been professionally bricked up (the new brickwork will have been "toothed-in" to the original bond), then you need to consult a builder or fireplace specialist.

The dramatic pillars supporting the mantelshelf turn this plain modern fireplace into a dramatic statement. Always integrate the fireplace into the room's overall decorative scheme.

CHIMNEY BREAST INVESTIGATION

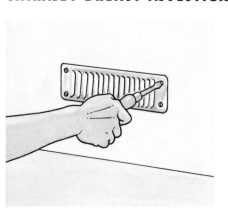

STEP 1 If your fireplace has been boarded up, there should be a ventilation grille in the closing panel. Remove it.

STEP 2 Cut the plaster back from around the opening and lever the closing panel from its supporting framework in the fireplace.

STEP 3 Remove the wooden framework and clean up the opening ready for a new fire surround. Be prepared for a lot of mess.

YOU WILL NEED:

- **3 WIDE BOARDS FOR FIRE OPENING**
- **VERTICAL/ HORIZONTAL BOARDS FOR SIDES AND TOP**
- **PAINT**
- **MOLDINGS**
- **PINS**
- **DRILL AND DRILL BITS**
- **HEAVY-DUTY ANCHORS AND NUMBER 8 SCREWS**
- **SHELF**
- **FLUTED DOWELS**
- **GLUE**
- **VARNISH (IF REQUIRED)**

PROJECT
Making a fire surround

Constructing your own fire surround is cheaper than buying one and it enables you to produce a unique decoration that will complement the style and decor of the room. The basic principles for creating a wooden fireplace surround are outlined here. You can paint and varnish the surround to your taste.

Fire surrounds

Second-hand fire surrounds are widely available, from specialist dealers and architectural salvage yards. If a period piece is your ideal, just make sure it fits before parting with your money. Buying a cast-iron fireplace full of character that doesn't fit the fire opening is an expensive mistake. Wood surrounds, on the other hand, merely need to be of the correct proportion to the breast; a separate fire basket fits the opening. Plenty of reproduction wood surrounds are available too.

Making a wooden surround

An interesting project idea is to create a hand-made wood surround. All you need is a grid on the wall, and a firm fixing for the initial lengths of wood.

- Measure up and draw the template grid on the wall.
- Depending on the dimensions of the surround you are intending to build, you'll need to buy about 10 ft./3 m of 1 in. x 2 in./2.5 cm x 5 cm, 1 in. x 4 in./2.5 cm x 10 cm, 1 in. x 6 in./2.5 cm x 15 cm and 1 in. x 8 in./2.5cm x 20cm.
- Fix the first lengths, 1 in. x 8 in./2.5 cm x 20 cm, to the wall with heavy-duty anchors and countersunk 2 in./5 cm number 8 screws.
- Butt the horizontal piece to the inside of the uprights, but don't miter the corners.
- The principle here is layering; each wood piece added to the surround hides the previous screwhead.
- Each completed layer can have its own color.

The widespread popularity of central heating led to many fireplaces being closed off, especially in bedrooms. But a fireplace gives a bedroom a wonderfully cozy feel.

INSTALLING THE FIRE SURROUND

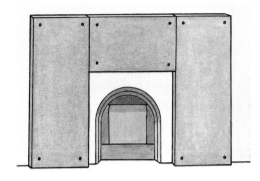

STEP 1 Begin the installation of this "stepped" design of fire surround by screwing a wide board to each side of the fire opening. Then screw a third board above the opening between the first two.

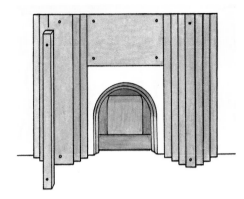

STEP 2 Add the vertical boards to each side, fitting progressively narrower pieces to hide the fixing screws of the previous boards fitted and create "fluted" columns. You can color the boards as you add them.

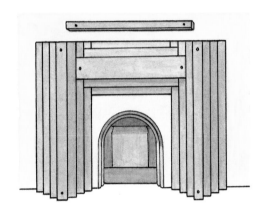

STEP 3 Continue by adding the horizontal boards. Again, use progressively narrower boards to gain the stepped effect, but note that each is longer than its predecessor to fit between the side boards. Conceal remaining screwheads with pinned-on moldings.

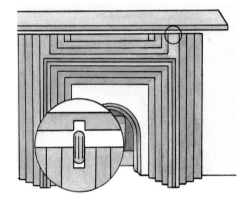

STEP 4 Cut the shelf to size and center it on the surround so that you can mark the positions of the fixing dowels. Drill holes for these in the underside of the shelf and the tops of the side columns. Apply glue to the dowels and fit them in place together with the shelf.

If you wish, simply apply an individual water-based mix as you proceed.

- Fix the largest size to the wall, then fix the remaining wood pieces to each other, centering the uprights in descending order of size, countersinking the 2in./5 cm number 8 screws.
- The horizontal wood pieces are fixed in the same order, and following the same principle, but you will note that each piece fitted is longer than the previous piece by the width of the step at each side.
- Screwheads in the final wood pieces can be covered by a centered molding or edging strip pinned into position—or hidden with filler.
- The two vertical sides act as supports for the mantelpiece, and can be cut from the 1 in. x 4 in./2.5 cm x 10 cm stock, or wider if you prefer.
- Secure it with glued fluted dowels into the top of the side supports and the underside of the mantelpiece.
- If you have colored the wood pieces, several coats of varnish are needed to protect the finish. If not, use any paint finish of your choice.

PROJECT
Tiled finishes in working areas

There is a huge choice of tiles for decorative purposes, lining walls in living quarters, or tiling surfaces that reflect light patterns. Hand-made and decorated terracotta, unglazed, iridescent glass, stoneware, three-dimensional, metallic, and retro are all available; the challenge is to match into your color scheme.

Tiles for use in a working area, in particular on kitchen surfaces, need to be both decorative and functional. Tiles that will be part of a work surface must not stain easily, must be strong and not crack, must be suitable for wet areas and easy to clean. Crazed and cracked tiles that harbor dirt must be avoided because they are a health hazard.

Tile selection

Tile makers—mass manufacturers and individual craftspeople alike—use many different clay types and glazes. The density of the clay and the glaze used affects the strength of the finished tile. For example, white and near-white glazes are much stronger than colored ones. For this reason most specialized suppliers have a "suitability chart," grading their tiles in terms of strength and color, to ensure that you make an appropriate selection. Before you make this selection, consider carefully the function the tile will have to perform. On working surfaces in a kitchen you will need the strongest tiles available in a color that will resist staining by food and its preparation. Special-effect tiles, such as iridescent glass or metallic, are not practical, however attractive they may look. Mosaic sheets need careful consideration, too. They are easy to install on a work surface because the backing sheet can be shaped to fit, but again, you will need the strongest tiles available. They require a lot of grouting, too, with a special epoxy grout recommended for kitchen surfaces.

Updating your kitchen

Refurbishing a kitchen or working area is not simply a matter of decorating walls. Storage areas and worktops must be upgraded as well, or they will detract from the finished scheme. Storage units can be fitted with new doors that are simple to make. Plywood cut to size and edged can be tiled to match a worktop style in the same way that the combination storage doors matched the tiled shelves (see page 155). TGV doors pinned to a softwood frame will help create the feel of a country kitchen. Even a partial paint job on the original doors can suffice, if it is combined with a new wood stain or a simple stenciled motif.

TILING A WORKING AREA

STEP 1 When adding a tiled finish to an old worktop, work over the surface with coarse abrasive paper to provide a key for the adhesive.

STEP 2 Set out the tiles "dry" so that you can determine the best arrangement of colors and work out where you will have to cut tiles to fit.

STEP 3 Be prepared to revise your arrangement, change colors and patterns until you achieve the best layout before bedding the tiles down.

The really noticeable difference, though, will result from a new worktop surface, and tiling over the existing top will be the most effective economically.

A new top

Select your tiles carefully. A tough glazed stoneware tile with a good color range would be ideal, but, depending on your surface size, they ought not to be too large.

- To avoid unpleasant visual discrepancies when cutting strips to fill, a 4 in./10 cm square would be small enough yet still allow for fairly simple grouting.
- Make sure the worktop is clean and dry.
- Abrade the surface with coarse aluminum oxide (40 grit) to provide a "key" if it is very smooth.
- Using a tile as a template, set out on the surface so that you achieve the best arrangement.
- Ensure cut tiles are at the back, where the wall meets the surface, not at the front.
- Allow space at the front edges for a wood edging strip if desired, although edging strips

fixed at the sides of the worktop are best, protecting the top better and letting tiles be set flush against the edge.

- Spread the waterproof adhesive and bed down the tiles as you would on a wall, cutting to fit.
- Leave to set for 24 hours.
- Before you grout the surface, make sure that your retailer has supplied the correct epoxy grout essential for these surfaces.

Finishing with wood

- Select a wood strip for the worktop edge. An astragal molding is ideal; it has no right-angled edge to knock against.
- Mark and miter to fit.
- Fix into position with 1¼ in./3.2 cm number 8 countersunk screws. Drive home the screws, setting them well below the surface of the wood.
- Fill the hole with a joint compound that can be sanded flush when dry.
- Alternatively, bore each pilot and shank hole in one go with a combination screwsink that leaves a counterbored hole, and drive the screw in.
- The hole is filled by a wooden plug, cut to the correct screw size from the same wood by a plug cutter, and glued in place.
- When set, cut the plug as flush as possible with a sharp chisel, and sand to leave a professional finish.

LEFT: **Mosaic panels can be used to good colorful effect in a kitchen, although they do not provide the ideal surface for a worktop since they are unlikely to be thick enough.**

STEP 4 Protect the perimeter of the worktop with wood strips the same depth as the tiles. Cut to size, mitering the ends and check the fit.

STEP 5 Pin the strips in place, overhanging the edge. Fix a reinforcing strip underneath the lip.

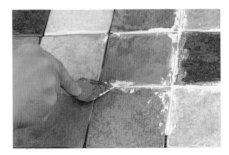

STEP 6 For reasons of hygiene, kitchen worktop tiles must be grouted with a two-part epoxy grout. Use a small trowel to press it into the joints.

YOU WILL NEED:

SHELVING SYSTEM:

• **WOOD**

• **SAW**

• **MARKING KNIFE**

• **THIN CHISEL**

• **GLUE**

• **CLAMPS**

• **PLYWOOD BACKING**

• **HAMMER AND PINS**

PROJECT
Storage box sections

Whether you need to reinforce sagging shelves with vertical supports or make up a self-supporting unit with stepped sides, the same simple wood joint can be used. Halving joints let the shelves slot together at right angles, forming a strong, unseen bond which can also be used as a decorative feature.

Weight for support

Shelving systems, constructed from 1 in./2.5 cm boards or ¾ in./1.8 cm plywood machined to size, are ideal for fixing in an alcove. The recess will generally be less than 6 ft./1.8 m wide and the shelf length, if supported on cleats to the side and rear, will be perfectly stable. Longer lengths, needed to span a gap where, say, two rooms have been knocked into one and the resultant distance between chimney breasts is over 10 ft./3 m, are liable to sag, particularly if they are 1 ft./30 cm in width. Front support pieces, glued and screwed under and flush with the front edge of each shelf, will help, but heavy weights will still cause problems.

It is reasonable to assume that a long, wide shelf will be used to hold larger, heavier items than a small shelf, so it must be constructed with more support. Load-bearing shelves can have brackets screwed underneath, either as separate fixed items or as part of an adjustable shelving system, where removable brackets are slotted into steel uprights screwed to the wall. There are many adjustable systems on the market, all using the same principle, and the heavy-duty ones are very strong indeed. The wall fixings must involve no less than 2¼ in./5.6 cm number 10 countersunk screws driven into heavy-duty wall anchors. The uprights should be spaced 2½ ft./75 cm apart. Heavy-duty adjustable shelving is available in only very basic colors, mostly suitable for workrooms, garages, or outbuildings. You can paint it yourself but the effect isn't exactly subtle. There is a better, much more attractive, load-bearing support system for a living area which you can construct yourself.

A self-supporting box system

This is a simple wooden unit that relies on horizontal and vertical boards meeting at a series of halving joints and providing mutual support. A halving joint is simple to cut and, when accurate, extremely strong and virtually invisible. The principle behind halving joints (also called half-and-half joints or half-laps) is that where the wood meets or overlaps at right-angles, one exact half of each piece is cut and removed to let the pieces slot together. The wood can be clamped securely, marked out with a knife, and cut together so that the housings are the same width as the thickness of the wood, and cut back with a chisel to a shoulder half the width of the wood. Always saw on the waste side of the marked line when cutting halving joints. If you don't, the housings will be too wide by the width of the saw blade, and the joint will be loose.

A modular box-section storage system can provide a versatile means of containing and displaying a wide variety of domestic objects. Such systems can be tailored to meet your specific needs.

MAKING A SHELVING SYSTEM

STEP 1 Cut the first half of the joint in one board. You can subsequently use it as a template to mark the matching half with your marking knife.

STEP 2 Cut the joint by making a series of saw cuts through the waste to the bottom of each of the slots. Then remove the waste with a thin chisel.

STEP 3 Then check the fit of each of the joints. They should all be snug, and making saw cuts on the waste side of each marked line should ensure this.

STEP 4 Glue inside the housings of the corresponding joint halves and carefully assemble the boards.

STEP 5 Clamp and wipe off excess glue. The unit can be strengthened by gluing and pinning on a plywood backing.

Custom building

Any size of unit can be constructed in this way. A drawing dividing the wall space into compartments is a good start. These can be any size, but square is easy and uniformly attractive. Consider using measurements that turn the unit into a series of cubes: if your chosen timber is 12 in./30 cm wide, use the same figure for the internal dimensions of each box. A scaled-down model made of card will give you a better idea of how it will look—slots cut in the card will join together in exactly the same way as the wood.

The top of the unit need not reach the ceiling. A long top shelf for houseplants and ornaments is created by forming outside corners, which are simply one-sided halving joints. Your unit is floor-standing, so you need to consider a plinth for the base, and this should be the height of the baseboard. Flush at the front and sides, the plinth can be set forward the width of the baseboard at the back of the base, so that the unit back is flush with the wall.

Securing and backing

If you are making a small unit, clamping it square as you glue the joints will ensure it is stable enough. Larger units can be glued in sections as you proceed, but any "play" in the halving joints will result in undue pressure being placed on the unit's square corners. A support cleat glued and screwed under the top back edge of each top corner box will hold that corner square, and let you drill through and fix the unit to the wall. If you prefer, you can attach a back panel, placing the unit face-down on the floor, and confirming that it is square.

Cut ¼ in./6mm plywood to fit the outside back, and glue and pin into position with brads. Make sure that the best side of the plywood is visible from the front. The unit is now stable and free-standing. Screws driven through the backing into the wall can be used to provide extra security, sensible if it is to hold heavy items.

Floors

The choice of a floor covering is usually a vote

for practicality over style and fashion. Heavy traffic areas,

potentially wet areas, outdoor access areas, and more intimate,

friendly areas all have their own separate requirements which take

precedence over decorative style. Expensive wall-to-wall carpeting is

not compatible with large, muddy boots, while cold quarry tiling is

not suitable for the children's playroom. Given today's lifestyles,

versatility must be an important issue when deciding on your

flooring; indeed, many modern flooring materials are described

as multifunctional. In a modern living environment, choosing

which floor covering to put where has never

been more important.

Designer's notes

A floor serves a single purpose; it is there to be walked on. Therefore, the first principle of flooring and floor covering is practicality. There is a wide range of flooring materials to choose from. Depending on the purpose of the room, you may want warmth and softness underfoot, or a more hard-wearing surface suitable for heavy traffic.

NEAR RIGHT: **Fitted carpets provide a soft and comfortable floor covering that creates a harmonious link between one room and another.**

FAR RIGHT: **Vinyl flooring is very hard-wearing and ideal for use in areas of heavy traffic, such as a hallway. It is also easily cleaned.**

To begin, decide on floor plans from a purely cosmetic viewpoint, and then look at the consequences. Stripped boards can allow drafts, especially if the house has a cellar. Light-colored or plain carpeting shows every mark. Scatter rugs can trip people up. Tiles can be cold in areas where people are likely to walk barefoot, as can lino and vinyl. Stockinged feet slide on polished floors, and thin woodstrip veneers wear out quickly in heavy human traffic. The way you choose to treat your floors has not only a decorative impact, but a noticeable effect on the quality of life around you. Don't overlook the effect a poor decision can have on your bank balance, either, should you be faced with the prospect of replacing expensive flooring that proved unsuitable.

Work with what you have

Replacing a floor is an arduous task, and one that should not be undertaken lightly. Quite apart from the floor surface, the baseboards will have to be removed and possibly replaced, damaging the wall surface and the decorative finish.

Unless you are renovating a property from scratch, or the existing flooring is beyond redemption, try to work with what you have inherited. This need not mean covering up an area with carpet or vinyl, relying on the "out-of-sight-out-of-mind" theory. Instead, identify the positive and workable characteristics of the floor.

If you have original floorboards, check them for rot and damage. If they are sound, you have an opportunity to sand, varnish, colorwash, stain, or simply leave them with a plain scrubbed finish. Broken, damaged, or rotted boards need replacing. Note the width and depth of the wood and its type (pine, usually) and seek out a local architectural salvage yard.

Modern floors tend to be chipboard, an artificial board of no visual worth in itself, but which provides a sound base for painted designs. A piece of woven matting placed centrally can be effectively emphasized by a painted border in contrasting colors. Chipboard is also a good base for vinyl floorcoverings, and for supporting interlocking boards of hardwood veneer on a backing of softwood or plywood, known as woodstrip flooring.

Period houses may have slate, marble, or flagstone floors, particularly in kitchen and washroom areas. Slabs are available from specialty suppliers, but they tend to be quite expensive. Imitation flagstones, made of concrete, can be bought at a fraction of the price.

Tiled floors can be refurbished, and encaustic tiles are available from specialty suppliers for repair purposes. Dull floors can be stripped and repolished. Quarry tiles were also popular throughout the ground floor and outhouses, and if you discover a damaged floor you, can easily replace individual tiles.

Start at the bottom

When you have identified the advantages inherent in your existing flooring, try to visualize the rest of the walls and ceiling in a finish that emphasizes these qualities. It may seem odd working up from the bottom, but if you can start from the point of a natural and practical asset, then you are much more likely to achieve a pleasing result that benefits the entire household design scheme.

Flagstones were often found in the kitchens of period houses. If you want to recreate the look of the past, they are ideal, and you can buy modern imitations, but they will be cold underfoot.

FAR LEFT: Rugs can be used to provide colorful accents on a floor, but they can also be trip hazards. Use special rug grippers to prevent them from moving and causing an accident.

YOU WILL NEED:
- DRILL AND DRILL BIT
- JIGSAW
- BACKSAW
- ELECTRICIAN'S BOLSTER
- CLEAT
- SCREWS/NAILS
- NEW BOARD

PROJECT
Basic skills: identifying boards

Recognizing wooden floor types and sizes is not a particularly difficult skill to acquire, but dealing with defects and problems, sometimes caused by neglect or bad workmanship by previous owners, can be hard and time-consuming. Replacing floorboards may involve sourcing second-hand materials from salvage or reclamation yards.

Basic, traditional floorboards will be made from softwood—usually pine. You may find them as bare wood because many older properties preferred scrubbed floors, or they may have been varnished to imitate a darker, more expensive wood. Using cheap timber and varnishing it to deceive was a Victorian trick. This has found popularity again, although today's colors, stains, and varnishes give a much subtler finish. You may also find painted boards, either across the entire floor, or just at the edges where they would be visible if the room had a central carpet.

Boards were laid in a number of sizes, originally 1 in./2.5 cm thick timbers, in widths of 5 in./13 cm, 6 in./15cm or 7 in./18 cm. Genuine old hardwood floors are rare, and the timber width will be significantly less than softwood. Be careful you don't mistake veneer strip flooring for the real thing.

Infestation

Check the condition of the floor carefully. If you have removed old carpets and underlays, or ripped up hardboard pinned or stapled in position, remember that this will have stopped the floor "breathing." Inadequate ventilation, combined with damp conditions, can lead to wood rot, so examine the entire area carefully, including baseboards. Dry rot can often be present in a lumber with an apparently unaffected surface, although small splits may be visible close up. If you are suspicious, prod the wood with a blade—dry rot gives easily. Wet rot is found only in saturated conditions, and thus tends to be more obvious. Both cases are solved only by cutting out the infected timbers, drying out the surrounding area, and treating it with a wood preservative. You must remove the cause of the damp and ensure proper air circulation, or the problem may return. Woodworm is a constant concern in wood-framed properties. If you find tiny flight holes in the floor, inject them with woodworm fluid. If the problem is far-reaching, you must call in a professional.

Repairing and lifting boards

Repairs to basic floorboarding are relatively straightforward, and they do not require many specialized tools. You will need a keyhole saw and electrician's bolster, but these should be part of your household kit anyway. A floorboard saw is useful if a lot of board cutting is needed. The first task is always to identify the cause of any particular problem. More floor damage is caused by previous attempts to access pipe systems and wiring runs than any amount of footwear. Access panels that are to be retained in the floor should be screwed down, not nailed. Screwing down a

BELOW LEFT: **Wet rot is caused when timbers are exposed to constant damp conditions. The wood begins to crumble and so loses its strength. The only solution is to cut out the damage and replace it with new wood, after having found and cured the cause of the original damp.**

BELOW RIGHT: **Attack by woodworm can be identified by the small flight holes left when the insects bore their way out of the wood. Small areas of damage can be treated with fluid; large areas should be dealt with by cutting out and renewing the infected timber.**

REPAIRING BOARDS

STEP 1 Identify the joist position (the fixing nails will help) and drill a hole at the edge of the board just to one side of the joist.

STEP 2 Insert the blade of a jigsaw through the drilled hole and use it to cut across the floorboard alongside the joist.

STEP 3 Drive the blade of an electrician's bolster into the saw cut and use it to lever the cut end of the board upward.

STEP 4 Lift the board sufficiently to wedge a length of cleat beneath it so that it is held clear while you cut the other end over a joist.

STEP 5 Screw a short length of cleat to the side of the first joist, and flush with the top, to support one end of the new board.

STEP 6 Cut the new board to size and set it on the cleat and second joist. Nail it down or use screws for easy removal in future.

wooden board rather than nailing it should cure any annoying creaks under carpeting that are caused by movement. If the board is man-made (chipboard) it should ideally have been screwed down in the first place.

Check to see if the boards are anchored on all joists, and none is missed. Creaking, exposed floorboards that are to be varnished can also be screwed down, but the screwheads need to be hidden. Either countersink the heads and fill with an appropriate colored plastic joint compound, or counterbore a hole and cover the head with a chamfered wooden plug.

To remove a damaged section of board, or to gain new access, locate the nearest joist and mark a pencil line alongside it. The floorboard nails will be your best indicator. Drill a hole to the side of the joist, large enough to start the cut with a keyhole saw blade, then use a floorboard saw. Alternatively, use a jigsaw, cutting the board parallel with the joist.

Lever up the end with the electrician's bolster, lift it, and slide a wood cleat under as support while you cut the other end, directly in the middle of a joist. Use a backsaw for this cut; on no account try using a jigsaw, because you have a solid joist underneath and will snap the blade immediately.

Screw a cleat to the side of the first joist, to act as a support for the access panel or a new piece of board. It is important to bear in mind that if the boards are tongue-and-groove, you will have to saw down one length to cut through the tongue and release the board.

YOU WILL NEED:

• SCRUBBING BRUSH

• HOT WATER

• HOUSEHOLD
  ABRASIVE CLEANER

• BRUSH

• FLEXIBLE BLADED
  KNIFE

ALSO USEFUL ARE:

• WIRE WOOL

• ALUMINUM OXIDE
  ABRASIVE

• SILICON CARBIDE
  (WET-AND-DRY
  PAPER)

• SANDING BLOCK

PROJECT
Preparing exposed floors

Old wooden floors that are recolored if necessary and varnished for protection look good in almost any situation. You don't always have to machine sand the boards, either; thorough cleaning is often all that you need to do before the application of a decorative finish and a coat of varnish to seal them and make them hard-wearing.

The pros and cons of sanding

Sanding floors and varnishing them has become very popular, because the finished floor will look good with any room scheme, and is as versatile an asset as you could wish for. If some of the floorboards are damaged, they can be replaced by new ones. And, since the whole room is being sanded back, there will be no discernible difference in the surface color. However, one drawback to sanding is that it reduces the thickness of the wood: floorboards that were once ¾ in. to ⅞ in./1.8 cm to 2 cm, providing solid support and a fair insulation against sound, are reduced by ⅛ in. to ¼ in./3 mm to 4 mm, depending on the uneven nature of the floor. This may be no problem for you, but in houses with a cellar or exposed beams underneath, the noise level will be increased, as will the draft. If the boards are currently bare and in reasonable condition, consider washing them down and adding color instead of sanding them back. Replacement second-hand boards can be found at architectural salvage yards, if needed; and even a new board or two can be matched in.

Try experimenting with oil-based stains on a scrap of (new) board, mixing them together, then diluting them with solvent. When you have a reasonable match, brush it onto the new floorboard and sand it down. Oil-based stains penetrate deeper into the wood, so don't try this with water-based stains.

Removing a ceiling to expose the floor joists of the room above can be very effective. Bear in mind, however, that sound and drafts can travel up through gaps between the floorboards.

WASHING AND FINISHING

STEP 1 Clean old boards thoroughly by scrubbing them with hot water and household abrasive cleaner, working with the grain.

STEP 2 When the boards have been left to dry, brush on the desired finish, again working with the grain and maintaining a wet edge.

Cleaning and preparing

Plain wooden boards in period properties were scrubbed vigorously with a mix of sand and water, often resulting in a delicate-looking gray sheen. Elbow work is still required, but modern cleaners and abrasives give every assistance and an impressive result. Start as you would any dirty job, using hot water, abrasive cleaning cream, and a stiff brush. Work the brush into and with the wood grain, not across it, and clean small areas of board at a time, washing down immediately with clean water. Clean the entire floor, leave it to dry, and repeat the whole process if necessary.

You can now see if any problem areas remain, such as stains, plaster lumps, or splashes of paint. Plaster, softened by the cleaning process, will lift off with a flexible-bladed knife. Stains and old paint need brushing with a water washable paint remover. Wait until the paint blisters, and then scrape it off with a flexible blade. Repeat the brushing process if a paint residue is left, but use wire wool for the best finish and for getting into the grain beneath a stain. You may now be left with a fairly rough board surface. If this is so, it is because the water used in cleaning down has raised the wood grain, and the board needs sanding slightly by hand. Wrap a fine grade of aluminum oxide abrasive (120 grit) around a

sanding block and gently sand with the grain on dry boards. If the floorboards are smooth after the cleaning process, which they will be if they have been varnished some time previously, they can be "keyed" to accept a new finish. Gently abrade the surface with a fine grade silicon carbide (wet-and-dry paper) used wet, again working along the grain.

The next stage

Take time out to review your plans. Is the floor in good condition? If it is, all you need to do is decide on a wood finish. If it isn't, and the boards have shrunk slightly, leaving gaps, or boards have been carelessly lifted by tradespeople, then you have to decide whether or not to proceed. Entire board lengths can be replaced, but finding a lumber match for second-hand boards is becoming more and more difficult. Gaps between boards can be filled with chamfered wooden fillets glued, hammered into place, and left to dry. In both these cases you would do well to consider sanding down the floor with a rented industrial sander.

A blue colorwash can look good on washed floorboards, the blue blending with the grayish tint of the old pine. You can use thinned latex paint provided it is sealed with a varnish.

YOU WILL NEED:

- MATERIALS TO PREPARE THE SURFACE (E.G. ABRASIVES OF DIFFERENT GRADES)
- INDUSTRIAL SANDER/EDGE SANDER (IF REQUIRED)
- NAIL SET OR PUNCH
- HAMMER
- HARDBOARD AND NAILS (IF REQUIRED)
- COLORWASH (IF REQUIRED)
- SEALER
- WOOD FINISH OR VARNISH
- FACE MASK AND PROTECTIVE GLASSES

This will achieve a level and color-matched surface. On the other hand, you may find that the gaps do not bother you. As long as there is no cellar or basement with exposed joists beneath, electric light will not filter up through the gaps, which can ruin the effect of any stripped floor. If you have access to the joists from the cellar, however, it is a simple enough job to nail hardboard to the underside of the floor, between the joists. Cut the hardboard into long strips that fit neatly between the joists. Tack into position with ¾ in./1.8 cm tacks, at 6 in./15 cm centers. Don't be tempted into using longer tacks, unless you check first to make sure that the points won't break through the surface of the boards of the floor above.

Colors on washed boards

The gray appearance of old scrubbed boards can be accentuated by using a gray-green or pale blue colorwash. Two teaspoonfuls of latex paint stirred into a quart/liter of water will provide a wash that sinks into the grain, but can be wiped off the surface if desired. This wash can be repeated until the color effect is satisfactory. Then, the board can be varnished or left unsealed. If you want to put color back into the bleached wood, try a wash of dark red, highlighting the grain, followed by an oil-based pine varnish. Dilute the varnish with white spirit so that it can be applied more easily, sinking into the wood surface. Now seal with a clear floor varnish.

Machine sanding

Rental centers will rent out two types of sander for your floor: a large machine that looks like an old-fashioned lawnmower with a dust bag attached, for the main floor area, and a small belt or disk sander for getting in close to baseboards. They will supply all the necessary abrasives, and, most importantly, face masks and protective

ABOVE RIGHT:
A properly sanded and boarded floor makes the most of the beauty of the wood grain.

glasses. Make sure you understand how both machines work before you take them home.

Your first job is to hammer down all the nail heads, well below the surface of the floorboards, using a nail set or punch. If you don't take on

MACHINE SANDING

STEP 1 Begin by making a series of diagonal passes with coarse abrasive across the boards. Then work diagonally in the other direction with a medium-grade abrasive.

Make sure you are wearing a protective mask and goggles when you start up the machine.

- Run the sander diagonally across the floor at 45 degrees to the boards, using coarse abrasive paper.
- Change to a medium-grade abrasive, and again sand across the floor, but this time at right angles to your first run.
- Then sand up and down, following the board direction.
- Change finally to a fine-grade abrasive, and finish off sanding with the grain.
- The small sander reaches into baseboard areas, doorways, and alcoves where the larger drum cannot reach. Here again, start with the coarser abrasive, finish with the fine.
- Clean dust from the boards before sealing and varnishing.

Sealing and varnishing

Clear varnishes are readily available but they are expensive. Make sure you have the best quality, and that the varnish is recommended for flooring. Cheap polyurethane varnish intended for internal woodwork is not tough enough for everyday wear and tear, and is a false economy. It may crack under pressure of furniture castors, and you could be faced with the prospect of a repeat job.

this tiresome task, the nail heads will rip the abrasive sheets on the drum sander. Sanding a floor raises a lot of dust, and despite the dust collecting bag, a lot gets into the air surrounding where you are working.

STEP 2 Next work up and down the boards using medium-grade abrasive. Then fit a fine grade of paper to the machine and repeat the process, working in the direction of the grain.

STEP 3 Using progressively finer grades of abrasive, work up to the baseboards with an edge sander.

STEP 4 After removing all dust and debris, treat the boards with a sealer and apply a varnish to them.

PROJECT
Special effects on wood floors

Many of the paint and dye effects used on purpose-built joinery, items of furniture, and wooden frames can be used successfully on floorboards. The main consideration remains—that floors are there to be walked on—and therefore any scheme must be permanently sealed in order for it to be considered practical and hard-wearing.

Visual effects can work well on both scrubbed and machine-sanded floors. The rule of thumb is that the darker colored schemes will tend to suit the scrubbed, darker boards, while the pale-colored finishes are best on newly revealed surfaces on sanded floors. Unless the reason for machine sanding was a very uneven surface, time and energy are wasted if the intention is to apply an overall dark finish.

Suitable finishes

Wood stains and varnishes will alter the color of the wood surface, grain, or both, and decorate and protect the timber. What they will not do is alter the basic visual characteristics of the wood and its grain. A pine floor is still a pine floor, no matter what stain is on it. Just as the Victorians failed to disguise cheap pine doors by applying a dark varnish resembling mahogany or dark oak, you will be unable to give the impression of expensive boards by brushing a can of rosewood stain onto a softwood floor. A basic rule of wood finishing is that cheap lumber with an applied stain of oak does not look like oak: it looks like cheap lumber with an oak stain on it. You will achieve a satisfactory result only if you apply a finish that complements the wood's natural colors and character. If you seek to obliterate it, you can simply paint it.

Water- and oil-based stains

Water-based stains are perhaps more suited for use on machine-sanded floors, their versatility being emphasized by a lighter wood surface.

A strong-colored stained wooden floor with a deep gloss finish greets visitors with a sense of opulence and warmth.

They can be bought in convenient-sized cans, and are available in bright colors as well as natural wood shades. In a concentrated form they are not very subtle, but the addition of water makes for pleasing tints. They do not penetrate the timber as deeply, and, when used diluted, can be wiped or sanded off the surface leaving only the grain colored.

Oil-based stains are strong, penetrating deeper into the wood fibers. A dark stain applied to a surface needs much sanding to restore the surface to its natural state and leave the grain colored. Colored varnishes are available, combining color and sealer in one coat. However, one coat of sealer is not enough, so these types of varnish are best used to produce a decorative effect, with a clear varnish applied on the top as a hard-wearing finish.

As with any wood, the natural color will alter the stain slightly and an experiment on scrap wood is always a good idea. Blues and greens diluted and washed onto scrubbed boards work well on the fairly gray surface. Different strengths of the same basic color, achieved by dilution ratios or repeat coats, can set up a floor of striped boards. Squares and checkered patterns can be achieved by simple measuring and masking with painter's tape. Test the wood first, however. If it is very absorbent, brush the stain up to, but not over, the tape or it will bleed underneath.

Any color you apply will require a protective varnish. Polyurethane will yellow slightly, so make sure your blues don't end up as greens by testing them first. Reds, though, improve when varnished because subtle shades of orange appear, so make sure you include the final seal in your color calculation. This is particularly important if you use a colored varnish decoratively before the finishing clear varnish, where, for example, a yellow pine finish is used over a diluted red. Red color is strong in the wood grain, but the surface

is influenced by the pine and appears as a patchy yellow-orange. The yellow content will increase slightly with time since finishing coats of varnish react to the sun's rays in a well-lit room.

Paint and varnish combinations

Oil-based enamel paints are tough enough for floor finishes in some lesser used areas: in bedrooms, for example, where scatter rugs are the featured covering. Heavy traffic areas are different. Constant wear and tear, particularly from external entry points, will quickly damage the floor surface. These areas—hallways, corridors and even "through routes" in living rooms—need a very heavy-duty finish.

Special floor paints are on the market, but outlets are limited, as is the range of colors.

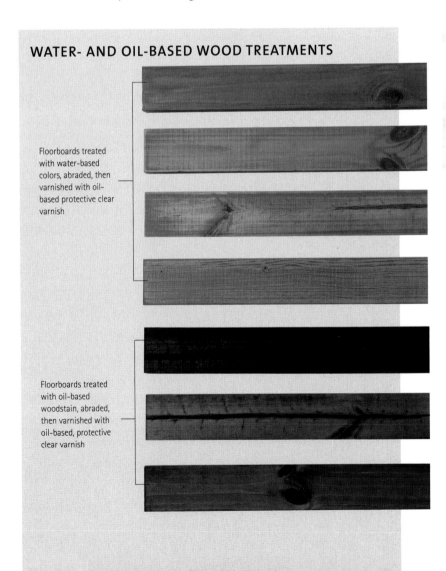

WATER- AND OIL-BASED WOOD TREATMENTS

Floorboards treated with water-based colors, abraded, then varnished with oil-based protective clear varnish

Floorboards treated with oil-based woodstain, abraded, then varnished with oil-based, protective clear varnish

However, if you are lucky and the color scheme is suitable, they are a good solution. Otherwise, choose your color from any paint source, and apply a flooring-quality clear varnish on top, building up a protective layer that needs to be at least two and possibly four coats thick, depending on the anticipated usage. Any design or color combination can be used because you are treating the paint finish in the same way as a colored stain. Remember, however, that the varnish will tend to add a yellowish cast to the colors, which may produce an effect that you had

Combining lumber treatments can produce some wonderful effects, such as this combination of a pale blue wash and pine stain. Don't be afraid to experiment, but try out your ideas on scrap wood first.

not intended or wanted. Recreate your intended scheme on scrap pine board and apply the required number of varnish coats. You may find that changing the base colors slightly will produce the effect you want. Many interesting marriages of stain and paint are thus open to you. Try painting the board with latex, and removing part of the surface when it is dry, revealing the wood grain underneath. A sander can be used for this, or work by hand to achieve a casual effect, using wet-and-dry silicon carbide paper (used wet) instead of sandpaper.

Try experimenting with wax resists. This is an old technique relying on the principle that oil (the wax) and water (the latex paint) will not mix.

- Start by washing a diluted pale blue stain along the board, and leaving it to dry.
- Use steel wool to rub a clear wax, available from art suppliers and home centers, along parts of the board, creating a random pattern.
- Before the wax is dry, overpaint the entire board with a mid-blue water-based latex paint, and this time let it dry out completely.
- Rub down the areas of the board that you waxed with coarse steel wool; they should appear slightly darker than the rest. The top paint will come off with the wax, leaving

You can lighten scrubbed boards further by bleaching them with a proprietary, two-part wood bleach and neutralizer. Here, the bleached board has been treated with a simple varnish.

patches of pale blue stain showing through.

- The top paint can be blended in more subtly if it is still wet when you rub it—the patches are less obvious since the paint tends to spread along the board.
- As with all combinations, the colors chosen give very different effects. Two-tone blues and greens are not as vivid as a mix of pine yellow and a dark red or brown, so test the scheme on scrap wood before you start.

Different wood colors

A rustic appearance can add to the appeal of bare wooden floors in smaller rooms, when the glazed look of expensive flooring found in town houses seems inappropriate.

Scrubbed floorboards can be further lightened by bleaching them. This technique should be used sparingly, however, perhaps one board in four across the floor area. Adding a pale gray wash and a pine stain at random to other boards, leaving the rest with a scrubbed finish, gives a pleasing range of tones. Proprietary wood bleaches are available from good hardware stores, and are usually applied in two parts with a special brush available from the same source. When the bleach has dried out, the wood needs to be washed, first with a recommended neutralizer and then sparingly with warm water. A pine varnish on some of the other boards needs thinning slightly to sink into the surface. When it dries, sand back the top surface to remove any trace of a sheen.

The floor can be left as it is, varnished once to seal it and then sanded by hand gently to remove any surface sheen. Alternatively, to ensure maximum protection, the floor can be varnished in the conventional manner.

YOU WILL NEED:
- DILUTED STAIN
- CLEAR WAX
- WIRE WOOL
- BRUSH
- WATER-BASED LATEX
- SEALER
- GLOVES

CREATING DIFFERENT COLORS

STEP 1 Using wax resists to create attractive colored finishes on wood is an old technique, but one worth investigating. Basically two colors are applied, but areas of wax prevent one color completely obliterating the other. Begin by brushing on a diluted stain, working along the grain. Leave it to dry completely.

STEP 2 Form a small pad from wire wool and use it to apply random areas of clear wax to the stained wood, creating an abstract pattern. Again work in the direction of the wood grain. You can buy the wax from home centers and art suppliers. Work quickly as you must apply the second color before the wax has a chance to dry.

STEP 3 Apply the second color, a water-based latex, which can be a darker or lighter tone of the base color or perhaps a contrast. Experiment on scrap timber first. Brush the color along the grain, making sure the entire board is covered. Then leave it to dry.

STEP 4 Use coarse wire wool to rub down the waxed areas of the wood, which will appear a different tone from the rest. The paint on top of the wax will come away with the wax, leaving areas of the base coat showing through. Finally, seal the finish in the usual way.

YOU WILL NEED:
- ELECTRICIAN'S
  BOLSTER
- HAMMER
- CLEAT

PROJECT
Fitting a floor, fitting baseboards

Renewing a boarded floor should not be undertaken lightly, as it involves a considerable amount of work and disruption. However, replacing a damaged baseboard board is a job that can be undertaken as a weekend project. Care and accuracy are required as always, but normal household life can continue around the work.

Fitting a new softwood floor onto joists, replacing one that is too badly damaged to repair, keeping it square with the room sides, and finishing with a replacement baseboard in the house style, is a major undertaking. This task is best left to a specialist, unless you have some previous experience. Irrespective of whether you tackle the job yourself or not, it is helpful to know what is involved: the room will be out of commission for a considerable time. You must make allowances for time spent not only on the floor itself, but in making good the room. Wall damage is likely to occur when removing the baseboards, and this may involve plastering or papering. If you have two rooms knocked through into one, measure the size of the baseboards in each half of the new area—they may be two distinctly different styles. Period houses generally had a larger, more ornate baseboard in what was referred to as the Sunday room, than in the back or "living" room. If these rooms are now joined, the baseboards could differ in height by as much as 5 in./13 cm. A consistent baseboard size will be needed. If you fit the larger size to stay in period, you merely need to be as careful as possible during removal. If you are fitting a smaller size, a great deal of making good will be needed to tie in to the wall. Remember the finish, too. Quite apart from any paint effect, three coats of protective varnish will be needed, each requiring 24 hours' drying time.

Removal

- Hammer an electrician's bolster between the top edge of the baseboard and the wall, near the end of a length, opening up a gap.
- Prise the baseboard away from the wall. If excessive levering is required, protect the wall surface with a wood off-cut.
- The baseboard length may be nailed directly to the masonry, or nailed or screwed to sawn lumber blocks inset into the wall, or nailed to vertical studs if you have a stud wall.
- If the boards come away from the wall leaving well-secured nails still in place, it may be easier to hammer them in rather than risk more damage trying to get them out.
- Once the baseboard is out of the way, start at one end of the room and prise up the first few boards only.
- Removing boards only as you replace them means that you always have a floor surface to kneel or stand on, lessening the risk of an accident.

In period houses baseboard boards can be of considerable depth, making a strong visual statement around the edge of the floor. However, they are vulnerable to knocks and may need replacing.

REMOVING BASEBOARDS

STEP 1 Drive an electrician's bolster behind the baseboard, near one end, to begin freeing it from the base of the wall.

STEP 2 Work along the baseboard, levering it from the wall and trying to minimize the damage to the plasterwork.

STEP 3 If any fixing nails pull through the board as it is removed, hammer them in rather than trying to pull them out.

- Remove the floorboard or cut nails with the claw of the hammer during the process of removing the board; don't hammer them down.
- Clean off the joist when it is revealed and then you are ready to lay the new floorboards.

New for old

Unless you plan to fit a reclaimed wood floor, possibly utilizing some undamaged lengths from the old one, you will find that the board widths will not be exactly the same as the ones that you have just taken out. Actual metric sizes of finished lumber have replaced the old imperial nominal sizes, so board widths will be close, but not exactly the same. Because the entire floor is being replaced, this is not important, and it gives you the opportunity to select TGV boards, giving the floor overall additional strength and minimizing the risk of warping and lifting.

Measure the floor carefully, in the direction the boards run, and make sure when you order the wood that there will be enough boards of that length or longer to complete the job. This avoids cutting and shutting on the main part of the floor, and looks much neater because no break appears in the run of the wood grain. If this seems overly fussy, remember that

unmatched joins will be more noticeable if you intend to use a decorative paint or stain finish.

Alcoves or bay areas with shorter lengths can be cut from longer stock on site, but remember when making your calculations that bays may need miters. Begin at the end of the room; you may be able to use the old boards as templates for cutting the new, particularly if you have to start in a bay. Otherwise, transfer angles for cutting lines directly from a sliding bevel. Notice that the boards stop slightly short of the wall. This allows for any small expansion of the wood and helps air to circulate between the floor and ceiling. This gap will be covered by the baseboard.

REMOVING FLOORBOARDS

STEP 1 Lift the first floorboard by driving an electrician's bolster into the gap between the boards and levering upward.

STEP 2 Once you have the end lifted high enough, slip a cleat underneath and begin to drive it along below the board, which will be sprung free.

MEASURING AND CUTTING

STEP 1 Measure the floor carefully to calculate the number and length of new boards required. Try to keep joints in runs to a minimum.

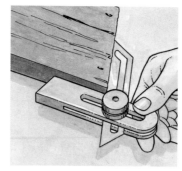

STEP 2 If the ends of boards need to be cut at an angle, use a sliding bevel to transfer the angle accurately to the new boards.

YOU WILL NEED:

MEASURING/ CUTTING:
• **MEASURING TOOLS**
• **SLIDING BEVEL**

CLOSING FLOORBOARDS:
• **NEW BOARDS**
• **CLEATS**
• **CLAMPS**
• **NAILS**
• **HAMMER**

Closing up the floorboards

Whether you use TGV or straight-sided boards, they need to be clamped together tightly. This will not only maximize the strength of the TGV join, but also minimizes the gaps that inevitably appear when using conventional boards, as the wood dries out fully even if it has been fitted after acclimatization. You must help this process by placing the lumber lengths in the room for a few days before installation. It still won't stop small gaps appearing over time, but it will tend to reduce the shrinkage.

As with all bought softwoods, the worst problems occur when cold, damp lumber is cut and joined, and the central heating is turned on.

For this reason, really top-quality floors are relaid, closing up the boards, after six months or so.

• Lay half a dozen boards in position, leave a 2 in./5cm gap, and place a wooden cleat across the joists, either nailed down or held against the old boards yet to be taken up.

• Make up two identical wedges, about 1 ft./30 cm long. Place them in the gap and hammer them together, tightening up the floor.

• Leave the wedges in place while you nail down the floor. In high-quality TGV work, where the floor is to be left exposed, one board at a time must be laid and wedged tight, so that the invisible fixing (a 2 in./5 cm lost-head or finishing nail) can be made through the tongue and then hidden by the subsequent board. With TGV boards it is important not to damage the tongue when wedging, or subsequent grooves won't fit very easily. Cut a scrap piece of TGV in half, fit the grooved half over the tongue as protection, and hammer your wedges against that.

Putting back a baseboard

The size and form of a baseboard will often date a property, so make sure the one you pick is suitable, and not at odds with the rest of

CLOSING FLOORBOARDS

STEP 1 Lay six of the new boards in place, leaving a space between them and the old boards yet to be removed.

STEP 2 Nail a stout wooden cleat across the joists about 2 in./5 cm from the edge of the last new floorboard laid.

STEP 3 Cut two long, narrow wedges. Drive them between the cleat and floorboard to clamp the boards together to nail to the joists.

NEW BASEBOARD

STEP 1 Measure up for the new lengths of baseboard, beginning at the door opening and working toward the nearest corner.

STEP 2 Nail the board in place. At an inside corner, mark the profile of the baseboard on the adjoining board so that it fits over the first board.

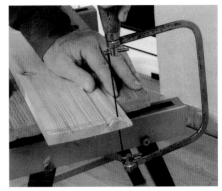

STEP 3 Use a coping saw to cut the profile in the end of the board. Its thin blade will be able to follow any intricate pattern with ease.

STEP 4 At an outside corner, mark the board for length, then miter the end outward from this mark. Do the same with its neighbor.

STEP 5 Nail the boards to the wall on each side of an outside corner. Then pin through the end of one board into the other.

STEP 6 You can attach the baseboard by using the original method, nailing into the wall or wooden wedges, or screw it in place.

your decor. Larger, more ornate molded baseboards give a period feel to the room, and usually appear to be part of the wall, not the floor. Smaller, modern baseboards, often found with a two-sided profile so that they can be fixed either way around, tend to appear as part of the flooring, particularly if they have been treated with the same finish.

- When you have made your choice of molding, start from the door opening (a right-angled cut).
- Measure and cut right into the first corner, flush against the adjacent wall.
- Butt up the next board, mark the molding profile onto it and cut it to fit. All internal corners should be cut this way.

- Outside corner turns should be mitered—after fixing the first length, mark the inside of the next miter on the reverse side of the next board. Remember that the cutting line should run outward from the back face of the baseboard, as the 45-degree joint with the adjoining board runs out from the corner.
- Fix the baseboard in place either re-using the method that was employed in fixing the old one, or screw the baseboard into position, covering the counterbored heads with wooden plugs, cutting flush with a knife, and sanding. This fixing method is recommended if you intend to give a stain and varnish finish to the baseboard.

YOU WILL NEED:

NEW BASEBOARD:
- BASEBOARD
- HAMMER
- PINS AND NAILS
- DRILL AND SCREWS
- PENCIL
- COPING SAW
- MITERING TOOLS
- STAIN AND VARNISH

PROJECT
Staircases

Staircases come in a range of shapes and styles from the purely functional to the elaborate and ornate. Get to know your staircase type and its functional parts; for example, whether it is a straight, sweeping, half-turn, quarter-turn, or dog-leg style staircase, and whether it has a closed or open string, or open tread.

Types of stairs

Modern staircases tend toward one style, the closed-string stair, which takes up the minimum of space, usually against a wall, and is the most economic to construct. Other styles in wooden staircases include the open-string, where the strings are sawn to the profile of the steps, and the stair treads sit on the cut-outs, or the open-tread, where the risers are omitted altogether. Other staircases, such as spirals, are often functional space savers installed to gain access to loft rooms or basements.

If you own a period property, you will already know that, historically, the staircase was much more than a functional way of changing floors—it was a status symbol. The Victorians, in particular, favored elaborate, decorative stairs and their house design emphasized ornate hallways, where the stairs could be admired by a visitor to the front door. By the time the stairs reached the servants' floors, however, best-quality joinery lumbers were replaced by cheap pine, painted or varnished a darker color as an attempted disguise. Whatever the age of your staircase, it is made up of the same functional parts, all of which are individually replaceable.

Basic staircase repairs

Creaking stairs are usually caused by loose-fitting treads or risers. Under foot pressure the loose part moves against an adjacent fixed piece. The repairs are fairly simple, however:

- Locate the source of the creak, and check the wedges that should hold the tread and riser firmly in position.
- If one is loose, remove it, checking that it is not broken or split. If it is, use it as a template to make up a new one. Replace the wedge, hammering it into position with a wooden mallet.
- Check the glue blocks, regluing if necessary.
- On troublesome treads, you could try screwing and gluing a cleat of 1 in. x 1 in./2.5 cm x 2.5 cm underneath the complete width, joining the tread and riser together.
- Countersink 1¼ in./3.2 cm number 8 screws—don't use longer ones or you risk them coming through on the other side.

REPAIRS

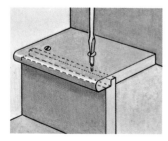

STEP 1 Screws can be driven down through the tread and into the riser below to reinforce the joint.

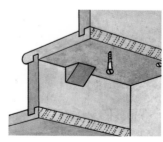

STEP 2 From beneath the stairs, drive more screws through the tread into the riser above.

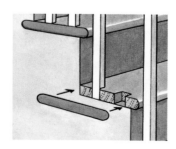

STEP 3 Return nosings can be prised off and replaced. They also give access to the baluster base.

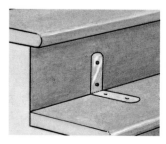

STEP 4 If access to the underside of the stairs is impossible, reinforce the treads and risers with L-brackets

STAIRCASE TERMINOLOGY

1 **Tread:** the part you stand on as you ascend or descend the stairs, and which usually overlaps the riser with a rounded or semirounded front.

2 **Nosing:** separate molding on the tread front, or the rounded tread front itself. (Return nosing is the same as the nosing, but hiding the end grain of the tread and side base of the baluster on staircases built with open strings.)

3 **Riser:** the vertical lumber joining the back of one tread to the front of the next.

4 **Strings:** the sides of the staircase. Against the wall side, the inner string forms part of the continuous baseboard. The outer string, which can be open or closed, holds the balusters in place.

5 **Balusters:** usually decorative turned sections of wood acting as banister supports. (Balustrade is the collective name of balusters.)

6 **Banister:** hand rail, running on top of the balusters.

7 **Newel post:** anchored support post, at the stair foot, and where the stairs turn.

8 **Glue blocks:** positioned at the back of the joint between riser and tread, as reinforcement.

9 **Wedges:** positioned underneath, securing both tread and riser to the string.

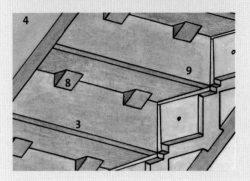

- Still underneath, drive the same screw size up into the bottom edge of the riser through the back edge of the tread.

- If you cannot gain access to the underside (if the soffit is plastered, for example), approach the problem from the front.

- Your only choice at the back of the tread is a right-angled metal support bracket to hold it to the riser.

- Mark the position with a pencil and carefully chisel the depth of the metal out of the wood.

- Screw into position with ½ in./1.2 cm number 6 screws.

- At the front of the tread, countersink 1¼ in./3.2 cm number 8 screws down through the tread, into the riser edge, at 4-in./10-cm intervals along the length.

Finishes on wooden staircases

If you have been forced to repair a tread from the front, using visible brackets and screws, you will have to fit a carpet or runner. Functional and conventional, coverings reduce the noise of feet on the stairs. Closed string cases suit a fitted carpet, but open strings encourage the use of a centrally positioned stair runner, letting both exposed sides be varnished or painted.

There is no reason why stairs in good constructional condition should not have a paint and varnish finish. Try a combination of royal blue or dark green with a clear varnished natural wood, where the balusters and the risers are painted and the banister, tread, and nosings varnished. The different woods of banister and stair contrast well with each other and the painted parts.

Use a top quality floor or yacht varnish on the treads, applying four coats as a minimum and sanding gently between coats. Don't reverse the stair scheme, though. Paint on the treads won't last long unless it is over-varnished, which rather defeats the object.

PROJECT
Overlaying floors

There is no better floor in any home than a wooden surface in good condition—it can be the center of attention. Its good looks ensure that it fits well with any decorative style. Wood flooring, as well as making a statement about your lifestyle, invokes memories of an age when floors were part of the decorative scheme in houses.

A popular choice

Current market research indicates that real wood and real wood veneer flooring will remain as a popular choice with property owners for the foreseeable future, being hard-wearing, stylish, and relatively "low maintenance." Real wood floors are perceived as warm and inviting in cold winters and as having a cool feel to offset hot summer days. Health is an issue, too, as carpeting of any kind harbors dust mites, and asthma and hay fever sufferers can benefit from the low dust retention qualities of this replacement flooring. Strip wood manufacturers have been quick to promote good environmental policies, too, claiming not to fell any endangered tropical species, and to take supplies of hardwood only from controlled areas where the rate of replanting equals the rate of harvesting.

Strips and tiles of real wood

Real hardwood floors can still be laid, using solid boards that are machined from oak, elm, chestnut, and ash, among others, often from controlled European stock. Specialized workshops will supply and fit a new floor, and often take on restoration projects. The cost can be prohibitive, though, and the rise in popularity of laminate wood flooring is testament to this fact. Solid hardwood strips will always be the top of the range, expensive to source, and very time-consuming to lay, but offer a finish that will last a lifetime. Current layering technology now offers a good-looking alternative, at a price closer to the average budget. Real wood veneers form the top layer of a composite construction, which includes a shock-absorbing middle layer and a stabilizing base. The three different layers comprise wood strips laid at right-angles to each other, to minimize expansion and shrinkage of the floor panel as it experiences different climatic humidities. The veneered panels are finished with up to five coats of varnish offering ultraviolet protection, with a pore sealer, and as a first impression offer the same visual qualities as solid floors. Planks of veneered flooring are tongued-and-grooved, and are priced per square yard (meter), but often sold in packs

BELOW: **The beauty of a real wood floor will set off any room's decor to perfection. The richness of the color and grain pattern will provide a feeling of warmth in winter and coolness in summer.**

covering 10 ft./3 m or more, and they can be fairly simply installed as "floating floors." The veneer thickness, about ¼ in./4–5 mm, allows the laid floor to be sanded down and finished in the same way as a solid floor, and as the years pass it will age and color in the same way. The same sanding and varnishing technique is needed for most wood-tile floors, although a few manufacturers supply prefinished units. Wood tiles consists of five or more strips of wood joined along their longest edge into a square, then bound together at right angles to similar units on a cloth backing to form a square tile. The small strips may be solid hardwood, but more often than not are veneers on a softwood or man-made backing board. Wood tiles offer a wide choice in wood types and are sold in bundles, again priced per square yard (meter). The main difference between these tiles and the strip flooring panels is that the tiles are glued into position conventionally, while the panels are joined to each other and not to the subfloor.

Laminate flooring

If real wood veneer-laminated flooring is the economic alternative to a traditional hardwood block floor, then laminate "wood effect" floor panels are the cheap alternative to real wood veneers. The top layer is a photographic effect, a fairly good plastic representation of a hardwood finish, either in colors pertaining to real woods such as cherry, chestnut, and ash, or in plain blues and greens. These easy to fit tongue-and-grooved panels are sometimes glued and sometimes snapped together, but always need a flooring underlay and an installation kit. Be aware that the top "wood effect" layer is very thin, and will not tolerate heavy traffic. Again priced per square yard (meter), laminate flooring is available in packs usually covering about 2 square yards/meters. A fair indication of its quality is the price tag. You will pay about 20 percent of the price of real wood floor, and it would be more realistic to offer this product as an alternative to linoleum or vinyl.

Whatever type of flooring you choose, bear in mind that looking at small areas will not necessarily give you a good idea of the impression produced by the finished floor; some finishes may become overpowering over a large area.

LEFT: **Laminate flooring provides an inexpensive alternative to real wood flooring and can be very effective. The panels snap together and have a synthetic finish representing various different woods.**

Wood tile flooring comprises square panels of wood strips on a cloth backing, which are laid like tiles. The strips may be cut from solid lumber, softwood, or board faced with veneer, and offer a range of hardwood finishes.

LEFT: **Plastic laminate flooring boards offer a cheaper alternative to real wood.**

RIGHT: **These real oak laminate boards are tongued-and-grooved for jointing.**

YOU WILL NEED:

FLOATING FLOOR:
- **FLOOR PANELS**
- **SAW**
- **GLUE**
- **HAMMER/MALLET**
- **PENCIL**
- **WOOD SLIVERS**
- **PROTECTIVE BLOCK**
- **MEASURING TAPE**
- **ANGLED METAL STRIP**
- **COPING SAW**

Parquet flooring strips are traditionally laid in a herringbone or basketweave pattern. The latter lends itself to mosaic panels.

Locating the right floor

Always consult with your supplier to ensure the flooring panels of your choice are suitable for the domestic location you have in mind. Depending on the manufacturer's recommendations, certain panels may be deemed unsuitable for bathrooms (wet areas) or kitchens (high-humidity areas), or be classified as suitable for entrance halls or bedrooms (high- or low-traffic areas). Some boards are unsuitable for heated floors, such as beech, whereas some woods are ideal for humid areas where high dimensional stability is required. Bamboo, for example, has a low moisture content and works well in bathrooms.

Preparing to lay a floating floor

As usual, the hard work in laying a floor is unseen, being underneath. Preparation is the key to a good floor, while the actual laying of the panels should proceed reasonably quickly, permitting an ever-increasing view of the final result. The preparation must include leveling of the existing floor, if necessary. A basement with a solid floor may need screeding with a concrete mix, or sealing to prevent damp problems. Slightly uneven or pitted concrete floors can be made good by pouring on a self-leveling compound; hardboard can be pinned over floorboards. Cleating and fitting a TGV chipboard under-floor is a good idea in a basement; however headroom is often a priority

in these areas, and if height does not permit cleating, then you must work on the concrete floor. If your room has a baseboard, consider whether or not you wish to remove it for laying, or replace it altogether with a matching wood finish. Floor panels must have a ⅜ in./1 cm expansion gap all around the perimeter of the room, to facilitate absorption and loss of moisture, covered either by the new baseboard or by a strip of beading pinned to the old one. Finally, prepare to lay your hardwood panels on a dry, level surface called a subfloor, which is an underlay on a roll that can be supplied with the boards. The cushioning effect of this underlay disguises any (small) defects in the old floor surface, and lets the new floor "float" on top of the old one.

Floating the floor

When you are happy with the subfloor, set out the hardwood panels. Lay the panels with the tongues facing into the room, following the direction of the longest wall, unless the room is square, when you should set out in the direction of the incoming light. Don't lay the panels in a strict grid; offset to make sure the butt joins do not line up across the floor. Make sure your first row of boards is straight—remember that the wall may not be—and use ⅜ in./1 cm blocks to create the expansion gap. Saw the last panel in the row to fit, using its offcut to begin row two.

Glue the panels to each other, at the sides and end, by running glue into the upper side of the groove and gently tapping with a hammer or mallet and protective block. Panels will probably need cutting to fit lengthwise when you reach the final row: mark the cutting line with a pencil by placing them on top of the previous row. Remember to include the expansion gap, and that your calculation must include the tongue-and-groove joint. Glue the final row of panels to each other, position the expansion blocks, and leave to dry. Finally fit the baseboard to cover the expansion gap after removing the ⅜ in./1 cm blocks or, if the baseboard has been left in place, fit a decorative beading such as quarter-round molding or similar.

You may find that you have to fit the flooring around central heating pipes, in which case take careful measurements of each pipe's position and transfer these to the appropriate board. Bore a hole in the board, making it large enough to clear the pipe, then make cuts from the hole to the board edge. Retain the off-cut. Fit the board in place around the pipe and glue the off-cut back behind it. If the flooring is to stop at a doorway, fit a hardwood threshold across the bottom of the frame and lay the boards up to it. Use a profile gauge to copy the shape of the crown molding, or make a paper template, and transfer this to the flooring, cutting around the shape with a coping saw.

Lay out the wood panels, working away from one wall with the tongues facing into the room.

A FLOATING FLOOR

STEP 1 Maintain a ⅜in./1cm expansion gap by inserting slivers of wood between the wall and boards.

STEP 2 As you work, glue the panels together by applying a bead of glue into each panel groove.

STEP 3 Tap the panels together, using a hammer and protective block to avoid damaging the edges.

STEP 4 When you reach the far wall, measure for the cut board, allowing for the expansion gap.

STEP 5 Transfer the dimension to a board, making allowance for the tongue-and-groove joint; cut it to width.

STEP 6 Use an angled metal strip to tap the cut boards into place. Then cover the gaps with beading.

YOU WILL NEED:
- DRILL WITH MIXING ATTACHMENT
- SELF-LEVELING MORTAR COMPOUND
- PLASTERER'S TROWEL
- BUCKET

PROJECT
Basic skills: tiled floors

Tiles are more popular than ever before as a decorative floor covering. This is due in part to the array of options now available, from basic ceramics from a discount warehouse to diamond-sawn slate from a specialized supplier. They can be easy to clean, hard-wearing, and, of course, very good-looking.

Tiles used for a decorative flooring effect in period houses were well made and extremely hard-wearing, surviving decades of abuse from working boots with nailed soles and heels that tramped in street dirt. Encaustic tiles in basic colors were used to make patterned floors in hallways and corridors; older houses sometimes had flagstones or slate tiles in kitchens and laundry rooms downstairs, but quarry tiles were more common in these areas. If you uncover a tiled floor in an older property that is basically sound, consider using it as a room feature rather than replacing it. Old cleaning principles and techniques can restore the look of a tiled floor

Stone tile

Cork tiles

Natural slate

Quarry tiles

Marble tile

Stone tile

Flagstone tiles make for a practical, hard-wearing yet attractive floor in a kitchen or hallway. They are easily cleaned, retain their color and pattern well, and require no maintenance.

simply and cheaply, soda crystals in hot water will take off grime and grease, and traditional polishes are still available from specialized suppliers. Encaustic (where colored clays are burnt in) and geometric tiles (natural clay fired into simple shapes and inserts) are available again, and it may be possible to match a tile design if floor damage has occurred. An independent tile workshop or supplier can advise you, or consult a restoration specialist.

Types of tile

If you intend to lay a new floor, several tile options are open to you. Specialized shops offer diamond-sawn slate, marble, and many types of natural stone slabs, and reclaimed terra cotta in tile form polishes up beautifully. Quarry tiles are functional, good-looking, and easy to keep clean, if rather cold to the touch, and ceramic floor tiles are as easy to lay on a floor as a wall. Other options are presanded cork tiles, laid with adhesive but requiring a sealer, or presealed cork that is easy to maintain. Vinyl floor tiles are usually self-adhesive, and come in a wide variety of color schemes, but if vinyl is your choice,

LEFT: **Encaustic tiles with simple patterns were commonly used in the hallways of period houses. Modern versions are available, making the restoration of this kind of flooring a viable proposition for those seeking to recreate an original look for their homes.**

need a homemade strike-off board to level the mortar bed, and this in itself will level a slightly uneven floor as the job proceeds. Otherwise a self-leveling mortar compound can be used. This is supplied dry, usually in 55-lb./25-kg packs, for self-mixing. Mix the contents in a bucket, according to the directions, so that the fairly liquid, lump-free compound can be poured onto the floor. It finds its own level, but you need to assist it by troweling it out to a thin layer with a plasterer's trowel. The compound dries hard and smooth fairly quickly but you must leave it a day before attempting to lay a floor on it.

Concrete that has cracked or has deeper surface damage can be patched: use a strong mortar mix (3 parts soft sand to 1 part cement), wetting the cracked area first and leveling off with a trowel. Slightly damp floors can be treated by brushing on two or three coats of a proprietary damp-proofing liquid, but if the floor is wet enough to indicate a failure of the damp-proof membrane under the surface, this will not solve the problem. A new membrane stretched onto the concrete can be covered with flooring-grade tongue-and-groove chipboard, creating a dry "floating" floor surface. Ideally, the membrane should be continued up the walls to meet with the damp-proof course.

consider loose-laid sheet vinyl, available in many designs and colors but often found as imitation wood or tiling complete with three-dimensional effect and colored grouting. Similar to sheet vinyl is linoleum, sold the same way by linear yard (meter) off a wide roll. A wide range of decorative patterning is available, to suit any room area, but particularly a children's play area because it is tough and easy to keep clean. Its drawback is that it is more difficult to fit, being stiffer and less easy to manipulate, and more awkward to cut.

Repairing and leveling solid floors

No matter what tiling system you intend to lay on a solid floor, the floor itself must be level. Quarry, stone, or any tile bedded in mortar will

LEVELING A SOLID FLOOR

STEP 1 Fixing a mixing attachment to an electric drill will speed the mixing up of self-leveling compound.

STEP 2 Trowel the compound into small shallow depressions, making sure you fill them completely.

STEP 3 Pour the self-leveling compound directly from the bucket into large depressions in the floor.

STEP 4 Feather the edges of the compound with the trowel and leave it for a day before starting further work.

YOU WILL NEED:

- TILES
- ADHESIVE
- NOTCHED TROWEL
- STRINGS AND CHALK
- GROUT
- TILE CUTTING
  EQUIPMENT
- DAMP SPONGE
- SQUEEGEE
- DOWEL
- SOFT CLOTH

Heavy tiles

These need to be bedded in mortar, and a concrete (solid) floor is ideal. Floorboards or chipboard over joists (a suspended floor) may not take the extra weight and are not really suitable for this type of tiling. Vinyl, cork, or a veneered floating floor would be more sensible, but if you really must have heavy quarry tiles or similar on a suspended floor, check with a professional builder first.

Laying ceramic tiles in adhesive

First set out a dry run: simply place the tiles on the floor to find the best arrangement or sequence before any permanent positioning is done (remember to leave a gap for the grout). Setting out corridor shapes, long and thin, can often be done by eye, following the longer dimension, but regular room shapes should be started at the center. The room center can be determined by using lengths of string to join the central points of opposing walls, forming a cross where the strings meet. To confirm that the grout pattern is square when you open the door, run a third string from the door frame to the opposite wall, forming a 90-degree angle. A right angle should occur where all the strings cross; if it does not, then the room is out of square. If this is the case, use the string from the door frame as the starting guide, and adjust the center point strings to form the required right angles. When you are happy with the setting out, either chalk the strings and snap them to the floor surface, leaving a guideline, or if you are confident that they are fixed securely, you can use the strings themselves as guides. Spread the adhesive to the required depth, using a notched spreader. The notch size is designed to spread different thicknesses. Your specialized tile supplier will advise you, and ensure you have the

LAYING FLOOR TILES

STEP 1 Set out the tiles dry first to establish a starting point for the rows and determine where cut tiles will be necessary. You may have to rearrange them several times until you are happy with the plan.

STEP 2 As when tiling a wall, use a notched trowel to spread a layer of adhesive on the floor. The notches ensure a uniform amount is applied.

STEP 3 Only cover a manageable section of floor at a time with the adhesive, otherwise it will begin to set before you can lay all the tiles.

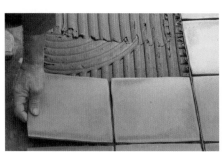

STEP 4 Bed the tiles in the adhesive, working away from your guide strings. Keep checking that your work is straight.

STEP 5 Remove excess adhesive from between the tiles. Grout the joints when the adhesive has set.

BORDER TILES AND GROUTING

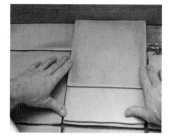

STEP 1 Lay a tile on the last whole tile laid and butt another against the wall to mark the cutting line.

STEP 2 Score along the line and snap the tile in two in the same manner as when working with ceramic wall tiles.

STEP 3 Tile nippers are ideal for making small cut-outs in tiles to fit around pipes and other obstructions.

STEP 4 Spread adhesive on the back of a cut tile and press it into place. This will protect the adjacent tiles.

STEP 5 When the adhesive has dried, mix up the grout and spread it into the joints.

STEP 6 At the edges of the floor, work the grout into the joint between tiles and wall.

STEP 7 Use a damp sponge to wash off all traces of excess grout before it has a chance to dry.

STEP 8 When all the excess grout has been removed, polish the floor with a soft cloth.

STEP 9 Make sure you remove any powdery deposits left in corners by the sponging.

correct adhesive, flexible on a suspended floor, water-resistant in potentially wet areas. Don't spread too much adhesive at one time; start with a square yard/meter or so, until you are sure that you can work more quickly. Line up the first tile with the guides, press the tile firmly into the adhesive bed, and place tile spacers (or wooden match sticks) to ensure correct positioning and spacing of the next tiles.

As you proceed across the floor, check that the work is level, using a straightedge. When the floor is covered with complete tiles, leaving only the borders to cut to fit, clean the joints and remove excess adhesive.

To measure the border tiles for cutting, lay a complete tile directly on top of the last one laid in that row, place a tile on top, butted to the wall or baseboard, and mark the gap with a line on the tile underneath. Cut the tile by scoring and

snapping, or by using a tile cutting machine which you can rent by the day. Fix the cut tile in place, and follow the same sequence in the next row. When the entire floor is completed, clean down the area and leave it for 24 hours.

Grouting and finishing

Spread the grout on the tiled surface, and force it down between the tile edges into the joint lines using a squeegee. Use a damp cloth to wipe the tile surface clean, rinsing the cloth regularly. The lines of grout now need to be smoothed out; you can use a grout finisher, available from your specialized supplier, or a short length of dowel will do just as well. When you are happy with the result, and all tiles are free of excess grout, polish the surface with a clean, dry cloth.

The finished floor will give many years' service and will maintain its good looks throughout.

YOU WILL NEED:

HARDBOARD:

- **NAIL SET AND HAMMER**
- **HARDBOARD PINS**
- **PANEL SAW**

CORK TILES:

- **SELF-ADHESIVE CORK TILES**
- **CORK SEALER (IF REQUIRED)**
- **PINS**
- **TAPE**
- **PENCIL**
- **STEEL RULE OR STRAIGHTEDGE**
- **STRINGS AND CHALK**
- **SHARP KNIFE**
- **SCISSORS**
- **SANDPAPER**
- **CORK BLOCK**
- **CLEAR VARNISH**

PROJECT
Laying vinyl and cork tiles

Good setting out and a level surface are the keys to successful laying of cork or vinyl tiles on a suspended wooden floor. Gaps between floorboards will show through the tile, even if level; covering the boards with hardboard is the only way to achieve the flat surface needed. TGV chipboard floors that are not uneven need sanding at the joins to ensure a smooth surface.

A hardboard subfloor

Before you lay hardboard sheets onto conventional floorboards, you need to punch the existing nail heads below the surface; otherwise the overlaid sheets will not lie flat.

Use a nail set and hammer, just as you would if you were sanding down the floor. Use the largest size of sheet that you can conveniently handle, to cut down the number of joints, and fit each shiny side down onto the floor. The textured face provides a good key for the tile adhesive.

You will need to stagger the joints from row to row, so that you do not create a line across the room, but as hardboard cuts easily, either with a saw or knife, this is a fairly simple job. Secure the sheets with hardboard pins, punched in at 4 in./10 cm centers and 4 in./10 cm intervals along all the edges, or use an industrial staple gun.

Setting out and laying the tiles

Set out the tiles following the guide for solid floors, finding the room center and drawing a cross on the floor. This centers the arrangement in the room, but, if this leaves a narrow border that does not suit the decorative design on the tile, you can adjust it. It is easier if you use string to make the initial centered cross, dividing the area into quarters. The string can be tied to pins driven into the floor, or secured with tape. If the tiles are patterned, ensure the design matches up as you place a dry run of two rows of tiles from the center to the baseboard, butting the tiles to the stringline. If there is a narrow gap at odds with your tile design, adjust the strings so that complete tiles butt to the wall in two directions. When the arrangement is satisfactory, rub chalk onto the strings and snap them against the floor to leave accurate marks or leave them in place to use as guides. Peel off the backing of the tiles (if they have one). Position, working along the guidelines to the wall. Some cork tiles use adhesive, which is spread on the hardboard (not the tile) with a notched spatula. Lay one tile at a time, pressing it down firmly. Cutting tiles to fit is a matter of overlaying on the gap and marking the waste, then cutting the tile with a sharp snap-blade knife held against a steel straightedge. Use a tile offcut as a cutting mat.

HARDBOARD SHEETS

STEP 1 Before covering a floor with hardboard sheets, drive all the nail heads below the surface of the floor.

STEP 2 Use a panel saw to cut sheets to size as necessary and stagger the panels from one row to the next.

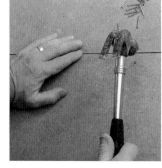

STEP 3 Staple or nail the hardboard sheets to the floor. You should space the fixings at 4 in./10 cm centers.

CORK TILING

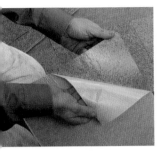

STEP 1 Some cork tiles are self-adhesive, so you just need to peel off the back and press them down.

STEP 2 Press the tiles into place on the floor, aligning the first rows carefully with strings.

STEP 3 Center the tiles on the floor, using two strings at right-angles to maintain the alignment.

To fit a tile around a bathroom fitting, make a paper template and transfer the shape to the tile.

STEP 4 Mark tiles for cutting by laying one over the last tile laid and butting another against the wall.

STEP 5 Using a steel rule or straightedge as a guide, cut the tiles to size with a sharp knife.

STEP 6 Press the cut tiles into place around the edge of the floor to finish the job.

Cork tiles can provide a stylish, attractive, and warm floor covering for almost any part of the house, including the kitchen.

Unusually shaped objects such as pedestals may need a template of paper to aid fitting. Tape scrap paper to the floor and cut a series of slits into the pedestal shape from the edge. Press a fold line around the shape with scissor points, remove it from the floor, and cut out around the fold. Tape the template onto the tile and follow the outline with a snap-blade knife.

Sealing the floor

Plain cork tiles are easy to fit. They need sealing after laying, but vinyl-coated cork does not. When the plain cork floor is finished and the adhesive has set, lightly sand rough areas at the edges of the tiles with fine-grade sandpaper wrapped around a cork block. Brush away dust, and wipe the floor with a rag dampened with mineral spirits. Use two or three coats of cork sealer or clear polyurethane varnish to finish the job.

Woodwork

Wood surfaces about the home need a sympathetic treatment if they are to look their best. Fashionable finishes are beneficial if they add to the character of the original wood, but if they disguise it, they are merely doing the same job as a lick of paint, commonly used by builders to cover new wood with well-marked growth rings and carrying defects. Traditional treatments like color waxing, intended for the best quality stock, and combinations of paint and stain washes will have a different visual effect depending on the wood surface. They can be used to emphasize and exaggerate lumber defects, resulting in a unique, abstract patterning.

Designer's notes

The decorative scheme you apply to the woodwork in your property should be viewed as an important finishing touch—if not exactly reflecting the period of construction, then certainly not being at odds with it. There are so many different finishes to choose from, whether you want to let the natural grain pattern show through or disguise it with solid color.

Intricate moldings and panels must be treated with sympathy.

Older-style houses have more elaborate moldings, crown moldings and frames than modern properties, and the use of bright, glossy, modern paint schemes can detract from their elegance. Enamel paints of any color can reflect both natural and controllable artificial light alarmingly, causing flare and highlight in moldings and recesses where none was intended, often appearing to change the shape of the wood and destroy the joiner's intended subtlety. Original period moldings were painted with "flat" oil colors and varnishes, the lack of any sheen on the finish emphasizing the decorative qualities of the joinery. Today, "dead flat oil" is again available as a paint finish from specialized

RIGHT: Paneled doors can be painted with solid colors, which let the shapes of the panelwork show through. Too fussy an effect would produce a confusion of shapes and patterns.

suppliers. Attractive alternatives include water-based effects and finishes which can be sealed with a mat varnish, or oil-based low luster paint that can be partially rubbed down and "distressed" before a sealer is applied. In this way, bright colors can be used together without causing light to flare across molded surfaces, and the original integrity of the joinery can be maintained. Whatever the period, always seek to enhance the natural characteristics of your property, rather than work against them. Modern housing, often having smaller, plain, or chamfered wood surrounds, is more suited to simple enamel treatments; often the narrow, minimalist frames match the glossy, plastic feel of PVCu window systems. These styles are based around advanced technologies, where expensive woods have been replaced with metals, plastics, laminates and manufactured boards. The increased use of metals has led to innovations like hot baseboards, where metal snap-on sections carry electric heating next to the floor. Standard panel radiators, so often a room design problem, can now be replaced with a variety of space-saving linear sculptures like multicolumns, and heating art designs such as continuous coils. As with period properties, work with the technology, not against it: powerful primary colors on narrow, plain surrounds complement minimalist room sets and provide defining borders for large wall areas.

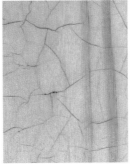

FAR LEFT: **Shutters make an interesting addition to any window. In period houses the original shutter boxes may remain, needing only new shutters to be made. However, they can also be added to more modern homes.**

MIDDLE: **Crackleglaze is a two-part varnish that can be applied to wood to produce an aged look.**

ABOVE LEFT: **Doors offer all sorts of possibilities for decorative finishes, whether they be stains or paint.**

Dealing with doors

Modern technology has changed the look and installation of many room features, and paint and decorative systems have adapted too. The basic reason for entry doors, storage doors, and shutters still remains the same, however, and this is an area worth exploiting decoratively.

Entry doors, either new or reclaimed, that are made from solid wood can be color stained and varnished to emphasize the grain structure. Cheaper modern doors that have plywood panels or other manufactured inserts benefit from a combination scheme: insert panels can be painted a solid color, and the real wood frame washed with a tint of the same color. Seal or varnish to protect the finish. Try matching up closet or storage doors in the same color system as the main door, or consider commissioning or building shutter doors to replace drapes. They can be constructed to the same basic door style fairly simply, and the same combination paint scheme will result in a coordinated wood finish. Bear in mind, too, the other woodwork in the room, such as baseboards, chair and picture rails, valances, and wall paneling.

Same technique, different area

Using the same paint effect on different door types and sizes, irrespective of the wood grain or board surface, is fairly logical because it achieves an overall pattern in the room. What isn't quite so obvious is that the majority of effects can be made to work on any wood surface, irrespective of where you may have seen them used, and the only limit is your imagination.

Techniques based on the principle of oil and water not mixing together, for example, as in wax resists used to distress floorboards, can be equally effective on moldings. Soft, solvent-based wax can be rubbed onto the top relief surface of a molding, and the entire crown molding painted with water-based paint. Rubbing down with steel wool takes the paint off the surface molding, but leaves it in the recesses. Wax resist techniques, often used to distress furniture, can look good on baseboards, especially when an underlying color is revealed. Likewise crackleglazing, which is usually associated with small areas such as picture frames, can also be used on inset door panels with a matching tint varnish on the frame of the door. Always remember that paint effects on wood can be applied to more than just one area, and, as long as the finishes are practical in the areas that you intend to use them, are versatile and interchangeable.

FAR LEFT: **Choose from a variety of paint effects to cheer up various old cabinets that are around the home.**

LEFT: **A rubbed, oil-based, wax-resisting red latex and an abraded green colorwash.**

YOU WILL NEED:
- ABRASIVE PAPERS
- SUGAR SOAP SOLUTION
- SANDPAPER
- SPONGE
- GLOVES
- BRUSH
- PRIMER
- UNDERCOAT
- OIL-BASED ENAMEL PAINT

PROJECT
Basic skills: wood

In any decorating job in the house you must decide what finish you desire before you prepare the surface. Paint on woodwork must cover defects such as holes and knots; therefore they must be filled and sealed, or stains and varnishes can be used creatively to emphasize them, if this is appropriate for your chosen decor.

Wood may be stripped in two ways: with a chemical paint stripper (left) or a blow torch (right). Both methods need care as they are potentially dangerous.

Preparation of surfaces

The surface preparation for the job will obviously depend on how you have visualized the finish. Wood only offers two basic choices, putting paint on, or taking it off. If you intend to repaint, and the existing paint surface is sound, you do not need to strip it off, only to remove the sheen completely using a medium-grade silicon carbide paper (wet-and-dry paper) soaked in a hot solution of sugar soap and water. Abrade the surface using plenty of liquid until the area is of a dull mat appearance. Switch to a fine grade of paper to achieve a smooth finish if necessary. It is important, after using wet abrasives and washing down, to let all surfaces dry out thoroughly.

You can now overpaint directly with an oil-based enamel if the color is similar, but a totally different scheme, such as dark blue replacing a pale yellow, will require the paint maker's recommended undercoat. If the existing paint surface is unsound, however, showing obvious visual defects like cracking, flaking, blistering, peeling, or chipping, then the paint must be stripped back to reveal the bare wood.

Stripping wood

Stripping paints and varnishes off wood surfaces is a time-consuming, dirty job. Unless you are stripping a door, which can be taken off its hinges, the job must be taken on in situ. Paneling, frames, and baseboards are best tackled with a burner and gas bottle; a flexible blade or shavehook follows the flame through softened paint and scrapes it off the surface. Hot-air strippers (or heat guns) are also suitable, but they

PREPARATION

STEP 1 Old paintwork should be rubbed down with abrasive paper to provide a key for the new paint.

STEP 2 Wash down the paintwork with a sugar soap solution. Leave to dry completely.

STEP 3 Areas of bare wood should be primed, and the surface sanded back where they join.

STEP 4 Undercoat, then apply one or two top coats. Keep a wet edge to prevent obvious joins.

are heavy, and as they must be held in the "wrong" hand (the "right" hand is holding the scraper for greater accuracy) are tiring to use. Paint strippers are another option; chemical action causes the paint to blister and bubble so it can be scraped off easily. They are recommended for crown moldings where delicate moldings can be stripped by the use of steel wool, rather than damaged by a clumsy blade. If paint stripper is your choice, use the water-washable kind, and keep a bucket of warm water beside you. Liquid chemical strippers are corrosive and must be handled wearing protective clothing; wash off any splashes immediately. Another option for removable doors is dipping in a caustic tank. Small firms offering this service will often collect and deliver, solving any transport problems, but the drawback is that caustic solutions tend to eat into the glued joints as well as stripping the paint. When your door is returned, be prepared to reglue the joints and clamp the door with sash clamps overnight. The door will need sanding down as the grain will have been raised by the stripping process, and the wood will appear dry and dull. If you prefer a natural wood finish, apply Danish oil with a soft cloth to replace the natural oils taken out in the caustic tank.

Filling

Wood preparation includes filling or sanding irregularities, old fixing holes, dead knot holes, splits, or cracks. If the wood is to be varnished, that is the grain and color will be part of the finish, the filler applied must match the wood color. Plastic wood filler can be bought to fill different woods, labeled pine, oak, mahogany, and so on. Slightly overfill the hole with a small flexible blade, to allow for some shrinkage and for sanding flush when hard. If the wood is to be painted, joint compound can be used, which is easy to sand when dry. When filling window frames and other occasionally exposed wood areas, an oil-based stopper or putty should be used, and this should be applied after the primer coat, not before. Otherwise, you risk the unsealed wood surface drawing out the oil, the filler shrinking and consequently falling out.

Paneled walls offer a range of decorative possibilities, whether you stain and varnish them or apply a solid paint scheme.

Knots in painted wood surfaces

The treatment of resinous knots must not be ignored if you are to achieve a first-class finish. Brush the knot with genuine shellac knotting, available from your decorating supplier, and leave to dry before applying the primer coat. Knots literally weeping resin must be scraped clean, and dried out as much as possible with a burner flame before sealing. Resin stains already covered by paint will eventually show through a fresh paint film. To prevent this problem, scrape the paint off back to the bare wood, apply shellac knotting, and repaint. Simply painting over resin stains is no good.

Holes can be filled with joint compound. It should be left proud and rubbed down when dry.

Treat knots with shellac knotting to prevent them from bleeding resin through your finish.

YOU WILL NEED:
- PAINT
- BRUSHES
- PAINTER'S TAPE
- LADDER
- OIL OR WATER-BASED
  PROTECTION

PROJECT
Painting doors and windows

Interior doors that are to be painted or varnished do not need a weatherproof finish. You can use oil-based finishes for protection against knocks, or the water-based variety. Windows, though, are exposed to wet conditions, cold in winter with condensation on the inside, and humid in summer, and they should be given a tough finish.

Door sequence

Paneled doors

Remove the door furniture and paint the door edges first. If you are only painting one side of the door, wedge it open. If the door opens toward you, paint the leading edge only. If it opens away from you, then you should paint the hanging (hinged) edge. Wipe off any paint that has fouled the other face of the door. Now paint the panel moldings and then the panels, taking care that any excess paint in the molding channels does not "run" onto the panels or rails. The horizontal rails are next, followed by the vertical center rails or muntins, and then the outer stiles.

Flush doors

Remove the door furniture and paint the edges as before, but there the similarity in techniques ends. You need to treat flush doors more as you would a small wall area, dividing the area into thirds and painting one third at a time. Lay the paint off toward the edges as you finish each section, and work quickly enough to maintain a wet or "live" edge so that the sections join together easily without leaving an obvious join. Leave the door wedged open until the paint is dry, and do not raise any dust in the room, as this is liable to stick to the paint film and ruin the finish. When the paint has dried, replace the door furniture.

SEQUENCE FOR PAINTING DOORS

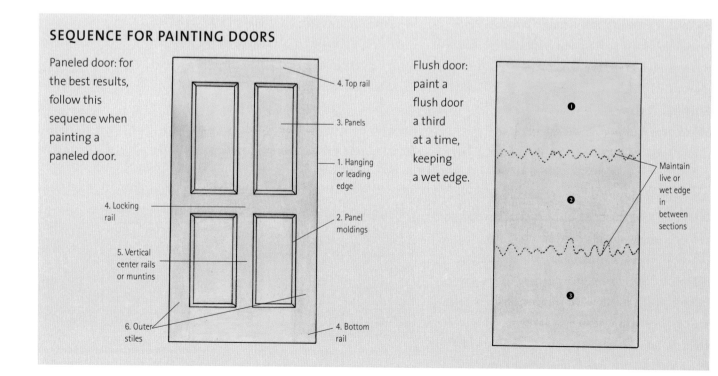

Paneled door: for the best results, follow this sequence when painting a paneled door.

4. Top rail
3. Panels
1. Hanging or leading edge
4. Locking rail
2. Panel moldings
5. Vertical center rails or muntins
6. Outer stiles
4. Bottom rail

Flush door: paint a flush door a third at a time, keeping a wet edge.

❶
❷
❸

Maintain live or wet edge in between sections

SEQUENCE FOR PAINTING WINDOWS

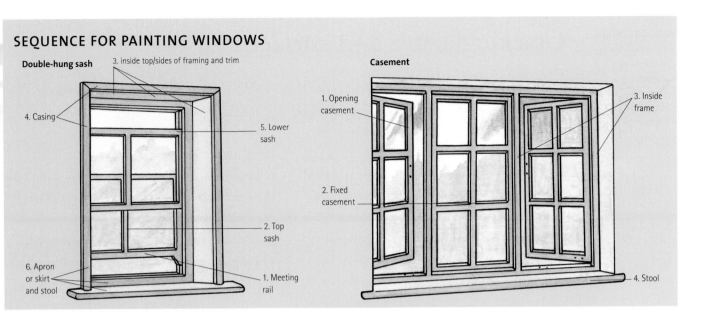

Double-hung sash

3. inside top/sides of framing and trim

4. Casing

5. Lower sash

2. Top sash

6. Apron or skirt and stool

1. Meeting rail

Casement

1. Opening casement

3. Inside frame

2. Fixed casement

4. Stool

Window sequence

Double-hung windows

Lift the lower sash and pull down the top sash so that the meeting bar can be painted first, giving it the longest drying time. Paint the top sash, then use a stepladder to reach and paint inside the top of the box frame and side runners, making sure no paint gets on the sash cords. Reverse the sash positions, and paint the casing and surrounds, completing the stepladder work. Now paint the lower sash, apron or skirt, and stool. Be careful when painting up to the glass in the two sashes: the paint should be cut in to overlap the putty slightly, forming a seal and preventing condensation from entering any gap between putty and glass.

Casement windows

Remove the window furniture, and paint the opening window first. Start with the glazing bars and edge moldings, then the face and hanging edge of the casement. Follow the same sequence for the fixed casement, then paint the external frame and center frame members, and the rabbet for the opening window. Lastly, paint the stool. If you have used painter's tape to get a clean edge, remove it as soon as the paint is touch dry.

Though functional, like doors, windows can contribute positively to the decor of a room.

PROJECT
Crackleglazing and surface resists

Cracked and crazed finishes are frequently used for special effects, paints, and varnishes being specifically applied so that the film tears or breaks during drying. This crazed effect can be used to give an antique-style finish to varnished woods, or, if combined with paints, a rustic finish. The aim is to age wood, in this case imitating cracked, well-worn, and weathered surfaces. These techniques usually rely on the incompatibility of consecutively applied coats. Surface resists also have as their origins a mistake in application, or paint defect, where a second coat will not adhere to the previous layer. Waxes are a prime example—oil-based wax rubbed indiscriminately onto a molding and then painted with a water-based latex paint will give a patchy torn-up finish that can be further emphasized with wire wool. In this case the oil base has rejected the subsequent coat of water-based paint.

Crackleglazing or cracklefinishing

This is the result of the difference in drying time, elasticity, and flexibility between an oil-based varnish and a water-based varnish brushed over it. Artists working usually in either oils or water-based paints found that mixing the two caused problems if they were applied in the wrong order; oil could be brushed over acrylic and water bases but not vice versa. Historically, in the paint-finishing trade, a top coat or finish preferably needed to be slightly more elastic than the preceding coats, unless a crazed finish was required by the client.

The introduction of proprietary paint systems where paint-makers supply primers, undercoats, and finishing coats ready-mixed has all but eliminated this problem. Crackle finishes are rare as mistakes, but commonly employed as special effects, often using oil- and water-based varnishes supplied in kits, complete with all directions. In today's decorating marketplace, what concerned yesterday's paint finishers is a practiced art form.

Using a cracked finish on wood

Cabinet doors or shutters are a good surface for a cracked finish. They are not too large an area to appear as an overpowering effect, and they provide a choice of cracked color or wood surface. The surface must be sealed, either by varnish or paint, depending on your scheme. Brush on a coat of oil-based varnish and leave it until it is just touch dry and therefore slightly tacky. Now brush on the water-based varnish, thinly for subtle crazing,

CRACKLEGLAZING

STEP 1 Brush on oil-based varnish. While tacky, add a water-based varnish and speed dry it.

STEP 2 To make the cracks more obvious, rub in a contrasting colored oil paint with a soft cloth.

STEP 3 Leave the oils to dry for 24 hours, and seal the finish with oil-based varnish to protect it.

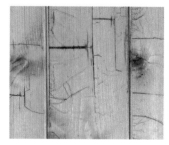

STEP 4 Here is very obvious cracking. Thinner varnish coats can produce more subtle effects.

more thickly for obvious cracks, and leave the surface near a source of heat. A hairdryer can be used at this stage, but care is required not to wrinkle the entire surface accidentally as the cracks start to appear. The cracks can be left as they appear on a painted base, or have a contrasting color rubbed into them, using an artists' oil paint applied with a soft cloth. If the scheme has cracks formed on a natural wood surface, they can be emphasized using black oil paint, or a coat of contrasting latex paint applied over the top. Use a wide brush or roller, and make one pass only; otherwise, the top coat will sink into the cracks, ruining the effect. Whichever you choose, when the surface is dry, seal with a clear coat of varnish.

Wax resist on wood

Most effectively used on moldings and crown moldings, solvent-based wax is rubbed onto the molding top surfaces, but not into the recesses. Paint the entire surface with water-based paint, and let it dry out. Rubbing the waxed areas with steel wool takes the paint off, leaving the top surface moldings looking as if the paint has worn off during the passage of time. Thinner surface streaks can be removed by substituting a candle for the solvent-based wax.

Small projects

Smaller areas, such as built-in cabinet doors that already have a varnish applied, can be given a period feel without a base coat. Simply "key" the surface using a fine abrasive paper. Otherwise, seal bare wood with two coats of clear oil-based varnish and leave it to dry. Apply a coat of oil-based crackleglaze, brushing it out well over the surface to give a thin, even coat, and let it dry out until the surface has a "tacky" feel. This usually takes about two to three hours, depending on conditions. Now brush on the water-based crackleglaze. A thick layer will take

longer to dry out than a thin one, and the resultant cracks will be more obvious. You can gently warm the surface with a hairdryer. Don't hold the dryer too close and stop as soon as the cracks start appearing. Rub an oil-based artist's color into the cracks with a soft cloth to aid definition, selecting a contrast to your original wood color. Oil- and water-based varnishes and the oil colors used in this technique are available from artists' suppliers.

Basic principle

Crackleglazing is intended as a wood finish, suitable for paneled doors and frames. The basic principle involved, which is the different drying times of water- and oil-based varnishes, can also be applied to large wall areas.

Large projects

For larger areas you will need to substitute color latex paint for water-based varnish. The oil-based crackleglaze lets the base color show through the cracks in the top latex coat. This effect works best with contrasting colors, so try brushing on a dark base color, and leave it to dry. Apply the crackleglaze, followed by a top coat of contrasting pale latex paint, which should be watered down. The effects in this technique vary from the subtle to the obvious so it is best to experiment first.

ABOVE: **Wooden furniture can be given an attractive period feel by the use of "distressing" techniques such as crackleglazing.**

Crackleglazing effects on lumber with contrasting color cracks.

YOU WILL NEED:
- FINE SANDPAPER
- FRENCH POLISH
- BALL OF LINT-FREE WADDING
- COTTON CLOTH OR RAG
- LINSEED OIL
- METHYLATED SPIRIT

PROJECT
Waxing and french polishing

Waxing and french polishing are restricted in their use today to small craft studios and homeworkers. Sourcing of materials for traditional practices is more difficult, but still possible, and using the techniques on simple projects is a welcome and challenging alternative to mass-produced finishes.

Completing any joinery project about the house will cause you to consider a choice of decorative and protective finishes, although experienced craftspeople may well have preselected a finish, and therefore sourced a wood accordingly. Wood finishes on simple shelving and paneling jobs can vary from straightforward clear varnishes, taking a minimum of effort, to more time-consuming decorative effects. A great number of these can be produced using modern paints and varnishes in a variety of combinations, and all materials can be found in neighborhood stores. While this has the advantage of convenience, it gives no historical perspective to colors and finishes painstakingly crafted by hand in days gone by.

Waxing

This was once a very popular finish. As well as protecting, it slightly darkened the surface of the wood, and the oils in the wax stopped the wood from becoming dry. A rise in popularity of french polishing sent waxing into decline, but today the versatility of this finish is recognized, and clear, neutral, white, and colored waxes can be found in artists' suppliers and hardware stores. Original waxes were easy to apply and gave a luster finish not dissimilar to low luster; today's waxes should contain a color that can be worked carefully into the woodgrain and slowly polished off the relief surface. White wax, for example, worked into the raised grain of a rich colored wood with steel wool and polished, gives a limed finish.

French polishing

This is a considerably more difficult application than waxing, and although it is a finish popular among traditional craftspeople, particularly on bespoke furniture, it is rarely seen elsewhere. Second-hand furniture pieces inherited or sourced from antique shops may be finished in this way, and it may be of interest to know a little about the basic technique, for restoration purposes or even as a matching finish for a bookshelf or bookcase project. French polishing will seal and fill in the woodgrain, stabilizing the surface, resulting in an easy-to-clean, hardwearing finish. Kits are available from specialist suppliers.

POLISHING

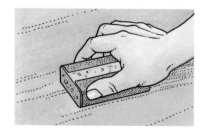

STEP 1 Sand the item to be french polished with fine abrasive paper to ensure a smooth surface.

STEP 2 Prepare the surface by fadding, applying a thin continuous film of polish to seal it.

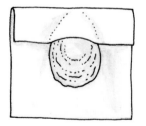 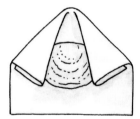

STEP 3 To make a rubber you need a ball of wadding and a square of clean, lint-free cotton cloth. Place the wadding in the center and fold over the top two corners to form a point.

Polishing a surface

French polishing involves layering thin films of shellac onto a wood surface. It is difficult to master, so practice first on a piece of hardwood.

Sand the surface smooth with fine sandpaper, and remove dust. Form a key between wood surface and polish by "fadding" (the fad is a folded piece of lint-free wadding dipped in polish) covering the surface with a thin film of polish. Let the surface dry completely, then sand down with fine sandpaper, again removing dust. Then apply polish with a rubber over the surface, working with the grain. A "rubber" is used instead of a brush to keep the surface as flat as possible. It is made from lint-free wadding wrapped in a square of cotton rag.

Place the wadding in the center of the rag and fold over the two top corners. Fold over the rest of the rag into a ball shape, and shape the top point so that the reverse side is pear-shaped.

Open the rag, and pour french polish onto the wadding until it is fully "charged," refold and gather up the rag, squeezing polish through to the rag face in the process.

Apply polish by passing the rubber over the wood surface, from end to end, with the grain, squeezing the rag ends so that polish comes through in a continuous moist film. Slide the rubber on and off the surface, making sure the runs of polish all join up. Wait until the polish is dry before applying a second coat. After three coats, leave to dry, and lightly sand down.

Finish bodying-up by polishing in small circles over the surface. If the rubber starts to stick on the polished surface as you work, use a little linseed oil to lubricate the rubber face. As the shine begins to appear, the bodying is over, and the surface needs to dry overnight. Lightly sand the surface, and again remove any dust.

Finish by applying polish in the same way, using long gliding strokes with the grain, exerting less pressure each time, and leave the surface to dry for about an hour. Now add a little methylated spirit to the rubber, diluting the polish that is left, and pass lightly and quickly over the finished surface, removing any traces of linseed oil that may remain.

Make sure the finishing rubber is not too wet, glide on and off the surface as before, and don't stop the stroke on the surface, as this will ruin the finish.

LEFT: **French polish is a common finish on quality period furniture. It produces a hard, glossy finish to wood that lets the beauty of the grain shine through, but it requires skill to apply it properly.**

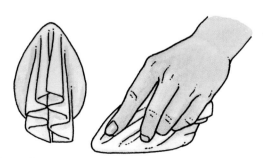

STEP 4 Gather the rest of the cloth so the reverse shape looks like a pear. The pointed end will reach into corners as you polish.

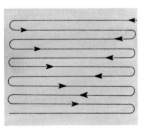

STEP 5 Apply polish with the rubber by working with the grain.

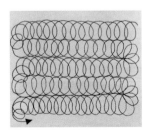

STEP 6 Finish off by bodying-up, applying polish with small circular motions.

YOU WILL NEED:

- 2 IN. X 1 IN./5 CM X 2.5 CM SOFTWOOD TGV
- 1½ IN. X ⅜ IN./3.8 CM X 1 CM SOFTWOOD
- SAW
- DECORATIVE MOLDING
- 2 IN./5 CM NUMBER 8 SCREWS
- 1 IN./2.5 CM NUMBER 6 SCREWS
- COMBINATION SCREWSINK
- BRASS SCREWS
- 3 IN./7.5 CM BRASS HINGES
- CLAMPS
- SCREWDRIVER
- HAMMER AND PINS
- CLEAR VARNISH
- SAW
- MOLDING PINS
- MITERING TOOLS
- SANDPAPER
- SANDING BLOCK
- WOOD GLUE
- SPACKLING COMPOUND

PROJECT
Simple wooden shutters

Internal wooden shutters were an integral part of window design in Georgian and Victorian period houses. The shutters were paneled, often had moldings that matched the panelwork in and around the bay recess, and folded neatly away into shutter boxes at the sides of the window. They provided security, privacy, and noise reduction.

If you have a period property that has had the shutters removed, but still retains the side boxes, seek the advice of a local joiner. You could have pine shutters made up to fit and match, consequently restoring the window area to its former glory. Period shutters are normally associated with double-hung windows, either full-length and covering the glazed area from floor to ceiling, or more usually covering the lower part of the window only. They look at their best in recessed bays, but were and still can be stylish and functional at any window, and there is no reason why you cannot fit them to modern double-hung and casement windows. Sashes can still be fitted with any height of shutter, but casement window styles look better with full-length screens, having no meeting bar to form a visual parallel to a half- or three-quarter-length shutter.

Made to measure

To install simple shutters to a window, first measure the opening carefully, and look to see if you need to fit wood cleats vertically inside the recess to hinge onto. If so, remember to subtract this measurement from the calculation. Small windows can accommodate two shutters easily, which gives you a nicely balanced scheme, but if the window is too large, or you prefer smaller shutters, then measure up for two hinged together on each side, or a total of three with one side doubling up. In this scheme, three shutters span the gap, with one side having two shutters hinged to neatly fold back to back. Check all your measurements twice, then cut to size 2 in. x 1 in./5 cm x 2.5 cm lumber for the inner support frame, TGV boards for the shutter body, an external frame that overlaps the front edge from 1½ in. x ⅜ in./3.8 cm x 1 cm wood, and a decorative molding.

Glue and screw the inner support frame first, using right-angled butt joints, driving home 2 in./5 cm number 8 screws. Use a combination screwsink to counterbore a hole enabling you to drive the head into the middle of the woodpiece at right angles. Fix a centered cross-piece for

MAKING THE SHUTTERS

STEP 1 Begin by assembling the inner support frame, using right-angled butt joints. Glue and screw the joints for maximum strength.

STEP 2 Mark the position of the centered cross-piece on the uprights and drill to accept the reinforcing screws. Glue and screw the piece in place.

STEP 3 Cut lengths of TGV boards to size and screw them to the front of the frame, countersinking the fixing screwheads, flush with the surface.

STEP 4 Attach the outer frame so it projects at the front, using glue and molding pins, which should be punched below the surface of the wood.

STEP 5 Cut lengths of panel molding to fit inside the projecting lip of the outer frame, mitering their ends for neat corners. Pin them in place.

STEP 6 Fill any defects and pin-heads, using a matching spackling compound if a clear varnish will be employed, and sand down the wood to a smooth finish.

extra strength, and then screw the TGV lengths to the front of the frame, using 1 in./2.5 cm number 6 screws. Countersink the heads just flush with the surface, and make sure their position will be covered by the molding that you will add later. Glue and pin the outer frame in position, counterpunching 1 in./2.5 cm molding pins below the surface, flush at the back and overlapping at the front. Finally, measure and corner-miter the molding to fit neatly into the rabbet created at the front, pinning it with the same molding pins.

Fill all pin holes prior to sanding down the surfaces. If you choose to paint the frame and molding, a joint compound is good enough here; if you intend to varnish the work, use a matching spackling compound as the wood and grain will show through even if it is colored. A painted frame and molding with a similar color varnished TGV inside makes a good combination effect. Attach the shutters to each other and to the frame with 3 in./7.5 cm flush hinges in a brass finish, using brass screws.

You could adapt the basic framework of these shutters to make louver shutters that will let cooling air into the room in summer while shading it from the sun. You would need to rout a series of slots into the inside of the frame at an angle to accept the slats.

BELOW: **Louvered shutters are very practical in the heat of summer, shading the interior from the sun. Here they are used to divide a room.**

YOU WILL NEED:
- MEASURING TAPE
- WOOD FOR VALANCE
- JIGSAW/PLANER
- GLUE
- NUMBER 8 SCREWS
  AND WALL ANCHORS
- SANDPAPER
- PANEL PINS
- MOLDING PINS
- DRILL/DRILL BITS
- JOINT COMPOUND
- BRUSH AND VARNISH

PROJECT
A customized valance

It is possible to completely transform a window and drapes arrangement by simply fitting a valance. A decorative front and customised wall brackets are easy to make from lumber stock. Using solid lumber may mean that more support is needed, but you can then pin to the front interchangeable seasonal arrangements, such as dried lavender.

Measuring and cutting

Measure the width of your window, and the drawn drape positions, then check to see if you have enough space to let you fix into the frame surround or whether you need to drill into the wall. In either case, the made-up brackets should be positioned to allow an overhang at each end of 1 in./2.5 cm. The principle is that two fixed brackets support, but are not permanently attached to, a valance that is designed to be fixed to the wall itself in a hidden position at top dead center. This allows for easy valance removal, for frame painting for example, by taking out one screw and lifting down, rather than removing bracket screws neatly but inconveniently hidden inside the valance. This is a difficult job which calls for small hands and

a stubby screwdriver. The cut bracket must be made up to fit exactly inside the internal right-angle of the valance. For example, if the valance is cut from 4 in. x 1 in./10 cm x 2.5 cm nominal size wood, planed to a finished size of 3¾ in. x ¾ in./9.5 cm x 1.8 cm, the inside dimension is 3 in./7.5 cm. Cut the bracket to this size at the top and part of one side, forming the support, then cut back to form a rabbet.

A section of wood ¾ in./1.8 cm wide and deep, and 4¾ in./12 cm long should be left, and this takes the wall screws, as shown in the diagram. Shape the bottom edge of the valance into a design of your choice with a jigsaw. Glue and screw a wooden support, 1 in. x 1 in. x 4 in./

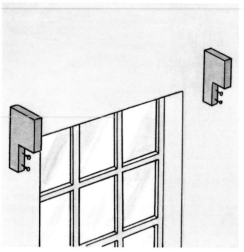

ABOVE: The upside-down L-shaped brackets take the weight of the valance and are screwed to the wall on each side of the window opening.

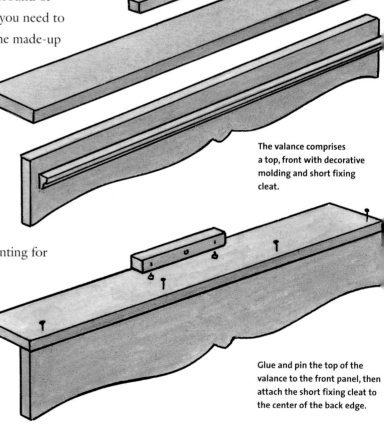

The valance comprises a top, front with decorative molding and short fixing cleat.

Glue and pin the top of the valance to the front panel, then attach the short fixing cleat to the center of the back edge.

2.5 cm x 2.5 cm x 10 cm with a centered fixing hole onto the top center of the valance so that you can screw through into the wall.

Joining together and fixing

Make up the valance by gluing the top to the front, and pinning with 1½ in./3.8 cm panel pins. On the front face, directly butting the join of top and front, pin a decorative strip molding, using ¾ in./1.8 cm molding pins, which disguises the butt join. Now attach the wall brackets, using a suitable length number 8 such as 1¼ in./3.2 cm if you are fixing to the wood surround, or a countersunk 2¼ in./5.7 cm number 8 screw into a wall anchor if you are driving into the wall. Position the valance, and equalize the side overhangs, then fix the top center support to the wall, again countersinking a 2¼ in./5.7 cm number 8 screw into a wall anchor.

Finishing

Fill the screw holes and sand the surfaces smooth. Again, select a filler that is suitable; decorator's fillers are fine if the surface is to be painted, but a matching wood-colored spackling compound is needed if the wood grain is going to be visible under a varnish, as this will tend to "disappear."

Clear or colored varnishes will certainly look good on the valance, but you could also consider painting the brackets to complement the wall color, blend in with the wall decoration, or to match exactly the wood surround. In this way the brackets are disguised slightly and full prominence is given to the wood finish on the valance that will support your choice of seasonal floral decoration.

Using seasonal flowers and foliage to decorate a window opening provides a means of extending the garden into the house, blurring the distinction between the two areas.

ATTACHING THE VALANCE

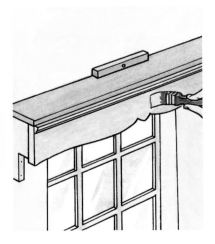

STEP 1 Position the valance on its brackets, screw to the wall through the top cleat and varnish.

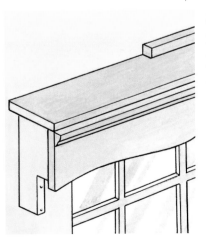

STEP 2 The finished valance is designed to accept seasonal floral decoration pinned to the front.

YOU WILL NEED:

TGV MATCHBOARDING:

- SPIRIT LEVEL
- TAPE MEASURE
- HAMMER
- 2 IN. X 1 IN./5 CM X
  2.5 CM WOODSTOCK
  FOR HORIZONTAL
  CLEATS
- 2 IN./5 CM NUMBER 8
  SCREWS/WALL
  ANCHORS
- TGV CLADDING TO FIT
- ³⁄₄ IN./1.8 CM
  MOLDING PINS
- 1¹⁄₂ IN./3.8 CM LOST
  HEAD NAILS
- 2 IN. X ¹⁄₂ IN./5 CM X
  1.2 CM WOODSTOCK
  FOR TOP PIECE
- 1 IN./2.5 CM MOLDING
  PINS
- DECORATIVE MOLDING
- BASEBOARD
- WOOD FILLER

PROJECT

Lower wall paneling or matchboarding

Protecting the lower portion of a wall, in an area of heavy human traffic, by easily cleaned wood panels finished with tough exterior varnish, is both visually attractive and practical. Utility rooms, hallways, and landings are all suitable areas, although this finish, particularly if it is stained wood, will look good as a decorative scheme anywhere.

Home centers sell paneling kits, with all necessary parts including chair rail and baseboard, primed and ready to fix. If you intend a painted finish, or a paint effect that uses a flat color as a base, then this is an option worth considering. Real wood finishes, however, are worth constructing yourself, and two basic schemes are described here.

Tongue-and-groove paneling

Mark out your wall area, using a spirit level to ensure verticals and horizontals are true. Fix two horizontal cleats to the wall, parallel with the baseboard, out of 2 in. x 1 in./5 cm x 2.5 cm wood-stock, countersinking 2 in./5 cm number 8 screws into wall anchors. Cut TGV boards to fit, measuring from the floor to the top of the upper cleat, and pin it to the baseboard and the

TGV cladding boards are suitable for a wide range of decorative jobs around the house. Use them in a bathroom to give a period feel to the room. However, make sure they are treated with yacht varnish to protect them from the steamy atmosphere.

top and middle cleat lengths. Start in the corner with the groove to the wall, and pin the first piece through the face; thereafter invisibly pin each piece through the tongue, covering the pin heads with the next groove. Use ¾ in./1.8 cm molding pins driven in at an angle. You can face pin the bottom fixing if preferred, as this will be concealed by a new baseboard, itself nailed in place with 1½ in./3.8 cm lost-head nails, with the heads counterpunched below the surface and filled. Cut a straight top piece from 2 in. x ½ in./

TGV MATCHBOARDING

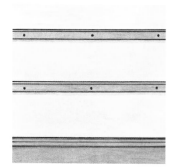

STEP 1 For vertical boards, attach horizontal support cleats to the wall above the baseboard.

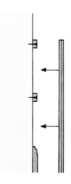

STEP 2 Invisibly pin the boards to the cleats, using the existing baseboard as the lower support.

STEP 3 Work along the wall, slotting the tongues and grooves of the boards together.

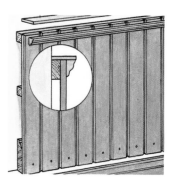

STEP 4 Finish off the top edge of the boards with a decorative molding and pin on a new baseboard.

5 cm x 1.2 cm woodstock, and pin it on top, using 1 in./2.5 cm molding pins, covering the end grain of the TGV lengths. The top overlaps slightly, and a final piece of decorative molding is pinned in position directly underneath, again with 1 in./2.5 cm molding pins, the heads being counterpunched and filled in the same manner as before.

Wood panels

More difficult and time-consuming to construct, this paneling uses a top cleat and the existing baseboard as before, but has additional vertical cleats equally spaced along the wall. These cleats are wider, being 3 in. x 1 in./7.5 cm x 2.5 cm, but are fixed in the same way.

Plywood panels are pinned to the cleats with ¾ in./1.8 cm panel pins, butting together on the vertical cleat center line. Plywood panels ¼ in./ 6 mm thick can be bought from home centers with a hardwood veneer facing, 2 ft./60.7 cm wide, requiring the cleat centers to be this same distance apart. If this is too wide for your scheme, cut the panels to your preferred size, and adjust the distances between the cleats.

The panel height is from the bottom of the baseboard to the top of the upper cleat. Fix the baseboard piece into position as before, but use a straight length of 4 in. x 1 in./10 cm x 2.5 cm lumber, as a top molding is not needed.

Using 2 in. x ½ in./5 cm x 1.2 cm woodstock, frame each panel on the remaining three sides, using the center line of the wall cleats as your guide at the sides and sitting flush with the panel edge at the top. Pin with 1 in./2.5 cm molding pins, countersink the heads and fill. To finish, measure and corner-miter a molding of your choice to fit inside the panel frame on all sides, and add a top piece from 2 in. x ½ in./5 cm x 1.2 cm woodstock. Pin in position and counterpunch the heads as before, and fill all holes with a wood filler.

WOOD PANELS

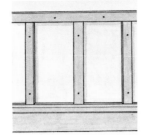

STEP 1 Plywood paneling needs a grid of upright and horizontal support cleats screwed to the wall.

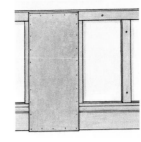

STEP 2 The uprights must be placed so that each supports the edges of neighboring panels.

STEP 3 Decorative moldings are pinned in place to conceal the joints between neighboring panels.

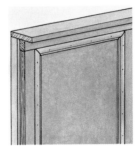

STEP 4 Add a decorative molding to each panel, mitering the ends for neat corners.

Stain the softwood so that a match is achieved with the veneered panels, and seal the surfaces, or apply any decorative paint finish that suits the remainder of the area.

YOU WILL NEED:

WOOD PANELS:

- SPIRIT LEVEL
- TAPE MEASURE
- HAMMER
- 2 IN. X 1 IN./5 CM X 2.5 CM WOODSTOCK FOR HORIZONTAL CLEAT
- 2 IN./5 CM NUMBER 8 SCREWS/WALL ANCHORS
- 3 IN. X 1 IN./7.5 CM X 2.5 CM VERTICAL CLEATS
- 2 FT./60.7 CM WIDTH X ¼ IN./6 MM THICK PLYWOOD PANELS
- ¾ IN./1.8 CM PANEL PINS
- 4 IN. X 1 IN./10 CM X 2.5 CM LUMBER LENGTH
- 2 IN. X ½ IN./5 CM X 1.2 CM WOODSTOCK FOR FRAME
- 1 IN./2.5 CM MOLDING PINS
- 2 IN X ½ IN./5 CM X 1.2 CM WOODSTOCK FOR TOP
- DECORATIVE MOLDING FOR CORNERS
- MITERING TOOL
- BASEBOARD
- WOOD FILLER

LEFT: Wooden wall paneling adds a touch of elegance to a dining room, especially when teamed with ornamental moldings framing panels of hand-blocked wallpaper.

Furniture facelifts

Many special decorative finishes are considered unsuitable for large wall surfaces, either because they are messy and difficult to control given the size, or because the result is simply too overpowering. They can be ideal for small projects, though, like table tops, cabinets, and chairs, irrespective of age. Bare wood knock-down, self-assembly pieces are suitable, as are traditional auction and flea market finds, but best of all, and the most economical, are those long forgotten items from the past stored in lofts and cellars. So, before you hunt for that expensive new piece to take pride of place in a new environment, consider what a makeover will do for an old friend. You may be surprised at the transformation.

YOU WILL NEED:
- VARIOUS ABRASIVE PAPERS
- ALUMINUM OXIDE SANDING BLOCK
- SCREWDRIVER
- CLEAR WAX
- COLORED PIGMENTS
- FINE STEEL WOOL
- LINT-FREE POLISHING CLOTH
- WOOD GLUE

PROJECT
Kitchen shelves

An old self-assembly pine unit that had fallen apart and been discarded provided a perfect set of surfaces for subtle waxed finishes, each one looking as if it were reflecting a different colored light into the room—a great improvement on the original polyester finish.

HOW TO DO IT

STEP 1 The unit was loosely reassembled, and the original surface removed using medium grade, followed by fine grade, wet silicon carbide abrasive paper.

STEP 2 The finish residue was removed from the dowel holes using an old screwdriver, and the surface sanded using 240 grit aluminum oxide around a sanding block.

STEP 3 Clear wax mixed with color pigment was rubbed into the grain of the wood with fine steel wool.

STEP 4 The waxed surfaces were well polished to achieve a fine sheen using a soft, lint-free cloth.

STEP 5 Wood glue was run into the dowel holes, before the fluted dowels were reinserted into the wood.

STEP 6 Reassembly—the different color-waxed shelves were glued to the other half of the dowels.

YOU WILL NEED:

- PAINT STRIPPER
- STEEL WOOL
- SCRAPER
- SUGAR SOAP
- PAINT BRUSH
- ALUMINUM OXIDE
  SANDING BLOCK
- COLORED LATEX
- WOODWASH
- WATER-BASED DYE
- VARNISH
- LIMING WAX
- CLEAR AND COLORED
  WAXES
- SOFT CLOTH
- BRASS FITTINGS AND
  SCREWDRIVER
- GLOVES
- STUBBY SCREWDRIVER

PROJECT
Wooden cabinet

Several different finishes—paint, colorwash, stain, varnish, and wax—are used, together with replacement glass and simple brass furniture, to give this well-made but badly neglected cabinet and drawer combination unit a new lease of life.

HOW TO DO IT

STEP 1 The old multilayered paint finish is removed using a scraper to take off blistered paint after applying water-washable paint stripper. Remember to wear gloves!

STEP 2 When all the paint is removed, steel wool dipped in sugar soap is used to clean the surface thoroughly. Always rub in the direction of the wood grain.

STEP 3 The door is removed and cleaned, and old glass bead and putty discarded. A coat of white latex is "distressed."

STEP 4 The inside of the cabinet needs to reflect a warm, friendly glow; orange latex from a sample pot is ideal.

STEP 5 Diluted woodwash (available in small cans) is painted onto the base and top of the unit. Here turquoise is used.

STEP 6 The multifinish theme continues—diluted ultramarine water-based dye is put on the side grain, avoiding the front edge.

STEP 7 The front will remain as bare wood, cleaned up with 240 grit aluminum oxide around a sanding block.

STEP 8 The waxed drawer is tested to ensure it slides well. Blue and white waxes have been applied and polished.

STEP 9 New brass drawer and cabinet door furniture is fitted to replace the old plastic knobs. Small hands and a stubby screwdriver are needed to gain access to the inside of the drawers.

YOU WILL NEED:

- ALUMINUM OXIDE SANDING BLOCK
- T-SQUARE
- YELLOW PENCIL
- TILES
- HAMMER
- RAGS AND CLOTHS
- RULER
- MITERING TOOLS AND SAW
- WOOD GLUE
- MOLDING PINS
- COUNTERPUNCH
- WOOD FILLER
- TILE ADHESIVE
- RIBBED SPREADER
- GROUT
- GROUT SPREADER
- BRUSH
- LATEX
- CLEAR VARNISH

PROJECT

Table mosaic decoration

The octagonal shape of this table is emphasized by the softwood angles that form corner triangles. The cross is tiled with different shades of blue mosaic, the dark blue pieces matching the triangles, and contrasting with the pale blue colorwash on the softwood.

HOW TO DO IT

STEP 1 The top is abraded to remove all traces of sheen and to provide a "key." Aluminum oxide is used around a cork block and abrades the surface.

STEP 2 Guidelines are drawn for the wood pieces, using a soft yellow pencil so that they can be clearly seen.

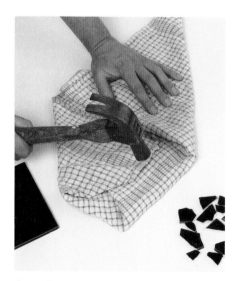

STEP 3 A cloth is wrapped around a tile. The tile is then broken into small pieces using a hammer.

STEP 4 The design is checked and the tile pieces sorted to see whether there are enough pieces of the right colors.

STEP 5 After mitering the wood pieces, they are glued and pinned following the yellow guidelines.

STEP 6 The tile adhesive is spread ⅛ in./3mm deep with the use of a ribbed spreader.

STEP 7 The tile pieces are then carefully positioned in the adhesive.

STEP 8 After the adhesive has set, the spaces between the tile pieces are grouted.

STEP 9 The mosaic is polished and the table is then painted and varnished.

YOU WILL NEED:
- SUGAR SOAP
- ABRASIVE PAPERS
  SUCH AS SANDPAPER
- SANDING BLOCK
- RED LATEX PAINT
- BLUE LATEX PAINT
- BRUSHES
- PENCIL AND
  MATERIALS FOR
  TRACING
- ARTISTS' ACRYLIC
  PAINT
- FINE ARTIST'S
  BRUSHES
- CLEAR SATIN VARNISH

PROJECT

Revamping a wooden chair

A small chair found in the loft, dirty from its travels, could be considered ideal for a child's nursery. A distressed paint scheme is envisaged for the chair. The scheme will match the room decor and a hand-painted design on the seat and back support will give the chair its own individual character.

HOW TO DO IT

STEP 1 The wood surface is sanded down using medium followed by fine sandpaper, to give a smooth finish prior to painting. The chair was cleaned with sugar soap first, so that dirt and grease wouldn't clog the abrasive and the paint would then go on evenly.

STEP 2 The entire chair is painted, using a first coat of red latex paint.

STEP 3 A second coat of pale blue latex is painted over the top of the first coat.

STEP 4 The surface is abraded so that the red paint shows through the blue second coat.

STEP 5 The design, which is a bright, colorful tree, is traced onto the seat.

STEP 6 The tree design is painted using artists' acrylic paints and a number 5 artist's brush.

STEP 7 Flowers and leaves are added using a finer brush and bright acrylic colors.

STEP 8 Finally, a protective coat of clear satin varnish is brushed onto the chair.

Stylish space savers

The modern living environment and time-specific lifestyles require the best use to be made of limited available space. Traditional lofts and cellars are often converted to form part of the living quarters where once they were dark, cold, long-term storage areas rarely visited. The clamor for personal space in a smaller world is thus one of the contradictions of our time, and householders face a difficult task attempting to maximize potential space while retaining a personal decorative style and concealing everyday items that are unattractive but necessary.

Hanging racks and containers

Hanging racks and wall boxes save space around the home because the floor or worktop space below them can be utilized for another storage purpose. Often cookware was hung on butcher's hooks from ceiling-mounted racks, but modern low ceilings and the dangers of falling pans have relegated even kitchen racks to a wall mounting.

BELOW: **Extra storage space is always useful in the kitchen. Open shelving is easy to fit into small corners and can be used to add an informal country feel. It's also a good way to show off attractive pans and implements, as well as having things close to hand for the cook.**

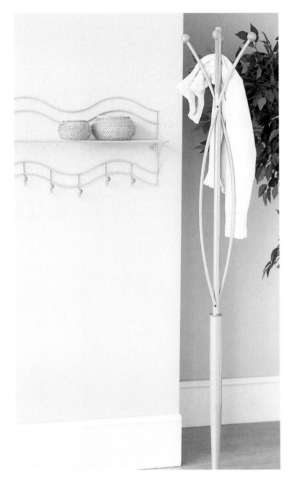

Storage in a hallway should be both practical and look good. In a small space a simple hat stand and shelf unit provide places for guests to hang their coats; in larger spaces closets can be built-in for all the family's needs.

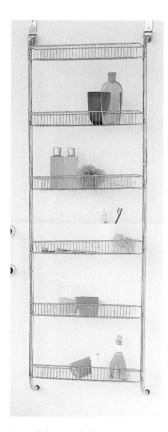

Open shelves in a bathroom give you a chance to show off expensive and beautifully packaged items.

ABOVE: **Displaying towels on open shelves adds a touch of warmth and softness to metallic modern design.**

Bathroom shelving comes in a variety of styles and materials so you can easily find storage to suit your bathroom decor. Wicker storage boxes give a natural feel, as well as hiding the clutter of personal items.

Shelving systems

The fittings of the modern home have advanced, none more so than the humble shelf, which has evolved from a rectangular unit holding books and ornaments to a multipurpose linear structure. Today's systems support all manner of audio and visual electronics, and must display designer qualities themselves, as well as showing off decorative accessories.

RIGHT: **Book shelves can be far more than an easy way to store books; they can also act as an attractive means of displaying them and a range of other items.**

RIGHT: **Modern style shelving can be made out of lighter, less obtrusive material than wood. Lightweight shelving such as this gives the room a modern feel.**

ABOVE: **Shelf units today are so beautifully designed that they can be used as a feature of the room, not just for practicality. These small shelves let you display mementoes in a stylish and imaginative way.**

LEFT: **Window sills can be used as an alternative to more traditional shelving, but don't think practical, think beautiful. Sills can be used not only to display the occasional objet d'art but a great place to grow things. Let seedlings thrive by placing them on a warm sun-filled window ledge, and reap the benefits of bringing your yard indoors at the same time.**

RIGHT: **Long narrow corridors may feel like a waste of valuable space, but with some thought and imagination you can utilize even the narrowest hallway both for storage and to add interest. A clever mix of stored items will provide a talking point in any hallway.**

Storage screens: fabric

Fabric screens can be simple lengths under a sink, hiding the household necessities, or complex three-way, self-standing frames used as changing screens or simply to indicate an area of privacy. The free-standing, folded fabric screen is both stable and lightweight; its portability and decorative qualities make it functional, fashionable, and very versatile.

ABOVE AND RIGHT: **Fabric screens do so much more than hide ugly clutter, they are also attractive additions to any room. Screens are widely available, but also easy to personalize to suit individual taste and decor. The true versatility of fabric screens, however, lies in the fact that you can position them wherever you want.**

ABOVE: **Even hard furnishings like closets need no longer be "hard." Use lengths of fabric draped over a frame, or hung like drapes around a small space, to add an exotic feel to your bedroom. Choose silks and velvets in bright and luxurious colors to create a spice trail feel, or white cheesecloth to bring a touch of softly flowing colonial days.**

Under-the-sink drapes bring a special charm to any kitchen or bathroom, making a sink a feature, not just a fixture. An ideal way to add color to a room, they hide necessities and add a finishing touch to soft furnishings. Choose your fabric carefully and make sure that you allow enough not just to cover but to drape attractively. Reminiscent of early twentieth-century homes, with the right fabric under-the-sink curtains can be brought up-to-date while retaining that country feel.

Storage screens: wood

Much heavier and less portable than fabric screens, wood screens are often used as room dividers to cordon off large areas into more user-friendly spaces. Traditionally, screens with solid, jointed frames made by craftsmen were inlaid with veneers of exotic and rarely seen woods, and some were exercises in grain pattern, mirror imaging, and picture marquetry.

BELOW RIGHT: **Wood always adds warmth and texture to a room. Wooden screens bring character but also have a highly practical function as room dividers. With an amazing variety in design and wood types to choose from, they can really bring your room alive.**

BELOW: **Lighter screens can add an attractive feature to a bedroom. Choose a type of wood and style to complement your existing furniture. You can even stain the wood to match your decor. Wooden screens are a great way to hide clutter, to divide rooms, or simply to add a feature.**

RIGHT: **To give an exotic oriental feel to a room, choose a darker wood. Filigree work in the wood turns a room divider into a piece with character and interest. Screens are an ideal way to change the function of a room, turning an everyday kitchen-cum-diner into a sophisticated and romantic dining-room.**

Boxes and containers

Storage boxes are more than a place to store unwanted clutter. From coffee tables to seating, strong wooden boxes have become a fashionable feature in many modern homes.

Storage chests are traditional favorites, a fashionable way to store items in a piece of wooden furniture that looks good in any room. Fabric-covered boxes, the lid doubling as a seat, can match room decor in a coordinated scheme, and wicker laundry baskets will assume a new identity if they are stained in bright colors and sealed with sprayed varnish.

Wicker boxes are highly fashionable nowadays and are a distinctive way to store anything from dirty laundry to letters, newspapers, and magazines.

The ottoman is the traditional place to keep bedding. Still placed at the bottom of the bed, this ancient piece of furniture has been given a modern make-over through the use of new materials and modern colors.

LEFT AND RIGHT: A collection of wicker baskets not only provides storage for knick-knacks and larger items but also makes an attractive feature. They can also offer a handsome hideaway for your dirty laundry if you don't favor the more modern canvas laundry bins (right) that can be equally appealing.

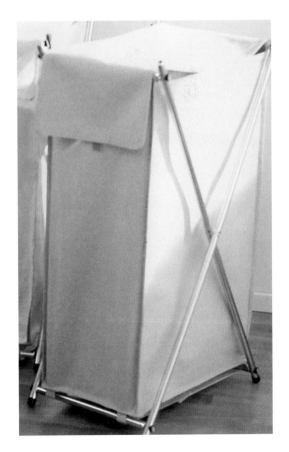

Accent accessories

If the decorative style of a room is largely dependent upon the characteristics of the building, seeking to emphasize original features and disguise less attractive areas, then the accessories around the room depend on and reflect the character and interests of the occupants. Vases, containers, lamps, boxes and frames can all underline a particular personal curiosity, be it historical or geographical, classical or modern. Accessorizing can vary from subtle frame distressing, reflecting an interest in traditional woods, to hand-painted floor coverings that pay homage to other cultures.

PROJECT

Painting a vase

A very satisfying project is to create your own designs on a pot. Enliven a plain vase by decorating it with ceramic paints, available from arts and crafts suppliers. Decant the paint into a small kettle or pot and sponge on tint combinations of the same color, or be more adventurous and mask out an area for hand-painting. In this way you could match your pot into the color scheme of a room, or show off your artistic talent by creating a picture.

HOW TO DO IT

STEP 1 Draw a sunflower head on clear sticky-back plastic film and carefully cut out as a mask.

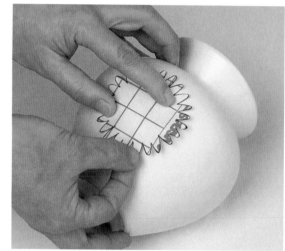

STEP 2 Hold up the mask to the vase to check the size and the position.

STEP 3 Using a natural sea sponge, put on the first tint of the color.

STEP 4 Sponge on the second tint, to start the build-up of the broken color effect.

STEP 5 Now add the third, darker shade; this gives a three-dimensional feel to the design.

STEP 6 Peel off the sunflower head mask and the vase is ready for hand-painting.

STEP 7 Paint in bright yellow petals using a number 5 artists' brush. The shadow detail in orange will require a thinner brush.

STEP 8 On a mid-brown base, touch in the minute black detail in the sunflower center with a number 1 brush.

YOU WILL NEED:

- ELECTRICIAN'S
  SCREWDRIVER
- SILICON CARBIDE
  PAPER (WET-AND
  DRY)
- 1 IN./2.5 CM BRUSH
- EMULSION
- CLEAR GLOSS
  VARNISH
- PAINTER'S TAPE
- STRING
- MARKER PEN
- FLAT ARTISTS' BRUSH
- ROUND ARTISTS'
  BRUSH
- SMALL BRUSH
- STAMP
- ARTISTS' ACRYLIC
  PAINT (DILUTED)

PROJECT

Revamping a lamp

An old lamp base that was spray finished in black, hiding the wood grain, and sporting a plain cream basic shade, was worthy of a stylish makeover designed to emphasize, not disguise its character. The shade was vignetted, creating colored stripes, and a simple symbol designed to complement the wood grain exposed on the base was added.

HOW TO DO IT

STEP 1 Separate all the parts to allow access to the base. Disconnect the electrical components, remove, and store carefully.

STEP 2 Remove the original finish with medium and fine abrasives.

STEP 3 Emphasize the grain pattern on the base stem with a pale orange wash.

STEP 4 Sand down the outer base and give a first coat of latex, in bright orange.

STEP 5 Distress the entire base using moistened fine-grade silicon carbide paper.

STEP 6 Apply black latex to the outside of the distressed orange base, matching the original finish left in the grooves.

STEP 7 Remove the black top coat with fine abrasive when dry. It remains in the grain structure, and the orange shows through.

STEP 8 When the distressed finish is satisfactorily completed, protect the entire base by brushing on a clear gloss varnish.

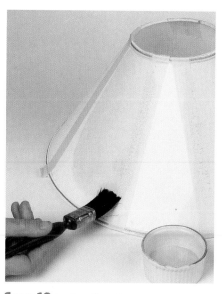

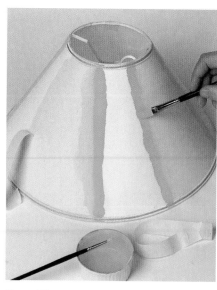

STEP 9 Divide the shade into equal segments, using string as a measure, and mask off.

STEP 10 Apply a diluted pale yellow wash to alternate segments of the lampshade. This will bleed at the edges.

STEP 11 Add an orange stripe, and use a number 6 flat brush dipped in water to vignette.

STEP 12 Wash the color to achieve a smooth gradation.

STEP 13 Test the tree symbol stamp and green color on scrap paper.

STEP 14 Press the stamp firmly onto the (supported) shade, in the center bottom of alternate segments.

STEP 15 The symbol in position. If the pressure applied is insufficient, you will need to retouch with a small brush.

YOU WILL NEED:

- FINE SANDPAPER
- SILICON CARBIDE (WET-AND-DRY) PAPER
- WATER-BASED WOOD DYE
- LATEX (DILUTED)
- 1 IN./2.5 CM BRUSH
- CLEAR SATIN VARNISH

PROJECT
Two-tint distressing

A clear-varnished wooden picture frame with rounded molding creates shadows from sidelighting on its surfaces. In this simple project, two tints of the same color form half the frame each, and are distressed with white and abraded to emphasize these side shadows. The result is a beautifully subtle finish that will show off a picture to great effect.

HOW TO DO IT

STEP 1 Remove the original finish using sandpaper. Fold it over to sand inside the molding.

STEP 2 Brush over two sides of the frame with a strong red water-based dye.

STEP 3 Using a more dilute mix of the same color, complete the other two sides.

STEP 4 Distress the frame with fine sandpaper until bare wood appears on the surface.

STEP 5 Brush on white latex diluted half and half with water and leave to dry.

STEP 6 Using wet silicon carbide, abrade the surface and inside molding detail.

STEP 7 Apply a coat of satin varnish to darken the distressed wood areas for a subtle finish.

YOU WILL NEED:

- ARTISTS' CANVAS
  TO SIZE
- DESIGN REFERENCE
- STRAIGHTEDGE
- TAPE MEASURE
- BRUSH
- PENCIL
- SCISSORS
- IRON
- DOUBLE-SIDED
  CARPET TAPE
- SET SQUARE
- COMBINATION
  SQUARE
- COLORED LATEX
  PAINTS IN SAMPLE
  CANS
- PAINTER'S TAPE
- ACRYLIC PRIMER
- ARTISTS' BRUSHES
- BROWN PAPER

PROJECT
Floor cloth: painting canvas

Hand-painted, individually designed canvas floor coverings owe their origins to the early New World pioneers, who reputedly reused their boat sails as the raw material. The design on this canvas continues on an historical American theme, using colors and shapes used by native peoples of the south-west desert states.

HOW TO DO IT

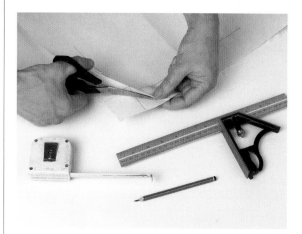

STEP 1 "Square up" the raw canvas, leaving a 2 in./5 cm border to be folded over, and cut the corners diagonally.

STEP 2 Fold the border to conceal the rough edges, and iron in the crease after damping down the canvas.

STEP 3 Use double-sided carpet tape (available from hardware stores) to secure the folded border permanently in position.

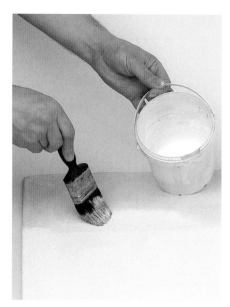

STEP 4 Some canvas is sold preprimed, some raw. If you buy yours raw, give it a coat of white acrylic primer.

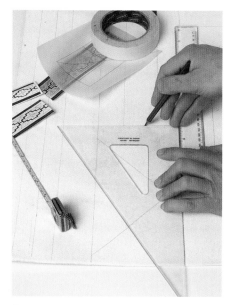

STEP 5 Pencil your geometric design onto the canvas, using set square, tape measure, and straightedge to keep it symmetrical.

STEP 6 Painting: use a number zero artists' brush to fill in the corners.

STEP 7 Use painter's tape to achieve an accurate, straight side stripe.

STEP 8 Use brown paper to protect the finished areas as you work.

Appendices

Don't skip this section just because it's the last bit of this part of the book, because these appendices cover important general safety aspects of decorating work. Many readers will rightly regard the advice as no more than common sense, which it is, but it also contains more specialized tips for protecting people and machines from accidental damage. The acquisition of a basic tool kit, always open to question, and the age-old problem of materials sourcing, particularly in the second-hand marketplace, are discussed at some length, as are the fundamentals and practicalities of artificial lighting.

Safety

Whatever your style or type of property, living and working in it with the minimum of risk to yourself and others is always a priority. Safety issues in the home can vary enormously, from keeping sharp kitchen knives out of the reach of small children, to making sure that your power tools have a circuit-breaking plug fitted between you and the electric power supply.

Different types of glove will help protect your hands from chemicals, paints, stains, splinters, and other sharp objects.

Accidents in the home account for a vast number of hospital admissions, particularly in the springtime, when there is a rush to take on home improvements. To avoid accidents, however, all you need to do is to take sensible precautions and follow some simple guidelines, many of which are little more than common sense.

Working safely in the home

Whatever the task about the house, here are some useful guidelines:

• Move obstructions such as furniture, decorative items and toys—don't "work around" them. If you were "on site" elsewhere, you would ask for a clear working space, for fear of damage to the contents of the room, so do the same in your own house. Working in an area that is cluttered and not easily accessible leads to over-reaching and losing control of the tool, and on a stepladder can result in overbalancing.

• Position your stepladder safely, so that you can reach the job height and width without stretching. Home improvement jobs are not always conveniently sited for a person standing on the floor. The requirement is likely to be of differing tasks at a variety of heights.

• Position the tools for the job on a temporary table surface, never on the floor.

• Route cables from power tools around the sides of the room, not across the middle.

• Clear up as you go.

• Work in a tidy area so that you can easily see and check all aspects of the job in progress.

Safety in the workshop

• Make sure that small children do not have access to your tools, whether your equipment is left in a cabinet when not in use or is stored in a dedicated workshop in a garage or basement area.

• Store cutting tools and potentially dangerous power equipment sensibly, that is to say, with protective sleeves and guards in place.

• Never leave power tools "live"; disconnect the supply or remove the battery, and if possible keep them in carrying cases or secure boxes.

• Quality handsaws and chisels come with protective sleeves; if you lose one, make up another from card and adhesive tape.

• Store planes on their sides with the blades retracted, and never leave snap-blade and marking knives with the blades exposed loose in a drawer where they could cut hands.

• Invest in a good-quality, solid tool box, or a tool bar that can be fixed to a wall to store your valuable equipment.

• Keep the workshop area clean and tidy.

• If you use a bench to cut, plane, shape, and

drill wood pieces, make sure that a fire extinguisher is within easy reach, as wood shavings burn easily.

- Keep the workshop floor free from obstruction.
- Store bolts, screws, nails, and pins by type and size in marked containers so that they can be easily found. Don't leave them lying on the bench, where they could scar your woodwork.

Power tools

- If the tool has a lead, fit a circuit-breaking plug, and always isolate from the power when changing the bits in a drill or blades in a saw.
- Always make sure you know where the lead is, and keep it behind you if you can.
- If you prefer battery power, remember that the tool is continuously "live." Disconnect the battery when changing bits and blades.
- Use the correct bit for drilling, and make sure that the saw blade is suitable for the material you intend to cut, and that both are sharp.
- It is dangerous practice to force bits and blades, and there should be no need.
- When drilling, back off the hole and stop the drill before removing it; likewise with a power saw, back off or stop the cut, and let the blade stop completely.
- Always read the manufacturer's instruction manual carefully before using any tool, and familiarize yourself with its operation.
- Do not switch on any piece of power equipment unless you know how to turn it off.

Protective clothing

- Site workers always wear safety clothing: protective shoes, overalls, and helmets all the time; safety glasses, ear defenders, and dust masks when required. As you are doing a similar type of work, you should wear the same types of clothing, most of which have obvious functions.

- Shoes need to be strong with reinforced toe caps in case you drop something heavy.
- Gloves will protect your hands from chemicals and corrosive liquids as well as from paint and oil stains.
- A helmet may not be needed in the house, but consider wearing one in the loft where the roof clearance is minimal.
- Overalls are better than old clothes, because they are designed in one piece so nothing gets caught up in machinery, and all the pockets are in the right place and can hold useful items.
- Try wearing a tool belt: all the heavier hand tools can be supported around your waist, so they are instantly accessible, and this is very useful on a stepladder.
- Dust masks are recommended in home improvement stores as a matter of course when you buy materials and equipment for a dirty, dusty job, but wear one even when just sweeping out the work area.
- Use ear defenders for heavy-duty masonry drilling and other noisy jobs, but always ensure that you can still hear warning noises.
- Protect your eyes when working; if you find that goggles tend to mist up, impairing your vision, try safety glasses (which can be worn over reading glasses), but make sure they have side protectors. Slivers of wood, particles of rust, and lumps of masonry can fly from any angle, not just straight at you.

Take a break

- Plan a sensible working schedule, with breaks for drinks (non-alcoholic) and food.
- Don't start early and finish late in the hope of completing the job quickly; working long hours leads to mistakes and sometimes accidents as the attention wanders.

Safety goggles are essential for some jobs to protect your eyes from flying debris and dust. Some fit over normal spectacles.

Always wear clothing that is appropriate for the job. Overalls will protect your clothes, gloves will save your hands from damage, while a cap will keep dirt and dust out of your hair.

Basic tool kit

This is a somewhat misleading title, as anyone who has attempted to assemble a basic tool kit will testify. It is perfectly possible to put together an impressive array of expensive tools, and still find that your door handle undoes with an allen key that you do not possess, instead of the screwdriver bit that you have in the basic tool box.

This is an unfortunate fact of life, and you must inevitably add items to your kit every time you take on a job around the house. Don't be tempted to "make do" with what is in the tool kit, either, because home improvement disaster lurks just around the corner. Using the wrong tool for the job can result in an accident; at best it can make the problem you are trying to solve considerably worse. Buying the correct tool for the job lets your basic tool kit grow with your experience and become a comprehensive tool kit, and before too long you will have a kit that you are confident of using.

For starters

A few basic items will be found in all domestic tool kits: measuring and marking tools, cutting tools, a drill and set of screwdrivers, a hammer, pincers or pliers, tools for making good, and basic painting equipment.

Measuring and marking

- A retractable steel tape that measures to 16 ft./5 m is a real asset; measuring shorter distances is simple with smaller tapes, but they won't run the length of a room. This forces you to add dimensions together, which can lead to miscalculations.
- A small spirit level can fit comfortably in an overall pocket.
- An engineer's square is essential for checking right-angles.
- A soft pencil should be included in your basic tool kit for use on wooden surfaces.
- A waterproof pen offers a very useful way of marking gloss-painted surfaces.

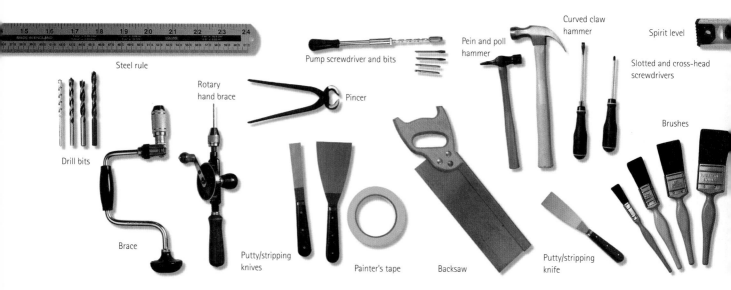

Steel rule

Drill bits

Rotary hand brace

Brace

Pump screwdriver and bits

Pincer

Putty/stripping knives

Painter's tape

Backsaw

Pein and poll hammer

Curved claw hammer

Spirit level

Slotted and cross-head screwdrivers

Brushes

Putty/stripping knife

Cutting tools

- A snap-blade or general-purpose knife.
- A small saw: pick a medium-sized backsaw to start with; it can be identified by a heavy-duty brass or steel strip on the top edge of the blade, keeping it straight. It is simple to use, and can cut large pieces of wood as well as make smaller, more intricate cuts for joints. Always use the protective teeth guard.

Drills and drivers

These are needed for plugging walls and driving screws.

- Drills: Whether your choice is mains-powered or cordless is entirely personal, but in either case, don't buy cheap. Home centers are full of "bargains," but don't be tempted. Cheap, badly made, noisy, inaccurate equipment is no investment; it will not last and will prevent you from doing a good job. Try to find a tool that will satisfy all requirements—wood, masonry and screwdriving—and which has variable speed control.
- Bits: An extensive range of bits is available for power driving, but consider a quality manual tool as well, such as a small spiral ratchet driver with interchangeable blades.
- An electrician's screwdriver.

- Hammer: Its role is self-explanatory, but there are several types. A curved claw hammer would be the most useful starter, the claw able to extract nails and pins. In confined spaces, a pair of pincers will do the job of the claw.

Gripping work

- A pair of combination pliers and an adjustable wrench are called for in gripping work, but it is worth including long-nosed pliers because they can sometimes reach where conventional pliers cannot, and are useful when undertaking electrical work.

Tools for making good

Tools for making good include:

- a scraper
- a flexible knife
- a putty knife
- a roller and tray combination
- a selection of small and medium size brushes.

Boxing clever

Whereas some consumer items are replaceable because they simply wear out, the majority of your tools will be with you a long time, particularly if you buy quality ones. Invest in a toolbox that will protect your equipment.

Marking pen

Roller

Try square

Mains-powered drill

Snap-blade knife

Hacking knife

Carpenter's pencil

Measure

Paint tray

Roller brushes

Battery-powered small drill

Lighting principles

Buildings of every type experience a series of different visual moods as the sun describes an arc from sunrise to sundown. They may be cool and aloof in the morning shade, and warm and friendly in the afternoon sun. Nothing is quite as dramatic, however, as the difference between day and night. Here we discuss how to make the best of the light your room receives.

Lighting-up time

How you see an object, how you define its visual balance and shape, whether or not the angle of the light has caused distortion, or whether the color is enhanced at all by the light depend on the position of the source. During daylight hours this is the sun, its movement causing long shadows and distortions early and late in the day, and a flattening effect when it is high in the sky. Colors that can seem washed-out at midday intensify at the end of the day as the sun sets, and contrasts temporarily increase before darkness descends. Artificial lighting assumes the same role: that of the source, flattening or emphasizing areas, objects and decorations depending on its position in the room.

Add or subtract

As a result of the sun's movement, a house will experience differing visual moods in its south-facing rooms than in its north-facing accommodation. The lighting designer can work with the natural elements, enhancing the effect, or seek to rebalance, adding artificial light to darker, colder areas and throwing highlights onto angles and edges. Just as the afternoon sun casts a warm glow onto a wall, the designer can carefully position wall washers of differing power to throw graduated light onto the area in the same way. Conversely, in rooms where the sun

ABOVE RIGHT:
Lighting should set the mood in a room. Using strategically placed table and standard lamps will produce soft pools of light and create an intimate, relaxing atmosphere.

makes only fleeting contact, the designer can employ hidden lighting techniques combined with light-sensitive switching, warming up what was once a cold, unfriendly environment.

Create the right mood

Try to select lighting that enhances the feel of the room and creates the type of environment that suits the family members that use it. Lighting does not have to be merely functional;

it can also be atmospheric. Centrally sited lighting can be used to great advantage in rooms with dark or rich colored walls, as they absorb a lot of light rather than reflecting it, and the low-key mood can be added to by low-level lamps, up- and downlighters or flicker lamps. Conversely, centrally placed lighting in areas with white or pale colored walls and ceiling can look austere to the point of unfriendliness; wall lights would throw light and shadow onto each surface simultaneously. Lights recessed in an alcove would create more interest still, adding to the wall's shape. If your decoration has involved a special finish, emphasize it by throwing light on the wall. If it is a textured finish, use the lighting to cast long shadows, increasing the three-dimensional effect.

Practicalities

Each member of the household will remind you of individual needs, be it lighting suitable for working on a computer, or reading by the fire. Your lighting arrangements should allow for all necessities, but at no detriment to anyone else. For example, reading lights positioned behind a bed should let one partner read without disturbing the other. Two separately switched directional lamps are needed here.

Areas used by everyone must be well and continuously lit, especially stairwells. Sudden changes in light levels can be hazardous, and for this reason lighting for a stairwell and lights along a corridor should be operated by the same switch. These areas will benefit from a nightlight, too, if you have children or elderly relatives who need to visit a bathroom in the early hours.

Kitchen areas pose a particular problem, in that food preparation and washing-up tasks are usually performed at perimeter units. Consequently a central light will force kitchen users to work in their own shadow. A series of

Stairways should always be well lit to prevent anyone from missing their footing in the dark. Placing downlighters beneath a handrail provides the answer without having to resort to harsh overhead lighting.

downlighters is a good solution, each positioned over a work area—sink, stoves, or hob, work surface, and any appliance in regular use, such as a washing machine. Two separately switched parallel tracks of interchangeable, directional spotlights offer another alternative.

The bathroom needs to have a central enclosed light for background illumination, which should be operated by a pull cord if the switch is inside the room. The basin area needs a separate light for shaving or the application of make-up; arrange it so that the user is illuminated, not the mirror. Remember that no one in the house will thank you for installing lighting that has an abrasive and inaccurate fluorescent effect when they are using the bathroom early in the morning.

Lights with a purpose

Always make sure your lights perform the function they should, and review the situation as your needs change. Good planning will ensure that your system is versatile enough to be multifunctional, providing ambient light for background, directional light for atmosphere and decorative highlights, working light for specific jobs around the home, safety light in heavy traffic areas, and security light as a deterrent to crime.

Wall lights create warming pools of light that emphasize decor.

Materials

Quality specialist materials are best sourced from an outlet
that trades specifically and knowledgeably in that area of supply,
and is therefore in a position to offer help and advice on requirements,
amounts, techniques, and tools needed, based on experience gained in the field.

Buying materials

The rise of home centers in recent years has led
the home improvement enthusiast to believe that
all the materials for any job can be found under
one roof. However, many of the materials for
special projects around the home can be sourced
from smaller suppliers who have specialized
knowledge in particular areas.

Lumber and joinery materials

Superstores and larger hardware or decorating
stores often offer "packs" of shrink-wrapped
lumber, but the packing can make it difficult to
check the quality. The alternative is to buy
from a lumberyard. Pick a yard that offers a
machining service, and that lets you select and
cut your own lengths from properly stored
woods. This will let you select lengths that are
not warped or twisted, and do not suffer from
sap or wet stain, or have shakes and splits.
Lumbers should be racked horizontally, and be
kept under cover. Finally, as price is always a
consideration, remember that cheap lumber can
actually become very expensive if you have to
throw half of it away because of defects or
substandard machining.

Specialized suppliers

Basic paints and varnishes
can be found in your local
decorating store, but these stores
cater for all tastes, and space is limited.

As a result, particular effect paints and glazes are
not usually a priority, and you must source from
a specialized outlet. Many of these suppliers can
be found in the classified pages of consumer
magazines and trade journals. The supplier may
be nowhere near you, but will offer a telephone
or internet buying service, and a delivery service,
except, of course, where the product is a fire risk.

Many small specialized suppliers have the time
and the knowledge to advise you, both on the
products they sell and the technique you are
about to employ. They are usually able to supply
materials needed for any project—for example,
french polishing, in the form of a kit.

Buying economically

Don't automatically assume that you can save
money by buying in bulk. True, it costs little
more for a 55 lb./25 kg bag of cement than for a
small bag of sand/cement mortar mix, but what
exactly are you going to do with what's left over?
If you store it in even a mildly damp place, it will
be useless, and you will end up throwing it away
a few weeks later.

Larger quantities of paints, varnishes, plasters,
cartridge sealants, and adhesives must be sealed
and stored correctly to be of any use at a later
date. A cellar will be cold and damp, an outside
shed prone to frost, and the garage (if it's big
enough) probably has no heating. Lumber
lengths must be racked level, and at room
temperatures, too; if you take wood from a cold

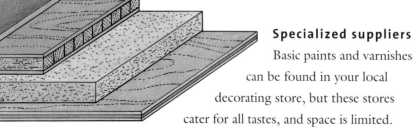

shed into a warm room, you will have no straight lengths to build anything with. So, unless you have the luxury of good storage facilities, think twice before chancing the often false economy of bulk buying.

Reclamation yards

Probably associated more with restoration projects than home improvement tasks, the reclamation yard is nonetheless a good bet for stripped doors, old fire surrounds, old pine floorboards, and all sizes of second-hand lumber. Old lumber sourced here will be of better seasoned stock than new woods, and if you have access to a machine saw, can be resized to live a new life. Don't pass by a builder's garbage container without having a good look, either; it's amazing what gets thrown in them. Just make sure you ask permission before removing something that takes your fancy.

Measurement conversion tables

The lumber supply industry is a worldwide industry and you might find you have to convert from imperial to metric measurements or vice versa when you are sourcing materials to redecorate or revamp your home. Here are two tables that might be useful to you. The first shows the metric sizes that wood comes in, with the equivalent imperial measure and the nearest traditional lengths. The second is a general feet/meters conversion table. The figure in the central column refers to meters if you are converting to feet and feet if you are converting to meters. For example, in the first row of figures the number of units is 1. If you look in the left-hand column, you will see that this means 1 meter converts as 3.2808 feet. If you look in the right-hand column, you will see that this means that 1 foot converts as 0.3048 meters.

WOOD: METRIC AND IMPERIAL LENGTHS

Metric	Equivalent Imperial	Nearest Traditional Length
1.8 m	5 ft. 10⅞ in.	6 ft.
2.1 m	6 ft. 10⅝ in.	7 ft.
2.4 m	7 ft. 10½ in.	8 ft.
2.7 m	8 ft. 10¼ in.	9 ft.
3.0 m	9 ft. 10⅛ in.	10 ft.
3.3 m	10 ft. 9⅞ in.	11 ft.
3.6 m	11 ft. 9¾ in.	12 ft.
3.9 m	12 ft. 9½ in.	13 .ft
4.2 m	13 ft. 9⅜ in.	14 ft.
4.5 m	14 ft. 9⅛ in.	15 ft.
4.8 m	15 ft. 9 in.	16 ft.
5.1 m	16 ft. 8¾ in.	17 ft.
5.4 m	17 ft. 8⅝ in.	18 ft.
5.7 m	18 ft. 8⅜ in.	19 ft.
6.0 m	19 ft. 8⅛ in.	20 ft.
6.3 m	20 ft. 8 in.	21 ft.

CONVERSIONS: FEET/METERS

Feet	No. of Units	Meters
3.2808	1	0.3048
6.5617	2	0.6096
9.8425	3	0.9144
13.123	4	1.2192
16.404	5	1.5240
19.685	6	1.8288
22.966	7	2.1336
26.247	8	2.4384
29.528	9	2.7432
32.808	10	3.0480
36.089	11	3.3528
39.370	12	3.6576
42.651	13	3.9624
45.932	14	4.2672
49.213	15	4.5720
52.493	16	4.8768
55.774	17	5.18163
59.055	18	5.48644
62.336	19	5.79125
65.617	20	6.0960
68.898	21	6.4008
72.178	22	6.7056
75.459	23	7.0104
78.740	24	7.3152
82.021	25	7.6200
85.302	26	7.9248
88.583	27	8.2296
91.86	28	8.5344
95.14	29	8.8392
98.42	30	9.1440

Paint and paper charts

Use the chart below to find out what sort of paint(s) will be required for your redecoration plans. Remember that it is a basic guide and that the amount of paint you will use will depend on the porosity of the walls and how much paint you put on. Always use high quality tools and equipment— a roller will tend to give a more uniform finish. When you work out the amount of wallpaper you will need (see right), take note of the pattern drop; a large pattern drop will mean more rolls of paper are required.

PAINT: TYPES AND USES

Primers/Undercoats	Base	Thinner (Cleaner)	Surfaces
Stain-blocking primer	Oil	White spirit	Wood knots, resin channels, resin stains
Wood primer	Oil	White spirit	All softwoods; softwood veneered boards
Aluminum wood primer	Oil	White spirit	Hardwoods, oily lumber, resinous woods, powdery surfaces (old plaster)
Alkali-resisting primer	Oil	White spirit	New plaster, fire-resistant boards
Penetrating stabilizing primer	Oil	White spirit	Crumbling, powdery surfaces of brick or plaster
Red oxide primer	Oil	White spirit	All ferrous metal surfaces
Acrylic primer/undercoat	Water	Water	Interior softwoods; softwood veneered boards
Oil/resin undercoat	Oil	White spirit	All softwoods, hardwoods, and boards

FINISHES/TOP COATS

	Base	Thinner (Cleaner)	Surfaces
Vinyl mat latex	Water	White spirit	Walls and ceilings
Vinyl silk latex	Water	Water	Walls and ceilings
Enamel	Water	Water	Interior wood finishes, small walls
Low luster	Oil	White spirit	All types of wood, metal finishes
Low luster emulsion	Oil	White spirit	Woodwork, walls, and all smooth surfaces
Enamel latex	Water	Water	Woodwork, walls, and all smooth surfaces
Smooth masonry paint	Water	Water	Brick and mortar finishes
Floor/Tile paint	Oil	White spirit	Concrete, brick, tile, cement, mortar

ESTIMATION OF NUMBER OF ROLLS OF WALLPAPER NEEDED

Height from skirting to coving/ceiling (feet)	Total measurement around walls (feet)							
	28	36	44	52	60	68	76	84
7–7½	4	5	6	7	8	9	9	11
7½–8	4	5	6	7	8	9	10	11
8–8½	4	5	6	7	8	9	10	12
8½–9	4	5	6	8	9	10	11	13
9–9½	4	6	7	8	9	10	12	13
9½–10	5	6	7	9	10	11	12	14
10–10½	5	6	8	9	10	12	13	15
10½–11	5	7	8	9	11	12	13	15

KEY

- Match height of wall (right-hand column) with total horizontal measurement (top row) to identify number of rolls needed. For example, a 10 feet high room 76 feet around would require 12 rolls.

- Each roll is assumed to be 33 ft./10.05 m long, and 20½ in./52 cm wide.

- Measurement listing includes average window and wall recess (door) areas. Increase/decrease as needed.

- Large (wasteful) patterns will need an increase of 1 roll in 5.

1 liter will cover	Recoatable in	Notes
N/A	N/A	If wood is very resinous, combine with aluminum wood primer.
11–12 m²	16–24 hrs.	Use oil with oil-based undercoat and finish. Clean surface with white spirit before application.
14–16 m²	24 hrs.	Leave for 24 hours before recoating.
9–10 m²*	Overnight	* Figure quoted for hard plaster surfaces; more porous surfaces will use more primer.
6–8 m²	16–24 hrs.	Sticky and splashable: wear eye protection and gloves at all times.
9–10 m²	16–24 hrs.	Clean off rust stains with wire wool; best base for oil-based finishes.
12–13 m²	1–2 hrs.	Inside use only; suitable for water-based gloss finishes. Not as durable as oil-based paints.
16–18 m²	16–24 hrs.	All-purpose undercoat, use with oil-based gloss. Manufacturers color-match undercoat with gloss.
12–14 m²	2–4 hrs.	Cannot be wiped clean—unsuitable for kitchens.
10–12 m²	2–4 hrs.	Washable/wipeable finish.
9–10 m²	3–6 hrs.	"No undercoat" versions available; not as hard-wearing or as glossy a surface finish as oil-based enamel.
16–18 m²*	16–24 hrs.	The ultimate paint finish for wood/metal. Smooth, shiny, tough, and permanent. Use inside and out.
19–20 m²	16–24 hrs.	Semi-gloss finish. Also found as silk, luster or satin finish. Good base for paint effects on walls. Needs no undercoat.
10–12 m²	2–4 hrs.	Not as hard-wearing as oil-based eggshell.
9–10 m²	6 hrs.	Limited colors; intended for external walls, but ideal for cellar walls.
10–12 m²	16–24 hrs.	Limited colors. Ideal for red ceramic tile floors, conservatories, and utility rooms.

Color in
your home

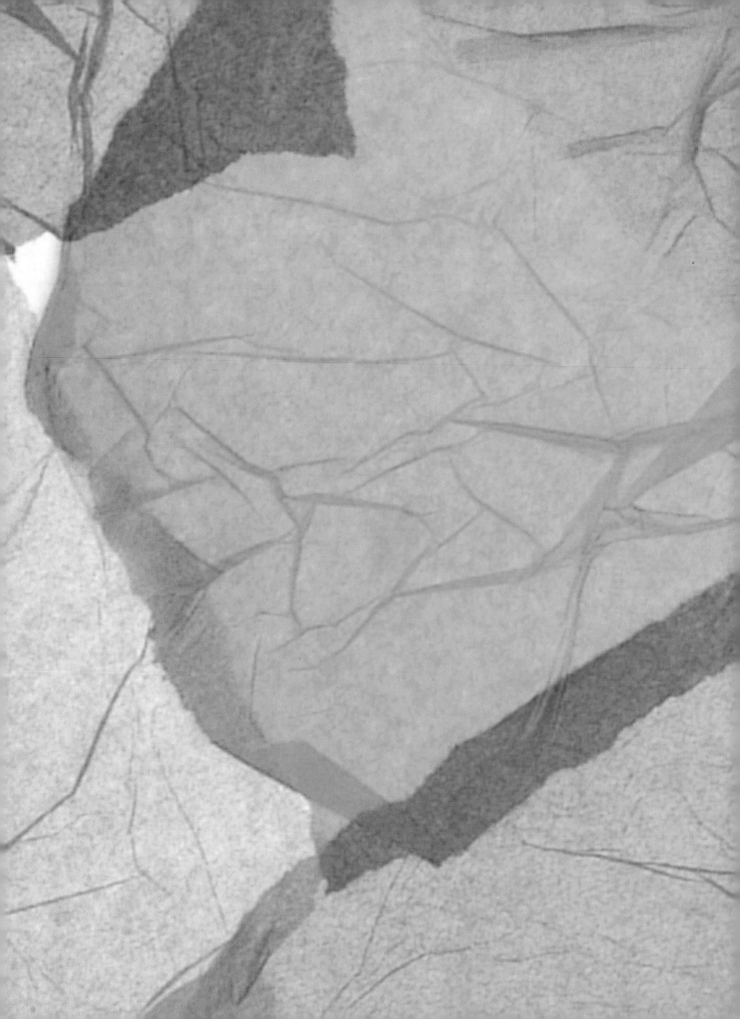

Introduction

Seeking a little natural inspiration for color schemes is always a good idea – after all, nature is without inhibition, and rarely gets it wrong. A stroll in the country at different times of the year will provide endless possibilities.

FAR RIGHT: Use of a bold primary color on nearly every surface may not appeal to everyone. However, if the color is applied with confidence, the results can be stunning. The vibrant red used here brings life to an otherwise austere kitchen, and light flooding in through the window makes the room glowing and cosy.

Color is something we take for granted because everything we see has a color as well as a shape and size. This section will help you to look beyond the paint charts and fabric swatches for inspiration and discover how to use color to make your home a more comfortable place to live.

Color choices

This part of the book aims to help you make the color decisions that suit you and your lifestyle best. If, for example, you work hard and need a relaxing environment to come home to, then aquamarines, lilacs or shades of blue will provide you with a calm and comforting atmosphere.

The first chapter explains the basics of color theory and how all colors are derived from the three primary colors red, yellow and blue, from which are then created the secondary colors of orange, green, and violet. In the second chapter we explore the relationship between color and our emotions. Color has many cultural and religious associations, and we also have instinctive preferences—positive associations and memories persuade us to choose one color over another. Understanding our influences will help us to make the color choices that suit our personalities.

In the third chapter we look at textures and special effects, and how they can be used to add depth to our decorating. The next chapter offers practical projects that will help to transform your home and presents ideas for adding focal points of color to a room.

All colors exist naturally in an enormous range of variations, and a glance at a summer garden in full leaf will reveal that each species of plant is a different shade of green. When we describe colors to each other without the benefit of a photograph we use all kinds of references to conjure up a picture in the mind's eye. A certain shade of pink may be described as looking like the inside of a seashell or as the color of unpainted plaster or of bougainvillaea flowering on a white

wall. We store color and texture memories; it is often the combination of the two that brings a color to mind.

Inspiration for color schemes can be drawn from many sources other than the conventional magazines or color swatch cards. Look at the colors of fruit in the market or of tropical fish in an aquarium. You may find that you are drawn to a painting or perhaps just one area of it because the colors look so good together.

Choosing a color scheme that is the height of fashion has many advantages —the paint colors will be readily available, your home will look fresh and up-to-date and the shops will be full of color co-ordinating accessories. Home color fashions change less often than they do for clothes, but there is a strong connection. The colors you see on the catwalks one year may just turn up in the DIY store the next.

This part does not deal only with ideas and theories about color; there are also plenty of practical, easy-to-follow projects, all of which are based around a color theme. Each one has been designed to be quick and easily accomplished and to give maximum impact for minimum effort. There is a range of soft furnishing, painting, craft and styling projects, so there should be something to suit all tastes. I hope that you find it useful, stimulating and fun to read and that you turn to it often for inspiration.

Fruits and vegetables come in a whole range of marvellous colors, from the hot, vivid red and fresh, bright green of chillies to the soft orange of the inside of a mango or the sumptuous, rich purple of an aubergine. Spend some time in a vegetable market for some great decorating ideas.

Color and design

Choosing the right color combinations for our homes will undoubtedly help us to create rooms that make us feel good. We all have personal favorites; for example, we choose our clothes from a mixture of our instinctive color preferences and what is currently fashionable. Where decorating is concerned, however, the stakes are higher, because mistakes can be both expensive and time-consuming. It makes sense to use some of your planning time to find out more about color and how it can be used to the most positive effect in your home. The first chapter introduces the basic principles of color theory, explaining why some colors blend comfortably when seen alongside each other, while others appear to vibrate and create visual friction.

Understanding the color wheel

Color breathes life into a home. It can warm or cool, calm or excite us. Clever use of color can make small rooms look more spacious or cavernous rooms feel cozy. It can blank out unsightly features and bring the ornate and interesting ones sharply into focus. It has the potential to elevate and energize all your interior decorating. Never before have home decorators had this much color choice, and the ranges just keep growing—often leading to more confusion and indecision. How can we select colors that are right for us?

Color theory

Knowing some basic color theory will help you to make color choices that go beyond your gut reaction to a color scheme, although that is also hugely important. Basic color tricks and rules exist, and it is certainly useful to take some time to understand them, even if in the end you decide to break all the rules. Color has always been a tool for self-expression!

Three hundred years have passed since Sir Isaac Newton shone pure white light through a glass prism onto a neutral background and was delighted to see a continuous band of merging color ranging from red through orange, yellow, green, blue, and violet. In essence he had captured a miniature version of the rainbow, which is created by light passing through drops

Yellow, red, and blue are the primary colors on which the color wheel is based.

of rain, causing the spectrum colors to be projected like a giant color slide across the sky.

When colors are arranged as a color wheel, it helps us to understand their relationships to each other and the different effects that are produced when they are used alongside and opposite each other. Secondary colors are produced by mixing two primary colors:

• yellow + red = orange
• yellow + blue = green
• blue + red = violet.

Tertiary colors are made by mixing a secondary color with an equal amount of the color next to it on the wheel:

• yellow + orange = yellow orange (golden yellow)
• red + orange = red orange (burnt orange)
• yellow + green = yellow green (lime green)
• blue + green = blue green (turquoise)
• blue + violet = blue violet (indigo)
• red + violet = red violet (crimson).

It is also useful to discover how much or how little of one color is added to another to make a third color. Try making your own color wheel.

THE COLOR WHEEL

The color wheel is the standard way to explain color mixing by separating the spectrum into twelve different colors. At the center of the wheel is a triangle divided into three equal sections of the primary paint colors—red, yellow, and blue.

These three colors are called primary because they can not be obtained from a mixture of any other colors. Along with black and white, they form the basis of all other paint colors.

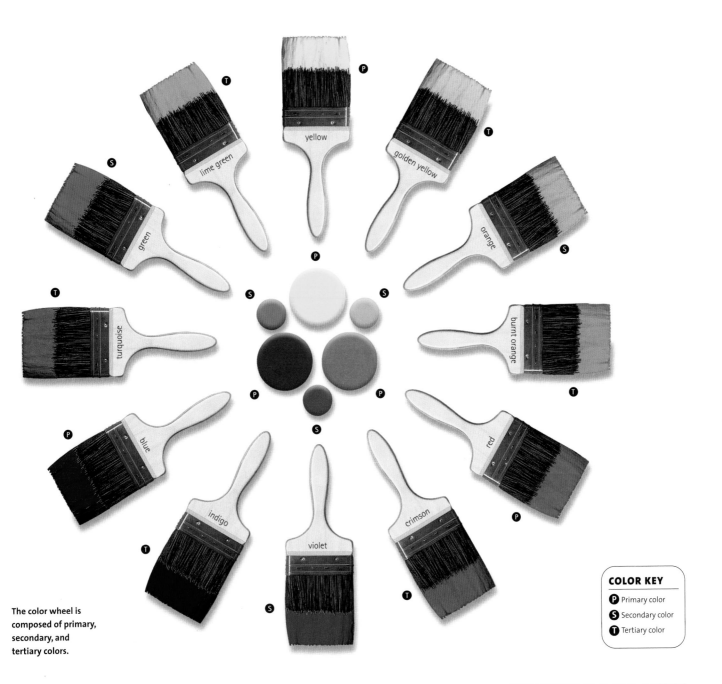

The color wheel is composed of primary, secondary, and tertiary colors.

HOW TO MAKE A COLOR WHEEL

1 Begin with a large dab each of primary red, yellow, and blue paint in the middle of a white plate, with yellow at the top, red lower right, and blue in the lower left. These are the primary colors and will form the basis of your color wheel.

2 Now mix an equal amount of primary color into the one next to it, around the outside of the original three colors. You will produce orange, green, and violet. These secondary colors fill the spaces midway between each two primaries.

3 Place a dot of each primary color on the plate rim opposite its central position. Do the same with the secondary colors. Leave a space between each, big enough for the tertiary colors (mix a secondary color with an equal amount of the color next to it on the wheel).

Color—our visual experience

Color is a very powerful tool that can be used effectively to help signs or signals convey their message. Our experience of color varies depending on the amount of light available, so the use of color varies accordingly. During daylight hours, for example, we experience the contrast of yellow and black very strongly, and these colors may be used for warning signs. At night we can see red without making any adjustment to our eyes, so it is ideal for warning lights on cars and to show "stop" at traffic signals.

Signs and signals

Our eyes experience colors as wavelengths of light, with each color having its own frequency that is recognized and interpreted by the brain. The paint colors used for public information signs, logos, advertising, and packaging are not chosen at random. They have been deliberately selected, using scientifically proven data, to be the most effective color for the purpose and situation.

In daylight, for example, yellow is most instantly readable and yellow and black give the strongest contrast, so these colors are used on construction vehicles, barriers, and warning signs.

Green on white, red on white, white on blue, and black on white also have immediate impact. Poor combinations in daylight are red on blue, red on green, and blue on green.

On its own, red-orange grabs our attention, and this makes it ideal for sea rescue craft. Red also advances, and is transmitted on the highest frequency of all colors; it is immediately recognized, making it the obvious choice for the stop sign at the traffic signal.

We see colored light in different ways, and in daylight yellow/green is brightest; in low light blue/green is most visible; but in extreme

darkness our eyes see red light clearly without having to make any adjustment, and this is why red light is used for controls and warnings that need to be clear at night.

A trick of the light

The existence of color depends entirely upon light. Try placing a red vase on a table in a room directly lit by a standard tungsten bulb. Turn the

RIGHT: **It is possible to drive a car safely at speed along a busy highway at night because of colored rear lights. The red lights are easily read by our eyes in darkness, making it possible immediately to recognize and react to brake and indicator lights.**

LEFT: **Here mother nature's warning colors yellow and black are used to reinforce the skull and crossbones danger message.**

ABOVE: **A red circle with a line passing through it is universally understood as a prohibition message. Red signals danger and the precise nature of the message is described by the black icon.**

light off and the vase looks just as black as everything else in the dark room. The color of any object is a visual experience and not a fact! We see this every day when the sun sets and darkness falls outside the window, yet the simple statement that color is just a trick of the light is almost impossible to accept.

It is all to do with the power of a surface to absorb or reflect light particles. Red appears to be red because it absorbs all the other colors of the spectrum and reflects only the red. Shine a green light onto a red object and it will no longer be red but black.

Anyone who has made the mistake of buying all red lights for their Christmas tree will confirm the strangely deadening effect they have on the green of the tree, and the way they rob the ornaments of their sparkle.

Color is a powerful tool that works on many different levels—and the more you know about color, the more chance you have of using it to its full potential.

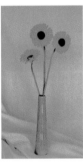

A red light intensifies the red flowers and knocks out the green.

A green light enriches all the parts that are green such as the vase and the stems.

In a blue light the red flowers lose their red glow; the vase becomes more turquoise.

Yellow light warms the red to orange and turns the vase a sickly green. It is never flattering.

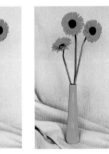

Halogen lights are bright and give off a bright white light that does not affect color.

Tungsten lights are no-frills everyday light bulbs. They give out a pleasant warm glow.

Color terms

The language used to describe color includes some specific terms that you may not have come across before unless you have studied art or interior design. The few terms that are explained here are those that are most likely to be mentioned within the context of home decorating. Some specialized terminology will come in handy and make it much easier to communicate your thoughts and ideas about color when dealing with professionals in the industry.

RIGHT: **Golden yellow and mauve clash with each other, producing a kind of visual discomfort.**

BELOW: **Blue and orange appear directly opposite each other on the color wheel and are known as complementary colors.**

Additive color

This is the color of light, where adding all the colors together creates white light.

Clashes or discords

This describes two colors of equal intensity, which cause visual discomfort. Think of them as musical harmonies and discords. Designers and artists sometimes make use of this effect to create a disturbance and give the color scheme an "edge," and color clashes were most famously used in the rebellious 1960s—bright orange and shocking pink, for instance, or golden yellow and mauve.

Complementary colors

Colors opposite each other on the color wheel are called "complementary." These are colors of equal intensity. When they are combined in equal proportions, they make a neutral gray. When placed alongside each other, they achieve maximum intensity and compete for attention.

Contrasts

Hue

The simplest contrast to understand is that of hue, which describes the difference between undiluted colors seen alongside each other. The primary colors (yellow, red and blue) are the most extreme example.

Hot and cold

Some colors are hot—red, yellow, and orange; some are cold—blue, green, and violet. The most extreme hot/cold contrasts are red-orange and blue-green.

Light and dark

Light and dark contrast is clear when you look at a color and a black-and-white version of the same photograph. Red and green have the same tonal quality and show up as an equal gray. Yellow and violet are the most extreme examples of this contrast (apart from black and white, which are not colors, but tones).

Hue

A hue is one of the pure colors of the spectrum, like red or yellow, and it can be used to describe the character of another color—for example, lavender has a violet hue, olive has a green hue, or pink has a red hue.

Harmonies

A harmony is a combination of colors that lets the eye travel smoothly between them with no sharp contrasts at all. Colors that are close to each other on the color wheel will naturally harmonize—yellow, orange, and red, for example.

Intensity

This describes how much pigment is in the paint. The more pigment there is, the stronger and less diluted the color will be. Another word used to describe color intensity is saturation.

Neutrals

The neutral colors are black, white, gray, beige, and cream.

Surface color or paint color

This is color that is mixed from pigments, where adding all the primary colors together creates black. This is the color we deal with when we are decorating. It is different from the colors of light. When all the primary colors of light are combined, the resulting light is white, not black.

Tints and shades

The addition of white to a color produces a tint, which we call a pastel color. According to the terminology, when black is added to a color, it produces a shade.

LEFT: In the black-and-white half of this picture the light foreground and dark background are very clearly defined. In the colored half the tonal contrasts are not as obvious because the glow from the bright yellow illuminates the wall.

LEFT: These three blocks are an example of subtle tints and shades. The central color has been lightened by tinting with white (left) and darkened by adding a small amount of black (right).

Classic colors

The colors people choose to decorate their homes are usually muted, light, and easy on the eye. This type of decorating does not follow fashion and has been around for decades. Classic combinations like pale blue and white with yellow highlights or terra cotta and blue-gray with cream almost carry a guarantee of success. These schemes work because the colors look good together, balance each other, and are easy to live with. The colors can be arranged in many different ways.

RIGHT: **The walls have been color-washed with a pale blue over cream and the main furnishings keep to the blue theme. The floor is of honey-toned parquet tiles and the natural wooden furniture has been kept light, to give a pleasant, harmonious effect.**

Tried and tested color schemes

These color schemes combine harmonious colors with similar tonal values, usually with pale neutral or white for the woodwork. Any deeper colors are introduced by way of soft furnishings and accessories, for example, drapes and cushion covers. These are tried and tested color schemes. The effect is pleasing and easy to live with.

Complementary color schemes

Complementary color schemes built around contrasting hues only work well when one color

is dominant and the other is used to complement it—for example, red lampshades and cushions in a predominantly green room.

Magnolia—pale beige with a hint of pink— is famously inoffensive. But it was too successful; new designers railed against safe colors, and magnolia became equated with being boring.

Monochromatic or single-color schemes rely on using one hue in different tones and intensity. This creates a strong sense of style, but requires a disciplined lifestyle and adequate storage space, as colorful clutter tends to detract from the look.

RIGHT: **The deep emerald green walls create a warm atmosphere. The drapes and cushion fabric picks up the green and the bright red adds a complementary balance. Pools of light from the lamps and the fire's glow make this room cozy.**

In North Africa, house exteriors tend to be painted with earth colors, but the interiors are a riot of jewel-bright colors. Decoration features elaborate geometric tiling and paneling based on traditional Arab influences and designs. Deep intense blue, viridian green, golden yellow, and rose pink are painted onto walls and used in geometric patterns.

India, of all places in the world, is most associated with brilliant colors. Like the beautiful colors of traditional clothes and jewellery, the color combinations that exist on the exteriors of houses can be literally dazzling to look at. Peppermint green, vivid mauve, and shocking pink seem to look perfect next to emerald green, carmine red, and saffron yellow. The rules are that there are no rules—and it looks divine.

LEFT: **A house in the Greek islands, painted white to deflect the heat of the sun, and looking superb against the bright blue sky.**

Color and climate

Climate has a big effect on color choices. In countries nearest the equator, decorators use the most brilliant colors because of the bright sunlight—pale colors and subtle tones and shades would not be visible under such intense light. In the northern countries, where the sunlight is less powerful, bright colors seem harsh and brash, but pale, more subtle colors look their best. This is why attempts to recreate a paradise island on a chilly hillside in the north of Scotland are doomed to failure.

In the Greek Islands (pictured above), where it is hot in summer, houses are painted white to deflect the heat of the sun. Windows are small, and often shuttered, which makes interiors quite dark and gloomy, but it keeps them cool. The traditional color for woodwork is bright blue, which the sun fades to aquamarine. The sight of bright pink geraniums blooming on balconies and doorsteps alongside this blue and white is simply beautiful.

In Scandinavia, the popular decorating style is minimalist. In traditional homes, walls are painted pale blue or white, with pale natural wooden floors. The modern Swedish style retains the clean open look, but uses brighter colors, especially yellow.

Colors that go together

The question most people ask when wading through color charts is: "Do you think these two colors will go together?" A good approach to the answer is to leave the technicalities aside and look at some tried and tested color schemes. Look somewhere other than a paint chart. If you see a gray slate rooftop against a pale blue sky or a purple wisteria plant tumbling over a soft yellow stone wall, make a mental note of the colors that appeal to you and consult the paint charts with this image in mind.

COLOR KEY

1 Ink blue
2 Light blue
3 Sunshine yellow

Contemporary

Yellow and blue are a positive, uplifting and friendl[y] combination of colors. The walls here are a bright sunflower yellow, which glows under the spotlights and is complemented by the deep blue of the table top. The yellow looks equally good with the enameled surface of the light-blue cooking range, the natural wood, and the reflective chrome. The kitchen is busy and filled with interestingly shaped objects wrapped up into one harmonious package by the glowing yellow backdrop.

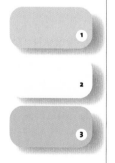

Traditional

This elegant room has been decorated in a classic pale blue, white, and gold scheme. The fireplace, ceiling and built-in cabinets are all mat white set against duck egg blue walls. The room has a good floor that has been stripped and polished and, along with the faded antique rug, it provides the room with warmth. The combination of black and gold candlesticks, gilt frames, wire mesh cabinet doors, and the gilded chair give the room a classic French style, which provides an understated background for well chosen elements.

COLOR KEY

1 Ice blue
2 Mat white
3 Yellow ocher

Natural

Where flowers grow in their natural habitat, the colors are in harmony with their surroundings. The colors of the landscape and plant life are a source of constant inspiration. Think of heather on the moors set against a pale sky, daisies in the grass, bluebells carpeting the woods, primroses on mossy banks, or the place where the ocean meets the shore. You just can't go wrong if you choose your color scheme this way.

COLOR KEY

1 Deep blue
2 Aqua
3 Apple
4 Pale apple

COLOR COMBINATIONS IN NATURE

Two light neutrals and one strong color
- White + gray + yellow
- Cream + stone + Sienna red
- Sand + cream + sky blue

Similar subdued tones of contrasting colors with a light neutral
- Sage green + brick red + light stone • Wedgwood blue + apricot + creamy white

Similar tones of harmonious colors with a deep tone of one
- Pale blue + lavender + deep purple
- Apricot + shell pink + deep ruby red
- Sage green + yellow-cream + deep green

Different tones of a single color with a light neutral
- Mid blue + pale blue + cream with gold highlights
- Mint green + emerald green + white
- Deep + pale orange + soft gray

Earth tones
- Yellow ocher + brown + red ocher + pale honey
- Stone + gray + black + yellow ocher + red ocher

Naturals
- Light + deep olive green + mud-brown + off-white
- Cream + dark brown + pale straw + silver green

Personal taste

If you were to start with a clean slate and were able to reinvent your personal taste, the result is likely to be as sterile as a hotel room or a room set in a furniture showroom. These rooms, designed to make many different people feel at home, always lack the character of personal expression. Taste evolves with us, whether as a result of rejecting our parents' taste, or being strongly influenced by fashion or a particular era's decorating style. Our taste in colors also builds up over the years and is developed from an accumulation of influences that go back to childhood.

The detail of this fine old chair would be lost if set against a bright patterned wallpaper. Design your color schemes to flatter the furniture or objects you already own.

RIGHT: This rough distressed wall finish is a perfect background for a contemporary folding chair. The different textures create a contradiction that gives the image energy. The very old and very new can often make good companions.

A background to your life

Visualize a living room with a white ceiling, pale blue walls, white woodwork, and natural polished wood flooring. This is a traditional classic color scheme, chosen to provide an unobtrusive background for elegant furniture—perhaps some antiques, paintings, and a chandelier. Now place your own furniture in the room and imagine how it will look.

Picture the same room with the baseboards and window frames painted a deep turquoise blue and the walls sunshine yellow. Is this more your sort of look? This is an extreme version of a very useful exercise, because the things you already own and love can provide the best clues when you are looking for a new color scheme.

The front door makes the first statement about who lives behind it, and your color choice can advertise or conceal your personality. Vivid orange, bright golden yellow, or scarlet announce flamboyance and sociability; and deep green suggests a much calmer welcome.

Busy rooms—like family kitchens, where there is a constant flow of traffic and activity—benefit from bold colors and strong contrasts, which add to the room's dynamism. Hallways look inviting in warm yellow or burnt orange, whereas a

bedroom is more relaxing if painted a calming green, meditative blue or lilac.

The way your house functions is improved by choosing the right colors for the various rooms and connecting areas.

Favoritism

We all favor certain colors, and consequently no amount of theoretical knowledge is going to convince someone to paint a room purple if they are of a pastel pink persuasion.

Vive la différence! Each of us is unique, and personal taste varies enormously.

Following fashion

Decorating has always followed fashion. Fashions used to be dictated by kings and queens and ignored at your peril. Scarcity of certain pigments played a large part in how and where they were used, until the Victorians invented synthetic color dyes. Initially pigments were made from earth, minerals, or plants; some were rare and expensive. Blue and purple are two colors whose rarity ensured that they were reserved for royalty and deity, and they still hold these associations today. These are two examples from recent history of periods of fashion:

Art Deco

In the 1920s the Art Deco style was one of symmetry, stepped shapes, vertical lines, and smooth surfaces. The style was influenced by the Cubist art movement and the arrival of the movies and the great ocean liners. Chrome, glass, ceramics, marble, and leather were some of the

most popular ingredients. This was an era when "having style" was considered a top priority.

Diner-style

The 1950s style is bold and fun. In the 1950s, decorating celebrated the return of color after the drab war years, and many of the innovations that had focused on the military were at the disposal of designers for the home market. Chrome was in fashion and the plastics industry celebrated with colored laminated surfaces and molded plastic shapes and this was reflected in the style of people's homes.

Fashions today

These days we are more likely to be influenced by top fashion designers, whose work often encompasses interiors and home accessories. This cross-over has introduced an aspirational feeling to interior decorating and spawned many magazines. Fashion is fun and, because it is ever-changing, it is also refreshing. The latest color scheme can certainly bring a drab room right up to date, but it is important to avoid being a fashion victim. Decorating is big business—to keep the tills ringing, paint companies also ring the color changes every season. But stick to what you like and what suits your room—unless you feel like a change!

COLOR KEY

1 Ketchup red
2 Gloss white
3 Black

ABOVE LEFT: **Chrome kitchen appliances echo the shapes of streamlined cars and planes, and black-and-white checked patterns add style.**

BELOW LEFT: **This room features a classic 1920s fireplace.**

COLOR KEY

1 Cream
2 Plaster pink
3 Warm orange

Pattern and texture

A colorful room without textural contrasts would look strangely sterile. The texture of an object is one of our key descriptive tools, and a surface pattern can be used to enhance a shape or carry a color scheme. When solid color seems heavy and overpowering over large areas, a patterned version can give a much lighter feel. The dense texture of a carpet means a plain color often works well on the floor but patterns might work better for drapes or wallpaper.

Faux linen: denim blue is a good color for upholstery.

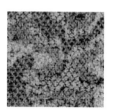

Faux snakeskin: chenille printed in a python pattern.

Woven chenille: a flat weave fabric with a very soft texture.

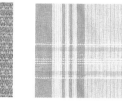

Woven check: in harmonious orange, yellow, and cream.

Cotton/linen: embodying the English country-house style.

Kasbah: this pattern motif works well with a traditional style.

Jacquard weave: a hard-wearing fabric good for upholstery.

Leather: the most hard-wearing of all upholstery material.

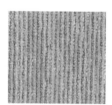

Gold chenille: a rich loose-weave chenille with a corded texture.

Woven dobby: fabric that has the look of brushed denim.

Suede fabric: the look of real suede with a smooth texture.

Pattern

Interior decorating styles follow catwalk fashions, and most of the top clothes designers now also have home ranges that include furniture, carpets, fabrics, and paint colors. So it is possible to coordinate every area of your life in the style of someone with impeccable design credentials! In real life, few of us would go that far—but it is useful to keep an eye on fashion, where you will find clues to new color trends. Pattern has been kept to a minimum for a long time, but that is about to change, and this is good for home decorators. Pattern is a great way of introducing more color into a room.

Texture

The texture of a color can change its appearance more than you would imagine. Some colors look bland and dead when painted in a mat latex paint. Terra cotta is a good example of this, as it only comes to life on a rough rustic surface or when used as a patchy colorwash. Mint green is another example—it looks fresh and fantastic in a chalky finish, but safe and dull in a flat latex

paint. Some colors benefit from having a reflective sheen, especially in combination with a contrasting mat color. Mat chocolate-brown woodwork with a glossy cream wall looks really delicious, and red always looks better with a sheen. The deep green of glass bottles is stunning with light shining through it, but the color is nothing without transparency and light. Experiment with sample pots if you are unsure about which texture of paint will give the look you're after.

A room style based on a natural palette where there is little color variation is brought to life by different textures, such as woven wool, linens and cottons, sisal matting, sheepskin, leather, bleached wood, and glass. A very little color will go a long way when a rich variety of textures provides the visual interest.

In this room the chalky texture of the walls has been emphasized by the use of a high sheen paint for the dado rail. Chalk finish paints dry to a paler version of the applied color and have a soft, powdery surface bloom. Any type of paint can be given a glossy finish by applying a coat of clear gloss varnish.

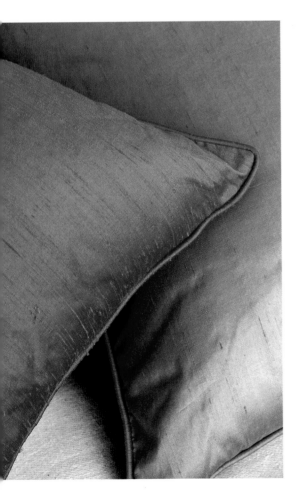

LEFT: Cushions are the easiest way to introduce different textures and colors to a room. Look for cushion fabrics with an obviously contrasting texture to the furniture upholstery, such as these shiny shantung silks against the unbleached rough linen of the sofa.

Contemporary color schemes

If you follow fashion and want the latest look, a fresh coat of paint is the cheapest, quickest, and easiest way to change the look of a room. Think about the atmosphere you want in your room, and choose the colors accordingly. Most paint companies produce ranges of coordinating colors with different contemporary theme names—tropical, spicy, natural, ethnic, and so on. If you are after a contemporary style, then look no further; these ranges represent the most popular looks of the moment.

Paint effects

Paint effects no longer require specialist materials—most companies have a range of products that enable beginners to apply color in effects such as metallic, denim, linen, suede, rustic, or antique. It's time to strip the varnish off the pine kitchen cabinets and update them with colored woodwash.

Metallics

Zinc, chrome, stainless steel, and copper have all crossed over from the factory into the home, providing a fresh, young style that does not cost a fortune. Metallic doesn't have to mean cold hard steel any more either, as there are several excellent metallic acrylic paint ranges on the market that can be used on most surfaces, including walls and furniture. Look no further than this if you have a boring chest of drawers in need of an update. In this picture (see left) the handles have been replaced with half-moon cut-outs, and the wood surface painted shimmering silver.

COLOR KEY

1 Aluminum
2 Deep lavender
3 Pale lilac

Chalky colors

Chalky colors create a soft, mat texture. They are usually mixed with water before application, and you can vary their strength from a thick textured mat covering to a soft colorwash. The colors dry lighter, with a soft bloom on the wall's surface. Bright chalky colors give a youthful, Caribbean island look—imagine a bright but sun-bleached beach house porch, bright blue sky, and palm trees. Pale chalky colors (see picture, right) are cool and sophisticated.

COLOR KEY

1 Powder pink
2 Sherbet yellow
3 Faded denim

Jewel-bright colors

Jewel-bright colors make a fantastic impact, and they look fabulous with unfussy furniture and equally vibrant fabrics, such as Indian sari silks or South American woven textiles. The best way to use jewel colors is to choose mainly harmonizing shades like crimsons, reds, and oranges, using them alongside just small amounts of equally intense contrasts.

Avoid using equal amounts of intense contrasting color like orange and blue or red and green, as they can actually cause visual discomfort. You should keep the colors flowing through the room by picking them up with various accessories such as cushions, throws, and lampshades (see picture, left).

COLOR KEY

1 Rich red
2 Salmon pink
3 Deep golden yellow

Creating an illusion

Color can be a magical tool if you have awkwardly proportioned rooms, as often happens when houses are converted into apartments. When big rooms are divided up, high ceilings can make them look smaller than they are. This is where clever use of color comes in useful. If a room has unusual proportions, color is the cheapest way to improve it without structural alterations. Light colors reflect the most light, making rooms appear bigger and brighter, while dark colors have the opposite effect.

Faced with a room with fine proportions like this one, it would have been a pity to spoil the symmetry by boxing in pipework. The far more sympathetic and successful alternative was simply to paint the pipes to match the background. This works particularly well with a mat paint finish because the shapes don't catch the light.

Tricks of the trade

A very high ceiling can be made to look a lot lower if a light color is used on the walls up to the height where the ceiling would be in proportion with the room, then a dark color is used above it for the top part of the walls and the ceiling. Fix a chandelier to hang into the room below the dark top section and the high ceiling will "appear to disappear." If you prefer not to have a central light, then make a feature of the lighting by using sculptural contemporary lights to create focal points where you choose to have them, or large table lamps that shed pools of light to give a cozy atmosphere. Look out for the new rechargeable colored balls of light—the charge lasts about four hours, and nobody will ever notice your high ceiling!

A low ceiling will look higher if the walls are painted in a dark color or papered with a "busy" patterned paper up to chair rail height, then painted a very light color above it, including the ceiling. Lighting and color can help exaggerate the illusion of space. Harness blue's receding quality and use subtle washes of light from uplighters to add the most height, like looking up into a pale summer sky. For a fantastic contemporary design solution, try soft washes of slowly changing colored light on a white ceiling to turn your low ceiling into an art feature. Specialized lighting shops have the equipment, and they are a lot less rare than they used to be.

Optical illusions

- If the room is long and narrow, it can be made to look wider by painting the longer walls with a cool pale green or blue, so that the walls appear to recede. The narrower walls will appear to advance if you paint them in a deep, warm shade of red or red-brown.

- Paint corridors to harmonize with the room color and remove doors to create a more open-plan sense of space in a small flat.

- Make "small" a virtue by painting walls and ceilings of tiny rooms in deep warm colors for a wrap-around coziness.

- Blot out unwanted details like pipework or damaged plaster features by painting them the same color as the surroundings.

- Add interest to a square plain room by creating optical illusions with blocks of color. Drop-shadows, stripes, or stenciled moldings can all be used in contemporary or traditional ways.

LEFT: One way to create a harmonious home is to link the colors of one room with the corridor, stairway, or a feature in the next room. Here the staircase is painted to match the woodwork in the foreground and a band of the blue along the top of the baseboard echoes the room's wall color.

You can make a low ceiling seem higher by painting the walls in a dark color and the ceiling in a pale color or white.

Painting the ceiling in a darker color than the walls of a room will appear to reduce the height of the room and provide a much more intimate atmosphere.

Color and light

The appearance of a color depends on the quality of the light it is seen in. Most of us share the experience of being unable to tell navy blue from black inside a store but once outside the blueness is revealed by daylight. Every color can be enhanced, softened or highlighted with lighting. The combination of a warm color scheme and soft lighting can create a relaxing environment, and cool colors with sharp contrasts and bright directional light can give a dull space an energetic uplift.

Here, the muslin drapes soften the sunlight that would otherwise dazzle in a white room. The floor is painted concrete and the walls whitewashed plaster yet the room has atmosphere created by the combination of a cotton rug, an attractive chair, and the quality of the light.

RIGHT: Concealed neon tubes below the wall units illuminate this cool modern kitchen. Kitchens are often too bright but here the task lighting is concentrated on the work surfaces.

Getting the lighting right

The boldest or most subtle color scheme in the world looks the same in the dark—so it follows that getting the lighting right is absolutely vital. This means making the most of the natural light as well as using the best sort of artificial light for the effect you are after. Anyone who has visited a night club during the day will understand the magic of clever lighting, as daylight reveals what the lighting conceals.

If your living room is the children's playroom during the day, then clever lighting tricks can help to create a more sensual atmosphere in the evening. Dimmer switches, uplighters, and concealed lights will create soft ambient lighting conditions, and table lamps make pools of light that add intimacy to a room. Try focusing spotlights on the tabletop to throw the rest of the room into shadow and create a sense of intimacy for an adult meal. Task spotlights can be used for "work" areas such as hi-fi, TV, and games consoles. Use small spots to accent flowers, art, or any other features.

Yellow is the lightest and brightest of the primary colors; it glows with reflected light. A cool, north-facing room can be infused with warmth and light if you paint the walls warm light yellow, and any room will look lighter if you paint walls opposite the windows white or any other very light color. If the windows are small, the natural light in the room will appear to double if the frame, recess and immediate surround are painted white.

LEFT: Rich red walls and a dark rug surround this dining table. The high chair in the background gives a hint that this room adopts a very different character during the day.

BELOW: The yellow walls in this room infuse it with sunshine and warmth. The use of pink in the room beyond has an enticing effect when framed by the yellow.

Colored glass or sheets of adhesive color film applied to windows can be applied in order to change the room color during the day. A white room can glow with pink, yellow, or green when the sun shines through the glass, only to return to white again. In the same way, colored lights can be used at night to change the mood and color of a room. One London hotel has a range of colored lighting options in every room, so guests can choose the room's color mood for themselves.

Planning color schemes

The starting point here is inspiration, and this could come from a room style seen in a magazine, a classic period style such as Regency, or the regional colors seen on a vacation overseas. Or it could be a combination of colors on a piece of fabric, in the corner of a painting, in a bunch of flowers, or in a bowl of fruit or sugared almonds —anything at all that pleases your eye and could be translated into colors for a room. Analyze the source of your inspiration to discover which of the colors will create the right mood for your room.

This lovely rustic Mediterranean home is furnished with an eclectic mixture of art and country furniture. The room is whitewashed and the beams have been picked out in the brilliant blue typical of the region. Blue and white predominate for walls and woodwork, but the bright furnishings, pictures, and flowers create a much more multicolored look.

Selection factors

If the walls are to be all of one color, then it should work in context with all the above

considerations. Lighter and darker versions of the same color may be a better option, letting some areas appear more prominent than others.

Patterned wallpaper could also be used to add texture and variety without introducing another main color. Bold patterns are back in fashion, and the right ones will certainly bring a room right up to date.

If you decide to base your color scheme on an historical or regional style, the color choices will be restricted to particular palettes. The colors simply have to be combined in the traditional way, and success is assured. Everything does not have to be innovative and original, and with color schemes it is generally better to look at something that works well, then copy it.

Decide upon the main colors for the room. The walls, the ceiling, the floor, and the woodwork are the key areas. Unless you are looking to create the illusion of a lower ceiling, then this should be the lightest color in the room. The wall color or colors can be either mat or have a slight sheen. The reflective sheen is best for pale colors where you want to increase the light in a room. Mat gives the most sophisticated look. Gloss is an unusual choice for

Sometimes in a small room a more spacious effect is achieved by simply painting them the same color as the walls, using a semigloss or satinwood paint. A large room, however, may benefit from the unifying effect of strong bands of color at baseboards, chair and picture rail height.

LEFT: Inspiration for planning your color scheme can come from a wide variety of sources in your environment; make a collection of inspiring objects.

Flooring

A new wooden floor will give any room a clean, contemporary look, and the cost need not be vast if you choose one of the cheaper laminates. It will provide a good base for colorful rugs, and the "click" type of floorboards do not require glue and can be easily lifted and relaid elsewhere. If existing wooden floorboards are in reasonable condition, they can be painted or stripped and stained. This style of flooring is popular at the moment, and it can always be carpeted over in the future, so there is nothing to lose.

If new flooring is not an option, then the color scheme will have to be chosen to take the existing flooring into account. If you have a rust-colored carpet, for instance, choosing a contrast color like light turquoise or ice blue for the walls will give you a much fresher, livelier effect than a more conventional choice of harmonious yellow, cream, or orange.

walls but it is very practical for hallways and stairways, especially when there are children in the house.

Window frames

Window frames are conventionally painted in a lighter color than walls, as this reflects more light into the room. Unless they are an attractive key feature in the room, such as lovely old double-hung or huge plate glass windows, the frames look better when kept light and neutral, as color will make a feature of any defects.

Baseboards and chair rails

Baseboards and chair or picture rails in older houses provide an opportunity for horizontal bands of color to divide the walls in clean lines. But just because these features exist does not mean that they have to be picked out and contrasted with the wall color.

Patterns

If you would like to use a pattern, there are a few basic rules worth considering. Large patterns work best in large areas and small patterns are best suited to small areas where they can be appreciated. A small floral pattern will read as a texture from a distance, whereas a large floral repeat in a small area is far too overwhelming.

Geometric patterns have recently made a big come-back and, as an alternative to hanging wallpaper, a wall can be treated as a giant painter's canvas with stripes, circles, and squares of color.

Making a swatch board

Not only is this a useful exercise, but it is also great fun. It will help you to make the right choices if you are dealing with something tangible. Begin with your source of inspiration, whether this is a scrap of fabric, a postcard, or a photograph you took on vacation. Place this on a white background to isolate the colors. Take it with you to the paint store, and collect sample paint swatches that match, harmonize or contrast with it. Look at several different manufacturers' ranges as the colors vary a lot.

Painted swatches

If your budget stretches to it, then also look at specialized ranges where the colors and finishes are often more unusual. Look out for painted swatches, which are far more accurate than the printed versions. If you are sensitive to chemicals, or simply wish to follow an environmentally kinder route, then send away for the "greener" paint companies' color cards.

Once you have found your colors, buy sample pots and paint them onto a piece of white board (at least 12 in. sq./30 cm sq.) so you can see what the color looks like, and whether it is true to the color card. Placing the board opposite the window, and in a dark corner, will help you judge whether you could go lighter or darker without changing the color. See what it looks like with the things that you are not planning to change in the room as well.

Take the color swatch with you when choosing fabric, wallpaper, and carpets. Get samples of anything you like and put them together on the swatchboard. Once you have carpet, fabric, and wallpaper, you will be able to see how the textures affect the colors. Refer back to your original inspiration and compare the colors to the ones that inspired you in the first place. If you haven't managed to find the right colors and you have

time for more research, then you just need to keep looking. There are more paint companies out there than you think, and it is usually the smaller, more specialty shops that deal in the desirable, unusual colors.

RIGHT: **This swatch board was created for a long sunny sitting room with a dining area at one end. The two main colors were used to homogenize the space; differences in texture defined the areas. A detailed swatch board like this makes it easier to visualize the finished room.**

Bringing it all together

When you have established your basic color scheme (walls, ceiling, flooring, woodwork, soft furnishings), you can experiment with other textures, patterns, and colors for the accessories. It may be that a very muted color scheme needs a vibrant accent of color to set it off, or conversely that a gaudy background cries out for a plain neutral rug or sofa. A newly painted bare room can look unbearably bright until all your possessions are back in place. Walls can be broken up with pictures, lighting, and shelves, and key wall colors can be picked up on small items like vases, picture frames, cushions, and lampshades to create a more unified color scheme.

A beautiful room

Above is an example of the successful use of color in interior design. The walls are warm yellow-green; the same shade appears in the landscape painting. The pictures are hung along a level base line. The natural yellow pine floor is highly polished to reflect and enhance the natural light, and the rug frames the sleeping area. The off-white grid pattern of the rug diffuses the intense indigo blue, creating another level of low-key pattern and color interest. The bed linen in a contrast of muted gray/white stripe and hot salmon pink is a seductive focal point. The shapes of the spiky bulrushes and the black lamp balance each other perfectly.

This room is a wonderful example of harmony, balance, and style.

The influences
of color

Color has a strong role to play in our lives, and can affect us
both physically and psychologically. This chapter explores the ways
different colors make us feel, and how a deeper understanding can
help us to make positive use of this powerful tool. In the short term it
can lift our spirits or help us to feel instantly relaxed, and in the long
term it can be life-enhancing and even healing. We may change the
colors of our surroundings as an outward display of our personalities
and preferences—this chapter offers a
deeper understanding of color selection.

Psychology of color

Color affects our state of mind; some even believe in its power to cure illness. Whether or not you believe in the more cosmic theories about color, there is certainly scientific proof that color can warm us up or cool us down. Using obvious literal associations, sunshine yellow makes us feel warm and deep blue cools us down. When the eye sees that lovely yellow, the brain interprets and associates it with warm sunshine, and the opposite happens with a cool icy blue—it's mind over matter.

Facts and feelings

A scientific experiment involved a control group spending time at the same level of activity in the same workroom, painted first in cold colors and then in warm colors. The room temperature was gradually lowered; the level at which the people first felt cold was 52°F/11°C in the red-orange room and 59°F/15°C in the blue-green room. It was concluded that color has the power to increase or decrease the circulation. This research shows that it makes sense to paint a cold room in warm colors.

Scientists and psychologists have studied the subconscious aspects of color's influence for many years. Colors have both positive and negative associations—the positive side of yellow is warmth and sunshine, but it can also represent jealousy and cowardice. There are different cultural associations too—yellow is associated with spirituality in Buddhist countries, while in the Muslim world the holy color is green. In France red symbolizes masculinity, but elsewhere masculine is shown as blue.

Everyone understands that the expression "feeling blue" means feeling unhappy, in the same way that "seeing red" explains a feeling of rage. Other colors associated with moods and emotions are "green with envy," "in the pink" (feeling flushed with good health)—and who can forget "mellow yellow"?

Color therapists believe in the healing power of colored light. The treatment involves shining colored lights on to the affected part of the body, with each color having its own specialized area of healing activity. Color is used for emotional, physical, and spiritual healing, often in combination with crystals, astrology, acupuncture, and traditional Eastern healing techniques.

If you paint a cold room in a warm color, such as red, you will create a room that is psychologically warm—it will be associated with flames, heat, and fire.

Color associations

RED
- love • life • power • flames • heat
- rubies • roses • berries • blood
- danger • strength • hot chiles
- fire engines • sealing wax • Christmas
- revolution • sex • cherries

ORANGE
- oranges • tangerines • Chinese lanterns
- pumpkins • clay • lentils • spices
- goldfish • marigolds • sunsets
- terra cotta • fall leaves
- amber • marmalade • rust

BLACK AND WHITE
- the 1920s • the 1960s • tiled floors
- newsprint • photography
- chess boards • piano keys
- penguins

GREEN
- grass • leaves • ferns • cool • calm
- sea • hills • ecology • planet • growth
- tea • peppers • olives • avocados
- lizards • cacti • vegetables
- mint ice cream

AQUA AND TURQUOISE
- oceans • dreams • imagination
- sensitivity • freshness • vacations
- summer • mountain streams
- Navajo jewellery • Ancient Egypt

BLUE
- sea • sky • freshness • mountains
- cold • aquamarines • sapphires
- sadness • bluebells • ribbons • jeans
- berries • birds • heaven • duck eggs
- intelligence • calm

PURPLE
- robes • violets • plums • heather
- heliotrope • eggplants • passion
- sky • lilac • lavender • mourning
- luxury • grapes • psychics
- the 1960s

PALE PINK
- softness • baby girls • face powder
- meringues • sugared almonds
- strawberry ice cream • piglets • roses
- clouds • candy floss • fresh plaster
- sea shells

HOT PINK
- passion • heat • tropics
- celebrations • exotic flowers
- lipstick • Indian saris
- spices • seaside rock
- lobsters

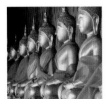

METALLICS
- wealth • glamour • worship
- marriage • opulence • celebration
- luxury • solidity • weight • shimmer
- good luck

YELLOW
- sunshine • gold • straw • saffron
- bananas • custard • daffodils
- canaries • primroses • warmth
- ducklings • the moon

BROWN
- wood • coffee • chocolate • dogs
- horses • toffee • mushrooms • earth
- comfort • security • skin • velvet
- nuts • cookies

Calming and Relaxing
Aqua and Turquoise

Aqua and turquoise fall between blue and green, and carry with them all the positive aspects of those two colors. Aqua takes its name from the greenish blue of shallow water where the sea meets the sand, and shares it with a transparent gemstone of the same color. Turquoise is the blue-green color of an opaque semiprecious stone found in the Arizona Desert. Although the two colors are similar and often confused, one is fluid and transparent and the other opaque and solid. The blue-greens are highly adaptable and look good both inside and outdoors, where their sparkle is not diminished by bright sunlight. Aqua is the more dreamy of the two colors, and looks especially good with colors that have similar relaxing properties, such as the whole range of lavenders. This is a favorite color for bathrooms, and cosmetic products are often packaged in shades of aqua for those wanting a coordinated look.

Aqua and Turquoise:
Great Combinations

Turquoise blue looks soft in pastel shades, and light turquoise has a contemporary edge when combined with rich earthy brown. Full-strength turquoise is best used on small areas where it packs a punch teamed with its complementary red-orange. Other earthy colors that look good with it are ocher yellow and sienna red. Aqua works well for large areas, especially with a textured broken or chalky paint finish. In contrast, pale warm pink and terra cotta suit it very well—and it looks great with icy sky-blue woodwork.

Naturally calm

The water in this mountain lake looks the purest transparent aquamarine. The clarity is a result of the fresh water being so clean and calm that it becomes a perfect reflector of the sky above. The pine trees around the edge of the lake are also reflected in the water and so add green to the blue, giving the water its aquamarine color.

COLOR KEY

1 Prussian blue
2 Aqua
3 Apple
4 Pale lavender blue

Creating riches

These decorative papier-mâché containers have been painted with a combination of green and blue paint to create a rich turquoise effect. The color can vary greatly, from a pale watery green to an intense bright blue. The effect is often lighter and purer if the colors are applied separately in glazes or washes rather than being premixed. Metallic gold is the perfect complement to shimmering turquoise.

COLOR KEY

1 Cobalt blue
2 Duck egg blue
3 Deep aqua
4 Hot pink

Tropical tones

The color of the sea surrounding this tropical island is the most brilliant turquoise blue. The sand below is white and in the shallows the color lightens to a pale aquamarine. These are the romantic colors of castaways, vacations, and dreams.

COLOR KEY

1 Aqua
2 Turquoise
3 Cobalt blue

Aqua and Turquoise:
Setting the Mood

Aqua as the main color in a room gives it a cool, modern quality without any sense of there being a chill in the air. The touch of yellow in turquoise blue warms and mellows it, making it a very comfortable color to live with. These colors are restful for our eyes and flattering to plain, uncluttered spaces. Keep to harmonizing colors to preserve a restful atmosphere, or add a splash of complementary orange as a visual wake-up call. Aqua, yellow ocher and terra cotta create a warm Tuscan mood.

A touch of drama

This kitchen with aqua blue units and matching shades set against a warm cream background is a good example of uncluttered, contemporary style. The strong ultramarine blue tiling adds depth with a flash of brilliance and the bright bowl of peppers provides a strong color focal point. This is a good example of how dramatic but temporary colors of fruit or flowers can be introduced to create a new dynamic in a room. The calming aqua is the main feature, with the jazzy color of the peppers appearing in a cameo role.

COLOR KEY

1 Shaker blue
2 Aqua green
3 Creamy white

Clouds of color

The intense aqua color on the wall behind the lovely Art Nouveau style fireplace below has been created by applying an emerald green glaze over a blue latex base coat, using a technique that is called "clouding." The glaze is spread with a soft cloth in a semicircular motion to make subtle cloud-like shapes. The transparent color glaze adds depth without obscuring the blue. The purple thistles and bright blue vase add lively sparks of color to the black and white mantelpiece.

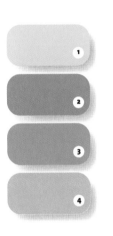

COLOR KEY

1 Pale aqua
2 Purple
3 Shaker blue
4 Mauve pink

Simply aqua

The all-over aqua blue, ceiling lights, and spiky-leaved desert plants give the room above the underwater atmosphere of an aquarium. The furniture style is ideally suited to the room. Imagine this setting in a house in the desert and you will appreciate the powerful influence that color has on our senses. Stepping out of the heat and into this room would be instantly cooling and calming.

COLOR KEY

1 Aqua
2 Sage
3 Deep salmon
4 Warm gray

Soothing and Rejuvenating
Pale Pink

Pale pink brings a warm glow into any room. The color is associated with sweetness and innocence and it is a life color, a signal of health and well-being. Pink is well-suited for use over large areas. Its character is influenced by other colors—with dove gray, it is sophisticated; with pale lemon yellow, white, and powder blue, it is nursery soft; but with faded aqua and terra cotta red, it is typically Mediterranean. Pink is the natural color of freshly plastered walls, a warm earthy pink with a rustic character that is enhanced by deeper terra cotta shades, natural wood, and deep greens. Mixed with verdigris and ocher, it is reminiscent of faded pink villas on Tuscan hillsides. Rosy pink is softer and sweeter, the color of cascades of rambling roses around cottage doorways. Pink can be very bold and striking in the deeper salmon shades that are tinged with orange.

Pale Pink: **Pleasing the Senses**

It is easiest to imagine a color when we have several sensory references. We recall the taste, smell, appearance, sound, and texture and create a perfect image in our mind's eye. It is impossible to think of sweet peas without also conjuring up their scent. Each of these pale pinks tickles the senses in a different way. Rose pink mixes well with deeper reds, white, sky blue, and pale and mid green. Salmon pink, black and cream create a smart look. Pale pink looks equally delicious in chalky distemper paint or high gloss.

Purely pink

The shape and texture of a meringue are unique. These sculptural mixtures of sugar and frothy egg whites set hard and crisp but dissolve at first bite into a chalky crumbling sweetness. The color is a pale and pure mix of white sugar tinted with pink food coloring that always looks like the prize exhibit in the bakery window.

COLOR KEY

1 Plaster pink
2 Rosy pink
3 Salmon
4 Cool pale pink

Sweet inspiration

Sugared almonds in a bowl almost look as if they could have been laid by an exotic bird rather than made in a candy factory. The set sugar coating has the smooth glazed appearance of marble and the pink seems to be tinted with a touch of cool blue. The paint equivalent of the surface is a satin finish that has a slight sheen but none of the vulgarity of a full gloss. This pink looks lovely alongside other pale pastels and white.

COLOR KEY

1 Pale lemon
2 Pale lavender
3 Rosy pink

Baby soft

Only the softest of fabrics should be used to wrap up a tiny baby, and this pale pink blanket conjures up those delicate first months of life. It is a color of life and of gentle energy.

COLOR KEY

1 Pale soft pink
2 Rosy pink
3 Pale pink

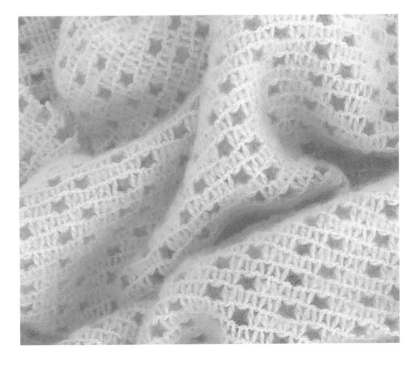

Pale Pink: **Soft or Sophisticated**

Pale pink is an undemanding color to live with and is useful for softening hard edges and creating a rosy glow. It is an adaptable background color that feels equally at home in the nursery or the office. Baby pink looks sweet with white or cream and other pastel shades, but it can also look sophisticated alongside steel gray, or funky with a sharp lime green or turquoise. Pale pink with black shouts 1950s glamour, pink gingham has a cute French style, and plaster pink is popular in the Country Style palette.

COLOR KEY

1 Pale ocher yellow
2 Orange sorbet
3 Plaster pink
4 Hot pink

Deliciously pink

This is a beautiful combination of pink and pale blonde wood that conjures up a vision of a strawberry ice cream with a fan-shaped wafer. The creamy pink is warmed by the soft light from above and by the reflected yellow tones of the wood. The chalky mat black pot adds a third but unobtrusive color to this harmonious combination. The pale yellow twig arrangement is a perfect color match for the wooden doors and their scratch patterned frame echoes the shape of the twigs.

Cool pink

Pale pink is given a contemporary treatment here by being teamed with gray woodwork and a simple pale pink curtain. The three pendant lights with brilliant blue glass shades create a cool modern look and the color is picked up with the arrangement of blue glass on the window ledge.

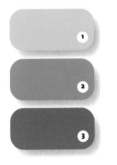

COLOR KEY

1 Plaster pink
2 Deep turquoise
3 Ultramarine

Pretty in pink

It would be difficult not to feel soothed and pampered in this pretty room. The walls are painted a very soft shell pink that reflects a soft pink glow onto the white bedstead. The bed linen is a mixture of harmonious pink and white stripes and florals.

COLOR KEY

1 Shell pink
2 Pale creamy yellow
3 Rose pink

Passionate
Hot Pink

Passionate pink is hot, feminine, and spicy, a courageous choice that will grant a room instant sex appeal and vitality. In nature it is the color of brilliant desert cactus flowers, where maximum visibility is needed to attract pollinating insects; it is also seen in luscious bougainvillea trailing down whitewashed villa walls around the Mediterranean. Pigments of the color have been made in India and the Far East for centuries, giving it an exotic appeal to Westerners. The intensity of hot pink is seen at its best in Indian saris, Chinese silks, and shimmering satins. Needless to say, it is the perfect color for a love nest, but it is also a fun color to use in other rooms. Hot pink will appear to shrink a room, so it should only be used where that is the desired effect. In the East pink is often used with gold, but this should be done sparingly, or the effect will be too brash. Keep the heat turned full on by mixing pink with other strong colors.

Hot Pink: **Causing a Sensation**

Walls painted with hot pink will advance to make a room look smaller. The pink will be "grounded" and the room's original proportions restored if pale moss green is used on the woodwork—these colors work very well together. Hot pink with other jewel-bright colors like purple, emerald, and peacock blue creates a vibrant ethnic look. Patterns of swirls, geometrics, and stylized flowers in hot pink, yellow, orange, apple green, and white proclaim an allegiance to 1970s' revival style.

Irresistibly pink

Bright passionate pink flowers are the first to catch the eye in the garden. The color leaps forward to demand attention and needs to be used with some discriminaton if it is not to overwhelm a flowerbed. Hot pink anemone flowers with their large fringed black centers set against feathery green foliage on succulent stems are a gorgeous sight and are not meant to be resisted.

COLOR KEY

1 Bright red
2 Hot pink
3 Violet
4 Racing green
5 Black

Slipping into pink

Inspiration can come from random color combinations. This bright pink slipper brings out similar tones in the floral rug, showing how the choice of an accessory color can influence the way we see a multicolored pattern. Our eyes seek out the matched color and it becomes more visually important than others in the pattern.

COLOR KEY

1 Hot pink
2 Shell pink
3 Mauve pink

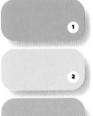

Exotic pink

This strong pink fabric embossed with a gold border and pattern motif was inspired by the beautiful saris worn by women in India. The hot pink originates from India, where the skill of manufacturing brilliantly colored dyes predates that of Western civilization by thousands of years.

COLOR KEY

1 Hot pink
2 Golden yellow
3 Creamy yellow

Hot Pink: **Some Like it Hot**

Hot pink is a tropical color most at home in brilliant sunshine, surrounded by other vibrant colors. Think of an Indian street scene with the women's saris a riot of clashing colors. Or South America, where woven textiles are colored with natural dyes to produce the most brilliant range of colors, including a startlingly vibrant pink. Outside the tropics this color is best suited for use in a room where there is limited natural daylight or where the room is mainly used in the evenings.

Perfect harmony

In this very feminine room the walls have been painted in the most brilliant shade of pink and then softened by using pink, white, and lavender floral prints to diffuse the impact of the shocking pink. The same bright pink appears in all the prints so that the effect is entirely harmonious.

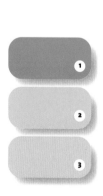

COLOR KEY

1 Hot pink
2 Pale lavender
3 Pale mauve pink

Pink shock

Hot pink hits you right between the eyes. Also called shocking pink, it is one of the most energetic colors you can buy in a can. Ten years ago the color was impossible to find but now it is all the rage and most paint companies have produced a version of it. Children adore this color; it is slightly wicked yet feels very positive and full of fun.

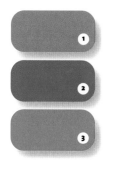

COLOR KEY

1 Bright red
2 Bright purple
3 Hot pink

Tots to teens

The hot pink walls in this young girl's bedroom give it a funky style that is extremely popular at the moment. The accessories and soft furnishings are perfect for the under-tens and with a strong color such as this one you always have the welcome option of giving it a more teenage look with new accessories and bed linen when the time comes.

COLOR KEY

1 Hot pink
2 Warm pink
3 Palest pink

Bright and Lively
Red

Red makes a powerful statement. It is the color of lifeblood and the center of a flame; of danger, anger, excitement, strength, and fire. It is a powerful, alarming, extrovert color, associated with physical activity and passion. It can be aggressive, and has some negative associations. Red has many different characters. It can look innocent with white in a gingham check; rustic with orange and brown; seductive as satin and velvet; or cheerful in candy stripes. Red is a favorite color in Western folk art, where the heart and the rose are popular motifs. In the Far East, red and gold are used in ceremonies. Decorating with red needs careful consideration, but that is no reason to avoid it. Red is an attention-seeker, good for details and accessories. Red stimulates the appetite, making it ideal for a dining room. It has traditionally been the color of love and sex, so it may be perfect for a bedroom if sleeping is the last thing on your mind!

Red: **Attention Seeker**

Red gives out a signal and demands attention. We use red as a warning color to indicate imminent danger but red in nature is more likely to suggest ripeness. Red can be a delicious color and perhaps our decorating should be inspired by visions of a pile of red strawberries surrounded by a moat of cream. Red draws our eyes to it so that anything red will be the first thing we notice in a room. If this effect is too powerful for everyday use, save it for a special occasion when a vase of red flowers will give an instant impact.

Stunning sunset

A sunset like this is one of those precious moments when it is impossible to ignore the breathtaking truth that we are living on a planet in space warmed by the heat of a burning fireball. Everyday life in the Western world may conspire to have us forget this awe-inspiring fact, but somewhere out there, right now, the fiery red sun is setting in the inky blue sky.

COLOR KEY

1 Deep violet
2 Golden yellow
3 Scarlet
4 Pure red

Chile hot

The rich red of these chile peppers provides a clue to their nature. These are burning pods of fire to be handled with care. The beauty of red chile peppers has always been appreciated in countries like Mexico where they are strung up like bunting to dry in the sun. If your kitchen needs warming up, a string of chile peppers could do the trick.

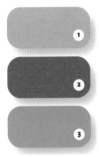

COLOR KEY

1 Orange
2 Pure red
3 Deep lime green

Red alert

When birds wish to be noticed, they smarten up their plumage and this scarlet ibis would be unmissable on land or in the air. A flash of a scarlet cushion, lampshade, or bowl of bright red flowers will attract the eye in just the same way.

COLOR KEY

1 Rich red
2 Hot pink

Red: **Going Red**

Decorating a room in red is making a statement. Pure scarlet is red at its brightest, full of youth, and fun. It's the red of checkered tablecloths, tomato-shaped ketchup dispensers, and 1950s diner-style barstools. Red-brown has a more comforting effect in the form of the natural red of quarry-tiled floors and polished mahogany. Deep crimson red is richer and contains blues and browns to give it warm and cool aspects. It's a luxurious, sexy red that oozes relaxed comfort and confidence.

Red heat

Red, black, and orange create a hot mood in this bar area. The burnt orange ceiling and reflective red varnished floor intensify the hot pink wall, making the area pulsate with vibrant color. This is a sophisticated look, which says clearly that this is a place where the grown-ups come to play. The cane bar furniture is early 1960s in style, and the slatted wooden shades cleverly keep up the room's temperature by implying the need for shade.

COLOR KEY

1 Scarlet

2 Hot pink

3 Black

Cherry red

The red in this kitchen is the color of ripe cherries. The gloss painted surface picks up all the irregularities in the old plaster and the shape of the wooden panels, while also reflecting the creamy yellow tiles and chrome chair. A deep red such as this benefits from a gloss finish, which has the effect of knocking it back where it would otherwise advance. This is a brave color choice for a kitchen; it works extremely well here because of the room's proportions and the light that floods in through the tall window. Keeping to just two strongly contrasting colors makes a powerful statement.

COLOR KEY

1 Cherry red
2 Pale pistachio
3 White

Night and day

Red is a highly stimulating color, ideal for a home office where action is the name of the game. Working from home is convenient but you miss out on the transition travel period when you have time to adapt yourself from home to work mode. Red will signal the change-over in an instant. Red with cream is a more sophisticated color combination than red and white, and with this cleverly concealed office-in-a-cabinet, the room could easily convert into a cozy, intimate dining area for the evenings.

COLOR KEY

1 Rich red
2 Creamy white

Stimulating
Blue

Stimulating blue is cool, spatial, and invigorating.
Blue is associated with peace, masculinity, intuition, cleanliness, trust, authority, and intelligence. In some shades blue is balancing, calming, and rejuvenating. It absorbs light and makes a room appear considerably darker than it would if painted with a light-reflecting color such as yellow. Walls painted blue appear to recede, so put blue to work when space is at a premium. The eye perceives blue as having a blurred edge, so it is useful for softening hard edges in a room. Bright blue and white are a crisp combination because white sharpens up blue edges, while blue makes white look cleaner and brighter. Indoors, this combination needs a shot of balancing orange or golden yellow to warm it up. Blue is good to use outdoors, providing a resting place for the eyes in bright sunshine. The shade beneath blue parasols looks the coolest and most inviting of all.

Blue: **Heavenly Blue**

Pure bright blue is a heavenly color. It can freshen a space, making it feel cool and airy. It is a meditative color, good for focusing the mind on higher things. Pale blue is soft, relaxing, and gentle. Ultramarine is the deep intense blue of the night sky. Its depth can be disturbing and needs to be balanced with a warm, positive color such as gold, yellow, or orange. Blue mixes well with other colors, and the resulting shade may be interesting or unusual but it will never be unpleasant. Blue is the most popular color.

Sky, sea and sand

The deep, almost Prussian, blue sky and turquoise sea set against white sands present an example of how to decorate on a grand scale. The yellow starfish in the foreground provides a welcome color and textural contrast. To recreate this spatial effect in a room, make use of the receding quality of a deep blue with an advancing pale yellow.

COLOR KEY

1 Prussian blue
2 Pale mint
3 Aqua
4 Peachy pink

Country fresh

One of the most stunning sights in early summer are the acres/hectares of brilliant yellow rapeseed flowers set against a clear blue sky. The sky looks bluer and surrounding green fields look greener under the influence of this brilliant yellow. A bright yellow throw, shade, or tablecloth can similarly brighten all the colors in a room.

COLOR KEY

1 Deep pure blue
2 Primrose yellow
3 Bright leaf green

Shades of blue

The layered blues of this mountain scene have an intense unreal beauty. In the moments between day and night before the light fades, the blues in the landscape achieve their fullest intensity.

COLOR KEY

1 Light blue
2 French blue
3 Prussian blue

Blue: **Freshen Up**

Blue is the color to reach for when a room needs refreshing. Blue can brighten and expand a room and a small area of blue can make a big difference. The spatial qualities of blue are invaluable and the color gives the perception of a lower temperature, which makes it very useful for an office where it helps concentration and stimulates ideas. A blue kitchen will feel more comfortable when the heat is on and a blue bathroom will provide more refreshment than relaxation.

Blue contrast

Here is a room mostly decorated in the neutrals black, white, and gray, given an overall effect of being more colorful than it is by the introduction of two bright blue areas. The stimulating effect of blue is vividly illustrated by the column in the foreground and echoing block of blue at the far end of the room. The blue provides the room's energy and everything else revolves around it. The scarlet of the poppies is the exact complementary color to this blue.

COLOR KEY

1. Bright pure blue
2. Black
3. Scarlet
4. White

Bright blue

This is the bright blue of a beautiful cloudless Mediterranean sky, the deep end of the swimming pool, and the striped awnings outside a seaside café. Yellow and white look great beside it. Notice how the deep blue intensifies the color and the yellow attracts the eye and provides relief from the intensity of the blue. When using a strong color like this, it is always important to introduce a small area of another equally bright color to provide some visual balance.

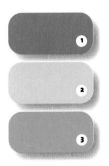

COLOR KEY

1 Pure blue
2 Lemon
3 Deep lime

Soothing space

The wood paneling and beautiful window make this a very special space indeed. The simple table and two chairs in natural pale wood look especially inviting surrounded by this beautiful shade of blue. This is a place to sit, talk, and share. The blue color scheme would create a similar effect if used on the interior of a conservatory or porch area, where you are protected from the elements and have the sense of being inside yet outside.

COLOR KEY

1 Ice blue
2 Soft aqua
3 Pale lavender

Energizing
Orange

Energizing orange is attractive, positive and full of zing; sociable, direct, creative, and secure. Orange is a warm, cheerful color, symbolizing prosperity, and both physical and mental energy. It is associated with brilliant fall leaves against blue skies and the warmth of leaping flames. Orange is light-reflective and can considerably increase both the light and our perception of warmth in a room. It is a good choice for entrance halls and rooms where people gather to socialize. The freshest shade of orange is the color of the skin of the ripe fruit. Bright orange can cause a sensory overload and needs balancing with a cool color such as aqua, blue, or green. The addition of white will remove most of orange's vivacious impact but none of its warmth, creating a more subtle, mellow color. Orange was all the rage in the 1920s and again in the 1970s, and orange is now back in fashion again.

Orange: **Outstanding orange**

Burnt orange is one of the richest natural earth colors. It is versatile and can mix with other deep natural pigments, or be the focal point in a sophisticated minimalist room. Sharp orange is vivacious. It refuses to be taken seriously and is the one to choose for a witty retro-fashion statement. Pale orange is a creamy, mellow color that is warm and welcoming. It feels hospitable and looks fabulous with its opposite number—icy blue. Pale orange's warmth matches the coolness of stainless steel, chrome, and glass.

Autumnal hues

Fall does not last very long but during those weeks, especially if skies are blue, we see some of the most stunning colors that nature has to offer. The sun is low in the sky and the leaves are lit up at tree level. A deciduous New England woodland like this one has every shade of orange leaves, from pale yellow right through to brilliant scarlet.

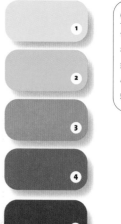

COLOR KEY

1. Custard yellow
2. Orange sorbet
3. Burnt orange
4. Brick red
5. Barn red

Hot and spicy

The spice colors of turmeric, paprika, and cayenne are warm and earthy. The bright orange-yellow turmeric is ground from a root and cayenne is powdered, dried chile peppers. These spices have been the most recent source of inspiration for paint colors in many shades of orange.

COLOR KEY

1 Paprika
2 Pure orange

Sun over Africa

This extraordinary picture of children herding cattle in the African sunset reveals the scale of the dry, flat landscape, about to be plunged into darkness. The sun dominates life in the semidesert, seeming larger and more brilliantly orange at sunset here than it is anywhere else on earth.

COLOR KEY

1 Luminous yellow
2 Burnt orange
3 Bright red

Orange: **Bold and Brave**

It comes as no surprise to find that orange is one of the favorite colors used by professional interior designers for living rooms and entrance halls. The color gives a room fresh energy and it is a choice that requires a certain amount of bravado. A designer's job is to have that sort of confidence and they know that if they can influence a client to have orange the room will be a great success. Orange may look brash in the can but it's great on walls and for soft furnishings.

Energetic orange

This is a good example of the way orange can work its magic in a room. The alcove shelving next to the fireplace here is functional and the objects on display are a very personal, homely collection with no coordinated style. It is the choice of broad orange and white striped fabric for the attractive curtain that makes the room rather interesting by adding a ripple of colorful energy.

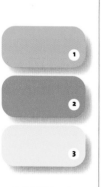

COLOR KEY

1 Earthy orange
2 Red/orange
3 Jersey cream

A warm welcome

The use of inviting, welcoming orange in an entrance hall immediately gives out the message that the occupants of the house are warm, friendly, sociable people who care about their environment and their friends. There is a suggestion of opulence in the elegant display of objects on the desk and the stunning flowers dramatically reflected in the ornate mirror behind.

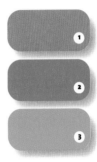

COLOR KEY

1 Cinnamon
2 Rose red
3 Warm orange

Full of bravado

The bravado of using so much orange in one room is justified by the resultant warmth, energy, and sense of security it provides. If you imagine this to be a cool basement apartment without any access to direct sunlight, then you will appreciate the power of color to radiate heat. This is a literally brilliant treatment for a cool dark room.

COLOR KEY

1 Sunflower yellow
2 Pale apricot
3 Pure orange
4 Deep orange

Serenity
Purple

Being surrounded by lilac and purple is said to help achieve serenity. Purple is linked to creativity and is favored by those living a Bohemian lifestyle. It is believed to have a negative influence on people with susceptible temperaments, so those prone to depression should avoid it. The color ranges between blue and red, with blue-violet at one end and maroon at the other. Violet is the darkest and deepest color of the spectrum. The more red a purple contains, the warmer it becomes. Deep purples are too heavy for large areas, but are good for adding depth, richness, and color accents to a room. Pale lilacs, lavenders, and violets have the opposite effect, and are excellent for walls and ceilings. Used in harmonious color schemes, their effect is cool but comfortable; they are ideal for bedrooms and studies. In a room used for sociable activities, the colors work best with warm contrasts, such as earthy oranges and deep yellows.

Purple: **Sumptuous Purple**

Royal purple is the color of robes and pageantry. It is associated with wealth and luxury of the highest order. The look and feel of silk, velvet, and satin are well-suited to purple. Violet is the deepest spectrum color. Decorating with this color indicates confidence with contemporary style. Lavender is a soft pale purple, which is infused with relaxing meditative powers. It can be masculine or feminine, and is enhanced by the proximity of blues and greens.

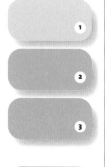

COLOR KEY

1 Cool pale lavender
2 Pinky mauve
3 Lilac

Lovely lilac

The lilac blossom is one of the first memorable garden scents of early summer. The flowers appear in many shades of purple from almost white to the deepest rich violet, warm purple, and pink. The leaves are pale yellow-green and glossy. Let nature inspire your choice of colors.

Night skies

Red sky at night produces wonderful color effects as the sun sets over the blue sea. Purple waves are a rare and extraordinary sight. This depth and range of liquid colors would be impossible to replicate in paint, but the colors could be introduced using iridescent fabrics like moiré satin or silk.

COLOR KEY

1 Dusky blue
2 Lilac
3 Pale aqua
4 Sand yellow

Lavender blue

A lavender field in full bloom presents one of the most attractive views of cultivated land. The bushes are grown in rows giving the effect of a very large purple quilt when seen from a distance. The smell is heavenly and should definitely be included to enhance the atmosphere as part of any lavender color scheme.

COLOR KEY

1 Deepest lavender
2 Bright apple green
3 Deep avocado green

Purple: **Purple Trends**

In Victorian times purple was considered to be the color of mourning, and this association took a long time to wear off. It was in the Swinging Sixties that purple first became associated with youthful rebellion and rock 'n' roll. It graduated into mainstream fashion and decorating, usually in muted shades of eggplant. Purple is back on top of the adventurous decorator's list now, thanks to TV make-over programs. It is a color to use boldly to make a statement or in small amounts to add drama to a neutral color scheme.

Stress relief

These walls have been treated with the most effective stress-busting color of all. This deep lavender purple is associated with the mind's higher thoughts and meditations. If your office environment needs to be more focused and less frantic, then this is the color to choose. The combination of deep color for the walls, pale natural wooden furniture, and an efficient open storage system gives the office a cool, contemporary look.

COLOR KEY

1. Lilac
2. Pale pink
3. Lavender blue

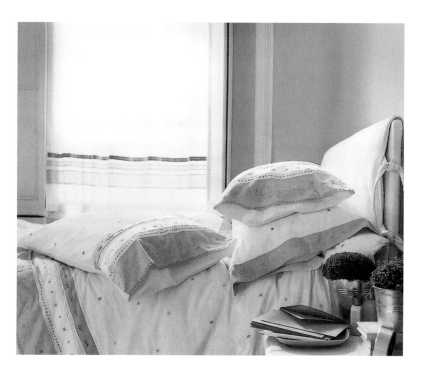

Lilac echoes

The placing of one color alongside another will always influence the way it looks. The color of the bedroom walls here is picked up on the border of the bedlinen along with bands of soft aqua and pink. The white separates the colors ensuring that they remain pure and fresh.

COLOR KEY

1 Lilac
2 Bright rose pink
3 Light bright turquoise

Cool kitchen

This vast old kitchen with its high ceiling has been transformed in a contemporary homely style with a coat of lilac paint. The combination of lilac, cherry red, and white with chrome and stainless steel gives the room a cool youthful style that mixes current fashion with 1950s revival. The color is affected by its neighbors, looking pale near white and more magenta alongside the red. It appears most intense in the shaded areas where it deepens to a much richer shade of violet. Lilac is tremendously popular and the stores are filled with lilac accessories and soft furnishings.

COLOR KEY

1 Lavender
2 Pale lilac
3 Deep salmon pink

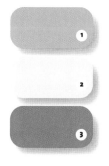

Sociable
Yellow

Yellow is a color that makes us feel happy. It glows and reflects light, which makes it a useful color for rooms with a northerly aspect. It is the brightest of the true colors and carries with it all the positive qualities of brilliance and light. Symbolically, yellow is associated with intellect, understanding, and knowledge. Yellow is strongly affected by the colors used alongside it—with black it is at its most luminous; with violet it looks hard; with orange it appears purer; and with green it radiates life and energy. Yellow and blue can be an uncomfortable combination unless the shade of blue is softened with gray. Red and yellow are celebratory colors. Use yellow in a large kitchen where meals are prepared and served—you will be guaranteed a lively atmosphere at meal times. In a playroom it will encourage generosity and good behavior, and in a work room it will encourage imagination, creativity, and communication.

Yellow: **Warm and Friendly**

Sunshine yellow radiates warmth, confidence, and goodwill. This effect is intensified and energized by a glossy reflective surface. Pale primrose yellow has a soft feminine character. Deep mustard yellow is heavy and rich, a match for powerful colors like scarlet and purple. Creamy custard yellow goes with everything—it is comforting, warm, friendly, and unchallenging. Lemon yellow has a hint of sharp green in it, and brilliance but no warmth. Its coolness can impart an air of sophistication, especially when used with black.

Mellow yellow

Banana yellow can be tinged with green or dotted with brown. The banana itself is a pale, creamy yellow and it is the skin color that grabs the attention. The color has none of the brashness of golden yellow or coolness of citrus yellow. This color must be the original mellow yellow.

1

2

3

COLOR KEY

1 Deep orange

2 Golden yellow

3 Sharp yellow

Floral tones

The fragile perfection of yellow rose petals is not easy to capture with a paint color. The outer petals are pale and translucent, while the closely furled inner petals have a richer, deeper color. A fresh bunch of yellow roses will brighten any room.

COLOR KEY

1 Jersey cream
2 Pale spring green
3 Golden yellow

Soft as down

Ducklings are a wonderfully pure, soft yellow. The downy texture lets the light shine through the young feathers and reveal their delicacy and softness. To paint walls this softest shade of yellow, begin with a mid-tone of yellow as a base coat, then apply a pale yellow using a dry brush and random short strokes to imitate the texture. Keep the effect subtle and the brush strokes light.

COLOR KEY

1 Orange-yellow
2 Lemon curd
3 Palest apricot

Yellow: **Convivial Color**

Decorating a room with yellow is like sending out an "open house" invitation. This color is associated with warmth, goodwill, and sociability. It is very reflective and on a bright day will infuse a room with yellow light. Earthy yellow is warm and looks good in a farmhouse setting or a sophisticated living room, while primrose yellow is fresh and suits a light, airy contemporary style. Citrus yellow is the coolest shade with a lime green cast. It's sharp as a lemon and works well with bold contrasts. Each yellow is unique but all are convivial.

Instant sunshine

Corridors, passageways, and entrance halls seldom have a natural light source—unless there is a skylight in the roof. These are areas to make the best use of yellow's light-enhancing properties. The brilliant yellow here has been used on the walls and ceiling to maximize its power, and the space vibrates with color. The tulips are an extravagance, but the effect is dazzling.

COLOR KEY

1 Pure orange
2 Sunshine yellow
3 Creamy white

Colorful fun

Have some fun and celebrate the spectacular contrasts of shocking pink and bright yellow. Turquoise is the true complementary contrast here, but with an overpowering blast of color like this it is difficult to pick out any one color as dominant. The effect of yellow here is to brighten all the other colors.

COLOR KEY

1 Hot pink
2 Scarlet
3 Pale peach
4 Citrus yellow

Attract a crowd

A kitchen this size will always be a social space where friends and family gather to chat over cups of coffee or to watch as the meal is prepared. The walls are a rich buttercup yellow that looks light and airy next to the solid natural wood cabinets and granite work surface. The stainless steel and chrome add sparkle and the balancing color is picked up with the large mauve pompon alliums. A kitchen yellow will always attract company.

COLOR KEY

1 Pistachio
2 Custard yellow
3 Bright mauve
4 Violet blue

Harmonizing
Green

Harmonizing green is the color of youth, growth, ecology, relaxation, balance, recovery, and optimism. It connects us to nature. Green soothes disturbed emotions and provides restful sleep, which makes it the ideal color for a bedroom. It is a favorite color in hospitals. Green is the perfect foil for most other colors, but when using several greens together it is best to keep to light and dark tones of the same green. Sea green and olive, for instance, make a sickly combination, as do yellow green and pine. Although green is a cool color, it will not make a room feel cold so long as there are some warm contrasts. The lighter greens feel most youthful, refreshing, and full of positive energy, just like new growth in springtime. They look good in a contemporary-style room with plum-purple and chocolate-brown. Olive, moss, lime, and lichen are other unusual shades of green with a contemporary edge.

Green: **Nature's Color**

Sage is a soft green-gray which is very easy on the eye—a most restful, cool, meditative color. Sage itself is the herb associated with wisdom and memory. Muddy green is thought to be depressing because of its associations with decay in nature, and lime green can induce feelings of nausea. Leaf green is the color of new shoots, full of freshness, hope, and energy. Pine green can be cold unless brightened with strong contrasts. A deep green looks good with burnt orange and cream.

Fern effects

This cool and shady forest scene is filled with green—some shades are so deep they appear as black. The five-fingered ferns in the foreground create a three-dimensional effect with their fresh light color against the deep green background. This idea could be used on a wall with a receding dark green as a background and a light-infused yellow-green leaf stencil as a pattern.

COLOR KEY

1 Forest green
2 Leaf green
3 Light leaf green

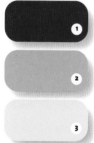

Fabulously fruity

The shine on the surface of a buffed green apple is always quite enticing and provides us with a clue as to how to make the most of this color. A flat mat green will always be more of a pea soup than an apple color. Lift the green with a reflective glossy varnish or provide shimmering accessories to lighten its mood.

COLOR KEY

1 Apple green
2 Pale fern

Lush green

What could be greener than green frogs seen through a lush green leaf in the jungle? Using inspiration like this for your color schemes is a lot more fun than choosing from a paint card. To create a luminous green like the leaf color, apply a strong lemon yellow beneath a wash or glaze of fresh green. The yellow will illuminate the green from below.

COLOR KEY

1 Tropical green
2 Yellow green
3 Light avocado

Green: **Simple Harmony**

The "green room" in a theater is the place where actors relax before a performance, and although not always literally green any more, the color association remains. To appreciate green's harmonizing effect, think of a garden filled with many different colored flowers. It is the green foliage around all these colors that lets them blend so well together. Use green in the same way when you decorate, and you will find that the results are invariably harmonious.

Cool and calm

This small home office area has been created from a "dead space" between rooms in a small apartment. Painting walls, ceiling, and woodwork in shades of olive green has defined the space and made another room. The combination of olive tones and chrome are cool and contemporary and the area has a calm, concentrated atmosphere.

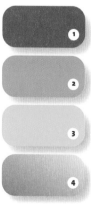

COLOR KEY

1 Deep avocado
2 Olive
3 Fresh green
4 Silver grey

Mix and match

Here a background yellow provides a perfect foil for the many shades of green in this room. The rustic style of the green dresser is echoed in the handpainted wall pattern, which in turn resembles the open pattern of the metal furniture. Mixing greens can be difficult, but here it has been successfully achieved by limiting the room palette to just two harmonious colors.

COLOR KEY

1 Light apple green
2 Mustard yellow
3 Yellow-green

Good companions

Green can be a difficult color to match, but when brown is used alongside it the task is made easier. Brown is green's companion in nature, and it has a mellowing effect, easing out the minor differences in tone and intensity of two shades of green. Here the boldness of the wallpaper design is balanced by the elegant simplicity of the chairs and the splendid cactus centerpiece.

COLOR KEY

1 Pale sage
2 Deep avocado
3 Barn red
4 Brick red

Comforting
Brown

Comforting brown is the color of so many of the good

things in life—polished wood, leather, crumbly earth, dogs and

horses, freshly baked bread, coffee beans, and chocolate.

It is a color of great variations, but is always warm. Brown appears in

most rooms as the color of polished wood, but is often not credited as

being a part of the color scheme. Brown dominated homes in

World War II, in a very drab way. In the 1970s, orange

and brown was the hippest combination, and right

now brown is back in fashion as a part of the natural palette.

Use dark brown in an eco-style room with soft sap green, taupe,

and olive; or mix contemporary dark wooden furniture with pale

jade and deep plum walls. Deep chocolate brown and cream striped

walls look delicious in a dining room, and red-brown

floor tiles infuse a kitchen with warmth.

Brown: **Nature and Nurture**

Brown is the color of the earth, rocks, roots, and tree trunks. We associate brown with stability, comfort, warmth, and nurture. The natural browns around us vary a great deal, but paint charts usually offer little choice. The best way to get the brown you want is to have a color specially mixed. Your color match could be anything from driftwood to a mushroom. A flat brown looks better than one with a sheen and the color is more suited to an opaque fabric with some texture than a sheer fabric.

Feel-good

Chocolate contains a unique blend of feel-good chemicals which most of us find difficult to resist. Although the texture and delicious aroma present a problem, the warm color of chocolate can translate into wall, floor, and furnishing colors to give a similarly comforting effect.

COLOR KEY

1 Rich brown
2 Brick red
3 Copper brown

Back to nature

The pine cone is one of mother nature's designer objects that falls from the trees and begs to be put on display in our homes. Pine cones are perfectly formed and have a fresh forest scent. They are rich in natural oils, which deepen their color, and they fade to become paler as they dry out. A display of pine cones in a basket or pot creates a sculptural focal point in a room, especially when the room's color scheme is inspired by nature.

COLOR KEY

1 Chocolate
2 Deep rose
3 Soft grey

Urban chic

The color of coffee beans is a sharper, fresher, redder brown than cocoa. At its purest it is lively and exciting but like the drink it becomes more mellow when diluted with white to a creamy latte shade. This is a sophisticated urban brown.

COLOR KEY

1 Mahogany
2 Dusky rose
3 Dark chocolate

Brown: **Brown is Back**

Brown is always to be seen in wooden objects, floors, doors, and furniture, but as a decorating color it is either the height of fashion or not used at all. It was huge in the 1970s when everything from bathroom suites to sheets, carpets, and curtains was brown. It became ubiquitous and was forced into hibernation for two decades, but now it's back. It fits well with the popular natural decorating style. It looks good with khaki greens and creams and also bright tropical colors and cool shades of lilac and turquoise.

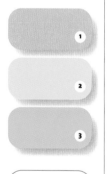

COLOR KEY

1 Soft rose pink
2 Palest peach
3 Tuscan yellow

Calm and neutral

The cool suede-look wall is actually a sand finish painted in a soft shade of mushroom brown, creating the perfect background for the contemporary style of bedroom furniture. The pale curved and polished wood presents an interesting textural contrast to the roughened wall and the overall effect is extremely calm, neutral, and natural.

Textural delight

Coffee-brown walls in this stylish kitchen are a deliciously textured background for the stained wooden fitted kitchen. The room features many shades of brown with an interesting mixture of brickwork, beams, and natural wooden floorboards. Everything coordinates, yet the brown does not overpower owing to the textural interest and superb natural light.

COLOR KEY

1 Dusky pink
2 Shell pink
3 Coffee brown

Tasteful tones

This elegantly proportioned room is blessed with a good natural light source and fine floorboards. Chocolate brown is a very sophisticated color choice as a background to this room where every object confirms the owners' good taste and design sense. The rich warm polished pine floor forms a harmonizing base for the colonial style cane and polished wooden furniture. The rich brown walls manage to create a sense of intimacy in a very large room.

COLOR KEY

1 Bitter chocolate
2 Palest lilac
3 Creamy custard

Sophistication
Black and White

Black and white present such a strong contrast that they are used over large areas only by the very brave. Black and white became popular in the late 1950s and early 1960s, when artists painted their studios white to reflect the light, and young people adopted the style for their homes. This style is still as cool as ever. The dramatic effect of black and white can be stark and cold unless handled with sensitivity. The secret of success is to have lots of colorful ethnic artefacts and interesting paintings to display against the pure white background. Japanese style is gaining popularity in the West and, although the black used is often a very dark brown and the white has the slightly yellow cast of unbleached paper, the style is one of stark contrasts. The Japanese have perfected the art of minimalism and use very few pieces of exquisitely shaped furniture whose shape is revealed by the sharp contrasts between the dark objects and their light background.

Artistic balance

This bathroom feels light, airy, and balanced with heavy black low down and pure light-reflecting white everywhere else. Black is the best choice for blending shapes and masking unwanted features such as exposed pipework. Here black and white have been used to make a very simple but artistic style statement.

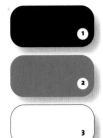

COLOR KEY

1 Black
2 Bright French blue
3 White

Simply striking

Black and white is a sophisticated choice for a kitchen where any color deviation will become the center of attention. Food packaging is designed to be noticed and has no place here, so everything is hidden behind closed doors. White walls and cabinets dominate, with black defining the space. Shape becomes very important when strong contrasts are used, because all edges are hard. A background like this provides a great opportunity to make bold but temporary color statements. A bowl of oranges or a plate of red peppers would be sure to make an impact.

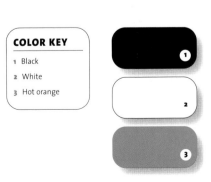

COLOR KEY

1 Black
2 White
3 Hot orange

Metallics
Gold

Gold is the most glamorous metallic color. The fashion for gold comes and goes. During the Regency or Empire period it was used as decoration on black ebony furniture. Chinese lacquered furniture in red and black with fine gold filigree patterns influenced artists and designers in the late Victorian era. In the 1980s gold made a big comeback in interior decorating, and this time it was more sassy than classy. Gold, white leather, mirror tiles, deep shagpile carpets, and perhaps a tented ceiling sent out all the right signals, but the look was never meant to last. In the contemporary home gold is most likely to appear as part of an ethnic-inspired color scheme such as one from India, Thailand, or Morocco, where fabrics and accessories are often patterned with gold. A magical array of modern products creates very convincing shades of gold. The most important thing about gold is that it gleams by day and sparkles in candlelight and, being fake, it should not take itself too seriously.

Thai style

Thailand has a lush green landscape peppered with temples and golden Buddhas. The mixture of green and gold evokes the countryside; the saffron, deep orange, and gold are the traditional temple colors and brilliant color mixtures of jade, fuchsia, electric blue, and gold are the colors people wear on the street.

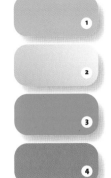

COLOR KEY

1 Golden orange
2 Pale gold
3 Turquoise
4 Bright mauve

Going for gold

When you want to make a big impact, choose gold. Inspired by the multicolored sofa, this room has been painted a vibrant blue with a golden yellow ceiling and burnt orange floor. Faced with this riot of color, the angelic finishing touch is a stroke of brilliance with the lustre of pure gold.

COLOR KEY

1 Gold
2 Lavender blue
3 Burnt orange

Metallics
Silver

Silver is the moon's color and it is thought, by association, to have a balancing, feminine influence on us. It flatters most other colors and is very easy to fit into a color scheme. Silver is cool and sharp with a reflective mirrored surface that picks up surrounding colors. It is the color of pewter, stainless steel, zinc, tin, chrome, aluminum and galvanized iron. In the past decade, since the arrival of the industrial style, many of these silver metals have been making a big impact on home decorating. Silver is most likely to dominate in the kitchen, where "catering style" demands professional-style cooking ranges, stainless steel work surfaces, sinks, and appliances. Chrome is popular for items such as kettles, toasters, and food processors. Elsewhere, painted silver walls look good with colors such as purple, lilac, cool blues, and rosy pink and with soft fabric textures like velvet and silk that share silver's reflective qualities.

Industrial chic

This metal platform provides a sturdy sleep area in a loft-style apartment. The look is very popular but can be hard and cold to live with. As an alternative, there are now several impressive brands of water-based metallic paints that can be used to give a tired wooden platform bed a new industrial chic style. Accessories really make a style like this and there are plenty of chairs, lamps, mirrors, and bins around that will help to pull the look together.

COLOR KEY

1 Silver
2 Black
3 Cream

Reflected glory

Chrome and stainless steel pick up all the light and color in a room while retaining their own distinctive color. These materials are mostly used for utility objects, like these espresso machines and teapots. The shelf arrangement is practical and decorative and sets the style of the room.

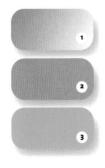

COLOR KEY

1 Silver
2 Pale coffee brown
3 Aqua

Textures and effects

The introduction of texture changes the appearance
of a color. The highs and lows of a pattern bring an element
of light and shade to a wall, and provide another level of visual
interest. Until recently texture, in the form of thick wallpaper or
swirling plaster patterns, was often used only to conceal structural
problems, but now applied texture has emerged as a serious
contender in contemporary-style decoration. Paint effects are
also making a comeback, being used to create areas of
textural contrast or to add all-over wall patterns in a
linen, denim, or damask effect.

Introduction

In this chapter we explore texture and the ways it can be used to add depth to a decorating scheme and enhance the impact of the colors. Several step-by-step projects are included that will help add character to a new house. There are contemporary ideas for white and very pale rooms where the main color theme is neutrality. There is a mat and glossy white-on-white stenciling project and one showing how to make the softest floor cushion with a cover made from a baby's cot blanket or fleece fabric.

Natural wood flooring, a sheepskin rug, and a bowl of vibrantly colored oranges—a simple combination, but very pleasing to the eye.

Eco palette

The eco palette consists of a range of earthy, muddy, and dull green colors, which look wonderful when combined with natural fabrics and materials such as linens, cottons, rush matting, and earthenware. We include a project that uses two different muddy pale browns to decorate a wall and another that shows you how to make dramatic drapes with unbleached calico and a staple gun. Liming wax is used to transform an old chair by restoring the beauty of the grain, and some very basic upholstery skills are used to re-cover the seat pad with tactile suede.

Color contrasts

Color contrasts can be used to create some very dramatic special effects but color can also be used in a practical sense to alter visually the proportions of a room or to disguise features that you would prefer people not to notice. One project in this section shows how to use two vibrantly contrasting complementary colors to create an energetic wall effect. There is also a project showing how to use a simple shadow to create a three-dimensional box and another that borrows a pattern from patchwork quilting to

One project produces a random patchwork of color that is created by applying torn and creased pieces of bright tissue paper to a pasted wall area. This is a fairly time-consuming project and is best suited to a small area such as an alcove rather than an entire wall. Another project has an eco theme, showing you how to apply cane or bamboo screening to the lower half of a wall. The cane or bamboo can either be left natural and varnished to a high sheen, or can be painted to match the wall and accentuate the change in texture.

The final project in this section creates a soft comfort zone for a small child but could also be used to define a sleeping area in a studio apartment. This project uses brightly colored fleece fabric to make cool hard walls softer, gentler and more appealing.

LEFT: **Centrally heated homes no longer need heavy drapes to keep out cold drafts, and contemporary fabrics reflect the trend toward a light, airy feel. Textures and colors are new and exciting, and they make decorative statements that can be echoed throughout the entire room.**

Stone can add interesting texture to any room, whether highly polished and brightly colored, or rougher and neutrally colored.

create the illusion of a three-dimensional frieze running all around the room.

Wall coverings

Textured wall coverings are now back in fashion, although the new patterns lean more toward a mixture of rough and smooth geometric patterns, 1970s style, than the original Victorian styles.

Natural materials, such as split bamboo, raffia, hemp, and linen, provide the textural contrasts that are so important when you are using the neutral palette, and in addition there are imitation pressed steel patterns that will give a room an industrial look at the swish of a pasting brush.

Wall textures

The last three projects in this section of the book all deal with the challenge of changing wall textures, and three different materials are used to this end.

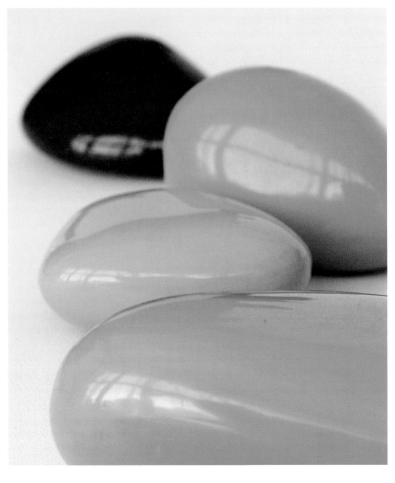

Texture

The way we choose and combine different textures for decorating is as much affected by trends as by our color choices. Felt, once used only as a protective barrier, padding, or cushioning under a more decorative fabric, now makes a serious fashion statement. Plastic used to be seen as horrible, tacky, and cheap, but now it's the last word in urban chic. Concrete was strictly functional and best kept hidden until minimalists rediscovered its potential. Brightly colored laminated worktops are now back in demand.

Here there is a corded carpet on the horizontal, with woven baskets on the diagonal to create an energetic textural contrast. The papier-mâché bowl breaks up the pattern and the even smoother stick adds a tactile finishing touch.

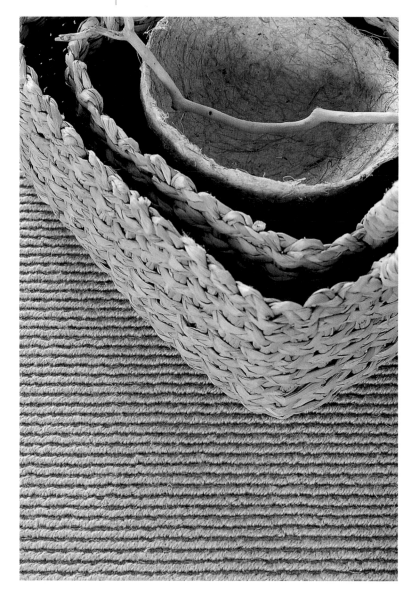

Creating interest

Texture does not only replace color—it can also be used exclusively for its tactile and visual qualities. The roughness, smoothness, or spikiness of a surface describes its texture. There are endless variations and combinations of textures that can be brought into play to make your home environment a more interesting and stimulating place.

Houses are being built faster than ever these days, with less attention to detail, and wherever we live most of us do it in an arrangement of smooth-sided, interconnecting box shapes. Old houses are more likely to have interesting architectural features to break up the monotony of plain walls, such as plaster moldings, high baseboards, and chair and picture rails. In their absence, there are many wall coverings and specialty paints that can be used to add interest. Anaglypta is a wall texture that has been around for more than a hundred years. The raised patterns were often used in heavy-duty areas such as hallways and staircases, where they adhered with such ferocity that any attempt to remove them brought most of the plaster off the wall as well. The original company still produces textured wall coverings, and has new ranges that look perfect in contemporary rooms. A more recent arrival is a wallpaper range with a raised texture in metallic finishes, which mimics aluminum flooring. It makes the full industrial look much more accessible and less of a permanent commitment, as the surfaces can be painted over with ordinary latex paint. Other new textures in wallpaper are a mixture of rough and smooth geometric patterns, widely spaced medallion shapes, and ranges of natural materials such as bamboo, linen, or woven reed panels. Cork is another warm, interesting natural texture due for a comeback—it looks good with dark wood, leather, and chrome furniture in sculptural modern shapes, and as a bonus it provides excellent noise insulation.

One of the reasons that the colors we choose from a paint chart surprise us by looking different on our walls is that any variation in texture will introduce elements of light and shade to alter the regularity of the color. Clever use of texture can really add depth to a color scheme, making the difference between an ordinary and an exceptional room.

Our eyes are constantly traveling over surfaces and colors to evaluate and balance what we see. Clever interior designers understand this, and provide interest and relaxation in equal measures, making a room as visually satisfying and comfortable as possible.

This bathroom has an enameled iron bath with chrome faucets and wood-paneled walls. The starfish, shells, sponges, and pebbles recreate a sense of the shoreline.

FAMILIAR TEXTURES

Some of the instantly familiar textures used in the home include: leather • suede • linen • cotton • wool • rattan • paper • rubber • corrugated cardboard • silk • velvet • wood • slate • glass • stone • shell • glazed and unglazed ceramics • cork • marble • PVC • fleece • fake fur • hard plastic • stainless steel • wire mesh • concrete • chrome • rough and smooth wood • foam • feathers • bamboo

LEFT: Slate gray walls with an extreme rustic finish could look dark and gloomy, but the fine wooden table gives a sophisticated effect. The lilac-glazed ceramic bowl and the shiny green apples add more textures to this intriguing environment.

YOU WILL NEED:

WOODGRAINING:

• DRY PAINTBRUSH

• OIL-BASED GLAZE

STENCILING:

• SNAP-BLADE KNIFE

• CARD

• SPRAYMOUNT
  (REMOVABLE)

• BRUSH

• PAINT

• PAPER TOWELS

SPONGING:

• PLASTER-BASED
  PAINT

• BRUSH, COMB, OR
  SPONGE

PROJECT
Paint effects

Paint effects have come a long way in recent years—not only do contemporary paint effects look better, but successful application is also a lot easier to achieve. The big paint companies have all produced ranges of special effect products, which are easy to use and guarantee good results. There is a textured paint to make new walls look like those of an old farmhouse. There are shiny, metallic paints that simulate hard metal, and there are even textile finishes to make your walls look like faded denim jeans.

Easy effects

Paint effects are fun, and there are several that require no specialized training.

Woodgraining and dragging

Essentially woodgraining and dragging are the same kinds of effect; they are both created by dragging a dry paintbrush through an oil-based glaze in the direction of the woodgrain. The difference is that in woodgraining you can create effects beyond that of imitating the pattern of the grain.

Stenciling and sponging

It comes as no surprise that stenciling is staging a comeback, because it is the easiest and least expensive way of applying a pattern. Everyone can cut a simple stencil, and there are thousands of more complex designs on the market. Stenciling is something most of us tackle as children but feel wary of trying on the walls. The first secret of stenciling success is using a removable spraymount on the back of the stencil so that it sticks to the wall as you apply the paint. The second one is to dip your brush in the paint,

then wipe it on paper towels to remove all the moist paint and just leave a dry coating of color. You can always apply more color, but too much will cause blobbing and runs. The same rule applies to sponging, when paint should be applied with a light touch. The textured finishes are applied as a thick coating of plaster-based paint, which is then worked on with a brush, comb, or sponge to score into the surface and lift some of the coating.

ABOVE RIGHT: You can use a graining comb to make attractive patterns by dragging the comb through an oil-based glaze.

RIGHT: A denim-effect wall finish is a soft blue finish available in kit form. The wall is first coated in pale blue, then rolled over in a denim blue glaze, which is dragged with a long-haired brush.

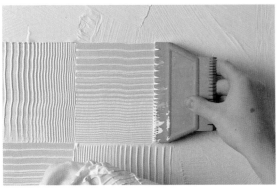

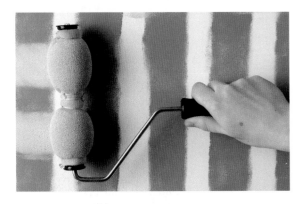

ABOVE: **Stencil cutting is easier if you stick the pattern onto the card or plastic with a removable spraymount. Use a very sharp snap-blade knife, inserting the point and cutting away from any corners. Protect the work surface with a cutting mat or cardboard.**

TOP LEFT: **Sponging can be done with a natural sponge and paint should be applied quite sparingly. Here a contrasting color is used to demonstrate the technique and a subtler effect can be achieved with a softer combination of colors. Rotate the sponge as you work to avoid a repetitious pattern.**

SECOND LEFT: **Use a comb or piece of plastic cut to size to create a pattern. This can simply be directional or geometric as here, with one square vertical one horizontal, or you could design your own effect.**

THIRD LEFT: **A sponge dabbed onto a textured base will create a simple raised pattern. This can look good in a rustic-style room, and can also be repainted with a foam roller.**

BOTTOM LEFT: **Roll a set of vertical stripes onto the wall from bottom to top and then paint a set of horizontal stripes in another color with a roller to create this check effect.**

Shades of white

White comes in a great many subtle variations of color and tone. Just one white standing alone is easily described. It is simply—white. A selection of whites seen together reveal that tones of white can be warm, cool, dull, bright, old, faded, blue, brown, and many more possibilities besides. Brilliant white is the most reflective of all of the whites, and can be hard and dazzling when compared with a color such as bone white, which is warm, soft, and natural, or blue white, which is fresh and cool.

The many white variations that we can now buy as named paint colors have been created to meet the popular demand for color-free decorating schemes based on the idea of a "pure" and simple style. Color and synthetics have no place in this white world; only natural fabrics and materials in a variety of white textures used together to create a harmonious, peaceful environment.

The only acceptable color here is the natural wood used for furniture and flooring, or the living green leaves of an indoor plant. It may sound like an impossible dream, but if the style is used in just one room, it is simplicity itself. A bedroom or bathroom will be easiest, but good storage is essential because if you have colorful clutter lying around the room, it will ruin the effect.

Bedroom sanctuary

Use a chalky white distemper paint for the walls. Floors can be sanded and polished if the wood is pale; otherwise floorboards can be painted white. Scattered sheepskins or white flokati rugs are the perfect way to create islands of warmth on wooden floors, and make the most deliciously soft bedside rugs. Sheer, floaty white curtain panels, white wooden shutters, or natural linen

shades are all suitable for windows—much depends upon the aspect and the shape of your windows.

Almost any style of furniture, old or new, can be used, so long as all the fabrics in the scheme are natural. A regular bed can be transformed into a four-poster by building a simple wooden frame surround and draping it with white muslin tab-topped curtains.

Bathroom sanctuary

This could be achieved with the most basic home improvement tool kit and skills.

If your bathroom suite is white, then you are already halfway there, and white-painted wood paneling or white tiles and towels are all that you need. Textural contrasts will make the room look more interesting—mat for woodwork, gleaming tiles, polished chrome, and folded soft fluffy towels.

Flooring could be a good white marble-effect vinyl, or pale gray and white checks with white cotton-twist rugs. Frosted windows with a slight green tint will add extra freshness to a bathroom, and you could hang up a pretty voile curtain panel to add a softening touch. If any color is used, stick to the very palest shades of gray, fawn, or aqua.

RIGHT: **Using different shades of white gives a clean, fresh look to a room. The contrasting chocolate brown blanket stitching on the cushion and neat wall stenciling complete the effect.**

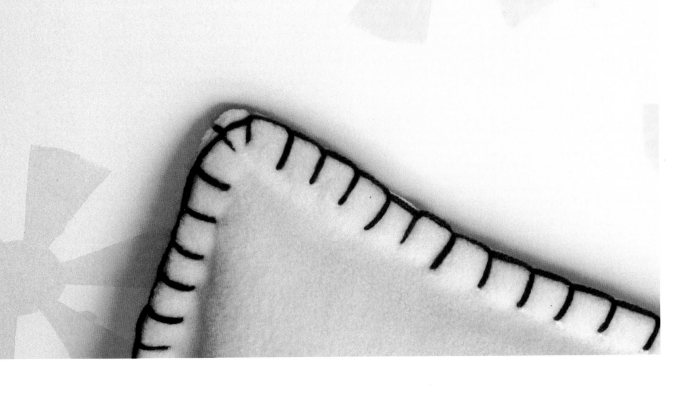

YOU WILL NEED:

Background color
(choose one of the
shades below) to
apply to all wall
surfaces first

- **TWO SHADES OF
  WHITE PAINT WITH
  CONTRASTING
  FINISHES (SUCH AS
  SATIN AND CHALKY
  FINISH)**
- **PAINT BRUSH**
- **STENCIL MATERIAL**
- **A PHOTOCOPY OF
  THE PATTERN**
- **SPRAY ADHESIVE**
- **SNAP-BLADE KNIFE**
- **BROAD STENCIL
  BRUSH**
- **CLOTH**
- **PLUMB LINE
  (OPTIONAL)**
- **SPIRIT LEVEL
  (OPTIONAL)**

PROJECT
White-on-white stencil effect

The idea is to stencil a pattern of contrasting textures, which can either be rough/smooth, chalky/glossy, or mat/glitter. The pattern is based on a geometric shape that is easy to enlarge and cut out. It can be stenciled in a regular grid pattern, or used randomly for a more casual effect. A compromise between the two is best for large areas, moving a plumb line along a wall at regular intervals as a guide and stenciling in a half-drop pattern. Decide on the distance between the motifs, and stagger the rows so that in each alternate row the first motif falls half-way between those in the row before.

RIGHT: **A stencil
effect can add a
delicate feature to
a wall surface and
can give a room a
contemporary feel.**

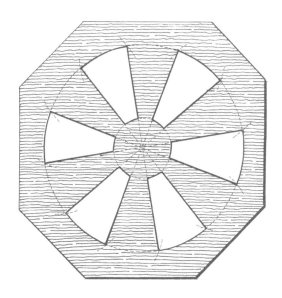

TEMPLATE

This pattern can be made either by using a pair of compasses and a ruler or, simpler still, by making a photocopied enlargement of this diagram to the size of your choice.

HOW TO DO IT

Stenciling a grid of bold shapes on the wall is simple and will give a very contemporary look to any room. To divide a wall into a grid, use a plumb line to mark the verticals and a ruler with a spirit level for the horizontals.

STEP 2 Cut out the pattern with a snap-blade knife, always cutting away from the corners toward the middle.

STEP 1 Enlarge the pattern and apply a light drift of spray adhesive to the back. Stick it onto a sheet of stencil card or mylar (the clear plastic stencil material).

STEP 3 Paint the wall with the mat white paint and leave till bone dry.

STEP 4 Spray the back of the stencil with spray adhesive and set aside. It should dry to a tacky finish that will stick to the wall when you are stenciling but be easily removed without leaving any sticky residue.

STEP 5 Place the stencil on the wall and use the chalky paint undiluted, applying a generous coating through the stencil with a broad stencil brush.

STEP 6 Lift the stencil and wipe the edges before repositioning it.

PROJECT
Floor cushion

YOU WILL NEED:

- A FOAM/FEATHER OR POLYSTYRENE BEAD FLOOR-CUSHION PAD (LOW BUDGET SUGGESTION: BUY A CHEAP FLOOR CUSHION AND RE-COVER IT, OR MAKE A CALICO LINER AND FILL IT WITH A PAIR OF OLD PILLOWS).
- A CREAMY WHITE COT BLANKET OR 1 YD./1 M OF FLEECE FABRIC
- SCISSORS
- SEWING MACHINE
- IRON
- CLOTH
- BEIGE TAPESTRY WOOL AND A LARGE NEEDLE FOR FINISHING IN BLANKET STITCH
- WHITE THREAD AND NEEDLE

In the white-on-white style, the floor is a very important part of the decorating scheme. Floor cushions are comfortable for lazing about on the floor. The project is simple and relies upon finding an interesting textured fabric and the right trimming. The cushion cover in the project can be made from a cot blanket, which is the perfect shape as well as being wonderfully soft and inviting, or you could use one yard/metre of fleece fabric. The cover is made in the most basic way, being machine-sewn on three sides and slip-stitched closed with the cushion pad inside. The blanket stitching suits the material perfectly.

This beautifully soft floor cushion is ideal for lounging on the floor. It is made from baby-soft fleece, which gives a warm and comforting feel.

HOW TO DO IT

This project is quick and easy, requiring only the most basic cutting out and sewing skills. The result is a smart and wonderfully soft floor cushion.

STEP 1 Fold the fleece in half lengthwise and cut it to make two equal-sized pieces.

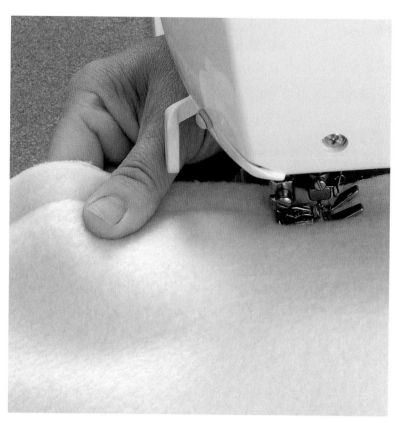

STEP 2 Cut off any edgings (which may be simple stitched folds of satin). Lay the two pieces on top of each other and stitch them together on three sides, ³⁄₄ in./2 cm in from the edge.

STEP 3 Snip across the corners, then turn the other way out to conceal the seams. Press flat, using a damp cloth underneath the iron to protect the fleece surface from the direct heat.

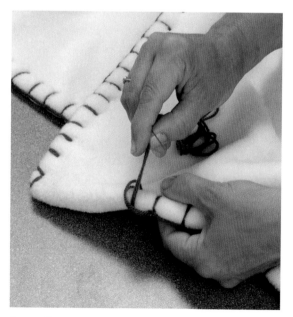

STEP 4 Thread the large needle with tapestry wool and sew a large blanket stitch on the three closed sides. Put the cushion pad inside and slip-stitch to close the open end. Continue the blanket stitch along this seam.

Neutrals

The term "neutral" applies to a range of indistinct tones and shades derived from mixtures of black and white with brown, gray, or sometimes with lesser amounts of muddy green, yellow, or blue. A neutral color scheme might be based around soft blue-toned gray or pale khaki brown, but whatever the slight color cast, there will always be a high proportion of white. The neutrals are usually taken from the color of a natural material such as parchment, sand, stone, or marble, and work well with natural textures and materials.

A neutral color scheme does not have to omit color altogether, but the proportion of any other colors used should be small enough so as not to override its basic neutrality. Pattern is one way that a color can be used without overpowering a scheme that is intended to be seen as neutral. This will work particularly well if the pattern combines the predominant neutral and a color.

A color scheme based around a single neutral does not have to look monotonous if an interesting mixture of tones and textures is used.

Sophisticated beige

A mid-beige vinyl silk paint on walls, with a dead flat darker mushroom beige on all woodwork and an almost white ceiling, does not sound all that thrilling. But add, for example, rough woven matting flooring, a large brown-and-white cowhide rug, loose weave drapes, and a slatted wooden shade, a pale linen covered sofa with dark beige suede cushions and a mohair throw, and the room has become the epitome of contemporary sophistication. Exactly the same theory can be applied to any neutral decorating scheme.

Tranquil haven

A neutral color scheme is superbly restful on the eyes. If you spend your days in an industrial environment or in the heart of a busy city, then this sort of room will be a haven of tranquility at the end of the day. If a room is mainly used in the daytime, a pale neutral scheme will make the most of any natural light, which can be filtered using sheer muslin panels over the windows.

If a room is inclined to feel cold, make your selection from the warmer neutrals with yellowish tones, like cream, sand, and pale straw. They look very good with pale grays or gray-greens. The cooler stone grays can be warmed up by the inclusion of a pinky beige.

Neutral backgrounds may be safe, but they certainly don't have to be dull or boring. A room painted in tones of stone gray on walls, ceiling, and floor is like a vessel waiting to be filled. Strong color statements can be saved for soft furnishings, contemporary furniture, paintings, and dramatic lighting, even flower arrangements. Imagine the gray room with purple floor-length curtains, leather, and chrome classic chairs, a red sofa, a row of colored neon tubes, and a giant cactus plant.

RIGHT: **In this room, which has no particularly interesting features to pick out, interest has been created by painting the wall in two harmonious tones. The bright seat cover contrasts beautifully with the neutral color of the wooden chair.**

YOU WILL NEED:

- UNBLEACHED CALICO, WIDE ENOUGH FOR TWO CURTAINS TO COVER THE WINDOW —MEASURE FROM FLOOR TO CEILING AND MULTIPLY BY FOUR (THIS IS TO ALLOW FOR A GENEROUS DRAPED HEADING AND SOME BILLOWING OF THE DRAPES ONTO THE FLOOR)
- STAPLE GUN AND STAPLES
- IRON-ON BONDING TAPE OR DOUBLE-SIDED TAPE FOR HEMS
- STEPLADDER
- TIE-BACK HOOKS

PROJECT

Calico drapes

This is a project for those who enjoy a touch of drama with their decorating. It requires no sewing; it can be managed without a pin or a pair of scissors—but you'll need another pair of hands and a stepladder.

It is an unconventional but effective and economical way to drape a large window.

The idea is simple enough—to use a single, long length of unbleached calico as two drapes and a draped heading, which is attached to the window frame using a staple gun.

If there is no wooden window frame, a cleat fixed above the window would serve the same purpose.

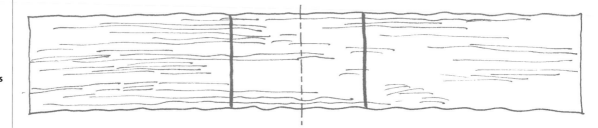

 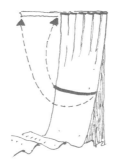 

TEMPLATE

Divide the length of fabric in half and mark the center line (see above middle). Measure the window width; transfer the measurement to the fabric, the center line running down the middle.

Hold the length of fabric up to the cleat and staple the two corners of the first marked line to the cleat (see above right). Now pleat it (see above right and the photo on the right).

With one side pleated and stapled, pick up the length at the second marked line on the far edge and staple it up to the end of the cleat (above, right). Staple the near edge to meet the first drop. The curtains are tied back during the day using tie-back hooks fixed in the window frames.

HOW TO DO IT

This is such a stunning window treatment and much easier to do than to explain! It's like riding a bicycle—once learned, never forgotten.

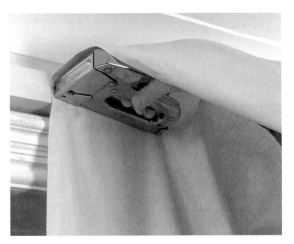

STEP 1 Hem one raw edge, and with a generous amount of this end resting on the floor on the left side of the window, take the rest of the fabric up the ladder with you. Line the fabric up with the top of the window frame and fold it over, letting the excess drop. Staple the fabric to the frame to overlap the center of the window frame by 1 in./2.5 cm, then staple the other side to the window frame on the left. Much will depend on the type of window frame, but aim to conceal the top of the frame under the fabric.

STEP 2 If the fabric's width is much greater than half the window, then you will need to pleat the curtain. To do this, find the middle and staple it to the middle of the frame. Do the same again on each side of it, and then again, until all the slack is taken up in evenly stapled pleats. Now move the ladder to the other side of the window.

STEP 3 Drape the length of fabric across the top of the window until you reach the right edge of the frame. The line between the corners should fall in a gentle curve (see middle diagram). Now twist the fabric over, taking the right edge under the drape and into the center, so that the rest of it falls to make the second curtain. Staple this right-side drape, pleating across the top in the same way as the left side.

STEP 4 Finish off the draped heading by gathering up and stapling the fabric in the middle, so that it falls in even drapes. Make sure that all the staples are concealed by the folds of fabric. Finally, fix tieback hooks into the sides of the window frame so that the curtains can be gathered up and tied back during the day.

YOU WILL NEED:
- PAINTER'S TAPE
- SET SQUARE
- STRAIGHT-EDGE WITH SPIRIT LEVEL
- PENCIL
- PAINT ROLLER AND TRAY
- 2 IN./5 CM PAINT BRUSH
- TWO SHADES OF KHAKI BEIGE

PROJECT
Two-tone neutral wall

This project will be most suitable for use in boxy rooms that have no particularly interesting features to pick out. The idea is to create energy and interest by painting a wall in two harmonious tones of khaki beige. The two colors meet with a zigzag line at the height most complementary to the shape of the room. In a tall room keep the line in a low position, in a short one move it up, and in a long thin room it might be best to divide the wall vertically, with two thirds of the wall painted in the lighter shade and the remaining third painted a few tones deeper. This will appear to bring the room more into proportion.

In this room, interest has been created by painting the wall in two harmonious tones. The pale drape and natural wood chair look perfect with the two tones of khaki beige used on the wall.

HOW TO DO IT

Taping the zigzag on the wall is the most time-consuming part of this project, but the result makes it all worthwhile.

STEP 1 Decide on the height where the zigzag color meeting point will be, then paint the top half of the wall in the lighter shade to roughly 1 in./2.5 cm below the lower point of the zigzag. Leave this overnight to dry—this is important to prevent the painter's tape from lifting the paint as it is removed.

STEP 2 Measure the height to where the top point of the zigzag will be and make a mark. Do this along the wall, and draw a soft pencil line to join the marks. Check it with the spirit level.

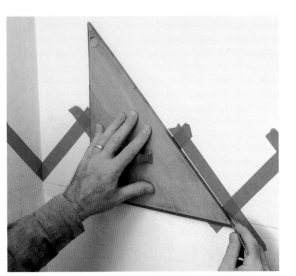

STEP 3 Place a strip of painter's tape at a 45° angle from the line to the wall edge. Now place another one at 90° to the first. This is the shape and size of the zigzag pattern. Each following piece is placed at 90° to the previous one and trimmed to give a neat point.

STEP 4 Paint the lower section of the wall using a small roller or brush to paint over the edge of the painter's tape. When the paint is almost dry, lift the painter's tape carefully, breaking off and disposing of manageable sections as you go along. This way you are less likely to become entangled in a web of painted tape! Use the paint brush to touch up any pencil guidelines that remain on the lighter shade.

YOU WILL NEED:

- A WOODEN (OAK OR PITCH PINE) DINING CHAIR IN NEED OF RESCUE
- GLUE
- A PIECE OF SUEDE LARGE ENOUGH TO COVER THE SEAT OR A SUEDE GARMENT TO CUT UP AND RE-COVER THE SEAT
- WIRE BRUSH
- LIMING WAX
- FURNITURE WAX
- FINE STEEL WOOL
- SOFT POLISHING CLOTH
- SCISSORS
- STAPLE GUN

PROJECT
Chair liming and re-covering

It is always worth looking out for a chair with potential for a make-over. The ideal chair for this project is oak or pitch pine with a drop-in seat pad. Oak is a beautiful hardwood, whose characteristic grain was often disguised with dark stains and heavy varnish. Strip off all the old coatings to reveal the natural wood beneath.

The liming is done with a liming wax. Once the wood has been treated, the chair seat is given a new look with a covering of soft suede—either imitation, or real suede from a leather dealer. An alternative is to use recycled suede from an old skirt bought from a charity shop or flea market.

This chair was picked up cheaply in a second-hand shop and given a make-over. After treating the wood, a new seat cover was made to give the chair a fresh, modern look.

HOW TO DO IT

Bring out the true beauty of oak with this simple liming treatment, then add a new seat cover and transform an old dining chair into a contemporary piece of furniture.

STEP 2 Dip the steel wool into the liming wax and rub the wax into the wood, both with and against the grain.

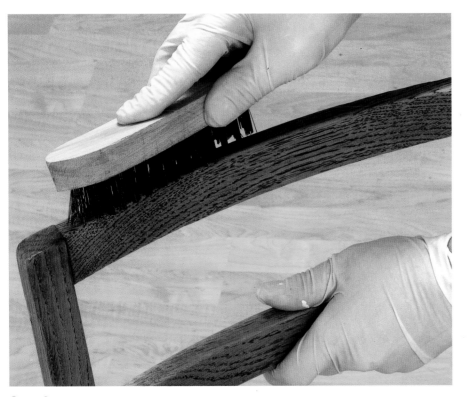

STEP 1 Save yourself the pain and have the chair professionally dipped in a paint-stripping tank. When it has dried out, check all the joints and re-glue where necessary. Push a wire brush along the surface following the direction of the grain. This is called raking out, and it will get rid of any soft wood or dust trapped in the grooves.

STEP 3 Leave it to dry for about a half hour, then dip a fresh piece of steel wool in furniture polish and rub it over the surface to lift off the liming wax. The grain will show up white where the lime has remained in the grooves. Buff the surface with a soft cloth.

STEP 4 Trim away any thick seams, zippers and buttons from the garment, leaving any attractive seaming, which can be used as part of a deliberate design on the seat.

STEP 5 Lay the seat base on the suede and use one staple in the middle of each side to attach the suede to the seat frame.

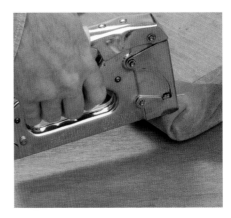

STEP 6 Staple the suede all the way around the seat frame, pulling it taut and trimming away any excess. Fit the seat back into the chair frame.

3-D effects with color

Color can make a wall shimmer, fade, dazzle, or confuse. The most obvious 3-D effect is produced by using a light/dark contrast to create a drop shadow. This can create illusions such as simple raised panels, recessed niches, or intricate plaster moldings. Colored shapes can be shaded to give them form and the shape of a room can be dramatically changed by the introduction of a false sense of perspective. Once you understand the advancing and receding qualities of different colors, you can produce very convincing effects.

The Ndbele tribeswomen in South Africa paint their simple mud huts externally with architectural features such as columns, pediments, archways, and castellated walls. The background is whitewash, with black outlines and patterns that are filled in with brilliant colors. It is an idea that can be seen in many parts of the world where paint is used in bold and creative ways in order to imitate ornate architecture.

In Mexico, houses are painted vivid colors with striped bands of contrasting colors. Wall paintings often create 3-D effects and murals are an important part of the local culture.

Trompe l'œil

Expert trompe l'œil painters create convincing illusions such as:

• walls of shelves stacked with books

• doorways where they don't exist

• windows looking out on panoramic views and many other special effects.

There is no need to be as ambitious as this, but there is fun to be had by using 3-D effects to add life and interest to a featureless room.

A painted frieze of light and dark geometric shapes can be drawn out with templates, and if the angles and the direction of the light are plotted correctly, the effect will be absolutely stunning.

The first of the 3-D projects included in this section shows you how to paint blocks of color with dropped shadows. This is a very basic 3-D effect that can be used in a striking way or in a very toned-down way, depending on which room in the house you choose to use it.

It can be a popular choice in living rooms, but it may be best to use small blocks of subtle colors—large blocks of primary colors may prove difficult to live with.

The second project offers a major color contrast that is only slightly toned down with the use of the feathering paint technique to soften the edges of the blocks. This, too, is an effect that is very easy to achieve but has a stunning result. Because the colors contrast so vibrantly, the blocks will seem to float.

The third project is ideal for use as a wall frieze or door surround and involves painting three diamond shapes to produce a convincing cube effect, which relies on each of the diamonds being a different tone.

Go on, let your creativity loose and dive into the world of 3-D!

RIGHT: **By using bright, bold shapes on a wall in a contrasting color to the main decor, you can dramatically alter the look of a room and create a stunning effect.**

YOU WILL NEED:

- RULER OR STRAIGHT-
  EDGE WITH SPIRIT
  LEVEL
- PENCIL OR CHALK
- PLUMB LINE
- SET SQUARE
- PAINTER'S TAPE
- COLOR FOR BLOCKS
- SHADOW COLOR
- SMALL ROLLER
  AND TRAY
- 1 IN./ 2.5 CM PAINT
  BRUSH

PROJECT

Blocks of color with dropped shadow

This is the simplest three-dimensional effect, the impact of which increases with the size of the shapes. The colors chosen for the blocks can be as subtle or bold as you choose. If the room style is based around neutral colors, then using two tones of stone gray will create a subtle paneled effect. On the other hand, primary colors with black shadows on a white background will make the blocks of color appear to leap off the wall. Much depends upon the room's shape, size, and purpose. But it is important to exercise caution—a bedazzling optical effect could soon become very tiresome in an everyday living room.

These large green shapes, with the black dropped shadows, produce a really impressive 3-D effect that is ideal for brightening up a child's nursery.

HOW TO DO IT

Treat your wall as a blank canvas and create this dramatic effect in the boldest of colors.
A 45° set square and ruler or straight-edge are the essential tools for the job.

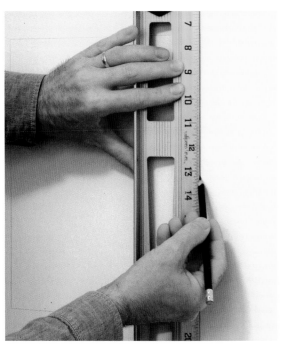

STEP 1 Measure the area and calculate the size and positions of the color blocks. Drop the plumb line to use as a vertical guide and use the straight-edge to mark out rectangular shapes in pencil.

STEP 2 Place a strip of painter's tape around each of the shapes, then apply the color with the small roller. Leave to dry, then peel off the tape. Leave overnight until bone dry.

STEP 3 Use the set square to draw a shadow box at 45° on one side and the base of each block. Place a strip of painter's tape around the shadow area, including the two inside edges of the color block.

STEP 4 Paint the shadow with the brush and leave the paint to dry before peeling off the tape.

YOU WILL NEED:

- BACKGROUND COLOR (SKY BLUE)
- BLOCK COLOR (BURNT ORANGE)
- CARDBOARD TEMPLATE OF BLOCK SHAPE
- PENCIL
- ROLLER AND PAINT TRAY
- 3 IN./7.5 CM HOUSEHOLD PAINT BRUSH
- SOFTENER BRUSH FROM PAINT-EFFECTS STORE

PROJECT
Vibrant contrasts

This project shows the power of intense color contrasts, but softens the impact by using a more painterly approach. The paint is applied with a large brush used to feather the edges of the blocks to avoid hard edges.

The orange and blue contrast is sharp and funky. Other vibrant contrasts are yellow and violet, red and green, and lime and purple. Cool colors retreat; warm ones advance.

First paint the wall with the background color, then draw outlines for the color blocks using a template. When you fill them with a vibrantly contrasting color, they will actually appear to float.

The bright shapes really do appear to float on the contrasting color behind them. If you are feeling courageous, you may want to experiment with other vibrant contrasts, such as lime and purple.

HOW TO DO IT

A template can be any shape or size. Have fun designing your own or simply follow the pattern used here. This dazzling effect is sure to be a real talking point.

STEP 1 Paint the wall the background color. Leave to dry.

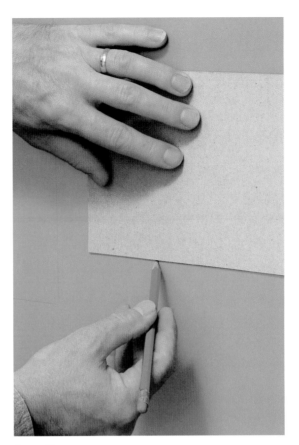

STEP 2 Hold the template against the wall and draw outlines for the color blocks.

STEP 3 Paint the blocks burnt orange up to the pencil line.

STEP 4 Feather the edges of the blocks before the paint has a chance to dry. Do this by running the softener brush lightly over the paint edge so that it spreads and fades.

YOU WILL NEED:
- UPHOLSTERY FOAM
- 3 X PHOTOCOPIES OF THE DIAMOND SHAPE
- SPRAY ADHESIVE
- SCALPEL
- PAINTER'S TAPE
- A LIGHT COLOR; A MID TONE AND A DARK SHADOW COLOR LATEX OR ACRYLIC PAINT
- 3 SMALL FOAM ROLLERS
- 3 WHITE DINNER PLATES
- STRAIGHT-EDGE WITH SPIRIT LEVEL
- PENCIL OR CHALK

PROJECT
Baby block pattern

This is a traditional patchwork quilt pattern in which three diamond shapes are fitted together to resemble a cube. The illusion relies on the top diamond being a mid-tone, the left side being light, and the right side a darkened tone. It creates an extremely effective illusion, and a line of these cube shapes makes a good wall frieze or a door surround. The pattern is printed on the wall using diamonds of upholstery foam, but it could also be stenciled if you prefer that kind of effect. The printing method gives the sort of variety seen in a marble mosaic, as each print is different but the three colors remain exactly the same.

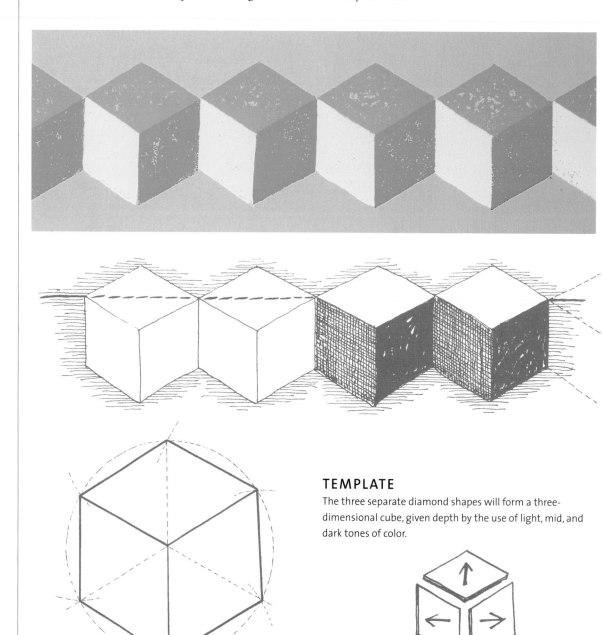

TEMPLATE
The three separate diamond shapes will form a three-dimensional cube, given depth by the use of light, mid, and dark tones of color.

HOW TO DO IT

Buy an off-cut of upholstery foam to try out this effect.

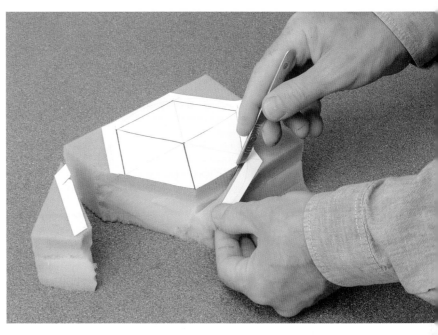

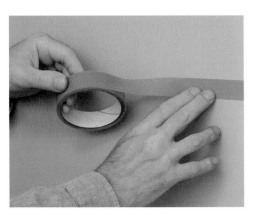

STEP 1 Apply spray adhesive to the photocopies and stick them onto the foam.

STEP 2 (Above) Carefully cut out the three diamond shapes. Try to cut each side in one continuous line for a neat edge. The full thickness can be cut through afterward—it is the printing edge that needs to be straight.

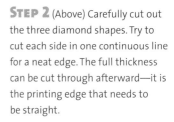

STEP 3 Measure and mark out a top line position for the frieze.

STEP 4 Check with the straight-edged spirit level that the line is straight.

STEP 5 Put the mid-tone color on a plate and run a small roller through it. Coat one of the diamond shapes and print the shapes lengthwise with the point on the line.

STEP 6 Put the other two colors on plates and use a separate roller for each one. Coat the remaining diamonds with the light and dark tones.

STEP 7 Beginning with the dark color, print a dark diamond below the mid-tone along its lower right edge. Then print the light tone alongside the dark one. Continue to the end.

Tactile surfaces

We not only need to see a variety of textures, we also need the tactile experience, and we feel soothed, reassured, excited, or energized when in touch with different textures. Silk, satin, suede, and velvet are warm, sensual, and luxurious, whereas cotton, linen, and muslin are cool, fresh, and practical. There are more textures than there are words to describe them. Some are there for practical and safety reasons—for instance, nonslip bathroom flooring. Hard, soft, smooth, or rough, we need a balance of textures in our home.

Man-made fabrics, floorings and furniture are best when they are being themselves rather than a cheap imitation of the real thing. One of the problems with man-made fabrics is that they are of a consistent quality and so lack the characteristic imperfections that make a natural product so attractive.

Seating

Most seating is a combination of hard frame with soft padding, with extra layers of comfort added by cushions, rugs, and throws. This is where texture can be used to best effect, either instead of, or as well as adding other colors. A loose-weave mohair throw, a large corduroy bolster, a soft suede cushion, or a silk shawl on a sofa will each generate a different layer of comfort. Pashmina shawls are one fashion item that is equally desirable as clothing and soft furnishings, being at home on both shoulders and armchairs. A neatly folded shawl or rug over the arm of a chair looks smart but also offers potential coziness should you need it. Contemporary style is very much about hard and soft areas, contrasting cool open spaces with soft islands of comfort.

Flooring

Flooring is often the largest area of texture, color, and pattern in a room. Walls and ceilings can be rough, chalky, or shiny without physically affecting us, but the floor we walk on has to be comfortable underfoot. There is tremendous choice in flooring, but essentially it needs to be suited to the room's purpose, easy to clean, and not too dominating. If you have beautiful wooden boards or polished parquet blocks, then color and texture can be added with rugs, and after that fitted woven matting is the most homogenous choice. Rush and coir mats do the same job as wooden floorboards for living rooms, not making too strong a statement yet providing a warm, comfortable, natural, and neutral base for most furniture styles and color schemes. Colored carpets are the ideal flooring for bedrooms, where bare feet touch the floor. They also have less through traffic and are a good place to use light colors and soft-textured carpets which would be impractical elsewhere. The ultimate is cream shagpile carpet, once considered a fashion crime but now back in the style magazines again—and a lot more fun than bare floorboards.

RIGHT: **Fleece is a perfect fabric to incorporate in a young child's bedroom; it is soft, warm, and comforting, available in bright colors, and very easy to work with.**

YOU WILL NEED:

• TISSUE PAPER
• WALLPAPER BRUSH
• WALLPAPER PASTE
• ROLLER
• CLEAR MAT VARNISH
• A BRUSH TO APPLY
  VARNISH

PROJECT
A colored tissue-paper patchwork wall

The color range for tissue paper is really gorgeous, ranging from hot pinks and purples to soft pastels and all the primaries. Choose a palette of four or five colors and tear random shapes so that none of the paper has a straight-cut edge. The idea is to overlap shapes, building up a collage of color on an area of wall.

The background color will show through the tissue paper, and should be used to set the overall color you would like for the wall. Tissue paper is very fine and will tear or wrinkle, but this is part of the effect, so you don't need to try to make it look perfect. The end result will be textured as well as colorful.

The variety you can achieve with this kind of patchwork is endless, and since it is so simple to do, you can easily change it in the future if you tire of the color scheme.

HOW TO DO IT

Making tissue paper patchwork is not difficult and the transparency gives it a stunning effect reminiscent of stained glass. There are lots of colors to choose from; the pieces can be made smaller or larger if you prefer.

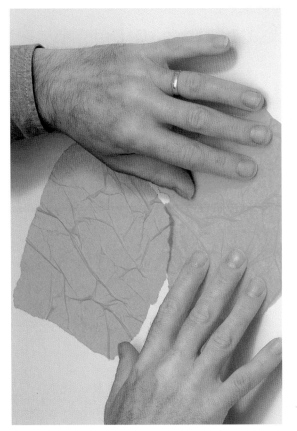

STEP 1 Tear the sheets of paper, reserving enough straight-cut edge pieces to go around the edges of the wall (think of a jigsaw puzzle!).

STEP 2 Paste the wall area to be covered with a thin, even coating of wallpaper paste.

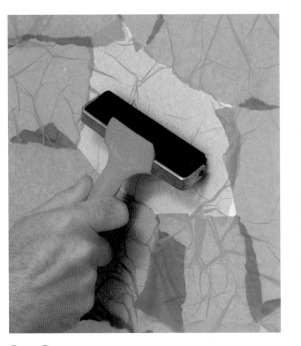

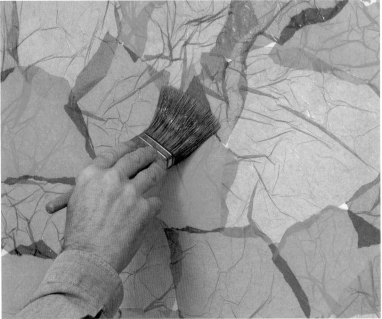

STEP 3 Beginning in the middle of the wall, apply different colored shapes to overlap each other slightly so that the wall is covered.

STEP 4 When you reach the edges of the wall, use the reserved straight-edged shapes to make a neat edge. When the wall is bone dry, apply a protective coat of mat varnish.

YOU WILL NEED:

- SPLIT CANE OR
  BAMBOO PANELS TO
  FIT THE LENGTH OF
  A WALL
- MOLDING TO
  FINISH OFF
  EDGES OF THE PANELS
  TO FIT THE LENGTH OF
  THE WALL
- SNAP-BLADE KNIFE
- PENCIL
- DRILL AND FINE
  DRILL BITS
- STRAIGHT-EDGE WITH
  SPIRIT LEVEL
- STAPLER GUN
- BRADS
- SMALL HAMMER

PROJECT
Cane or bamboo wall panels

One of the hottest new looks around is applied texture, especially using various kinds of natural materials to line interior walls. Cane and bamboo are both ideal materials for this kind of home decoration project. The garden centre is the best place to look for cane or bamboo panelling. It is sold in a large range of heights and lengths and is not particularly expensive. Other options for this kind of project include willow and reed panels.

You could fix the panels to wall battens that can be easily removed or, as has been done here, use a staple gun and panel pins to attach the panels to the wall.

This cane paneling is easy to fix on to the walls. Team it with natural-style furniture, such as the wickerwork chair shown here.

HOW TO DO IT

Bamboo or cane panels are not expensive but will quite easily transform a room. Before you start this project, paint any areas of the wall that are not going to be covered with bamboo or cane.

STEP 1 Measure and cut the required lengths of bamboo or cane. Use the fine drill bit to find the positions of the studs in the wall.

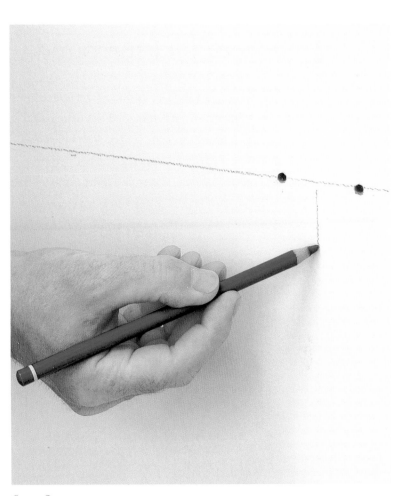

STEP 2 Mark the positions on the wall and above the height of the panels so they can be found once the panels are in place.

STEP 3 Smooth the panel up against the wall and use a staple gun or brads to fix it to the studs in the wall.

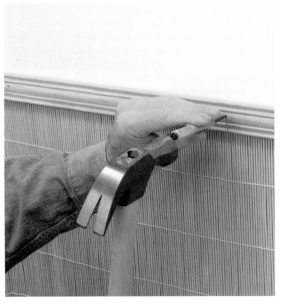

STEP 4 Fix the moldings along the top and bottom of the panels with brads and a small hammer.

PROJECT
Fleece bed surround

This project is an extension of the cot bumper, and it is intended to create a wall softening transition zone for toddlers when they make the move from sleeping in a cot to a proper bed pushed up against a wall. Fleece is made in a wide range of bright colors and is very easy to work with because the edges do not fray and will not need to be hemmed. Choose the fabric and braid in a contrasting color to the wall, or go for a deeper shade of the wall color, perhaps with a contrasting edging braid. Keep the trimming simple if the child is very young because a fringe or baubles will not withstand very much tugging!

This attractive fleece bed surround makes the bed area warm and cozy and can protect a child's head from accidental bumps against the wall. It will certainly ease the transition from cot to bed.

HOW TO DO IT

The fleece is attached to the wall using white school glue. If you prefer not to glue the fabric directly onto the wall, glue the fabric to a sheet of hardboard or ¼ in./6 mm plywood first and fix it onto the wall with screws.

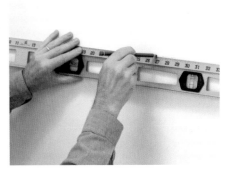

STEP 2 Draw the shape on the wall in pencil, checking the vertical and horizontal lines with the spirit level.

STEP 1 Measure the area to be covered and cut the fleece to an average of 3 ft. x 5 ft./1 m x 1.5 m —depending on the child's bed size. You need to cover the wall area about 20 in./50 cm up from mattress height. Trim the fleece to the same size.

STEP 3 Spread an even coating of white school glue onto the wall, starting in the middle of the shape and working outward. Pay special attention to the edges. The glue dries fast so aim to work quickly.

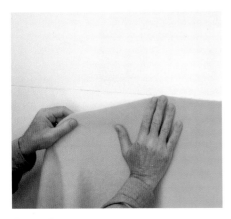

STEP 4 Smooth the fleece onto the white school glue with the flat of your hand, keeping pressure light and even so that the fabric does not stretch and distort the shape.

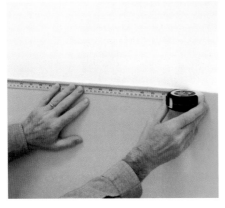

STEP 5 Measure and cut the lengths of braid or trimming ribbon needed for the edging.

STEP 6 Apply fabric adhesive to the back of the braid then run it around the edge of the fleece so that it overlaps slightly onto the wall and completely conceals the raw edge of the fleece.

Color highlights

Flashes and splashes of color in any room will attract
the eye and create a more energetic environment. The secret of
color highlighting is that the strongest impact is achieved when the
highlight color is used in moderation. Too much and it becomes
a feature, too little and it might be overlooked. In this chapter we
take a look at the different elements that go to make up a decorating
scheme, and how their colors can be used to add focus to a room.
Paintings, plants, rugs, lamps, and window treatments are
the key areas we focus on.

Introduction

The idea of a highlight is to attract attention and perhaps at the same time distract the eye from a less deserving area. If color is to be effective as a highlight, it has to be seen against a neutral or tonally similar background. It will obviously not work in a room that is already a riot of color. A highlight does not have to be a strongly saturated color—a flash of pale apricot, for instance, seen against dark gray, would be as effective as a violet purple against baby pink.

A simple clear glass vase filled with luscious lilies will inject a sense of grandeur into any room. Choose flowers for their colors, their shape, and their glamour.

Creating the extraordinary

If the room is mainly used for daytime activities, any color highlights should be placed within reach of the direct natural light coming from windows, skylights, or doors. A room for evening use can be fitted with directional spotlights, as light is imperative to bring any color to life.

The highlight should stand out and be quite different from the surrounding color, and its effect should be uplifting. Choosing colors to use in this way provides an opportunity to follow our color instincts and introduce our favorite colors. These are often the stronger shades that produce an immediate physical response when we see them, and as this reaction is so subjective, it is best to avoid using them over large areas. Many interior designers have built their reputations on their bold use of certain colors in public places or other people's homes, but are revealed to have chosen a neutral palette when their own homes feature in interior design magazines. Large areas of a favorite color can be too stimulating and exhausting to live with, whereas a small area can be deliciously attractive, bringing the eye back again and again to take pleasure in its beauty.

The right combinations and arrangements of color are like food for the eyes, and good food makes us feel better. We need to balance what our eyes see in the same way as we do our diets, providing a balance of colors to satisfy our senses without over-indulgence, which leads to the visual equivalent of indigestion.

The color of the background will help decide which highlights will work best. A strong contrast is important, but the contrast could be one of tone as well as color. Complementary colors from opposite sides of the color wheel, such as orange and blue or red and green, create exciting highlights, but they must be used in the correct proportions to one another or they will be too competitive. A sage green room, for instance, will be enlivened by a bowl of scarlet dahlias but would be completely overpowered by a large red rug. Remember that it is with flashes of brilliance that we turn the ordinary into the extraordinary.

LEFT: **Cushions can be a stylish and effective means of giving a room color highlights.**

A checkerboard floor can provide a colorful and charming feature.

Adding focus

The process of decorating involves a lot of visualization, preparation, shopping, and plain hard work. The inspiration for a color scheme or room style may have come from something seen in a magazine, on vacation, or in someone else's home, but the results are disappointing because, although the general look is the same, something is missing. The room has changed, but with all the hard work completed an extra something is needed to pull the look together. This something is the room's focus.

This circular rug has radiating colored lines that attract the eye to its color, shape and size. A bare floor is fine for dancing, but rugs make a room much more homely.

The creative path

Most rooms will have some individuality, a feature such as the fireplace, a doorway, an attractive floor, or perhaps a style of window that becomes the natural focal point.

If nothing is striking enough to become an area of focus, then you can create a focus point using color. This can be done with paint; it could be as simple as painting a contrasting colored shape on one of the walls, or painting blocks of color as broad borders for framed pictures. More often, though, it is done by introducing a carefully chosen new element, which could be a painting, a sculptural piece of furniture, a rug, a special bunch of flowers, or a wonderful plant.

This does not necessarily mean spending a lot of money. The art could be a row of pebbles from your last shoreline vacation, arranged in a straight line; a strangely shaped piece of driftwood displayed on a bright background, or a pile of pine cones sprayed shocking pink. A canvas floorcloth can be painted and stenciled for a fraction of the cost of buying a brand new rug, or you could paint a rug directly onto the floor. It is important to enjoy the decorating process, and taking the creative route is always much more rewarding than shopping—well, nearly always!

Keeping things in proportion

Proportion is very important, as there is a big difference between attracting attention and dominating a room. An exuberant palm in a ceramic pot looks great—as long as it's not so great as to infringe on your space! In just the same way, something that is far too small in proportion to its surroundings doesn't work either. A small handmade designer rug will still attract attention in the middle of a large open expanse of floor, but it will look mean.

Smart but simple

Choosing wisely does not always mean spending a lot of money. One idea which works very well is repetition. Instead of buying one large vase, buy four in the same style but in different colors, and arrange them in a straight line. This will create a color rhythm and focus. The same could be done with something completely free, like green-tinged cola bottles, which are design classics. A line of them becomes a sculpture in the right setting.

Fresh flowers are the most reliable way of adding instant focus to a room. Depending on what you choose, flowers can be used to change the mood of the room—they can even be used to reflect your own mood, if you like! For instance, if you're feeling romantic, choose roses; and if you're feeling full of the joys of life and you don't care who knows it, go for lilies. Many flowers come in a whole range of gorgeous colors, so you should have no problem working with your room's color scheme, and changing the atmosphere throughout the year. An arrangement of striking seedheads from the garden can also make a really stunning display.

If a bunch of flowers seems too much of an indulgence, just buy one or two single stems and angle a spotlight their way. This little trick creates a tremendously cool, contemporary effect.

This is a good way to make more of a picture and bring out a color within it. Here the blue-green color at the center of the flower has been used as a border color.

Window treatments

Window frame colors or drapes should create a perfect frame for a fabulous view like this one, with either a strong contrast as an outline or a harmonious shade to create a natural progression from room to view.

Windows are one of the main focal points in any room because of the light coming in and the view of the outside world that they reveal. Windows also give us an opportunity to introduce color and pattern that will flatter the room's color scheme and pick up on colors used elsewhere in the room. The biggest mistake is to treat the window in isolation without taking the rest of the room into account, because the right window treatment will make any room look a hundred times better.

The right treatment

There are so many different ways of covering windows, and some solutions will only suit certain situations. Consider whether the room is mainly to be used during the day or at night,

what the room's purpose is—or various purposes if it serves more than one—and if there are any practical limitations on the type of window treatment that would suit the room. In a room which has direct early morning sunlight, drapes will need black-out linings or shades; one that is overlooked by other windows will need muslins or nets for privacy, and windows opening onto a busy street will soon make drapes grimy and the chosen fabric will need to be one that will not deteriorate with regular washing.

Sometimes, the view from a window is simply too stunning to conceal—a view of city lights at night, for instance, can be hundred times better than the same view during the day when it would be better obscured by slatted shades, which would also soften and filter the light. A large picture-window view over a garden or fields will be the room's best feature in daylight, but can make the inhabitants feel too exposed after dark, when thick drapes would make the room feel more intimate. Ruling out specific window treatments is helpful as this will help to narrow down the options and let you focus on what will look best.

When in doubt, do something creative and temporary while you decide. If there is a curtain rail, use cotton sheets or saris, draped or with curtain clips.

Subtle coordination

The over-coordinated decorating style where the same fabric is used for furnishings and drapes is very dated, and looks as impersonal as a hotel or a furniture showroom. Try picking up a theme instead with, for instance, sari-style fabric used for drapes and embroidered silk cushions in matching colors, making a link between the furniture and the window treatment. A crochet white lace panel pinned across a window in a simple Mediterranean-style bedroom will echo the lace cloth on a bedside table. A bright orange roller shade will warm up a shaded north-facing window, and something as simple as a bowl of oranges will match the color and balance its brilliance in the room.

Simple roller shades are one of the most economical window treatments and are simpler to install than traditional drapes, although they do not provide their warmth. You can buy roller shades fairly cheaply as kits or you can even make them yourself. Roller shades have the added benefit of obscuring only a small part of the window surface. This means that they can be adjusted to let maximum light into a room when needed or pulled down to reveal the pattern and provide privacy in the evening.

ABOVE: **A simple roller shade, partially raised to let in the sunlight.**

LEFT: **It would be a pity to hide a deep window recess like this one. The wooden paneling creates the perfect frame for the flower arrangement. Painting a deep recess in light gloss paint brings more light into the room.**

Drapes and Shades

If walls are painted in plain colors, then drapes can be patterned in harmonious or contrasting colors, but when using pattern proportion is extremely important. As a rule, large patterns need large areas and small patterns work best when they are seen at close range.

This light and harmonious living room has been designed around a single shade of lilac. The furniture, woodwork, and soft furnishings all match and the gingham and plaid check of the curtains prevent the effect from becoming too bland.

Colored transparent fabrics look pale with daylight shining through them, but their color looks stronger in the evening, especially if the windows are fitted with roller shades.

Shades are a good way of adding color to a room, and a contemporary-styled room with a row of windows looks good with a different color shade in each one. A shade fitted into the

window recess can remain in place if drapes are added, but will also look good on its own.

Roman shades are very easy to make—they hang in folds, and can be made in most fabric weights from heavy canvas to soft voile. They are also the most economical treatment as they hang as a flat panel to match the dimensions of the window.

When in doubt, choose a plain neutral color and a classic window treatment rather than something wildly fashionable if you are buying a good quality fabric, as this will not date. If you are on a tight budget, investigate alternative fabrics, especially from street markets near garment-making districts, e.g. unbleached calico, bed sheeting, felt, fleece, or suit linings.

Shades can be very useful for glazed doors that are frequently used, for example, a kitchen door leading out to the garden.

Try teaming up a Roman shade with simple drapes; the door can be left open to admit the light on sunny days, or closed with the shade down and drapes closed to provide shade when the temperature rises. The key element here is flexibility.

ABOVE: **Full-length yellow drapes frame this window. When drawn, the drapes almost fill the wall.**

LEFT: **Floral Roman shades with a dark border are teamed with simple sprigged muslin curtains for these glazed doors.**

Soft furnishings

Soft furnishings are the fabrics we use in the home to add character and instil our own personalities. As very few of us undertake the making or even reupholstery of sofas, armchairs, or beds, it's the cushions, shawls, throws, lampshades, tablecloths, and bedspreads we add that change something mass-produced into something uniquely ours. To make the room look more attractive and increase the level of comfort, choose soft fillings and fabrics that are tactile as well as beautiful.

Choose cushions of the same style in different colors to give a harmonious look. These embroidered cushions in purple and olive are exotic and inviting against deep rose chenille upholstery.

Ring the changes

Soft furnishings can be changed with the seasons, creating a light, airy style in summer and a warm comfort zone for the winter. A sofa can be covered with a fleece throw for winter and cotton for summer. In the days before central heating, this was a normal part of home life, with flannel sheets and woolly rugs for winter and cotton sheets and light floor mats in summer. Winter drapes were thick to block out the cold drafts, but summer was a time for lace and cheerful cotton prints. Nostalgia can be fun and there is always room for retro style in fashion.

Color has a huge role to play in soft furnishings, especially if the room is decorated in plain colors. A room could be painted off-white with unbleached muslin drapes and chair covers, but still be seen as colorful if the sofa and chairs were piled with an assortment of vividly colored cushions, the floor boasted a bright dhurrie, and the table lamps had equally vibrant shades. To see how soft furnishings can alter a room's character, first imagine a golden yellow bedroom with an iron bed draped with a rich red velvet bedspread and bolster cushions, then change the bedding to a blue and white striped duvet cover. The whole mood has swung from luxurious and exotic to fresh and breezy. Put the idea into practice by using different fabrics and accessories in your bedroom to spice it up or cool it down to suit the mood.

Color coordination

A monochrome color scheme can look bland without the right type of soft furnishings. One solution is to choose a range of patterned fabrics that are not usually seen together, in a single color. This could mean mixing classic patterns such as toile-de-jouy, stripes, tie-dye circles, and floral damask to make a set of unmatched cushions. Keep the rest of the room neutral and leave the cushions to make the color statement. The beauty of this style of color coordinating is that you can usually buy remnants of expensive fabric in amounts sufficient for cushion covers at a fraction of the cost of buying it off the roll. Make it a rule always to have a rummage in remnant bins anyway, and build up a treasure chest of fabric for future soft furnishing projects.

LEFT: **Rich, varied textures and weights of fabrics in shades of yellow.**

ABOVE: **The success of creating a Japanese look means taking a no-frills, minimalist approach to both color and design. Cream, red, and black are all the colors you need.**

LEFT: **A thick gold and red curtain softens the hard edges of the doorway, and the same colors are picked up in the soft covers of the dining chairs in the background. A band of contrasting color could be used to join short remnants of superior quality fabrics and create a luxurious draped curtain like this one at a bargain price.**

Painted floors

Painting a floor is a popular and inexpensive option. A floor often needs only a light sanding to prepare it and many paint companies have added special floor paints to their product ranges. If you use conventional paint, add a couple of coats of strong polyurethane varnish to keep the color fresh or, for a more lived-in style, just let the wear and tear show through.

Preparing the floor

If you need to dispose of carpets or old vinyl, first have a peep underneath to assess the condition of the floorboards. If the flooring has been stuck to the boards with carpet tape, you will need to use a sander to remove the sticky tape. If the floor would benefit from a good sanding, then it would be best to rent a machine for a day. The sanding machine rent is not hugely expensive but the cost of the special sandpaper can add up, so do make it clear in the rental store that you are sanding to prepare for painting rather than to expose the true beauty of the natural wood. Using a sanding machine does not require great effort but it creates a lot of noise and dust and you have first to remove everything from its path. Once the floor has been sanded, it can be wiped over with sugar soap and left to dry before painting.

The most important thing to remember when painting a floor is to begin in the far corner and end in the doorway! A standard paint roller and tray do the job very well unless you are painting the boards different colors, when it is advisable to use a small foam roller or a paint brush. The paint is best applied in thin coats with adequate drying time between.

Patterned floors can either be stenciled or marked out in chalk and filled in with a paint brush. One of the most timeless painted patterns is a simple checkerboard which can be painted directly onto floorboards or onto sheets of hardboard tacked over the boards if you prefer a smoother "marble" finish.

There are several ways of painting a checkerboard, which can be done diagonally or horizontally. Painter's tape can be used to outline the squares. It makes painting easier, but mask and paint only a few squares at a time because it can cause confusion and ruin the pattern over a large area. The simplest method is to mark out the floor in pencil or chalk by drawing around a square template. The stark contrast of black and white can be very unforgiving of any wobbly edges, so choose gray, coffee brown, or sage green and off-white instead for a softer but very stylish flooring effect.

Special floor paints

You can now buy paint made specially for vinyl floors, which means an end to the days of putting up with nasty patterns when you move into a new place, just because the flooring is in too good a condition to justify replacing it. All you need is a pot of paint and a roller to transform a bad floor with a tasteful mat dusky blue, sandy yellow, or barn red. Now that's progress!

There are also specialized paints for concrete floors that give a more finished, homely look. Concrete is a cold indoor flooring material suitable only for warm climates or conservatories.

PROJECT
Painting a floor

O nce you have decided to paint a floor, everything will have to be removed from the floor area. Examine the floorboards closely, checking for any protruding nails, which should be banged in using a hammer with a nail punch. Splintered boards must be sanded and any holes filled with a good quality wood filler. Sand the floor lightly, then sweep up all the dust and wash the boards with a sugar soap solution to get rid of any grease. A proper floor paint will give the best finish and last the longest; otherwise, apply two coats of floor quality varnish after the paint.

HOW TO DO IT

Painting a floor in a single color could not be simpler. It does not take long and the effect will be one of instant freshness.

YOU WILL NEED:

- PRIMER FOR BARE WOOD OR UNDERCOAT
- ONE COLOR OF FLOOR PAINT (OR USE EMULSION PAINT WITH HEAVY-DUTY POLYURETHANE VARNISH)
- 2IN/5CM HOUSEHOLD PAINTBRUSH
- A LARGE ROLLER AND TRAY FOR THE PRIMER AND VARNISH (IF USING)
- CLEAR HEAVY-DUTY MATT OR GLOSS VARNISH
- MASKING TAPE

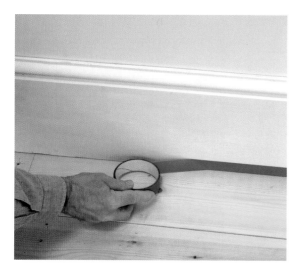

STEP 1 Mask off the baseboards to floor level.

STEP 2 Begin with the brush, painting the primer into the edges of the floor, right into the corners and up to the painter's tape. Apply the primer to the rest of the boards.

STEP 3 When the primer has dried, apply the floor paint. It should not be applied too thickly, and two thin coats will always give a better finish than one thick one.

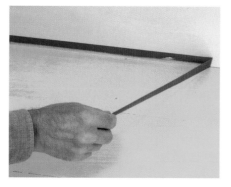

STEP 4 When the paint has dried, remove the painter's tape that was used to protect the baseboards.

YOU WILL NEED:

- PRIMER FOR BARE WOOD OR UNDERCOAT
- THREE COLORS OF FLOOR PAINT (OR USE LATEX PAINTS WITH HEAVY-DUTY POLYURETHANE VARNISH) PASTEL PINK, LILAC, AND POWDER BLUE ARE USED HERE
- 3 SMALL ROLLER TRAYS
- 3 SMALL FOAM ROLLERS OR A 2 IN./5 CM HOUSEHOLD PAINT BRUSH
- A LARGE ROLLER AND TRAY FOR THE PRIMER AND VARNISH (IF USING)
- CLEAR HEAVY-DUTY MAT OR GLOSS VARNISH
- PAINTER'S TAPE

PROJECT
Stripes of pastel colors

Floorboards are arranged in a striped pattern, which makes it very easy to pick them out in different colors and create a special feature floor. The floor must be prepared in the usual way with a thorough washing, sanding, filling, and priming. The colors should be chosen to suit the room's purpose and they do not need to be strong or even obvious contrasts. A child's playroom can be painted in bright primary colors or perhaps in seaside pastels, for example. A very gradual tonal color change will produce the effect of fading or shading, or you might want to introduce a pattern in the room by reversing the colors.

HOW TO DO IT

A transparent color like a woodwash is applied directly onto the wood without a primer or undercoat. This will let the grain show through.

STEP 1 Run painter's tape around the baseboard at floor level, then apply a coat of primer or undercoat and leave it to dry.

STEP 2 Begin by applying the pastel pink to the floorboard farthest from the door. Paint each third board in this color and leave to dry.

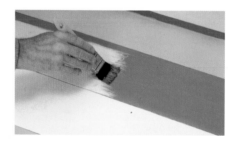

STEP 3 Paint the lilac next, carefully cutting in along the painted board edge. Paint all the lilac boards, then leave them to dry.

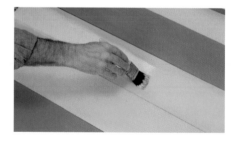

STEP 4 Paint the blue boards last, cutting in carefully along both edges. Leave the floor to dry overnight.

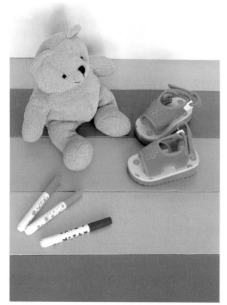

STEP 5 Apply one or two coats of clear mat or gloss varnish. Take care not to apply the varnish too thickly. Two thin coats are stronger than one thick one.

STEP 6 Finally, peel off the painter's tape around the baseboard edges and stand back to admire your masterpiece.

PROJECT
Painting a checkerboard floor

There are several different approaches for painting a checkerboard floor. If the room is a regular rectangle, it is important to center the pattern, dividing the room into quarters and beginning the pattern with a block of four squares in the center of the room. However, if you are painting an irregular hallway or a small room, this is not as important. The design can be arranged as a horizontal grid or on the diagonal—here it is horizontal, making use of the shape and grain of the floorboards. In order to create an integrated look, it is a good idea to paint the baseboards and any other woodwork in one of the floor colors.

YOU WILL NEED:
- FLOOR PAINT OR WOODWASH IN TWO COLORS
- PRIMER OR UNDERCOAT
- 12 IN. X 12 IN./30 CM X 30 CM THICK CARDBOARD FOR A TEMPLATE
- RULER
- STRING
- SNAP-BLADE KNIFE TO CUT OUT THE TEMPLATE
- CARPENTER'S PENCIL OR A CHALK/PENCIL
- PAINTER'S TAPE
- 2 IN./5 CM BROAD HOUSEHOLD BRUSH
- ½ IN./1.2 CM SQUARE-TIPPED BRUSH OR ARTISTS' BRUSH FOR EDGES

HOW TO DO IT

The effect is charming and must look deliberately painted, so don't be tempted to fill gaps between old floorboards.

STEP 1 Draw a square onto a piece of stiff cardboard (the width of two floorboards for a large square or one for a small pattern) and cut it out with a strong snap-blade knife.

STEP 2 If you are using a primer or undercoat, apply this to the floor first. Leave it to dry.

STEP 3 Apply the lightest color to the whole floor surface next and leave it to dry.

STEP 4 Find the centerpoint of the room by running two pieces of string between the opposite corners. Draw the shapes at the intersection, using the template and a pencil.

STEP 5 Paint the edges of the square first using the small square-tipped brush.

STEP 6 Use the broader brush to fill in the square and continue in the same way. If you are using a protective varnish, apply with a large foam roller when the squares are dry.

Picture gallery

The pictures you choose to put on the wall can say more about who you are and what you like than almost anything else in the room. The idea may sound intimidating, but it is far more important to surround yourself with images and colors that give you pleasure than to woo any would-be art critics. Don't restrict your displays to the conventional paintings, prints, and photographs—be adventurous and let your creativity flow freely.

Fun on the wall

Hang up anything you like—this could be clothing, hats, games boards, plates, travel tickets, tea packets, circus posters, or old property deeds. Try photocopying and scanning —it's a great way to obtain arty images for the walls. Big enlargements of small copperplate signatures and seals make superb graphic images, and small sections of photographs of landscape or flowers can be blown up to make abstract color compositions.

Original art does not have to cost a fortune, and it is well worth patronizing art college shows and local galleries. Black-and-white photographs are often more dramatic than color. Use fine black frames to show them off.

Picture-hanging tips

- If you are only hanging one picture on a wall, it will either need to be large enough to fill a wall on its own or to be hung off-center, otherwise it will look out of proportion.
- Never hang a large, heavy picture above a small one.
- When hanging a single row of odd-sized pictures along a wall, fix them so that an imaginary horizontal center-line runs through them all. The heights will vary but the eye level remains constant.
- Make even more of a favorite picture by surrounding the frame with a painted colored border on the wall.
- Framed pictures need to create a balanced effect on the wall, so perhaps one medium-sized picture in one half of the wall is set against a group of three small pictures on the other side.
- A wall filled with pictures needs to have a mixture of small and large set out in a pleasing way as well, so that the frames are not too weighty in any one area.

This colorful corridor contains many small pictures. The pictures are mostly photographs hung at eye level and above it, which is practical when space is limited and the subject matter demands close examination.

- Don't hang pictures too high up the wall, or too low down—keep them around eye level.
- When you group pictures together, try to see them as colors and tones rather than subject matter. If you half-close your eyes, this will help to block the detail and reveal the "bigger picture."
- Lay a group of pictures to be displayed together out on the floor first before putting any fixings in the wall so that you can plot the shape and spaces of the whole arrangement.
- Begin by examining the walls, checking for pipework and electric cables. There will be water pipes near the radiators, and electric cables run horizontally or vertically near any plugs and switches.
- Different walls need different fixings, and you need to tap the wall to discover whether it is a cavity wall or plastered brickwork.
- On a cavity wall use screws with fixings that grip the back of the wall panel as the screws are tightened. If using a hook, fit it onto the screw before you tighten it; the backing drops into the wall cavity when you remove the screw.

- A solid wall is suitable for single or multiple brass hooks fitted with masonry nails, which enter the wall at an angle. The shallow three-prong plastic hooks work by spreading the weight, but are only effective if the plaster is in good condition, so check this out before buying the hooks.
- Heavy pictures are best hung from bolts fitted into drilled and anchored holes.
- Picture-hanging hooks come in a range of shapes and sizes. It is very important to make sure that the fixings you use are strong enough to support the weight of the picture to avoid a nasty accident.
- Fit D-rings or screw eyes to the back of the picture and thread with taut picture wire. It is vital that these are perfectly aligned for the picture to hang level.
- Position the picture on the wall and make a mark at the top center. Measure the distance from the taut wire to the top of the frame and make a mark below the first one. This is the wall fixing position.

Arranging art on a wall can be an art in itself. This room has pale neutral walls with an interesting arrangement of pictures in a wide variety of styles, colors, and media. A perfect sense of balance has been created here.

Creating a style
with color

The rich variety of historical and cultural influences in our world, as

well as the differences between urban or rural environments and hot

or cool climates, have ensured that certain color combinations have

become synonymous with particular places. Regional traditions often

begin when people use materials available locally, such as lime for

whitewash or earth pigments for coloring. A familiar local style

is established, which people follow even after other

choices have become available.

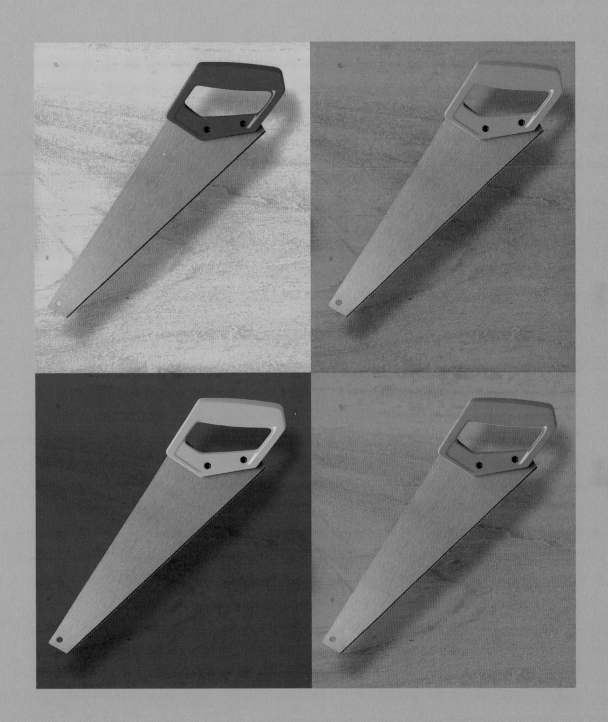

Introduction

Colors can evoke such strong memories and associations that they transport us to faraway places. In this chapter there are projects designed to help you create a sense of place. Whether you prefer the faded earthy colors of walls in the back streets of Venice to the gilded grandeur of its hotels along the Grand Canal, or the perfumed lavender hills of Provence to the palm trees, striped awnings, and pink umbrellas of Cannes, getting the colors right is the vital first step toward recreating the style.

Indian colors defy all the rules and succeed every time. The stamped detail on the wall is easy to create and looks superb.

RIGHT: The spirit of Provence conjured up with color and pattern. The green of the wall has been created by layering three different colors: yellow, blue-green, and yellow-green.

Country styles

The chapter begins with a focus on country style. The most urban, modern take on the country theme emphasizes muted, soft background colors and natural fabrics. The country theme is carried on into New England, with a Shaker peg rail and a set of star sconces. Shaker-style features peg rails around the walls of every room, and of course, no American country home would be quite complete without some reference to the United States flag. Then we include an English country look, a combination of new and old country-house style. The colors are bright and modern but the country garden atmosphere remains the same.

Styles from around the world

Scandinavia is a collective name for the countries around the Baltic Sea and the Arctic Ocean. The colors used here often reflect the sky and the landscape—white, gray-blue, and yellow. There is a tradition of bold wall painting, and the roller stripe pattern could be made more ornate with hand-painted spots or flowers.

Moroccan colors and style are used for the Moorish Casbah projects, with an arched bedhead painted onto a wall and, because tiling is so much a part of Moroccan style, there is a simple mosaic mirror frame project.

Most Moorish colors are made using natural earth pigments and the most typical shades are pink, orange, terra cotta, and blue-green. The deep intense blue is the one color we most associate with this style and is worth seeking out from a specialized paint company. Assemble a mixture of Moroccan textiles and pierced tin lanterns for the full casbah effect.

The Indian room is brilliantly colored, inspired by bright sari fabrics with a touch of pure gold in the stamped detail and border pattern. The key to decorating in this style is to use highly saturated color at its full intensity.

If it looks too bright in the tin, then it's going to be perfect for the Indian look!

Romany and rustic styles

Next up is Romany, which mixes Eastern European folk art and bargeware style. The folk patterns of all traveling people have a lot in common, and the two window projects included here show how to give your kitchen window the Romany treatment.

The rustic farmhouse colors of Tuscany are based on earth pigments and reflect the colors of the fields. The rich red brown, yellow ocher and pale faded viridian green are typically Tuscan. There is an easy woodwork project here, showing how to make a key cabinet for the hallway that looks like a small shuttered window set into a rustic wall. The heat of Provençe is offset by the brilliant blue Mediterranean Sea and the colors here are bright and lively. The pattern on the chair is traced and hand-painted in the traditional way. Tablecloths are a key feature of the Provençal kitchen style and, trimmed with simple yellow rickrack braid, this one is very easy to make.

Eco, urban, and beside the ocean

The next projects have more to do with a style than a particular place. The Natural Palette is inspired by eco style. Soft, muddy colors, chalky finishes, and natural materials are combined in a cool, calm, and contemporary way.

The Urban Minimalist combines few possessions with perfect taste and a limited color palette. Here the color lilac is chosen for its calming effect and the floating shelf lets nothing interfere with its horizontal line. Industrial Modern is a take on loft living style, where a home is made inside an industrial space. Here steel flooring, pulleys, and exposed metal girders are the state of the art. The projects show you

how to give your floor an unusual make-over using strips of hardboard nailed into the existing floor and how to make a shelving unit supported by breeze blocks.

Beside the Ocean shows how to give your dining area a beach hut vacation feeling with shiny white wood paneling surrounded by plenty of fresh bright colors. And if your idea of a vacation is more Ocean Drive than bucket and spade, the final Miami Pastel projects could be just what you're looking for.

We are all unique individuals with our own personal color preferences and passions. The projects in this chapter reach out in so many directions and cover a wide range of decorating ideas, skills, and challenges. Be inspired and take this opportunity to nail your own favorite colors to the mast.

This bedroom has been fitted out in Moorish style, using pink, orange, terra cotta, and blue-green. The mosaic mirror, arched bedhead and Moorish-style fabrics complete the colorful look.

Modern country

Country style is about blending in with your surroundings, bringing the outdoors inside and creating a comfortable, harmonious living space. Traditionally, this took place on a farm or around the edge of the town where suburbs and fields merge, but now urban country style proclaims everyone's right to a piece of the country—even those with high-rise city homes. Modern country is about choosing the right colors from a limited traditional palette and combining them with weathered textures and homespun accessories.

Colors like buttermilk, moss green, rust red, and blue-gray all promote a calm atmosphere and are good choices for the country look. Plaster pink, soft golden yellow, and terra cotta add warmth, and dark green and brown are good deep natural colors.

This is not a cluttered look, although a few genuine country pieces like a birdhouse, stoneware pottery, or a weathervane will give an air of country authenticity. The trick is to celebrate simplicity and craftsmanship without resorting to the coolness of minimalism.

Strip and wax the floorboards if they are worth exposing, or paint them if not. In a large room where the floor is less than perfect, you could try a painted checkerboard floor. They are quite easy to do and look great in soft colors like pale green or gray and white.

Keep it natural

Walls are painted in pale country colors to make the most of the room's natural light. Patterns can be introduced with simple graphic stencils, but avoid anything fussy or overtly pretty. Keep the color scheme natural and save the stronger colors for accents in the room, rather than making a feature of them.

Perfect accessories

Modern country patterns are stripes, checks, and plaids, and the key motifs are letters, numerals, stars, and simplified natural shapes like fruit, vegetables, animals, and flowers.

Textures include basketweave, wrought iron, linen, and genuinely distressed old pieces of furniture or vintage textiles. The combination of good modern design and carefully selected flea market finds are what give this style its charm. Look out for wooden kitchen chairs—a mixture of chairs in different styles can be coordinated by painting them using the same shade or several different but harmonious colors.

If your window frames are new and far from country in style, then drape the real windows with fine muslin. Look out for an old wooden window frame in a salvage yard which can be fitted with a mirror and hung on the wall as a fake window feature—the effect is surprisingly good, especially if you choose what is reflected with care. Don't be afraid to use good modern design with this look—old and new are fine together, just combine good country colors, natural materials, and interesting one-off objects to create your very own individual modern country style.

RIGHT: **The greens used here on the walls and the wooden table are perfect for creating the calm feel of the modern country look. You can incorporate interesting items picked up in flea markets that fit with the style.**

YOU WILL NEED:

- A BENCH — OR
  5 BOARDS TO
  CONSTRUCT
  YOUR OWN
- RUST RED/ORANGE
  PAINT IN ANY MAT
  FINISH
- TURQUOISE MAT
  PAINT
- GLOSS VARNISH
- WHITE CANDLE
- MEDIUM GRADE
  SANDPAPER
- STEEL WOOL
- 2 IN./5 CM PAINT
  BRUSH
- BACKGROUND
  COLORS:
  BUTTERMILK CREAM
  FOR WALLS, NATURAL
  BOARD OR MATTING
  FLOOR, OLIVE GREEN
  WOODWORK

PROJECT
Painting a five–board bench

The bench used here has been constructed to a traditional pattern using rough timber, to create an instant country antique. These benches have been made all over the world in many shapes and sizes—essentially they have a nice smooth plank top, two ends cut into legs at the base, and two side pieces. It is a simple design that endures because it is easy and it works well.

These days they are displayed as country antiques, but once every home would have had a small five-board bench that would double-up as a seat for a small child and a single step for reaching high shelves.

A bench is easy to make. Here rust red paint was used with a turquoise second layer; part of the top layer was rubbed away to give the worn look of a sturdy piece of furniture well used over the generations.

HOW TO DO IT

Use colors with a good contrast in order to make the most of this fun painting technique.

STEP 1 Apply one coat of the rust red paint. This thick covering coat must be bone dry before the next stage.

STEP 2 Rub the candlewax on all the edges of the top plank, plus lightly across two "sitting" areas on the surface. Also rub along the edges of the legs and the side planks. The candlewax will resist the next coat of paint, although this will not be obvious at first.

STEP 3 Apply a single coat of the bright turquoise paint, and leave the bench to dry.

STEP 4 Using the steel wool, rub away the paint in all the areas where you rubbed the candlewax. After initial resistance it should come off quite easily. Now use the sandpaper to rub away some of the red below to reveal some of the wood. Don't rush this job—the aim is to replicate the effect of many years of family life, so it is worth taking a little time over it!

STEP 5 Apply two or three coats of gloss varnish to the turquoise parts, leaving the rubbed areas matt. This will enhance the illusion of layers applied over the years.

YOU WILL NEED:

- IRON
- IRONING BOARD
- SCISSORS
- TAPE MEASURE
- PENCIL OR CHALK
- RULER
- 1 IN./2.5 CM WIDTH
  BONDING TAPE
- 5 FT./1.5 M CURTAIN
  WIDTH MUSLIN
  (PREFERABLY)
- 20 IN./50 CM OF
  SAME WIDTH GREY
  LINEN OR FINE
  COTTON LAWN
- PINS
- CURTAIN POLE
- POLE SUPPORTS

PROJECT
Muslin no-sew drapes

Butter muslin or cheesecloth is soft and not too transparent. It filters the light and obscures the view both into and out of a room. The unbleached cream fabric has just enough weave to be interesting, and lets in just enough light to show this off. The muslin is a very lightweight fabric and as such is ideal to use with bonding tape and an iron. The drapes are hung from a pole threaded through a fold-over casing at the top and finished with a binding hem of dove-gray linen which adds just the right amount of weight to ensure that the drapes hang really well.

These beautiful soft muslin curtains give privacy but let light pass through. They can be made very quickly and easily and are perfect for those who cannot sew.

HOW TO DO IT

No-sew muslin drapes can be made very quickly and the finish is often neater than stitching. Take time to measure and turn the hems evenly and avoid touching the bonding tape with the iron.

STEP 1 Measure the window. The drapes should not be too full, so allow the width plus half again to give a slightly gathered look. Measure the length from the pole to the floor and add 4 in./10 cm for the fold-over casing. At the bottom the raw edge will be enclosed in the band of linen. Place the drape lengths on the ironing board and press a folded ¾ in./2 cm hem.

STEP 2 Draw a line 3¼ in./8 cm from the first fold. Iron the bonding tape on the line. Peel off the backing and fold the top section over. Press to bond the two sides together.

STEP 3 Cut out the gray binding strips and turn over and press a small seam to fold in the raw edges.

STEP 4 Place a strip of bonding tape along each of the folded seams and press with an iron to bond. Now fold them in half lengthwise and press along the fold.

STEP 5 Place the raw bottom edges of the muslin inside the folded linen edgings. Pin them in place. Peel off the backing, one side at a time, and iron to bond the fabrics.

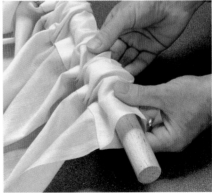

STEP 6 Press the drape lengths and feed them onto the pole.

New England

The New England style contains elements of the Maine coast, Shaker, Amish, and American Folk Art, and could also be called New Yorker's Retreat style — simplicity as interpreted by the wealthy. The East Coast of America is where the European settlers first landed and cultures merged. There is a mixture of preserved European traditional crafts, local materials, and new world aspirations. In the countryside, picket fences surround clapboard houses with rocking chairs on their porches.

Pay a visit to the library to look at books on the Amish and Shakers, whose quilting and furniture-making skills are at the heart of this style. The furniture has a simple elegance and the quilts were constructed within the strict religious boundaries that forbade unnecessary decoration. This pared-down approach to design gives their work a contemporary feel.

The Maine coast style is light and airy, with lots of pale wood, flag and lighthouse references, handhooked rugs, slatted wooden chairs, and painted canvas floorcloths. The style is comfortable and casual. There is a real reverence for anything old, from farm stall signs to iron gates or vintage quilts, but this lifestyle relies on just the right mixture of old, new, and repro to provide the minimum housework and maximum leisure time.

Mellow warmth

To get the New England country look right, you should use historical American colors in shades reminiscent of those originally derived from earth, mineral, and plant pigments — rich, deep rusty red, blue-gray, sky blue, deep green, golden yellow, red-brown, cream, and yellow ocher.

Combinations of deep red, black, and yellow, or cream and rust red with deep brown woodwork, give a delicious mellow warmth. Keep the main colors slightly muddy and add accents of brilliant colors with tinware, rugs, cushions, and pictures.

Seaside style

The seaside style is lighter and brighter, making use of a lot of white to reflect the sun and sea. Faded seaside colors like pale sea green, gray and sky blue combine well with rich bright red and deep navy blue. Driftwood or polished light natural wood looks good, but dark wooden furniture is too heavy for this style. Windows can be shuttered or draped with plain cotton canvas. If drapes are needed for warmth at night, use blankets with contrasting blanket-stitch edges at the windows. Limit your paint color palette to a selection of those mentioned, and look out for authentic coastal collectables such as shell pictures, ships in bottles, ropes, anchors, etc. But remember to keep it quite bare with a few key objects, and avoid clutter or your airy Maine style will start to resemble a Cornish pub!

RIGHT: **This Shaker style peg rail adds a decorative touch without being overly ornamental. This style has become very popular during the last decade.**

YOU WILL NEED:

• 2 IN. X 1 IN./5 CM X
2.5 CM PAR TIMBER,
THE LENGTH OF YOUR
WALL

• WOODEN PEGS OR
6 FT./2 M OF
1 IN./2.5 CM DOWEL

• 1 IN./2.5 CM SPADE
BIT

• DRILL

• MEDIUM GRADE
SANDPAPER

• WOOD GLUE

• STRAIGHT-EDGE WITH
SPIRIT LEVEL

• TAPE MEASURE

• PENCIL

• WALL ANCHORS

• NUMBER 6 MASONRY
AND COUNTERSINK
BIT

• 2½ IN./6 CM
NUMBER 6
COUNTERSINK
SCREWS

• SCREWDRIVER

• SAW

• WOOD FILLER

• PRIMER

• SHAKER BLUE PAINT

• PAINT BRUSH

PROJECT
A Shaker-style peg rail

The Shakers were a religious group who lived communally. They needed plenty of clear floor space for their meetings, where they performed a peculiar shaking dance, so they hung their chairs from rails on the wall. The Shakers are famous for their simple but beautifully crafted furniture, much of which was "built in" to keep the rooms plain-looking, although they found ways of adding decorative touches without breaking the religion's strict guidelines on having ornaments. Shaker style has become very popular in the past decade and fits in really well with the modern trend for de-cluttering.

ALTERNATIVE COLOR SUGGESTION:
Deep cherry red on a yellow ocher wall

The peg rail is equally at home in the bathroom for hanging up toiletries and in the bedroom for coats and children's toys. It is a great way to keep clutter off the floor and surfaces.

HOW TO DO IT

Peg rails can be positioned at the most useful height for any room — high up in the bathroom or low down in a child's bedroom.

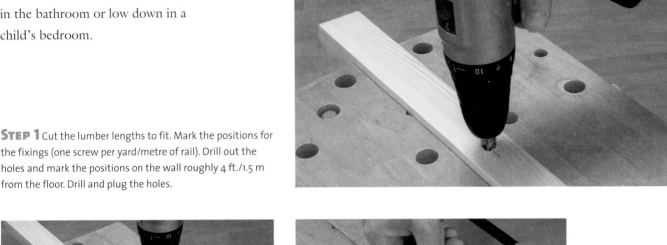

STEP 1 Cut the lumber lengths to fit. Mark the positions for the fixings (one screw per yard/metre of rail). Drill out the holes and mark the positions on the wall roughly 4 ft./1.5 m from the floor. Drill and plug the holes.

STEP 2 Mark out the positions for the pegs along the rail. They should not be too close together; consider the room's proportions and allow a spacing of 12 in.–20 in./30 cm–50 cm. Fit the spade bit to the drill and make the holes for the pegs (at an angle of 45°).

STEP 3 If using dowel, cut it into 4 in./10 cm lengths for the pegs. Smooth the exposed ends to a neat rounded finish and rub the sides of the "sinking" ends on the sandpaper to slim them slightly so that they fit snugly into the drilled holes.

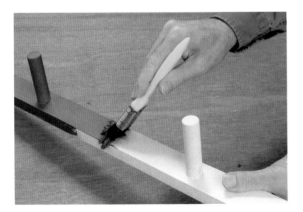

STEP 4 Paint the pegs and the rail before you fit them together or attach them to the wall. When the paint has dried, squeeze wood glue into the holes and coat the sinking ends of the pegs. Tap them in position, then wipe away any excess glue. Leave to set.

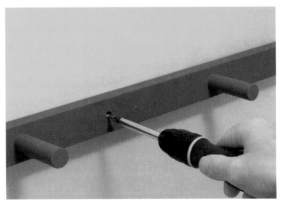

STEP 5 Finally, screw the peg rail onto the wall, then cover the screwheads with wood filler and touch up with paint once it has dried.

YOU WILL NEED:

- 10 IN. X 10 IN./
  25 CM X 25 CM PIECE
  OF OLD PINE FOR
  STAR, PLUS SMALL
  OFFCUT FOR SHELF
- STAR PATTERN
  TEMPLATE
- BENCH WITH A
  CLAMP
- BACK SAW OR A
  JIGSAW
- DRILL WITH A
  NUMBER 4 BIT
- MEDIUM GRADE
  SANDPAPER
- 2 X 2 IN./5 CM
  NUMBER 6 SCREWS
- CHERRY RED PAINT
  (ACRYLIC)
- DEEP-BLUE PAINT
  (ACRYLIC)
- WHITE PAINT
  (ACRYLIC)
- BEESWAX POLISH
  AND A BRUSH TO
  APPLY IT
- PAINT BRUSHES
- A PIECE OF WIRE AND
  A NAIL FOR HANGING
  UP THE STAR

PROJECT
A painted folk-art star

Stars and stripes appear in many forms in American decorating. Genuine folk-art is wonderful, but reproduction objects like this star are fun to make, and help to reinforce the Maine coast theme. Make just one large star or a group of smaller, different-colored ones. The project shows how to make the most of the grain of an old piece of wood by painting, then rubbing back the star and waxing it, or you can use new pine and give it a similar treatment by applying two different-colored paints, then rubbing back the top coat with sandpaper in places to reveal the color below. Stark color contrasts are always best for this effect.

TEMPLATE

Draw a pattern based on this star shape. The star made here measured 8 in./20 cm from point to point and the small shelf for the candle was 3 in./7 cm square.

SUGGESTION

Make a group of small stars in the flag colors and hang them together on the wall as candle sconces (never leave candles in a room unattended as they present a fire risk).

HOW TO DO IT

A jigsaw makes short work of cutting out these star shapes. Practice your cutting technique on scrap wood before you go on to the real thing.

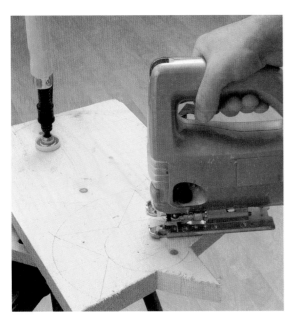

STEP 1 Transfer the pattern onto the wood. Clamp the wood to the bench and, using the back saw or jigsaw, carefully cut out the star shape. If you are using a jigsaw, then it will be easiest to drill holes at the inner points, insert the blade, and cut outward away from them.

STEP 2 Sandpaper the edges of the star to round them off a bit and to tidy up the inner and outer points. Mark the position for the small shelf and drill two screw holes through the star, then fix it in place from the back using 2 x 2 in./5 cm number 6 screws.

STEP 3 Apply a coat of red paint and leave to dry.

STEP 4 Rub back the paint around the edges and also rub gently with the grain so that the ridges are revealed. Fix the wire to the back of the star and hang it from a nail, folk style.

English country

The English country cottage is a very cozy and welcoming place where there are roses and honeysuckle around the door in summer and usually a freshly baked cake for tea. In the winter time there will always be a log fire burning in the grate and a soft wool shawl draped over the back of the sofa for that little bit of extra warmth. If you get the look right, visitors should immediately feel so at home that they flop down in a comfortable chair, put their feet up, and ask for a cup of tea. In fact, you may have to use force to evict them!

English country style is eclectic, and only really works well when old and new are mixed together. Aim for the impression that furniture and accessories have been passed down through the family for several generations. If you are starting from scratch, shop around at antique markets, garage sales, and craft fairs. The right framed mirror or china bowl can make all the difference and need not cost a fortune—imperfections, chips, and worn edges actually enhance the look.

Pattern is one of the key ingredients, and many different styles can be successfully combined, including woven woollen plaids, Indian and Turkish rugs, tapestries, plain and floral cotton chintz, damask, and lace.

Old and mellow

Floral patterned fabrics are now produced in soft faded colors, or you could search out genuine vintage fabrics at charity sales or flea markets. One old chintz curtain can make a whole set of plump cushions if you're handy with a sewing machine.

In old country cottages with exposed beams, walls are usually rough plaster painted white, pink, or creamy yellow. Low ceilings and small windows can make rooms dark and gloomy, but by painting window recesses glossy white you can virtually double the amount of incoming natural light. Another trick is to position mirrors opposite windows to reflect the light back into the room.

Faking it

If you don't have a sweet little beamed country cottage, but still want to decorate in the English Country style, the first thing to consider is the proportions of the room. Even the most boxy plain room can be made to look a lot cozier with the right wall treatment, colors, and lighting. Walls can be tongue-and-groove paneled up to picture rail height with a shelf running above the paneling. Or apply a rough textured paint to give the impression of an uneven surface and rough plasterwork. Stenciling works well on rough surfaces and is perfect in a country setting. Patterns can either be cut at home, taking inspiration from textiles in the room, or bought ready-cut.

The key colors are taken straight from the cottage garden: soft powder blue, cream, all shades of pink, pale, moss and grass green, brown, and brick red.

RIGHT: **You should be able to find an old second-hand chair fairly easily. Once you have repainted and varnished it, choose a floral-patterned fabric that will give the feel of an English country cottage.**

YOU WILL NEED:
- POWDER BLUE PAINT FOR BACKGROUND
- SAMPLE POTS OF TWO PINKS
- SAMPLE POT OF GREEN
- STENCIL MATERIAL (MYLAR OR STENCIL CARD IF YOU PREFER), OR BUY A READY-CUT ROSE STENCIL
- SPRAY ADHESIVE
- SCALPEL OR SNAP-BLADE KNIFE
- 3 STENCIL BRUSHES
- 3 WHITE SAUCERS
- PAPER TOWELS
- PLUMB LINE
- SQUARE OF CARD (TO MARK DISTANCE BETWEEN MOTIFS)

PROJECT
A rose-stenciled wall

If you like pattern and have uneven walls, then stenciling is the best method for you, as wallpaper requires walls that are smooth and even. This is a very romantic, feminine style for a pretty bedroom. The blue rose-patterned walls have a look of faded textiles and combine well with lace, muslin, and plenty of vintage floral fabrics used for cushions and bed covers. The walls provide a perfect backdrop for traditional bedroom furniture like dressing tables, Lloyd Loom chairs, iron bedsteads, and closets. Keep a look-out for pretty old vases, mirrors, and lamps that will add authenticity to the look.

TEMPLATE
Copy this pattern or enlarge it using the grid system. We used the rose pattern at the size of 2½ in./6 cm across. The stencil can be cut from waxed card or special stencil plastic available from craft stores.

HOW TO DO IT

Stenciling a wall pattern is quicker than putting up wallpaper and also a lot cheaper. Use the smallest amount of paint on your brush and practice on paper before you tackle the wall.

STEP 2 Peel off the paper pattern, then spray the back of the stencil with spray adhesive and leave it to become tacky.

STEP 3 Hang the plumb line 10 in./ 25 cm from one corner of the wall and position the card with the line running through two corners. Make a pencil mark at each corner, then move the card down, placing the top point on the lowest mark, and repeat to baseboard. Mark up the whole wall in this way.

STEP 1 Make the pattern for the stencil. Coat the back of the pattern with spray adhesive and stick it onto the stencil material. Use a sharp snap-blade knife and cut out the stencil carefully.

STEP 4 Position the stencil and smooth it onto the wall. Put the paints on the saucers and dab off brushes with paper towels so little remains on the brush.

STEP 5 Begin stenciling with the dark pink in the middle of the rose, then move on to the pale pink for the outer petals. Lift the stencil to check on the result as you go.

STEP 6 Use the green paint for the leaves and stem. Lift the stencil to check the result. Position it on the next mark and repeat the pattern until the wall is covered with roses.

YOU WILL NEED:

CHAIR:

- **A CHAIR TO MAKE OVER**
- **MEDIUM GRADE SANDPAPER**
- **PALE GREEN PAINT**
- **WHITE MAT ACRYLIC PRIMER**
- **PAINT BRUSH**

CUSHION COVER:

- **FLORAL FABRIC TO COVER YOUR CHAIR SEAT**
- **SCISSORS**
- **PINS**
- **THREAD**
- **SEWING MACHINE (OR JUST A STAPLER IF THE SEAT IS A DROP-IN TYPE)**

PROJECT

A painted chair with a new cushion cover

First, look for an old chair in need of some tender, loving care. It should be easy to pick up a bargain, as dealers go for matching pairs or sets of four or more. The ideal chair would be wooden with a pretty shape and an upholstered seat. A Lloyd Loom chair is another option, and you could make a frilled loose cushion if the seat is not upholstered. The chair used here is a traditional bentwood design with a hard round seat in need of a soft cushion. If your chair has an upholstered seat, cut out a new one using the previous cover as a pattern and staple it in place.

PAINTING THE CHAIR

Decide where you are going to put your chair before you buy it, and choose one that will suit the space. It is not necessary to strip all the old paint or varnish from the chair—simply rub it down for painting.

STEP 1 Give the old paintwork a good rub down with sandpaper, not removing all the paint but scratching the surface to provide a key for the primer. Apply a coat of white primer.

STEP 2 Apply one or two coats of the green top coat. If your upholstery fabric has green in the pattern, then try to match the chair color to it. Use satin or low luster paint or latex paint with a protective coat of varnish.

MAKING THE CUSHION/ SEAT COVER

Choose a fabric that will look good with the rosy wall, something genuinely old or an offcut of soft furnishing fabric in a floral chintz. If the chair has a drop-in seat, remove it and use the seat itself as a template for the fabric. If you are making a loose cushion, follow the directions below. Round cushions are simple to make but the stitching must be done slowly to keep to the curve. A feather-filled round cushion pad is ideal for a bedroom chair.

STEP 1 Cut out two matching round pieces of fabric, adding a 2 in./50 cm seam allowance all around the edges.

STEP 2 Pin the pieces together, right sides facing, leaving an opening for the cushion pad. If you would like a lace frill or piped edge, then this has to be inserted and pinned at the same time.

STEP 3 Sew around the pinned seam line. Notch a seam allowance all around the cushion, then turn it the right way around.

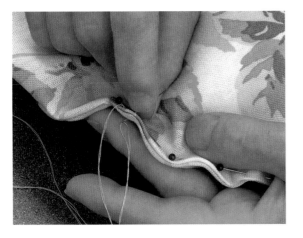

STEP 4 Place the cushion pad inside the cover and neatly slip-stitch the opening.

Pure Romany

Romany style is most suited to people who prefer to keep one foot in the past and whose idea of bliss is a country kitchen with a cooking range. Rich, dark background colors are decorated using the light touch of single freehand brushstrokes, with each pattern being composed of a mixture of stripes, swirls, dots, and curves. Romany inspiration comes from the countryside and nature; flowers are the most popular decorative motif. Red, green, black, and white are the main colors, but many other colors can be used for the decoration.

The colors explode with all the fun of the fair. Bright canal barges, decks piled high with vividly patterned tinware, fairground stalls, and painted gipsy caravans are the inspiration for this look. Painting patterns were handed down through Romany families, and as traditional lifestyles changed, many of these painting skills disappeared.

Fortunately the lazy, slow, canal-boat lifestyle appealed to people looking for an escape route from the fast pace of modern life, and since the 1970s many canal boats have been restored and brought back to their former vivid beauty. The main patterns used include flowers, leaves, castles, bridges, horses, playing cards, scallops, and striped bands of color. Lettering is often part of the design, spelling out the name of the barge or its owner.

Free style

If the idea of living in a painted horse-drawn caravan or a canal boat sounds appealing but impractical, then why not settle for bringing some of the color and atmosphere into your home? The bright colors are set against a dark background of either black, dark green, or blue, and all the patterns are painted freehand.

It is a true peasant painting style, which is great fun to do as it requires the type of loose, confident brush stroke that is best achieved after a glass or two of wine!

If you love the patterns but find the brilliance of the colors too overwhelming, try artificially fading them with a milky glaze of varnish tinted with a small amount of white. This effect will be more like an old sun-bleached painted caravan needing a fresh coat of paint. If this appeals, then you could take the illusion a stage further and rub back some of the paint to simulate years of wear and tear.

Small is beautiful

On a large scale the pure Romany style would be quite overpowering for a main room, but it is perfect for a small cubby-hole of a room, or just as part of a room. These two projects show how to build and paint a pelmet and make curtains to hang below it. The window treatment will look equally good as the focal point in quite a plain room, as one of many patterns in a busy kitchen, or to add a touch of fantasy in a child's playroom. And a painted window-box filled with flowers outside the window is the perfect finishing touch.

RIGHT: **Flowers are the essential ingredient in the Romany look. The floral pattern here is made by cutting out the flower shapes from felt and gluing them onto the curtain.**

YOU WILL NEED:

- A LENGTH OF 6 IN. X 1 IN./15 CM x 2.5 CM SHELVING PLANK (MEASURE THE WIDTH OF THE WINDOW PLUS 4 IN./10 CM
- SHELF BRACKETS
- TAPE MEASURE
- SPIRIT LEVEL
- DRILL
- SCREWDRIVER
- MASONRY BIT AND WALL ANCHORS
- SCREWS FOR THE BRACKETS
- A LENGTH OF HARDBOARD 6 IN./ 15CM WIDE OR ¼ IN./6 MM MDF— ENOUGH FOR BOXING IN THE TWO ENDS AND THE LENGTH OF THE FRONT
- HARDBOARD PINS
- SMALL HAMMER
- SAW
- WHITE CHALK PENCIL
- BLACK BASECOAT PLUS A SELECTION OF ACRYLIC COLORS
- STRIPS OF PAPER
- SMALL DECORATOR'S BRUSH
- LONG-HAIRED ARTISTS' LINING PAINT BRUSHES (FINE, MEDIUM, AND BROAD)
- CURTAIN ROD AND 2 END FITTINGS

PROJECT

A painted wooden valance

A valance like this will look best fitted above a medium- to small-sized window. It is really easy to make, being basically a shelf on brackets with a strip of hardboard pinned onto the front and sides.

Valances are not especially fashionable at the moment but they do suit a folksy, traditional project like this, and the combination of valance and drapes is effective in creating a bold Romany-style statement.

One other bonus of making a valance is that it creates another shelf in the kitchen and provides a perfect place to display painted plates, pitchers, or even a vase of flowers.

The completed valance, which provides a handy shelf for displaying folksy objects such as this painted plate.

TEMPLATE

These patterns are the outline shapes for the freehand painting. Either practice by copying them freehand or enlarge the patterns to the desired size and trace their outlines onto the valance. Do this by rubbing the back with chalk or using a chalk transfer paper.

HOW TO DO IT

Make a simple valance out of hardboard or MDF, paint it black, and cover it with colorful Romany patterns.

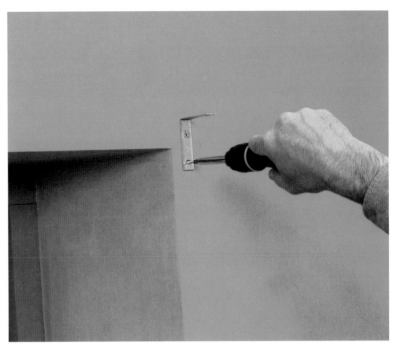

STEP 1 Measure and mark with a pencil the valance position 2 in./5 cm above the window recess. Check that it is straight using the spirit level. Mark the screw positions for the shelf brackets on the wall and on the shelf plank.

STEP 2 Drill all the necessary holes, insert wall anchors and fix the brackets to the wall.

STEP 3 Cut the end pieces from the length of hardboard, then lay all three pieces flat and apply the basecoat. Leave to dry, then apply a second coat.

STEP 4 Roughly mark out the pattern with the chalk pencil. Avoid using a ruler—use strips of paper as measuring guides where you need them.

STEP 5 Paint all the bands of color and leave them to dry. Practice the base patterns on paper first, and when your hand has loosened up, move on to paint the pattern details.

STEP 6 Paint as much decoration as you like, then fix the hardboard to the shelf front and sides. Screw the rod fittings into the inside ends. Use a small brush to touch up any pinheads or exposed edges, then fix the valance to the brackets.

YOU WILL NEED:

- COTTON DRILL:
  2 X DOUBLE THE
  WINDOW WIDTH
  X THE HEIGHT PLUS
  4 IN./10CM
- FELT IN 4 OTHER
  COLORS (FOR
  EXAMPLE, GREEN,
  WHITE, BLACK,
  YELLOW)
- BUTTONS FOR
  DECORATION
- THREAD
- LINING FABRIC—CAN
  BE COTTON SHEETING
- SEWING MACHINE
- RUFFLETTE TAPE FOR
  CURTAIN HEADINGS
- CURTAIN RINGS
- FABRIC GLUE
- A BRUSH
- PENCIL/CHALK
- PINS
- SCISSORS
- IRON
- NEEDLE AND THREAD

PROJECT
Felt appliqué drapes

Felt decorations can give drapes a stylish, brightly colored Romany look. Felt pattern shapes can be cut out and stuck down with glue. Although felt does not wash well, the colors are bright and will stay fresh-looking for a couple of years. The drapes are backed with a plain cotton lining.

Romany style has always included a variety of textiles—hand-dyed, woven, embroidered, and appliquéed. The main pattern theme is a flower treated in a stylized way. These floral patterns are taken from Eastern European folk art and arranged in a typical way for decorating a long skirt or an apron.

The completed drape with its cheerful flowers. Try out this pattern or use your imagination and create your own flower template.

TEMPLATE

Draw these patterns or copy them (enlarged to the desired size) and cut them out of thin paper. Then pin the patterns to felt and cut out the shapes.

HOW TO DO IT

These drapes are lined and headed
with a simple tape and curtain rings.
The decoration is glued in place with
strong fabric glue but could also be
fixed in place using a contrasting
blanket stitch.

STEP 1 Cut out all the drape and lining
lengths. Draw the pattern shapes and cut
them out of the colored felt.

STEP 2 Arrange the pattern shapes on the background, then
glue each one in position (if you like hand-sewing, these can
be edged in contrasting running stitch or blanket stitch).

STEP 3 Turn over a narrow hem on the lining side seams,
then pin the linings onto the front of the drapes along the top
edge, allowing roughly 1 in./2.5 cm for the seam. Stitch, then turn
the lining over onto the back and press the top seam flat.

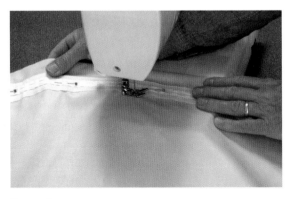

STEP 4 Pin the heading tape to the lining about 1 in./2.5 cm
from the top edge, then stitch it using the same color thread
as the felt drape so that the stitching is invisible on the front.

STEP 5 Fit the curtain rings onto the heading tape and
hang the drapes from the rail. Pin up the hem with the lining
tucked into the seam, then loosely slip-stitch the hem (this
can be done without taking the drapes down).

Provençal

Provence in the south of France has a wonderful climate, perfect light, and absolutely stunning scenery. The Mediterranean sea and sky provide a vibrant blue background for the old buildings with their tall windows, balconies, shutters, and awnings. Palm trees line the coast and the countryside is rocky and rugged, peppered with bushes of wild lavender, thyme, and rosemary. There are olive groves and citrus orchards on the hillsides, and purple fields of lavender down in the valleys. Yellow mimosa trees with their feathery leaves are grown all around this beautiful region.

Provence is a mixture of extreme wealth and high fashion in the popular French Mediterranean coastal resorts of Nice and Cannes, co-existing alongside a traditional rustic lifestyle in the hills. Marseilles, France's main port, has a large population of North Africans, who have brought their own culture and decorative traditions with them. The regional style in Provence can be compared to a busy marketplace where many delightful influences converge and where the overwhelming feeling is that life is good.

Landscape colors

The predominant colors used for decorating are those that appear in the landscape—a range of earthy yellows and red browns used with bright blues and viridian greens. Terra cotta is always there too, as clay plant pots and the rippling patterns of sun-bleached tiled rooftops. Walls are often painted using two colors, a deep shade below with a lighter one above. The bright sun soon fades exterior paintwork producing soft, muted, harmonious shades. Houses are decorated to feel cool inside, with tiled floors and pale-colored walls.

Typically Provençal

Green is popular for its cooling effect, and ferns are the favorite house plant. The wall-painting style is often quite rustic, rough, and distressed in contrast to elaborate decorative wrought iron, stained glass, carved or painted furniture, lace drapes, and richly patterned colorful fabrics. The distinctively complex Provençal floral and paisley fabric style is based on old Indian patterns that were brought back to Marseilles by sailors returning from Eastern countries in the eighteenth century. The French version of the fabric is still produced in the region, although the old handblocking and vegetable dyes have largely been replaced by modern textile printing methods and inks.

In a typical kitchen there will always be some colorful printed fabric, perhaps as a tablecloth or place mats. Displays of colorfully decorated plates and enamelware line the walls and shelves. Large cabinets, known as *armoires*, with wire mesh and gathered fabric door panels, are favored over the modern fitted kitchen. Herbs hang from racks, vases are filled with flowers, and the smell of coffee hangs in the air. *C'est magnifique!*

RIGHT: **The walls in this Provençal kitchen are a bright green, one of the colors of the Provence landscape. Colorful printed fabric is a must; the attractive tablecloth with accompanying napkins make the perfect complement to a continental breakfast.**

YOU WILL NEED:
- A PINE TABLE
- A WOODEN KITCHEN
  CHAIR
- SANDPAPER
- HOUSEHOLD BLEACH
- SCRUBBING BRUSH
- PROTECTIVE GOGGLES
- RUBBER GLOVES
- YELLOW PAINT
- PATTERN FOR CHAIR-
  BACK DRAWN ON
  TRANSFER PAPER
- PENCIL
- PAINTER'S TAPE
- TUBES OF PALE AND
  DEEP BLUE PAINT FOR
  DETAIL (ACRYLIC)
- 2 IN./5 CM
  HOUSEHOLD
  PAINT BRUSH
- ARTISTS' PAINT
  BRUSHES
  (ONE MEDIUM AND
  ONE FINE)

PROJECT
A painted kitchen table and chair

Preparing meals and eating together form a central part of the Provençal lifestyle. For this project a plain pine kitchen table is given a new, more decorative French style with a scrubbed top and painted legs, and the wooden kitchen chair has been given a new coat of bright yellow paint and the finishing touch of a typical French Provençal motif. Look out for a country-style kitchen chair with a shapely backrest and, if you're very lucky, a rush seat. Some peeling paint or chipped enamelware is part of this look, and will give the room a sense of history.

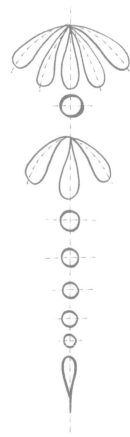

TEMPLATE

Trace this pattern twice to use across the back of a chair with an extra dot between them. Chalky-backed transfer paper is ideal for this task and can be bought from art suppliers.

HOW TO DO IT

Give a pine table some character with a scrubbed top and brightly painted legs and paint a wooden chair to match.

STEP 1 Prepare the table legs and the chair for painting by sanding away any loose paint or varnish. Sand the top to remove all traces of varnish, then scrub it thoroughly with a 50/50 solution of bleach and water. Protect your eyes with goggles. You may wish to protect your hands with rubber gloves.

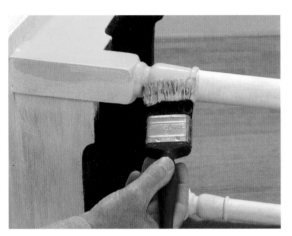

STEP 2 Apply a coat of primer, then two coats of yellow paint to the table legs and top rails.

STEP 3 Prime the chair, then apply two coats of yellow paint. Latex is used here for a mat finish, but gloss could be used instead for an easy-clean surface.

STEP 4 Trace the pattern twice to make a symmetrical pattern for the chair-back. Insert transfer paper between pattern and chair.

STEP 5 Tape the transfer paper and the pattern onto the chair-back. Go over the pattern in pencil.

STEP 6 Paint the pattern on the chair-back using free-flowing brushstrokes and two different-sized brushes.

YOU WILL NEED:
- FABRIC FOR THE TABLECLOTH AND 6 NAPKINS: 90 IN./2.25 M OF 48 IN./1.2 M WIDTH FABRIC
- 13 YD./12 M OF CONTRASTING RICKRACK BRAID
- THREAD
- PINS
- SCISSORS
- SEWING MACHINE

PROJECT
Tablecloth and napkins

The French lifestyle revolves around mealtimes, and in the south the lunch table is likely to be spread with one of the locally produced bright floral cloths. Square tablecloths and napkins are easy to make—all you need is a suitable piece of fabric and a border trimming. Genuine handblocked Provençal fabric can be bought in specialty stores, but there are many machine-printed versions. Better still, take a vacation in Provence and bring back examples of the real thing! The trim that is used here is called rickrack, but color coordinated cotton fringe would also look good around the tablecloth.

The tablecloth and napkins are made from simple squares of cloth, cut to shape and fitted with a trimming in a contrasting color. The blue fabric is reminiscent of clear blue Provence skies.

HOW TO DO IT

This is sewing at its simplest
and the biggest effort will
involve getting the sewing
machine set up.

STEP 1 Cut out the square tablecloth by
taking one corner of the fabric across to meet
the other side. Align the edges, smooth the
triangle flat, and cut the fabric using the
top edge as a guide. This will provide an
accurate square.

STEP 2 Divide the remaining fabric into six
10 in./25 cm squares.

STEP 3 Fold over a narrow hem on the cloth and napkins,
and pin, then machine them using zigzag stitch.

STEP 4 Pin the trimming around the edges of all the pieces
and topstitch in a matching thread. Use a straight stitch and
pay special attention to folding in the trimming ends;
otherwise they could fray.

Tuscany

Tuscany in summer presents the perfect antidote to a gray winter spent in a city—the effect is instantaneous and unforgettable. Italy, like every other industrialized society, has moved away from old-style farming and many Italians choose new, problem-free housing with all mod cons over the tumbledown old farm buildings that fire the visitor's imagination. The restoration of farmhouses and villas in the Tuscan countryside has largely been undertaken by outsiders, for whom it was a case of "love at first sight."

It seems that another culture's rural lifestyle always has more appeal than one's own, doubly so when the weather is good. The outsiders who have bought second homes in Tuscany have rescued what the locals would have thrown out in the name of progress, and craftsmen have found their traditional skills in great demand.

Tuscany has a treasury of art, architecture, and culture in cities such as Florence and Siena, where the climate has helped to preserve its beauty. The colors of marble, earth, and clay predominate, with the sun playing its part by fading fresh paint to blend seamlessly with the colors of older buildings.

The Tuscan climate is hot and dry, and houses are built of local stone with curved earthenware roof tiles. Windows have wooden shutters and the coloring of the buildings lets them blend into the landscape.

Simple and functional

Inside, the houses have tiled floors and plastered walls painted in pink, shades of faded blue green, or ocher yellow. There are no baseboards in the Tuscan style, but the lower parts of the walls are painted in a darker color in order to hide the scuff marks made by the broom. The small windows shield interiors from the scorching heat of the summer sun and the cold winter nights. Curtains are rare, but wooden shutters are fitted inside the windows, making it easy to block out the light during the afternoon rest hours. Window ledges are tiled, and the broad bands surrounding windows and doorways are picked out in softly contrasting colors.

The paint used in Tuscany is always limewash tinted with pigments. This is the perfect paint for the climate, and the chalky finish is essential for the authentic Tuscan look.

The furnishing style is simple and functional, as most entertaining takes place outside on the terrace. In Italy, furniture is often arranged against the walls rather than in the center of a room to keep an open, spacious feeling. A few pieces of wooden furniture, some hand-painted ceramics, pot plants, Turkish rugs, and table lamps are all in keeping with this style.

Terra cotta floor tiles are practical in an entrance hall and a kitchen, but are only suitable for living rooms in warmer climates. Polished floorboards and rugs look good and feel warmer underfoot. The key to success here is to keep it very simple.

RIGHT: The Tuscan look is easy to create using a Mediterranean paint for the walls that dries to a chalky finish. A textured wall surface is achieved by using a special textured paint. The shallow key cabinet gives the impression of a shuttered window.

YOU WILL NEED:

• LUMBER (SEE LUMBER
  REQUIREMENTS,
  RIGHT) PLUS SMALL
  SCRAP OF WOOD TO
  MAKE A CATCH
• SANDPAPER
• SANDING BLOCK
• 4 x HINGES
• 1 x IRON BOLT
• SMALL BRADS
• WOOD GLUE
• HAMMER
• HANDSAW
• SCREWDRIVER
• SMALL SCREWS
• AWL
• 6 CUP HOOKS
• 2 MIRROR FIXINGS
• RUST RED PAINT
• PAINT BRUSH

PROJECT
A small shuttered wall cabinet

This shallow cabinet looks just like a wooden shuttered window you would find in a farmhouse. On the wall in an entrance hall it creates the illusion of a window, when it is actually a key cabinet. Recycled wood gives the most rustic effect—or you could use part of a small louvered door. The idea is to make a box with a decorative lid that you can hang on the wall. For the backing plate, use wood that is thick enough to allow for hooks to be screwed in. The traditional colors used for shuttered windows are red-brown or blue-green, both of which soon fade and mellow when exposed to bright sunshine.

LUMBER REQUIREMENTS

Back: 11½ in. x 13 in./29 cm x 33 cm

Sides: 2 x 1 in. x 1 in./2.5 cm x 2.5 cm, measuring 11½ in./29 cm;

Top/bottom: 2 x 1 in. x 1 in./2.5 cm x 2.5 cm, measuring 11¼ in./28.5 cm

Doors: 5½ in. x 12½ in./14 cm x 32.5 cm

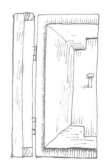

Panelling:
2¾ in./7 cm wide x
11½ in./29 cm long
(mitered)
2¾ in./7 cm wide x
4⅞ in./12.5 cm long
(mitered)

TEMPLATE
Draw a template based on these designs. The cupboard made here is 11½ in. x 13 in. x 1 in./29 cm x 33 cm x 2.5 cm , but adapt your template to the size you require.

HOW TO DO IT

This idea can be adapted to suit your needs or the lumber you have available. The cabinet is simply glued and pinned together.

STEP 1 Cut all the pieces to size (see lumber requirements, opposite). Sand as necessary.

STEP 2 Make up the shallow box with simple butt joints, using wood glue and brads to secure the sides and fix them to the back.

STEP 3 Make up the two front doors, adding extra panels and cross bars to give the shutter style (if required).

STEP 4 Attach the doors to the box base using two hinges for each door.

STEP 5 Fix the iron bolt onto the front to joint the doors in the middle.

STEP 6 Apply two coats of paint. When the cabinet is dry, screw six hooks (or more) into the back of it, then fit the mirror fixings onto the back and fix the cabinet onto the wall.

PROJECT
A painted wall finish

The Tuscan decorating style uses weathered, textured, and harmonious color with no hard lines, startling primary colors, or sharp contrasts. The look is not difficult to reproduce with Mediterranean paint that dries to a chalky finish. A slightly textured wall surface and colorwashed effect will intensify the Tuscan flavor, and the rough texture can be effectively applied with a special textured paint in a sand or farmhouse finish. The color here is also used to surround the small key cabinet to add to the illusion of it being a shuttered window.

The bright colors of this Tuscan-style wall give a feeling of zest and energy. The terra cotta stripe should be painted freehand. Then choose plants that will look fresh and lively against your wall.

HOW TO DO IT

Keep the brush strokes fresh and energetic and use chalky water-based paint for an authentic Tuscan wall finish.

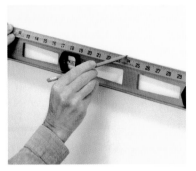

STEP 2 Measure 3 ft./1 m up from the floor and mark the wall at intervals. Draw a line along the length of the wall.

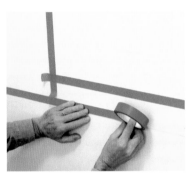

STEP 1 Measure a border of 4 in./10 cm around any window, doorway, or fitted feature, such as a cabinet, and mark this in pencil.

STEP 3 Place painter's tape on the lower side of the 3 ft./1 m line and inside the border line.

STEP 4 Dilute the paint and apply it to the lower wall and inside the inner border for the feature using random brushstrokes. Then leave it to dry.

STEP 5 Renew the tape and paint the top part of the wall and the outer border of the feature using the second diluted paint. Peel off the tape and paint a freehand stripe in terra cotta across the wall.

Moorish casbah

The Moorish style comes from the north of Africa where Morocco nestles between the Atlas Mountains and the sea. This meeting point of African and Muslim culture has a rich artistic and cultural tradition. Islamic art and decoration is based on geometric patterns as the religion forbids the making of images. Houses are built around inner courtyards with plain, fortress-style exteriors; all of the decoration is on the inside. The courtyards are lined with open balconies, often with rows of columns and elaborate arches.

One of the most stunning features in Moorish homes is the tiling. Tiles are used on walls and floors to create elaborate interwoven shapes and patterns. The star features in most patterns, usually in the center of a radiating trellis-work of star patterns. The main colors used are blue, white, black, pale green, and terra cotta. Colors are jewel-bright, whether on walls, tiles, or woven in textiles.

Domes and arches

Other important features in Moorish design are domes, arches, and water; these are features from traditional Arabic architecture. Doorways are arched and windows are usually covered with decorative metal grilles. Walled rooftop terraces are the most popular place for evening entertaining. Walls are either topped off with stepped patterns or simply castellated and whitewashed to reflect the searing heat. Pools and fountains cool the courtyards, and date palms provide shade.

Pierced lanterns, leather pouffes, carved tea tables, and intricately woven rugs are typical furnishings. Low couches are spread with rugs and silk cushions in all shapes and sizes. They provide comfortable seating for guests to drink tea and enjoy delicious sweet delicacies. This is a style that encourages relaxation and a more exotic, sensual way of living.

Moroccan style is not expensive or beyond our reach thanks to the market culture which exists at the source in Morocco and in all major cities in Europe. The hippy trail led straight to Marrakesh in the late 1960s, and people soon discovered that they could finance their nomadic lifestyles by buying Moroccan goods and selling them back home to fund their next visit. As a result, the markets were flooded with folding tables, rugs, lanterns, trays, and ceramics, many of which can still be picked up at reasonable prices in flea markets today. The ethnic decorating style which has been popular recently has brought a new wave of stylish Moroccan imports, but there are also plenty of beautiful and inexpensive pierced tin lanterns, sets of tea glasses, textiles, and rugs on offer through homestyle stores and mail order catalogs.

Exuberant palette

Travel guides for the area and books on Moorish architecture and interiors show this to be a rich mixture of sophisticated building and decoration enhanced by an exuberant ethnic palette.

RIGHT: **The Moroccan look is easy to achieve because the accessories are readily available and inexpensive. The headboard is painted on the wall and the mosaic mirror frame is handmade.**

YOU WILL NEED:

- DEEP-BLUE CHALKY FINISH PAINT
- PINK PAINT
- DEEP TERRA COTTA PAINT
- 2 x 4 IN./10 CM SQUARES OF THICK FOAM
- STAR PATTERN TEMPLATE
- SCALPEL
- SPRAY ADHESIVE
- BROWN WRAPPING PAPER FOR THE ARCH TEMPLATE
- SCISSORS
- CHALK
- LARGE BRUSH TO APPLY MAIN COLOR
- SMALL PAINT BRUSH FOR EDGES
- PLATE

PROJECT
A painted arch bedhead

Turn your bedroom into a scene from *A Thousand and One Nights* by painting the walls a warm pink stone color and painting a typically Moorish arch at the bedhead in deep ultramarine blue with a stamped tile surround. Enhance the casbah atmosphere with metal lanterns, candles, urns, and striped woven textiles. All the other colors in the room should be rich and warm so that the effect is one of looking up at an inky blue Moroccan night sky. If this effect appeals to you, why not also paint a distant sickle moon and stars on the blue arch shape?

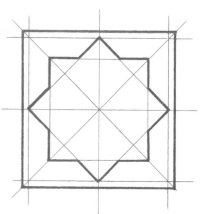

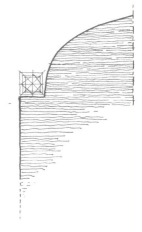

TEMPLATE
Draw the star pattern so that it fits neatly into a 4 in./10 cm square following the method shown in the diagram.

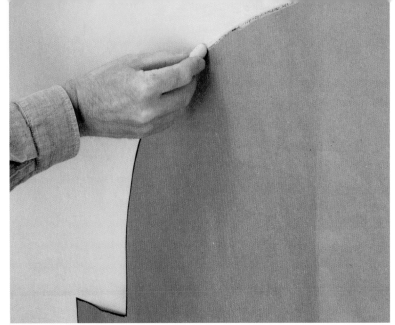

HOW TO DO IT

This arched bedhead does not take long to paint, and the stamped tiles are simple, bold, and effective.

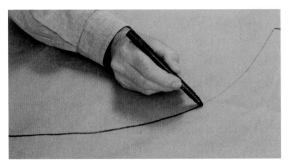

STEP 1 Enlarge and draw one half of the arch pattern onto the brown wrapping paper, either in sections on a photocopier or by squaring up. Cut it out and spray a light coating of spray adhesive on one side.

STEP 2 Stick this onto the wall and draw the shape with chalk, then flip the template over and repeat these steps to create a complete arch.

STEP 3 Enlarge the star pattern to 3¼ in./8 cm wide and stick the pattern onto one of the foam squares. Carefully cut out the shape to the depth of about ⅝ in./1.5 cm. Cut outward from the middle every time. Peel off the background to ⅝ in./1.5 cm, leaving a star-shaped stamp.

STEP 4 Paint the arch in deep blue, using the small brush for a neat finish around the edges.

STEP 5 Put some of the terra cotta paint onto a plate and coat the square tile stamp. Stamp a tile border around the edge of the arch, leaving the top triangle for now. Leave to dry.

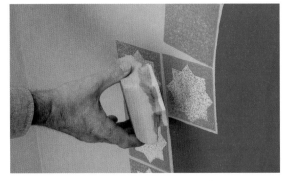

STEP 6 Now coat the star stamp in pink and place one star in every tile shape. Cut a foam stamp in a triangle shape to fill the gap at the top and on each side where the arch meets the straight supporting column. Fill in the gaps with this stamp using the terra cotta color.

YOU WILL NEED:
- ½ IN./1.2 CM
  PLYWOOD BASE
  16 IN. x 10 IN./40 CM
  x 25 CM
- ½ IN./1.2 CM
  PLYWOOD FRAME
  PIECES, 2 x 2 IN. x 14
  IN./5 CM x 33 CM
  AND 2 x 2 IN. x 8
  IN./5 CM x 20 CM
- MIRROR, CUT TO SIZE
- WOOD GLUE AND
  CLAMPS
- TILE ADHESIVE
- TERRA COTTA-TINTED
  GROUT
- MOSAIC TESSERAE
- MOSAIC SNIPPERS
- WHITE SCHOOL GLUE
- BRUSH
- MIRROR FIXINGS
  AND SCREWS
- SOFT CLOTH

PROJECT
Mosaic mirror frame

Tiling is very much a part of the Moorish style, and a mirror framed with tiles will look perfect in this setting. If you have never made a mosaic before, then this is the project to start with. Mosaic is not difficult, and there is always a wonderful surprise at the end when the grouting is wiped off and the bright jewel colors are revealed. Choose colors that would appear in Moroccan tiling such as blue, white, orange, and black, and either adapt an existing frame or make a new one one from plywood with a raised beading edge. A cut-down border of tiles around the inside edge of the mirror creates the illusion of depth.

This project is simple enough for those who have never done a mosaic before. A mirror framed with tiles is an essential part of the Moroccan style and looks fantastic.

HOW TO DO IT

Begin by making a simple plywood backing with a wide frame stuck on it as a recess for a mirror. Mosaic tiles are then arranged, stuck, and grouted to stunning effect.

STEP 1 Glue the frame pieces onto the base as shown, then clamp and leave until the glue has bonded. Outline the pattern on the frame in pencil.

STEP 2 Lay out the pattern, gluing each piece as you go. This is a very simple pattern and you should not need to trim any of the pieces.

STEP 3 When the frame pattern is laid, glue the mirror into the middle with a large squiggle of glue.

STEP 4 You may need to cut tiles to fit into the area between the mirror and the surface of the mosaic. Glue uncut tesserae to the outside edge of the frame so that they align with the surface of the mosaic. Grout the mosaic, making sure that the grout fills all the gaps, then polish the tiles and mirror with a soft cloth.

India

The subcontinent of India is a huge country of many distinct characters. The Buddhist north is mountainous with a cold climate, and to the west lie the farmlands and deserts of Rajasthan and Gujarat, which border the Arabian Sea. The Hindu south has the hottest climate and the most relaxed lifestyle, and here the economy is based around the traditional creative industries of textile printing and carving. The east has the River Ganges, jungles, mangrove swamps, and Calcutta, the most overpopulated city in India.

There is no such thing as one Indian style, but one thing all the regions of the subcontinent have in common is that they mix brilliant colors in ways that break all the Western rules defining "good taste" and color combining! The result is vibrant, energizing, and uniquely Indian. Colors are flung together with great confidence, and their impact is stunning. Different areas of India are famous for their skills in specific crafts such as embroidery, textile printing, pottery, or carpet weaving, but there is no area where most of these traditional skills are not practiced anyway.

Brilliant work

It is clear from the dress, homes, and jewellery of the craftspeople who produce these items that they have a genuine love for the patterns, colors, and motifs they reproduce, even though they are poorly paid for the work that they do. Most of the work is produced for the home market. Houses in cities are painted in brilliant colors; temples are adorned with carvings and bronze castings, and each festival generates a hive of industry producing all the necessary deities, offerings, and accessories that are needed for a proper celebration.

Seeking out the style

Many of the styles we recognize as our own have their origins in India. The paisley shawl, floral chintz, Madras check, Provençal prints, and damask cottons all originally came from India. Nowadays, several charitable organizations have Fair Trade arrangements with communities of craftspeople in India who supply goods directly for sale in their downtown stores, so it is really easy to buy genuine handmade accessories, textiles, and ornaments to give a room the right feel.

The sari stores found in the local shops of Asian communities sell lengths of fabric ranging from plain vibrant muslins for everyday wear to the finest exquisitely embroidered cloth for wedding saris. Sari lengths are ideal for draping over curtain poles at windows or as exotic drapes for a four-poster bed.

You will find that most paint companies produce vibrant color ranges. Choose the mainstream latex paints for children's rooms, where Indian-style brilliant color schemes are always sure to find an appreciative audience. Alternatively, you could buy a Mediterranean-style paint that dries to leave an authentic powdery bloom.

RIGHT: **The key element of this look is to incorporate all kinds of brilliant colors. The red, blue and pink on this wall defy notions of Western decorating taste, but combined with the bindi stamps and patterned border the effect is amazing.**

YOU WILL NEED:

- CHALK FOR MARKING
  UP THE WALL
- STRAIGHT-EDGE AND
  SPIRIT LEVEL
- BRILLIANT PINK
  LATEX PAINT
- BLUE-VIOLET LATEX
  PAINT
- RED LATEX PAINT
- PAINT ROLLER
  AND TRAY
- SMALL PAINT ROLLER
  AND TRAY
- 2 IN./5 CM PAINT
  BRUSH

PROJECT
Wall painting with borders

Brilliant pink is very typically Indian, especially when seen with crimson red and blue violet. Saris have bands of decoration at each end, and this is the source of inspiration for the project. The border edges are painted freehand —don't worry if it waves and wanders a bit, as it will look softer that way. To carry on the Indian theme, hang a real sari at the window as a drape with a beaded necklace or belt for a tie-back. Indian trinket boxes, ornaments, brightly colored woven baskets, and rugs can all be bought from stores that specialize in ethnic goods.

The middle band of color should be painted carefully but the freehand effect is right for this look, so don't be concerned if it isn't perfectly straight.

HOW TO DO IT

Take time to measure and mark the wall before applying each color. The small foam roller is just the right width for the border and creates a nice soft edge to the stripe.

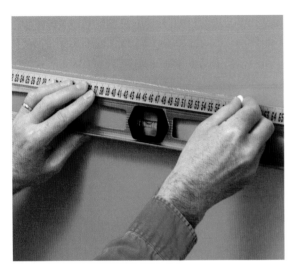

STEP 1 Measure and mark the wall at 30 in./75 cm and 3 ft./ 1 m height from the floor. Mark all the way around the walls, then draw lines in chalk—use a dark color for light walls.

STEP 2 Paint the top section of the wall first, using the roller to apply the bright pink color. If you overlap the guide line, let the paint dry, then draw the chalk line again.

STEP 3 Move to the lowest section, which can also include the baseboard. If the wood has been painted with gloss it should be rubbed down or primed with an all-surface primer prior to painting. Paint this section red and leave to dry.

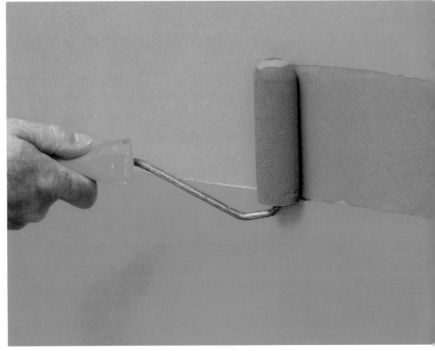

STEP 4 Use the small foam roller with the blue-violet paint and carefully paint a band of color between the red and the pink.

YOU WILL NEED:

- HIGH DENSITY FOAM
- CRAFT KNIFE
- COPIES OF THE PATTERNS
- SPRAY ADHESIVE
- SIZE (SPECIAL GLUE)
- TABLESPOON
- PLATE
- SMALL FOAM ROLLER
- PLUMB LINE MARKED AT 12 IN./30 CM INTERVALS.
- 2 OR MORE PACKS OF GOLD LEAF— (THE SQUARES CAN BE CUT IN HALF WITH SCISSORS OR A CRAFT KNIFE, TO AVOID WASTE)
- SOFT BRUSH
- CLOTH

PROJECT

Bindi stamps and a border stamp

Very few textiles escape having some extra form of decoration beyond color dye in India. It is as if they simply cannot resist adding another pattern, thread, or ornament.

These little teardrop shapes are inspired by the decorative marks which Indian women paint or apply to their foreheads, called bindi.

The shape is stamped onto the wall using a clear glue called size, then when it is almost dry a sheet of gold leaf is rubbed over it. The result is a gleaming gold shape. The pattern for the border is larger and can be applied either in the same way or with a bright pink paint color as shown here.

The bindi stamps and border pattern are just the beginning when creating your Indian-style room. Look for bright accessories and a bunch of flowers to add to the riot of colors.

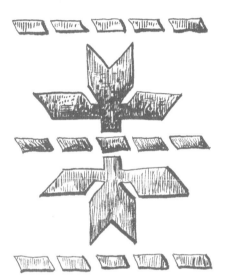

TEMPLATE

These are the actual size patterns for the foam stamps and can be traced from the book. Use thin paper that will be easily cut through when you make the stamps.

HOW TO DO IT

Foam stamps can be made from any firm foam, but cutting needs to be done slowly and accurately to get the best effect.

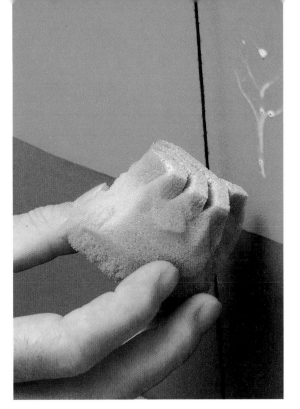

STEP 1 Make copies of the patterns and stick them on the foam. Cut them out carefully, using a craft knife. Practice cutting on an offcut to judge how much pressure is needed. Cut at an angle so the base of the pattern is wider than the top; this makes the stamp stronger.

STEP 2 Put 1 tablespoon of size on a plate and run the foam roller through it. Coat the bindi and stamp it onto the wall at 25 in./60 cm intervals using the plumb line as a guide. Stamp the next row, starting 12 in./30 cm from the ceiling to make a half-drop pattern.

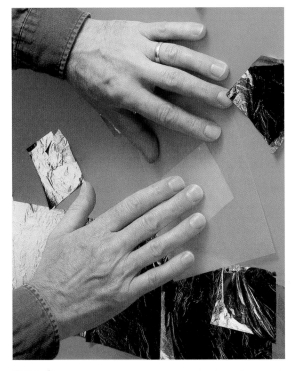

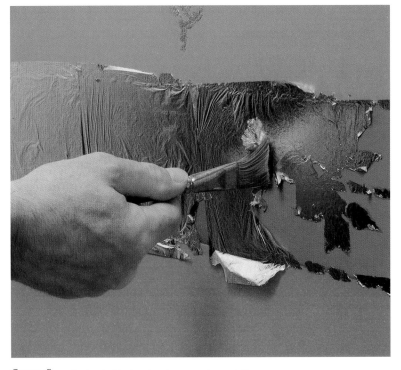

STEP 3 Take a sheet of gold leaf with its backing sheet and rub it gently onto the stamped size. The leaf will cling to the size, but easily brush away from the surrounding wall. Don't worry if the motifs are not sharp-edged—this is typical of the hand-blocked style.

STEP 4 Apply size to the border stamp and repeat the pattern along the deep violet band. Complete the whole length of the wall, then apply the sheets of gold leaf. Brush away the excess, then burnish the gold with a soft cloth.

Africa

The African continent is one of many contrasts, divided in half at the equator by a band of heavy forests. To the north is the massive Sahara Desert with the huge countries of Egypt and Sudan. Egypt is one of the great ancient civilizations, whose past is well documented compared to the other African civilizations. In contrast, there are still tribes who lead a Stone Age existence as hunter-gatherers deep in the equatorial forests, or as nomadic huntsmen in the southern deserts.

East Africa borders the Indian Ocean and the Red Sea, and trade with India and the Arab countries over the centuries has made north-east Africa more Arab in style than African. There are white domed buildings, minarets, date palms, and bustling markets. Southern Africa has the grasslands, lakes, mountains, semi-deserts, and wildlife; people traditionally lived off the land as herdsmen and farmers. Much of Africa's rich heritage of art, crafts, and architecture was undermined by colonization, and only recently has a pride in true African style re-emerged.

Updated traditions

The textiles of West Africa are amazingly varied. Traditional fabric patterns were tie-dyed or patterned using the mud-resist technique, and colored with indigo or other organic plant dyes. Modern dyes are used now, with mixtures of old and new designs. Some of the most interesting feature objects such as bicycles or clocks as design motifs set within traditional border patterns. Utility objects such as baskets, rugs, or pottery remain unchanged. Authentic African goods including textiles and household goods have been added to beadwork, trinkets, and wood carvings for the export market. The abstract patterns and simple shapes fit in well with contemporary interiors.

African color

The Southern African color palette comes from the earth. Red ocher, yellow, burnt orange, and black dominate, with any other available color used to riotous effect. In some places telephone wires are split open and the multicolor wires used to weave baskets; in others tin cans are recycled to make storage trunks, lamps, and toys.

Creating an authentic African-style room should not be difficult or expensive. The look is simple and relies on a few well-chosen objects, shapes, and colors. The walls are roughly textured and painted in bands of color, dark at the bottom and light above. Patterns are loosely geometric and rhythmic. There are specialty stores that deal in African furniture and crafts; baskets, masks, woven wall hangings, and soapstone carvings are always on sale in Oxfam's stores and it is always worth exploring flea markets and junk shops for stools, tables, or curios.

RIGHT: **The African-style look has been created by stenciling a pattern on the wall; you may like to roughen the wall a little first to make it more authentic. The cushion cover is printed by potato printing, which is great fun.**

YOU WILL NEED:

- EARTHY ORANGE, GOLDEN YELLOW, MUD BROWN, AND WARM TERRA COTTA PAINTS IN SAMPLE SIZE FOR STENCILLING
- MAT BLACK LATEX PAINT (SMALL CAN)
- SHORT-PILE ROLLER
- BROAD PAINT BRUSH
- 1½ IN./4 CM PAINT BRUSH
- 1 IN./2.5 CM PAINT BRUSH
- STRAIGHT-EDGE AND SPIRIT LEVEL
- PENCIL
- STENCIL CARD
- SPRAY ADHESIVE
- CRAFT KNIFE
- SHORT, FAT STENCIL BRUSH

PROJECT
African walls

The walls in African homes have undulating surfaces that are rough in places and shiny smooth in others. Smooth walls may need roughing up a bit to achieve the look. There are several ways to do this. The cheapest is to apply a skim coat of plaster with a wooden trowel, but this is a specialized job. A thin, uneven coat of filler can be mixed 50:50 into white latex paint and applied with a plastering trowel or a large brush; or special-effect paint can be applied with a short-pile roller and given random criss-cross strokes with a decorating brush.

ABOVE RIGHT: **The browns and yellows of the wall and stenciling give a genuine African feel. Try to find African artifacts to match the style.**

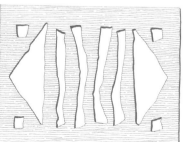

TEMPLATE
This stencil imitates stick printed patterns, so keep the lines irregular when you cut it out.

HOW TO DO IT

Stenciling is easy and effective so long as you use spray adhesive to hold the stencil in place and remember to use only the smallest amount of paint on your brush.

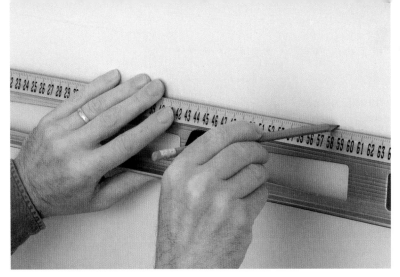

STEP 1 Measure and mark the wall at 30 in./75 cm and 3 ft./1 m height at 3 ft./1 m intervals around the walls and draw guidelines for the three bands.

STEP 2 Paint the top and bottom parts of the wall first and leave to dry.

STEP 3 Paint the dividing band with your chosen latex. Paint the lines freehand using the narrower brush along the edges and filling in with the broader brush.

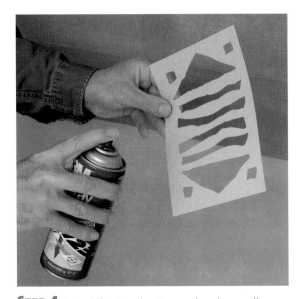

STEP 4 Cut out the stencil pattern and apply a small amount of spray adhesive to the back of it.

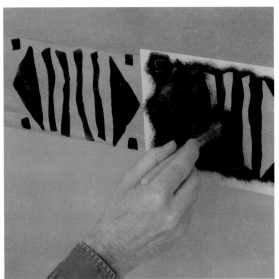

STEP 5 Stencil the pattern in the center band in your chosen color.

YOU WILL NEED:
- **LARGE POTATO**
- **PATTERN**
- **SHARP KITCHEN KNIFE**
- **RULER**
- **PLATE**
- **SMALL FOAM ROLLER**
- **FELT-TIPPED PEN**
- **CRAFT KNIFE**
- **LINO CUTTING TOOLS (SCOOP AND V-SHAPE GOUGES)**
- **FABRIC PRINTING INK**
- **A PLAIN CUSHION COVER**
- **NEWSPAPER**
- **PAPER TOWELS**
- **IRON**

PROJECT
Cushion cover

The charm of this type of African textile pattern lies in the slight irregularities that are so much a part of the process of printing by hand.

This type of pattern would usually be stamped onto fabric using a carved wooden block, but this one is produced with a potato cut. Potato printing has a liberating, youthful quality—you probably enjoyed doing it as a child—and it is particularly well suited to the African style. The same pattern is quite versatile; here it is used in an all-over pattern for a cushion, but it could be used to make a border for drapes or a throw.

A potato stamp has a limited life but can be saved overnight in a pitcher of cold water, then dried well before being used again.

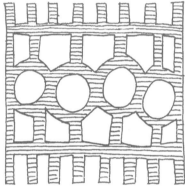

TEMPLATE
Draw the template to fit the surface of your halved potato.

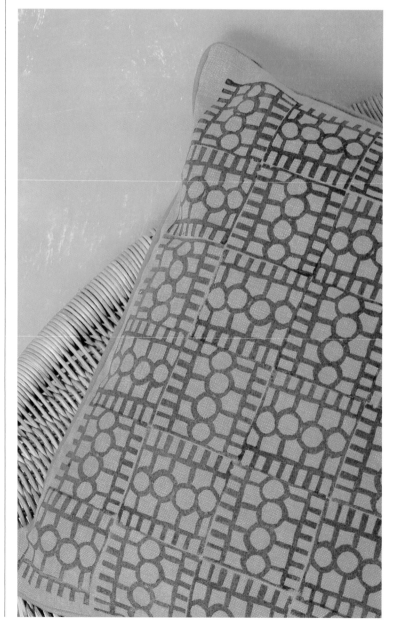

The irregularities of hand printing are an essential ingredient of the African style; the result should not be too perfect.

HOW TO DO IT

Potato printing is great fun but large potatoes can be tricky to hold. Cut out a notch on each side of the potato to make a handle, as shown in the picture for Step 4.

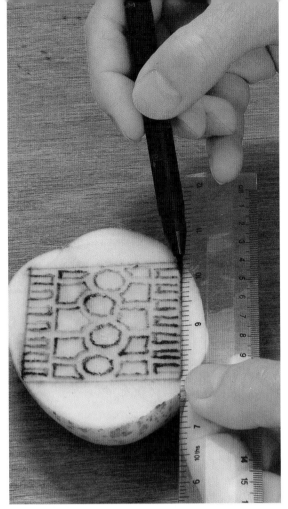

STEP 1 Cut the potato in half using the kitchen knife, and draw the motif onto the surface with the felt-tipped pen.

STEP 2 Cut around the motif edges using the craft knife, then scoop away all the background using lino-cutting tools.

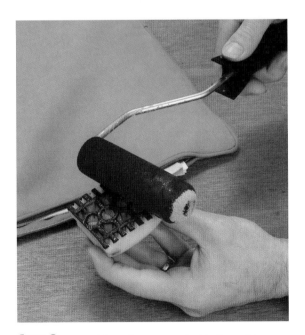

STEP 3 Put a padding of newspaper inside the cushion cover. Place some of the printing ink on the plate and use the roller to coat the potato stamp. Stamp once or twice onto paper towels, then re-coat the stamp and stamp onto the fabric.

STEP 4 Stamp the pattern in rows, then iron to fix the ink following the manufacturer's directions.

Scandinavian simplicity

The North European countries of Norway, Sweden, Denmark, and Iceland are collectively known as Scandinavia. Much of the area lies inside the Arctic Circle, and the sea separates four of the countries from mainland Europe. Although each country has preserved its own national identity, the similarities in climate, landscape, and building materials make it possible to bind the regional differences together as Scandinavian style—bright colors on the outside, and cool, sophisticated colors on the inside.

Wood is Scandinavia's traditional building material, used both inside and out. The extensive pine forests provide a ready supply of construction lumber, and country houses are still built in traditional styles and painted in vivid color combinations. The colors used to decorate the outside are very likely to be stronger than those used on the inside. Houses painted rich brick red with bright blue, yellow ocher with sea green, or bright blue with yellow and white all rub happily up against each other. It is a practical solution in these cold, northern countries where the landscape is often snow-covered and houses need to stand out to be seen.

City style

City buildings are grander, built in an elegant, classically influenced style. Scandinavia was slow to become industrialized and therefore managed to avoid the chaotic frenzy of building that took place around most big cities. Having held back initially, they were able to take a more structured, aspirational "lifestyle" approach to the design of their towns. Their sophisticated exterior design awareness extended to the interior design, incorporating furniture, glassware, ceramics, and traditional crafts.

The Gustavian style is named after King Gustav III, who fell in love with English and French interiors in the late 18th century. In those days, what met with the King's approval became the fashion of the day, and Gustavian remains one of the most recognizably Scandinavian interior styles.

Minimalist meets traditional

Furniture is upholstered in soft blue or yellow checks; walls are pale blue, sometimes striped with white; floors are polished pale pine; and elegant chandeliers provide the lighting. This style has found grace with people who admire the minimalist approach in principle, but still hark after a more traditional style of interior decorating. It combines the best of both worlds, being perceived as modern for its cool, calm, uncluttered style and limited color palette, and traditional for the inclusion of accessories such as antique chandeliers and gilded mirrors, which are central to a successful Gustavian look.

Unclutter your life and try a little Scandinavian chic.

RIGHT: **To get the Scandinavian look, go for a popular wall treatment such as hand-painted wall stripes. Add some renovated wooden chairs with re-upholstered seats, or make your own small frilled, skirted cushions for them.**

YOU WILL NEED:
- A WHITE-PAINTED WALL
- 3-PACK OF SMALL FOAM ROLLERS AND TRAY
- PLUMB LINE
- PALE BLUE LATEX PAINT
- PALE GRAY LATEX PAINT
- SMALL PAINT BRUSH
- PAPER
- 1 IN./2.5 CM PAINTER'S TAPE
- CRAFT KNIFE

PROJECT
Easy wall stripes

Hand-painted stripes, borders, and panels are popular Scandinavian wall treatments. The more detailed patterns feature twisting ribbons, floral posies, bows, and garlands, often painted in a naturalistic, three-dimensional style. This project shows how to paint broad stripes with a roller. The roller can be trimmed to make thin stripes for a more detailed pattern. Choose calm colors to complement the style, such as pale yellow and white or blue and white. The bold colors used in this large light and airy room might be overpowering in a small space; they could be toned down for a more subtle effect.

These bold stripes look fantastic in a large, airy room but you could choose more subtle tones for a smaller area. You will need some practice to work out how to get the stripes just right.

HOW TO DO IT

Painting stripes with a foam roller is easy, but there is a knack to getting the right amount of paint for a whole stripe and using the right pressure. Begin on a part of the room that will not be the focus of attention.

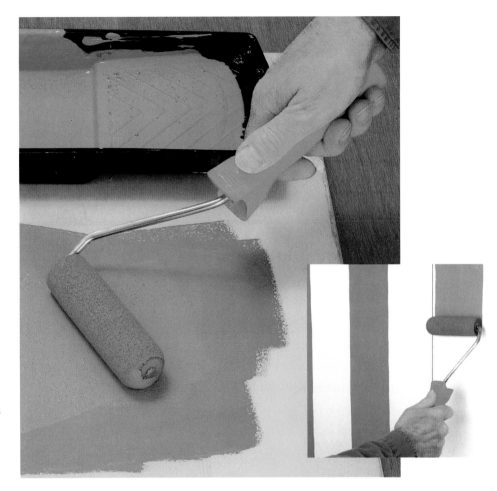

STEP 1 Fill the tray with blue paint and run the roller through so that it is evenly coated. Test this on paper first to judge the pressure needed for good coverage and no runs.

STEP 2 Hang the plumb line from ceiling height about 12 in./30 cm in from one corner. Paint a stripe from ceiling to baseboard. The roller leaves gaps at top and bottom that can be filled in with the paint brush. Leave a roller's width between stripes and move the plumb line as you go.

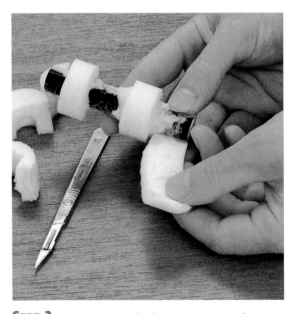

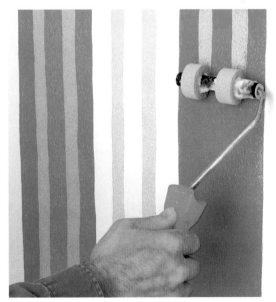

STEP 3 Divide up a new roller by wrapping painter's tape around each end and the middle section. This will leave two foam pieces showing. Use a craft knife to cut down the edges of the tape and to remove the taped pieces. You will be left with two foam ridges.

STEP 4 Fill the tray with gray paint and run the roller through it. Test the twin stripes on paper first. Run the roller down the white stripes and the blue stripes to add a double gray stripe. Fill in the small gaps at the top and bottom with the paint brush.

PROJECT

A Scandinavian dining chair

This project requires you to visit a few junk shops in search of a suitable chair to rescue and revamp. Look for a well-proportioned wooden dining chair that could have a tall rounded or short square back and a drop-in seat. The shape should be elegant but not overly decorative. If you find one with a nice back and legs but a plain wooden seat, buy it and make a tie-on cushion in place of reupholstering the seat. A popular treatment for dining chairs in Sweden is to make small frilled, skirted cushions. Before you renovate the chair, strip away any old paint or varnish by hand or have it dipped professionally. Let it dry before re-painting.

RENOVATING A CHAIR

Renovating a wooden chair is a very satisfying make-over project. The clean-up, painting, and upholstery are all enjoyable, and the result can be remarkable. Take care to remove all traces of the old varnish and make repairs before you repaint.

STEP 1 Rub the edges of the chair-back and any raised pattern on the wood, the curve of the legs, and the seat corners with the candle. A light stroke will be enough.

STEP 2 Apply two coats of the white paint, leaving the correct drying time in between and after.

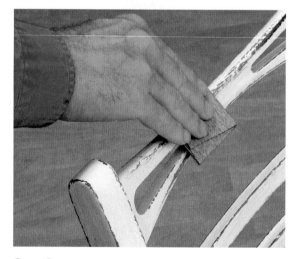

STEP 3 Rub the waxed areas with sandpaper. The paint should lift away easily, so that the bare wood shows through in places. It is important not to overdo this effect as it is meant to simulate natural wear and tear.

STEP 1 Lay the seat face down on the lining fabric and cut out the shape, adding an extra 2 in./5 cm on all sides to allow for the seat depth and turning under. Using this as a pattern, cut out the checked fabric.

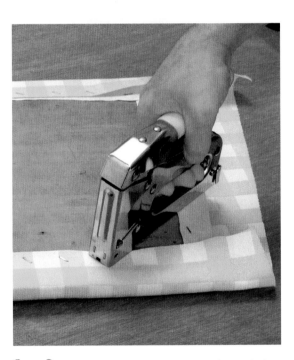

STEP 2 Lay the fabric face down on a flat surface with the seat on top. Pull it round to the back of the seat and staple half-way along one side. Pull tight and staple the opposite side. Do the same with the other two opposite sides. Fold the corners over and staple them flat. Now pleat the fabric on each side of the corners and staple that down. Add several more staples along each side to secure the new cover. Drop the seat back into the frame.

UPHOLSTERING THE SEAT

This is the simplest of all upholstery tasks—all you need is a pair of scissors, a stapler, and a spare half hour. Discard any tatty old upholstery, but if the padding and cover are intact, simply place the new one over the old.

Miami pastel brights

Miami Beach at the tip of Florida has a style all of its own. The resort was built between the 1920s and 1940s in the Art Deco style, which was popular in New York and Chicago, but in Miami they gave the look a unique twist by choosing a very different range of colors for their buildings. In Miami the buildings were painted with bright tropical pinks, sunny yellows, purples, blues, and greens. The colors were not primaries but bright pastel ice-cream colors, perfect for a vacation city.

The buildings echoed the shape of streamlined ocean liners, with the main body of the building painted white and color used to highlight the horizontal banding. For a while Miami was the most glamorous vacation destination, but it fell on hard times in the late 1950s. In the 1980s a massive renovation plan was set in motion, and now Miami outshines its former glory. The buildings are freshly painted and are a little brighter, with less white and more entire buildings painted bright colors; the chrome is polished and neon signs light up the night. The interiors are decorated in a similar style, using colors to stress the geometric devices in the design such as columns, stepped parapets, and windows with narrow horizontal glazing bars. Also synonymous with Miami are palm trees, tropical flowers, nautical themes, flamingos, and unrestrained elegance.

Art Deco Miami-style

Miami is a top vacation resort and its stylish hotels and boulevards are favorite locations for films and fashion photography. Creating your own piece of South Beach (SoBe) should not be too hard because a distinctive color scheme will do most of the work for you. Look out for one or two genuine Art Deco pieces of furniture, either from specialized dealers or flea markets.

Miami used Art Deco shapes but applied its own color scheme—you can do the same with bright pastel upholstery. If you have no luck finding original furniture, buy a plain sofa with a streamlined shape and dress it up with contrasting cushions piped in Miami colors.

A touch of fun

Neon lighting is very much a part of the Miami look, and a pair of colored neon tubes would add an authentic glow at night. These can be bought as colored sheaths to fit over standard tubes. Chrome wall or table lights will also fit in well, and there are plenty of good reproduction Art Deco lights around.

Miami has a fun side, and if this appeals to you, then a fake flamingo or two and a few stylized sunset pictures are a must! In Miami, the sun shines all year and most residents are on permanent vacation. Adopt this style at home so that, even if work occupies the day, every evening will feel like a vacation.

RIGHT: Miami style is fun and bright with tropical colors; these bands of color will liven up any room. If you can find some genuine Art Deco furniture to go with the decor, then all the better. With the Miami look, your home will benefit from a vacation feel all year round!

YOU WILL NEED:

Background color
(choose one of the
three below) to
apply to all wall
surfaces first

- **PINK, YELLOW, AND
  SEA GREEN PAINT**
- **PENCIL**
- **LONG RULE**
- **STRAIGHT-EDGE
  WITH SPIRIT LEVEL**
- **PLUMB LINE**
- **PAINT BRUSH**
- **ROLLER AND TRAY**
- **SMALL FOAM ROLLER
  AND TRAY**
- **PAINTER'S TAPE**

PROJECT
Miami deco walls

The geometric and streamlined shapes associated with Art Deco can be used mural-style, drawn onto a wall and painted using the Miami palette of tropical bright pastels. The most important lines to emphasize are the horizontals, which should wrap around the room in smooth streamlined stripes. Vertical columns topped off with stepped parapets can be painted around doorways or windows. Miami is very style-conscious but fun is also high on the agenda, so use the basic shapes and colors but feel free to interpret the style in your own way.

These bright pastels give the impression of delicious ice-cream flavors. Once you've done the walls, search for suitable accessories and work on the lighting. Neon lighting is part of the style so look out for reproduction Art Deco lights.

HOW TO DO IT

Wrapping your walls with these bands of Miami color will liven up any room. It's fun, but don't rush it as the paint needs to be dry before you apply the tape.

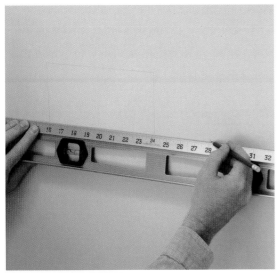

STEP 1 Draw the streamlining stripes by measuring up from the floor, and marking, then drawing pencil lines. Check that they are level. A plumb line may help.

STEP 2 Run painter's tape around the outside edge of the lines.

STEP 3 Paint the bands of color inside the painter's tape using a brush or rollers.

STEP 4 Leave until almost dry, then peel off the tape.

PROJECT
A piped cushion cover

Cushion-making is something of a mystery until you actually make one. You then realize how much difference a fresh set of cushions can make to a room, and how inexpensive they are when you make them yourself. You also have the pleasure of choosing exactly the colors, sizes, and fabrics that you most want. Make a set of different colored cushions on the Miami color theme, choosing four bright pastel cottons and using the main color of each one to pipe one of the others. These cushions are simple to make and the cover is slip-stitched closed using matching thread to give a neat finish.

Even if you can't manage to find a Miami-style sofa with bright pastel upholstery, you can buy a plain sofa and add cushions in Miami colors with contrasting piping.

HOW TO DO IT

The secret of making successful piped cushions is no mystery, but you need a zipper foot on your machine so you can get up close when stitching the piping in place.

STEP 1 Fold the fabric in half and cut it into two square pieces. Pin the piping to the right side of one of the pieces, with the flat edges aligned and the cord on the inside. Snip it up to the stitch line at the corners.

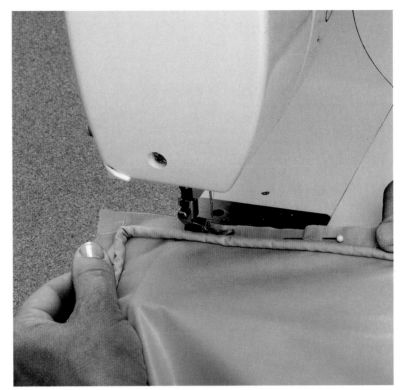

STEP 2 Stitch the piping to the fabric using the zipper foot to get right up to the cord.

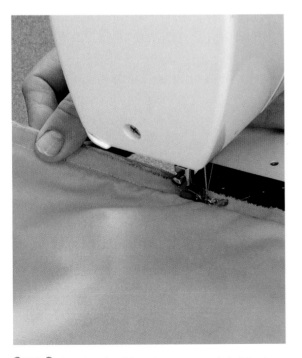

STEP 3 Place the other fabric piece on top and pin it in place. Stitch it to the piped piece, once again using the zipper foot to get as close as possible to the piped cord. Leave one seam open.

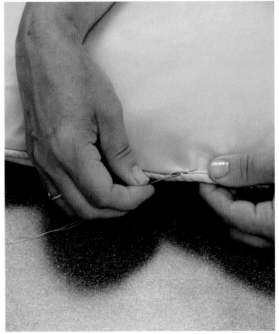

STEP 4 Turn the cushion cover the right side out and press lightly. Insert the cushion pad, then slip-stitch to close.

Urban natural

This is a style that has emerged from industrial chic, a 1990s phenomenon that began in New York where young people broke away from the traditional property market and moved into vacant loft and warehouse spaces. Loft-living has now become the height of fashion. The lifestyle has spread worldwide and resulted in the regeneration of many a run-down dockland or industrial area. At first the hard-edged look was cool with plenty of open space, exposed metal beams, steel staircases, and very few home comforts—but then cool started to feel a bit cold and there was a new yearn for comfort.

This is where the urban natural style comes in. Hard surfaces can be mellowed down with soft chalky distemper-based paints in natural colors. These are old-fashioned, water-based paints which can be applied directly onto brick walls or bare plaster, and being porous they let the walls breathe. Wooden or matting floors seem far more feet-friendly when scattered with sheepskins, felt, or woven rugs. Those large leather sofas can be softened with soft cashmere throws or piles of soft cushions with lamb's-wool covers. Windows are dressed down with pleated paper, calico, wooden Venetian, or vertical slatted shades. Drapes are simply made from pale, plain fabrics such as loose-weave linen, fine cotton, or fine voile.

Understated style

Lighting is low, subtle, and ambient, concealed behind green-tinted glass screens or under shelving. Scented candles, tea lights, or large multi-wicked candles are a compulsory feature. House plants contribute to the natural style so long as they also make a design statement—think orchids, sculptural desert cacti, or luscious ferns. And if the budget doesn't stretch to orchids and cashmere, we can compromise and enjoy the best-looking bits of the urban natural style without losing too much sleep about whether our throws are actually cashmere or a polyester/wool mix. It's a chill-out style, where comfort is king.

Look out for mohair shawls and hand-knitted sweaters to convert into cushion covers. Large unbleached-cotton decorator's drop cloths make great drapes or sofa covers. Make use of natural textures like stone, wood, glass, and leather. Stick to the key colors of dark brown, tan, mushroom, stone, olive, spring green, and—yes, even beige!

Avoid strong contrasts by having progressively darker or lighter shades alongside each other, so that the whole look is harmonious and easy on the eye. Repetition can look very stylish—a long galvanized metal container planted with a perfect row of African violets, for instance, or a row of pebbles on a window sill. The effect should be more meditative than passionate, creating a calm environment to ease the stresses of city living. With the background to your life in place, it's time to light a scented candle, put on some music, and—relax.

RIGHT: Urban natural decor should create a calm environment to ease the stresses of daily life. Soft natural colors are used for the walls, and the correct lighting is essential—it should be very subtle. A few well-chosen house plants will contribute to the natural style.

YOU WILL NEED:

- 3 HARMONIOUS
  PAINT COLORS—
  SAGE GREEN, PALE
  COFFEE, AND LIGHT
  BEIGE (CHALK FINISH
  PAINTS USED HERE)
- PAINTER'S TAPE
- CHALK/PENCIL
- TAPE MEASURE
- STRAIGHT-EDGE
  WITH SPIRIT LEVEL
- PAINT BRUSHES/
  ROLLER AND TRAY

PROJECT
Painting bands of harmonious colors

Simplicity is the key to success in this style of decorating. It is minimalism with a soft edge, so be selective with the accessories and furniture, and make a statement on the walls. Horizontal bands of color look best in medium- to large-size rooms, so this is a look for the living room.

The depth of the color bands can be altered to make the most of your room proportions. If the room is tall and you want to bring the focus down, make the two lower bands the same size with a much wider one above. Here, the chalky finish of the paint enhances the subtle colors.

This wall has been painted in three harmonious colors; this treatment suits a reasonable sized room, so try it out in in the living room. You will need to be careful with the accessories you choose so as not to spoil the dramatic effect of the stripes.

HOW TO DO IT

The secret of success is painter's tape, but patience is needed as the wall must be bone dry before you apply the tape to outline the middle band of color.

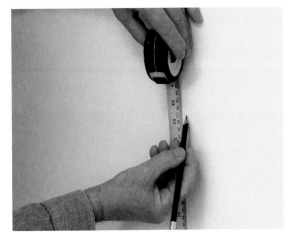

STEP 1 Divide the height of the wall by three to get three equal-sized bands. Measure and mark the divisions using the tape measure, then check the horizontal with the straight-edge and level, and draw soft pencil lines.

STEP 2 Run painter's tape along the top of the lower line and do the same below the upper line.

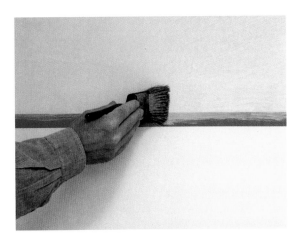

STEP 3 Paint the top section of wall with light beige. Then paint the lower section of the wall sage green, slightly overlapping the painter's tape so that you get a straight line when it is peeled away. Leave both to dry overnight. The paint must be bone dry.

STEP 4 Apply a line of painter's tape along the top of the sage green section (if the paint is not bone dry, the tape will lift the new paint). Do the same along the edge of the light beige, then paint the mid-section pale coffee. When the paint is dry, peel off the painter's tape.

YOU WILL NEED:

- A CONICAL OR CYLINDRICAL FABRIC LAMPSHADE
- PAINT IN A PALE COFFEE COLOR—OR YOUR CHOICE
- DAMP SPONGE
- FINE-BLADED SAW
- CLEAR STICKY TAPE
- A BRUSH
- BUNDLE OF BAMBOO FROM GARDEN CENTER
- STICKY TAPE
- A COLUMN-STYLE LAMPBASE WITH GOOD WIRING
- PAINTER'S TAPE
- GALVANIZED WIRE
- PLIERS

PROJECT
Customizing a lamp

When you have a brand-new color scheme, everything has to change, and if you are a trendsetter rather than a follower, it can be difficult finding accessories to match. However, when it comes to lampshades you don't need to—just paint them with the same latex paint you use for the walls. It could not be simpler, and it really suits this sort of color scheme when you are working with a limited color palette. Once the paint is dry, the lampshade can be trimmed with a darker or contrasting shade of velvet ribbon, suede fringe, or textured braid. Use any lamp base—just follow the wrapping directions.

Why buy a new lamp when you can adapt one you already own? Once you have painted the lampshade with leftover latex from the walls, try making this bamboo wrap. When fashions change, you can easily replace the wrap.

HOW TO DO IT

Transform a boring old table lamp in an afternoon with a coat of fresh color on the shade and a bamboo wrap around the base.

STEP 1 Clean the lampshade with a slightly damp sponge. Apply two coats of your chosen color, being careful not to splash any inside the lampshade, which will be a special fire-resistant material. Leave to dry.

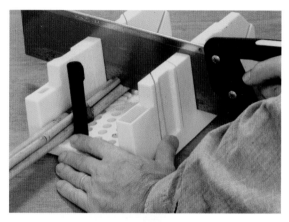

STEP 2 Tape several pieces of bamboo together and use a fine-bladed saw to cut them to size. The lengths should completely cover the existing base and extend at least 2 in./ 5 cm above it. Work out how many you need to surround the base, and cut the required amount.

STEP 3 Sand the ends, then lay the pieces flat, close together and perfectly aligned. Hold them together top and bottom with a length of clear sticky tape.

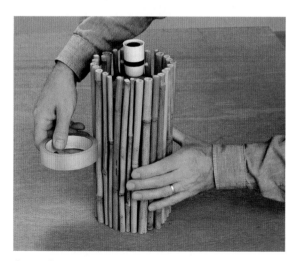

STEP 4 Wrap the bamboo around the lampbase and secure temporarily with a length of clear sticky tape.

STEP 5 Wind the galvanized wire (rafia or twine are alternative options) around the bamboo and use the pliers to twist the ends together neatly and fold them flat against the bamboo. Do this both top and bottom, then fit the shade onto the lampbase.

Industrial modern

The industrial look is one that was born out of necessity, when young people in big cities like New York, Paris, and London went looking for places to live and found themselves priced out of the market. The empty properties that attracted their attention were dockland warehouses and abandoned factories whose businesses had long since closed down or moved out of town to escape the traffic-clogged streets. The buildings presented an opportunity for a whole new way of living, and loft style was born.

One of the most essential aspects of industrial modern style is to retain as much of the fabric of the original building and any specialized associated material as possible. A large winch with an iron hook, for instance, would be seen as sculptural and retained, as would a metal staircase, steel shutters, or a ventilation shaft. The idea is to retain the best of the building's original character, but also to make it work as a comfortable home.

Fabulous fittings

Once the factory and warehouse spaces had been colonized, the next step was to make use of factory fittings, office furniture, and items of industrial scale that could be converted for use in the home. Galvanized iron shelving, movable storage units on hefty rubber casters, and cafeteria tables were put to immediate use, and aluminum waste bins, metal filing cabinets, catering ovens, and sets of lockers began appearing on the pages of magazines. Floors were covered with aluminum sheeting or painted with industrial paints; brickwork was exposed, and scaffolding poles were used to create mezzanine sleeping decks in the middle of vast open spaces.

Lofts and warehouses have now moved up to the top end of the market—but the industrial modern style is here to stay. Aluminum flooring, stainless steel units and catering ovens are readily available. There are aluminum and steel acrylic paints that will make any surface look like cool metal, and there is a range of textured wall covering that looks just like factory flooring. Metal storeroom-type shelving, track lighting, and bare concrete used for seating, tables, shelving supports, and planters are all a part of this pared-down style.

"Islands of comfort" are another vital ingredient—cool hard surfaces look fabulous, but everyone needs to curl up and feel warm and comfortable as well. These comfort zones are furnished with generous leather sofas, soft mohair or lamb's-wool throws, deep pile rugs, and low coffee tables. Even in a vast space, clever lighting can create a sense of intimacy if kept low and concentrated by using floor and table lamps to cast warm pools of light. Use the same basic concepts to create an industrial modern style in any room—keep the style utilitarian and the space cool, open, and uncluttered, but make sure you always include soft areas for comfort and indulgence.

RIGHT: **This shelf unit is made from concrete breeze blocks, which give the impression of a modern sculpture. Once created, it is guaranteed you will spend ages adjusting the items on the shelves!**

YOU WILL NEED:
- 6 CINDER BLOCKS
- 2 x 14 IN. x 6 FT. X
  ³/₄ IN./35 CM x 2 M X
  2 CM PLANKS
- PRIMER
- MAT BLACK PAINT
- PAINT BRUSH
- STRAIGHT-EDGE WITH
  SPIRIT LEVEL
- SET SQUARE

PROJECT
Cinderblock shelving

Concrete cinderblocks have replaced bricks as the basic construction material in most new houses. They are regular-sized, strong, and inexpensive, but they don't make beautiful-looking walls, so bricks are still used as a facing material. The rough gray texture of the blocks takes on a sculptural quality when taken out of context and used indoors as shelf supports.

The planks used here are painted black wood but other materials would also look good. Glass, steel mesh, or galvanized zinc are all very much a part of the industrial modern style.

You can use black painted wood for the shelves, as here, or choose from glass, steel mesh, or galvanized zinc, all of which are equally in keeping with the industrial modern style.

HOW TO DO IT

The sculptural style of this shelving unit relies on the positioning of the cinderblocks. Use a set square to align each one at the correct angle.

STEP 1 Apply a coat of primer to the shelving planks. Leave to dry, then apply two coats of black paint.

STEP 2 Space two base cinderblocks to stand 2½ in./6 cm from the wall, 20 in./50 cm apart, angled at 45° to the wall. Stand the first shelf on top with 10 in./25 cm overlap at each end.

STEP 3 Place two more blocks on the shelf above the lower ones, this time angled at 90°, the narrow side facing forward.

STEP 4 Stand the second shelf on top, again with 10 in./25 cm overlap at each end, and position the final two blocks angled at 45°. Put the third shelf on top. Note: this shelving unit should only be used in rooms with solid floors and where it is unlikely to be knocked.

YOU WILL NEED:

- **HARDBOARD SHEETS**
- **PANEL ADHESIVE**
- **SNAP-BLADE KNIFE**
- **CRAFT KNIFE**
- **STRAIGHT-EDGE WITH SPIRIT LEVEL**
- **HAMMER**
- **¼ IN./6 MM TACKS**
- **A STRIP OF CARDBOARD—SHOE BOX TYPE**
- **CLEAR FLOOR VARNISH**
- **PAINT BRUSH OR FOAM ROLLER AND TRAY**

PROJECT

Hardboard flooring

Hardboard has many enduring qualities which are not to be found in more modern manufactured boards. It is kind of compressed cardboard that is rough on one side and shiny on the other. It is inexpensive, comes in large sheets, is bendable, can be cut with a heavy-duty knife, and feels warm underfoot. The brown color deepens and can be improved with varnish. Hardboard makes a low-budget, industrial-style floor covering that is suitable for laying onto unattractive wooden floors or for covering shabby vinyl or even concrete.

Hardboard flooring is a quick and inexpensive way to give a floor a make-over. If you make sure that the tacks line up neatly, they will look quite attractive and add to the look of the floor.

HOW TO DO IT

Hardboard flooring is hardwearing and feels good underfoot. Using the nail guide will ensure that the lines stay straight and look decorative.

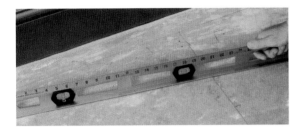

STEP 1 Make sure the existing floor is dust-free and level. Floors can be leveled with a proprietary leveling compound or with sheets of newspaper. Lay the first sheet of hardboard into one corner without adhesive to check that the walls are square.

STEP 2 Apply a long squiggle of panel adhesive to the back of the board and lay it in position. Apply foot pressure so that the adhesive grips onto the base.

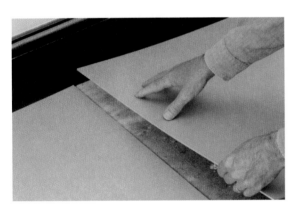

STEP 3 Butt the next sheet of hardboard up to the baseboard and the first sheet. If it all fits neatly, then apply adhesive and repeat the same procedure. Cover the floor in this way, measuring and making any adjustments to the final piece with a snap-blade knife before laying it.

STEP 4 Decide on the width between the tacks. Mark a series of 1¼ in./3 cm measurements along the straight edge of a piece of card. Cut a 2 in./5 cm notch to mark each one. For a large floor you may like to widen the gap a little.

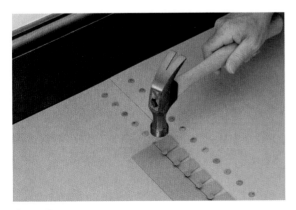

STEP 5 Line the notched edge of the card up with the edge of the hardboard and place a tack in each notch. Tap the tacks half-way in, then slide the card away and hammer the heads flush to the hardboard. This way all the tacks will line up nicely!

STEP 6 Fill the paint tray with varnish and, beginning in the far corner, apply one coat. Leave to dry, then apply a second coat.

Urban minimalist

The key elements for this look are open space, good color and only a few well-designed pieces of furniture. Floors are left bare with either painted or waxed floorboards. Ornaments are out—instead, choose really stylish utility objects that are sculptural in their own right. We all need radiators, but the urban minimalist goes for fabulous columns, swirls, or ladder-style "rads." Everything makes a style statement, and for this look you really do have to maintain a disciplined attitude to tidiness, because clutter is definitely out.

The furniture you use for the urban minimalist look can be from any period as long as it is in good condition and has a design pedigree—some of the most contemporary looking chairs and loungers were actually designed in the 1920s by the famous community of designers at the Bauhaus in Germany. Chairs from any of the key decades in the last century can be reupholstered in plain contemporary colors to flatter their shape. Brand new technology sits comfortably alongside retro pieces, so long as the good design ethos remains paramount.

Urban color

Light interiors are always enhanced when a good proportion of white is used, as it reflects and doubles the room's natural light. Leave windows bare when possible and paint window frames and surrounds white. If the windows are small then create the impression of bigger windows by painting a broad white border beyond the frames and below the sill down to floor level, which will create the impression of full length windows. Folding wooden blinds look wonderful, but if they are likely to blow the budget, choose plain white shades instead.

The urban minimalist look consists of just a few equally important elements, and color is one of them. Consider the room's function and any existing color that appears in furnishings, paintings, or accessories when choosing a wall color.

Adding accents

A meditative lavender or pale powder blue creates a relaxing atmosphere in a sitting room, and pale mushroom brown looks good with white and deeper browns, especially if bright colors such as spring green or red are used for upholstery. Just one or two permanent colors are needed, and others can be added as color accents with cushions, vases or flower arrangements.

Fresh flowers are very much a part of the urban minimalist look, and a whole new style of floristry has emerged to complement it. Single variety arrangements or indoor plants are favored, such as vibrantly red or orange dahlias in tall glass tubes; rows of pink orchids growing in moss-covered containers; zinc tubs planted with white marguerite daisies—or, alternatively, a giant earthenware pot filled with very tall wild grasses.

RIGHT: **Every single item in the urban minimalist environment must be carefully selected to fit in with the style. A few bright flowers in a glass vase and some cushions provide accents of color.**

YOU WILL NEED:

- FLOATING SHELF KIT
  —INCLUDING SPECIAL
  FITTINGS, SCREWS,
  AND WALL ANCHORS
- TAPE MEASURE/LONG
  RULER
- STRAIGHT-EDGE WITH
  SPIRIT LEVEL
- PENCIL
- DRILL AND THE
  CORRECT DRILL BIT
  FOR YOUR WALL
  (MASONRY OR
  WALLBOARD)
- WALL ANCHORS AND
  SCREWS

PROJECT
Floating shelves

The essence of the urban minimalist style is that rooms should appear to be more empty than they actually are. Create the impression of open space by fitting shelving that seems to float in the air without any visible support system. There are several different systems on the market that work very efficiently, so instead of "re-inventing the wheel" the project shows how to use one of the existing designs. The shelves come in a range of sizes, the one used here being the shortest. Choose a length to suit the proportions of your walls and the things you wish to display, as it is important to keep to the open uncluttered style.

This shelf is perfect for the minimalist look. The wall supports are attached to the wall and are covered by the shelf, leaving no visible fixings. Nothing will detract attention from the items you have chosen to display.

HOW TO DO IT

Simple to fit and a minimalist's dream, these shelves are magical. But, as with most tricks, the explanation is quite simple.

STEP 1 Having decided on the best position for the shelf, measure and mark it on the wall lightly in pencil.

STEP 2 Hold the wall support up to the wall and check it with the spirit level. Mark the correct position.

STEP 3 Attach the wall support, making sure that the screws are firmly attached.

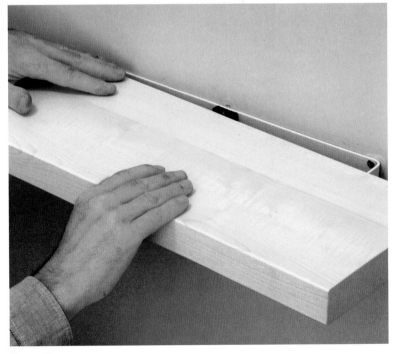

STEP 4 Fix the shelf onto the wall supports.

YOU WILL NEED:

- A BOLSTER
  CUSHION PAD
- ROUGH SILK FABRIC
  IN A BOLD COLOR—
  ENOUGH TO WRAP
  AROUND THE BODY
  OF THE BOLSTER PLUS
  TWO CIRCLES FOR THE
  ENDS. CUT THEM TO
  ALLOW FOR A
  ⅝ IN./1.5 CM SEAM
- MATCHING THREAD
- PIPING CORD (CUT A
  STRIP OF FABRIC AND
  FOLD IT OVER THE
  CORD, THEN STITCH
  CLOSE TO THE CORD
  USING THE ZIPPER
  FOOT, AND CLIP
  ALONG THE SEAM
  ALLOWANCE SO THE
  CORD BENDS EASILY
  INTO A CURVE)
- A ZIPPER TO FIT
  LENGTH
- SCISSORS
- PINS
- SEWING MACHINE
  WITH ZIPPER FOOT
- IRON

PROJECT
Making a bolster cushion

A bright silk bolster cushion on a sofa or chair can be used to add an accent of color to the room. Bolsters are long, firm tubular cushions whose shape and proportions suit the minimalist look but they have a real sense of style. These cushions were a popular feature of the design-conscious Regency and Biedermeier styles in the 19th century, and Le Corbusier's famous leather and chrome lounger has a bolster neckrest, which certainly confers it with top design credentials.

The secret of success is to take the sewing slowly so that you keep turning the fabric in a smooth curve.

The bolster cushion is made from a rough silk fabric with piping around the edge. Choose a bold, bright color and this cushion will make a great contribution to your urban minimalist project.

HOW TO DO IT

Fit a zipper foot to the sewing machine so that you can stitch up close to the piping and the zipper.

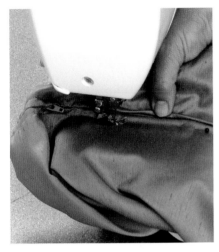

STEP 1 Turn over a small hem and stitch the zipper into the seam of the main body fabric. Undo the zipper so you can work on the cover.

STEP 2 Sew the piping onto the round ends before you stitch them to the main body.

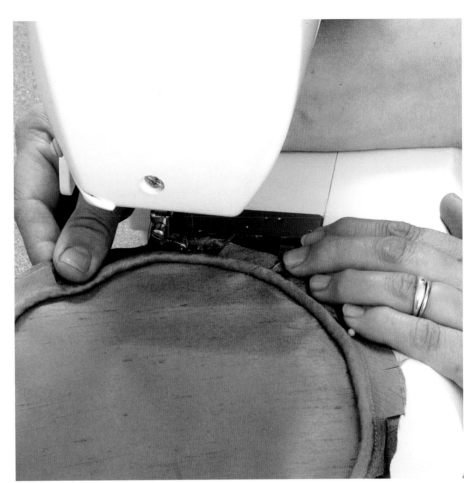

STEP 3 Snip out ⅜ in./1 cm notches every 1¼ in./3 cm around the end pieces. Pin the ends in place and stitch them using the zipper foot to get close up to the piping cord.

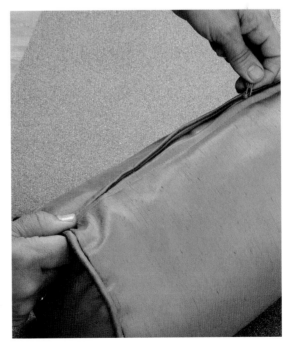

STEP 4 Press the seams lightly and turn the right side out. Fit the cushion pad inside and close the zipper.

Beside the ocean

Living where the land meets the sea brings light into your life. The color of the sea is affected by the weather—when the sun shines in a cloudless sky on a summer day, it is a perfect bright blue, while on a stormy winter's day both sea and sky turn a deep gray-violet. Sunlight reflects off the sea, brightening everything along the shoreline, and there is always a vacation feeling whether the beach is soft sand, shingle, or pebbles. This is what draws people to live by the sea, and the way homes are decorated reflects this relaxed feeling.

Anyone with a home overlooking the ocean will know that a room with large sea-facing windows barely needs decorating at all. What could compare to the scale of a view like that? The best you could do is have window seats, comfortable chairs, a telescope, and an open fireplace for cool nights. Wherever people live near the ocean, they collect the treasures that come in on the tide—shells, pebbles, and strangely shaped pieces of driftwood—and display them on windowsills and shelves.

Local color

There is often a definite local style that gives a town or village a unique character. This could be the use of a limited color palette, particular flowers in window boxes, a local stone used for house building, or something ingenious like the rows of houses built from old rail road cars with added porches that are found on the English south coast. In places with lighthouses, fishing fleets, or a strong sailing fraternity, the boat theme will never be far away, and in traditional seaside resort towns the weatherboard huts, shops, and houses with their fresh white paint and colorful window frames declare that every day is a vacation.

Coastal props

To get the look, you will need some seaside props, and the best place to find them—and the inspiration you need—is by the sea. Souvenir shops crammed with shells, anchors, buckets, and spades, seagulls and sailing boats are worth investigating. A single seagull and a row of pebbles may be all your room needs to give it seaside character, so don't go overboard and clutter the room. Removing stones from beaches is no longer permitted, but they can be bought in garden centers. Chandlers sell everything you need for sailing, including a wonderful selection of ropes, sail cloths, and eyelets. Taut steel sail cables can be used as tracks with canvas curtains, and a coil of fat rope is pure sculpture.

Choose color to suit the location. Rooms are often painted white to make the most of the fabulous light that comes off the ocean, and this creates a brightness that works well with either primary colors or soft colors that look as if they were once bold but have faded in the sunshine. Sea greens, powder blue, sugar pink and lemon sherbet all fall into this category. Stripes, fishy prints, or simple florals can suit the seaside mood. When in doubt, let simplicity rule the day.

RIGHT: **A couple of pictures, a model boat and a fish— just a few objects can successfully give the impression of the seaside and recreate that relaxed vacation feeling for you to enjoy every day.**

YOU WILL NEED

- TONGUE-AND-GROOVE PANELING TO FIT AROUND THE WALLS (BEADED PANELLING IS USED HERE)
- 3 LENGTHS OF 2 IN. X 1 IN./2.5 CM X 1.2 CM CLEATS FOR EACH WALL LENGTH
- SHELF 3 IN. X 1 IN./7.5 CM X 2.5 CM PLANED SOFTWOOD TO FIT AROUND THE ROOM (MEASURE THE LENGTH REQUIRED)
- SUPPORT BRACKETS FOR SHELF—TO BE SPACED 24 IN./60 CM APART
- ¼ IN./6 MM WALL PLUGS
- BOX OF 2 IN./5 CM NUMBER 6 SCREWS
- BOX OF 1 IN./2.5CM BRADS
- SMALL HAMMER
- SPARE PIECE OF WOOD
- DRILL WITH ¼ IN./6 MM AND ⅛ IN./3 MM PILOT BITS
- FINE NAIL PUNCH
- MITER SAW OR BLOCK WITH HANDSAW
- SCREWDRIVER
- STRAIGHT-EDGE WITH SPIRIT LEVEL
- PENCIL
- ENAMEL OR LATEX PAINT SEALED WITH MARINE QUALITY VARNISH

PROJECT

Paneling a wall with tongue-and-groove

Wood paneling is very much a part of beach house style, whether the home is in the Outer Hebrides or Montego Bay. The panels are light, easily transportable, simple to fit, and they cover a multitude of sins. The best thing about them, though, is the instant beach style they bring along with them. Tongue-and-groove can be bought in kit form or as long lengths from a lumberyard, which you can then cut down to a size to suit your room. The paneling can be fitted from floor to ceiling or, as described in the project here, on part of the wall, topped off with a shelf to display your most interesting beach-combing finds.

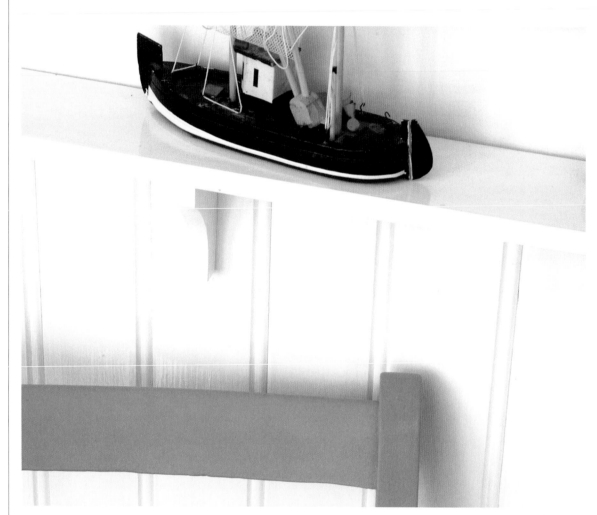

ABOVE RIGHT:
Wooden paneling looks great with a shelf above it; you don't necessarily need to panel the whole room to achieve the effect.

FOR TONGUE-AND-GROOVE PANELING

Either: Measure the width of one plank and divide this into the length of the wall area to be covered. Multiply this figure by the height of the paneling to find out how much wood you will need. Or: Buy made-up paneling kits to fit the length required.

HOW TO DO IT

Once the cleats are up, the paneling grows really fast. Finish it off with a shelf to hide the raw edges and display your seaside finds.

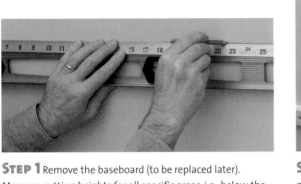

STEP 1 Remove the baseboard (to be replaced later). Measure cutting heights for all specific areas, i.e., below the window or above any fitted units.

STEP 2 Using the rule with the spirit level, mark three positions for the cleating on the wall to align with the top, middle, and bottom of the panels. Drill and insert wall anchors spaced 20 in./50 cm apart, then screw the cleats onto the wall.

STEP 3 Beginning in one corner, place the end plank against the wall and check the vertical with the spirit level. Hammer a pin through the inside edge of the tongue, angled slightly inward. Use the nail punch with the hammer to drive the pinhead below the surface.

STEP 4 Fit the groove of the next plank into the tongue of the first. To ensure a tight fit, place a spare piece of wood along the edge and tap it with the hammer to prevent damage to the plank's tongue. Continue in the same way to complete the paneling.

STEP 5 Cut the shelf planks to fit the wall lengths, mitering the ends for a neat fit in the corners and at any joins. Check and mark the shelf position on the wall with a spirit level. Drill pilot holes in the planks and the panels for the brackets.

STEP 6 Screw the brackets into the front of the paneling and down through the shelf into the top of the brackets. Prime and paint with gloss or latex paint sealed with marine quality varnish.

YOU WILL NEED:

- HEAVYWEIGHT COTTON CANVAS
- LARGE BRASS EYELETS
- IRON-ON BONDING TAPE
- IRON-ON FABRIC STIFFENER FOR A 4 IN./10 CM DEPTH BAND ALONG THE TOP OF EACH CURTAIN
- SCISSORS
- HAMMER
- SCALPEL
- PENCIL
- METAL RULER
- ROPE TO LOOP THROUGH EYELETS— ALLOW ABOUT 8 IN./20 CM BETWEEN EYELETS PLUS AN EXTRA 6 IN./15 CM FOR A KNOT AT EACH END
- CURTAIN POLE
- IRON

PROJECT

Curtains with eyelets

These stylish curtains with eyelets are very easy to make, and no sewing is involved. The fabric is hemmed using an iron-on bonding tape, and the headings are strengthened with an iron-on fabric stiffener.

Once the eyelets are in place, the curtains can either be threaded straight onto a chrome rail or threaded with rope to add an extra nautical touch and suspended from any curtain pole.

The eyelet fixings will require a heavyweight fabric such as cotton canvas to ensure the curtains will hang in neat folds when drawn back. The eyelets come in a range of sizes, as do curtain poles.

The combination of the heavyweight cotton canvas and the rope used to hang these curtains gives a real nautical feel to the room.

HOW TO DO IT

You need to allow plenty of time for pressing with a hot steam iron in order for the tape to bond, because the fabric is quite thick.

STEP 1 Measure the drop for the curtains, adding a 4 in./10 cm. turn-over at the top and 2 in./5 cm to be turned up as a hem at the bottom. Press a ⅜ in./1 cm fold-over along the bottom, then iron on the bonding tape to fix the hem in place.

STEP 2 Iron the fabric stiffener onto the wrong side of the curtain tops. Peel off the backing paper, then turn it down and press with a hot iron to bond the stiffened section, making a double thickness header along the top of each curtain.

STEP 3 Mark the positions for the eyelets roughly 4 in.–5½ in./10 cm–14 cm apart, depending upon the curtain width. Fix the eyelets in place using the tool, which is supplied with the pack.

STEP 4 Fix the rope through the eyelets. Thread the curtains onto the pole, then arrange them to drop in neat folds.

Designing
new rooms

Introduction

In the past, decorating was seen as a necessary chore, but these days it has become one of the most popular leisure activities. The aim of this book is to make decorating your home simple, inexpensive, and more fun than ever before. We live in the age of the make-over, and there has never been more choice available to the home decorator than there is now. There are more materials, books, television programs, and magazines about decorating and interior design than there have ever been before, and the only downside is that there is often too much choice when it comes to deciding what you want! It is easy to make a decision about a color if there are only ten to choose from, but if you are faced with 200 subtle variations of blue, it is enough to confuse even the most experienced of decorators.

The best way to stay sane and enjoy the decorating process is to have a clear idea of what you want and what you are going to do before you hit the stores. This means taking time to decide on color, style, and content by watching the television programs, looking in magazines and stores, then finding out how to get the look you're after by following the well-designed and inspirational step-by-step projects in this book.

This section takes you through the entire home, offering a choice of traditional or contemporary ideas for each room. Many of the ideas will easily translate into other decorative styles,

A 1950s breakfast bar is just one of the many inexpensive projects you can do by following the step-by-step directions in this section.

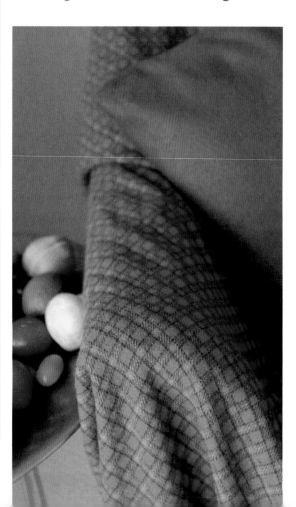

You don't need to go out and buy new furniture to give a room a new look. A new throw like this one on an elderly sofa can introduce strong color contrasts and a more relaxed style, as well as covering marks on old upholstery.

and can be adapted for use in other parts of the house. As many techniques are covered as possible; for example, the various flooring options that are available have been allocated to certain rooms, but the process of painting a wooden floor will be the same, whether done in a kitchen or a bathroom. You may well find that the ideal storage solution for your kitchen is one that is suggested in the nursery section, so be sure to have a look at all the projects before making up your mind.

The step-by-steps have been kept as clear and concise as possible—it is usually the case that too many directions are as confusing as too few. As most decorating products come complete with their own set of directions, these have been taken as read in many cases and the step-by-steps just show how to put the actual idea into practice. The most vital product and tool directions and advice to follow are those that relate to your safety. The statistics for accidents when making home improvements show that many could have been avoided if

only the safety advice on many of these tools had been followed.

So, if you plan to do up a whole house, decorate a room from scratch, or just make stylish improvements, we hope this section gives you all the inspiration and information that you will need.

Practical storage solutions like this disguised drawer on casters can be adapted for different rooms in the house, from the office to children's bedrooms.

Kitchens

The kitchen is often regarded as the heart of the home.
It is the room where meals are prepared and is often a place to eat,
gather, and socialize, so function plays a large part in the style. This
chapter shows you how to transform your kitchen into three different
styles: Country, Contemporary, and 1950s. Every kitchen can achieve
these styles, whatever its size or shape, but an additional section
shows you how to make the most of a galley kitchen. The three step-
by-step projects will start you off, and a few accessories and a fresh
coat of paint will do the rest. Have fun!

Country kitchen

For most of us, country living is a bit of a daydream, and if there is one aspect we would like more than anything, it is the traditional country kitchen. The idea of sitting at a large, scrubbed pine table, with the smell of baking and jars of homemade pickles and conserves on the shelves is very appealing, especially when your own kitchen has fitted melamine with all the charm of a cafeteria! Don't despair, though; that country kitchen of your dreams may not be possible, but there is a lot that can be done to inject any kitchen with all the key ingredients.

Begin by listing the top ten features that say "country" to you, loud and clear. They might go something like this …

1. Gingham
2. Baskets
3. Pine table and chairs
4. Old-fashioned sink with brass faucets
5. A wooden dish drainer
6. Drapes instead of shades
7. Open shelves or a dresser
8. Solid-fuel stove
9. Busy walls with a display of plates
10. Quarry-tiled floor

Realistically, your existing kitchen may be too small for a table and chairs, the floor may not be strong enough to support a solid-fuel stove, and you may have to make do with your stainless steel sink and the vinyl floor, but this doesn't mean that you can't go country in other ways. There are loads of things you can do to make a practical modern kitchen feel more homely.

Natural colors

Start with the color. If it is bright white and shiny, it can be mellowed with a soft yellow wash;

if it is too boring and beige, it can be spiced up with rusty red. Country colors are never harsh and tend to echo nature and the countryside. Stenciled patterns make a very good background to the busy look that is so typically country style. And more is definitely better when it comes to hanging pictures, plates, and kitchen utensils on the walls.

Soft lighting

Lighting can also make a real difference. You certainly need to see what you're doing and there is no denying that spotlights are useful, but they are also real atmosphere killers. A simple wrought-iron candelabra or a frosted-glass shade hung low over the table will create a more relaxed feeling, especially when fitted with a dimmer switch to vary the brilliance.

On display

A key aspect of the country look is having lots on show. You may not own a large Welsh dresser loaded with crockery, but a couple of wide plank shelves above a base cabinet can soon be dressed up to look like one. Simply paint the wall, shelves, and cabinet below the same color. Add rows of cup hooks below the shelves and brass drawer handles,

A pine table and chairs, a solid-fuel stove, and open shelves of crockery are features of a typical country kitchen, but there are other ways you can adopt the country style and give your kitchen a more homely feel.

and then make a display of your kitchen crockery. You can buy rolls of self-adhesive vinyl in gingham checks, using it to line drawers and shelves. Invest in a good quality, checked PVC tablecloth, and look around for odd wooden chairs in junk stores, and then paint them all the same color to make a nonmatching set.

Distressed paintwork

Distressed paintwork is still one of the key features in the country style because it gives the impression of having both a family history and a relaxed attitude. Fake it by applying contrasting colored paint in two coats, and sanding away the top coat in places to simulate wear and tear. Use mat paint and finish it off with a topcoat of beeswax polish, which looks and smells heavenly.

Country kitchens should also feel cozy in the evenings, so ditch the shades and choose drapes instead. Shaker-style patterned fabric featuring ticking stripes, tiny checks, or plaid patterns will all look good in the kitchen, and if you have a sewing machine, a simple plain border and some hand-stitched button detailing will add a contemporary touch. Some matching drape ties in the same fabric will complete the look.

THE PROJECTS

The three projects on the following pages will help you achieve a country-style background in your own kitchen. A few carefully selected accessories, a fresh coat of paint, and some warm, relaxed lighting will do the rest.

More is better than less in a country-style kitchen, so have as much as possible on display. Cover wall space with shelves of crockery, cups on hooks, and small wooden cabinets, and replace modern drawer handles with brass versions.

YOU WILL NEED:
- ³/₈ IN./9 MM MDF
- FINE-GRADE SANDPAPER
- FACE MASK
- JIGSAW
- ¹/₁₆-IN./2-MM DRILL BIT
- ⁵/₁₆-IN./8-MM DRILL BIT
- ALL-SURFACE PRIMER
- PAINT (VYNYL SILK OR LOW LUSTER FINISH)
- ENAMEL ROLLER AND SMALL ROLLER TRAY
- ¹/₂-IN./1.2-CM WIRE NETTING (OR NEAREST GAUGE TO THIS)
- WIRE CUTTERS
- SMALL HAMMER
- STAPLE GUN

PROJECT

Replacing existing doors with wire netting, framed in MDF

This project is suitable for wall-mounted kitchen or base cabinets. If you like the look you could use it throughout the kitchen, but remember that you can see through wire netting and not everything in a cabinet makes a good display.

Begin by emptying the cabinet and unscrewing the door. Kitchen cabinet hinges tend to leave large holes, which will need filling if you are changing the style. Clean the inside of the cabinet with a grease-cutting detergent and paint it a country color—pale moss green or slate blue, for instance. Melamine will need to be primed first, ideally with an all-surface primer. If you are lining the shelves, do it at this stage before the door is replaced.

Replacing existing cabinet doors with wire netting suits the country-kitchen look because it puts more of your kitchen on show. It's a good idea to plan the contents of the cabinets before you put them on display.

HOW TO DO IT

STEP 1 Place your outgoing door on top of the MDF. Use it as as a template, drawing the outline onto the MDF. Clamp the MDF on a workbench, and wear the mask as you cut it to size, and sand the edges lightly.

STEP 2 Draw the cut-out shape onto the MDF. Drill a hole in one corner of the shape, using a ⁵⁄₁₆-in./8-mm drill bit.

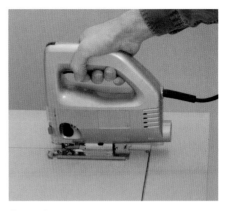

STEP 3 Clamp the MDF to the workbench and jigsaw out the inside shape. Keep the jigsaw's foot in touch with the surface of the MDF, and move with the saw.

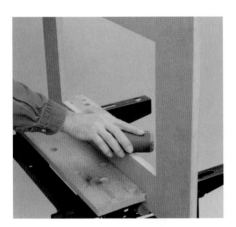

STEP 4 Use sandpaper to smooth the edge on the inside and outside.

STEP 5 Give the door two coats of primer, following the drying times as directed on the can. Use a foam roller to apply the paint because it will give a better finish than a brush, and painting takes half the time. Apply the top coat in the same way.

STEP 6 Cut the wire netting to the size of the cut-out shape leaving an extra 1 in./2.5 cm all around the edge. Turn over a seam of ³⁄₈ in./1 cm and flatten it with a hammer. Lay the MDF face down with the wire netting in position at the back. Staple the panel at the four cardinal points first, then add more staples in between until it is perfectly secure. Re-hang the door.

TOP TIPS

• Wire netting, even with a folded seam, has sharp pointy edges. As long as the shelves in the cabinet are set back from the door, it is a good idea to cover up these edges with a simple wooden molding.

• Measure the lengths, then miter the corners and use brads to secure them.

• Wear a mask when using sandpaper to stop you breathing in harmful particles!

YOU WILL NEED:

• SCREWDRIVER

• WOOD FILLER

• MOLDING

• MITER SAW (OR BACK SAW AND MITER BLOCK)

• MEDIUM-GRADE SANDPAPER

• CONTACT ADHESIVE

• MOLDING PINS

• NAIL PUNCH

• SMALL HAMMER

• ALL-PURPOSE PRIMER

• PAINT (IN A SUITABLE COUNTRY COLOR)

• SMALL FOAM PAINT ROLLER AND TRAY

• WILLOW BASKETS

PROJECT
Removing cabinet doors and adding willow baskets

Any base cabinet or kitchen cabinet can be given a real country look by removing the doors, and using willow baskets on the shelves as pull-out drawers. In fact, it may require a leap of the imagination to convert a standard beige melamine cabinet into something beautiful, but it can be done! All you need do is whip off the doors, fill the holes and pop in the baskets, but a few trimmings will make all the difference.

A melamine cabinet can be painted after suitable priming, and the facing edges of the cabinet can be covered with a wooden molding. They come in a range of styles, from twisted rope and oak leaves to simple half-moon and square edge. The inside of the cabinet will look good painted in a contrasting color to the outside, and there is also the option of adding a drape on a simple net wire. Checked gingham or even linen dish towel drapes look a million times better than old melamine, and they can be tied back to reveal the baskets inside.

Willow baskets as sliding, pull-out shelves transform standard melamine cabinets. Paint the insides and outsides of the cabinet first, and add wooden molding to the facing edges.

HOW TO DO IT

STEP 1 Unscrew the existing doors and remove the fittings. Fill the holes with wood filler so that the filler stands slightly proud of the surface. Once it has dried, sand the filler level.

STEP 2 Measure the frame, then cut the molding to fit, mitering the corners. Apply contact adhesive to the frame.

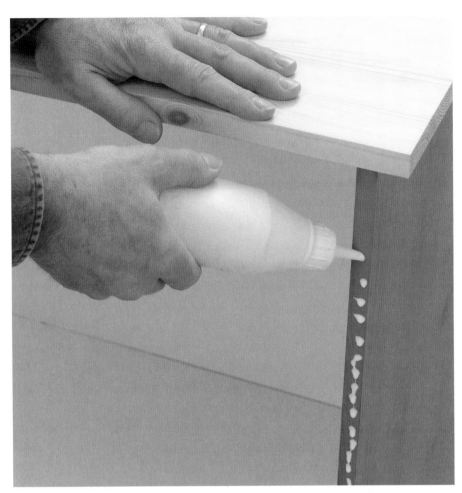

STEP 3 Stick the molding down and then add a few pins along each length. Tap the pinheads into the molding with a nail punch, then fill the holes and sand smooth.

STEP 4 Prime the cabinet and then paint it inside and out. If you are using two different colors, paint the inside of the cabinet first and let it dry before painting the area where the colors meet.

BASKET HANDLE IDEAS
You can use any of the following:
- Baggage labels tied on with string
- Checked ribbons
- Stitched tubes of fabric
- Threaded beads or buttons on twists of wire
- Rope loops
- Buckled leather straps

STEP 5 Buy willow baskets to fill the space widthwise, leaving just enough room for them to slide easily in and out. Many baskets have handles attached, but if not there are plenty of ways to make your own.

YOU WILL NEED:
- "HOCKEY-STICK" MOLDING (MEASURE THE DEPTH OF THE WORKTOP AND ADD TO IT THE DEPTH OF THE TILE PLUS ⅜ IN./ 1 CM OF ADHESIVE FOR THE MOLDING HEIGHT, AND ALL AROUND THE EDGE OF THE WORKTOP FOR THE LENGTH)
- CONTACT ADHESIVE
- FINE BRADS
- NAIL PUNCH
- SMALL HAMMER
- MITER SAW (OR BACK SAW AND MITER BLOCK)
- WOOD FILLER
- TILES
- CERAMIC TILE ADHESIVE
- SPREADING TOOL
- GROUT
- SPONGE

PROJECT

Tiling a worktop

One thing you won't find in a perfect country kitchen is a vinyl laminated worktop. Wood or tiles are the look to go for, but the wood has to be well seasoned and solid, which is expensive. Tiles are the better option, and laying them on a flat surface is not only easy but fun. They will give you the country look for next to nothing and have maximum make-over power. The worktop is edged with a "hockey-stick" molding, which has a flat edge and a rounded top resting on top of the tile, giving a very neat, professional finish.

Choose traditional-style, plain deep greens or blues, or cream for the dairy look. Quarry tiles are another option, but grease will mark them, so keep them away from the cooking area. A cheap and cheerful idea is to buy a range of different-colored tiles that are all the same size. End-of-line tiles are often sold off cheaply and can be laid to look like a patchwork-quilt pattern. Most importantly, measure the area that needs tiling carefully and buy the correct number of tiles to fit the space.

Tiles are one of the easiest and cheapest ways of giving your worktops a country-kitchen make-over. Edge them with a "hockey-stick" molding to give them a neat, professional finish.

HOW TO DO IT

STEP 1 Have a trial run by laying out the tiles to get an idea of their spacing. Ideally you will have bought tiles that fit snugly to the edges of the worktop. If you do need to do any cutting, borrow a good tile cutter because it will make the job so much easier.

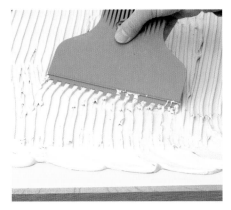

STEP 2 Spread ceramic tile adhesive over the surface to an even depth of about ³⁄₈ in./1 cm. Comb the surface of the adhesive into ridges with a spreading tool.

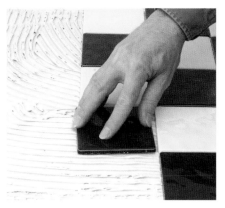

STEP 3 Press the tiles into the bed of the adhesive, beginning at the front corner, working along the front, and then filling in the rows behind. Aim to leave an equal gap between the tiles. Wipe off any adhesive that squeezes out while it is still wet, and then leave to set.

STEP 4 Apply a generous amount of the grouting mixture, working it into the gaps between the tiles. Wipe off most of the excess with a damp sponge and leave to set. Wipe again when it is semidry.

STEP 5 Measure the lengths of molding you need, and cut the adjoining pieces to a 45° angle with a miter saw. Only the front corners need mitering if the worktop is to stand against the wall.

STEP 6 Apply contact adhesive to the front edge of the worktop. Rest the top of the molding on the tiles, and flatten it down onto the adhesive at the front. Fit two sides the same way, then tap in a few fine brads to help secure them and punch their heads below the surface with a nail punch. Fill the small holes, and then paint or varnish the molding.

Contemporary kitchen

The contemporary kitchen is a fusion of professional catering style and the comforts of home. This is the antidote to clutter and the minimalist's idea of heaven. It may seem impossible to maintain this chic modern look, keeping worktops free of clutter, but with well-planned storage space and a little daily discipline, it can be easier than you think to achieve the contemporary style.

At its most extreme, the look is cold and industrial with steel, concrete, glass, and large no-frills appliances that mimic a restaurant kitchen. However, in the same way that haute couture inspires main street fashion, the extreme version of industrial chic is the inspiration for a more practical, comfortable, and achievable home style. The top ten elements to go for are ...

1. Stainless steel appliances

They echo the catering style, but are scaled down to a more realistic size, while worktops are granite or marble, or resin compounds that look the part but are not as heavy or expensive as the real thing. Accessorize with stainless steel handles, utensils, light fittings, and sink units. Small details like stainless steel outlets and shelf supports will also make a big impact.

2. Pale wooden cabinets

Plain, pale wood like beech or ash provides a perfect complement to steel, and this is where the homely look breaks ranks with industrial chic, because wood is warm and organic. Keep the doors plain with steel handles, and avoid drawers above cabinets if you can. A set of drawers on their own are actually more practical, and the look is more contemporary.

3. Floating wooden strip floor

This is laid on top of the existing floor—what could be simpler? All that's needed is a dry, level surface, a polystyrene sheet underlay, and enough laminated floorboards to fit the room. The boards come in a range of wood finishes and the quality will be reflected in the price, which, with luck, includes a free fitting.

4. Frosted glass shelves

Frosted glass is cool. Use the reinforced version for shelves, supported by stainless steel brackets, as panels in doors, or design and make your own frosted window with painter's tape, templates, and etching spray.

5. Limited color range

When it comes to choosing color, think pale and interesting. Bright white is too stark and reflective, but pale gray, off-white, duck-egg

The best tables in a contemporary kitchen are simple fold-aways or small, round café-style versions, which do not interfere with the clean lines.

Stainless steel appliances and granite or marble worktops bring the professional catering style into the home. Stainless steel handles, utensils, light fittings, and sink cabinets add to the impact.

blue, or light sea green all suit this look. For a subtle toned effect, pick a color and its immediate neighbors on the chart. Try and avoid strong contrasts and go for harmonies instead.

6. Slatted shades
Shades provide the neatest window treatment, but only if they fit perfectly and work efficiently. Roller shades are neat and good value, but the ideal shade for this look is the slatted Venetian shade. Aluminum or light wood both look fabulous, and you can adjust them in several ways to filter the incoming light.

7. No clutter on worktops
The no-clutter rule has to be strictly enforced if this look is to succeed! Real life is not a clutter-free zone and the only way to achieve this is by being very organized, with good storage and a place for everything. Lighten the look with a vase of freshly cut flowers or a row of herbs in matching pots.

8. Chrome rods with matching utensils
Utensils don't belong in drawers, but they do need to be visible and well within reach. The best way to arrange them is by hanging them on a fitted rail above the worktop. This type of rod with hooks can be bought in a range of lengths and styles, or follow the simple directions in the project and make your own.

9. Contemporary kitchen table and matching set of chairs or stools
The table is not the main attraction in a contemporary kitchen. A small, round café-style table or a simple fold-away version is an extremely good idea, especially in small spaces, and it avoids cluttering up the no-frills look. Chairs are now very much in fashion, and there are so many new designs to choose from.

Whether you go for lightweight, cast aluminum chairs, smooth beech with chrome legs, or folding metal and polypropylene in jelly colors, it is hard to go wrong.

10. Recessed downlights in ceiling, or halogen spotlights
To see what you're doing in the kitchen, a combination of good task lighting and an ambient glow is ideal. Recessed ceiling lights look great, but there are restrictions on their use. Better still, use strip lights fitted below the wall cabinets or you could opt for a row of halogen spotlights angled to illuminate the work area.

Worktops are kept clutter-free in a contemporary kitchen, so good storage space and planning a place for everything are essential.

THE PROJECTS
The three projects on the following pages will help you achieve a contemporary background in your own kitchen. A few stainless steel accessories, a fresh coat of paint, and some halogen lighting will do the rest.

YOU WILL NEED:

- READY-MADE DOOR OR A SHEET OF BEECH-FACED MDF
- SANDPAPER (IF YOU ARE MAKING A NEW DOOR)
- STEEL DOOR HANDLE WITH SCREWS
- NEW SPRING-LOADED HINGES (ONLY IF THE OLD ONES NEED REPLACING)
- SCREWDRIVER
- HANDSAW
- SCREWS
- $^1\!/_{16}$-IN./2-MM DRILL BIT FOR PILOT HOLES
- DRILL
- SPECIAL 1$^3\!/_8$-IN./3.5-CM SPADE BIT (IF YOU ARE RE-FITTING CONCEALED HINGES)
- PENCIL
- SPIRIT LEVEL

PROJECT

Replacing existing doors

A change of doors on the kitchen cabinets is a quick way to create a new look. Fitted kitchen cabinets are made to a standard size and, although the hinges look quite complex, they are not difficult to fit. Ready-made hardwood doors are widely available and it makes sense to use them if the style is right. The other option is to make them yourself using beech-faced MDF. You get the best of both worlds with a material like this. The MDF backing makes it easy to work with, and the beech facing has all the beauty of the natural grain. You can buy it from good lumber merchants in sheets measuring 48 in. x 96 in./ 1.2 m x 2.4 m in a ¾-in./1.9-cm thickness.

Replacing kitchen cabinet doors is one of the quickest ways to create a new look. Since fitted kitchen cabinets are made to a standard size, you can buy them ready-made. Add chrome handles to complete the look.

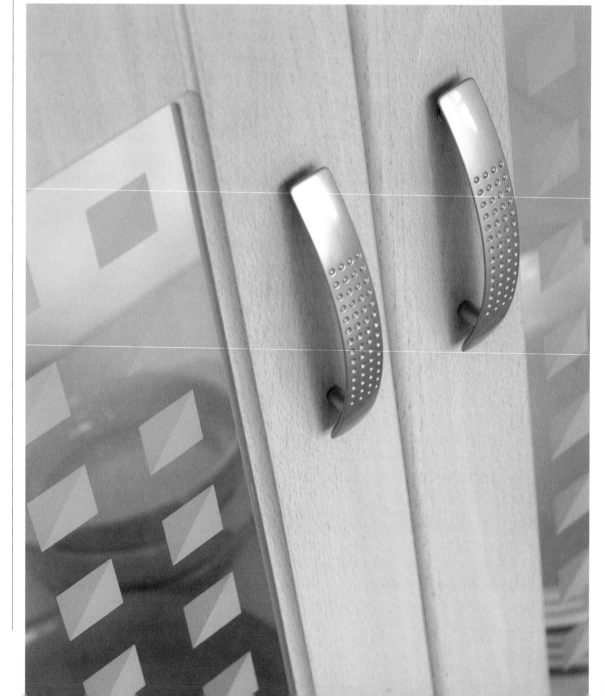

HOW TO DO IT

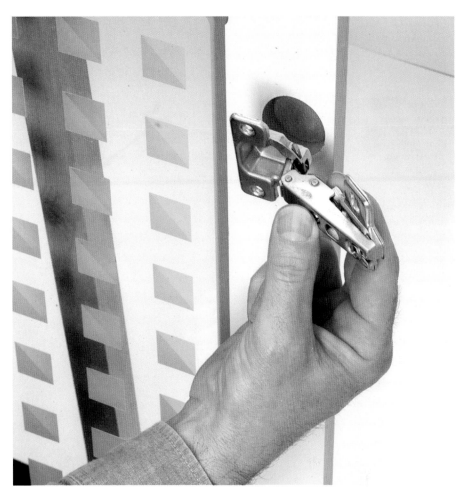

STEP 1 Support the door as you unscrew the hinges to remove it. If the screws are in a good condition, save them to reuse in the new door.

STEP 2 If you are making a new door, use the old one as a template to draw around. Check the rightangles and the measurements, then cut out the new door with a handsaw and use sandpaper on the edges.

STEP 3 Mark the positions for the hinge fittings, and drill out the recess with the spade bit.

STEP 4 Hold the door in position with the hinge mechanism fitted into the recess, and mark the screw positions. Drill small pilot holes.

STEP 5 Screw the hinges to the doors. The fit of the door can be adjusted using the two screws on the hinge inside the cabinet. Loosen the screws, move the door slightly, and re-tighten them. Repeat this sequence until the fit is perfect.

STEP 6 Measure the positions for the screws or bolts accurately. The handles on all the doors must be perfectly aligned, so double check and use a spirit level. Drill holes for the screws or bolts and fit the handles.

YOU WILL NEED:
- STEEL OR CHROME ROD WITH HOOKS (OR TWO CHROME TOWEL ROD HOLDERS AND A LENGTH OF ROD)
- LONG RULE WITH SPIRIT LEVEL
- PAINTER'S TAPE IF THE WALL IS TILED
- DRILL
- CORRECT SIZE MASONRY DRILL BIT FOR THE SCREWS (E. G. SCREW AND BIT SIZE NUMBER 6)
- WALL ANCHORS

PROJECT
Fitting a chrome utensil rod to the wall

The first thing you need to discover is what your wall is made of: the usual suspects are painted or tiled brick or wallboard, and they require different wall fixings. There is also a knack to drilling holes in tiles successfully. Use a small strip of painter's tape, which has to be placed on the tile before you mark the screw position. The tape stops the drill bit from skidding off as it spins. Whether you buy a ready-made rod or make one yourself by customizing a chrome towel rod, the actual task of fitting it to the wall will be the same.

Chrome utensil rods can be bought ready-made or you can make them by customizing a chrome towel rod. When you are deciding which height to fit it at, hang the longest utensil from the rod to make sure it's high enough.

HOW TO DO IT

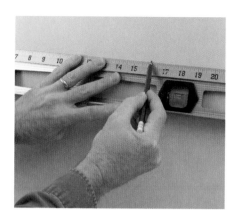

STEP 1 Using the long rule with spirit level, decide where you would like the rod on the wall and mark the position in pencil. Hold up the rod to the wall. Make certain that the rod is level, then accurately mark the positions for the screws.

STEP 2 Drill the holes for the wall anchors. Hold the drill at a right angle to the wall and apply firm pressure as you drill.

TOP TIPS

• Chrome rods can be clamped to a workbench or a table edge, and cut down to size with a hacksaw.

• Wooden doweling rods can be used with chrome towel rod fittings to give a softer look. They are especially suitable if you have wooden floors or cabinet doors.

• Buy butcher-style hooks, without sharp points, from kitchenware stores.

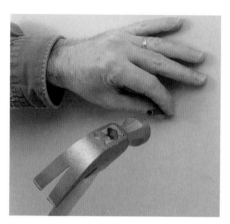

STEP 3 Push the anchors into the holes, tapping them lightly with a hammer if necessary. They should fit snugly and stay in place. If the hole is too big, you may need to go up a size with both wall anchors and screws.

STEP 4 Screw in the top screw on each side to support the rod as you tighten the other screws.

YOU WILL NEED:

• SCREWDRIVER
• WOOD FILLER
• SANDPAPER
• SET OF NEW
  HANDLES
• SPIRIT LEVEL
• DRILL FITTED WITH
  A BIT TO MATCH THE
  BOLT SIZE

PROJECT
Changing handles

This is an easy project to provide an instant lift. Fashions change, thank goodness, and at the moment knobs are out and long thin steel handles are in. They are usually fixed with bolts that screw in from the back of the door. It is a style that suits only plain doors and drawers because the look emphazises clean lines and good design. If you have doors with moldings and panels, you might want to consider replacing the doors altogether, or facing them with hardboard or ¼-in./6-mm MDF stuck down with panel adhesive.

Fitting new handles on kitchen cabinets provides an instant lift. Long, thin steel handles emphasize clean lines, so they suit only plain doors.

HOW TO DO IT

STEP 1 Unscrew the old handles or knobs and fill the holes. When the filler has dried, sand it flat and touch up the paint or varnish. You may decide to take this opportunity to refresh all the paintwork.

STEP 2 Decide on the position for the new handle. This can be fitted horizontally or vertically about 1 in./2.5 cm from the door edge—both ways look good. Check it with the spirit level, then mark the fitting positions.

STEP 3 Drill the holes for the bolts. Check each hole against the next mark with the spirit level before you drill the hole.

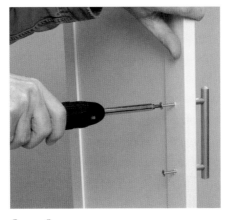

STEP 4 Tighten the screws or bolts from the back of the door; you can hold the handles if it makes it easier.

TOP TIP

If you are changing the handles on a row of cabinets, it is vital to fit them in a straight line. Make a cardboard template with the bolt positions drilled out. This can be placed against the back of each cabinet to make sure that the handle positions do not vary.

The 1950s kitchen

Sometimes it seems that color was invented in the 1950s because everything before that was photographed in black and white. In truth, homes were pretty dull during the war years, but it was also a time of great advances in technology and design. When all the brainpower and new materials were no longer needed for the war effort, thoughts turned toward the commercial world.

Formica worktops are a key element in any 1950s-style kitchen, along with contrasting colors, such as primrose yellow used with black. Streamlined, rocket-shaped bins and other appliances complete the look.

The 1950s kitchen is a part of the "American dream," fitted with bright Formica worktops, shiny chrome appliances, colorful plastics, and checked linoleum flooring. It started in America, but the look took off across the Atlantic as soon as it was seen in Doris Day movies. Look out for 1950s cook books in second-hand book stores because they offer a wealth of inspiration. Genuine 1950s kitchen cabinets are collectors' items, but you can still pick up kitchen accessories in junk stores and specialized stores. The 1950s revival is always simmering away on the back burner, and kitchen furniture with that look features in many contemporary ranges, mixing chrome, leather, Formica, and fun. The top ten ingredients that make this style are …

1. Rounded, streamlined steel and chrome appliances

The streamlined style was inspired by the advent of the jet aircraft, and excitement surrounding space rocket missions. Sleek chrome striping was used to make stationary kitchen appliances look as though they were speeding! Everything from refrigerators to food mixers were given this look, and some of the best designs are still in production today. Look out for retro refrigerators, and toasters, chrome bins, kettles, blenders, kitchen clocks, and radios. Since they are still a popular style, they shouldn't be hard to find.

2. Red-and-white checkerboard vinyl floor

Some of the least expensive floor tiles on the market are slightly marbleized, self-adhesive, plain-colored vinyl. They have the look of authentic 1950s linoleum but at a fraction of the cost. Go for a big color contrast—red-and-white or yellow-and-black checkerboard floors may not appeal to the faint-hearted, but when you see them reflected in the chromework—wow!

3. Small black-and-white checkered borders

Small, black-and-white checkered borders seen on the sides of New York taxicabs often feature in 1950s-style diners. There are two ways to get the same effect without re-tiling the kitchen: one is to apply the checkerboard pattern on a self-adhesive tape strip, and the other is to print the border with a rubber roller stamp, bought from a specialized crafts' supplier.

4. Walls painted in contrasting colors

Color in the 1950s was all about contrasts. Pale colors like eau de nil (a light green) or primrose yellow and sky blue were often used with black. And you can't fail with red, whether it's just the plastic handles of cabinets and drawers or a whole wall painted in red enamel. Different-colored walls, or blocks of strong color on a part of a pale wall, are the look to go for.

5. Patterns—polka dots and stars

One of the most popular patterns for wallpaper back in the 1950s had small white stars or spots on a colored background, which would be used on just one wall. Tablecloths and drapes were made from polka-dot fabric reversed out, where the pattern color swapped over with the background color.

6. Formica

Formica is the plastic laminate that revolutionized kitchen worktops. It is one of the key elements in any 1950s-style kitchen. Choose bright yellow, cherry red, or sky blue for a big impact, and take it up the wall behind the worktop as a backsplash.

7. Tubular steel

If you ever see a set of old chrome steel kitchen chairs, buy them, regardless of the state of the upholstery. Re-cover the seats with soft vinyl stapled in place, edged with a row of chrome upholstery studs. These retro-style kitchen tables and chairs are back in fashion and are really expensive, so cheat if you possibly can.

8. Kitsch

Kitsch is the German word for bad taste, but sometimes bad taste is actually good taste, especially when it is entirely deliberate! Think of Elvis in *Blue Hawaii* with plastic fruit and flowers, sunsets, neon signs, flying ducks, laminated calendars, and anything plastic in the shape of a poodle!

THE PROJECTS

The three projects on the following pages will help you achieve a 1950s background in your own kitchen. A few kitsch accessories, some streamlined chrome appliances, and some black-and-white checkered borders will do the rest.

9. Colorful modern ceramics

Organic shapes, Picasso-inspired patterns, and bright contrasting colors give 1950s ceramics a highly distinctive look. These things are within everyone's budget, so you just need to get out there and start looking. Try inexpensive yard sales and junk stores but if you can't spare the time to trawl, find a market trader who specializes in 1950s ware.

10. Packaging and plastics

Quite a lot of cheap plastic ware that is manufactured in the Far East fits in well with this look. American mustard in a bright yellow squeezy bottle, or a large plastic tomato filled with ketchup helps to set the scene. You do have to be selective, but that is the fun of putting a themed look together.

Checkerboard vinyl floors can be bought as self-adhesive tiles at a fraction of the cost of authentic 1950s linoleum. The greater the contrast in color, the better.

YOU WILL NEED:

- SILICONE-CARBIDE
  SANDPAPER
- ALL-SURFACE
  PRIMER
- SMALL FOAM ROLLER
  WITH TRAY
- METHYLATED
  ALCOHOL (FOR
  CLEANING)
- VINYL SILK PAINT
  IN PALE GREEN
  (MAIN COLOR)
- STENCIL MATERIAL
  (CARD OR PLASTIC)
- SNAP-BLADE KNIFE
- TRACING PAPER
  (OR PHOTOCOPIES
  OF PATTERNS)
- TEST POT OF BRIGHT
  RED (BACKGROUND
  COLOR)
- TEST POT OF BLACK
  (FOR THE PATTERN)

PROJECT
Painting the kitchen cabinets

The idea that melamine kitchen cabinets can be painted is actually quite new. This has a lot to do with TV make-over programs and the popularity of home-style magazines. Once the make-over idea took off people started experimenting, trying different products and discovering new uses for old materials.

The problem with a shiny surface like melamine is that, without the right primer, the paint has nothing to key into and is easily scratched. The trick is to scratch the surface with a silicone-carbide sandpaper, then apply one or two coats of a shellac-based primer. It gives good coverage, is very strong, and leaves an ultra-mat surface.

Go creative on your kitchen cabinets! Melamine kitchen cabinets can be painted as long as they are prepared beforehand, using sandpaper to scratch the surface and primer to give an ultra-mat surface.

HOW TO DO IT

STEP 1 Clean the doors with a grease-cutting detergent or abrasive powder. Rub them down with silicone-carbide sandpaper to remove the shine from the surface.

STEP 2 Apply the primer with the roller and leave to dry (repeat if necessary). Apply the main color (repeat if necessary).

STEP 3 Enlarge the two stencil patterns and transfer them onto a stencil card or plastic. Cut them out with a snap-blade knife. Paint the background shapes first in the light color.

STEP 4 (Above) Use the second stencil to apply the pattern inside the shapes, and then apply two coats of clear enamel varnish.

Enlarge the stencils (left) and transfer them onto plastic or stencil paper. The guides to the left will help you position the two main stencils together on your kitchen cabinet door.

YOU WILL NEED:

• TAPE MEASURE

• SHEET METAL

• DOME-CAPPED
  MIRROR SCREWS

• DRILL

• NAIL PUNCH

• MASONRY BIT TO
  MATCH SCREW SIZE

• WALL ANCHORS TO
  MATCH SCREW SIZE

PROJECT
Fitting a stainless steel, zinc, or aluminum backsplash

Measure the size of the backsplash area, then visit a sheet metal dealer. They cut metal sheets to size and will usually have a stock of off-cuts suitable for small jobs like this. Explain what you will be using it for, and check that the type you have chosen will keep its shine and never rust. They have the right equipment, so ask for the sheet to be cut to size and for the edges to be buffed. There may be a charge for this service, but it will be worth it!

Metal sheets can be bought as off-cuts from a sheet metal dealer and cut to size with the edges buffed. You can drill holes in the sheet using the same bit as you use for wood.

HOW TO DO IT

STEP 1 Measure the backsplash area. Don't have it too narrow because it needs to be about one-third of the depth of the worktop. Mark the positions of the screws with a nail punch.

STEP 2 Holes can be drilled in sheet metal using the same bit as you use for wood. You will need to have a wall fixing approximately every 10 in./25 cm on a long strip. Drill all the screw holes in the metal, and then hold it in position as you mark the screw positions on the wall.

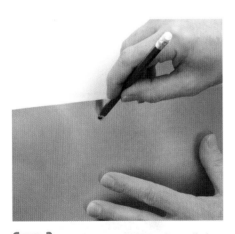

STEP 3 Drill the screw holes in the wall, then push in the wall anchors. If you are fitting this on a solid wall, use regular wall anchors, but for a stud wall you need cavity wall anchors that grip from the back.

STEP 4 Place the backsplash against the wall and screw it in place. Screw the domed caps into the screw heads.

TOP TIP
Acrylic sheet is a colorful option. It can be supplied cut to size.

YOU WILL NEED:
- ¾-IN./1.8-CM MDF
- JIGSAW
- SANDPAPER
- HACKSAW
- WORKBENCH
  OR TABLE WITH 2
  C-CLAMPS
- STICKY-BACKED
  PLASTIC (OR
  FORMICA AND
  PANEL ADHESIVE)
- WOODEN SUPPORT
  BRACKETS AND
  SCREWS
- CHROME CARPET-
  FITTING STRIP
- DRILL
- SPIRIT LEVEL

PROJECT
Creating a breakfast bar

The breakfast bar is just the thing for informal snacking. It is the very place to perch on a stool as you munch your toast and sip your espresso, or for a friend to have a drink while watching you cook. The 1950s styling means that you can have fun with the shape and cover it with shiny Formica or sticky-backed plastic sheeting, whichever the budget allows.

Breakfast bars make a convenient and space-saving place to have a snack, and this 1950s style version is fun and colorful. It can be made out of MDF and covered with Formica or sticky-backed plastic sheeting.

HOW TO DO IT

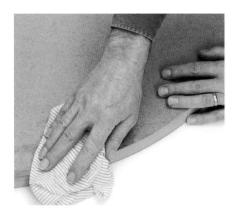

STEP 1 Draw out the shape of the pattern on the MDF. Cut the pattern out with a jigsaw. Hold the jigsaw firmly down on the surface and move with it. Sand the edge smooth, then wipe away any dust with a damp cloth.

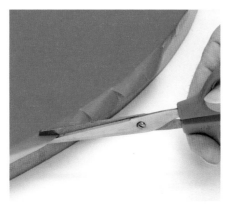

STEP 2 Cover the MDF with sticky-backed plastic, smoothing it flat as you roll it on. Snip notches on the curve of the table and fold over the edge so the plastic lays flat.

STEP 3 Cut the chrome carpet-fitting strip to size with a hacksaw.

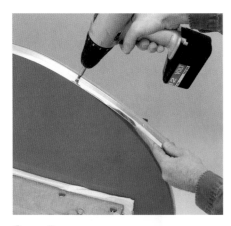

STEP 4 Drill pilot holes for the chrome strip and then screw into place on the edge of the table. Begin at one end of the curve, bending the strip as you go.

STEP 5 Drill holes for the bracket fittings in both the wall and the MDF. Mark the position for the fittings on the wall and drill the holes. Fit the appropriate wall anchors into the holes.

STEP 6 Screw the brackets to the wall first, then screw them to the MDF. Trim the edge. Use a spirit level to check the tops are level.

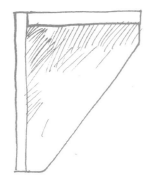

Check these illustrations when you are constructing and attaching the brackets to your kitchen wall. Always double-check that they are straight with a spirit level.

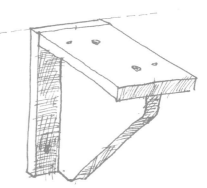

Galley kitchen

A small kitchen space should be seen as a challenge and not a problem. Believe it or not, squeezing everything into an area the size of a corridor can be an easier task than putting together a coherent style in acres of space. By using storage solutions that make the best use of the space available, galley kitchens can look extremely stylish.

Stools are an ideal seating choice for galley kitchens, although they may take up the same area of floor space as chairs, their height makes them less dense and claustrophobic.

Start by evaluating what you have in the way of major appliances such as the stove, refrigerator, freezer, washing machine, and tumble dryer. Some may be too big, and some you may not need at all. Do you only ever half-fill the refrigerator and freezer? Do you cook only under the broiler, in the microwave, or on the stove top, and would a mini-oven be better? Compact versions would certainly save a lot of space and money on fuel bills. Also make sure that all the kitchen's storage potential is being used, and that there is no "dead" space. Keep only essential equipment, and make sure that the things you use most are stored within easy reach. Remember, a galley kitchen must be functional, with as much floor space as possible, and easily accessed cabinets and appliances. A long, thin kitchen can afford to have the space trimmed down a bit and be fitted with wall-to-wall shelving around the door frame. Worktops need to be kept clutter-free, with the food and crockery hidden behind plain doors.

Gentle variations in color, or using the same color for worktops, walls, and cabinets, will make the space seem bigger, and brushed steel appliances and shiny backsplashes can help by reflecting light. There is so much that can be done with a can of paint, and the new, multi-surface paints have extended these boundaries even further.

A number of important points to consider when kitchen space is tight are …

Sliding or folding doors

A door opening into a galley kitchen will be using up quite a lot of space. One way of reclaiming space is to have the door re-hung so that it opens the other way, and another is to fit a sliding door on the outside. Sliding doors still need somewhere to slide to, and if you don't have this space, then think about a folding door. Concertina-style melamine panels with steel hinges look sleek, and take up only the space of the door area. Or you could make up a double-sided, heavy duty PVC drape with eyelets, and thread it onto a chrome tube rod.

Glass shelves over windows

Kitchen windows are usually quite a generous size, so they eat up potential wall and storage space. You can section off part of the window and fit it with glass shelves. The space above a window is an ideal place to store glassware; the natural light is not completely blocked, and glasses can sparkle within easy reach.

Plain flooring

Since the overall floor area of a galley kitchen is fairly small, it should not cost the earth to invest in some very flattering floor covering. All patterned flooring follows a repeat grid of some type, and the grid pattern will visually "shrink" the floorspace. Instead, choose a floating, wooden strip floor laid crosswise, or plain-colored sheet linoleum or vinyl flooring.

Storage—everywhere

Make full use of every bit of space. Kitchen cabinets are made to a standard depth, but most of us have things lurking toward the back that never see the light of day. Reduce the cabinet depth by 6 in./15 cm and you might have room to swing that cat! Create even more space in a shallow cabinet by fitting two shelves instead of one to make full use of the height. Fit a row of wall cabinets above eye level for things you use less often.

Task lighting

Draw the eye toward the action by lighting the worktops with an angled track of halogen spotlights. A small kitchen is no place to be stumbling about in the dark with hot oil, so make sure the work areas are bright when you need them to be. It is also best to have an ambient light source to soften the effect. Recessed, dimmable ceiling lights or even a stylish table lamp will offer a change of atmosphere when you want it.

Expanding space with color

When decorating a small room, it is best to work with a limited palette. Use one main color with perhaps a darker and lighter version. Earth colors work well if you have wooden doors and floors, blue is a receding color and will "expand" the space, and bold bright yellow is good with metal. Red will make the room look smaller but quite sexy, and white will dazzle. If you need to reflect

Glass and brushed steel surfaces reflect light around a galley kitchen, helping create a bigger sense of space.

natural light with pale walls, it's a good idea to choose a warm cream because it looks delicious with dark wood.

Fold-away counters

Think of caravans or yachts because they provide plenty of practical inspiration for the galley kitchen. Fold-down flaps, collapsible tables, high cabinets like airplane lockers, and pull-out breadboards are all good ideas to adapt with a touch of contemporary styling.

Stools instead of chairs

Chairs and stool legs may take up roughly the same area of floor space, but stools are less claustrophobic than chairs in galley kitchens. Perched on a high stool looking down on the worktops, the view is of the widest part of the kitchen.

THE PROJECTS

The three projects on the following pages are practical, space-saving solutions that will help optimize the space in your own galley kitchen. Think about adding a few homely touches of your own to personalize the effect.

Homely touches

Never forget that this galley kitchen is part of your home. Design tips can help you make the best of the space, but you should always feel free to introduce your personal style. Efficiently designed kitchens can look too clinical, so be sure to introduce some homely touches.

YOU WILL NEED:
- ¾-IN./1.8-CM MDF
  (OR LAMINATED
  WORKTOP OR A
  WIDE SHELF)
- JIGSAW
- STICKY-BACKED
  PLASTIC
- 1IN x 1 IN./
  2.5 CM x 2.5 CM
  SQUARE MOLDING
- BRADS
- NAIL PUNCH
- HAMMER
- TAPE MEASURE
- FOLDING BRACKETS
- LONG RULE WITH
  SPIRIT LEVEL
- DRILL
- MASONRY BIT (SIZE
  TO SUIT SCREWS)
- SCREWS
- SCREWDRIVER
- WALL ANCHORS
- PILOT BIT

PROJECT
Making a hinged breakfast bar

When space is limited, it is worth thinking about when and how the room is used. There is no need to allocate precious space to a permanent eating area if it is going to be used only for a quick croissant and coffee in the morning, or a bowl of noodles at night.

A fold-away bar like this one is ideal in this situation, and if you make one to match the color of the kitchen walls, it will virtually disappear when it's not in use. Alternatively, you could choose to make a feature of it and cover it with a bright color or pattern.

Wall-mounted, hinged breakfast bars are ideal eating areas that can be folded away after each use.

HOW TO DO IT

STEP 1 Cut the MDF to the size required and cover with sticky-backed plastic, snipping and folding the corners to make a neat edge.

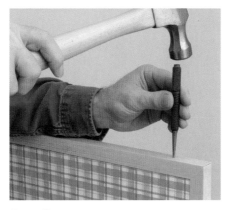

STEP 2 Cut and miter the molding, and use brads to attach it to the MDF. Use a nail punch to punch the brads home.

STEP 3 Determine the position of the shelf on the wall by using a tape measure and pencil.

STEP 4 Place the shortest end of the bracket on the wall and mark screw positions. Fix and tighten all the screws.

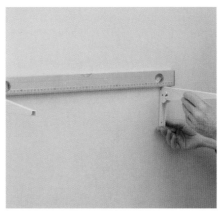

STEP 5 Align the second bracket with the long rule with spirit level. Check the horizontal. Fix the second bracket as described in step 4.

STEP 6 Fix the shelf to the brackets, leaving a ³/₁₆-in./5-mm gap between the wall and the shelf for easy folding.

TOP TIPS

• Drill a pilot hole using a ¹/₁₆-in./2-mm drill bit if you are screwing into MDF.

• Design the breakfast bar as an extension to the kitchen worktop, making sure that it doesn't block a cabinet door when folded down.

• Give up painting furniture with brushes and use small "enamel" rollers instead. The finish is far better and you avoid the drips.

YOU WILL NEED:

LUMBER AS FOLLOWS:

- 4 LEGS: 2 IN. x 2 IN./
  5 CM x 5 CM,
  23 IN./58 CM LONG
- 4 FEET: 1⅝ IN./4 CM
  WOODEN KNOBS
  WITH SCREWS
- 1 BOX BASE: ½-IN./
  1.2-CM MDF,
  30 CM x 30 CM/
  12IN x 12IN
- 2 BOX SIDES:
  ½-IN./1.2-CM MDF,
  12 IN. x 8 IN./
  30 CM x 20 CM
- 2 BOX SIDES:
  ½-IN./1.2-CM MDF,
  13 IN. x 8 IN./
  32.5 CM x 20 CM
- 2 SEAT FRAMES:
  ½-IN./1.2-CM MDF,
  13IN x 8 IN./
  30 CM x 80 CM
- 2 SEAT FRAMES:
  ½-IN./1.2-CM MDF,
  13 IN. x 31½ IN./
  32.5 CM x 80 CM
- 1 SEAT: 1-IN./2.5-CM
  MDF, 14 IN. x 14 IN./
  35 CM x 35 CM
- PENCIL
- TAPE MEASURE
- LONG RULE
- SAW
- WOOD GLUE
- DRILL WITH
  ¹⁄₁₆-IN./2-MM
  BIT AND
  COUNTERSUNK BIT
- BOX OF 1⅝-IN./
  4-CM NUMBER
  6 SCREWS
- PRIMER
- PAINT
- SMALL FOAM ROLLER
  AND TRAY

Not an inch is wasted by this high stool, which has a storage box in the base. Experiment with colors that either match or contrast with the rest of the kitchen.

PROJECT
Stools for storage

Remember the space rule and don't waste an inch of it. This high stool is easy for a beginner to make, and has a useful storage box in the base. The stool can be painted to match the kitchen if you want it to blend in, or try primary colors with black legs for a Bauhaus look.

HOW TO DO IT

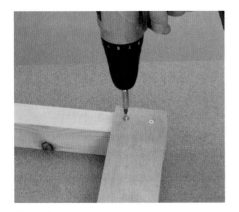

STEP 1 Make up the two shorter sides. Drill, countersink, glue and screw the 12 in./30 cm seat frame across the top of each pair of legs. Check that the legs are square to the seat.

STEP 2 Drill, countersink, glue, and screw the 12-in./30-cm box sides at the other end to overlap the ends of the legs by ½ in./1.2 cm and allow for the depth of the box base. Check that everything is square!

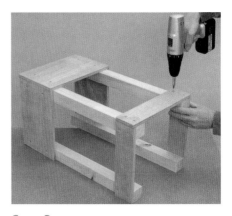

STEP 3 Join the two sides of the stool by fixing the 13-in./32.5-cm seat base and box sides between them.

STEP 4 Fix the base by screwing up into the legs from below. If this is a nice tight fit, it will add stability. Fix the seat on from the top.

STEP 5 Fill all the countersunk holes with wood filler, leave to set, and then sand them smooth.

STEP 6 Drill four pilot holes, then screw the wooden feet into the base. Prime and paint the stool using a small foam roller.

TOP TIP
You might need to plane a small amount of wood from the underside of each of the wooden knobs that are to be used as feet. Check how the stool stands on the floor and adjust the feet accordingly.

YOU WILL NEED:
- COPPER ROD
  AND HOOKS
- DRILL
- PILOT 1/16-IN./2-MM
  BIT
- SCREWDRIVER
- MITER BLOCK
- BACK SAW
- 12 IN./30 CM OF
  2 IN. x 2 IN./
  5 CM x 5 CM
  LUMBER
  FOR SUPPORTS
- 7/8-IN./2.2-CM
  SPADE BIT

PROJECT
Fitting a rod below a floating shelf

Shelves with internal brackets give the kitchen a contemporary edge, and by fitting steel rods for cups below the shelf, you can double its usefulness. If you are displaying glasses, cups, or mugs in this way, invest in a brand new matching set so that you can enjoy looking at them. Buy the shelves from a home improvement store: they will have full fitting directions and the fixings needed to complete the job. The design of the steel rod is best kept simple —as a rule the cheaper they are, the more elaborate —so shop around for a rod that pleases the eye. Some of them can be bought complete with hooks; if not, buy blunt "S" hooks rather than authentic butcher's hooks, which have lethal points.

Open shelves fitted with steel rods provide useful storage space without blocking out areas of the galley kitchen. Matching sets of crockery are preferable to odd sets, if you are putting them on display.

HOW TO DO IT

STEP 1 Use the backsaw and miter block to cut the supports for the rod.

STEP 2 Use the ⅞-in./2.2-cm spade bit to drill holes in the supports to take the rod. Drill to ⅝ in./1.5 cm depth.

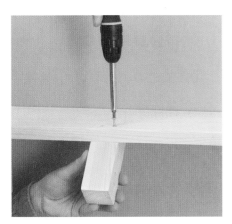

STEP 3 Drill a pilot hole through the shelf and screw the first support in place.

STEP 4 Fit the pipe into the hole of the fixed support and then fit the second support at the other end of the shelf. Screw this in position from above.

Living rooms

The living room is a space to relax, to read, and to watch television. It is also the place to entertain visitors; so, as the most public face of your home, it is an ideal room to reflect your personal style. This section shows you how to transform your living room into a choice of three different styles: Traditional, Contemporary, or Global. Most sizes and shapes of living rooms can achieve one of these three styles, but an additional section shows you how to make the most of a small living room. The three step-by-step projects will start you off, and a few accessories and a fresh coat of paint will do the rest.

Traditional living room

The traditional living room is a place to relax alone or with company, perhaps watch TV or listen to music, or curl up with a magazine or a good book and warm your toes in front of the open fire—somewhere to feel at home. If you live in an old building, the shape and height of the room probably suggest that you decorate it in a traditional way. Begin by choosing the right colors. Most paint companies now have a range of historical colors that are suited to different decorative periods. You don't have to recreate the past, but getting the colors right is important.

Comfortable sofas, colorful rugs, and a generous scattering of cushions make the traditional living room a comfort zone.

The great thing nowadays is that we have so much choice, not only in color schemes but also in lighting, furniture, and accessories. Gas-fueled open fires are more realistic than ever, and whether you're after chandeliers or gilded mirrors, you will find excellent reproduction versions in department stores or the genuine article in antique markets. If it's out there somewhere, there will very likely be a directory to help you find it.

One very good reason for decorating a living room in a traditional style is that you can mix old and new pieces of furniture. Furniture is passed down through families and whether they are priceless antiques or simply granny's lamp, they give a home a sense of history. And if the idea of granny's lamp fills you with horror, remember it can always be repainted and treated to a new lampshade. Comfortable old sofas can be re-upholstered or dressed up with colorful throws and cushions. Try mixing old with new even if you have to cheat and buy your "family heirlooms" from a flea market. They are often exactly what a traditionally decorated living room needs to settle it down, and turn it into that comfort zone. Ten points to consider that will help you to get the look are …

1. Open fireplace

There was a time when fireplaces were boarded up because they were too old-fashioned for the modern home. They were soon opened up, however, because living rooms seemed so much colder and less inviting without them. If you have the real thing, dress it up with a full log basket, a coal bucket, and a range of fire implements. Victorian and 1900s-style fireplaces are still made from the original designs, and today some of them don't even need a chimney. They can be gas fueled and lit from the comfort of your armchair via a remote control!

2. Fitted carpets

A traditional living room can have polished floorboards with a scattering of rugs or good old fitted carpets. Hard floors are fashionable at the moment, but you really can't beat wall-to-wall carpets for warmth and comfort. Choose a warm neutral color or a woven natural material like seagrass or coir matting, which matches most furniture styles.

3. Armchairs

There are lots of comfortable armchairs that look pretty dreadful, and fabulous-looking armchairs that weren't meant to be sat in. You should strike a balance, but looks must come into the equation. A brand new armchair can cost almost as much as a sofa, so look out for a second-hand bargain. Give an old chair new life by re-upholstering it to suit the rest of the furniture.

4. Rugs and cushions

Rugs are like pictures on the floor. They don't have to cost a fortune, but can become the focal point in a room. Plain floors can be brightened up with splashes of color, and rugs also provide soft islands of comfort on hard wooden floors. Cushions do the same job on furniture. Don't be mean with them—the more the merrier!

5. Throws

Throws are not really a new invention, they are just blankets with another name. We have all been liberated by them, though—no doubt about it! Before the throw came along, there was no alternative but to send for the steam cleaners or to re-upholster when accidents happened, but

now we chuck on a throw and hide a multitude of sins. Throws can also introduce strong, contrasting colors, and create a more casual, relaxed, and informal look.

6. Drapes

"Grown-up" drapes can be terribly expensive, and choosing the fabric is the only exciting part of the experience. The linings, weights, tracks, and hooks are not at all thrilling and they can be costly too. This explains the popularity of drape poles and tab-tops, which are simplicity itself to put up. Buy them ready-made for convenience or make them yourself. If you still long for a serious set of drapes there are specialized second-hand curtain dealers who are not cheap, but you do get totally authentic grandeur.

The traditional living room mixes the old with the new, so it is an ideal place to arrange your family heirlooms (even if you have to cheat and buy them from a flea market).

Wall uplighters and large table lamps are far better methods of lighting than central ceiling lights. They cast a warm, ambient light over the room.

actually flatter the room. It is difficult to get the proportions right, and the light is very often far too bright, which creates a stark atmosphere. Large table lamps are better all round. They can sit on tables and cast a warm glow onto the seating area. Picture lights or wall uplighters can be used to supply more ambient light to the room.

9. Comfortable sofas

There are so many cheap sofas and special offers in the stores, but for the traditional look it makes more sense to wait until sale time and spend as much as possible on a quality piece of furniture in a traditional design, such as a chesterfield. If you don't mind buying second-hand it is worth checking out local furniture auctions. They can be great fun and you never know what you might find. Factory outlets are also worth investigating because many sell end-of-lines and uncollected special orders at knock-down prices.

10. Bookshelves

Restaurants, bars and hotels have recently caught on to the fact that rows of books make the place feel like home. Fit a row of shelves into an alcove, and make a display of your favorite books. You can cheat a bit as well—think of them as accessories and buy sets of second-hand books just for their bindings. Book spines can be extremely decorative and charity stores always have large quantities of hardbacks to choose from.

7. Framed photographs, paintings, and prints

Traditional living rooms need art on the walls. This gives you something to look at while you are relaxing, and to talk about when friends drop by. Don't worry if you don't know your Picasso from your Leonardo, you can always cheat a little. Buy old frames from a flea market and revitalize them with gilding cream or an antique-gold spray paint. Look out for framed mirrors, prints, photocopied drawings or etchings, and old black-and-white photographs.

8. Lighting

Most living rooms have central lights that hang down from the ceiling, but very few of them

THE PROJECTS

The four projects on the following pages will help create a traditional feel in your own living room by adding soft, cozy furnishings on top of your existing items. Some old framed mirrors and prints with warm lighting will do the rest.

PROJECT
Throws

A throw is quite simply the most versatile of all soft furnishings. They are usually square, but there are no size or fabric restrictions. When it comes to throws, anything goes! Make a double-thickness throw using fabrics with contrasting textures and colors. This could be velvet and corduroy, fleece and cotton, or perhaps a color-coordinated patterned or plain fabric. Add extra style around the edge with a fringed, beaded, or blanket-stitched border.

YOU WILL NEED:

- **2 CONTRASTING PIECES OF FABRIC ABOUT 60 IN./1.5 M SQUARE (IF THE FABRIC IS TOO NARROW, STITCH 2 WIDTHS TOGETHER AND USE THIS MEASUREMENT FOR THE LENGTH AS WELL)**
- **TAPE MEASURE**
- **SCISSORS**
- **PINS**
- **SEWING MACHINE**
- **THREAD**
- **EDGE TRIMMING**

HOW TO DO IT

STEP 1 Trim the patterned fabric so it is 2 in./5 cm smaller than the plain fabric. Pin the two pieces together. Miter the corners.

TOP TIPS

- A dark-colored brushed cotton sheet is soft and wide, and makes a good lining fabric.

- If you have never sewn with fleece, try it! It is wide, inexpensive, the edges don't fray, it washes brilliantly, and it comes in a fabulous range of colors.

- Good decorative touches include tassels, buttons, twisted cord, piping, or a beaded fringe.

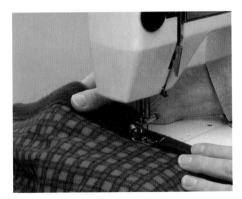

STEP 2 Sew a double row of stitches about ⅝ in./1.5 cm in from the edge, but leave a 1⅛ in./3 cm opening in the middle of one side. Turn the fleece over to form a border and zigzag the two together along the joining edge.

A new throw is a cheap and easy way to transform an elderly sofa or armchair, and can add a splash of warm color to the living room.

YOU WILL NEED:

- CUSHION PAD, FEATHER- OR POLYESTER-FILLED
- FABRIC
- PINS
- IRON
- TAPE MEASURE
- THREAD
- SEWING MACHINE

PROJECT
Cushions

A chair or sofa will always look more inviting if it's stacked with plumped-up cushions. Neutral, plain-colored covers for sofas and chairs are the most popular choice because furniture is a major expense and we want something that won't date. Cushions can be much more frivolous. A new cushion cover is quick, easy, and inexpensive to make, especially if you buy remnants of luxurious fabrics. These leftovers are sold at a fraction of the original price.

A splash of strong color on a neutral-colored sofa in the form of plumped-up cushions creates a very inviting and cozy look.

HOW TO DO IT

STEP 1 Cut one square of fabric to be the front of the cushion. Cut two pieces to overlap each other at the back. These two must measure as wide as the first square but be only two-thirds as long.

STEP 2 Turn back and zigzag a small hem along one edge of each of the smaller pieces. These two seams will overlap at the back of the cushion, making an "envelope" access for the cushion pad.

STEP 3 Lay the square flat with the right side facing upward. Place the two shorter pieces face down on it, one at each end so that they overlap one another in the middle, with the hem-stitched edges facing upward. Piped cord can also be sandwiched in at this stage, with the flat edge facing outward. Pin all round the edge.

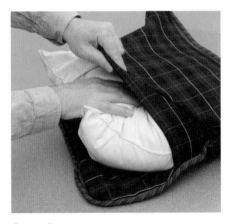

STEP 4 Sew the pieces together, about ⅝ in./1.5 cm inside the outer edge. Turn the cushion cover the right side out and press with an iron. Place the cushion pad inside the cover. For most fabrics, the overlap will not need any additional fixings, but soft, silky fabrics will hold their shape better with a press fastener, ribbon tie, or Velcro dot attached inside the overlap.

YOU WILL NEED:

- FABRIC (MEASURE THE HEIGHT OF YOUR WINDOW AND ADD 3 IN./7.5 CM FOR THE HEADER AND HEM, THEN MAKE EACH DRAPE TO THE WIDTH OF THE FABRIC)
- LINING (THE SAME AMOUNT AS THE FEATURE FABRIC)
- TAPE MEASURE
- IRON-ON STIFFENER FOR HEADING AND TABS
- BUTTONS FOR THE TABS (OPTIONAL)
- SEWING MACHINE
- IRON

PROJECT
Drape treatments

Let the proportions of your room and the size of your windows be the deciding factor when you choose your drape style. A large, high-ceilinged room with a bay window can look fabulous with a heavy valance and pleated drapes, but a smaller room would be overwhelmed by this sort of treatment and needs something lighter. A combination of plain shades and fabric draped over a drape pole can provide the best of both worlds. The window panes are covered by

the shades, while the hard lines of the frames are softened by the drapes.

If you have double glazing and don't need drapes for warmth, a drape rod with ring clips is the quickest solution. The row of clips is snapped on at regular intervals and will hold most light-to-medium-weight fabrics. Sheets, saris, and even large tablecloths can make the most elegant drapes. The project shows how to make simple tab-top, banner-style drapes.

Tab-top drapes give a lighter effect than valances and pleats, so they are ideal for slightly smaller rooms and windows. Choose between a wooden or iron pole.

HOW TO DO IT

STEP 1 Measure and cut out the drape panels and matching lining. Tab tops do not need to be much wider than the actual window width because they hang almost flat when pulled. Cut out tabs 1⅛ in./3 cm wide and 4¾ in./12 cm long. Calculate how many you need, spacing them 6 in./15 cm apart. Cut out the same shape and number of strips of fabric stiffener, and iron it to the wrong side of the tabs. Iron a 2 in./5 cm-wide strip of stiffener to the wrong side of the top edge of each drape panel.

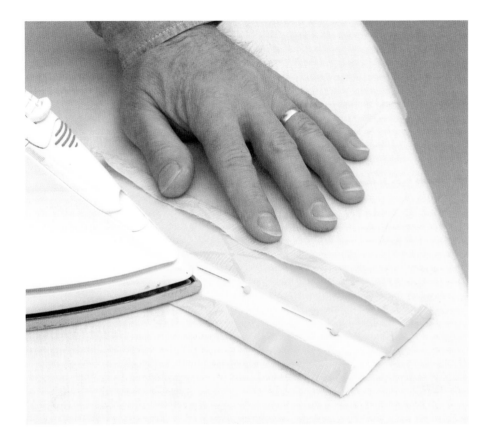

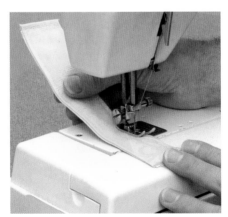

STEP 2 Sew the tabs into tubes with the stiffener on the outside. Turn them inside out and press flat. Fold each tab in half lengthwise and press.

STEP 3 Pin the sides and bottom lining and fabric together with the right sides facing. Stitch around the edge and then fold the right way round. Turn the raw edges over at the top and tuck them inside. Space the folded tabs along the top edge and pin them to the stiffened fabric. Sew a double row of stitching across the top to close the seam and attach the tabs. Press the panels.

TOP TIPS

• Stitch a button or wooden bead at the base of each loop.

• If you can't sew, buy iron-on tabs and press the seams with fabric bonding tape.

• Paint a cheap drape pole black, and use gold leaf or paint in bands to add a touch of glamour.

A folding screen
is a portable and
decorative way of
hiding modern
equipment such
as computers,
televisions, and
video recorders.

PROJECT

Making a two-panel screen to hide modern equipment

All your efforts to recreate the atmosphere of a traditional living room can be ruined by televisions, computers, and video recorders. They attract the eye even when they are not switched on. Furniture stores now stock antique reproduction cabinets to conceal high-tech appliances, but they do tend to be expensive and look cheap. If you watch a lot of television, it isn't practical to hide it in a cabinet, but you could take it off its stand and put it on something more in keeping with the room's style, such as a tin trunk or a wooden chest. If the room has an alcove, push the equipment back into it, and fit a wide shelf at least 12 in./30 cm above it. A shade or drape can be fitted along the shelf edge to conceal everything when not in use. A folding screen is an even easier solution, and it also offers more decorative possibilities.

HOW TO DO IT

STEP 1 Apply wood glue to the joining edges and assemble the frames. Screw to fasten. Paint the frames and the molding with a primer, an undercoat, and the final top coat.

STEP 2 Lay the frame over the fabric and cut, leaving at least 1½ in./3.8 cm as an overlap.

STEP 3 Stretch the fabric taut and staple it to the back of the frame. Place the first four staples halfway along each side, then staple the corners and several points in between.

STEP 4 Measure the lengths of braid needed to cover the edges. Miter the corners then apply fabric adhesive to the back edges.

STEP 5 Lay the two screen panels flat, butted up together, and place hinges 4 in./ 10 cm from the top and bottom, with one in the middle. Use the awl to make small pilot holes for the screws.

STEP 6 Small round feet can be added, using brass or wooden cabinet door knobs screwed into the base of the frames.

VARIATIONS

• Fit the sheets of woven cane in the same way as the fabric.

• Use small screws to secure the fretwork panels to the frames. You will need to drill clearance holes along the panel edges, and use an awl to make pilot holes for the screws. Paint the panels to match or contrast with the frames.

Contemporary living room

The really big influences over the past few years have been minimalism, modern art, and eco-awareness. And a more open-plan style of living has filtered down from Manhattan lofts, while the rediscovery of 1960s high-rise apartments has found its way into everyday decorating. It is also true to say that we may not all aspire to live in converted warehouses, but we can still appreciate the clarity of an uncluttered space furnished with a few interesting pieces.

We can even try glass bricks, which let light filter through to create an airy feel. In fact, comfort areas are more clearly defined than ever with sheepskin rugs on hard floors, huge sofas, low tables, and lighting directed toward the seating and decorative objects. The trick is to keep colors muted and natural for a really airy feel, and introduce them by masking off and painting blocks of color to break up the wall space. You should also add some contemporary art. This can be anything from an abstract painting to a large rock, a weather-beaten tree trunk, or a large desert cactus. Just do it with a

great deal of confidence! Sixteen sure ways to give your living room that contemporary style are …

1. Floating wooden floor

The new wooden floor looks different to stripped pine floorboards: the wood strips are narrower and the boards are butted up, leaving no gaps. The design principle is the same for most brands of strip flooring, although quality and price vary quite a lot. Tongue-and-groove boards are laminated with a veneer of real wood and are laid on top of existing-level flooring. This sort of flooring has the look and feel of wood, but is laid with the convenience of vinyl.

2. Glass shelving and wooden storage cubes

Glass is a strong, natural material and an essential ingredient in contemporary style. An alcove fitted with toughened glass shelves looks superb and can be used to display anything from a row of pebbles to a collection of magazines, but you will need to consider fitting concealed lighting as well. It's only when glass and light are combined that the full effect becomes clear. Use frosted glass or glass bricks as screening between rooms to create a barrier without losing the sense of space.

Muted, natural colors help the contemporary style by giving an airy feel. Soft throws folded over the backs of sofas add to the style.

Wooden floors are a must in any contemporary living room, but new, floating wooden floors make it easier than ever before to create this look.

3. Eco-friendly materials

Caring about the environment means being choosy about the materials with which you decorate your home. So many chemicals infect the air of the home these days, all in the name of treating mold, stains, bacteria, and good old wear and tear. If you want a more natural environment, there are organic and eco-friendly paint ranges, carpets, fabrics, and cleaning materials. They will do you no harm and may prevent allergies as well.

4. Rugs and fabrics

Hard wooden floors give a fabulous look, but they need to be comfortable, too, especially when walking barefoot. Rugs have made a comeback recently, and all fashionable furniture outlets have ranges of colorful or neutral designer rugs, ethnic kilims, natural matting, and soft sheepskins. Rugs can be used to define a seating or eating area in an open-plan room. Spend as much as you can on them and make a real feature of them by putting them on show.

Felt, wool, mohair, and rough-weave cotton are the key fabrics to use.

5. Blinds or sheer drapes

Flounces and frills are out, so fit wooden Venetian or handmade paper shades, or hang plain, tab-topped drapes from a pole. King-sized, white Egyptian cotton sheets look stunning clipped onto a rod, or to inject some spicy colors, drape sari fabrics or hand-blocked Japanese textiles from a curtain pole. Vintage patterned fabrics and brocades combined with plain bands of color are also chic and stylish.

6. Low coffee table

A long, low coffee table looks great, providing it is not piled up with clutter. Favorite styles also include designs with storage space beneath the table top. Chrome or aluminum legs with 1970s-style rosewood laminates, tubular chrome and glass, pale wood with industrial size casters, and roughly hewn African dark wood versions are all considered to be extremely cool.

If you have the space, over-size, dramatic house-plants like this one will add an organic feel to your contemporary living room, without making it seem cluttered.

7. Leather cushions, armchair, or cube

Classic leather and chrome chairs such as the Barcelona and Wassily chairs were designed in the first half of the last century and, although they have been copied, they have never been bettered. If your finances don't stretch to a designer chair, then a leather cube or even a cushion will show that you're on the right track.

8. Lamps and candles

Table lamps need to be quite large—think of large organic-shaped ceramic or wooden table lamps with plain, cream shades or tall and simple metal floor lamps. High-tech, tracked spotlighting systems are also fine for illuminating CD collections or books. Large multi-wick candles, or tealights in a row of matching glasses, are also good for creating an atmosphere.

9. Large, plain-colored sofa

Big, plain-colored sofas are very much part of the contemporary style living room. The most stylish sofas have a boxy shape, with ultra-generous seating and short legs. These sofas are made for putting your feet up and relaxing. Comfort is the essential antidote to all this fashionable minimalism.

10. Soft, folded, pashmina-style throws

The other concession to comfort comes from being able to drape your furniture and yourself in beautiful, soft woollen throws. Fold them over the arms of chairs or the back of the sofa and use them as comforters on cool nights. Pashmina shawls are the best, but anything from a fringed cot blanket, or a mohair stole, to a plaid travel rug will work if the colors are right.

11. Decluttering

This word may not be in the dictionary, but everybody knows what it means. It used to be called being neat or putting things away, but now we call it "decluttering." There are even stores, catalogs, consultants, and entire books dedicated to the art of tidying up your home. If you have a great deal of money, you can even hire someone by the hour to visit you and tell you to throw out most of your stuff and put the rest of it in labeled boxes. If you would prefer to "declutter" yourself, then read on ...

12. CDs

Free up space currently used to hold your CD collection by buying a wall-mounted CD storage cabinet. Make sure you buy one with more space than you need. Allow for at least a third more slots than the CDs you currently own, and edit the collection as new CDs are added.

13. Magazines

An acrylic or bent beechwood magazine rack will look perfect, and keep magazines and color supplements neat and tidy. Keep only the current editions in your rack and store back issues on a bookshelf in magazine box files.

14. Video tapes

Video tape covers are competitively garish on purpose so that they stand out from the thousands of other videos in the store. But they never look good at home, so put them away! Choose an easily accessible storage system suitable for the number of tapes you own. Woven baskets or heavy board boxes with lids are a good idea. If you own a lot of tapes, make long, plain MDF boxes with hinged flaps, which can be fitted onto the wall. Use a beech or maple-veneered MDF for the front, or paint it the same color as the walls.

15. Storage space down below

Choose a low table with compartments or drawers, and stand lamps on cubes or drums that can also be used to hide clutter—this works only if you go through it regularly and sort things out!

16. Fitted shelving units with doors and drawers

If there is one good lesson to be learned from minimalism, it is that not everything is worth displaying. Choose a few decorative objects for open, glass shelves and keep the rest behind closed doors.

The contemporary living room is clutter-free, which requires a little day-to-day discipline of putting things away behind closed doors.

THE PROJECTS

The projects on the following pages will help achieve the basic elements of any contemporary living room: the wooden floor and the coffee table. Some disciplined decluttering, a large, plain-colored sofa, and a big rug will do the rest.

PROJECT
Laying a floating wooden floor

Laminated flooring is a fashion that's here to stay. It's easy to lay, looks a million dollars, and is really easy to keep clean. It's made in average floorboard width and comes in a wide range of stained hardwood veneers, varying between ⅜ in./ 1 cm and ¾ in./1.9 cm in depth. The best are the most expensive—surprise, surprise. Laminates are stain-resistant, won't splinter, and because of their tongue-and-groove fitting, you avoid drafts coming up through gaps in the floorboards.

Existing floors need to be leveled before you begin. Concrete floors will need a heavy-duty PVC damp-proof membrane, and all floors need a good underlay of either ⁵⁄₁₆-in./7-mm felt boards or ⅛-in./2-mm foam sheeting. When you buy laminated flooring, you will also need a fitting kit and laminated flooring adhesive. The kit will contain fitting directions and spacers for between the floor and the baseboard, because the floor will expand after it has been laid.

Laminated flooring is stain-resistant, and also splinter- and draft-free. It comes in a range of stained veneers, the best of which are the most expensive.

HOW TO DO IT

STEP 1 Put down the underlay, butting the joints together.

STEP 2 Lay the first board with the groove on the edge next to the wall. Place spacers at the end and along the wall.

STEP 3 Lay another board loosely (without glue) at the end of the first, engaging the tongue-and-groove. Add another board or, depending upon the space, cut one to fit the remaining space, leaving enough room for a spacer next to the wall. Use a string line to check that the boards are straight; otherwise the other boards will be out of line as well.

STEP 4 Run a continuous line of adhesive along the tongue-and-groove.

STEP 5 Use the tamping block with a hammer to force the boards tightly together.

STEP 6 Immediately wipe off the excess glue, which will ooze out between the joints, with a damp cloth. Begin the second row with the off-cut from the first, providing it is at least 12 in./30 cm long. Lay the first three rows and leave the adhesive to dry before you continue. The last row of boards may have to be cut widthwise to fit into the space, and you must remember to leave room for the spacers. Finally, remove the spacers and fit the quater-round molding to the baseboard to cover the expansion gap.

YOU WILL NEED:

- 4 LENGTHS OF
  PREPARED LUMBER
  FOR THE TOP
- 2 SHORTER LENGTHS
  OF LUMBER FOR THE
  LEGS
- 4 CLEATS
- 6 SCRAPS OF WOOD
- WOOD GLUE
- 16 X 2-IN./5-CM
  NUMBER 6 SCREWS
- $\frac{1}{8}$-IN./4-MM DRILL
  BIT
- DRILL
- CRAMPS
- WOODSTAIN
- BRUSH
- METAL RULE
- COMBINATION
  SQUARE
- PENCIL
- SCREWDRIVER
- WAX POLISH
  AND CLOTH

PROJECT
Making a coffee table

The best coffee tables are long, low, and simply elegant, the focus being on a good shape and finish. This one is made from four main pieces of prepared lumber, with hidden cleats to support the legs. Construction could not be more simple, and the wood can be stained deep tan or dark brown to suit the contemporary room style that has been chosen.

This long, low, and elegant coffee table is easy to construct from just four main pieces of prepared lumber, with hidden batons to support the legs.

HOW TO DO IT

STEP 1 Butt together the four long planks of lumber on a flat work surface, and lace the three scraps between them to make narrow gaps. Mark 12 in./30 cm from each end and use the combination square and a pencil to draw a line across both planks.

STEP 2 Place a cleat across the lumber and draw in the halfway line (3 in./7.5 cm). Drill a hole through the cleat in each of the four planks of wood. Coat the base of the cleat with wood glue and screw it to the planks.

STEP 3 Draw a center guideline across the width of each leg.

STEP 4 Apply a liberal coating of wood glue to the base of each of the leg and to the side of the cleat, then, having lined them up with the gap, put the leg in place.

STEP 5 Now fix a second cleat to the other side of the leg to hold it firmly from both sides. Apply wood glue to the surfaces and screw the cleats to the planks. Leave to bond overnight. (This is very important, no matter what it says on the tube!). Repeat for the other leg.

STEP 6 Apply a coat or two of woodstain, tinted varnish, or wax polish.

Global living room

This is a room where color leads and everything else follows on. If you love color this is the way to proceed, and it's a very helpful approach if you are starting from scratch and don't know where to begin. Once you have decided on, say, burned orange, pale blue, and cream for the walls, then the furniture and accessories can be chosen because they look great against that background.

RIGHT: **This Moroccan-style room displays the elaborately carved furniture and exotic colors traditional to the region.**

Deep, earthy reds in a symmetrical pattern conjure up the heat of North Africa.

A color scheme can be inspired by anything that you see around you, from a bowl of fresh fruit to the background in a vacation photographs. In fact, it is easier to find paint to match a color that you have already chosen than it is to begin by staring at a paint chart for inspiration. Charts are fantastic once you know what you're looking for, but confusing when you don't.

Color ranges get bigger, brighter, and bolder all the time, and whereas a few years ago you could buy strong colors for walls from only an expensive paint specializer, they now appear in the home centers' own ranges at a fraction of the price. Test pots let you experiment with colors and are far more helpful than a small rectangle on a white background. And if you want only a small amount for an area of intense color, they do the job at a great price.

Tricks with color

There is no doubt that the TV decorating programs have had a massive influence on the way we think about using color at home. Most rules regarding good taste have been broken in the quest for more riveting TV, and this has actually been quite liberating. Now it's OK to say that you chose turquoise and lime with a splash of silver-leaf gilding because it tickled your fancy!

Also note that blocks of color can be used to create dramatic effects in a room. As a rule, red foreshortens a room, bringing the walls in closer, while blue recedes. This is the way our eyes read these colors, and you can use them to stretch or compact a space accordingly. Play visual tricks with color. For example, yellow brightens a room and is useful when a room doesn't get much natural daylight. Color also affects our moods, making us feel happy, tranquil, excited, or irritable, which is something to bear in mind when you are doing up your global living room.

THE PROJECTS
Color ranges have associations with different cultures and climates. This means that you can conjure up the mood of another place by using its characteristic colors. The following three projects show how you can use color to create an African, Moroccan, or Mediterranean style. A low divan bed, rough-textured wall, and a small table are the common starting points.

Cool stone floors, earthy colored textiles in bold patterns, and an open fire bring a taste of Africa to this living room.

YOU WILL NEED:
- **PAINT**
- **PAINTER'S TAPE**
- **BRUSHES**
- **DARK WOODSTAIN**
- **ACCESSORIES SUCH AS DRUMS, BEADWORK, EBONIZED WOODEN MASKS, SOAPSTONE CARVINGS, HIDE RUGS, AND FOLDING DIRECTOR'S CHAIRS**

PROJECT

The African room

The colors of Africa are drawn from the landscape: rusty reds and dark, mud browns of the earth, yellow ochers of the sun, and pale, sky blues are combined with the rich, ebony black of cooking pots on the open fire. The style is plain with organic shapes and bold patterns. Look out for woven and printed African textiles for throws and cushion covers, wood-carved figures, woven grass matting, clay pots, gourd bowls, and recycled African tin and wirework.

This African-style wall reflects the colors of the landscape—the rusty red of the earth, the soft, yellow ochre of the sun, and the blue sky between. A woven grass mat in a bold, spiral pattern completes the effect.

HOW TO DO IT

STEP 1 Stain the floorboards using a very dark woodstain. Measure and mark 39 in./1 m up the wall from the floor and stick up a line of painter's tape.

STEP 2 Paint the wall above the tape a soft, yellow-ocher color. Use random brush strokes to sweep the color in different directions.

STEP 3 Paint from the floor to the tape in a rich, earthy red.

STEP 4 Remove the tape and paint a freehand brush line using a pale stone-colored paint. Don't be nervous—it should look hand-painted.

STEP 5 Cover the divan with a rough-weave African cloth, tucked under tightly at the edges. Add cushions covered in dark brown and cream or indigo blue batik-patterned cottons, or fabric patterned like zebra, giraffe, or leopard skin.

STEP 6 Use grass matting on the floor, baskets woven from grasses, gourd bowls, a pendant light with an African sun hat as a shade, a small table painted black, and a top covered with a woven place mat.

YOU WILL NEED:

- PAINT WITH A BLUE
  PIGMENT
- PAINTER'S TAPE
- BRUSH
- STENCIL PAPER
- SNAP-BLADE KNIFE
- ACCESSORIES SUCH
  AS TOOLED LEATHER
  POUFFES, CAMEL
  SADDLE STOOLS,
  BEADED AND
  MIRRORED
  CUSHIONS, KAFTANS
  TO BE MADE INTO
  CUSHIONS. AND
  ENGRAVED
  BRASSWARE

PROJECT
The Moroccan room

The north of Africa has an Arab culture in which strong Islamic principles influence the decorative traditions. The homes have cool marble floors, arched shuttered windows, and mathematical patterns everywhere. The look is exotic, mysterious, and highly stylized. Look out for tasseled and mirrored textiles, kilim rugs, small, carved shelves, and Ali Baba pots.

This stepped, geometric pattern border stenciled at chair rail level shows the mathematical patterns typical of the Moroccan decorative tradition. Moroccan rugs, tasseled cushions, and an arched, framed mirror add to the look.

HOW TO DO IT

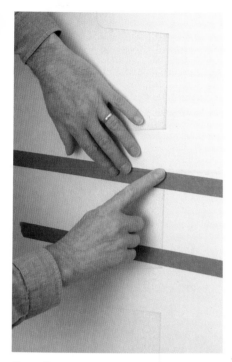

STEP 1 Mark a tile's-depth white border at chair rail level.

STEP 2 Paint the wall above the border in a deep blue paint.

STEP 3 Stencil the stepped, geometric pattern border along the wall (stencil pattern provided) in deep red.

STEP 4 Lay Moroccan rugs and durries overlapping each other to cover the floor. Hang an arched, framed mirror, beaded bags, mirrored cloth wall hangings, and small carved shelves on the wall.

STEP 5 Stand a date palm in an Ali Baba pot on the floor, and on the small table place a large brass tray laid with a set of Moroccan tea glasses.

YOU WILL NEED:

- PAINT
- CHAIR RAIL
- PANEL ADHESIVE
- COUNTERSUNK SCREWS
- STENCIL PAPER
- SNAP-BLADE KNIFE
- BRUSH
- ACCESSORIES SUCH AS GERANIUMS IN TERRA COTTA POTS, BRASS OIL LAMPS, BLUE-AND-WHITE CUSHIONS, PATTERNED PLATES, AND SMALL PICTURES IN FRAMES

The Mediterranean room

There are many countries and islands around the Mediterranean Sea, and each has its own distinctive decorating style. The influence of the warm dry climate is seen in the cool interiors with tiled floors and shuttered windows. White is the dominant color, its brilliance enhanced by the azure blue sky. The dry climate simplifies the decorating because no sealants are needed. Walls are painted with chalky distemper and wood is left unvarnished. There are different traditional embroidery, weaving, ceramic, and ironwork patterns throughout the Mediterranean.

This wall has been divided using a wooden molding painted a deep turquoise blue. The paint above and below has a chalky texture. A group of small pictures in frames and a grapevine stencil painted along the top of the wall complete the effect.

HOW TO DO IT

STEP 1 Divide the wall at the height that a chair rail would be, using a wooden molding. This can be applied with panel adhesive and strengthened with a few countersunk screws.

STEP 2 Paint the bottom half of the wall using a plaster pink, chalky finish paint.

STEP 3 Paint the top half with a creamy yellow, chalky finish paint.

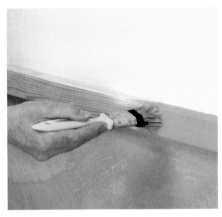

STEP 4 Paint the chair rail deep turquoise or cobalt blue.

STEP 5 Stencil a grapevine along the top of the wall. This does not have to look realistic in vine colors, just stencil it in one color to look like a shadow in dark green or terra cotta.

STEP 6 Cover the divan with a blue-and-white Greek embroidered bedspread, and hang up a Greek fisherman's lamp.

STEP 7 Hang a rustic, unvarnished wooden shelf and a group of small pictures in frames. Cover the table with a white lace-edged cloth and a vase of bright flowers. Add red geraniums in terra cotta pots, blue-and-white rustic ceramic wares, and a rush-seated chair.

Enlarge the stencil below and transfer the pattern to plastic or stencil paper. Cut out carefully using a sharp snap-blade knife.

Tiny living room

With a small room, you have to decide whether to accept it and decorate without deception, or to play tricks with color, light, and mirrors to create an illusion of a bigger space. Many apartment conversions have left rooms that are either tall and narrow, or low and long, but it's amazing what a few tricks of color, furnishings, and lighting will do to change the apparent shape of the room. Whichever you choose, you will have to maximize all the space you have by organizing your possessions and using every storage trick in the book, from disguised drawers to making the most of any nooks and crannies.

The first thing you need to think about is how many people will regularly use the living room. If it will be no more than two, then a small sofa and a place for the television, stereo, and coffee table are all that's really needed. If it's more than two, you need to get creative!

Small is beautiful

If you decide to make a feature of the room's diminutive size, it can be made into a very sexy, tactile space where the edges between furniture, floor, and walls are blurred. Remember the shagpile carpet. It must be due for a revival and wouldn't break the bank in a tiny room; an alternative option would be a long-haired rug like the flokati, another 1970s favorite, which is handwoven with a very thick, shaggy wool pile. A low couch, felt cushions, knitted throws, and fake fur rugs are other things to consider. A sheepskin-covered bean bag would be the ultimate accessory. The lower walls can either be covered with a soft-textured wallpaper or even be lined with fabric like a Bedouin tent. Emphasize the coziness by painting the room a dark color, such as deep red or chocolate brown, with gilded woodwork, and have plenty of warm, low lighting and thick drapes. Vintage velvets, draped felt, or dyed blankets buttoned over a pole all work well.

Think big

If you decide that the challenge is to make everyone believe that the room is twice its actual size, then your first accessory has to be a mirror. If an entire wall is lined with mirror tiles, the room will appear double its size, but there are more subtle ways of using mirrors that will make the space appear bigger, and make the shape look more interesting as well. You will need to watch the lighting, though, as the reflections can be blinding. A pair of wooden window frames fitted with mirrors will give the appearance of looking into another room; long mirrors placed across the corners of the room will make it look octagonal; and a large, arched, framed mirror will appear to be a doorway into an adjoining room. Plants in front of mirrors will also look twice as bushy thanks to the reflection. Use pale colors, playing around with two or three different tones of yellow, light blue, or green. The deeper shades will appear to recede and give shape to mat walls.

You can make a feature out of a small room like this one by deciding firmly what it will be used for before you start. This one is definitely a reading room. A long, low couch in neutral colors blends into the surrounding walls. Floor-to-ceiling book-cases complete the look.

Doors and windows

Windows are best played down by fitting shades or shutters into the frame. Keep the color the same or lighter than that of the walls. A half-glazed door or a window onto a passage way is a means of including the space outside the room. And if you could do without the door altogether, it could be removed to give a more open-plan feel to the room.

Tall rooms

In old buildings that have been converted into apartments, the ceilings are often very high. This is fabulous when the room is in proportion, but, all too often, large reception rooms have been sectioned off and the resulting rooms are narrow and tall. There are a few simple tricks though, which will help to squash the room into shape. Paint the ceiling and cornice down to picture-rail height using a dark mat color. Hang the lights so that they emerge below this level and cast the light downward. Use a patterned carpet or rugs to attract the eye

downward, and hang pictures a bit lower than you normally would. If you would prefer to do something more substantial, why not build a platform to raise one half of the room up to a different level? This would create useful storage space at the same time.

Short rooms

If your tiny room has a low ceiling and you need to raise the roof, similar tricks can be used in reverse. Vertical stripes have an elongating effect, and a white ceiling with no center light will give the room a lift. Use spotlights to pick out pictures or interesting objects, and wall uplighters for ambient light.

THE PROJECTS

The projects on the following pages show two ways of making the most of a small room. The first uses an aluminum-leaf wall to make a room look bigger, and the second shows how to make a drawer disguised as part of the baseboard.

YOU WILL NEED:

- SILVER MAT LATEX
  PAINT, WHICH MUST
  BE WATER-BASED
- ALUMINUM LEAF
  (SOLD IN ARTISTS'
  SUPPLIERS
  GENERALLY IN PACKS
  OF 25 SQUARE
  LEAVES)
- WATER-BASED GOLD
  SIZE (GLUE)
- ENAMEL OR SILK
  VARNISH
- ROLLER AND TRAY
- PAINT BRUSH
- SOFT CLOTH
- LONG RULE

PROJECT
Covering a wall with foil squares

A surface that reflects light will blur the boundaries as well. This project shows how to use squares of aluminum leaf to create a glowing wall in a small room. If you like the idea but would find a whole wall overpowering, why not begin by lining an alcove? Silver looks good with pale wood, frosted glass, and smart navy-blue furniture.

An aluminum-leaf wall reflects the colors around it, blending into the walls on either side.

HOW TO DO IT

STEP 1 Apply two coats of silver paint to the wall, leaving the correct drying times before and after the second coat.

STEP 2 Measure out a section of wall big enough for nine squares and apply the glue. Leave it for about 15 minutes, or until it feels tacky. Begin applying the leaf in one of the top corners, pressing the square gently onto the wall and rubbing the back lightly with your fingers.

STEP 3 Slowly peel the backing paper off from top to bottom. If any of the leaf remains on the paper, replace it and rub the back again lightly. Line the next square up to the edge of the first. Continue in the same way, fitting the squares in sections until the wall is covered.

STEP 4 Buff the leaf to a gleaming shine using a lint-free soft cloth. Apply a coat of silk or enamel varnish to protect your foil squares.

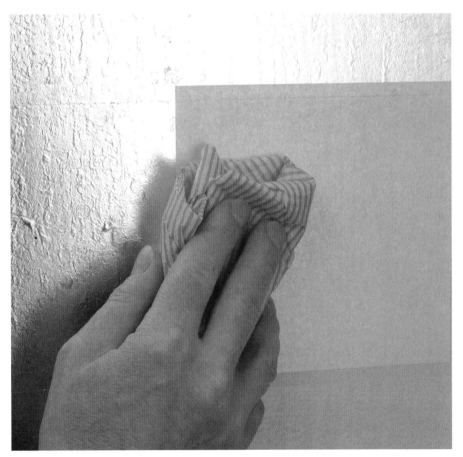

YOU WILL NEED:
- 8 SMALL CASTERS
- LENGTH OF BASEBOARD TO MATCH THE EXISTING ONE (IF IT CAN'T BE RE-USED)
- PANEL ADHESIVE
- 2 IN. X 1 IN./ 5 CM X 2.5 CM CLEAT
- ½-IN./1.2-CM MDF SHEET FOR SHELF
- ¼-IN./6-MM MDF FOR DRAWER BASE
- ¼-IN./6-MM MDF FOR 4 DRAWER SIDES
- BACKSAW
- THIN BRADS
- SMALL HAMMER
- PAINT AND A BRUSH
- SPIRIT LEVEL
- DRILL
- MASONRY BIT
- WALL ANCHORS
- ⅛-IN./4-MM DRILL BIT FOR WOOD
- 1/16-IN./2-MM DRILL BIT FOR PILOT HOLES
- SCREWS

PROJECT
Disguised storage

If you really want to disguise something, the trick is to make it look the same as everything around it. This project does this by building a boxed-in shelf with a drawer at floor level, and using a baseboard front to disguise it so well that it could almost be used as a safe. This is also a way to make the most of an alcove by building the shelf wide enough for the TV. If the alcove is not deep enough, it will need to be built out at the front, but the basic idea remains the same.

This drawer on casters has been built as part of a low, boxed-in shelf, and disguised with a baseboard front to blend in with the edges around it.

HOW TO DO IT

STEP 1 Measure the depth of the alcove. If it needs extending, take this into account and cut out two side-pieces of 2 in. x 1 in./ 2.5 cm x 5 cm to support the shelf. If the shelf height is 19³/₄ in./50 cm the sides will need to be at 19¹/₄ in./48.8 cm. Drill and screw to the wall and then check the level.

STEP 2 Cut the shelf to fit the alcove. Cut a U-shaped cable hole on the back edge. Apply a long bead of adhesive to the top edges of the sides and place the shelf on top. Use a hammer to drive in some brads to hold the shelf securely. If the alcove is wide, use the drill to add a supporting leg to the middle.

STEP 3 Make up the two drawers: cut the base of each drawer to fit snugly inside the alcove, leaving just enough clearance for it to slide in and out without catching.

STEP 4 Cut drawer sides to match the depth of the shelf, and a front and back to be butted into them.

STEP 5 Fit each of the four casters to the base of the drawer.

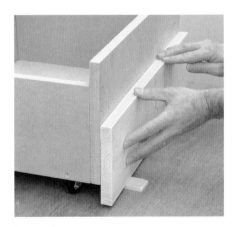

STEP 6 Cut the baseboard to fit onto the drawer front (and box-sides if the shelf has been built out beyond the alcove). Stick the baseboard onto the drawer front (and box-sides if built out) with panel adhesive. Do this so that the baseboard skims the floor, hiding the casters. Paint the sides and front of the drawers to match the walls and the front to match the baseboard.

Dining rooms

Good food, good wine, and good company are made even more special by a stylish dining room, but even the simplest of meals can be made into a special occasion by a beautiful setting. Since the dining room is all about eating, much of the style is down to the table and chairs, but flooring, lighting, and color can have just the same impact. This chapter shows you how to transform your dining room into one of three different styles: Traditional, Contemporary, or Living-dining room. The step-by-step projects will start you off, and a fresh coat of paint and some flexible lighting should do the rest.

Traditional dining room

The dining room is the place to indulge yourself. There was a time when most family life took place here—meals were eaten around the table, and that was also where children played and did their homework. Fashions change, though, and after the 1960s, homes were built with dining areas rather than separate dining rooms. In older houses, internal walls were knocked down to make kitchens bigger; and after that, walls were knocked down between living rooms and dining rooms, to make even larger open-plan spaces. Dining rooms became something of a luxury because only people with large houses still had them.

Wooden chairs with upholstered seats can be revamped with a fresh coat of paint and a change of fabric.

It has taken a while, but with the top two leisure activities now being cooking and decorating, there has been a natural progression toward reinstating the dining room. It is now thought extremely stylish to invite your guests into your dining room to serve them a lovely meal without a television or kitchen sink in sight. Traditional dining rooms also make it a lot easier to cheat with the cooking when the chef is out of sight next door.

Chairs

The key ingredients in a classy dining room are the chairs. You can always fake the table by using an elegant tablecloth to cover an old door on saw horses, but the chairs will be on show and should be as good-looking and as comfortable as they possibly can be.

The great thing about opting for the traditional style is that you can always pick up second-hand dining room chairs for a reasonable price in flea markets or at an auction. The trick is to buy them one, two, or three at a time, because they are always much cheaper than in sets of four or more. They don't even have to match, so long as they are of more or less the same period and

are in a similar style. In fact, a slightly mismatched collection of chairs can look really chic if you decorate them in the same way.

The Swedish Gustavian style is well suited to this treatment, and it is a classic look that manages to appear traditional and fresh at the same time. Paint the woodwork mat white and give it a "mildly distressed" look by rubbing the paint back to the bare wood in places with sandpaper. The seats can be covered with a red, yellow or blue gingham or stripe.

Wooden chairs with upholstered seats can easily be given a whole new style with a change of fabric and a lick of paint. Strip the wood of its old varnish and re-stain it a deep, rich brown, and then cover the seats with a warm-colored velvet or brocade fabric. Look out for remnants of good-quality upholstery fabric or even old drapes, which are often abandoned when people move house and find their new homes have different-shaped windows.

Tables

Tables are usually expensive and are one of the few pieces of furniture that seem to hold their value whether they are in fashion or not.

A chandelier over the dining table is the centerpiece of the traditional dining room. Traditional-style, matching cutlery, linen napkins and fresh flowers add a finishing touch.

Choose a table with the right proportions for your room—there must be enough space around it to pull out the chairs and serve a meal without having to hug the wall. Most traditional dining tables have hidden fold-out flaps so that they can expand from four or six to eight or ten settings. They are ideal for occasional entertaining. The only other furniture needed in a dining room is a console table, sideboard, or trolley for the food.

Colors

Colors can be rich, strong, and dramatic in dining rooms. Hang large-framed pictures and mirrors on the walls and go to town with the drapes and lighting as well. If you own a chandelier, this is the place to use it. Candlelight turns a meal into an occasion, and a candelabra hung over the table will bring an air of grandeur to even the simplest of meals. Keep a look out for an old chandelier in a flea market—it will often need mending and rewiring, but it will be worth it.

If the room is warm enough to do without a carpet why not try stenciling a border pattern on the floor instead? This is a good way to get the unifying look of an expensive carpet at a fraction of the price. There are some fabulous stencil patterns on the market, and with a few pots of stencil paint and a dash of confidence, you could paint anything from a simple folk-art border to a very convincing Turkish carpet in your spare time. And don't forget the finishing touches—a smooth, white tablecloth with matching napkins, traditional-style cutlery, sparkling glassware, and a pretty vase of freshly cut flowers.

THE PROJECTS

The two projects on the following pages show how to paint broad, vertical stripes in the traditional style, and how to revamp old dining chairs in the Gustavian (Swedish) style, complete with new, matching upholstery.

YOU WILL NEED:

- SMALL SPONGE ROLLER AND TRAY FOR THE STRIPES
- 2 COLORS OF LATEX PAINT
- WALLPAPER PASTE (MIXED)
- 1-IN./2.5-CM PAINT BRUSH
- ROLLER AND TRAY FOR THE BACKGROUND
- PAINTER'S TAPE
- FOAM WASHING-UP SPONGE
- PLUMB LINE (STRING AND A KEY WILL DO THE JOB)
- LONG RULE WITH SPIRIT LEVEL
- PENCIL

PROJECT
Painting broad stripes with a roller

There is no need to be restrained just because you have decided to decorate the dining room in a traditional style. If you are doing French Empire style, the stripes can be broad, bold, black, and gold; if your theme is Swedish, make them yellow and gray. Arts and Crafts colors are earthy, woody green, and rust red. Every traditional style has certain key patterns and colors, and these stripes are a quick and easy way to give your room a dramatic new look.

Broad, vertical stripes painted in colors to suit a particular traditional style are an easy way to give your dining room a new look.

HOW TO DO IT

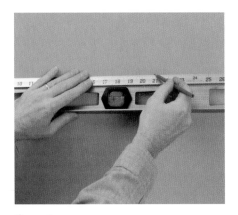

STEP 1 Decide whether you want the stripes to go the full length of the wall or just up to the picture rail. Here, we are painting a horizontal stripe at picture rail height. Room heights vary, so judge this by eye. Hang the plumb line above the height of the stripe, and use the long rule with spirit level to mark the stripe's position along the wall.

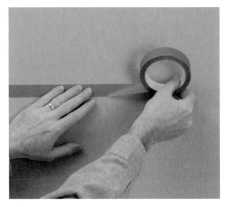

STEP 2 Follow the marks with a line of painter's tape between the corners. Paint the lighter background color between the baseboard and the tape, and leave to dry.

STEP 3 Put the second color in the small roller tray and mix it half and half with pre-mixed wallpaper paste. Run the roller through the paint until evenly coated.

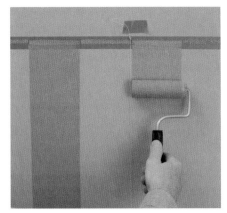

STEP 4 Make a stripe guide by marking the painter's tape with the roller, leaving a roller's width between the stripes. With the plumb line as a guide, run the roller down the wall in a straight line. Do not press too hard, but keep the pressure even. Stop just short of the baseboard and re-charge the roller. Continue in this way, moving the plumb line as you progress so that you don't drift off the vertical.

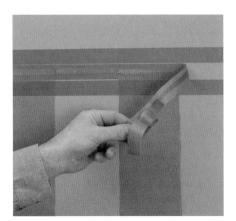

STEP 5 When the wall is finished, dip the small sponge into the paint and use it to stamp the rest of the line up to the baseboard (the roller will not reach this last bit). Remove the painter's tape and leave the paint to dry. Now run a line of painter's tape with its top edge along the top of the stripes, and then another 2 in./5 cm above it. Check it with the spirit level.

STEP 6 Use the brush to paint inside the painter's tape using the striping color, or a contrasting color to match the baseboard if you prefer. Peel away the tape when the paint has dried.

YOU WILL NEED:

- CHAIR WITH A PADDED SEAT, EITHER DROP-IN OR FIXED
- PAINT AND VARNISH STRIPPER
- PAINT BRUSH
- NEWSPAPER
- RUBBER GLOVES
- SCRAPER
- STEEL WOOL
- MINERAL SPIRITS
- MAT WHITE PAINT
- CANDLE
- PAINT BRUSH OR SMALL FOAM ROLLER AND TRAY
- SANDPAPER

PROJECT
Doing up a dining chair

Everyday furniture used to be far better made than it is now, so it really makes sense to buy a selection of old dining chairs with drop-in or upholstered seats. These are not expensive antiques, but chairs from the days when every home had a dining room table and chairs. A tall-backed design is best for this Gustavian (Swedish) style, and it is amazing how much of a set an odd bunch will look once they have been given a similar paint finish and upholstery.

Old dining chairs can be transformed into this Gustavian style using a distressed paint finish and re-upholstering in red, yellow, or blue gingham, or stripes.

HOW TO DO IT

STEP 1 Put on the rubber gloves and stand the chair on newspaper. Cover it in a thick coating of paint stripper and wait for the surface to bubble up.

STEP 2 Scrape off the paint or varnish, taking care to drop all the waste onto the newspaper.

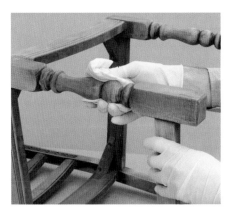

STEP 3 Dip the steel wool in mineral spirits and clean off the remaining paint or varnish. Leave to dry.

STEP 4 Rub the edges of the chair and any raised pattern on the wood, the curve of the legs, and the seat corners with the candle. A light stroke will be enough.

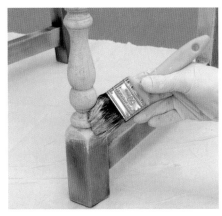

STEP 5 Apply two coats of the white paint, leavinging the correct drying time between and after the two coats.

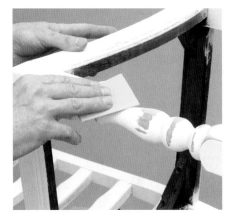

STEP 6 Rub the waxed areas with sandpaper. The paint should lift away easily, so that the bare wood shows through in places. It is important not to overdo this effect, because it is meant to simulate natural wear and tear.

YOU WILL NEED:

- TACK LIFTER
- SCISSORS
- CALICO
- CHECKED FABRIC
- STAPLE GUN OR
  TACKS AND A SMALL
  UPHOLSTERY
  HAMMER
- BRAID FOR EDGING
  (OPTIONAL)
- FABRIC GLUE
- PINS

HOW TO DO THE UPHOLSTERY

STEP 1 Strip off the old fabric and remove the old tacks and staples. Replace the seat pad if necessary.

STEP 2 Lay the calico over the seat and cut it to fit, leaving enough to fold down the sides and turn over a small hem.

STEP 3 Use the calico as a template and cut out the checked fabric, adding an extra ¾ in./2 cm on all sides so that it will overlap the calico on the seat. Turn over and press a small hem on both pieces.

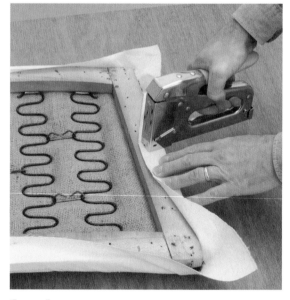

STEP 4 Lay the calico over the seat and fix it to the frame in the middle of one side first, then stretch it across and staple it in the middle of the opposite side. Do the same with the back and front.

STEP 5 Fold a triangle under at each corner and staple this flat to the frame on both sides. Do this on opposite corners, and then pleat the excess fabric over and staple it to the frame. Fix the calico all the way around the seat.

STEP 6 Fix the checked fabric to the seat in the same way. It should be fixed a bit lower than the calico so that it covers it completely, which also means that the staples will not conflict. If using braid, apply a continuous bead of glue to the back and, working from the center back, place the braid over the line of staples along the edge of the fabric. Pin to hold it in place until the glue has bonded.

Contemporary dining room

Fabulous contemporary restaurants provide terrific inspiration, and what a tasty way to research a look! The look is essentially pared down, clean, and uncluttered. The materials are natural and the line is simple. With this sensual style, any unnecessary decoration has been removed to be replaced with space, texture, and clarity.

The best flooring in a contemporary dining room is a floating wooden floor. The cheapest laminated types are good enough for this room. Alternated dark and light strips of wood give an effective look.

Some style magazines have named this "hotel chic" and there is an element of truth in the tag. But don't be put off: the hotels they refer to are top-of-the-range, contemporary establishments. They are more like lifestyle palaces, where those in the know choose to gather and socialize. Luckily for the rest of us, designs filter down faster than ever now, and most top styles can be recreated and accessorized at a fraction of the original cost. Everyone's doing it, and it's a lot more fun than being conventional. The nine key ingredients are …

1. Glass

A sheet of tempered, tinted glass resting on a pair of saw horses looks cool and makes a practical dining surface. It is easy to clean, won't scratch and costs less than wood. Suitable toughened glass with rounded corners and smooth edges can be ordered to size from a local glazier, and several contemporary furniture stores sell pairs of suitable saw horses.

2. Wood

Dark, stained wood has staged a comeback. Instead of the real thing, you can buy a sheet of 1-in./2.5-cm MDF and give it a rosewood finish with the help of some deep, red-brown paint and a rubber graining tool. Supported on saw horses, the result is amazingly realistic, and if you splash out on a sheet of glass to cover the tabletop nobody will be able to tell the difference.

3. Buying second-hand

Look out for second-hand furniture that can be updated with a dark stain. The lines must be squared off and boxy, with straight or tapered legs. If you have a large room, check out second-hand office furniture dealers, who sometimes have boardroom tables and chairs on sale. This is a way to get top-quality furniture at a very low price. And if you're not ready for dark wood or simply prefer a lighter look, then go for pale ash or beech with straight legs and squared-off edges.

4. Stainless steel

Stainless steel in the dining room is fine in small doses—for example, handles on the sideboard, cutlery, lampshades, and the pepper grinder and salt cellar—but too much will begin to look industrial. The trick is to get a balance between the hard and soft edges in the room. Keep it cool but comfortable.

5. Floors

Carpets are something of a liability when food and wine are being consumed. The best flooring in the contemporary dining room is a floating wooden floor. The least expensive laminated types are fine for a dining room and are guaranteed to be stain-resistant. If you can't decide between dark and light wood, then why not alternate them? Floor strips laid in stripes of different shades make a really bold, contemporary statement.

6. Chairs

There are many superb modern chairs to choose from, and the key questions to ask are how often you will be using them and for how many hours at a time. If there are just two of you most of the time, it makes sense to buy two really good chairs and a set of four others that will look good, but which won't break the bank. If you entertain a lot, then bite the bullet and buy a matching set of modern upholstered chairs because they are definitely the most comfortable.

7. Children

If children are going to use the dining room every day, the chairs need to be resilient and easy to clean. Shiny wooden floors can be dangerous for children who rock back on their chairs, so fit rubber tips on wooden chair legs or, better still, buy molded-polypropylene or plywood chairs with tubular steel legs, which are always rubber-tipped. And, since sitting at the table should never seem like hard work for kids, buy a generously sized, brightly colored PVC cloth which will protect the table top so that everyone can relax.

8. Lighting

The table is the only area that needs to be fully lit. The lighting should be good enough for everyone to see what they're eating without shining in anyone's eyes and blinding them, or being too ambient and not casting enough light. Consider frosted-glass wall lights, which can be used to provide an ambient glow, table lamps to add diffused light, and halogen spotlights directed onto the serving area or sideboard. And the table? You can't go wrong with candles. Look for the most contemporary styles, such as long rectangular blocks with six or more wicks, tall tapers, or clear glass tubes. There are so many to choose from.

9. Color

Choose a harmonious color scheme avoiding strong contrasts, but this doesn't mean it has to be safe or dull. Textured paint could be applied to one or two walls to give a linen, suede, rustic, or metallic effect. If you are searching for color inspiration, have a look in a contemporary cookbook. A café au lait with a slice of chocolate cake would give you cream, tan, or dark brown, and tandoori chicken with lime pickle and poppadums would give you deep red, burned orange and pale yellow. It's not a bad way to plan the dining room color scheme!

A sheet of toughened glass on a saw horse makes a stunning contemporary dining table. The glass can be ordered to size from a glazier, with the corners rounded and the edges smoothed.

THE PROJECTS
The two projects on the following pages show how to make a concealed wall uplighter for subtle, ambient lighting, plus a rosewood-effect dining table out of MDF.

YOU WILL NEED:
- 2 IN. X 1 IN./5 CM X 2.5 CM PAR LUMBER CLEAT FOR WALL FIXING—24 IN./61 CM/LONG
- 4 IN. X 1 IN./10 CM X 2.5 CM PAR LUMBER FOR SHELF—61 CM/24IN LONG
- 6 IN. X ½ IN./15 CM X 1.2 CM MDF FOR FRONT PLATE—25 IN./63.4 CM LONG
- 4 IN. X ½ IN./10 CM X 1.2 CM MDF, PLUS 2 END PLATES 8-IN. X 4-IN./20-CM X 10-CM CUT TO SLOPE BETWEEN THE WALL CLEAT AND THE FRONT PLATE
- 20³/₈-IN./52.5-CM SLIM FLUORESCENT LIGHT FITTING AND TUBE
- LONG RULE WITH SPIRIT LEVEL
- PENCIL
- ⅛-IN./4-MM AND ¼-IN./6MM DRILL BITS
- NUMBER 6 WALL ANCHORS
- NUMBER 6 SCREWS— 1⅝ IN./4 CM AND 2 IN./5 CM

PROJECT
Mood lighting using a concealed uplighter

Instead of buying several feature wall lights, this project shows how to make an uplighter that is fixed on the wall and painted to blend into it. It is in effect an upside-down valance that conceals one or more slimline fluorescent striplights as a low-voltage wall light. Make the box unit to fit the length of wall, or just long enough for a single light fitting (like the fittings usually used below kitchen cabinets). Get a qualified electrician to insert the wiring into the wall; any additional fittings can use the box so that only one wall access outlet is needed.

This subtle uplighter is made out of MDF and painted the same color as the wall behind. Inside it is a slimline fluorescent striplight. The uplighter can be made to fit a single light fitting, like this one, or made to fit the length of a whole wall.

HOW TO DO IT

STEP 1 Mark the position for the 2 in. x 1 in./ 5 cm x 2.5 cm cleat on the wall. Ideally this should be at eye level so that the tubes are completely concealed by the front plate.

STEP 2 Locate the studs in the wall and fix the cleat into them using the 2-in./5-cm screws.

STEP 3 Fix the shelf to the cleat, at a right angle to the wall, using 1⅝-in./4-cm screws.

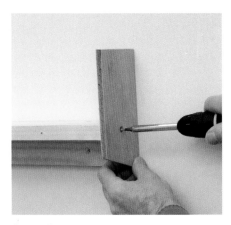

STEP 4 Place the end plates in position, and mark the angle to be cut away between the front and the cleat. Use a saw to cut the angle, then fix the end plates in position.

STEP 5 Fix the MDF front plate to the shelf front using a 1⅝-in./4-cm screw every 4 in./10 cm. Prime the unit, then paint it using the same color as the wall behind. Place the light fitting inside the unit and connect the wiring as necessary. There is no need to fix the light fitting inside the unit.

YOU WILL NEED:

- SHEET OF 1-IN./
  2.5-CM MDF
- PVA
- PAINT BRUSH
- DEEP RED-BROWN
  VINYL SILK AS THE
  BASE COLOR
- SMALL FOAM ROLLER
  AND TRAY
- WATER-BASED
  CLEAR GLAZE
- TUBE OF BLACK
  ACRYLIC PAINT TO
  TINT THE GLAZE (OR
  BLACK INK)
- 2-IN./5-CM BRUSH
- RUBBER OR PLASTIC
  GRAINING ROLLER
- SOFT COTTON CLOTH
- PLASTIC CONTAINER
  FOR THE GLAZE
- CLEAR MAT VARNISH

PROJECT

Rosewood graining an MDF table top

Rosewood has a deep-red base with a dramatic near-black grain. The real thing is very expensive, but it is actually quite easy to fake with the aid of a rubber graining roller. This can be bought in specialized paint stores and even some home improvement stores. MDF is an ideal material for this treatment because it has a perfectly smooth surface with no grain of its own. Buy a sheet of 1-in./2.5-cm MDF cut to a size that will suit your room and the number of people you need to seat, and support it on saw horses. If you have never tried woodgraining before, don't be put off; it is not as technical as it appears. You will need to practice with the graining tool and glaze, however, before you paint the table. You will soon discover the right amount of glaze needed and the technique for rocking the roller as you go.

This rosewood-effect dining table has been made out of MDF, using a rubber graining roller and a deep-red vinyl silk paint.

HOW TO DO IT

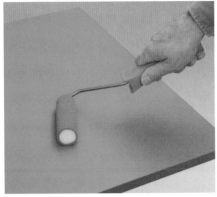

STEP 1 Paint the tabletop and edges with a coat of diluted PVA, 3 parts glue to 1 part water, to seal the surface.

STEP 2 Apply a coat of the red base color and leave it to dry. Check for coverage and, if it needs one, apply a second base coat.

STEP 3 Mix up the glaze using 4 parts glaze to 1 part black paint.

STEP 4 Paint the glaze over the red base coat, using a flat-ended paint brush. Gently wipe the cotton cloth over the wet surface so that only the thinnest layer of glaze remains. Don't scrub it all off, and leave a fine film of glaze for the graining.

STEP 6 Do the edges of the table top in exactly the same way. Leave the graining to dry and then apply two coats of clear mat varnish.

STEP 5 Hold the graining roller firmly with the ridges curving down. Beginning at one end, hold the roller on the glazed surface and gently pull it toward you, rolling it over as you go.

Having reached the extremity, begin rocking it back the other way, still pulling it toward you. Continue to the end and begin again alongside the first strip.

Living-dining room

The large room with a dining area at one end and sitting area at the other has been around for a long time. Large Victorian and 1900s houses often featured folding doors between the reception rooms, to be opened up for large social gatherings. The open-plan lifestyle began in the 1960s. For many years now, new houses have been built to an open-plan design downstairs to make them feel as spacious as possible. Recent trends have seen the dining area become more defined, with low walls, glass bricks, and screens being used to show that the room serves two different purposes.

Lighting is one way of subtly separating the eating from the seating areas. The sitting area needs relaxed lighting with table lamps or wall lights, while the dining table can be lit from above.

The seating and eating areas should ideally complement each other while being divided into separate areas. There is a number of ways to achieve this effect. Five areas you need to look at are …

1. Color

When choosing the color for the dining end of your room, you must look at the room as a whole, which means taking all the existing colors into account. The furniture, drapes, carpets, and paintings at one end must not look out of place with what you choose for the other. One of the projects in the following section shows how to use the same background color throughout, and then mask off sections of wall and paint blocks of a deeper, more intense version of the same color. This gives the dining area a different character while retaining a harmonious color scheme. For a more dramatic effect, use the same technique but with blocks of contrasting color.

2. Lighting

Clever lighting alone can define the different areas and make the same color look warmer, cooler, brighter, or more faded. The sitting area needs to have a relaxing atmosphere, which can be achieved with table lamps, wall lights and accent lights directed onto your favorite things. The dining table can be lit from above with a track of halogen spotlights, a chandelier, or candelabra, depending upon the furniture style.

3. Flooring

One of the clearest ways of saying one end is for comfort and the other is for eating, is to have different types of flooring. This could be linoleum or a floating wooden floor at one end and a fitted carpet at the other. If this idea sounds too fixed, then consider fitting one type of flooring throughout and using a large round rug as the focus point in the sitting room.

4. Screening

A screen describes a barrier other than a wall—it could be solid and transparent, such as a glass-brick wall, or something that you can see through, like cube shelving or a line of wooden rods. A semisheer drape on a decorative rod (as shown in one of the following projects) is a good compromise because it can be drawn to section off the dining area for special occasions, and, when drawn back, softly frames both sides.

5. Furniture and accessories

Dining furniture for a dual-purpose room
should be lighter and more compact than
something for a dining room. Choose a square
or circular table with extra flaps or panels so that
it can expand when necessary and not be too
obtrusive at other times. A sideboard is ideal in
a room like this because the plates, glasses, and
cutlery can be hidden away conveniently close
to the table. After years in the furniture
wilderness, the sideboard is now an absolute
"must-have" in contemporary homes.

THE PROJECTS

The two projects on the following pages show
subtle yet effective ways of separating the eating
from the seating areas of a sitting-dining room.
The first, a semi-sheer drape divider, is the
modern equivalent of 1900s or Victorian folding
doors between reception rooms. The second
project shows how to use color blocking to
separate the two areas while keeping the same
color scheme throughout the room. Incorporate
your personal style in the colors you choose.

Tables in living-
dining rooms need to
be lighter and more
compact than those
in separate dining
rooms, so they are
not too obtrusive
over the whole area.

YOU WILL NEED:

- STEEL CURTAIN RAIL (SUITABLE FOR CEILING MOUNTING)
- DRILL
- SCREWS
- STRING AND PAINTER'S TAPE
- CAVITY WALL ANCHORS
- FABRIC
- PLUMB LINE
- TAPE MEASURE
- LONG RULE WITH SPIRIT LEVEL
- PENCIL

PROJECT

Drape divider

The treatment you choose for your sitting or dining room must reflect your own lifestyle. There is little point in having a semisheer drape divider if you also own a large boisterous dog, no matter how much you like the idea! And avoid any fabric that has too much bulk and is too heavy, because the best drapes should hang as flat panels without any gathering at the top. Embroidered sari fabric will give an exotic look while muslin is modern and minimalist, but you could also use a light cotton canvas as a flat dividing "wall" of color.

This drape divider will subtly divide the seating and eating areas in a living-dining room. The best materials to use are light, so they hang as flat panels without any gathering. Semisheer fabric, muslin, embroidered sari fabric, or light cotton canvas are all ideal.

HOW TO DO IT

STEP 1 Measure an equal distance from the dining end to the center of the room on opposite walls, and mark these points on the baseboard in pencil.

STEP 2 Use a line plumbed to the baseboard. Take a vertical measurement up to the ceiling height (using a long rule with a spirit level) and make a pencil mark. Run a length of string across the ceiling between the two marks to be a guideline for the rail fitting.

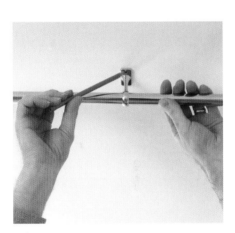

STEP 4 Slide the center fixing onto the rail and mark the position for the screws between each end in the center of the rail.

STEP 5 Drill out all the holes for the screws. Insert the cavity wall anchors. These are specially designed with claws to grip wall board from the back as the screws go in.

STEP 6 Clip the curtain rings onto the fabric or slip the curtain header tabs onto the rail.

STEP 3 Mark the positions for the screws to hold the rail fittings. The rails are supplied with fittings, usually one at each end with one in the middle.

YOU WILL NEED:
- PAINTER'S TAPE
- PLUMB LINE
- LONG RULE WITH
  SPIRIT LEVEL
- SET SQUARE
- PENCIL
- MATCH POTS (LATEX,
  METALLICS, OR
  TEXTURED PAINTS)
- PAINT BRUSH
- WALLPAPER PASTE IF
  COLOR-WASHING

PROJECT
Color blocking

The wonderful thing about this decorating idea is that you can use test pots for all the feature colors. The base color is applied throughout the whole room, then the dining area is enlivened with blocks of color. This can be done in all sorts of ways using different colors and textures. A multicolored wall of squares, a graduated color change from left to right, or deeper, more saturated shades of the background color are some ideas to try. Contrasts in texture can also be introduced with metallic paints, chalky distempers, or by thinning the latex paint with wallpaper paste to make a transparent glaze.

The wall of this dining area is decorated in multicolored squares, but the color scheme of the whole room is the same. You can introduce contrasts in texture by using metallic, chalky, or glazed paint.

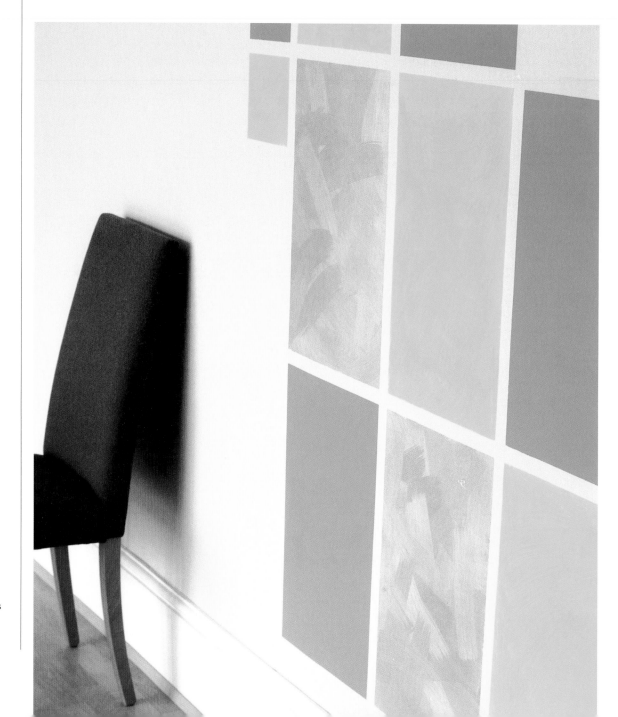

HOW TO DO IT

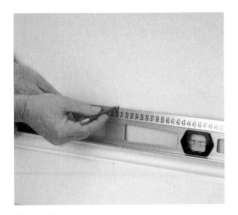

STEP 1 Having decided upon the shape, size, and position of the squares on the wall, mark the verticals along the baseboard in pencil (for instance, 12 in./30 cm—6 in./15 cm—12 in./30 cm—6 in./15 cm).

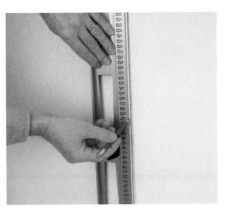

STEP 2 Hang the plumb line down the wall as a vertical guide, then use the long rule and a pencil to make guide marks for the same grid going up the wall (12 in./30 cm—6 in./15 cm—12 in./30 cm—6 in./15 cm).

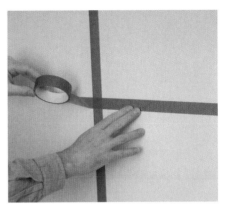

STEP 3 Run tape up from the baseboard in straight lines. Then, using the level to check that the corners are square, run tape horizontally across the wall, intersecting the verticals and completing the grid of squares.

STEP 4 For a color-wash effect, mix wallpaper paste into latex (half and half) and spread the glaze with random brush strokes.

STEP 5 Apply the color of your choice in all the large squares.

STEP 6 Once the paint has dried, carefully peel off all the painter's tape.

TOP TIP
You can use metallic paints as well, to catch the light and make the room appear larger. These are now generally available from home improvement stores everywhere.

Bedrooms

The bedroom should be a sanctuary, a place of rest, a temple of calm. But since it is also the room least on display to friends, it is easy to pay less attention to bedrooms than to other rooms. The bedroom has a range of practical functions, that need to be taken into account in any redesign. Apart from sleeping, it is a place for storing clothes, getting dressed, styling hair, reading, and perhaps watching television. Children's rooms have another set of functions that need to be taken into account, not least the children's own preferences. Above all, the fact that bedrooms are the most private rooms in the house means they are the perfect place to express yourself.

Traditional bedroom

Traditional style in the bedroom means grand, comfortable, and irresistible but certainly not old-fashioned in any way. This is the sort of room where you should feel very grown up, and, since it is also where you do most of your dreaming, it should be the room of your dreams. The star of the show is the bed, which should be as comfortable as your budget allows, with a good bedhead, a bedside table for your champagne or morning cup of tea, soft but effective lighting, and twice as many pillows as you really need.

Alcoves are ideal places for shelving, and to position dressing tables and mirrors. Look out for traditional furniture in local furniture auctions.

This style uses lots of traditional ideas—it could be very feminine, with lace, frills, and satin, or have the understated elegance of dark wooden furniture, monogrammed linen pillowcases, satin-edged blankets and a cream woven coverlet. And how about a four-poster bed with a plump eiderdown? As this is the one room in your house that people visit by invitation only, you can truly please yourself.

A low-ceilinged room would look smaller with a four-poster, but a similar lighter effect can be achieved by fixing drape rails above the bed hung with muslin or voile drapes. If the idea of being drapeed in sounds too claustrophobic, then a canopy on the wall behind the bed head with fabric drapes falling to the floor will frame the bed, giving a romantic but less enclosed look. The canopy can be fixed to something as simple as a wooden shelf fitted with a decorative molding.

You can really work wonders with fabric and a staple gun. Any existing headboard can be revamped with a new fabric cover, and a plain bed can be dressed up with a headboard of MDF covered with upholstery foam and fabric, which is then screwed onto the wall or hung from a drape pole. Trimmings of fringe, tassels, buttons, ribbons, lace, or fancy braids can be stitched on or attached with a glue gun.

Storage

Unless there is space for a separate dressing room, you will need a closet and drawers for clothes, somewhere for shoes and perhaps a dressing table. Make use of any alcoves for shelving or hanging space and, if you have a bay window, fit a built-in window seat with lift-off lids covered with cushions to match the bedcover or drape fabric, and storage space below. If closet are fitted, make sure that they suit the look of the bedroom. Wooden door panels can be removed and replaced with soft panels of gathered fabric on net drape wires. Visit local furniture auctions, where you can often find traditional bedroom suites. They really don't make furniture the way they used to, except at the top end of the market, but old wooden furniture given a new paint finish and upholstery can look fantastic, and will cost much less than similar new furniture in traditional styles.

Try a stripped-pine blanket chest to store out-of-season clothes. Give it a dark stain or try something like découpage or a crackleglazed effect. Boxes on casters under the bed are a good place to keep your shoes. But remember that all storage for items currently in use should be easily accessible, otherwise it just doesn't work. If there isn't enough floor space to pull out an underbed drawer, then keep the drawer for things that you won't need for a while.

Walls and floors

Choose colors that are easy on the eye and patterns that won't keep you awake at night. Don't try to match everything or the result could be a bedroom with no personality. Stripes, checks, and floral patterns can all be combined if the colors are similar, as can different textures like tweed, cotton, velvet, and linen. Don't use too many different colors, though: two or three main ones are enough with accents of contrasting colors in small amounts. Fabric trimmed with a ribbon border can be used on the walls in place of wallpaper, or hung from a picture rail around the bed. Pattern motifs can also be copied from textiles and made into stencils to decorate the walls or furniture. Floors should ideally be soft carpets, but if you prefer wooden floorboards, make sure you have "islands" of soft bedside rugs.

Windows

A traditional bedroom has drapes. Indulge in generous drapes, deep valances, and black-out linings. Generosity is the key, and it is better to use lots of cheap fabric like unbleached calico or suit lining, and dress it up with a boldly contrasting ribbon or deep fringe border, than to use small amounts of an expensive fabric.

Accessories and lighting

Have at least one good mirror on the wall and for a real touch of luxury, nothing beats a vase of fresh flowers. Think about the practical lighting you need for closet and drawers as well as pretty bedside lighting—if you have an overhead light, use a dimmer switch for a shadowy, sensual atmosphere.

Decluttering

Most of the clutter in the bedroom comes from newspapers, books, shoes, laundry (clean and dirty), make-up, accessories, and jewelry. It helps if you begin by having a place for everything, then all you have to do is keep up the good work. New stuff arrives all the time, so unless you constantly chuck out the surplus, things will begin to pile up.

Small cabinets

Give a small cabinet a traditional French country look by painting it green, blue, or deep pink, and replace its door panels with wire netting sprayed to match. Stretch net drape wires above and below the panels on the back of the doors with screw-in eyelets, and gather fabric panels onto them. Choose a fabric that you already have in the room.

A canopy fixed to the wall behind the bed head, with drapes falling either side, frames the bed in a romantic look that is less enclosed than the four-poster.

THE PROJECTS

The following projects show how to transform your bedroom into the traditional style using both decorative and functional ways. Some accessories and trimmings should do the rest.

YOU WILL NEED:

• STENCIL CARD

• TRACING PAPER

• SNAP-BLADE KNIFE

• CUTTING MAT OR
  PIECE OF THICK CARD

• SPRAY ADHESIVE

• STENCIL BRUSH

• RULER

• PLUMB LINE

• TEST POTS OR
  STENCIL PAINT

• PLATE

PROJECT
Stenciling a wall

Stenciling has been around for a very long time, but not everyone has the confidence to cut out a stencil and paint their bedroom wall. This little stencil motif will get you started, but be warned, once you realise how easy and effective stenciling can be, you won't want to stop! Stencils can be cut from any waxed cardboard or plastic specially formulated for this purpose. The advantage of plastic is that it is transparent and easier to align, but with a simple pattern like this one you can draw a vertical line through it, and visually line it up with a plumb line each time you move it. The pattern is stenciled with a half-drop on each second column.

This simple stencil motif is easy to paint and is very effective on a traditional bedroom wall. Choose the paint for the stencil in your favourite calm color.

HOW TO DO IT

STEP 1 Photocopy or trace the pattern and spray the back of it with spray adhesive. Stick it onto the stencil material. Place on the cutting mat, and cut out the shape using a snap-blade knife. Peel off the paper and draw a line through the middle as a guide.

STEP 2 Spray the back of the stencil with spray adhesive. This will make the stencil sticky enough to stay flat against the wall, and stop the paint from bleeding under the stencil. It will also peel off the wall leaving no residue.

STEP 3 Put some paint onto the plate and load up the stencil brush with paint. Now wipe most of the paint off on a sheet of paper towel (you need only a tiny amount of paint for stenciling).

STEP 5 Move the plumb line across and begin the second column 12 in./30 cm across from the first, but start this one 6 in./15 cm from the top of the wall. Stencil the next motif 12 in./30 cm below and continue in the same way as before. The third row is started 12 in./30 cm from the top, and the following one 6 in./15 cm, and so on.

Enlarge the stencil below and transfer onto stencil card or plastic. Line up the stencils on the wall as shown in the second sketch below.

STEP 4 The first line of stencil pattern is applied in a straight line 12 in./30 cm apart. Starting in one corner, fix the plumb line to the top of the wall, measure 12 in./30 cm across and down, and line up the top of the stencil. Check the center line with the plumb line, then apply the paint in a light swirling stroke. Begin at the edges and work inward. Don't overdo it because you can always return to add more paint once it is dry. Complete the first column.

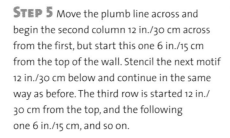

YOU WILL NEED:

- 4 UPRIGHTS—
  2 IN. x 2 IN./
  5 CM x 5 CM
- 2 TOP SIDE-LENGTHS
  (MITERED)—2 IN. x
  1 IN./5 CM x 2.5 CM
- 2 TOP END-LENGTHS
  (MITERED)—
  5 CM x 2.5 CM/
  2 IN. x 1 IN.
- 2 LOWER SIDE-
  LENGTHS (MITERED)
  —1 IN. x ⅝ IN./
  2.5 CM x 1.5 CM
- 2 LOWER END-
  LENGTHS
  (MITERED)—
  1 IN. x ⅝ IN./
  2.5 CM x 1.5 CM
- METAL RULE
- SAW
- SANDPAPER
- MITER SAW OR
  BLOCK
- DRILL
- ⅛-IN./4-MM
  DRILL BIT
- COUNTERSUNK BIT
- WOOD GLUE
- 2-IN/5-CM NUMBER
  6 SCREWS
- COMBINATION
  SQUARE
- PENCIL
- SCREWDRIVER

PROJECT

The four poster

This project shows you how to build a four-poster frame around a plain bed, and once the frame is in place you can choose a fabric to give the bed the look of your choice—floral chintz for an English country house style, or calico and gingham for an American folk look.

The first key step is to decide the height of your bed, which should relate to the ceiling height in your bedroom, and then follow the simple construction steps. The frame can be painted or varnished depending upon the style of your room.

A four-poster frame transforms a bed into the ultimate in romantic decadence. The choice of fabric will give the bed its look—whether it's floral chintz, calico, and gingham, or sheer white muslin.

HOW TO DO IT

STEP 1 Measure the length of the bed base and add 4 in./10 cm to allow for the width of the uprights. Miter the top and lower side-lengths to this measurement. Measure the width of the bed base, and miter the top and lower end-pieces to this measurement. Use sandpaper on all the cut edges.

STEP 2 The top ends and sides are fitted flush with the top of the uprights. To find the height for the broad lower planks surrounding the bed, measure the distance from the floor to halfway up the mattress. This is where the top of the lower planks should be fixed to the uprights.

STEP 3 Make up the bed ends first. Lay down parallel one set of uprights, with the top and lower end-lengths between them. Drill holes for two screws at each joint. Apply wood glue and screw the pieces together. Repeat to make up the other bed end.

STEP 4 Drill and countersink screw holes in all the top and lower side-pieces, and pilot holes in the uprights, making sure that these screws will miss the ones already located there.

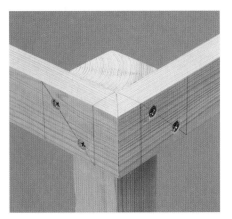

STEP 5 The top sides can now be screwed in place, with your assistant supporting one end while you stand on a stepladder and secure the other. The completed bed frame can be painted, stained or varnished, and hung with tab-top drapes.

STEP 6 Ask your assistant to hold the frame-end against the wall or prop one frame-end against the wall with the bed pushed against it. Support the lower sides at the foot-end while screwing them to the uprights at the head-end. Have your assistant hold the foot-end upright while you screw the lower sides to it.

TOP TIP

If you prefer a more gathered drape effect, fit a standard drape rail to the inside edge of the top frame and hang the drapes from it in the usual way.

PROJECT
Dressing table with storage space below

A plain table with a shelf below can be converted easily into a dressing table and storage area with the help of fabric, Velcro, a sheet of glass, and a freestanding mirror. Once you've made the floor-length fabric skirt for the table, add lace, ribbon, or braid edging and top it with a sheet of toughened, smooth-edged glass ordered to size from your local glazier.

A plain table with a shelf beneath can be easily transformed into a traditional dressing table, with useful storage for the less attractive cosmetic bottles and tubes you'd rather not have on display.

HOW TO DO IT

STEP 1 Measure the height from the table top to the floor, and then measure around the sides and the front, adding a bit extra for an overlap. If you want to pleat the "skirt," then allow more fabric. Divide the length into two.

STEP 2 Depending upon the condition of the table top, either cover it with fabric or a lace cloth, or paint or stain it with the color of your choice.

STEP 3 Stick the looped side of the Velcro around the table edge.

STEP 4 Turn back a hem on the top and bottom of the skirt, and sew or bond with iron-on tape.

STEP 5 Sew or stick the other side of the Velcro tape to the top hem of the fabric. Press the skirt onto the table edge. Have one piece overlap the other by about ¾ in./2 cm where they meet in the middle. Fix a small square of looped Velcro to fasten the overlap. And finally, place the glass on the table top. Add a vase of flowers and a mirror and hide all your undesirables behind the drape!

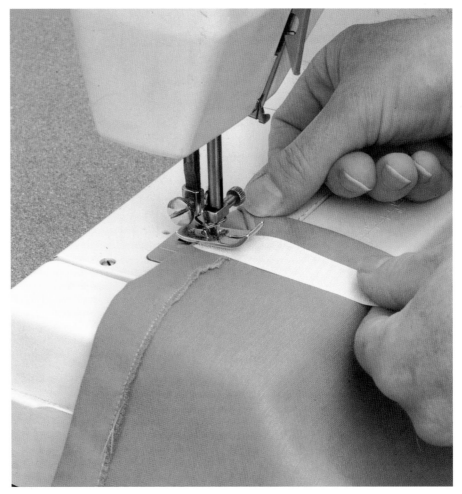

Contemporary bedroom

There are many different ways to create a contemporary look, but the style is predominantly about clean lines, clear space, and creating an atmosphere. This is the age of the senses, where aromatherapy and feng shui are considered mainstream, and natural colors, fabrics and decorating materials are understood to bring a feeling of well-being. Minimalism has been the biggest recent influence on home decorating, and the quickest way to get the contemporary look is to clear the surfaces, put away all your clutter, lay a wooden floor, and light some candles.

Ideally, the only furniture in a contemporary bedroom is the bed. Walk-in closets or separate dressing rooms are an effective luxury that keep the bedroom free of clutter.

Efficient storage is a must in the contemporary bedroom. It is the only way to keep clothes, shoes, make-up and jewelry out of sight and maintain the minimalist style. Ideally, clothes would be stored in a separate dressing room, freeing up the bedroom space of functional furniture, but in reality few of us have

this choice, so we have to be creative with our storage options. Five key things to consider when creating a contemporary bedroom are …

1. Furniture

The double bed is a very big piece of furniture, which will immediately dominate the room. If you give the bed a contemporary make-over, the rest of the room can follow. If you already have a good bed, it is worth keeping because they are very expensive. Give it a change of style by adding a drop-in headboard, which is one of the projects in this section.

Pine bed heads with turned spindles were popular, but now look very dated. They can be boxed in with sheets of MDF or plywood, and painted or covered with foam and fabric to make a really comfortable back rest. Basic upholstery like this can be tackled with a staple gun, double-sided tape, and a glue gun. Stick the foam to the MDF, staple the fabric over the top of it, and neaten the edges with a plain ribbon trimming stuck on with the hot glue gun. You can do it!

An alternative plain and minimal style is the Japanese look. If your budget is tight, and you don't mind sleeping on a futon, you can make a really cheap and stylish bed base out of a pair of

wooden pallets. The wood will need sanding to get rid of potential splinters and then you just put the futon on top. Keep bedside tables low, place woven grass mats on each side of the bed, fit paper shades and blinds, and hang framed Japanese prints on the walls.

If you are starting from scratch, go for a low-level platform bed with built-in storage below and reading lights in the headboard. There are some amazing new wooden beds available, which have a closet's worth of drawers built in, but be warned that they are very expensive. Iron bed frames are cool and popular, and there are loads of original designs made by small companies. Check out magazine classified advertisements if you are looking for something unique. Beds are also made in different finishes, aluminum being one of the latest materiels, and all the big furniture stores have their own ranges of metal beds. If you do choose a metal bed, be sure to

have plenty of pillows because they are cold and hard to lean against.

The Shaker style is now making a comeback, even though it's over 250 years since it first appeared in America (the Shakers were an offshoot of the Quakers). The Shakers lived in community houses without any unnecessary decoration or personal possessions, keeping the floor space clear and putting everything away in built-in closets. All of these ideas strike a minimalist chord, and the furniture is so beautiful that the reproduction Shaker style is now one of the most popular styles around.

Closets and chests of drawers are large enough to ruin any sense of space you have created by careful use of lighting and color, so think carefully whether you really need them. If you have only skirts, shirts, and trousers to hang up, fit double rods in a small closet and use the full height of it. Space below hanging clothes can

You can't go wrong with white as a color scheme—it reflects the light, is flattering to the complexion, and goes with everything. Off-whites look particularly good with wood.

If you've got windows to flaunt, make the most of them by fitting shades into the window recesses or make them more dramatic with floor-to-ceiling billowing muslin drops.

easily become untidy, so put in a shoe rack or storage boxes. Also check out new closets with frosted-glass doors, but be aware that they will look good only if everything inside is tidy.

If you are lucky enough to have a big room, think about having a false wall built to make a walk-in closet. This need not use up more than 3 ft./1 m of room space (including the partition wall). This storage space is just right for all your clothes and shoes, suitcases, and spare bedding. The only furniture needed in the bedroom would be the bed. Now that is luxury!

The way you decorate the bedroom windows depends on several things. Do you need to keep out drafts or traffic noise? Does the sun shine too brightly in the morning? Are the window frames attractive and do you have a nice view? Try thick drapes for absorbing noise and blocking drafts, making the room a lot more cozy. For a warm contemporary style, use blankets, felt, or lined fleece to make drapes. Block out the sun with black-out lining material, which costs a bit more than ordinary lining, but really is effective. If the window frames are a good feature, like the old wooden double-hung kind, they shouldn't be hidden away, and you can fit shades into the

window recess. There are some fabulous new materials and designs, including felt and denim for warmth, voile to let in the light, pierced patterns, and lots of variations on the classic Venetian blind.

2. Color schemes

Bedroom color schemes need to create a mood. A natural palette of greens, browns, and off-whites look fabulous with wood. It is a sophisticated choice and these colors are also harmonious and relaxing. If you feel a bit wilder, there are some wonderful rich colors to choose from. Bedroom colors can also be toned down or livened up for a change of mood by using the right lighting. Lilac, turquoise, and pink are a wonderfully feminine combination with a contemporary edge, while cinnamon, oatmeal, mushroom, and chocolate brown are warm, rich, masculine colors. Blue is spacious and dreamy, and white reflects the light, flatters the complexion, and goes with virtually everything.

3. Lighting

Bedroom lighting can be divided into three definite areas. The room as a whole might need a large, central chandelier-type light fitted with a dimmer switch. The bedside area needs reading lights, while task lighting will help you find things in the closet after dark. Choose lights that switch on when you open the door, or simple, battery-powered lights for occasional use.

4. Flooring

The flooring for the contemporary bedroom is best kept plain. If you have wooden floorboards, paint them with wood wash that is a lighter version of one of the colors used in the room. Pale wooden floors look good, and soft rugs can be used by the bedside to warm your toes in the morning.

Decorating this room is really very personal. It's a place to enjoy being wrapped in those colors, textures, and patterns that please you. And whatever you do, never sacrifice comfort for style in the bedroom.

5. Decluttering

Clutter can be everything. It's the mail that arrives in the morning and then sits next to the tea things and the hair slides, with your glasses case and the pen by the notepad right next to the phone. When it threatens to engulf us, it is time for some serious decluttering.

Try to clear the morning clutter when you leave the bedroom. Have a deep-sided tray for the morning tea or coffee and make sure that the mail, newspapers, and glasses from the night before are taken out there and then. Look out for a stylish bed tray or breakfast tray—they have two side compartments that act as legs, with a sturdy section

across the middle. A bedside magazine rack is a necessity, and once you have one, you may wonder why they are not considered standard bedroom accessories. Also buy matching boxes in a range of sizes—choose leather, wicker, clear acrylic, or canvas. Mount bookshelves on the wall in an alcove or as a series of modular cube shelving units. Keep videos in a box with a lid, because even if they are neatly stacked, their packaging still looks like clutter. Buy a wooden ladder to lean up against the wall—use a dark wood stain to smarten it up and use it as a temporary resting place for discarded clothes and towels. Buy a laundry bin and wastebasket to match the room style and finally an open shoe rack big enough for the shoes you wear all the time, keeping out-of-season and special occasion pairs stacked in matching shoe boxes. Decluttering is all about learning to be organized and stylish at the same time.

THE PROJECTS
The two projects on the following pages suggest how to start achieving a contemporary look in your own bedroom. A fresh coat of paint, some flexible lighting, and some disciplined decluttering should do the rest.

The natural colors of wood and the stone flooring, with the clean, clutter-free lines of built-in closets give this bedroom a contemporary look.

YOU WILL NEED

LUMBER AS FOLLOWS:

• 1 BACK:
  ³/₄-IN./1.8-CM MDF,
  1 SHEET OF
  8 FT. X 4 FT./
  2.4 M X 1.2 M

• 1 TOP SHELF:
  PAR SOFT WOOD,
  5³/₄ IN. X 8 FT./
  14.5 CM X 2.5 M

• 2 SIDES:
  ³/₄-IN./1.8-CM MDF,
  4 FT. X 2 FT./
  1.2 M X 61 CM

• 2 INNER SIDES:
  ³/₄-IN./1.8-CM MDF,
  19 IN. X 24 IN./
  48 CM X 60 CM

• 2 SHELVES:
  ³/₄-IN./1.8-CM MDF,
  19 IN. X 17 IN./
  48 CM X 43 CM

• 2 TOPS:
  ³/₄-IN./1.8-CM MDF,
  19 IN. X 19¹/₂ IN./
  48 CM X 50 CM

• BOX OF TWIN-
  THREAD 2-IN./5-CM
  NUMBER 6 SCREWS

• WOOD GLUE

• WOOD FILLER

• SANDPAPER

• PRIMER AND VINYL
  SILK PAINT

• DRILL WITH
  COUNTERSINK, AND
  ¹/₈-IN./2-MM PILOT
  HOLE BIT AND
  SCREWDRIVER BIT

• LONG RULE

• COMBINATION
  SQUARE

• PENCIL

• TAPE MEASURE

• SMALL FOAM ROLLER
  AND TRAY

This stunning bed
surround is practical
as well as chic. It can
be an effective way
of boxing in the
now-dated pine
bedheads, and you
can either leave the
surrounds painted or
attach basic
upholstery.

A drop-in bed surround

Building a box headboard with a shelf and two side tables sounds ambitious, but be assured, it is totally simple and the construction method is quite straightforward. It can be done with the most basic tool kit and it will make the bedroom look utterly chic.

The list on the left gives the sizes of all the pieces of MDF and softwood needed to make this surround to fit a 60-in.-/1.5-meter-wide double bed. Most lumber merchants will cut the wood to size for a small sum, which will save time considering the number of different lengths.

HOW TO DO IT

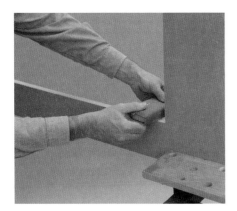

STEP 1 Cut out the waste from the two ends and sand the edges.

STEP 2 Draw positional guides for the assembly of the sides, back, and inner sides. Mark these very carefully with pencil lines.

STEP 3 Drill pilot holes for the screws and countersink them.

STEP 4 Screw the sides and inner shelves to the back.

STEP 5 Add the shelves and the tops.

TOP TIP
Unpainted MDF looks good varnished. If you don't intend to paint it, use brass screws with screw-cup washers rather than countersunk screws. They will be a visible feature and look better than patches of woodfiller.

STEP 6 Fill and sand the countersink holes. Seal, prime, and paint.

Use this sketch to help you position the surround correctly around your bed. You will need an assistant to help you drop it in place against the wall.

YOU WILL NEED:
- 6 FT./2 M CORDUROY FABRIC
- 60 IN./1.5 M ARTIFICIAL FUR FABRIC
- 60 IN./1.5 M OF 4½ OZ/125 g QUILT BATTING
- PINS
- THREAD
- SEWING MACHINE

PROJECT

Using textures to create a comfort zone

Most of the time we spend in the bedroom is in darkness, and this makes it perfect for exploring the use of different textures. These must change with the seasons if they are to be fully appreciated. Imagine stepping out of bed on a hot summer night onto cool woven-grass matting or onto a thin sheepskin fleece in winter. The summer bedroom should be airy, with billowing muslin at the windows and cool cotton sheets on the bed. In winter the bed is more of a cozy nest, with knitted hot water-bottle covers, soft velvet cushions, thick blankets, and flannel sheets. This bed cover, which is 50 percent throw and 50 percent quilt, combines two contrasting textures, corduroy and fake fur, to give 100 percent comfort! Choose a wonderfully soft and warm fabric such as artificial fur, fleece, or the more hard-wearing corduroy.

This bed cover combines fake fur on one side with corduroy on the other, each sandwiching quilt wadding, to create the ultimate winter warmer.

HOW TO DO IT

STEP 1 Lay the corduroy on a flat surface with the batting and fur fabric placed on the top. Place the two top fabrics 2 in./5 cm inside the top edge and on one side-edge of the corduroy.

STEP 2 Trim away the fur on the other two sides to make a 2-in./5-cm border all round.

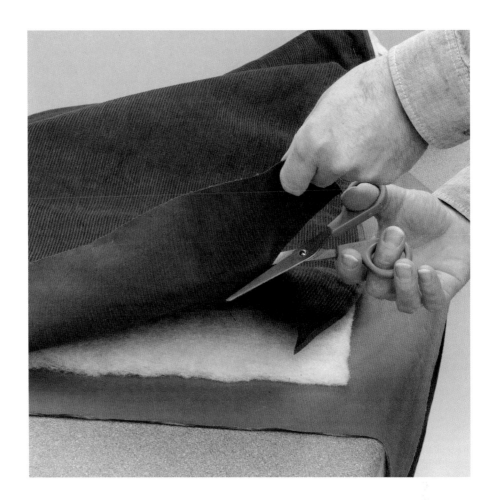

STEP 3 Miter the corners. When you fold them over, the two edges meet to make a neat finish.

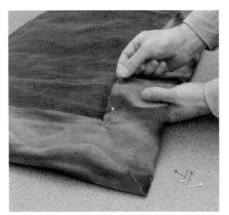

STEP 4 Fold the fur border over and pin it to the corduroy. Set the sewing machine to satin stitch, and sew all around the edge and up the middle of the miters so that all the cut edges are sealed and sewn.

TOP TIP

When making the quilt, the choice of fabric on each side is up to you. You could choose velvet, corduroy, brushed cotton, or even a knitted blanket. Check that the textures that you use together will be good companions.

Teenage boy's room

Forget about the stereotypical messy teenage boy, he's an urban myth. Boys want to live in nice surroundings just as much as girls do. They have strong ideas about color, fashion, and relaxation and will not thank you for making these decisions for them. Good TV decorating programs appeal to young people's imaginations, especially with their rule-breaking ideas. It may seem like a contradiction, but being seen as an individual matters just as much to a teenager as being in fashion. And who wants to do things the traditional way when you can get the same effect with panel adhesive in a fraction of the time? Unfortunately, what goes up will probably need to come down at some time, and this is where screws have the advantage over glues.

S tart the project with a conference. Decorating influences can come from all over the place—sport, music, fashion, and movies are the four most obvious ones and a good starting point. One way to do something original and fashionable is to mix ideas and decorate using the key features of recognizable brands of clothing. Think trainers, skateboards, surfing, snowboards, and other sports gear with a distinctive style and

Get teenagers involved in any redecorating from the start. They'll have strong ideas about the colors and style they want, and you might even get them to help...

you'll be on the right track. If he is into surfing, make a stencil of the logo on his surfboard. It doesn't have to be too literal, just the colors of a brand will be enough to make the statement.

So far it's easy, but the difficulty lies in keeping his enthusiasm alive during the boring preparatory stages. It is hard to be too enthusiastic about primers, undercoats, and filling, so you may have to resort to a good old-fashioned bribe. Try offering a coveted CD to listen to while working, or a new duvet cover, a cool bedside light, or a full-length mirror when the room is finished.

Color can affect moods, so try and talk him out of black walls because they are seriously depressing. And the advantage of another color is that it can always be painted over (unlike black). Just go with the flow! If the room is small, it's a good idea to paint the furniture the same color as the walls, and this is a good way to update closets and chests of drawers that have been around for a while. Whatever the room's dimensions, he will want to have friends stay over. A sofa-bed is ideal, but alternatives include a bed in a bag, a rolled-up camping mat that doubles as a bolster, or a

foam cube that unfolds to become a single mattress. A sleeping bag rolled up and tied with a belt makes a pretty good cushion, too.

Homework area

If the room is going to be used for schoolwork, it is important to make it easy for him to study. We all work in different ways, but an organized work area is always helpful. Even if he reads the books sprawled out on the floor, it is better if they are kept on a shelf rather than under the bed. And either buy a desk or build a work table with shelving and a good light source. Make it big enough for a computer, television, and stereo as well, then buy him a swivel chair and he can really get down to business.

There is one more thing that every teenager needs, regardless of his or her interests, and that is a huge noticeboard—kill two birds with one stone by covering a wall or all the walls with softboard. This is the material used to line school corridors so that work can be pinned up. It can be painted to look like any other wall, and used to display anything and everything. It is also great at noise reduction. It should be compulsory!

When it comes to flooring, it is best to choose something that won't stain but will be as soundproof as possible. A good padding will block out most of the beat from his stereo, and carpet tiles are good because they can be lifted and replaced if damage occurs. Hardboard is cheap and under-used as a flooring material. It can be laid in large sheets fixed down with lines of domed upholstery studs, and painted with floor paint to give a hard-edged industrial look. And if the floor is hard, make sure he also has a big soft rug to laze about on—because that's what he'll like best.

Traditional American culture is a firm favorite among teenagers, and if you're going to take it on, as with this floor-to-ceiling mural, you've got to think big!

THE PROJECTS

The two projects on the following pages give street cred to functional bedroom furniture. The first project shows how to make a bedhead out of scaffold poles, while the second adds a hip-hop stencil to transform a cheap desk.

YOU WILL NEED:
- 6 LENGTHS OF
  SCAFFOLD POLE CUT
  TO THE FOLLOWING
  LENGTHS:
- 4 LENGTHS OF
  20 IN./50 CM FOR
  THE UPRIGHTS;
- 2 LENGTHS OF
  39 IN./1 M FOR THE
  CROSS-PIECES
- 2 ELBOW FITTINGS
- 2 T-FITTINGS
- 2 END SOCKETS
- HEX KEY (USED FOR
  TIGHTENING METAL
  JOINTS)
- 8 FT./2.5M OF
  36-IN./91-CM WIDE
  MEDIUM-TO-
  HEAVYWEIGHT
  COTTON DUCK
  (COARSE COTTON
  OR LINEN)
- SEWING MACHINE
- THREAD
- SEWING MACHINE
  NEEDLE FOR
  SEWING DENIM

PROJECT
The scaffold pole bedhead

This project takes the building site into the bedroom by using scaffold poles to make a bedhead. You can also make a hanging rail in a similar way. There are companies who specialize in scaffold beds and platforms, but this project uses galvanized scaffold materials, bought from a builder's supplier, to make a serious, industrial-chic statement. A piece of coarse cotton or linen makes a comfortable back-rest. The items in the list on the left are for a single bed.

This industrial bed-head is made out of scaffold poles, with a section of denim for a back-rest. This heavy bedhead will need screwing into the floor due to its weight, so make sure that you are able to do this before you start.

HOW TO DO IT

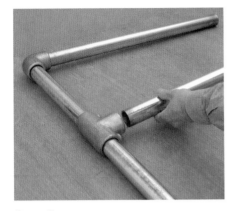

STEP 1 Slot the elbow fittings onto the end of one of the cross-pieces and add two 20-in./50-cm uprights. Fit the T-fittings on to the other cross-piece and fit it onto the uprights. Don't tighten anything up yet.

STEP 2 Wrap the fabric around the two cross-pieces and mark the position for a joining seam at the back with chalk.

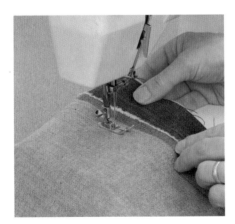

STEP 3 Fold the seam over at the back and sew it flat with a double row of stitching.

STEP 4 Loosen the joints at one side and slip the fabric over the two cross-pieces. Tighten up the fittings with the hex key.

STEP 5 Complete the bedhead by adding the two lower poles and the end fittings. Because this is a very heavy bed head, it must be well secured. Fix to the floor using large screws. And check that there are no water pipes passing underneath the fixing points!

YOU WILL NEED:
- 1 PLAIN AND VERY CHEAP DESK (SECONDHAND IS BEST)
- 1 LARGE CAN OF ALUMINUM PAINT, PLUS SMALL CANS OF OTHER COLORS (YOU WILL NEED TWO COLORS FOR EACH NUMBER STENCIL THAT YOU CHOOSE)
- STENCIL CARD
- PENCIL
- SNAP-BLADE KNIFE
- PAINTER'S TAPE
- SPRAY ADHESIVE

PROJECT

Customizing a cheap computer desk in the hip-hop style

Everyone needs somewhere to work, but that doesn't mean it has to look boring and worthy. This project takes a really cheap, white-laminated, fiberboard desk and gives it street cred. The numerals could be exchanged for letters done in the same shadowed style, and whatever pattern you choose, remember it doesn't matter if it's slightly off-center or if the spray drifts a bit at the edges—it'll still look good.

A basketball style stencil has transformed this cheap, white, fiberboard desk. Add stickers, labels and logos to complete the look.

HOW TO DO IT

STEP 1 Take a photocopy from a favorite sports sweatshirt.

STEP 2 Enlarge the numerals to about 11 in./30 cm in length and transfer the patterns onto the stencil card. Cut out two stencils. One should just be the letter outline, the other should have stencil bridges added on letters such as Os and Rs, to keep the shape intact.

STEP 3 Use a snap-blade knife to cut out the stencils. Spray the back with spray adhesive. One stencil is for the main motif, the other for the border.

STEP 4 Protect a well-ventilated area with lots of newspaper and then roller or brush the aluminum paint onto the desk.

STEP 5 Attach the first stencil to the desk with painter's tape.

STEP 6 Spray this with your first chosen color. Spray through the second stencil in the second color to create the border. Repeat this as many times as you like on the top, the outsides, and insides, and then add as many stickers, logos, and labels as you like.

Teenage girl's room

Decorating is influenced by changes in fashion, and never more so than in a teenage girl's room. The big problem is that fashion is an industry and in order to keep it ticking over, looks have to change with the seasons. What is totally "in" now might be totally "out" in six months' time. Do not despair, though: there are a few hardy perennials that manage to stay cool throughout, and denim tops the chart. The blue-denim theme runs through all the projects in this section, but apart from the cushion cover made from old jeans, the same methods could be used to suit different fabrics.

Plan any bedroom make-over together and make sure she gets to choose the style. If you absolutely hate the combinations she chooses, you could always try reverse psychology and pretend it was exactly what you were thinking for the room too...

If this is the first major make-over since childhood, take time to plan the decorating together. If you're stuck for inspiration watch TV decorating programs and look through magazines, color charts, and fabric samples. Leaving the toys and other childhood paraphernalia behind is a big step in a girl's life. It can be a bit much if everything familiar and comforting is suddenly whisked away, so don't make big changes when she's not there.

A teenager's bedroom is much more than somewhere to sleep. It is a room to entertain friends, experiment with clothes and make-up, listen to music, and study. Planned well, it can be all these things and more. A good way of planning room space is to cut out paper versions of all the furniture and move it around on a room plan. Do this to scale using squared paper and draw in all the fixed features, like radiators, windows, doors, chimney breasts, alcoves, and any built-in closets or shelves. If the room is small, a platform bed with a desk underneath may be ideal, because they are now being made in stronger materials. They are a brilliant solution if space is limited, because all the sleep and study space is fitted into a compact area, and the rest of the room can be geared toward leisure.

Dressing table

A dressing table is not strictly necessary, but will be appreciated. Most girls need somewhere to keep a lot of nail polish, make-up, and hair-styling equipment. They also need mirrors—a long one to see the whole picture and a small one for close-ups. She will be the envy of all her friends if you wall-mount a mirror surrounded by light bulbs in the movie star's dressing-room style—use low-watt, soft-glow type bulbs.

Clothes will pile up on anything that stands still, and a small clothes rail on casters is a really good idea even if there is a perfectly good closet in the room. This is more like the rail a model would have backstage with a selection of outfits for the runway. Encourage her to keep her school clothes on the rail at night instead of on the floor and to keep other clothes on the rail or in the closet the rest of the time.

If, like most teenage girls, she likes to dance, you could divide the floor space in two and have carpet in one half and laminated wooden floorboards in the other. This only works in a medium to large room, and a small room would look bigger and better with a laminated floor and rugs. Don't scrimp on the padding—whatever flooring you choose, this will act as soundproofing.

Color

Wall colors are a personal choice, and the best thing is to step back and only offer your opinion if you're asked for it. If you absolutely hate the combinations she chooses, you could try reverse psychology and pretend that it's exactly what you had in mind for the dining room! If that doesn't cause an instant rethink, bear in mind that in the end it's only paint, and mistakes can always be put right with a coat of something less alarming.

The style of window treatment will very much depend on the overall look of the room—if she likes the ethnic look, something floaty like sari fabric would be lovely. A trip to a market is always fun and they are often a good place to buy ethnic accessories like lamps, cushions, and throws. If she prefers a more contemporary cool look, shades are the best bet. If you don't live near any trendy furniture stores, shades can be bought by mail order and come in a wide range of materials, including denim and felt.

A new set of bed linen also works wonders and she'll be spoilt for choice. There are colors and patterns to suit every style and mood, so be adventurous and investigate all the possibilities before making a decision.

Storage

Storage is far less of a nightmare than it used to be, because there are so many good systems on the market. They range from matching boxes that take everything from CDs to shoes, through modular storage cubes that can be added to if you need more space, to wire-basket closet organizers with stacks of drawers on casters. Send for all the manufacturers' catalogs, set yourselves a budget for buying storage equipment and take your pick. Shelves are always a good investment, and a high shelf on one wall makes a good retirement home for all those cuddly toys from childhood.

Lamps

Lamps are now fashionable accessories, having crossed over from furniture stores to gift stores. You will find they are sold alongside novelty greetings cards, cushions, and candles. Young consumers are very well aware of the latest trends, and a wacky bedside lamp is frequently rated as a top birthday or Christmas gift. On a more practical level, think about getting an anglepoise lamp for studying; and additionally a closet light will be useful. Finally, when all the hard work is done and the room looks out of this world, step back and let her take the credit for her wonderful design and inspiration. It will be worth it!

Alcoves can make interesting spaces for wall-mounted desks and bookshelves, keeping the homework side of the room to a compact corner.

THE PROJECTS

Two of the three projects on the following pages focus on denim, the fabric that refuses to date and the ultimate in cool.

YOU WILL NEED:

• DENIM—MEASURE THE WINDOW AREA AND THEN ADD HALF THE AREA AGAIN, PLUS A ¾-IN./2-CM SEAM ALLOWANCE TO ALL EDGES. NOTE THAT DENIM COMES IN DIFFERENT WIDTHS AND WEIGHTS. WIDTHS CAN BE JOINED WITH A JEANS-STYLE DOUBLE ROW OF ORANGE TOPSTITCHING.

• STRONG SEWING MACHINE NEEDLE (SOLD AS SUITABLE FOR DENIM)

• GRAY THREAD, NORMAL THICKNESS

• NEEDLE FOR HANDSTITCHING

• PINS

• IRON

• TAPE MEASURE

• SCISSORS

• BIG, BRIGHT BUTTONS, ONE PER TAB

• SEWING MACHINE

• STAINLESS STEEL DRAPE ROD

PROJECT
Denim tab-top drapes

Tab tops are really easy to make if you have a sewing machine. In fact, this is the best way to do it because denim is a heavyweight fabric, and very difficult to sew by hand. To jazz the denim up, sew a bright button at the bottom of each tab—you could also use metal stars, which are also very "jeans." The drape rod is stainless steel and can be purchased from any home center, although you could use copper piping instead. Line the drapes with a lightweight fabric which could be a plain color, gingham, or a floral print.

You can't go wrong with denim tab-top drapes, which are easy to make if you have a sewing machine.

HOW TO DO IT

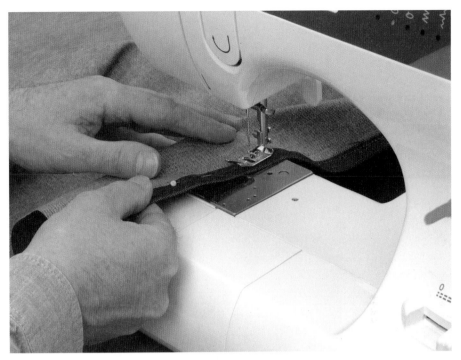

STEP 1 Cut a 6¼-in./16-cm-deep band the width of the fabric for the top of each drape. Cut two 10⅛ in. x 3⅛ in./26 cm x 8 cm strips per tab. They are spaced 4in/10 cm apart, so calculate how many you will need for your window. Cut the drape lengths to the drop, adding ¼ in./2 cm for turnover and an 3⅛-in./8-cm hem. Pin a ¼-in./2-cm seam down the sides.

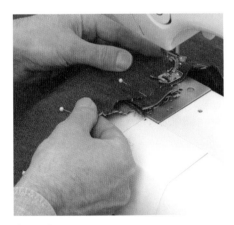

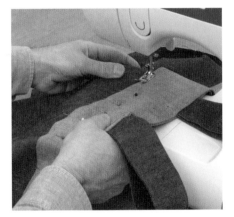

STEP 2 Stitch the side seams on the sewing machine using the gray thread. Turn over the hem and stitch this in the same way.

STEP 3 Place pairs of tabs together with right sides facing and stitch a seam on both sides. Turn them inside out and press flat with a hot iron. Fold them in half and press the fold.

STEP 4 Turn the drapes over and lay the tabs on top of the fabric with the raw ends slightly overlapping the top edge. Arrange them so that they are spaced 4 in./10 cm apart. Check that the folded ends form a straight line and the tabs are exactly the same length. Make any length adjustments at the other end.

STEP 5 Lay the 6¼-in./16-cm-deep band over the tabs on top of the drape with the dark side facing upward. Pin it in place keeping the tabs in their positions sandwiched between the two layers of fabric. Stitch all the way across, ¼ in./2 cm inside the top edge. Turn the band over. The tabs are now at the top, fully enclosed in the contrasting band. Turn the edge over and top-stitch the band to the drape. Sew a bright button on each tab.

YOU WILL NEED:

• A PAIR OF OLD JEANS

• SNAP-BLADE KNIFE

• BALL-POINT PEN

• RULER

• SCISSORS

• PINS

• SEWING MACHINE
  WITH NEEDLE FOR
  DENIM

• STRONG THREAD IN
  ORANGE OR RED

• POLYESTER BATTING

PROJECT
Cushion cover from old jeans

This is one way to immortalize your favorite jeans or, if the idea of cutting them up is too painful to contemplate, you could buy a second-hand pair from a charity store especially for the job. Extra trimmings can be added to spice the cushion up a bit—try a thick fringe, a broderie anglaise frill, velvet ribbons, or some metal stars.

Denim refuses to go away and fashion designers have given up trying to ignore it. They now bring out new variations, decorations, colors, styles, and hip labels. This cushion cover is made from an old pair of jeans.

HOW TO DO IT

STEP 1 Cut the legs of the jeans open along the front. Use a snap-blade knife to cut the stitching of the back pockets. Lay the fabric out flat.

STEP 2 Cut out a square paper pattern and pin this to the fabric. Cut out the two sides of the cushion in this way. Now re-stitch the pockets onto the center of each of the denim squares, using the strong orange or red thread.

STEP 4 Stuff the cushion with the polyester batting and slipstitch the seam closed. Sew on any extra trimmings, or pop a remote control into the pocket.

STEP 3 Lay the square down with right sides facing and pin a seam around the edge. Machine, sew the seam with a double row of stitches. Make sure that you leave a 4-in./10-cm gap open for the batting. Snip the corners up to the stitching and turn the cushion cover the right way out. Press the cushion cover with a hot iron.

YOU WILL NEED:

- ONE VARNISHED WOODEN DINING CHAIR
- PAINT STRIPPER TO REMOVE THE OLD VARNISH
- SCRAPER
- RUBBER GLOVES
- SANDPAPER
- STEEL WOOL
- WHITE WATER-BASE PRIMER
- LIGHT PINK AND DARK PINK LATEX PAINT
- 2-IN./5-CM PAINT BRUSH
- 20 IN./0.5 M FAKE FUR FABRIC
- STAPLE GUN
- FOAM PAD FOR SEAT
- SNAP-BLADE KNIFE
- CARPET-FITTING TAPE

PROJECT

Pink pony chair

In this project, an old wooden chair is given a funky fur make-over. Old wooden dining room chairs don't cost very much, and you can have a lot of fun searching yard sales for the perfect specimen. Look for a nice-shaped back and a seat that's in good condition.

Give an old dining chair a denim and fake-fur make-over for the ultimate in groovy chic. You could choose denim fabric instead of the fake fur, and paint the chair a toning denim-blue color instead of pink.

HOW TO DO IT

STEP 1 Begin by sanding the chair smooth. Use paint stripper to remove any old paint.

STEP 2 Prime the woodwork of the chair with white water-base primer.

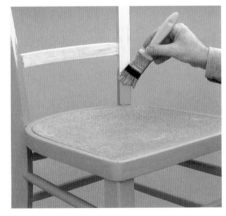

STEP 3 Apply the first coat of the darker pink paint.

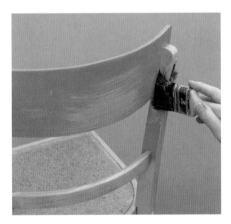

STEP 4 Lightly brush the second, paler pink color over the top of the first coat.

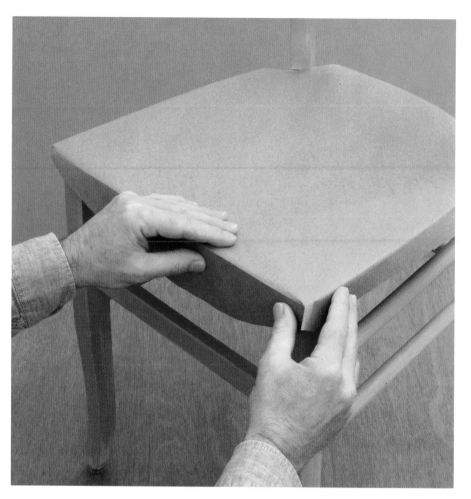

STEP 5 Gently wipe the paler top coat with a sponge to reveal parts of the dark pink paint.

STEP 6 When the paint is dry, fold brown paper over the seat, creasing at the edges, to make a template.

STEP 7 Cut out the paper template along the creases and place it on the foam pad. Cut round the template with a snap-blade knife.

STEP 8 Lay the paper template on the fur fabric and cut round it, leaving approximately 2 in./5 cm for the turnovers.

STEP 9 Cut notches in the fur fabric so that it will fit neatly around the curved foam seat pad.

STEP 10 Apply carpet-fitting tape to the foam pad. Peel off the backing.

STEP 11 Press the fur fabric onto the sticky surface, making sure there are no creases.

STEP 12 Stick down alternate notches as you go, easing the fabric around the curved edges.

STEP 13 Apply carpet-fitting tape to the seat of the chair, and stick the covered cushion down.

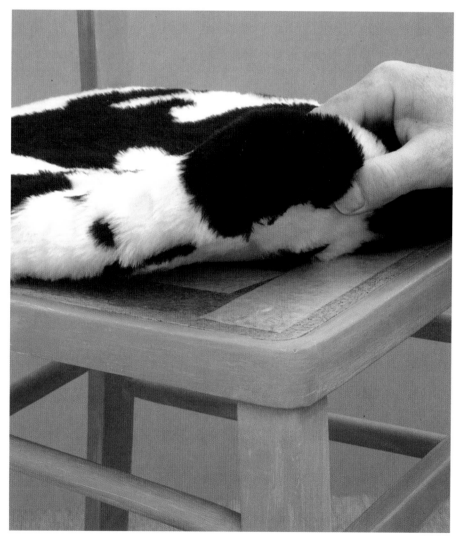

Children's bedrooms

Decorating a room for a child is brilliant fun. This is where you can experiment with paint effects, use bright colors, and live out all your own childhood fantasies. Whether or not you have a free hand will depend upon the age of your child, but you will know what they like best. All children have strong preferences for particular cartoon characters, animals, activities, and colors from an early age. The best thing is that children love to feel special, and decorating a room especially for them is always a big success.

Think about the effect of colors before you choose the wall paint. Yellow is sunny and happy, while blue is relaxing and dreamy. Avoid red walls at all costs!

Children grow out of any cozily decorated nursery quicker than you might expect, but there's more than just redecoration to do to a children's room. Five things to consider when revamping a children's room are …

1. Decorating

If the room is being redecorated for the first time since the nursery years, then it is time for a big change. The most obvious and the cheapest way to change a room is by painting it a fresh new color. Color is known to affect us psychologically, and this may be worth investigating before you reach for the primary colors. If the room is also going to be a playroom and workroom, color could be used to separate the areas. Green has calming, reassuring qualities; yellow is sunny, happy, and warm, blue is relaxing, and dreamy and for, obvious reasons, a good ceiling color. Red is far too powerful a wall color for a child's room but is good for fabrics and features. Boys often like orange, which is said to create a positive atmosphere, and all little girls have a pink phase, which may last for years: in fact, some never grow out of it! Also try Roman blinds because they are easy to make, and the design is basic enough to withstand rough treatment. Make them in nice bright fabric backed with black-out lining material so that the room can be darkened for bedtime.

2. Play areas

A school-age child will need some sort of work area for model building and painting. Kids need to feel they can relax and make a mess, and that you will not make too much fuss if they spill and scatter things. For this reason it is a good idea to have mess-friendly flooring such as vinyl, linoleum, cork, or laminated floorboards. Two colors of vinyl tiles can be laid as a checkerboard —white with yellow or grey looks good and not too overpowering. This sort of surface is good for all kinds of games as well—wheels speed across it and handstands can be done without slipping. Mats with a looped pile, more usually seen in the bathroom, are excellent because they come in lovely colors, are non-slip, and can be cleaned in the washing machine. If your child is older and wants a more sophisticated style, go for cork or laminated floorboards with a soft rug by the bedside, and colorful rugs to laze on.

3. Lighting

Good lighting is equally important because children like to see what they are doing clearly. They will also make a lot more mess if they can't find what they're looking for! Lights need to be fixed onto surfaces, otherwise there is the risk that they will be knocked over and cause a fire. Fix anglepoise lights to the worktop or wall above it, simple closet lights that come on when the door is opened, and a wall light above the bed for reading. A central pendant light is a "must" for brightening up the whole room, and small plug-in nightlights can be fitted into the wall outlets to give a soft glow.

4. Photographs

A frieze or pinboard on one wall will take care of all their favorite pictures, party invitations, paintings, and photographs. A closet door or section of wall could be painted with blackboard paint to make an instant chalkboard. Make it big enough for a few friends to work on at the same time and supply loads of brightly colored chalks. Also put a nice big mirror on the wall, and buy some easy-access frames so that photographs can be changed from time to time.

5. Books and toys

Keep bookshelves low down and accessible, but also have high, out-of-reach cabinets for storage. This is especially useful when young children go through the stage of pulling everything out of drawers and cabinets. Buy a set of matching toy boxes on casters, which can be pushed away under the bed or into the bottom of a closet. Also have separate places for paint brushes, construction kits, board games, and dolls with their clothes and accessories. If everything has a place, it is much easier to clear up. Try a row of pegs hung with orange plastic bags, which are great for small toys like bricks, cars, and marbles. If you can make a game of putting things away, it won't seem such a chore.

It is also worth buying or building a cabinet with deep shelves and a set of transparent plastic

crates. Label each crate with the name of an article of clothing, using a picture and the word, so that there is no confusion and everything stays in its own crate. Hooks on the back of the door or along the chair rail as shown in the project should take care of most things that you need to hang up. Child-size closets are also a good idea if you have a daughter with dresses—if the closet is adult size, fit an extra rod lower down for her to reach and the top rod can be used for out-of-season clothes.

When we have children, we often spend a great deal of time organizing their activities, lessons, and social events. It doesn't have to be this way all the time, though, and they also need to relax. Large floor cushions, beanbag chairs, or a small sofa-bed will also encourage them to think of the room as a place to snuggle down and think, read, and listen to stories.

A bed with storage space underneath is a good way of saving floor space. If the storage will be on show, like this bedroom, a matching set of brightly colored boxes will look fun, too.

THE PROJECTS

The projects on the following pages are a mixture of fun and function. Make sure you take your children's own preferences into account.

YOU WILL NEED:

- TONGUE-AND-GROOVE PANELING TO FIT AROUND THE WALLS (MEASURE AND BUY PANELING KIT PACKS TO FIT THE LENGTH REQUIRED)
- 3 LENGTHS OF 1-IN. X ½-IN./ 2.5-CM X 1.2-CM CLEATS FOR EACH WALL LENGTH
- SQUARE MOLDING TO FIT AROUND TOP OF PANELS (ONLY IF YOU ARE NOT FITTING THE PEG RAIL)
- ¼-IN./6-MM WALL ANCHORS
- BOX OF NUMBER 6 2-IN./5-CM SCREWS
- BOX OF 1-IN./2.5-CM BRADS
- SMALL HAMMER
- DRILL WITH ¼-IN./6-MM BIT AND SPADE BIT FOR PEGS
- FINE NAIL PUNCH
- MITER SAW, OR BLOCK WITH BACKSAW
- SCREWDRIVER
- LONG RULE WITH SPIRIT LEVEL
- PENCIL

PROJECT
Lining the walls with tongue-and-groove paneling

Wood paneling gives a very cozy, country feel to a room and the peg rail on pages 640–641 is such a useful addition that you will wonder how you ever managed without it. If you buy the tongue-and-groove paneling in kit form it will be pre-cut and ready to fix to the wall. If you cut the lengths yourself, you may like to make it slightly lower than usual, which has the effect of scaling down the room to the child's size. If you are impatient for the boarded effect, you can buy large panels of MDF that have been carved to give the effect of joined boards. They can simply be stuck to the wall using panel adhesive, although do bear in mind that removing them at a later date could affect the condition of the wall surface.

Tongue-and-groove paneling gives a children's room a cozy feel. The paneling can be bought in kit form and painted in your choice of colors. The "hockey-stick" molding on the top makes a useful shelf. For a wider shelf and row of pegs, see pages 640–641.

HOW TO DO IT

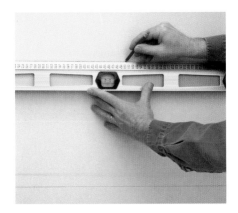

STEP 1 Using the long rule with spirit level, mark three positions for the cleats on the wall to align with the top, middle, and bottom of the panels.

STEP 2 Drill and insert wall anchors every 20 in./50 cm and then screw the cleats onto the wall.

STEP 3 Beginning in one corner, place the end plank against the wall and check the vertical with the spirit level. Hammer a pin through the inside edge of the tongue, angled slightly inward. Do this into all three cleats. Use the nail punch with the hammer to drive the pinhead below the surface.

STEP 4 Fit the groove of each subsequent plank into the tongue of the first. To ensure a tight fit, place a spare piece of wood along the edge, and tap it with the hammer to prevent damage to the plank's tongue. Continue in the same way to complete the paneling.

STEP 5 Fit a narrow cleat along the top edge of the paneling using brads and a nail punch.

STEP 6 Replace the baseboard, and then prime and paint the paneling in the color of your choice. If you are also fitting the rail and shelf, continue as explained in the steps overleaf, fitting the rail along the top of the paneling. If not, you will need to finish off the top of the panels with a square molding. This can be screwed into the wall or stuck with panel adhesive.

PROJECT
Fitting a peg rail and shelf

This can either be a continuation of the tongue-and-groove paneling project on the previous pages (pages 638–639), or a project on its own. If you decide against the paneling, you may not want to fit the peg rail and shelf on more than one wall. The directions allow for this, and explain the order and technique rather than giving exact measurements.

A row of pegs can make clearing up fun. Hang a row of brightly colored bags on the pegs to hold small toys like bricks, cars, or marbles, or hang the toys directly on the pegs themselves. The shelf above offers even more storage space.

HOW TO DO IT

STEP 1 Cut the peg rail plank to fit the wall lengths, mitering the ends for a neat fit in the corners and at any joins. Check and mark the rail position on the wall with the long rule with the spirit level. Drill clearance holes in the planks, then mark, drill, and plug the wall, and screw the peg rail in place.

STEP 2 Use the spade bit to drill holes for the pegs and then apply wood glue to their ends before pushing them firmly into the rail. If the pegs are to be painted different colors, it may be easier to do this before you fit them.

STEP 3 Screw the peg rail to the wall.

STEP 4 Add a shelf to the top of the peg rail. Screw the shelf to the peg rail and through into the wall cleat. Prime and paint.

YOU WILL NEED:
- **WHITE WOOD PRIMER**
- **2 BRIGHT-COLORED TEST POTS OF LATEX PLUS CLEAR VARNISH, OR 2 VINYL SILK OR LOW LUSTER COLORS**
- **WATER-BASE BLACKBOARD PAINT**
- **SMALL FOAM ROLLER AND TRAY**
- **PAINT BRUSHES**
- **SANDPAPER**

PROJECT
Painting MDF furniture and using blackboard paint

An ideal project to encourage your children's writing skills (or at least their naughts and crosses!) This is a small painting project that will make a big difference. Incorporate your children's two favorite colors to make it personal. You could apply the idea to any piece of furniture you already own, find a second-hand piece to makeover, or buy an unpainted MDF blank. Blanks are nicely designed pieces of furniture made especially for people who enjoy applying the paint themselves. They are sold by mail order, and the money saved by not painting them is reflected in the price. You will find an address in the directory at the back of the book.

HOW TO DO IT

STEP 1 Sand the old paint to create a good surface for the paint to key into.

STEP 2 Prime the whole unit using a white water-base paint.

STEP 3 If the furniture has panels, paint as shown. If not, draw a square on the front. Edge with painter's tape.

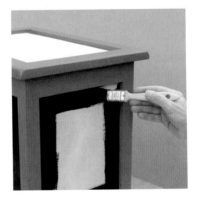

STEP 4 Apply two coats of blackboard paint and wait until dry before removing the tape.

PROJECT
Making photocopied fun cushions

T-shirt printing is available at most photocopying stores, and any image not protected by copyright laws can be photocopied onto a special film and transferred onto fabric. The image could be a photograph of your dog; a a cartoon figure; or an original drawing, cut-out, or pattern. Take a plain white square of cotton fabric to the photocopying store and ask them to transfer the image onto the fabric, then take it home and make up a cushion. The transfer film can also be bought for home use with a computer scanner and printer.

HOW TO DO IT

STEP 1 Cut out a square of white cotton fabric measuring roughly 16 in. x 16 in./40 cm x 40 cm. Choose an image to be photocopied and trim it to a square shape.

STEP 2 Mark the size and position for the print on the white cotton fabric, and take this to the photocopiers. Ask them to enlarge and print the image onto your fabric.

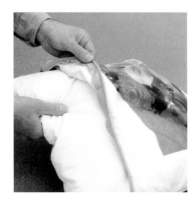

STEP 3 Fold back a small hem on the printed fabric and pin it to the front of the cushion cover. Slipstitch by hand, or machine-stitch.

Fantasy bedroom

Parents often find that having a young child gives them the opportunity to rediscover their artistic side, which may have been neglected since they left school. It's fantastic when you realize that the time has come to put all those skills learned in woodwork, art, and design lessons to good use.

Children's bedrooms are often also their playrooms, so fun is a number one priority. But apart from safety and comfort, there are no rules when it comes to decorating children's rooms, so you can let your imagination run wild!

A lot of the most exciting decorating programs on TV create rooms that are a mixture of window dressing and stage design adapted for the home. Children's bedrooms can be treated in the same way, and all you need are basic skills, time, and imagination. There is no reason why their beds have to look like beds—so long as they are safe and comfortable to sleep in, they can be anything from caves to castles. The same approach can be used to transform the whole room into a complete fantasy world.

MDF beds

Children's beds can be costly, but you can make your own from MDF. The design chosen for the project on the following pages is a castle, and whether you have a sleeping beauty or knight in shining armor, the bed is sure to be a hit.

The one good reason why MDF is so popular is that it has no grain. When you work with natural wood, the direction of the grain is very important, particularly when cutting and planing. This is because the wood splits along the grain. If, for instance, you insert a row of screws in a line along the grain, the wood is very likely to split. Softwood is most prone to splitting because it is harvested from fast-growing trees and the grain is less dense than with hardwood, which comes from slow-growing trees.

MDF is short for medium-density fiberboard. It is made from small, even-sized particles of wood, which have been mixed with a chemical compound to bind them together before being compacted into sheets. You should always wear a mask when sawing through MDF, because the dust contains those binding chemical compounds, which can be harmful, and it is best not to do the cutting work in your child's bedroom, where the fine dust will be difficult to clear away completely. Once MDF is cut out and painted, it presents no greater health risk than any other construction material. The good news is that MDF can be cut into all kinds of shapes with a jigsaw. A bed like a castle is easy!

The castle theme

Once you have made the bed, turn your attention to other areas in the room in order to extend the castle theme further. If you have shelving, it can be edged with strips cut out in the shape of battlements, and the bedcover could perhaps be decorated with appliqué shields or knight's heraldic flags. Drape poles can have arrow-head finials (securely screwed to the wall!), and the toy chest could be made to look just like a king's treasure chest.

If you are making the castle for a princess, she will probably also like the idea of a climbing rose winding its way up the battlements, with a

THE PROJECTS

The projects on the following pages show how to make and paint a castle bed. Some battlement shelving, a heraldic bedcover, and a king's treasure chest will complete the castle theme.

painted crown about her pillow and a silky bedcover to sleep under. Think of Queen Guinevere in Camelot, where ladies were wrapped in velvet trimmed with lace. However, if she happens to be more of a Joan of Arc, it might be wiser to stick to battlements and suits of armor!

Role play is a favorite children's activity, so if their bedroom is designed like a stage, with a number of different scenes and settings, they'll be in heaven!

YOU WILL NEED:

- **2 SIDES:**
  ¾-IN./1.8-CM MDF,
  78 IN. X 39 IN./
  2 M X 1 M
- **2 ENDS:**
  ¾-IN./1.8-CM MDF,
  34 IN. X 39 IN./85
  CM X 1 M
- **4 LEGS:**
  2 IN.X 2 IN./
  5 CM X 5 CM, PAR
  16 IN./40 CM
- **2 SIDE CLEATS:**
  1½ IN. X 1½ IN.
  3.8 CM X 3.8 CM/
  PAR 75 IN./1.9 M
- **8 SLATS FOR BASE:**
  1 IN. X 6 IN./
  2.5 CM X 15 CM PAR,
  32 IN./81 CM
- **WOOD GLUE**
- **WOOD FILLER**
- **SANDPAPER**
- **BOX OF 2-IN/5-CM.
  NUMBER 6 SCREWS**
- **FACE MASK**
- **JIGSAW**
- **DRILL WITH
  ¹⁄₁₆-IN./2-MM,
  ⅛-IN./4-MM AND
  COUNTERSINK BIT**
- **SCREWDRIVER**
- **TAPE MEASURE**
- **LONG RULE**
- **PENCIL**
- **COMBINATION
  SQUARE**

MDF is a perfect
material for
cutting out a
castle's battlements.
You could choose
a different kind of
building if you're
not so keen on the
castle idea.

PROJECT
The castle bed

This plan for the castle bed tells you what you need and exactly how it is made. This is the first stage of the project, and in the next stage there are ideas for how it can be painted. If you are keen to make a bed but not so keen on the castle idea, then the plan could be adapted. You could use the same basic construction method, but change the cut-out shape to give the bed a different theme. Cars and engines are always popular with boys. If your child has a favorite story or cartoon, that would be a good place to look for inspiration.

HOW TO DO IT

This makes a bed that will fit a standard 32-in./80-cm-wide mattress.

STEP 1 Support the MDF between two saw horses or tables and draw the cut-outs on the ends and the sides. Draw positional guidelines on the sides for the legs and the side cleats. Use the long rule to draw them as continuous pencil lines.

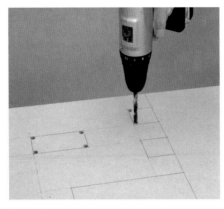

STEP 2 Drill holes in the corners of each of the cut-outs to access the saw blade.

STEP 3 Wear a mask! Use the jigsaw carefully to cut out the shapes, then use sandpaper to round off the edges paying particular attention to the sides of the bed where the child will be climbing in and out.

STEP 4 Drill the pilot holes and countersink holes for the screws.

STEP 5 Glue and screw the legs and side cleats in place.

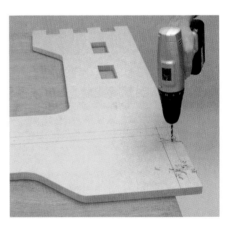

STEP 6 Draw positional guides on the two ends for the legs, and to mark where the bed ends meet the sides on the MDF. Drill pilot holes and countersink the screws.

STEP 7 Drill, glue, and screw the MDF panels to the legs of the bed.

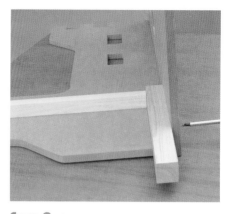

STEP 8 Glue and screw the ends to the sides.

STEP 9 Space out the base slats (mattress supports) and then drill pilot holes, and glue and screw them to the bed. Fill all the countersink holes and sandpaper smooth once the filler has set.

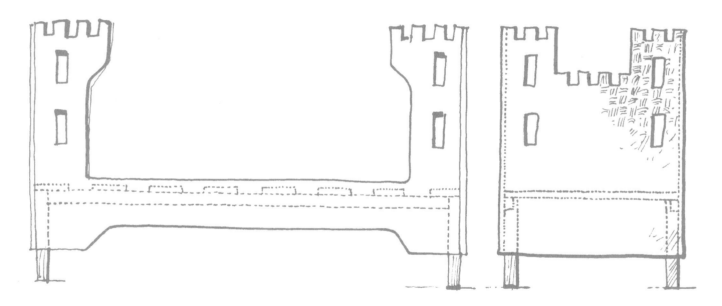

Follow these guidelines when you are making up your castle bed. Remember to measure everything properly and use a spirit level to check that everything is level.

PROJECT
Painting the castle bed

The method described here is just one way to paint the castle bed. There are other ways of painting it—you may prefer to paint it freehand, or all in one color (see picture on page 646).

This project shows a quick and easy way of giving the castle bed the appearance of weathered brickwork. You could use this method with another pale color, such as light blue.

YOU WILL NEED:

- FOAM OFF-CUTS ROUGHLY 2 IN./5 CM SQUARE
- PLATE
- SMALL FOAM ROLLER AND TRAY
- LATEX PAINT IN DARK AND LIGHT GRAY
- CLEAR MATTE VARNISH

HOW TO DO IT

STEP 1 Cut three or four foam squares into rough stone shapes. They can vary in size and be rounded off at the corners.

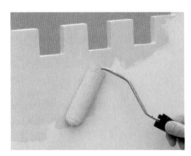

STEP 2 Use the foam roller to paint the entire bed in a base coat of light gray, or another pale color, such as light blue.

STEP 3 Thin the darker paint with water, 2 parts paint to 1 part water, then use the foam blocks to build up the castle brickwork. Cover with a coat of clear varnish when dry.

Nursery

When it comes to preparing for a new arrival, our instincts are like any animal's. We want to make a cozy nest and have everything ready for the big day. Nature is a wonderful thing, and even if you have never looked twice at a frieze of fluffy bunnies or frolicking lambs before, you will find the choice is suddenly a major one! A baby opens up a whole new world and it's amazing that something so small needs that much stuff. In truth, they don't but we do, and as long as we keep spending, manufacturers will keep coming up with new ideas to make life with a baby easier.

These flimsy drapes may look nice, but they will make it impossible to encourage a baby to sleep in the daylight.

Decorating a nursery for a first baby is one of life's luxuries. The baby won't mind how you decorate it, but it gives expectant parents something positive to do, and there are lots of things to look out for.

Colors

If you already know the sex of your baby, you may want to follow a traditional pink or blue color scheme, or the usual alternative, which has always been pale yellow. One good reason for sticking to these colors is that they are the colors of most products, gifts, and accessories for babies. Strong primary colors like red, yellow, and blue are great for later on, but they seem very harsh for a nursery. There are more gentle contemporary colors if you wish to avoid the pinks and blues, such as moss green, pale sea green, lavender, apricot, and buttery cream.

It may be difficult to imagine, but your baby will soon be a rampaging toddler and it is worth keeping this in mind when you decorate. Try to choose colors and styles that will either be appropriate later on, or which can be added to or adapted for a growing child.

Windows

The most important thing you need to know about nursery windows is that they need to have drapes or blinds that block out the light completely. This can be done by lining drapes with black or navy fabric or using special black-out lining fabric. Flimsy muslin drapes will do nothing to convince a baby that it's time to sleep if the sun is still shining outside!

Roller shades are fine for babies before they begin to investigate the way things work, but can be something of a hazard later on when the pulls are grabbed too hard or suddenly let go of so that they shoot out of reach. Roman blinds fold up and down and are a better bet because they don't need stiffening, can be lined with black-out, and are surprisingly easy to make.

Changing

Babies generate an incredible amount of washing and you will need one or two laundry bins. Two will enable you to sort out the more urgent toweling hot wash from the rest when you change your baby. Changing diapers and baby clothes can be a back-breaking task if you are constantly leaning over, and it will be a lot easier if you have a changing table with everything you need close at hand. Baby clothes can be kept handy in drawers or baskets below, with absorbent cotton, wipes, and diapers all being within easy reach on the table top.

Sitting

In the early months you will want a comfortable chair to sit in while you're feeding the baby. Have a small table with a lamp to read by as well, because you may want to consult any baby books you have or just need somewhere safe to put a drink down. Once your baby begins to crawl and climb up, everything that could topple over like a small table with a lamp should be removed from the room to prevent accidents.

Lighting

Central lights are the best and safest option in the nursery. Look out for a fabulous lampshade

that will give your baby something to gaze at. Safe nightlights made specially for a child's room can also be great fun, especially the ones that turn round and project images on the walls—babies love them.

Sleeping

The decision whether to buy a crib or a cot is a personal one. A cot is more practical because it will last for about three years, though tiny babies do look lost in them, but a crib is so sweet and it is almost impossible to wear one out. Full-size cots are adjustable to three different heights. If you decide to use one from the start, have it at the highest level to avoid too much bending and move it down as soon as your baby starts pulling up on the bars.

Pinks and blues are the colors of most baby products, gifts and accessories, so it makes sense to use these colors for the walls.

PROJECT

Painting a gingham wall

Gingham is one of the freshest fabrics around and it will never, ever go out of fashion. This project shows how to customize a small foam roller and give the nursery walls a gingham effect. You can do this on a colored background if you prefer, but white is traditional and always makes a room look bigger and brighter. Most nursery borders look good with gingham, and if you buy one first, you can coordinate the colors.

Gingham made easy—a simple trick with a small foam roller can transform a nursery wall, making it look bigger and brighter.

HOW TO DO IT

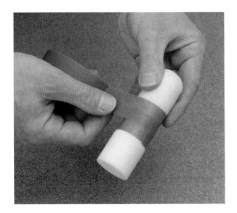

STEP 1 Wrap the painter's tape around the middle of the roller, dividing it into three equal parts.

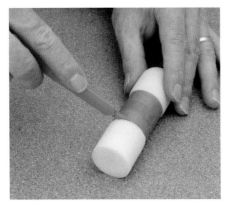

STEP 2 Cut down to the middle of the roller in a straight line following the edge of the tape. Turn the roller and cut all the way around, then once across between the lines.

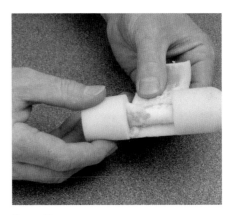

STEP 3 Peel off the middle foam section, then peel off the painter's tape.

STEP 4 Mix the wallpaper paste following the directions on the pack, and then mix it half and half with the latex paint in the roller tray.

STEP 5 Hang the plumb line from the top of the wall to give you a vertical guide to follow. Run the roller through the paint/wallpaper paste mixture and begin painting in one corner, applying a medium pressure and continuing to within about 2 in./5 cm of the baseboard. This final bit can be filled in with the offcut from the roller. Continue in this way to complete all the vertical stripes.

STEP 6 Place the spirit level on the wall and make some small guide marks for the first horizontal band of striping. The next stripes can be aligned with the first, but check with the level on each alternate row so that you don't drift away from the horizontal.

YOU WILL NEED:
- **1 BASE:**
  CUT FROM
  ¾-IN./1.8-CM MDF
  THIS SHOULD BE
  31 IN./78 CM-DEEP
  (FROM FRONT
  TO BACK) AND THE
  WIDTH OF THE CHEST
  OF DRAWERS PLUS
  ³⁄₁₆ IN./5MM ON
  EACH SIDE
- **1 CLEAT:**
  2 IN. X 1 IN./
  5 CM X 2.5 CM, THE
  WIDTH OF THE MDF
- **2 SIDES:**
  6 IN. X 1 IN. X 31 IN./
  1.5 CM X 2.5 CM X
  78 CM PAR
  SOFTWOOD
- **1 BACK:**
  6 IN. X 1 IN./
  15 CM X 2.5 CM PAR
  SOFTWOOD, WIDTH
  OF CHEST OF
  DRAWERS PLUS
  ³⁄₈ IN./1 CM
- JIGSAW
- BRADS
- WOOD GLUE
- NAIL PUNCH
- FILLER
- DRILL WITH
  ¹⁄₁₆-IN./2-MM
  PILOT BIT AND
  COUNTERSINK BIT
- 2-IN./5-CM
  NUMBER 6 SCREWS
- SANDPAPER
- PAINT

PROJECT
Making a removable changingtable top

The first few months with a new baby can be very tiring, and it is impossible to imagine how back-breaking diaper changing can be if you are constantly bending over. This project shows you how to make a table top that can sit on a chest of drawers, a small desk, or even a single kitchen cabinet at the right height, to make diaper-changing a thousand times easier. It has been designed to be used lengthwise with the back pushed up against the wall, and the supporting chest of drawers or desk pulled forward so that the front is level with the edge of the unit. Any foam-padded, sponge-cleanable changing mat will fit into the wooden frame. The exact dimensions will depend upon the size of the piece of furniture you are using as a base.

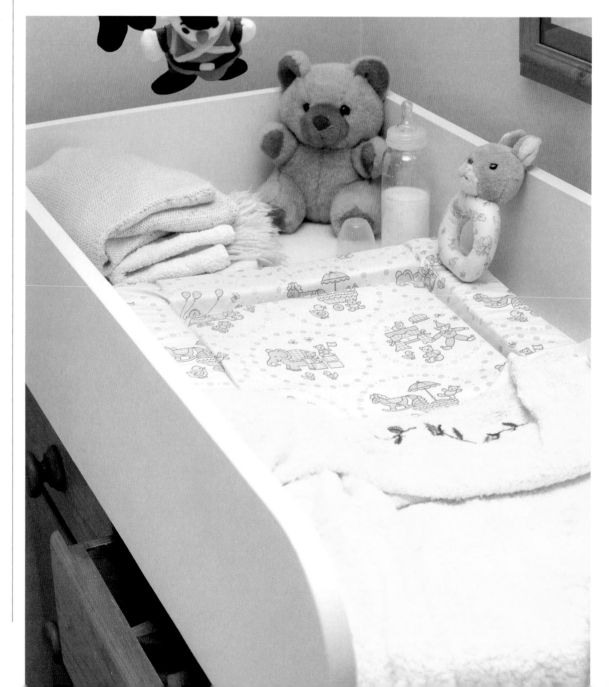

A portable table top for diaper changing makes the task far less back-breaking. Decide which piece of furniture you will use underneath before working out the dimensions.

HOW TO DO IT

STEP 1 Jigsaw all MDF to shape. Mark the base position on the back board and mark, screw, drills and countersink the screws.

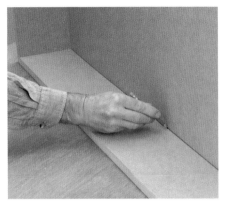

STEP 2 Place the top on your base in line with the front, and draw a line to mark the back edge.

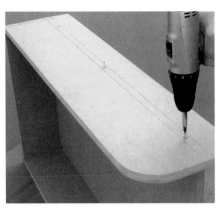

STEP 3 Draw location guides on the base for the sides and the back. Drill pilot and countersunk holes for the screws.

STEP 4 Fill the screw holes with filler.

STEP 5 Sandpaper all the edges of the unit to smooth and round them off, and then prime and paint the unit.

PROJECT
Fish mobile

There is one other essential ingredient to keep a baby happy in the nursery, and that is a mobile. It is made from simple felt shapes hung from three mobile wires on nylon thread. Make sure that the mobile is always well out of the baby's reach.

This colorful fish mobile, made out of simple felt shapes, will provide a welcome distraction for a baby in his or her cot.

HOW TO DO IT

STEP 1 Draw a fish shape onto a piece of card and cut it out. Use this as a template to draw fish shapes on the felt. Cut out the felt fish shapes and put them together in pairs. Sew around the outside, leaving a small gap for the stuffing. Stuff each fish with a small amount of cotton batting, and slipstitch around the edge.

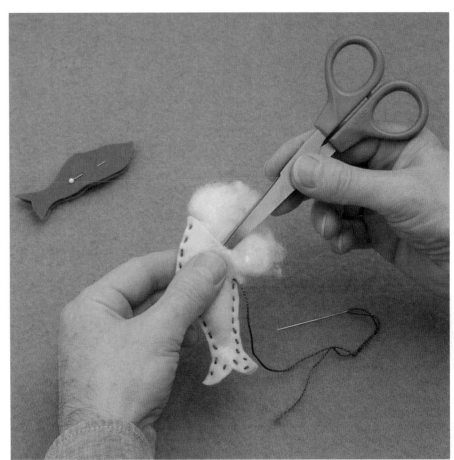

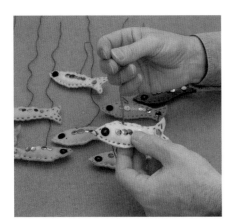

STEP 2 Glue the sequins onto the middle of the fish as scales. Sew two small buttons on each one for eyes. Stitch the gap closed.

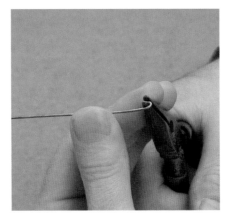

STEP 3 Twist lengths of wire over at both ends making loops. Thread a short length of fishing line onto a needle and attach a line to each fish. Tie the lines onto the wires. Screw a hook to the ceiling and hang the fish mobile over the cot or changing area.

Bathrooms

Today's bathrooms are more than simply a place to wash. They have

become sanctuaries for pampering and indulgence, a tranquil retreat

in which to relax and unwind, a beauty salon in your own home.

As one of the first rooms you see in the morning and one of the last

you see at night, it's no wonder the decor and style can make such a

difference to how you start or end the day. This section shows how to

transform your bathroom into one of two different styles, Traditional

or Contemporary, before looking specifically at the shower room.

Choose a style, choose a project, and go full steam ahead!

Traditional bathroom

The bathrooms that we now tend to think of as being traditional are actually early 20th-century in style, when the bathroom first became a feature in ordinary people's houses. Modern Westerners were a bit slow on the uptake as far as bathrooms went, but the Ancient Romans had stunning baths and flushing lavatories. There was a gap until the first bathtub was instaled in the White House in 1851, and there was no bathroom in Buckingham Palace when Queen Victoria was crowned in 1837. By the end of her reign, all kinds of bathroom fixtures had been invented, including stand-up showers, short and long bathtubs, flushing lavatories, mixer faucets and heated towel rails. And now there has never been more choice in bathroom fittings and fixtures, so whatever your idea of traditional may be, you can satisfy every whim.

A free-standing bathtub positioned in the center of the room with an old-style shower above looks wonderful. If you're buying an old iron bath, check your floor joists are strong enough to support it.

With such a huge choice of bathroom fittings and fixtures, it's a good idea to make a list of the things you would like in your traditional bathroom before you begin redecorating. Nine things to consider are …

Planning

If you are planning a complete bathroom refit, this is a good opportunity to move things around. Just because the bathtub is against one wall doesn't mean that this is the only place for it. Now is your big chance to give the bathroom a complete new look. The best way to begin is to visit a bathroom showroom—the most upmarket one you can find—and pick up all the latest catalogs. Always start by looking at the best designs and work backward to something that suits your budget. That way you will immediately be able to spot the best features in the cheaper range, and see where savings can be made without any loss of style.

Some bathroom catalogs include a planning section, but if not you can make one yourself using graph paper and scaled down cut-outs of the main fixtures. Mark the position of the window and door on your plan, and then see if the bathtub, basin, or lavatory are in the best places. If the door takes up space when open, perhaps it could be re-hung to open outward or even be moved farther along the wall. Pipes and the electricity supply can always be re-routed if a new arrangement makes more sense. And if you have a large bathroom, the bath could be moved away from the wall into the middle of the room. Plan the lighting at the beginning of the project, and make the most of any natural light by painting the window frames white and fitting shades into the frame recess. If you have a window with a view that is not overlooked, position the bathtub, so that you can enjoy the view from it. Mirrors should be placed in both useful and flattering positions!

Old v new fixtures and fittings

If you choose a period-style bathroom suite, you can opt for the real thing or a reproduction version. Many companies make reconditioned

Original wooden floorboards look lovely in a traditional bathroom, either stripped and painted with a waterproof floor paint, or simply stripped and varnished.

bathtubs and basins, or you could visit an architectural salvage yard, which is great fun and usually has lower prices than antique stores. Before buying an old iron bathtub you must find out whether your bathroom floor joists are strong enough to support its weight plus 242 lb./110 kg of water plus a person! Old faucets may look wonderful, but might not have the right-size pipe connectors for modern plumbing, so do find out what it will cost to have them updated before celebrating your bargain buy. Since most old styles of fixtures and fittings have been copied, it is often best to buy the repro versions. Old lace shelf-edgings, glass bottles, mirror frames, and shelves add to the atmosphere without costing a fortune. And treat yourself, at least once, to expensive bottled bath products to display on the shelves—you can always refill them with cheaper versions!

Showers

A separate shower room is ideal and it does not have to be much bigger than the average stall, but for most people a shower has to be fitted into the bathroom, either as a self-contained stall or over the bathtub. There are lots of options, and it is best to get advice from an expert. Begin by asking a plumber which system is best suited to your home. It will depend upon several factors, including the siting of your cold water tank, the water pressure, and your boiler type. Armed with this information, you will be able to pass on the technical details to the sales staff, and confine your efforts to your favorite style. If you are fitting a power shower unit over a bathtub, a shower drape will not be enough to protect the surroundings, and you will need to have a panel or folding screen, which can be quite costly.

Electricity

Never be tempted to do an electrical job yourself in the bathroom. Wait until you've got a few jobs that need doing and then employ a qualified electrician to instal new fittings and check old ones at the same time. All switches should be outside the bathroom, and an electrician will make sure that all the correct procedures are followed.

Lighting

Bathroom light fittings must have suitable sealed units for safety reasons. All switches must be pull-cords, and all fittings must be kept well clear of any potential splashes. The lighting should create a relaxing atmosphere, with efficient illumination where it is most needed.

Walls

Steamy bathrooms need walls with water-resistant surfaces, which is why glazed tiles are so practical around basins, lavatories and bathtubs. The damp that often occurs in bathrooms happens when they are not very well ventilated in winter and condensation becomes a problem. You can buy special paints for bathrooms made with added fungicides to combat mold, but if you don't want to introduce such chemicals into the atmosphere, then stick to an oil-based low luster or enamel paint, or latex paint sealed with waterproof varnish.

One of the projects in this section shows how to line a bathroom with tongue-and-groove paneling. Although it is an old idea, it has now become the most popular alternative to tiling. It is not necessary to remove old tiles when you change to paneling, or indeed when you change tiles because the new surface can simply be laid over the existing tiles. If you are re-tiling, do it in a brickwork pattern to give the tiles a brand-new look. If you want to refresh the tiling on a tight budget, use tile paint to change the color or simply re-grout the existing tiles to give them a fresh new look.

Floors

Bathroom floors get wetter than any other floor in the home, especially if you have young children, and there is no doubt that nonslip, sheet vinyl is the best option. This can be sealed along the edges with silicone so that no water can seep underneath. The range of patterns and prices is huge, and there will be something to suit all tastes and budgets. Small bathrooms could be tackled with off-cuts, so get measuring before you visit a showroom and check whether they have a selection of roll ends. If you prefer carpets, choose one with a rot-proof latex backing, and use a bath mat with waterproof backing as well. Floating wooden floors are not suitable for bathrooms, but original wooden floorboards look lovely stripped and varnished or painted

Wood paneling is an old idea, but for those not keen on tiling it is the most popular choice. The paneling can be laid over existing tiles to save work in removing them.

with a waterproof floor paint. A stenciled pattern or different shades or colors for the border create further interest.

Storage

All your hard work will be wasted if the bathroom becomes cluttered with shampoo bottles, lotions, and toothbrushes. Assess your space and make the most of any dead areas for storage. They include wall-to-ceiling space above the lavatory and the bathtub, and the wall under the sink. If extra towels are to be kept in the bathroom, they can be folded and displayed.

Essential luxury

A bathroom is a room for self-indulgence, somewhere to relax and recharge your batteries.

It is a room for indulging in small luxuries, and these should be included in the budget for your bathroom project. Scented candles, bubble bath, a large, fluffy towel on a heated rail, and a comfortable bath mat can make you feel as pampered as any supermodel. Remember that not everything in the bathroom has to have hard edges and, if you have the space for it, try to find room for an upholstered chair to help create a relaxed atmosphere.

Cabinets can help hide cleaning materials, spare bathroom rolls, and toiletry clutter in your bathroom. Look for some dead space in the bathroom, where you could fit a small freestanding or wall-mounted cabinet.

THE PROJECTS

The four projects on the following pages will help achieve a traditional background in your bathroom. Some period-style fixtures and fittings and a big pile of fluffy towels should do the rest.

YOU WILL NEED:

- TONGUE-AND-
  GROOVE PANELING
  TO FIT AROUND THE
  WALLS. (MEASURE
  AND BUY PANELING
  KITS TO FIT THE
  LENGTH REQUIRED)
- THREE LENGTHS OF
  1-IN. X 1½-IN./
  1.2-CM X 2.5-CM
  CLEATS FOR EACH
  WALL LENGTH
- SHELF 3-IN. X 1-IN./
  7.5-CM X 2.5-CM PAR
  SOFTWOOD TO FIT
  AROUND THE ROOM
  (MEASURE THE
  LENGTH REQUIRED)
- SUPPORT BRACKETS
  FOR THE SHELF
  TO BE SPACED
  24 IN./60 CM APART
- ¼-IN./6-MM
  WALL ANCHORS
- BOX OF NUMBER 6,
  2-IN./5-CM SCREWS
- BOX OF 1-IN./2.5-CM
  PANEL BRADS
- SMALL HAMMER
- NAIL PUNCH
- DRILL WITH ¼-IN./
  6-MM AND
  ¹⁄₁₆-IN./2-MM
  PILOT BIT
- FINE CENTER PUNCH
- MITER SAW OR
  BLOCK WITH
  BACKSAW
- SCREWDRIVER
- LONG RULE WITH
  SPIRIT LEVEL
- PENCIL

PROJECT
Lining the walls with tongue-and-groove paneling

This is a lovely style for a bathroom and can be given a country or seaside accent, depending upon the color and paint finish used. You may even like the idea of staining the wood dark brown to give it a distinctly masculine style. The shelf around the top of the paneling can have hooks screwed into it for hanging up small hand towels and face cloths.

Wooden paneling can be customized to the style you want by the choice of paint color—blues and greens for a seaside theme, or earthy browns and creams for a country feel. Dark-brown wood stain will give it a masculine style.

HOW TO DO IT

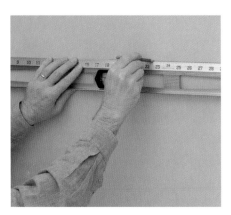

STEP 1 Use the long rule with spirit level to mark three positions for the cleating on the wall, to align with the top, middle, and bottom of the panels. Drill and insert wall anchors spaced 20 in./50 cm apart, and then screw the cleats onto the wall.

STEP 2 Beginning in one corner, place the end plank against the wall and check the vertical with the spirit level. Hammer a pin through the inside edge of the tongue angled slightly inward. Do this into all three cleats. Use the nail punch with the hammer to drive the brad head below the surface.

STEP 3 Fit the groove of the next plank into the tongue of the first. To ensure a tight fit, place a spare piece of wood along the edge and tap it with the hammer. Continue in the same way to complete the paneling. Planks will almost certainly need to be cut down to fit at the corners. Draw a line where this is required, clamp the plank in the jaws of a workbench, and cut with a backsaw or power saw.

STEP 4 Use a nail punch to knock the brad heads into the wood.

STEP 5 Cut the shelf planks to fit the wall lengths, mitering the ends for a neat fit in the corners and at any joins. Check and mark the shelf position on the wall with a spirit level. Drill pilot holes in the planks and the panels for the brackets.

STEP 6 Screw the brackets into the front of the paneling and down through the shelf into the top of the brackets. Prime and paint the paneling with enamel, or latex sealed with marine-quality varnish.

YOU WILL NEED:

- STRIP OF
  HARDBOARD ABOUT
  3 IN./7.5 CM DEEP.
  MEASURE AROUND
  THE BASIN FOR THE
  LENGTH
- 2 CLEATS TO HOLD
  HARDBOARD
- 4 NUMBER 10,
  3-IN./7.5-CM
  SCREWS
- ¼-IN./7-MM
  WALL ANCHORS
- HARDBOARD PINS
- DRAPE FABRIC—FOR
  GATHERED EFFECT
  BUY DOUBLE THE
  WIDTH
- STRONG SELF-
  ADHESIVE VELCRO
- STRONG CLEAR GLUE
  TO ATTACH
  TRIMMING
- DRILL WITH ¼-IN /
  7-MM MASONRY BIT
- SMALL HAMMER
- STAPLE GUN (ONLY
  IF YOU'RE NOT
  USING VELCRO)

PROJECT
Hanging a drape below a basin

This project makes a pretty addition to a traditional bathroom, and also provides a concealed storage area below the basin for cleaning materials. Basins are made to many different designs, some rounded and others square at the front. Hardboard is used here to make a curved strip, which fixes on to the wall behind the basin. The drape is attached with strong Velcro, but for a quick fix you could use staples instead, and then cover the staples with a braid or ribbon held in place with strong glue. This will make it harder to remove and wash.

A simple, curved strip of hardboard provides a drape rail around a basin, creating extra storage space beneath the basin as well as an attractive bathroom feature.

HOW TO DO IT

STEP 1 Mark the positions for the two wall cleats just below the outside edge of the basin, using a ruler and pencil.

STEP 2 Drill two holes to secure each cleat and fit them with wall anchors. Screw the cleats in position.

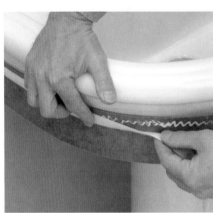

STEP 4 Attach one side of the Velcro to the hardboard, and the other side to the drapes. Allow one drape to overlap the other by about 1⅛ in./3 cm in the front so that the drapes don't gape (or staple the fabric to the hardboard, and then glue on a braid or ribbon to cover the staples).

STEP 3 Dampen the hardboard to make it more flexible and then attach it shiny side out, below the sink. Attach one side of the hardboard to the cleat with the pins, then bend the hardboard into a curve and attach the other side to the other cleat in the same way.

YOU WILL NEED:
- ABRASIVE POWDER
  AND CLOTH TO
  CLEAN
  THE BOARDS
- AN ELECTRIC SANDER
  WITH COARSE-
  GRADE SANDPAPER
- NAIL PUNCH
  AND HAMMER
- PRIMER
- THREE SHADES OF
  BLUE WOODWASH
  OR LATEX PAINT
- PAINT BRUSHES
- MARINE-STRENGTH
  CLEAR VARNISH
- SMALL ROLLER
  AND TRAY

PROJECT
Painting floorboards

If you live in an old house you will most likely have floorboards in the bathroom. A painted wooden floor looks nice, but a striped wooden floor is even better. The idea is to take one main color and two shades of it, one slightly deeper and one slightly lighter, giving an effect of subtle shading. Start painting at the far wall and work back toward the door.

Original wooden floorboards look great painted in stripes contrasting three shades of the same color.

HOW TO DO IT

STEP 1 Sweep the floor and then check all the nails, firmly tapping down any that protrude using the nail punch and a hammer.

STEP 2 Use the electric sander to get rid of any rough areas that could cause splinters. Don't spend too much time doing this because the paint and varnish will add a smooth finish.

STEP 3 Scrub the floor with an abrasive powder solution and leave it to dry.

STEP 4 Begin painting with the darkest shade next to the far baseboard. Paint the next board in the main color (this is likely to be used elsewhere in the room).

STEP 5 Paint the third color and then repeat this sequence back across the room toward the door. It will be easier to paint the last three boards once the rest have dried, letting you reach into the corners and up to the baseboard.

STEP 6 Finally apply at least two coats of clear varnish, leaving the correct drying time between coats.

YOU WILL NEED:
• **WINDOW CLEANER**
• **PAPER TOWEL**
• **THIN PAPER**
• **SCISSORS**
• **SPRAY ADHESIVE**
• **ETCHING SPRAY**

PROJECT
Decorating a window with an etched pattern

If you have a small bathroom or very little natural light coming in, it is a shame to block the window with drapes or shades. And when bathrooms are fitted with thick, obscuring glass designed to stop the neighbors seeing you in the bath, this is not always very attractive.

In both cases, and with plain glass, the window can be decorated with etching spray. This will let you keep clear glass in the top half of the window and stencil a frosted pattern of your own creation on the lower section to give you all the privacy you need.

A window decorated with etching spray is a subtle and attractive way of creating privacy without blocking out the light with drapes or shades.

HOW TO DO IT

STEP 1 Clean the window and leave it to dry. Fold four strips of paper (1⅛ in/3 cm wide) so they fit the length and height of the window into a concertina, then cut out a fancy pattern on one edge. Flatten the strips out and lightly apply spray adhesive to one side.

STEP 2 Fold another three strips of paper into 1⅛-in./3-cm squares concertina-wise, and draw simple motifs in the middle. Cut these out and spray one side lightly with spray adhesive.

STEP 3 Stick the borders around the window up to the desired height, and then arrange the motifs across the window pane in a geometric or random pattern. Mask out the surrounding area with paper to protect from the spray.

STEP 4 Spray on a light and even coating of etching spray. You can always apply a second coat if this is too thin and patchy, but it is best to apply one continuous coat first and then leave it to dry. Peel off one of the motifs to check the effect and apply a second coat of etching spray if necessary.

The contemporary bathroom

Big changes have been taking place in the bathroom. It began in new hip hotels, where minimalism took over from opulence—and before long, everyone was at it. This look is the antidote to Victorian and 1900s repro style, which was the last big style statement for bathrooms. The big thing to note is that fashions take longer to change in bathrooms for the obvious reason that you can't move things around or replace them on a whim. The second factor is cost because this is a room where expert help is definitely required, and plumbers, electricians, and builders don't come cheap. If you are going for a complete change, it may be worth asking an architect or specialized bathroom designer to advise you.

The contemporary bathroom replaces opulence with minimalism, giving domestic bathrooms the hip hotel look.

Plumbers and electricians often work together on bathroom installations and it is worth finding a pair who work well as a team. An electric shower, for instance, needs the expertise of a plumber and electrician at different stages. It is also a good idea to consult a plumber before you hire a designer because you need to know what the water pressure is, the type of boiler, and size of tank. The plumber will also be able to advise you, for instance, whether it is worth replacing an old boiler at the same time to accommodate a shower system, which would be more economical to run. And if you can find a "new wave" creative plumber who keeps up with what's new in bathrooms, you won't be needing any other bathroom design advice.

Store around

The first step is to get hold of as many top class catalogs as you can and make your style choice. Cut out your favorites and prepare to move downmarket in search of lookalikes. As with main street clothes stores, there are lots of budget versions of the latest styles, and home centers should be your first port of call. If you are on a tight budget, always go for the plainest designs because they will be the slowest to date.

There is also a booming mail order trade in bathroom fixtures and fittings, and you may be able to economize by getting hold of a plain bath and lavatory from a home center, making your style statement with accessories and a state-of-the-art sink. Bathroom cabinets, heated towel rails, mirrors, shelves, lights, and laundry bins can all be bought in coordinating contemporary ranges, and extra items can go on a birthday or Christmas gift list!

The best advice is to store around before you buy, because some copies of designer items are as low on quality as they are on price, and it may be worth waiting for a sale of the real thing, or buying last year's range from an outlet. That is particularly true because style changes take a long time to filter down to the cheap end of the market, sometimes taking two or three years.

Planning a brand-new bathroom

One of the most important aspects of planning is your budget, and it should include the cost of the main sanitaryware (bathtub, lavatory, bidet, basin, shower tray), the faucets, shower, and the screen or stall. Also include decorating materials such as tiles, paint, flooring, and essential accessories like storage units, lights, towel rails, mirrors, and shelves. Get quotations for the plumbing, electrics, and carpentry, and any decorating that you can't manage yourself, such as skim coating or replastering. If you add these up and are still smiling, skip the next paragraph!

Upgrading your old bathroom

If you like the idea of a new bathroom but not the price, it's time to take stock and take action. If the bathroom suite is outdated or plain ugly, it will have to be disguised. Materials to think about are pure-white laminated board, sheet acrylic, or sheet metal. If you like the look of an aluminum bath panel but not its price, then buy a sheet of marine ply and spray it with metallic aluminum spray paint. Spend money on the trim and it will look every bit as good as the real thing. Paint is still the cheapest way to make changes, and you can use it on walls, tiles, woodwork, and even vinyl flooring.

Pick a color scheme with a contemporary feel, something like ice blue, linen white, and café latte with accents of dull silver. Box in the bathtub and basin with ply, paint the walls ice

blue and linen white, paint the floor café latte, and fit matching colored blinds. Then change the lavatory seat, shower curtain, bath mat, bathroom roll holder, towel rail, and mirror. This doesn't necessarily mean buy everything new— keep a look out for things that can be transformed with paint, like woven laundry baskets or mirror frames. Galvanized metal is very cheap and has been taken up by some contemporary designers for mirror frames, candle holders, and small cabinets. Classic items like buckets and utility shelving can be bought from home centers and integrated with designer buys. In short, this is the sort of quick fix that you can do in a weekend. So what are you waiting for?

Designer catalogs can help you decide on the look you want, before looking for a budget version. Sometimes it's worth waiting for a sale of the real thing to prevent sacrificing quality for price.

PAINTING TILES AND FLOORS

In the 1990s, interior designers' quest for originality meant that products on the industrial side were taken up by the home sector. Nonslip floor paints were one of the first products to cross over from the factories and shipyards, and many other resurfacing products and specialized finishes followed. The next four projects show how to transform three shiny bathroom surfaces: tiles are primed and painted, vinyl flooring is given a whole new look, and a window is decorated with etching spray.

YOU WILL NEED:

- ABRASIVE POWDER OR WALL AND FLOOR CLEANER
- SCOURING SPONGE
- OLD TOWEL
- TILE PRIMER
- SMALL FOAM ROLLER AND TRAY
- PAINTER'S TAPE
- ENAMEL OR LOW LUSTER PAINT IN CHOSEN COLOR
- EXTRA ROLLER

PROJECT
Painting tiles

This is one of those miracles where doing and seeing what you've done is believing.

TOP TIP

If you want the tiles to look convincingly ceramic, then scrape out the old grout before you paint and re-grout the tiles afterward, following the steps shown in the tile grouting project.

HOW TO DO IT

STEP 1 Wash down the tiled area, and dry it well with an old towel to get rid of any surface water. Mask off the edges of the tiled area with painter's tape, and then pour some of the tile primer into the tray and apply a thin, even coat with the small foam roller. Leave to dry. If the tile pattern or color shows through, then apply one more coat. Clean the tray and fit a new roller.

STEP 2 Pour the feature-color paint into the tray and use the roller to apply it to the tiles. Leave to dry and then apply a second coat.

Old tiles can be transformed into ceramic lookalikes with a coat of tile primer and a coat of enamel.

PROJECT
Painting a vinyl floor

This may seem like a very lazy option, but don't knock it if it works! Vinyl flooring is the most practical and comfortable flooring for a bathroom, but some of the patterns on offer really let the material down. Until recently, the only options were to live with it or rip it out and fit new flooring, but there is now a third option, and that is to paint it. It is much cheaper and far less hassle than cutting out templates and replacing something that's practical, and in good condition, because you loathe the color or pattern. The paint that you need to use is a specialized type, but it is now available from several major home centers.

YOU WILL NEED:
- **VINYL FLOOR PAINT (0.21 GAL./ 1 LTR COVERS 150 SQ FT./15 SQ M)**
- **ABRASIVE POWDER**
- **LARGE SPONGE**
- **BUCKET**
- **SMALL HIGH-DENSITY SPONGE ROLLER AND TRAY**

HOW TO DO IT

STEP 1 Before you begin painting, the floor must be spotlessly clean. Fill a bucket with hot water and dissolve the abrasive powder as directed. Clean the floor and leave it to dry.

STEP 2 Apply the paint with the roller. Do not apply it too thickly because it will develop an unpleasant film. If, however, you apply it too thinly, it will wear off. For the best results, apply two to three even coats for a thorough covering. The first coat should be touch-dry in an hour, and the second coat can be applied in four hours, time. The paint can be walked on after six hours but will be even tougher if you leave it for a few days. It will provide a long-lasting finish.

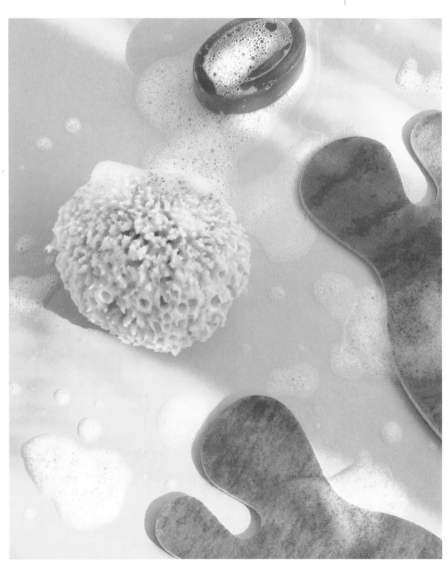

Transform those hated vinyl floor patterns with a couple of coats of paint. Try to leave a few days for it to dry; this will make it last longer.

YOU WILL NEED:

- **COLORED GROUT IN A COLOR OF YOUR CHOICE**
- **SCRAPER OR SMALL SCREWDRIVER TO CLEAN OUT OLD GROUT**
- **SPONGE WITH SCOURER**
- **FLEXIBLE GROUT SPREADER**
- **GROUT SHAPER (ROUND ENDED)**
- **SOFT DRY CLOTH**

PROJECT

Colored grouting

Grout is the filler between tiles, which can be used decoratively to make a very obvious grid of colored lines. It comes in a good range of colors and is easy to apply.

Colored grouting is a good finishing touch for freshly painted tiles, or it can simply be used to freshen up existing tiles.

HOW TO DO IT

STEP 1 Run the grout scraper (or another suitable tool) along the old grout and scrape most of it away. Don't let the scraper skid across the tiles and damage the surface, or dig too deep and affect the tile adhesive.

STEP 2 Dampen the scouring sponge and run it down the scraped gaps between the tiles to remove any loose material.

STEP 3 Use a flexible spreader to press the grout into the gaps so that there are no air bubbles left.

STEP 4 Use the sponge to wipe away any excess grout from the tiles and use a shaping tool to mold the grout into a slightly concave shape. Wipe away any smears, leave to dry, and finally polish the tiles with a dry, soft cloth.

YOU WILL NEED:

- **DE-GREASING WINDOW CLEANING SPRAY AND CLOTH**
- **ETCHING SPRAY**
- **PAINTER'S TAPE**
- **TAPE MEASURE OR RULE**
- **PLAIN PAPER**
- **SPRAY ADHESIVE**

PROJECT

Decorating a window with etching spray

This gives a cool contemporary look to a bathroom window, and obscures the view from outside. The design is more of a style statement, and the spray could also be used to make a matching border for a bathroom mirror. The same spray is used for a project in the traditional bathroom, so just follow the steps for the method.

Decorating a window with etching spray gains privacy without drapes or shades while adding a cool, contemporary look. Your own design would do just as well as the one shown.

HOW TO DO IT

STEP 1 Run a frame of painter's tape ¾ in./2 cm inside the edge of the window, attaching paper to protect the area around.

STEP 2 Enlarge the "h₂o" figures on a photocopier to fill an A4 sheet, then cut them out and apply spray adhesive to the back. Place the letters inside the masked frame and then frost the window with the etching spray. Peel off the tape and the templates.

Shower room

A home with a bathroom and separate shower room has the best of both worlds, letting you freshen up quickly or relax and enjoy a long soak in warm bubbles. En suite bathrooms are often shower rooms through lack of space. But even if space is not an issue, if you really prefer a shower to a bath anytime, it could make sense to get rid of the bathtub altogether and enjoy the luxury of a spacious shower room instead. And if, at a later date, you decide you do want a bathtub, one can simply be put in.

You can now find shower stalls small enough to fit into almost any space, so closets can become potential shower rooms.

In a small apartment a shower is more economical space-wise, and is also a good option as an en suite facility for teenagers. This idea could save many a row over how long certain people spend in the bathroom! However, babies and very small children usually hate showers and getting water in their eyes. Washing their hair under an overhead shower can be a nightmare, so stick to the sink for that job. Or try an adjustable shower that you can set at the right height so you don't splash water in their faces, which is what tends to cause all the fuss.

A range of possibilities

If you are starting a shower room from scratch, it is worth considering doing without a stall and tray and instead turning the whole room into a walk-in shower. You will need the help of a plumber, electrician, and carpenter. The shower fittings are fixed on the wall, and the floor will have to be raised slightly to create a slope to a central drain. The shower room can then be tiled, grouted, and silicone-sealed. Slatted wooden boards are also a good idea on part of the floor, to prevent slipping and minimize puddles. The luxury of a shower room like this could actually cost less than buying a new tray and stall.

If you are fitting a stall, tray, and shower in a small room that doesn't have a lavatory or basin,

try not to clutter it up too much, because space is one of the biggest luxuries in a shower room. Walls need to be tiled outside the shower unit only if it doesn't have glass on all sides, so the rest of the room can be decorated for comfort and convenience. Have a rail to warm towels over the radiator, or replace the radiator with a large, heated towel rail. A bathroom cabinet, shelf, and a mirror with good lighting are the other essentials. If the room is small and square, this might also be a good place to fit a false ceiling with recessed lights fitted with a dimmer switch, operated from outside the shower room. All lighting should be of the sealed-unit type suitable for bathrooms. And also make sure there is some ventilation, because steam needs to escape if you are to avoid condensation problems.

Adaptability

Shower manufacturers boast of making units that can fit into almost any space, and that can mean somewhere as small as a closet. And with new combination boilers, water is heated on demand without the need for a large hot-water storage tank in an airing closet. So if you are changing the boiler, why not investigate the possibility of fitting a new shower? Who knows, your airing closet may just be big enough for a shower with a folding door. Another good shower option is having one

near the back door. This is especially useful if you live near the shore, or on a farm; or have an occupation or play a sport that means you return home dirty and sweaty. It is also an ideal place for kids to be sluiced down as they come in from the garden. This is a no-frills sort of shower, with rendered and tiled stud walls and a heavy-duty PVC shower curtain on a rail. Fit a mirror, and a soap and shampoo tray inside and have a handy towel hook outside with a wooden duckboard to step out onto.

En suite shower room

An en suite shower room must be waterproof, warm, and welcoming. Privacy comes with the territory and you can afford to think more about the design and less about the barricading. Flexible MDF wood is a relatively new material that makes building curves possible. This could be used to create the base for a curved mosaic

wall instead of a glass shower stall. Mosaic tiles can be bought and applied in sheets, which makes tiling curves easier than you would imagine. Mosaics come in many other colors than "swimming pool" blue, and while you're at it, why not try your hand at a mirror frame or simple frieze? Be warned, though, the mosaic habit is a difficult one to kick. The best floor treatment for a shower room like this would be tiles or sheet vinyl, but do make sure that you always step onto a dry bath mat to avoid wet feet on the bedroom carpet.

If the en suite is for a teenager, make sure that there are plenty of hooks to hang up towels, and a radiator to dry the bath mat on. One day, they'll realize that towels and bath mats are revolting if they stay on the floor in a wet heap! It is also vital to make sure that the shower is totally watertight, and it may even be worth building a low, tiled wall that you step over at the entrance to the room. It is better to anticipate problems now than deal with them later.

There is one element to showering that hasn't really been mentioned, and that is the pleasure to be had from standing under a powerful stream of warm water. A power shower option is a really good idea for those times when you need kick-starting in the morning or when you need a blast to unwind after work. Ask your plumber about a power-shower pump unit, which can be switched on and off from outside the bathroom. This will let you conserve hot water and electricity when a regular shower will do, and will give you the option of having an exhilarating power shower when you really need it.

LEFT: **Only the walls inside a shower stall need tiling. The other walls can be decorated with paint.**

A refreshing wake-up shower in an en suite shower room is a perfect morning tonic, especially if you add the exhilaration of a power shower.

THE PROJECTS

The main issues facing you when decorating a shower room are what to do about the walls and floor. The following projects offer some ideas.

YOU WILL NEED:

- 8 x 2-¾ IN./7-CM LENGTHS OF 2-IN. x 1-IN./5 CM x 2.5 CM PAR PINE
- 2 x 1¾ IN./4.5 CM LENGTHS OF 2 IN. x 1 IN./5 CM x 2.5 CM PAR PINE
- BACKSAW
- MEDIUM AND FINE SANDPAPER
- COMBINATION SQUARE
- DRILL WITH COUNTERSINK BIT AND ¼-IN./ 6-MM BIT
- 16 x 2⅜ IN./16 MM NUMBER 6 COUNTERSINK SCREWS (NON-RUSTING)
- WOODSTAIN, CLEAR VARNISH, OR WAX
- STEEL WOOL
- BRUSH

PROJECT
A pine duckboard

Say goodbye to soggy bathmats or standing in a puddle on a wet floor, by making yourself this little deck to stand on when you get out of the shower. This duckboard is made from pine softwood, which is very easy to cut. The lengths can be sanded smooth and colored with an exterior-quality wood stain or just varnished to seal the surface.

This practical and stylish duckboard is easy to make from pine softwood, and finished with wood stain or simply varnished.

HOW TO DO IT

STEP 1 Cut all the lengths of pine then sand any sharp edges to round them off slightly. Pay particular attention to the sawn ends.

STEP 2 Line the lengths up and mark the positions for the two cross-pieces.

STEP 3 Drill a countersunk clearance hole for a screw at each end of all the lengths and screw the lengths to the cross-pieces.

STEP 4 Stain, wax, or simply varnish the duckboard. Apply the wax with a soft, lint-free cloth, leave to dry for 20 minutes, then buff with steel wool.

YOU WILL NEED:

- A PLAIN-COLORED PLASTIC OR NYLON SHOWER CURTAIN FITTED WITH A SET OF RINGS
- LIGHTWEIGHT FABRIC THE SAME SIZE AS THE CURTAIN OR, IF WIDER, IT CAN BE HEMMED
- APPLIQUÉ DAISIES
- FABRIC GLUE OR NEEDLE AND THREAD

PROJECT
A customized shower curtain

Plastic shower curtains aren't the most attractive sight in a shower room, but only one side of the shower curtain needs to be water-repellent, so why not use cheap plastic curtain trimmings as the lining for something more in keeping with your own bathroom style? The curtain is fixed to the liner at the top only, above the level where it will come into contact with any water, so the stitch perforations will not be a problem. Any lightweight fabric that is not too prone to creasing is suitable for this project and the decorative additions are up to you. The daisies can be stuck to the fabric with a good fabric glue, or hand-stitched if you prefer.

Practical plastic shower curtains can be made into attractive versions with just a covering of fabric, a choice of decorations, and a sewing machine.

HOW TO DO IT

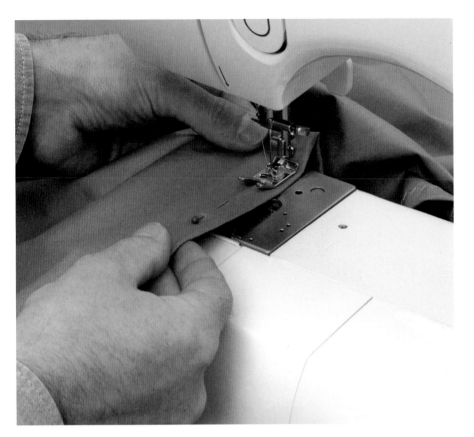

STEP 1 If the fabric is too wide, then cut it and hem it to match the size of the shower curtain. Measure the length against the shower curtain and sew a small hem at the top and bottom.

STEP 2 Line up the top of the cotton curtain with the top of the plastic curtain. Stitch the two together just below the holes for the shower rings. Use matching thread so that the stitches are invisible.

STEP 3 Arrange the daisies all over the curtain in a random "natural" lawn pattern. Stick them onto the fabric with the fabric glue and leave until it has dried and bonded. If you prefer, they can be slipstitched in place.

YOU WILL NEED:

- **WOODEN PLANK, ABOUT 20 IN. x 4 IN./50 CM x 10 CM DRIFTWOOD IS IDEAL, BUT NEW WOOD WITH AN INTERESTING GRAIN, SUCH AS AN OFF-CUT OF PARANÁ PINE OR A FRUIT WOOD, WOULD ALSO LOOK GOOD**
- **SOAP DISH**
- **2 HOOKS**
- **DRILL**
- **⅜ -IN./1-CM TILE BIT**
- **PAINTER'S TAPE**
- **PENCIL**
- **SPIRIT LEVEL**
- **NON-RUSTING SCREWS TO ATTACH COAT HOOK (SHOULD COME WITH SCREWS)**
- **2 x 3 IN./7.5 CM NUMBER 10 SCREWS TO FIX THE WOOD TO THE TILED WALL (THE SCREW LENGTH DEPENDS UPON THE DEPTH OF YOUR WOOD)**
- **WALL ANCHORS**
- **BRASS CUPPED SCREWS**
- **AWL**
- **STAIN OR VARNISH (IF REQUIRED)**

PROJECT
Shower caddy

Trying to locate the soap, shampoo, or sponge can be highly frustrating when water is cascading into your eyes. This simple solution should help to keep everything you need in one place, close to hand when you need it. It is ideally suited to a tiled wall and its beauty lies in the fact that only two holes are drilled through the tiling, with the rest going into the wooden support.

This shower caddy lets you have a range of fittings with only two holes drilled through the tiles. All the rest are drilled through the wooden caddy.

HOW TO DO IT

STEP 1 Find the ideal position for the caddy on the shower wall, making quite sure that there are no pipes behind the tiles where the screws will be located! Mark the positions for the components and the shelf.

STEP 2 Drill two evenly spaced holes in the shelf end.

STEP 3 Screw the top shelf to the back plank using brass cupped screws. Screw the hooks and soap dish into position.

STEP 4 Place the unit in position on the wall. Mark through the pre-drilled holes onto the wall using an awl.

STEP 5 Drill holes through the tiles using the painter's tape to stop the tile bit from skidding. Insert wall anchors.

STEP 6 Screw the unit to the wall using the brass cupped screws.

Fun & study

Working from home is many people's dream—
no traffic gridlocks, no train delays, no office politics. But whether
you're going to be working from home full-time or just a few hours a
week, your work area needs to be carefully planned so that you can
switch from a domestic to a work environment without one intruding
on the other. Home offices are also an opportunity to have fun with
design—at last you don't have to put up with gray metal filing
cabinets, because your office is to suit you, and you alone. This section
shows how to create stylish working spaces, either in separate offices
or in part of a living area. It also looks at creating a
teenager's study and a child's playroom.

Office-living space

The keyword in home office design is flexibility. Ideally you want to be able to put away your work in the evening, without leaving a trace, and to start again effortlessly the next morning. This might seem like a tall order, but with so many people working from home, there is a wealth of design expertise in this area. You can buy fantastic pieces of furniture that look like stylish closets, sideboards or bookshelves at night but open out into a full working office during the day. They are designed so that a full desk with computers and bookshelves can be closed without putting anything away. Wonders like this don't come cheap, but when you consider the cost of renting and fitting out an office, it puts the price into perspective.

Despite the age of the computer, there is still a lot of paperwork around, which means old-fashioned filing systems are not quite dead. If your home office is also your living room, it's worth making your filing system as attractive as possible.

If your office is to be at one end of the living room, a divider of some sort will let the room be used for both purposes at the same time. Modular cubed units are excellent for this, especially if you have a mixture of some open cubes and others with doors. Mix the cubes so that some face the office and some the living room. If you prefer something less solid, a screen is the best idea. There are lots of different styles in stores and catalogs, including minimalist Japanese, decoratively carved Indian, wrought iron, and bamboo and seagrass. Screens are not difficult to make and the basic construction technique described in the Traditional Living Room section could be used to make a larger office screen. Another option is to fit a Venetian blind. It will add a sharp, efficient look to the office and you can vary the level of exclusion from the rest of the room by adjusting the slats. At the end of the working day, you have the option of lowering and closing it to block the view of the office.

It is a good idea to have your office equipment, including the desk, on casters. This offers you maximum flexibility, because everything can be easily moved around or out of the room altogether if the occasion demands. A wall-mounted cabinet with sliding doors will look good and conceal loads of files, catalogs, and magazines, and a low sideboard is a perfect piece of dual-purpose furniture. If you have a dining room, you could use a dining table as your daytime desk and a sideboard for storing all your paperwork without anyone being any the wiser. It is only viable for tidy, organized people with very good memories.

The essentials

Top of the list is some sort of work surface that may be a proper desk or a table with a drawer unit. Begin by making a realistic list of all the things you will need in your home office, and if you use a computer, leave plenty of space for all the extra bits and pieces like Zip drives, scanners, and printers. Several stylish mail-order companies have ranges of contemporary desk units with all the proper shelves, including a low keyboard shelf, which is advisable if you are going to be using the computer every day. Ideally the monitor should be at eye level and your arms should be level with the keyboard. Desks don't have to cost much at all; in fact, they are often given away free when you buy a new computer. A pair of saw horses topped with a piece of MDF will also make a great desk, especially if you invest in one or two filing cabinets and drawer cabinets on casters, which can be wheeled out of sight when the office is shut. A proper office chair is essential for anyone spending more than an hour a day sitting at a desk. Aim to spend as much money as you can on the chair and economize elsewhere. To avoid backache and repetitive stress injury (RSI), you should sit with a straight back, your feet flat on the floor, and elbows at your side as you tap the keyboard.

Organization

If your working area also serves another purpose, you need to be really well organized. Computers were supposed to take the place of paperwork, but that hasn't completely happened yet, and most of us find that we still need an old-fashioned filing system. Then there are all the bits of stationery and bits and pieces you need for your work. A strong set of shelves for reference books, box files, and magazines could be fitted with a shade to hide them when you're not working. And a smart set of matching boxes to keep on display is particularly useful for clearing away all your clutter at the end of each working day. A notice board and calendar are also essential if you are to keep track of appointments, and there are some excellent programs for the computer, which act as notes and daily, weekly, and monthly diary pages.

THE PROJECTS

The project on the following pages is the ultimate in flexibility, letting you keep the clutter of a desk in organized compartments, which can be put away after use.

Lighting

The best light to work by is a directional light, angled to illuminate your desk area. In addition the room needs either good natural light, or artificial ambient light, for the evening or dull days, so that the contrast between the brightness of a computer screen and the rest of the room is never too great. Use overhead or wall lights to balance the lighting.

Pleasing yourself

One of the joys of working from home is that your office need not bear any resemblance to an office at all. So, be creative and remember that this is home first and an office second. A large wicker hamper is as good as a metal cupboard for keeping box files in, and polka-dotted tumblers can hold pencils and paper clips. Cookie barrels hold several rolls of tape and balls of string, and a CD storage rack takes care of the CD-Roms and Zip disks. A typist's chair can be re-covered to match the drapes, a vase of flowers will do more for the desktop than any executive toy, and when the day's work is done, why not treat your computer like a birdcage and cover it up with an attractive silk scarf?

A home office doesn't have to look like an office at all. Wicker hampers with compartments serve as useful storage space and you can never go wrong with a vase of fresh flowers.

YOU WILL NEED:

- A SHEET OF ³/₄-IN./
  1.9-CM MDF
  CUT AS FOLLOWS:
- BACK: 24 ³/₈ IN. X 35
  IN./62 CM X 89 CM
- TOP SHELF: 12.IN X
  35 IN./30 CM X 8 CM
- BOTTOM SHELF:
  9³/₄IN. X 12 IN./
  25 CM X 30 CM
- SMALL SIDE SHELVES:
  6 IN. X 6 IN. /15 CM
  X 15 CM (2 PIECES)
- LEFT-HAND SIDE:
  24³/₈ IN. X 26 IN./
  62 CM X 66 CM
- RIGHT-HAND SIDE:
  24³/₈IN X 8IN/62CM
  X 20CM
- LEFT UPRIGHTS:
  17⁵/₈IN X 12IN/45CM
  X 30CM (2 PIECES)
- RIGHT UPRIGHTS:
  17⁵/₈ IN X 6IN/
  45CM X 15CM
  (2 PIECES)
- 1¹/₂-IN./3.8-CM
  NUMBER 6 SCREWS
- WOOD GLUE
- WORKBENCH
- JIGSAW
- TAPE MEASURE
- COMBINATION
  SQUARE
- CARPENTERS' PENCIL
- DRILL WITH PILOT,
  SCREW, AND
  COUNTERSINK BIT
  (USE SIZE 4
  SCREWSINK BIT FOR
  ALL THREE)
- LONG RULE
- SANDPAPER
- SPIRIT LEVEL

When this desktop
unit is put on a
table, it creates an
instant work
surface. It keeps all
your desktop clutter
in an organized
space, which can be
quickly put away
after use.

PROJECT
A desktop unit

The work surface can be a table or simply a sheet of thick board supported on a pair of saw horses, but what turns it into an efficient desk are the drawer units, shelves, and storage space. This project shows how to build a freestanding unit to sit on top of the work surface. It includes space for the computer monitor, storage for CD-Roms and disks, two file compartments, a stationery tray compartment and a book-ended shelf on the top.

HOW TO DO IT

STEP 1 Hold the uprights, dividers, and shelves against the back section and mark out their positions in pencil on the back.

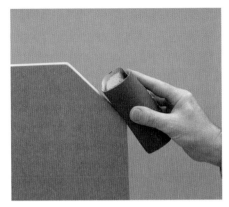

STEP 2 Draw, cut, and sand the mitered corners on the two sides.

STEP 3 Measure and draw a 6-in./15-cm square box at the bottom of the central section on the back piece. This will be cut out to serve as a channel for the computer cables.

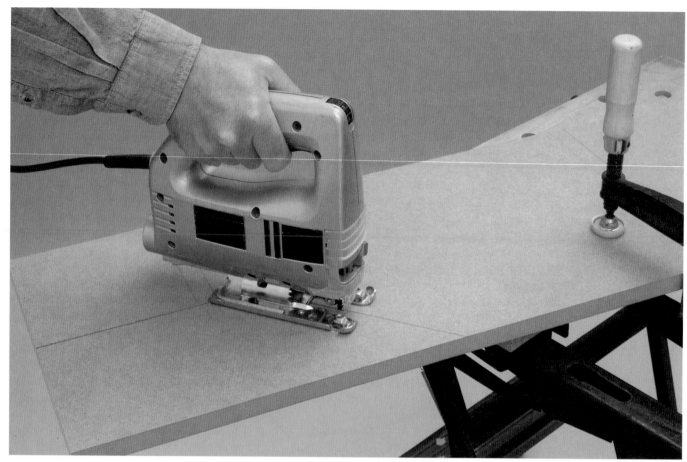

STEP 4 Use a jigsaw to cut out the cable box and the top shelf shape.

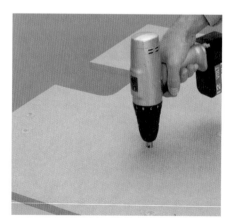

STEP 5 Drill clearance holes on the back section and countersink.

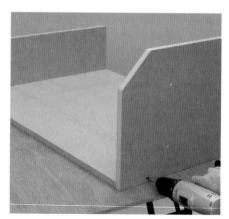

STEP 6 Fix the uprights to the back section.

STEP 7 Fix the sides to the two uprights. Fix the smaller shelves to the sides and back.

STEP 8 Fill the holes, sand, and paint in your chosen color.

Use this sketch to help you construct your desk. Remember to measure all the wood accurately, and use a spirit level to ensure that everything is level.

Home office

Computers have revolutionized our world to the point where many more of us now work from home. Why spend time commuting to and from the office when everything can be done here and not there? And if that's the route you are taking, it really is worth designing and decorating your new office.

The first thing you need to do when planning a new office in your home is to decide what you will use it for, for how often, and what equipment you will need to keep in it. Then you can look at what you would like in your home office, as well as what you will need. As the boss, you're in the lucky position of making all the decisions, so don't feel constrained by any preconceived ideas of how an office should or

When space is at a premium, or you only plan to work at home part-time, an area underneath the staircase can be an ideal working space.

shouldn't look. Six things to consider when planning your home office are...

1. Location

A spare bedroom or a dining room are the rooms most likely to be turned into an office, but when space is at a premium, you could make use of a landing or even a closet under the stairs. A lot depends upon how many of you share the home—if you're on your own or in a couple, it will be a lot easier to set the office boundaries than if you have a family. Working from home with young children is not impossible, but can be quite a challenge.

If you have an attic, garage, or outhouse with conversion potential, it is worth finding out what it will cost. If you plan to work from home in the long term, then an office slightly removed from the home environment could be the perfect solution. If you are planning to work only a few hours a day, though, you could make do with a very small but highly organized work area, and, for this, the space under the stairs is not as funny as it sounds. The idea is not to disappear into a closet and close the door behind you, but to think of your office area as part of an open-plan design. The best scenario is where the stairs run up the side of the room. Your desk, storage, filing, and bookshelves can be tucked into the space underneath the staircase while you actually sit in the room facing the desk, without being claustrophobic!

If you are at work in complete isolation, then arrange everything to suit yourself, but if you expect to see visitors, then the office should be as close to the front door as possible to minimize domestic intrusion. Maintaining a professional attitude is difficult enough at home without having strangers peering at your unmade beds and unwashed breakfast plates.

2. Electricity

One of the first things to consider is, do you need more electric and phone sockets? The fax and internet connections are best on a separate line so that they don't interfere with the home phone number. In fact, new phone line options are being introduced all the time, so seek advice from your phone company. With outlets, the basic strips can take four plugs, but you can also buy a more expensive version with eight outlets and two phone outlets. Be generous with your outlets allowance so that you avoid trailing cables in the work area. Computers should also be plugged into surge protectors, which block destructive power surges during electrical storms. Plan your lighting at this stage too, so that your work area is well lit and the rest of the room has a pleasant ambient lighting system. Having a good background light level prevents eye strain from a bright computer screen. Daylight bulbs mimic natural light and are reputed to be easier on the eyes, and getting the lighting right keeps you alert and prevents tiredness.

3. Fitting and furnishing

A flick through an office supplier's catalog will show you that there isn't just a gadget for everything, but different versions of each gadget. So be assured that whatever your special office needs, they can be met. And if it's just a desk, chair, and filing cabinet that you're after, they also come in a huge range of styles and prices.

Spend as much money as you can afford on a good adjustable chair to help you sit in the right posture when you're working. Ideally your back should be straight, with the lumbar region of your spine well supported, thighs parallel to the floor, and both feet flat on the ground. You may need a raised foot rest if you are not working at an ergonomically designed computer desk. To find out what the correct posture feels like, simply place a few books under your feet and a rolled towel in the small of your back.

Fully adjustable office chairs have levers for tilting and altering the seat and back-support height. Since they can be very expensive, it really is worth looking in a second-hand office supplies store. And because businesses regularly close down or have a change in office style, second-hand does not necessarily mean worn out. Filing cabinets, letter trays, and drawer units are other potentially expensive items that can be bought second-hand and given a make-over to match

A good adjustable office chair is one item of furniture you cannot afford to be without. Second-hand chairs can be just as good as new, so it doesn't need to break the bank.

your home-office style. In fact, these stores can be real Aladdin's caves, and you never know what you'll find. There is no need to surround yourself with dull, utilitarian gray or beige metal cabinets just because they are the only colors on offer. Buy the poor dull things and inject a bit of fun by giving them an uplifting color change with metal primer and enamel paints from an auto accessory store. If meetings or interviews are part of your work, you will also need to provide seating for your visitors. A lot depends on your line of work, and if it is quite buzzy and informal, stools would be fine. Otherwise, consider a smart, compact sofa-bed and then you will even be able to offer friends a bed for the night!

4. Walls

Decorating the home office should encourage you to spend time in there without any distractions. One of the most difficult aspects of working from home is being able to disengage yourself from any domestic jobs or other tasks that need to be done. The very last thing you want is to be constantly looking round and thinking that the room could do with a good coat of paint and a new set of drapes. Concentrate on your work. You haven't time for all that! Get the decorating done after the electrics and before the arrival of heavy desks and cabinets. Keep the style simple and wall colors light to make the most of the daylight, and don't be afraid to use white, which looks good with everything. Light colors expand spaces and prevent the office from looking crowded once all the equipment is in place.

5. Windows

When choosing a window treatment for your office, it is quite important to choose something that won't look out of place with the rest of your home when seen from the outside. Slatted blinds are the most versatile option because they can be adjusted to admit maximum daylight, filter bright sunlight, and block views, giving good security. They also look cool and contemporary. Vertical blinds are being used a lot more in homes these days and they do a similar job but with broader, vertical slats.

6. Floors

When it comes to flooring, you have the choice of a carpet or hard surface. As ever, your choice must be guided by your kind of work. Vinyl or linoleum is the most hard-wearing and easy to clean, and it also has the advantage over carpet when casters are being used. Cork is an inexpensive natural material that is coming back into fashion, particularly the dark stained version. The other hard-flooring option is a laminated floating floor. It comes in different quality grades

and two basic designs. Both follow the tongue-and-groove style with one type needing glue to join the planks, and the other using an interlocking design. The second type can be lifted and moved. If you choose carpet, it is a good idea to buy a clear plastic chair mat to go on top, which will let you move and swivel easily around your desk area.

Closets can be made into stationery cabinets or complete workstations. At the end of the day, the doors can be closed on anything resembling work.

PROJECTS

The three projects on the following pages focus on three essential parts of any home office: lighting, storage, and, of course, the desk space. But to make the most of the freedom offered by the home office, the emphasis is on fun as well as function, letting a bit of creativity be added to the work environment. A fresh coat of paint, a little disciplined filing, and a big vase of flowers should do the rest.

YOU WILL NEED:
- 4 IN. X 1 IN./
  10 CM X 2.5 CM
  LUMBER FOR BOX
  FRAME
- SPRAY ADHESIVE
- THIN ACRYLIC SHEET
  FOR FRONT
- 1.2-CM/½-IN MDF
  FOR BASE
- DRILL
- FLUORESCENT
  STRIPLIGHT TO FIT
  THE BOX SIZE
- ARROW SHAPE CUT
  OUT OF CARD
- SNAP-BLADE KNIFE
- ADHESIVE SPRAY
- 2 MIRROR FIXINGS
- RIGHT-ANGLED
  MOLDING
- BACKSAW AND
  MITER BLOCK

PROJECT
Lighting

If you are converting a bedroom or dining room into an office, the chances are that you will have to completely rethink the lighting. The two types of lighting needed in such an environment are ambient, which is the background lighting all around you, and task lighting, which is directional lighting illuminating your work area. If you also have a seating area for clients, this could be lit from above with a pendant lamp. We are all familiar with light-boxes, usually with the message "EXIT" on them. This project is a bit of fun along these lines. Use two dark-colored pieces of cardboard cut in arrow shapes, which will show through the acrylic sheet. The glass is then assembled in a box frame with a fluorescent tube inside.

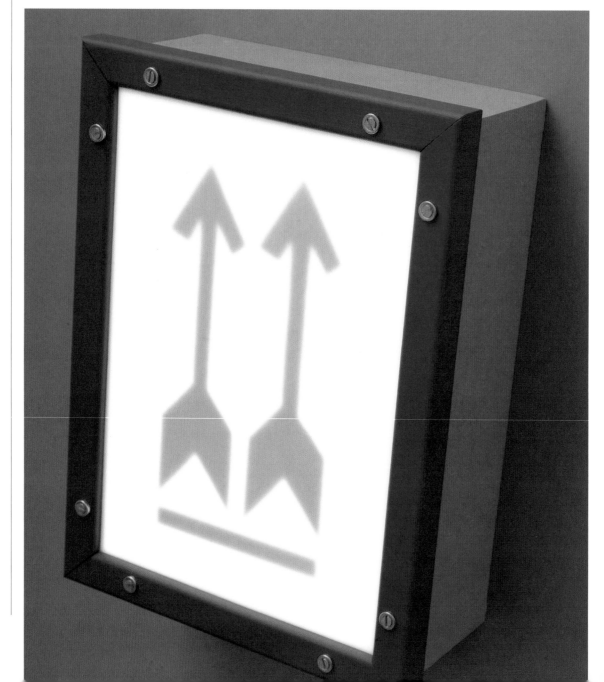

An exit sign with a difference! This novel light box uses an acrylic sheet in front of a fluorescent light tube. You can design your own pattern or lettering for a personal touch.

HOW TO DO IT

STEP 1 Have the acrylic sheet cut to size, and then cut the wood to size and sand the edges. Make a simple butt-jointed box, then glue and screw the joints.

STEP 2 Cut out the right-angle molding, using a backsaw and miter block.

STEP 3 Place the acrylic sheet on top of the box. Drill clearance holes through the molding and screw it to the acrylic sheet and the box frame.

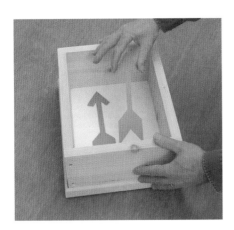

STEP 4 Cut out the arrow shapes. Use a spray adhesive on the back and stick to the acrylic sheet in the inside of the box.

STEP 5 Drill an exit hole for the cable in the back or the side of the box, and place the fitting and bulb inside the box.

STEP 6 Screw the back of the box in place, add the bulb and fixings, then attach to the wall. Paint if desired.

TOP TIP
You can use any motif or word in your light-box—just choose something that is personal to you.

YOU WILL NEED:

• 1 SHEET OF ¹/₄-
  IN./1.8-CM MDF
• LONG RULE WITH
  SPIRIT LEVEL
• TAPE MEASURE
• COMBINATION
  SQUARE
• PENCIL
• DRILL
• PILOT BIT AND
  COUNTERSINK BIT
• SCREWS
• 4 CASTERS
• WOOD GLUE
• SANDPAPER
• PAINT

PROJECT
Storage

There is no getting away from storage. Whatever type of work you do, paperwork mounts up, records must be kept and we all need somewhere to keep telephone directories and reference material. This storage unit on casters will take care of books, files and catalogues. The top is at desk height, so with a piece of MDF laid on top, it provides an extra work surface.

This handy storage unit on casters keeps books, files, and catalogs accessible, while they are neatly stored away. An optional top surface of MDF will make a useful additional work surface.

HOW TO DO IT

STEP 1 Cut the back of the unit from the sheet of MDF. It should be the height of your desk minus the height of the casters if you want to extend the desk area. Cut out all the shelves, dividers, and the top, sides, and bottom of the unit.

STEP 2 Draw the positions of the sides, top, and bottom, and all the partitions and shelves in pencil on the back. Use a length of MDF to do this so that you can see a flat plan of the unit on the back.

STEP 3 Drill clearance holes to fix all the pieces to the back of the unit. Hold each piece in position as you drill through the clearance holes to make pilot holes for the screws.

STEP 4 Assemble the outer frame first, applying wood glue to the joining edges before screwing them together through the back. Drill pilot, clearance, and countersink holes, then secure the corner joints by screwing them together. Fit all the partitions in place first, and then add the shelves. Drill, glue, and screw each one so that the whole unit stands firm.

STEP 5 Drill holes and fit the four casters onto the base of the unit.

STEP 6 Sand all the sharp edges smooth, then paint if required, or use it just as it is.

PROJECT
Curved desk

You can make a very smart desk from one sheet of MDF and a pair of saw horses. Or you can buy the legs in sets of four, as shown in this project, then simply attach them to the underside of the desk. This desk is ideal for someone whose work surface is always piled high, because it is shaped like a curve, so when you sit at it, everything is within arm's reach.

A simple curved desk made out of MDF is both stylish and functional. You can either buy a pair of saw horses or four, ready-made legs.

HOW TO DO IT

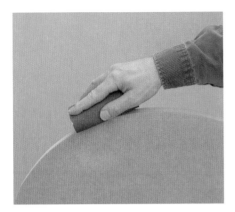

STEP 1 Support the MDF between two saw horses. Draw the curve in pencil, either from a pattern or to your own plan. Cut out the curve with a jigsaw, and sand.

STEP 2 Support the desk leg in the workbench and drill a vertical hole for fitting, using the correct drill bit for your screws.

STEP 3 The leg fittings consist of two parts —one post with a screw-fitting to fit into the leg and one to receive the post, which fits under the table top.

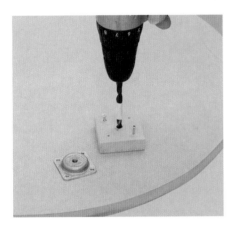

STEP 4 Screw the squares of wood to the underneath of the table, then mark the positions for the legs and all their screws. Drill pilot holes using a 1/16-in./2-mm drill bit.

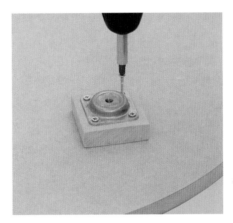

STEP 5 Screw the top receiving plate of the leg-fitting into the wood boss.

STEP 6 Screw each leg into position. Lift the table and turn. Seal the surfaces with MDF primer or a 50:50 dilution of PVA and water. Paint, or stain and varnish the desk.

TOP TIP

These table legs are sold in packs in home centers, and always have instructions included with them. If you prefer, you could use saw horse legs, which can also be found in home centers.

Teenager's study

Creating an environment to encourage a teenager to study is an interesting challenge, and one solution is to put the emphasis on relaxation, keeping a corner that is conducive to study. The best way to do this is to build in a worktop with all the shelving, drawers, and electrical outlets that the teenager will need for computers, CDs, and video games. There is little point in excluding these things because the object is to get kids to spend time in the room and make studying easier. Exclusion simply makes forbidden fruit taste sweeter.

The great thing about the home improvement boom is that there is a close link between fashion and decorating styles, with top clothes designers also designing home furnishing ranges. This means that teenagers today are far more conscious of interior design fashions than most of us were at their age. The key to success lies in parent and child working together as a team, doing everything from planning and shopping to making the changes. Sometimes as parents we think it is easier to do the work ourselves, but then we are denying our kids the satisfaction of working hard and joining in. Begin by asking for a wish list of everything they would have if money were no object, then set a budget and help to edit what is on the list. Try to include an extravagance like a fake fur beanbag or a really cool anglepoise lamp. Discuss color, furniture, lighting, and flooring, and look at as many style magazines as possible. Keep a look out for special features flagged on the front of home magazines, and buy any for home offices or studio apartments. If your teenager is likely to go to college, this room could build a bridge between childhood and student days.

Practicalities

If you are giving this room a make-over together, it is important that the whole process doesn't drag on too long. Paint the walls one weekend, and hire an electrician to fit extra outlets and sort out the lighting at the same time. When it comes to the flooring, the best tip is to use expensive underlay and cheap carpeting. The underlay will cut the noise level dramatically, and the carpet can be replaced once your fledgling has flown the nest. A tough, cord carpet can always be softened by a large rug for lounging on.

The best studies for teenagers are those that also include an element of relaxation and entertainment, to entice them into the work area.

Once the carpet is down, the workstation can be built. It should be custom-made to meet your teenager's specific needs. Drawer units on casters are a good idea because they offer more flexibility. And make the desktop wide and long enough with ample shelving for magazines and reference books, with smaller shelves for CDs and games. Fit strip lighting under the shelving and an angle poiselight on the worktop. If the area looks business-like, they will be more likely to get down to work. Set aside an amount in the budget for folders, boxes, files, notebooks, and a new mouse mat for the computer.

You should also buy a comfortable, adjustable office chair to encourage good posture. Most furniture stores stock them and it is also worth having a look at second-hand office furniture stores. They deal with businesses that close down, so second-hand does not have to mean old and tatty.

Comfort zone

Once the work side of the room has been taken care of, you can turn your attention to the comfort zone. Seating can be soft and low with cushions and beanbags. If you have an old sofa to put in the room, it can be covered with a fleece throw. Fleece comes in a wide range of colors and has the bonus of requiring no hemming and washing really well. Fake fur fabrics also make great throws, and are not expensive to buy by the yard. A decorator's cotton dropcloth covers most sofas, and can be machine-dyed to the color of your teenager's choice.

Coffee table

A low coffee table can be made from recycled wooden pallets. This wood is rough but soft, and is easy to smooth with an electric sander. The table surface can be faced with a sheet of hardboard edged with domed upholstery tacks, and four

Teenagers need storage space too, especially if their study is part of their bedroom. Make sure they have enough places to put everything, so they have no excuse for not tidying up.

large casters will give it a contemporary edge. Another option is to head down to the second-hand shops and find something to makeover.

Window dressing

Shades or shutters that block out the daylight are usually popular with this age group. A room should be as dark as a nightclub first thing in the morning. Roller blinds with black-out backing work best if they are fitted into the window frame recess.

Refrigerator

A small refrigerator may seem like a luxury, but it makes sense if long hours are to be spent in the room. Look for a studio or caravan refrigerator that will not take up too much space, and give it a color lift with auto spray paints.

PROJECTS

The four projects on the following pages combine a sense of work with relaxation, to make a teenager's study as appealing as possible. Make sure you work as a team from the start, so that personal touches can be added along the way.

YOU WILL NEED:

- 1-IN./2.5-CM
  WOODEN CLEAT FOR
  THE BACK OF THE
  FRAME
- 2³/₄-IN./7-CM-
  SQUARE POST TO
  SUPPORT
  THE CORNER
- 1 SHEET OF
  ¹/₂-IN./1.2-CM
  MDF FOR
  THE WORKTOP
- 3 IN. x 1 IN.
  7.5 CM x 2.5 CM
  FASCIA LUMBER FOR
  THE FRONT AND SIDE
- WOOD GLUE
- 1-IN./2.5-CM BRADS
- FINE SANDPAPER
- PAINTER'S TAPE
- WOOD PRIMER
- LOW LUSTER PAINT
- PAINT BRUSH, OR
  SMALL FOAM ROLLER
  AND TRAY
- LONG RULE WITH
  SPIRIT LEVEL
- TAPE MEASURE
- PENCIL
- DRILL
- ¹/₄-IN./7-MM
  MASONRY BIT
- ¹/₄-IN./7-MM
  WALL ANCHORS
- ¹/₈-IN./4-MM
  DRILL BIT
- 1¹/₂-IN./3.8-CM
  CHIPBOARD SCREWS
- SCREWDRIVER
- JIGSAW
- SMALL HAMMER
- MITER SAW OR
  BLOCK

PROJECT
Worktop

The big advantage of making a desk is that it can be made to fit the person and their specific requirements. If the desk is to be used for, say, a sewing machine as well as a computer, the outlets should be sited in a convenient position for both uses, with all electrical cables channeled behind the unit. When you plan a unit to your own specifications, it can be easily fitted under a sloping ceiling or in an alcove. This plan is for building a worktop into a corner; the right type of shelves can be attached to the wall above it.

A worktop made specially for teenagers can be painted in their favorite colors, making work seem less of a chore.

HOW TO DO IT

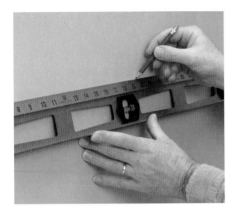

STEP 1 Decide upon the length and depth of the worktop, and then cut the wood to fit. Mark the position and height of the table on the wall. Use a long rule with spirit level to check that the cleat will be straight.

STEP 2 Drill clearance holes through the cleats approximately 10 in./25 cm apart, and then hold them up to the wall and mark their positions in pencil. Drill and plug the holes in the wall, and then screw the cleats in place.

STEP 3 Cut the leg to the correct height. You will need an extra pair of hands to support it while you rest the long rule with spirit level on the wall cleat to check that it is level before sawing it at the correct place.

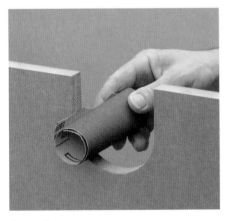

STEP 4 Cut the sheet of MDF to fit the top exactly, and then cut out a channel at the back of the worktop to take all the electrical cables down to the outlet. Sand smooth.

STEP 5 Drill clearance holes, then screw the top to the back cleat and the legs.

STEP 6 Measure two fascia strips to fit on to the front and side of the worktop. Mitering the ends where they meet will give a more professional finish. Apply wood glue, and then secure the strips with brads using the small hammer. Sand, prime, and paint the legs and fascia strips. The worktop can be protected with two coats of varnish, or a coat of paint. If you varnish the top, then run a line of painter's tape along its edge when you paint the fascia to guarantee a really straight line.

YOU WILL NEED:

- PEGBOARD OR
  SOFTBOARD
- MOLDING FOR
  FRAME SURROUND
- MITER SAW TO CUT
  FRAME CORNERS
- DRILL, WALL
  ANCHORS AND
  SCREWS TO
  FIX THE FRAME TO
  THE WALL
- PANEL ADHESIVE
  FOR SOFTBOARD
- 1 IN. X 1 IN./
  2.5 CM X 2.5 CM
  CLEATS FOR
  PEGBOARD
- HARDBOARD PINS
  AND SMALL
  HAMMER FOR THE
  PEGBOARD

PROJECT

Pegboard or softboard wall covering

Pegboard is perforated hardboard, which can be used to cover sections or complete walls. It not only looks good, retro, and funky but provides a really useful storage surface. The holes are used for hooks and pegs for hanging containers, small boxes, speakers, and other gizmos. An alternative, useful, and inexpensive material is softboard, as shown in this project. Softboard is usually used as a liner for school corridor walls. It is very lightweight, and can be stuck on to the wall with panel adhesive and then painted for use as a noticeboard.

Softboard makes an ideal noticeboard because it is lightweight, so it can be stuck on the wall with panel adhesive and painted a favorite color. A few pop-star pin-ups and other teenage collectables will do the rest.

HOW TO DO IT

STEP 1 Hold the softboard against the wall and mark the position of the corners. Apply panel adhesive to the back of the softboard and stick it onto the wall.

STEP 2 Hold the molding up to the wall for position. Mark, cut, and miter the molding. Drill clearance holes in three places along the length of each side. Mark the screw positions on the walls, and then drill and plug. Apply panel adhesive to the back of the moldings and screw them to the wall.

STEP 3 Paint the softboard to blend in or contrast with the wall color. Two coats may be necessary because it is highly absorbent.

YOU WILL NEED:
- HUBCAP
- DRILL
- CLOCK MOVEMENT AND HANDS
- BATTERY
- STEEL WOOL
- DETERGENT
- STICKY DOTS

PROJECT
A hubcap clock

Making clocks is incredibly easy, costs very little, and you can use any image you like for the face, including a photograph of someone, or a hubcap! For a graphic effect, apply brightly colored sticky dots to the clock face instead of numerals. You will also need a battery-powered movement and a pair of hands, which come in a range of styles.

It is easier than you might think to make a clock, and you can make one out of almost anything. All you need is a clock movement with hands and your choice of "clock face" (in this case, a hubcap), and you've done it!

HOW TO DO IT

STEP 1 Clean off any dirt using steel wool and detergent.

STEP 2 Drill a hole in the center of the hubcap for the clock movement.

STEP 3 Add the sticky dots to mark the hours.

STEP 4 Place the mechanism in the back and add the clock hands.

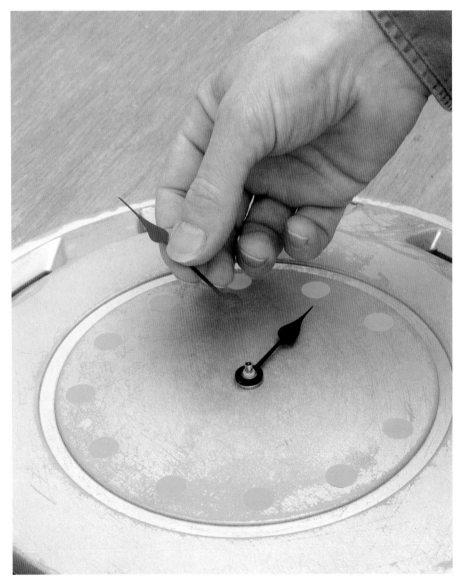

YOU WILL NEED:
- 30 IN./75 CM EACH
  OF ORANGE AND
  BLACK (OR ANY
  COLORS) OF FLEECE
  FABRIC
- THREAD
- SEWING MACHINE
- NEEDLE FOR HAND
  STITCHING
- BAG OF FOAM
  CHIPPINGS OR
  TWO PILLOWS
  PER CUSHION

PROJECT
Floor cushions

If you have a sewing machine and can sew in a straight line, there is no reason to buy large, expensive cushions. The best fabric for this sort of thing is fleece. It is inexpensive, comes in a wide range of funky colors, and is something of a miracle because it is made from recycled plastic bottles! Buy 30 in./75 cm lengths of two colors and then cut the two lengths in half. This will make two 30-in./75-cm square cushions, and you can use both colors on each cushion.

Fleece floor cushions are perfect for lounging on a study floor after a hard few hours' studying. Fleece is a cheap fabric that comes in a huge range of funky colors.

HOW TO DO IT

STEP 1 Place one dark and one light square together with fluffy sides facing. Sew a line of stitches about 1 in./2.5 cm inside the outer edge, but leave a 4 in./10 cm gap for stuffing. Do the same with both cushions.

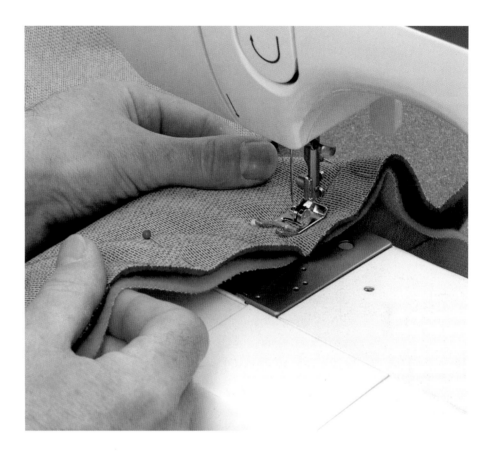

STEP 2 Fill the cushions with foam chips or a pair of pillows, and then use small slipstitches to close the gaps. Could anything be simpler?

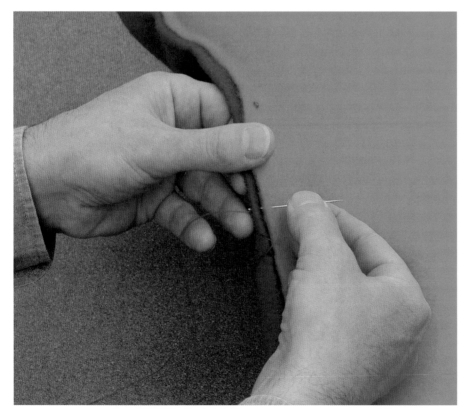

Child's playroom

If you have space for a playroom in your home, then everyone is a winner. The children will love having their own activity room, and you will be able to gear their bedrooms toward relaxation and sleep, avoiding reminders of daytime excitement. A playroom is not just for kids, though, it is somewhere for parents to relax with their children and friends without worrying about dangers or mess. The trick is to design a playroom that is virtually indestructible and danger-free, without making it look like a padded cell!

A children's playroom is a perfect excuse for letting your imagination run wild. This playroom has been transformed into an exciting Wild West setting, complete with its very own jailhouse.

To do this, you design with children in mind, excluding things like slippery floors, sharp corners, not quite out-of-reach shelving, trailing electric cables, and doors that can slam on small fingers. It is not that you want a child who is unaware of danger and is incapable of recognizing it, but more that the playroom should be a sanctuary from it: somewhere to let off steam, a place to be happy and uninhibited. Top ten things to have in a playroom might be…

1. Vinyl flooring

A cushioned vinyl floor with a good-quality underlay and a nonslip surface is the best flooring for a playroom. It has all the necessary qualities. Kids can safely scoot around, rollerskate, play with cars, fall on their knee and spill their drinks, while you have an easy-clean surface.

2. Bean bags

The original beanbag has been downsized for kids, and the same idea has been taken a stage further to make little armchairs with beanbag filling. Kids love sitting or lolling about in beanbags, and there are no hard edges to bump themselves on. As a security measure, stitch the metal end of the zipper flat onto the fabric cover to prevent the ultimate snowstorm when the little darlings discover how to fling out the polystyrene beads!

3. Sofa

The comfortable sofa is for the adults. This is where you sit with your friends, or with a child on your knee, watching a video or telling a story. An inexpensive sofa with a removable, washable cover in a bright color is the ideal choice.

4. TV and video

A television in a playroom may seem something of a contradiction, but television is definitely part of a young child's experience. If the television is surrounded by more hands-on, tempting things to do, then it will not always win the battle for the child's attention. Sometimes children are soothed by the repetition of their favorite story or cartoon video, or want to watch them with their friends. The television can always be kept behind doors if you prefer not to have it on show all the time.

5. Worktop for painting and drawing

Children love to paint and draw and they need access to paper, paints, and crayons. They learn the rudiments at kindergarten, and will delight in endlessly painting their favorite subjects. You will need one or two low tables and chairs, an easel, paint pots, large brushes, anti-spill beakers for water and paints, wax crayons, aprons, and a washing line with pegs to hang up the pictures to dry. Colored paper, glue, and safe scissors are the other must-haves.

6. Construction area

Children play with all kinds of building sets, beginning with basic wooden blocks before moving on to wooden trains, snap-together plastic bricks, and miniature models of everything from galleons to spacecraft. The most important thing to know about construction toys is that each type must be kept separate; otherwise they are never played with. This inevitably means a lot of hard sorting for parents, but you can make life easier by having an efficient storage system. Transparent plastic crates on casters are the perfect solution.

7. Shades or drapes

The playroom will mostly be used in the daytime, but it is still nice to have the option of cutting

Each set of games and construction toys needs to be kept separate, or they will never be played with.

If you don't have space for a separate playroom, here's an idea for creating a separate one inside a bedroom—is it a greenhouse or is it a playhouse?

FAR RIGHT: **A clever use of mural paint on the walls can create 3-dimensional mini-dramas in a playroom.**

out the daylight by pulling down the shades or drawing the drapes. They are particularly useful for afternoon naps on the settee, a game of hide and seek, shutting out the rain, or reducing dazzling sunshine. And winter evenings always seem more cozy with the curtains drawn.

8. Sink

If there is a water source nearby, have the pipes diverted and instal a sink in the playroom. You will not regret it. It means that children can be cleaned up after painting, eating, or accidents without leaving the room. The paint pots and brushes can be washed, cloths can be wrung out under the faucet, and all this without leaving the playroom. A low, square sink is ideal, but do have a thermostat on the hot faucet to prevent scalds. It is also wise to keep the plug on a high shelf to avert any catastrophic floods!

9. Easy-reach storage

One way to make short work of tidying up is to build a boxed seat along one wall with doors hinged along their top edge instead of on the side. They can then be lifted up like garage doors for putting boxes away. Another storage idea is to have a rail with pegs for hanging bags—plastic mesh bags are good because the contents are

visible. Buy the storage crates first and build the shelves to fit them. It is also essential to have out-of-reach storage for art materials, a first-aid kit, face paints, board games, and jigsaw puzzles —everything that you have out.

10. Bright lights

There is a difference between bright and harsh, and what you want is bright, jolly lighting. One or two 100-watt overhead pendant lights will illuminate the room, and a dimmer switch can be used to lower the light for quiet times. Anglepoise lights are useful for illuminating worktops, but use screw fittings to secure the lamp onto a shelf and avoid any type of lamp that could be knocked over.

When decorating the playroom, include one area of wall painted with blackboard paint. This is guaranteed to be one of the most popular places in the room. Supply a large box of colored chalks and a damp cloth to clean the board. Paint the other walls with bright, cheerful colors and use as many special effects as you can find. Glitter glazes and scented paints are just two fun finishes that kids will love. And one of the following projects shows how to print a mural using foam blocks. It couldn't be easier or more effective. Deciding whether to let children help with the decorating is up to you—there are definite pros and cons (it can be difficult for a young child to understand why it's OK to paint on the walls in one room but not in another!). The floor project shows how to stencil a bold pattern of stripes, balls, and stars on a painted wooden floor. This could also be done with vinyl floor paints to cheer up an existing vinyl floor. In a big room, the floor can be treated like a playground and painted with a roadway, hopscotch, snakes and ladders, or another favorite game. Let your imagination run wild—the more fun you have while decorating, the better it will look.

YOU WILL NEED:

- OFF-CUTS OF UPHOLSTERY FOAM
- SNAP-BLADE KNIFE
- BALL POINT OR FELT-TIP PEN
- SET SQUARE
- RULE
- A SELECTION OF LATEX PAINT COLORS
- PRE-MIXED WALLPAPER PASTE (DO THIS 5 MINUTES BEFORE YOU NEED IT)
- SEVERAL LARGE PLATES
- BRUSH FOR MIXING

PROJECT

Mural printed with large foam blocks

Children have been building toy towns from shaped wooden blocks for a very long time, and this project does the same thing in two dimensions instead of three. Look out for a store selling upholstery foam, and buy off-cuts. They are easy to cut with a snap-blade knife if you make the first cut along a drawn line, then bend the foam to open the cut and cut through the rest. Limit yourself to five bold shapes—a large square, a small square, an oblong, a triangle, and an arch.

A colorful mural printed with foam blocks is far easier than a hand-drawn creation, but can be just as inspirational.

HOW TO DO IT

STEP 1 Draw the pattern shapes on card, using the set square and rule to draw the geometric shapes accurately. Draw generously sized shapes in proportion to the wall width and height. Stick the shapes onto the foam.

STEP 2 Cut out the shapes. Make sure you have a sharp blade, and make the first cut in one go along the drawn line. The lower cuts to separate the foam pieces are not as important because they are not part of the printing surface.

STEP 3 Place a circle of each color on separate plates, and mix in the same amount of pre-mixed wallpaper paste. This will stop the paint from running if you have too much paint on the foam.

STEP 4 Dampen the foam, squeeze out any excess moisture, and then begin to print. Press the block into the paint and test the print on a sheet of paper.

STEP 5 Press the foam onto the wall to make a print. Build up the base blocks first. From this base, use the squares and oblongs to make a pair of pillars, and then print the arch shape over the top.

STEP 6 Top some of the squares with triangles, and keep on swapping the foam blocks and printing until the wall is covered with a toy town. A coat of clear varnish will help to protect and preserve the mural.

YOU WILL NEED:

- SHEET OF WAXED STENCIL CARD CUT INTO TWO 12IN. / 30CM SQUARES
- SNAP-BLADE KNIFE
- PHOTOCOPY OF EACH PATTERN
- SPRAY ADHESIVE
- LARGE STENCIL BRUSH
- TWO WHITE PLATES
- ABSORBENT TOWEL
- PAINT IN TWO CONTRASTING COLORS (EITHER LATEX AND VARNISH, OR A PREPARATORY FLOOR PAINT)
- CLEAR, STRONG POLYURETHANE VARNISH
- BRUSH TO APPLY THE VARNISH
- MINERAL SPIRITS TO CLEAN THE BRUSH

PROJECT
Stenciling a floor border

Stenciling on the floor is really easy, and you never get the problem of paint running, as sometimes happens on walls. For this project you need a 12 in./30 cm square as the repeat, with two different shapes cut out of stencil card and alternated to form a border pattern around the edge of the room. This could be done on vinyl floor tiles with special vinyl paint, or using a latex paint with a varnish to seal it on wood. If you want a solid border, then paint a 12-in./30-cm-wide background color, or alternate two colors that can then be reversed for the pattern.

A stencil pattern border can brighten up either a wooden or a vinyl floor. For vinyl, use a special vinyl paint. Use a few repetitive patterns to produce a balanced, geometric effect.

HOW TO DO IT

STEP 1 Photocopy the pattern so that it fills most of the stencil card—leave a ³/₄–1³/₈-in./ 2–3-cm border around the edges so the stencil is not too flimsy. Spray the back of the pattern with spray adhesive and stick it to the card.

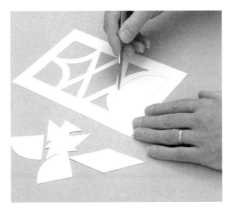

STEP 2 Use a snap-blade knife to cut out the stencils carefully. Always cut outward from the corners, and try to cut curves with one even movement to avoid jagged edges.

STEP 3 Spray the back of the stencil with spray adhesive and leave for 5 minutes. Put a blob of each color on the plates. You need a very small amount of paint for stenciling. Coat the brush with paint, and then dab most of it off on the paper towel.

STEP 4 Mark the guidelines in chalk if you are painting on to wooden floorboards; otherwise paint onto the colored background. Place the stencil on the floor and smooth it flat. Apply the first color.

STEP 5 Apply the second color in exactly the same way.

STEP 6 If you are painting a wooden floor with latex apply 1–3 coats of varnish when the paint is bone dry. Floor paint is tough enough not to need varnish.

Use this guide to help you cut out the pattern for the stencil and position it on the correct place on your floor.

YOU WILL NEED:
- SHEET OF ½-IN./ 1.2-CM MDF
- 2 LEGS FOR THE FRONT OF THE WORKTOP 2 IN. x 2 IN./5CM x 5CM
- CLEATS FOR THE WALLS 2-IN. x 1-IN./ 5CM x 2.5CM
- 2 IN. x ½IN./5 CM x 1.2 CM/ FASCIA MOLDING FOR THE TOP
- WOODFILLER
- NUMBER 6 WALL ANCHORS
- 1 IN./2.5 CM PINS
- WOOD GLUE
- SANDPAPER
- PRIMER AND ENAMEL OR MAT PAINT
- LONG RULE WITH SPIRIT LEVEL
- PENCIL FOR MARKING
- DRILL WITH A ¼-IN./6-MM MASONRY BIT
- PILOT, CLEARANCE AND COUNTERSINK BIT (USE A SCREWSINK FOR ALL THREE)
- BOX OF NUMBER 6, 2-IN./5-CM SCREWS
- BACKSAW
- SMALL HAMMER
- NAIL PUNCH
- PAINT BRUSH

PROJECT
Making a low worktop

Children's furniture can be expensive to buy, so if you are fitting out a playroom it is well worth building a low, stable work surface. Begin by buying small chairs to match a low work surface, increasing the size of both as the children grow. Think about placing the work surface in a convenient place for electric outlets or wall lights, or in good natural light.

A low work surface is probably the most important item in a children's playroom. It is essential for doing painting, drawing, coloring in and glueing, as well as other learning activities.

HOW TO DO IT

STEP 1 Mark the height for the cleat on the wall. Cut the cleat to the correct length and drill clearance holes every 8 in./20 cm Mark these as screw positions on the wall, and then drill and plug the holes.

STEP 2 Screw the cleat to the wall. Rest the worktop on the cleat and (with help) place the legs in position. Mark their cutting height, having first checked the worktop with the long rule with spirit level.

STEP 3 Measure the fascia against the top, and mark the position of the miters.

STEP 4 Glue and pin the fascia boards to the edge of the worktop.

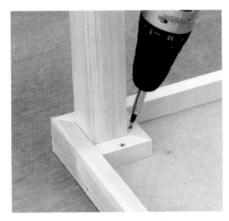

STEP 5 Miter two cleats to form a square collar to hold the leg firmly into the corner of the fascia. Screw into position.

STEP 6 Drill clearance holes and screw through the worktop to secure it to the wall-mounted cleat.

YOU WILL NEED:

• SHEET OF
 SOFTBOARD
 (STOCKED BY
 LUMBER
 MERCHANTS)
• PANEL ADHESIVE
• "HOCKEY STICK"
 MOLDING TO
 SURROUND THE TOP
 AND SIDES
• NUMBER 6
 1½-IN./3.8-CM
 SCREWS OR 2.5-
 CM/1-IN PINS
• WOOD FILLER
• ¼-IN./6-MM WALL
 PLUGS (IF USING
 SCREWS TO FIX)
• BACKSAW
• MITER BLOCK
• DRILL WITH NUMBER
 6 MASONRY BIT, OR
 A SMALL HAMMER
 AND NAIL PUNCH
• CUPPED BRASS
 SCREWS

PROJECT
Fitting a pinboard above the worktop

It is a very good idea to fit a pinboard that runs the length of the worktop. This means that paintings and drawings can be pinned up to dry and be admired. A pinboard can be made from cork tiles or softboard, which is inexpensive. It can be painted any color to match the room.

Softboard makes an ideal pinboard because it is lightweight, so it can be stuck to the wall with panel adhesive and painted a favorite color. Some paintings to be proud of will complete the look.

HOW TO DO IT

STEP 1 Measure and cut the softboard to fit. Cut the length of molding for the top edge with mitered ends. Cut the two side pieces, also mitered at the top and bottom.

STEP 2 Fix the lower mitered molding onto the wall first, using cupped brass screws.

STEP 3 Fix the rest of the frame to the wall. Apply a long squiggle of panel adhesive to the back of the softboard and attach to the wall.

Color & light

Selecting colors can be completely daunting—there's such a huge range of choice it can be difficult to know where to start. But everyone's got their favorites and it's important to be surrounded by yours. But a combination of color and light can also completely set the mood of a room, so it's useful to know about the qualities of different colors and the effects they can have. This section describes how colors can be used to create moods and different styles, and how a whole range of different lighting can enhance the function and atmosphere of a room.

Using color to create moods

Color can lift our moods, relax us, stimulate our senses, and even make us feel uncomfortable in certain combinations. According to color theory, there are three primary colors—red, yellow and blue—from which all other colors are derived. To test this, put a blob of each primary color on a white saucer and then mix equal amounts of two colors together. Red and yellow make orange; red and blue make purple; and yellow and blue make green.

Lilac is a calming color because it is a product of blue, which is said to have a meditative effect. Be careful not to go too dark though— darker shades of lilac, which become violet purple, can be depressing.

These are the secondary colors, and by adding black or white you can darken or lighten them. By mixing combinations of different amounts of the primaries and black and white you can, in theory, make any imaginable color. It is quite a science, though, and beginners soon discover that most combinations turn gray or muddy brown! The paint companies have taken the guesswork out of color mixing for us, and computers are used to dispense just the right amount of each component color so that we can rely on color number 3055b, for instance, to look the same every time.

Choosing colors

When choosing colors for a room, the first consideration should always be to choose a color that you like, regardless of fashion. That is not to say don't experiment, because otherwise you would probably never develop your own ideas. Try to raise your color awareness by noticing combinations of colors that you like. And don't restrict yourself to just looking at color in a decorating context, because you may find the best inspiration elsewhere, for instance in a cookbook. A plate of salad, a bowl of fruit, or heaps of vegetables on a market stall could equally provide the key to a brand-new look for one of the rooms in your house. Vacations are also inspirational times, because all our senses are more receptive to pleasure when we are relaxed and away from the pressures of everyday living. Take photographs of the landscape and buildings, the sea, and any unusual color combinations, and then see if you can pick out one color scheme that reminds you of that time and place.

Making a complete color change can be daunting, especially if your inspiration has come from a book or make-over television program in which a room has been professionally styled

with coordinating furniture and accessories. Strong colors invariably work well on television because the programs need to make an impact in a short time, and there is not much room for subtlety. In your own home, conditions are different, and you may find that the ideas which inspired you need to be toned down for everyday life. A strong color is useful for defining the shape of a room and creating an atmosphere. It will set the mood for the whole home when used in the entrance hall, and it is a good way of defining your own space if you are sharing the living space with other people. Blue is a most versatile color and was one of the last to appear in a full range of shades for home decorating because, until recently, the deepest shades were available only as pigments from artists' suppliers. This was also noticed with green because it

Red and yellow fabrics add warmth to a room with a wooden floor and create a modern country look.

derives from a mixture of blue and yellow. As the range of blues has expanded, so have the greens. The most obvious newcomer that has become tremendously popular is lime green. It is sharp, sassy, and youthful—the color that nobody grew up with! Also note that in hot countries the light is much brighter, and strong colors work better than they do in the pale gray of Northern light. In fact, color cannot exist without light, and colored light actually changes painted color. When darkness falls, all color disappears and red,

A cool room lacking natural light can be brightened by white, and this is the perfect background for a crimson spotlight to add a splash of color.

blue, and green become black—it's just a trick of the light!

Warming

If you have a cool room that needs warmth, use red, yellow, and orange—the effect is immediate and warming. The intrinsic power of a color is not lost in dilution either. A warm yellow could be a rich cream or an earthy ocher—these are the yellows that lean toward red and away from blue. In the same way, choose reds that contain yellow rather than blue, like deep, rusty brown, red ocher or deep, burned orange.

To keep a color scheme warm, avoid reds, purples, or pinks that contain a lot of blue. These exotic colors, like crimson, violet, and cerise, are good for highlights and flashes of brilliance, but they do not radiate warmth. A rosy pink with pea green and white is a natural combination that is fresh without feeling cool. Choose greens with a deep-yellow cast, like moss, pea, and olive, for warmth. Sage green is a neutral gray-green that can be warmed or cooled by the colors that surround it. Use it with deep reds and mustard yellow for a warm country look. Brown, rust, and deep greens all look good with natural wood and fabrics, and the effect does not have to be old-fashioned or heavy—mix woven fabrics like tweed with leather chairs, wooden flooring, and rugs for a modern country look.

Cooling

In the Northern Hemisphere we tend to choose colors for warmth, but sometimes we need the opposite effect. If the coolness of a room is pleasant and desirable, enhance the effect with pale greens, icy blue, or pale lemon-yellow. Think of the Swedish look, where the whites and grays of the landscape have been brought into the home. The style is cool and minimal. In the Mediterranean countries, houses are painted

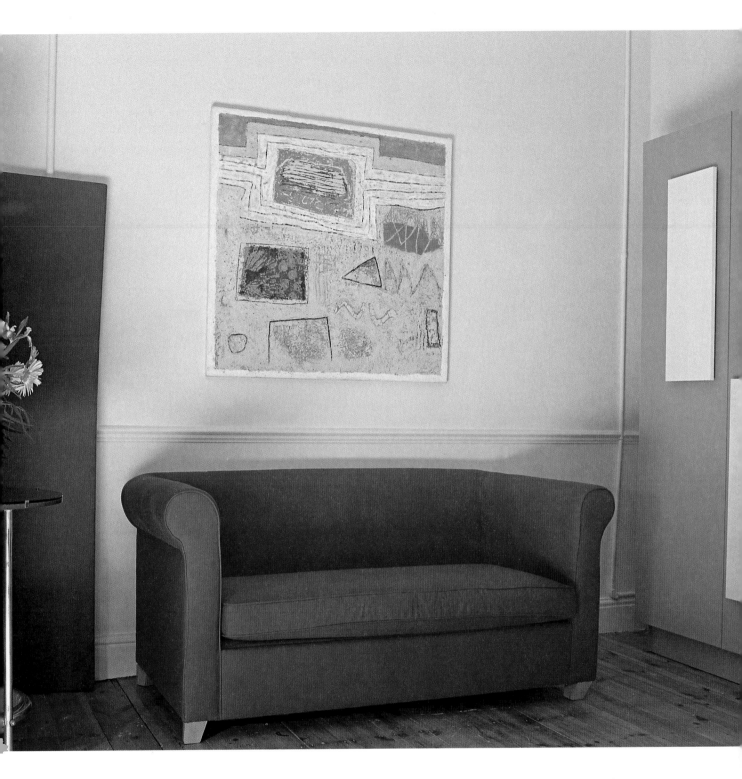

white to reflect the heat away from the house and keep it cool. Used indoors, white will brighten a cool room that lacks natural light without warming it, and help to create a tranquil atmosphere. All colors look good with white, but the really strong contrasts look best in brilliant sunshine, as in the intense blues and whites of buildings on the Greek islands. A pale sky or lavender blue and white have an altogether more calming effect.

Citrus yellow together with gray, black, and white gives a sharp, cool, and modern feel.

Red can add warmth to a room. Red and blue together, as two primary colors, make a strong contrast, which can look very effective.

It looks especially good with the reflective metals like stainless steel, chrome, or aluminum. Black and white are cool but hard, and being the ultimate contrast are best used where crisp lines are required on tiles or to make a traditional checkerboard floor.

Creating an atmosphere with color

Certain styles and color schemes are quickly recognizable, for example, New England, African, Caribbean, and Far Eastern. This makes it quite easy for us to recreate a particular atmosphere in our own homes, giving the living room the Moroccan look, or a dining room a dash of

Scandinavian, mostly with the use of color. Different historical periods are also known for their color schemes, which were sometimes more bizarre than you would imagine, and most paint companies produce historically correct colors for use in period homes. This does not mean living in museums and furnishing our homes with all the correct antiques. A Georgian or Victorian room returned to its original colors and furnished in a modern style can look elegant and seriously cool at the same time.

As a rule, light color schemes will provide a lighter atmosphere, and so on. If you want your bedroom to look like a Turkish lovenest,

LEFT: **Pinks and purples in these silk and satin cushions suggest an exotic Turkish bazaar.**

begin by getting the color right on the walls—a deep Alizarin crimson is as passionate a color as you can find and has its origins in the Ottoman Empire. Be inspired by color combinations in paintings, and textiles, and decorate with bazaar accessories like metal lanterns, scarves, beadwork, and wall hangings.

Blues and yellows

Deep ultramarine blue is cool and atmospheric, and a room with walls painted this blue will appear bigger. The effect is the opposite to that of deep red, which can make the walls close in! Blue is said to be the perfect meditative color, so choose this for a spiritual atmosphere. Yellow rooms are said to be stimulating to the senses and for this reason yellow is best avoided in bedrooms where it might prevent a good night's sleep. Yellow is a good kitchen color where its positive properties will give you the ideal start to the day. Lavender blue is the opposite—it is very calming, but taken several shades darker to violet purple, it can be depressing, so use purple sparingly unless it is contrasted with an equally powerful color such as lime green, which will neutralize its depressive qualities. Purple and lime green have become such an essential part of the modern decorator's palette that these colours will probably define our period of history as clearly as pale green, apricot, and cream did in the early years of the 20th century.

ABOVE: **The warm yellow of these walls is complemented by the Oriental purples of the lampshade, chair cover, and floor cushions.**

LEFT: **Green and white combinations have a fresh, cool effect. If you want a warmer green than the one shown here, choose one with a deep-yellow cast, like moss, pea, or olive green.**

Using lighting effectively

The first thing to consider when decorating a room is the amount of natural light it gets and also when it gets the sun. This proportion of natural light and sunlight, and the function of the room, will help you make the correct lighting choices. Lighting should never be an afterthought in the decorating process and is something to consider from the start, especially if new outlets and channels for wall lights are needed. Remember this and you will never have the depressing task of channeling into a newly plastered and painted wall to fit a wall light!

It is not just color that can affect mood—the way a room is lit can affect the whole atmosphere, so it is worth giving it as much consideration as you do the color, furniture, and accessories. Lighting has to be functional, but it is also esthetic, so think about the function of the room as well as the mood you want to set for it. Good illumination can be created by using several different types of lighting, each of which has a different function.

Task lighting

When you are planning the lighting for your room, first decide on which areas need strong light, or task lighting. These should be the work and reading areas, where it is essential for you to

RIGHT: **Table lamps create pools of low light, which make a room more cozy and intimate.**

FAR RIGHT: **Inspection lamps, spotlights, or just plain torches can be used to simulate lighting, so you can buy a type suitable for a particular room.**

be able to see what you are doing. You will also need occasional strong lighting in some areas to illuminate cabinets, bookshelves, hi-fi equipment, televisions, video recorders, or writing desks.

Ambient lighting

Ambient lighting is another way of describing the light that is all around us. This background lighting simulates the natural daylight and takes the glare out of direct task lighting. Ambient light reveals the shape and size of the room and the colors used in it. A pendant fitting or a wall light fits this description.

Accent lighting

This type of lighting is either purely decorative, where the light itself is the decorative feature, or is used to highlight and accentuate a piece of furniture or art in the room.

Buying lighting

Lighting is not an easy thing to buy because, unlike other products, it is difficult to look before you buy—if you go to a crowded lighting showroom with no idea of what you are looking for, it will be practically impossible to judge the effect of an individual light when so many others are turned on. The best idea is to decide what kind of light you need and experiment in your home before you go out and buy it. Look in lighting catalogs for the different kinds of lights available, and magazines for how they look in situ. Then experiment by using torches, plug-in spotlights, and inspection lamps to simulate wall washers, uplighters, downlighters, pendant lights, spotlights, and table lamps. This is a job for two or more people, so invite friends round with their torches and turn a task into a party! There are lots of good lighting catalogs that supply goods by mail order, so there is no reason to feel

limited to what is available locally. Most suppliers also understand the importance of seeing a lamp in your own room, and will be happy to offer an exchange or refund when you return a light for purely esthetic reasons.

Creating illusions

If you use a room during the day and it gets very little sunlight, you can make a room seem much sunnier by concealing white fluorescent tubes beneath valances above the windows. Daytime lighting is often necessary, especially in winter, but bulbs tend to create an unpleasant glare in natural daylight. Fit concealed halogen spotlights behind plants or furniture, and fluorescent striplights beneath wall cabinets to light worktops. Make any room appear more spacious by washing the walls with light from above or below. You can also try to disguise any features you dislike in a room by using angled spotlights to cast pools of light in another direction. A pendant light will appear to lower the ceiling height to where the light begins; use these lights in small rooms with high ceilings to change the proportions. A room will look more cozy and intimate with table lamps creating pools of low light.

Colored lights

Tinted bulbs are useful for creating an atmosphere. Pale yellow will warm the room and pink will create a rosy glow. Stronger-colored bulbs will knock out some of the colors completely —red or green cancel each other out, and blue will give a cool nightclub effect, which is perfect for summer parties. Red has the opposite effect, making a cool room seem instantly warmer. Christmas lights are also useful for adding instant sparkle, and use very little electricity. Put them around pictures, doorways, or in glass fishbowls as feature lights with a party feel.

Uplighters can make a ceiling look higher by casting it with light from below.

Candles

Candles give a room a unique atmosphere, and there has never been more choice than there is today. One candle can cost as much as a table lamp, but the perfumes on offer are so sublime that stores have trouble keeping up with the demand. The flicker of candlelight is the most romantic and relaxing type of light, and rows of nightlights bring a room to life.

Safety

There is one big downside to the candle boom and that is the rise in the number of house fires. Always use common sense when you site your candles, and never place them where there is the slightest chance of flames catching paper or fabric. It is also important not to leave candles burning unattended; we all love to walk into a candlelit room, but it is easy to ignore the safety advice. Very real danger comes from falling asleep or actually leaving the house with a candle burning: this should *never* be done.

FAR LEFT: **Halogen spotlights cast an ambient light, which can be angled to cast pools in different directions.**

Accessories

The finishing touches you add to a room are a chance to put a little of yourself into the style, whether it be in an arrangement of pictures, a choice of mirrors, a pile of cushions, or a display of flowers. These final choices are fun to make, and usually take the least amount of time and effort. But they can also make or break the whole effect. This section gives a few things to think about when you're choosing these final touches.

Accessories

The dictionary defines an accessory as "a thing that is extra, useful, or decorative but not essential." These are the finishing touches to have some fun with when the paint has dried, the flooring is down, and the drapes are up. This is where we can let our own individuality shine through, making our rooms reflection of our lifestyles and personalities.

Walls without pictures or mirrors can make a room seem cold and unfriendly. Pictures are an ideal way of adding a splash of individuality to your walls.

Magazines and mail-order catalogs all use stylists, who are to rooms what hair and make-up people are to celebrities. The stylist's job involves keeping track of everything that already exists and is new to the accessory market, and their real skill is in knowing how to accessorize to best effect. Thanks to these tireless hunter-gatherers, we get tons of visual reference and no shortage of shopping information. Treat yourself to a selection of different sources of inspiration—a good weekend color supplement, a monthly homes magazine, or a range of mail-order catalogs.

A room with individuality will often include a mixture of old and new objects, or at least things sourced from different places: a set of matching cushions from a chain store, for instance, used next to an unusual lamp from a specialized lighting shop. Similar objects in varying styles will create areas of interest that will catch the eye. Black-and-white photographs arranged in a block of four matching frames on the wall will look smart and stylish, but a bit cold and contrived. Add one brightly colored picture in an intricately carved wooden frame on a table top and the atmosphere will change immediately.

Not everything needs to be unique or expensive and it is worth perusing a few of the style magazine's "best-buy" pages for recommendations. Keep a look out for the price

comparison features, which show very similar designs with massive price differentials. You may fall in love with an impossibly expensive wrought-iron candelabra and be lucky enough to discover an almost identical version in a cheaper home center. Decorating has become very much like fashion and clothing in this way, with new styles sourced at the top end of the market, then copied and quickly reproduced for mass consumption. Great news for the consumer, not so good for the designers under constant pressure to change styles and create new looks.

Frames and pictures

Walls without pictures or mirrors seem to absorb energy and interest from the room and, depending on the wall color, they can also make a room seem cold and unfriendly. There are so many framing options that it can be very confusing, and the right frame can make an ordinary image look impressive or quite the opposite. As a simple rule, most things look best with some white space around them, and a small image needs the most space between it and the frame. Sets of matching frames can look brilliant with very simple images of fruit or flowers, bold colorful art postcards, or something more graphic, like letters of the alphabet or stamped numbers. The frames themselves can be the stars, especially if you

trawl through antique and bric-à-brac markets. An ornate molding can look fabulous around the most unlikely image. If you lack confidence, buy framed prints from a good furniture and accessory store or a small gallery. The actual act of looking for something to put on your walls will soon make you aware of what appeals to you and what doesn't. Ideally you should find something that will give you pleasure every time you look at it.

Cushions and throws

All you need to uplift an elderly sofa or chair is a new throw and a couple of cushions. Throws do a lot more than just disguising marks on the upholstery; they are also useful for introducing a strong color contrast, a more casual, relaxed style, and a real sense of comfort. A throw can be the same color as the sofa, but a very different texture, for instance, mohair on linen or velvet on leather. Cushions and throws can be co-ordinated in fabric, texture, or color, but beware of too many matching accessories—they can make a home look like a hotel. If you are short of money but want a new look, buy a large cotton decorator's drop cloth and a packet of machine dye to make a giant

throw to cover an old sofa. Spend any money left over on lovely cushions, or buy cushion pads and make the covers yourself. For color and sparkle at a reasonable price, buy Indian or Chinese fabric; for florals, buy an old chintz drape and add a nice trimming; for knitted woollens or plain cottons adapt old shirts and sweaters by cutting off the arms and sewing up the top and bottom seams— the buttons stay put.

Vases, flowers, and plants

If you allow yourself just one treat for the house once a week, make it a vase of fresh flowers. Vases can be square, round, tall, or short, and be made of glass or ceramic. Left empty, they still look good on a shelf. This is a way to add accent color that can be changed to suit your mood. If fresh flowers don't match your busy lifestyle, then get a plant or two. Very beautiful house plants are often low maintenance in the right position, which is usually near light and out of drafts. Larger, more architectural plants, like palm, bamboo, cacti, and the good old money plant, look good in contemporary surroundings. If you prefer something smaller with flowers, orchids are the current must-haves.

Throws are a good way of introducing a strong color contrast, a more relaxed style and a sense of comfort.

Mini projects

Starting big decorating projects can be daunting. It's best to begin with something small, so you can get your creative steam up; you will find that one thing leads to another. These projects do not take long to complete and do not cost much. They have been designed to give maximum satisfaction with minimum effort. A room can be perked up with new cushions, frames, and lampshades, and sometimes all that is needed is a make-over for your existing accessories.

MINI PROJECT
Lampshades

YOU WILL NEED:
- A SELECTION OF BUTTONS
- TUBE OF CLEAR GLUE
- LAMPSHADE

It is often difficult to find a lampshade to match the color scheme of your room. But there is no need to worry, because lampshades can be painted with ordinary latex paint, and a test pot of color will be enough to transform two medium-size shades or one large one. Plain colors look great, but patterns can be stamped or stenciled on, and you can also add trimmings such as a fringe, baubles, or beads in contrasting or harmonizing colors. The lampshade in the project is embellished with buttons that are stuck on with clear glue. Before the throwaway culture took over, every home had a button tin and these sometimes now turn up at flea markets and charity shops. Old buttons can be really beautiful and even the plain shell or mother-of-pearl types are well worth showing off on a lampshade or cushion cover.

Bases of lamps can be decorated as well as the shades. This seaside-style lamp base has been given a wet-sand effect with shells attached using strong glue.

HOW TO DO IT

STEP 1 Plan the arrangement of the buttons on the shade. Apply a blob of glue to each.

STEP 2 Hold it firmly against the shade until you feel the glue bonding. Continue with this until you have used all your chosen buttons.

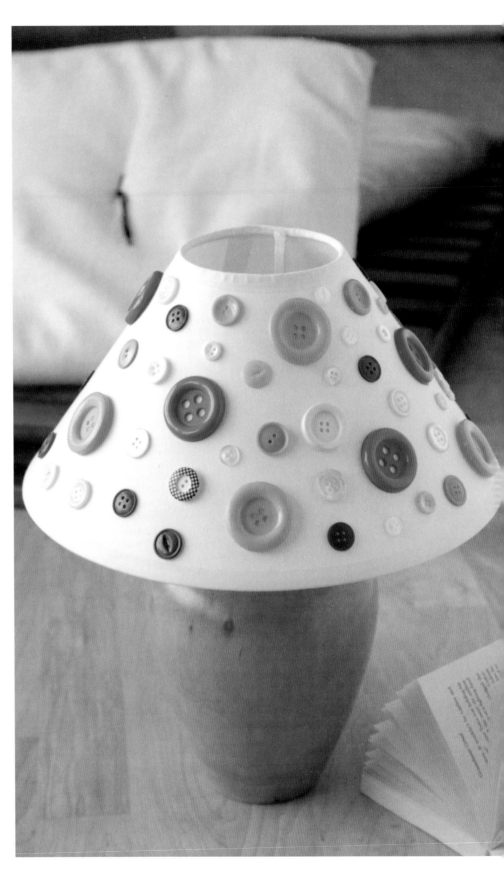

YOU WILL NEED:

- 19½ IN./50 CM FLEECE FABRIC IN COLOR A
- 19½ IN./50 CM OF COLOR B FLEECE FABRIC, WHICH IS HALF THE WIDTH OF COLOR A FABRIC
- CUSHION PAD
- LONG RULE
- CRAFT KNIFE
- SEWING MACHINE
- SCISSORS
- THREAD
- PINS
- CARDBOARD TEMPLATE FOR CUT-OUT
- PEN

MINI PROJECT
Cushions

There is no need to put up with grubby or faded cushions when a new set of covers is all you need to inject a bit of fresh style into the room. If your cushions feel lumpy, be bold and throw them away, then treat yourself to some new ones. Cushion pads are not expensive and fabric can be bought either in remnant lengths or by the foot. Check out thrift stores and markets for lengths of fabric or clothing that can be cut down to make cushion covers. Shirts and cardigans make great covers because they already have a buttoned opening and you simply have to sew across under the arms and then cut off the top and the bottom. Evening dresses can be transformed into wonderfully exotic cushion covers for the boudoir, and an odd velvet drape could be used to make a whole new set of cushions. There is also a lot of fun to be had with dyes and trimmings. If the bug really bites you, you could end up selling designer cushions from a stall of your own!

This stylish cushion cover can be made from fleece or felt, both of which do not fray when cut, so they will need no hemming. Fleece has the advantage of being washable, so is the best choice if you want the cushions to last a while, and if you use a washable pad, the cushion can go in the washing machine and tumble drier.

A two-colored cushion cover made out of fleece fabric is easy to make, and, if used with a washable cushion pad, it can be put in the washing machine and drier.

HOW TO DO IT

STEP 1 Cut out three squares of fabric in the same size—two in color A and one in color B.

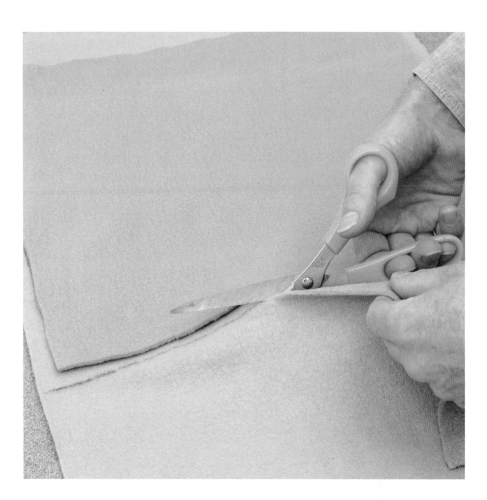

STEP 2 Mark the cut-out squares by drawing a grid on the back of the color B square to use as a pattern. Use the craft knife and long rule to cut out the shapes.

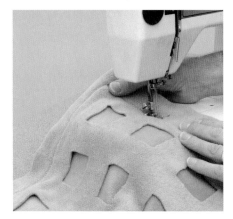

STEP 3 Place the color B square on top of the other two and sew a line of close zigzag stitches to join the three layers on three sides. Put the cushion pad inside, then sew up the fourth side.

YOU WILL NEED:

- FOIL WRAPPERS
  FROM CANDIES AND
  CHOCOLATES
- PVA GLUE
- A SIMPLE FRAME
- SCISSORS OR A
  SNAP-BLADE KNIFE

MINI PROJECT
Frames

Framed pictures on the walls make a house look like home, and there is no need to have bare walls just because you think you don't have any art worth framing. Make the frames into a focal point and pop anything inside them that fits in with the shape and color scheme. You will be surprised how effective this can look. If your frame is square, pay a visit to a card shop and check out all the square cards. Once everyday objects are framed, they assume a new importance, and can even become art! Try framing groups of bottle caps, buttons, labels, or some unusual foreign packaging—most of these things have been designed by experts, so why not put them on show? When it comes to the actual frames, these can be picked up second-hand for next to nothing at yard sales or from market stalls. New frames from discount stores can also be used, and sometimes all that is needed is a coat of paint to give them a new lease of life. Buy matching sets and paint them different colors, or buy lots of different frames and make them into a set by painting them a matching color. There are so many ways in which they can be improved— it's just up to you to do it.

This wooden frame was about as plain and cheap as anything new can be, but now looks a million dollars with its shiny jewel-colored covering. The metallic papers are candy wrappers (yes, you have to eat the candies first!), which are carefully smoothed out and stuck onto the frame in a patchwork pattern using PVA glue. This project is pure pleasure, from start to finish.

Old picture frames or cheap, new ones can be given this sparkling, jewel effect using candy wrappers and glue. Try framing everyday objects inside to create an original work of art!

HOW TO DO IT

STEP 1 Smooth out enough candy wrappers to cover the frame. They will need to overlap each other, and look best in a random patchwork pattern. Lay them out to decide on the color arrangement.

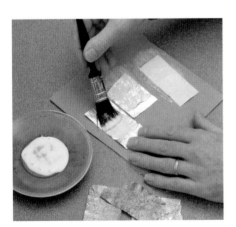

STEP 2 Apply a coat of PVA to the frame, and then leave it to become tacky. Apply a coat of PVA to the back of each wrapper.

STEP 3 Smooth each wrapper onto the frame. Take care not to rip the fragile foil as you flatten it around the shape of the frame.

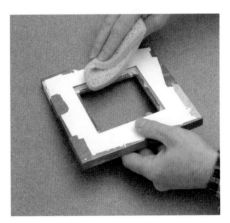

STEP 4 Use a sponge to ease the foil papers onto the frame and then wipe away any excess glue.

Making soft furnishings

Introduction

Making your own soft furnishings can be very satisfying and you can make the most of your individual taste.

Soft furnishings can really enhance a room and provide an attractive decorative atmosphere. You don't need to be an accomplished needleperson to attempt many of the projects in this section—there are simple make-overs that even the beginner can attempt.

There is a wonderful choice of fabrics from all over the world readily available to us nowadays, and modern, easy-to-use fixings make soft furnishing a craft accessible to everyone. Having such a choice, however, makes it difficult to know where to begin when making these important decisions regarding your home and lifestyle.

Changing the covers of chairs is an easy way to transform the decorative atmosphere of a room.

This section is designed to lead you through the different options available, from creating a color scheme and room style and selecting fabrics, to making up soft furnishings and recycling or making over the furnishings you have already. It is economical to make the major soft furnishings that are used daily, such as drapes, shades, table linen, seating, and bed-linen, and it is great fun to create the more decorative elements, such as cushions and lampshades.

You could have a theme running throughout your home or change the mood for each room, but take care that you do not overdo this, as too much contrast in the home can be unsettling. Consider also the architectural style of the rooms, as creative window treatments can show beautiful period windows at their best, or disguise characterless ones.

Color in the home

Color within the home affects our moods quite considerably. Different people benefit from different colors.

Unless you really want to go over the top, use red sparingly in the home. Orange is another vibrant color, but it also has earthy associations. Use terra-cotta shades if you want to suggest warmth but prefer less vitality in a room than a bright orange.

In many countries, yellow represents the power of the sun. It is a stimulating color that can overpower a small room, but its links to longevity and happiness make it a popular choice for family-oriented rooms.

Brown is literally a grounding color. It gives a sense of well-loved antiquity and has a stabilizing effect. Green is thought to calm the nerves and invoke feelings of safety. As it is such a balancing color, it can be used in most situations, but avoid it for offices, because too much calm does not induce one to work!

Blue represents the energy derived from water. It is a tranquil and serene color that is a popular choice for bedrooms, since it is believed to suggest sleep. Those prone to low moods should avoid too much blue in the home, which may literally give them the "blues."

Introspection, dignity, and artistry are all associated with the color purple. It is a regal color that is great for opulent styles in grand rooms. Purple is often chosen for meditative locations, as it has very strong links with spirituality.

Pink is a feminine and romantic color, and is a popular shade for bedrooms because it is calm and nurturing and is thought to be sedating.

Creative treatments can make the most of period windows and doors.

White can be calm and comfortable to live with. It can help to enlarge a small room and shows off other colors and features.

RIGHT: Yellow's association with the sun and happiness makes it a suitable color for bathrooms and other family-oriented rooms.

White is a superb backdrop to other colors. Shades of white and cream are comfortable to live with, whereas brilliant white is often too stark.

Gray is a neutral color that can be regarded either as harmonious or depressing. Use it thoughtfully, because it can appear dull.

Black absorbs all other colors and can be a stunning backdrop to any other color. Careful touches of black add a mysterious atmosphere of drama.

Inspiration board

When deciding upon a color scheme, consider whether you want to make a room seem larger or smaller.

Pale colors appear to enlarge a room, and dark colors make it seem smaller. Remember that colors look different during the day compared with the night, because sunlight and artificial light have different effects.

Study fabric swatches, magazine tear sheets, and manufacturer's brochures, and collect together your favorites. Imagine your own possessions among them, and a vision of your personal style will soon become clear. Add other sources of inspiration: a paint sample, a seed envelope, or the color of an item of junk mail can set you off on a whole new scheme, so don't rush into a decision that you may have to live with for a long time.

Your favorite swatches and pictures may be of a style you have always lived with, but you may also find colors and items cropping up that you initially thought were not "you." Perhaps this means that now is the time for change, so follow the instinct started by the inspiration board and say "out with the old and in with the new."

Be brave and do not stick to one color. Choose shades of different colors that blend together well and seem easy to live with. Different textures add interest, and there is a large choice of interesting, tactile fabrics available nowadays. Some, such as velvet, are problematic for a beginner to sew, but they can be used where minimal sewing is needed, and textured fabrics are shown at their best when worked in simple styles.

Modern techniques mean that many fabrics once regarded as difficult to work with are now more stable to use yet still retain their effect. Alternatively, replace a tricky fabric with a slightly more robust one. Chiffon, for example, is

Enjoy making soft furnishings in colors you may not have considered before.

hard to work with, but there are many sheer fabrics available that give a similar effect but are much easier to handle.

Creating your own fabric

You may have a beautiful fabric in mind for a particular project, but cannot find it in the stores or find that it is too expensive to buy. Do not despair—it is simple to create your own fabrics. The range of fabric paints available today is easy to use and hard-wearing, so you can apply your own designs to fabric or decorate it with trimmings. You can create an all-over pattern quickly with ready-made stencils and stamps. Pick a design motif from your wallpaper or other soft furnishings and apply it to your fabric with paints or fabric pens. You can dye a light-colored fabric to match a new color scheme, and even large items can be dyed successfully in a washing machine.

A few personal possessions added to your favorite fabric swatches, magazine tear sheets, or manufacturer's brochures will create a clear vision of your personal style.

Getting started

There are many practical considerations to think about when embarking upon a soft-furnishing project. This chapter outlines the fabrics and trimmings that are most commonly used. Basic equipment and notions are also explained concisely. You may have many of the most regularly used tools and standard notions already and will find that you do not need to invest in specialized equipment and extras.

Choosing fabrics

Choosing a furnishing fabric is a decision that must not be rushed. You will want to live with your choice for many years, so the fabric needs to be a pleasure to look at as well as being practical. Follow your instincts rather than current trends. Enhance favorite items bought on foreign travels with ethnic, patterned fabrics or colors.

Always get samples to look at in situ; maybe buy 1 ft. 7 in./50 cm of the fabric to be certain it is right for you. View the fabric in both daylight and electric light, and place it in its intended position. Sit on it if it is to be used for seating: see if it crushes easily and would therefore look creased and tattered very quickly. Hang drapes at a window. Look in from outside your window at night to see how much privacy they offer. See how the color looks combined with those already in the room. Take care when mixing patterns—they may all coordinate well together but not be restful to live with on a day-to-day basis. Up-to-the-minute fabrics are very covetable but will date, so use them for small items. Buy the best-quality fabric that your budget allows; it will last longer.

Furnishing fabric checklist:
Brocade

Originally made of silk, this luxurious fabric is now almost always made from synthetic fibers. Swirling, raised designs, often incorporating metal threads, are very characteristic of a typical brocade design. Brocade frays easily, so work double hems and neaten any seams. You can successfully use this fabric for drapes, upholstery, and cushions.

Broderie anglaise

This lightweight cotton or cotton-and-polyester-mix fabric has delicate designs punched out and then embroidered. The embroidery is often worked along a border, making it very effective on bed-linen and drapes.

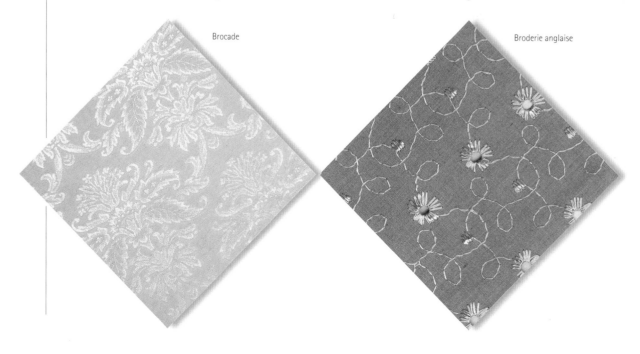

Brocade

Broderie anglaise

Canvas

A strong, coarse fabric made of cotton or linen, used for awnings and garden chair covers. Use for simple designs: it is heavy to handle.

Chenille

Fringed yarns are woven to create the soft pile of chenille fabric, which is made of cotton or cotton and man-made-fiber blends. Use chenille to make cushions, bedcovers, and loose covers. The pile will wear and flatten with heavy use.

Chintz

Chintz is usually printed with pretty floral designs. It is a fine, closely woven cotton fabric that is widely used for drapes because it hangs well. Plain chintz is very versatile and is recommended for lining fabrics when the lining must be of a good quality because it will be visible, on a bed canopy for example. Glazed chintz has a resin finish, making it resistant to dust and dirt. Dry-clean glazed chintz to preserve its finish.

Crewelwork

Wool embroidery is worked on thick cotton fabric, traditionally in designs of flowers, trees, and birds. This fabric suits drapes and cushions in an ethnic-style environment.

Damask

Damask, a very popular choice for soft furnishings, originates from fourteenth-century Damascus, Syria. The woven designs usually feature flowers, fruits, or figures, and are mostly self-toned, i.e. the design is the same color as the background. Linen damask is traditionally used for tablecloths because it is elegant and hardwearing. It can be boiled to get rid of stains, and starched. When calculating quantities, bear in mind that damask designs are usually one-way.

Gaberdine

A hard-wearing, closely woven, ribbed fabric made of cotton or wool and sometimes man-made fibers. Use gaberdine for upholstery.

Canvas

Chenille

Chintz

Crewelwork

Fabrics need to be practical as well as visually appealing. Look at a sample of fabric in situ to check its practicality and how it looks alongside other colors in the room.

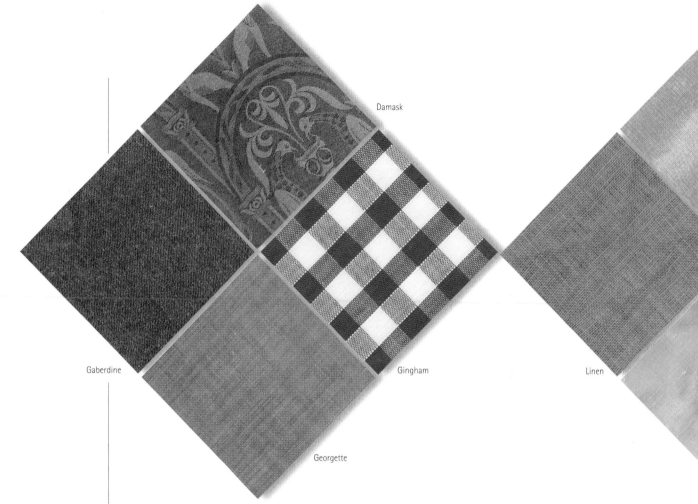

Damask

Gaberdine

Gingham

Linen

Georgette

Georgette

This fine, floaty fabric is made in a variety of fibers. It does not crease easily and can be used to make sheer drapes and soft blinds. It frays easily, so make double hems and neaten any seams.

Gingham

This colorful and hard-wearing fabric is usually white with woven checks and sometimes stripes of another color. It is a classic fabric for soft furnishings in children's rooms, for kitchen drapes and tablecloths.

Linen

This strong natural fabric is available in different weights. It is expensive and creases very easily, but drapes well and feels luxurious. It can be blended with polyester, which makes it easier to handle but of poorer quality. Linen is machine-washable. Press it damp on the wrong side with a hot iron.

Organza

This stiff, lightweight fabric is made from silk, polyester, or viscose. Metallic and hand-painted organzas can be used for dramatic effects. It creases easily, and the creases are difficult to remove. Use organza for sheer drapes, or lay it over another fabric and treat both as one to make cushion covers.

PVC

PVC is a thermoplastic material. Most fabrics called PVC are knitted or woven cotton that has been sprayed with polyvinyl chloride, making it water-resistant. PVC is firm to handle, does not fray, and can be used for simple shades, tablecloths, and outdoor furnishings. To clean, wipe over with a damp cloth.

Silk

Silk will bring a touch of glamor and luxury to a room. It is not a hard-wearing fabric, so use it

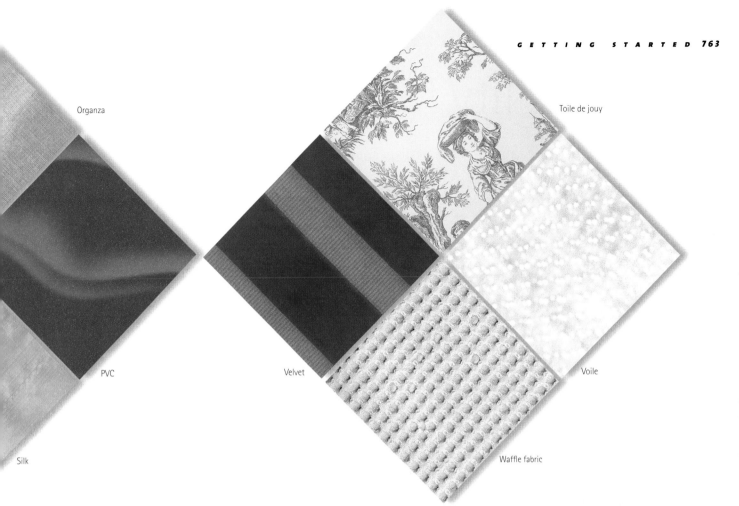

Organza

Toile de jouy

PVC

Velvet

Voile

Silk

Waffle fabric

decoratively rather than for items in regular use. It drapes well, but the colors will fade quickly in sunlight.

Toile de Jouy

Although this fabric originated in India, it has been made for the last two centuries in Jouy, France. Pastoral, engraved designs are printed in one color on natural-colored cottons. This is one of the few designs that works well when used entirely in a room, as a wallcovering, drapes, and upholstery or bedlinen.

Velvet

Velvet is available in a superb range of rich and luxurious colors, and has a wonderful pile that must always be used in the same direction. It is difficult to handle when making soft furnishings and should not be tackled by a beginner. If possible, baste and stitch all seams in the direction of the pile. If the fabric puckers, slip

tissue paper between the layers. Acrylic velvet rather than a dressmaking velvet is recommended for soft furnishings, especially for upholstery, because it is harder-wearing and resistant to fading. Never wash or spot-clean velvet, instead hang it on a rail and steam-clean it. Do not fold or hang it on a clotheshanger. This will create creases and break the pile; roll it instead.

Voile

Made from cotton, man-made fibers, and sometimes silk, voile is a soft, fine fabric used for sheer drapes and soft blinds. Cotton voile can be starched to add body.

Waffle fabric

The threads in waffle or honeycomb fabric form ridges and valleys on both sides of the cloth, making it very absorbent. It is therefore a practical choice for soft furnishings that can be used in the bathroom or kitchen.

Utility fabrics

A utility fabric has a functional purpose, but many of these fabrics are handsome enough to be used as attractive fabrics in their own right. Hardwearing canvas and ticking come in many bright colorways. They can be used to make cushions and drapes, and can cover items of furniture as well.

Brushed cotton

A soft, warm cotton fabric with a slightly fluffy, brushed surface. It is used to interline drapes.

Buckram

Cotton cloth that is made firm with size to stiffen pleats on drape headings. It is available in strips or by the yard/meter.

Bump

A mediumweight interlining for drapes, valances, and bedcovers, bump is a thick, fluffy cotton fabric.

Calico

This inexpensive, all-purpose cotton fabric is closely woven and available in various weights and widths. It washes and wears well but does tend to crease easily. Unbleached calico is cream-colored with occasional dark flecks. For practical purposes, use calico for undercovers and mattress covers, because it is very hardwearing, but it can also be used for any soft-furnishing purpose. It has become very popular nowadays because it harmonizes well with other fabrics, dyes efficiently, and is very cheap to buy.

Cotton sateen

This cotton fabric woven with a satin weave is smooth to the touch and has a pleasant sheen. It comes in wide widths, so it is often used both to line drapes and to make drapes. Allow extra fabric for shrinkage.

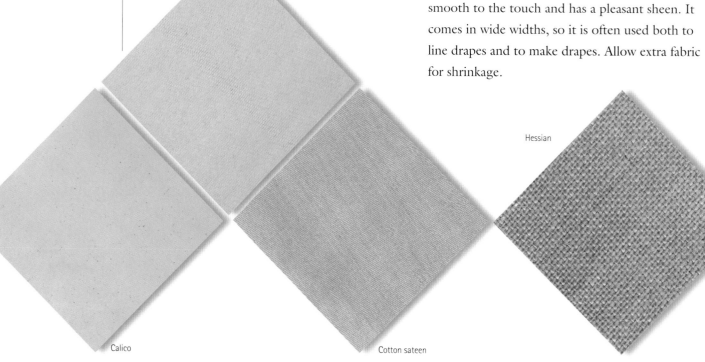

Brushed cotton

Hessian

Calico

Cotton sateen

Domett

A soft and fluffy, open-weave fabric made of wool or wool and cotton and used to interline lightweight drapes and bedcovers.

Hessian or builap

Usually a coarse, loosely woven jute fabric used for upholstery. It is available in finer weaves and can be used for sturdy drapes, shades, and wallhangings. Hessian frays easily. Dampen it to pull into shape—the grain can become distorted.

Interfacing

Use interfacing to stiffen drape headings, valances, and tiebacks. There are woven and non-woven varieties in different weights to match your fabric. They are sold in packs or by the yard/meter, 32¼ in./82 cm wide. Press-on (fusible) interfacing is pressed to the wrong side of the fabric with an iron.

Muslin

Use a piece of natural-colored muslin as a pressing cloth. Muslin is also a popular choice for sheer drapes because it is cheap to buy and hangs well, so it can be used in volume.

Self-adhesive stiffening

This is a self-adhesive card that is cut to shape for valances, tiebacks, and lampshades. Its backing is then peeled off revealing its adhesive surface, which is stuck to the fabric.

Ticking

This strong fabric is traditionally used for mattress and pillow covers because its close weave makes it featherproof. Its distinctive colored stripes on a white background are very striking, making it a very popular fabric for soft-furnishing purposes.

Batting

Place batting between fabrics to pad them for making quilts. Cotton batting is sandwiched between two layers of papery fabric. Polyester batting is more commonly used; it is much springier than cotton batting and comes in different weights, such as 2 oz./56 g, 4 oz./113 g, and 8 oz./226 g per yard/meter.

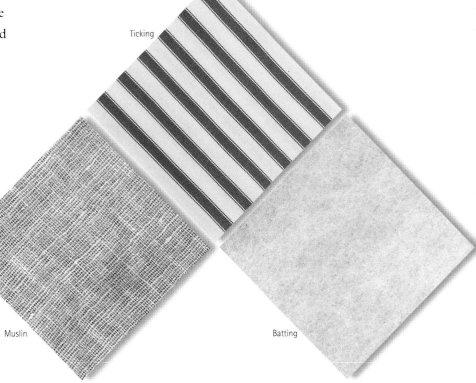

Interfacing

Muslin

Ticking

Batting

RIGHT: **Crevices between drape pleats collect dust and dirt. Use the soft-upholstery attachment of a vacuum cleaner to gently remove any dirt.**

PROJECT
Fabric care

Care for your soft furnishings and they will repay you by lasting for much longer. Gently vacuum-clean them on a light setting with a soft-upholstery attachment, paying particular attention to crevices between drape pleats or swags and seating where dirt and dust can gather.

Plump up pillows and cushions regularly to maintain their shape and shake off dust. Most soft furnishings must be dry-cleaned; washing will break up loosely woven interlinings and wreck special finishes on fabrics. Remove pet hairs with a de-fluff mitt or a wet rubber glove. Make a note of the fabric content and any cleaning instructions when you buy fabric, then you will know how to care for it and deal with any stains.

Stain removal

Deal with spills promptly. Read instructions on specialized cleaning preparations carefully before use, and test them on a discreet area or scrap of leftover fabric first. If possible, work on stains from the wrong side of the fabric.

Blood

If you prick your finger while sewing and drop blood on the fabric, immediately roll a small ball of thread from the fabric between your fingers and moisten it. Rub the ball of thread on the drops of blood to remove them. If the stain is large, apply salt to the surface to soak it up, then soak a washable fabric in cold water; hot water will set the stain. Sponge dry-cleanable fabrics with cold water containing a little liquid detergent. It is important to resist the temptation to rub at the stain.

WINE

STEP 1 It is important to treat the stain immediately; if you leave it, the stain will be much harder to remove.

STEP 2 Dabbing spilled red wine with white wine will thin it and make it easier to wash out.

STEP 3 Sprinkle the stain with salt to soak as much of it up as possible, then launder the item, ideally before the stain has time to set.

Coffee and milk

If you spill either of these liquids, dab the stain with liquid detergent diluted in warm water.

Fruit juice

On washable fabrics, stretch the stain over a bowl and pour warm water through it. Cover stains on silk and wool with borax, then wash the fabric in warm water.

Grease and oil

Slip a clean cloth under the stain and apply a proprietary stain remover. Dab washable fabric with liquid detergent.

Ink

Use a proprietary stain remover to suit the type of pen used. Use undiluted liquid detergent on washable fabrics, and ethyl alcohol on dry-cleanable fabrics.

Mildew

Spots of mildew can develop on fabric in a damp environment—particularly on drapes if they rest against a window covered with condensation. Mildew can sometimes be removed by soaking in bleach and water; always test out this treatment on scrap fabric first, because the bleach may fade the material.

Scorch marks

Brush off as much of the scorching as possible with a stiff brush. Mix salt and lemon juice and apply to the marks. Leave the item to dry naturally in the sun.

Water marks

Lightly sponge the entire surface evenly, then press. Carefully shake silk and velvet over steam from a kettle, covering the spout with a cloth to prevent it from spluttering.

TEA

STEP 1 If possible, soak the stain on washable fabrics with hot water before it dries.

STEP 2 Dab dry-cleanable fabrics with a wet pad or have the item dry-cleaned. Dried-in stains can sometimes be removed with glycerin, which can loosen them.

CANDLE WAX

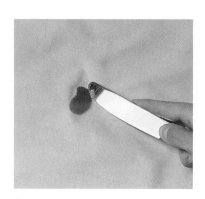

STEP 1 If spilled, scrape off as much as possible with a palette knife.

STEP 2 Sandwich the fabric between layers of brown wrapping paper and iron it to melt the wax onto the paper. Keep replacing the paper until all the wax is gone. When colored wax is removed, some color will remain on the fabric; dab this off with a little alcohol.

Decorative trimmings

A well-chosen trimming can make all the difference to an item of soft furnishing, and shows that thought has gone into the finishing touches. Always check to see whether the trimming has the same wash-care instructions as the fabric it is to be attached to; some trimmings are not color-fast.

There are whole stores devoted to beautiful beads, ribbons, braids, feathers, and trimmings of all kinds, so you will be spoiled for choice if decorative trimmings are your thing. A plain cushion or a lampshade edge can be transformed into a work of art with an exotic beaded trim, for example, or you can experiment with jolly pompons and ribbons.

Ribbons

Beads

There are masses of inspirational beads that can be used to trim soft furnishings. Tiny rocaille and bugle beads can be handsewn at random or to a definite design. Drop beads have a hole across the top or centrally along their length for sewing. Check the washing instructions, and avoid using glass beads, which may break or splinter.

Pompons

Braid

This straight-edged, woven trimming can be sewn, glued, nailed, or stapled in place, either purely as decoration or to hide seams or cover raw edges of fabric.

Eyelet lace

Buttons

Use buttons for decorative as well as practical use. There is a huge choice available, and the price range is just as huge. Don't forget self-cover buttons, which you can cover with your choice of fabric. Sew-through buttons have flat backs with two or four holes. Shank buttons have a loop underneath to sew through, and are best for thick fabrics and rouleau loop fastenings.

Cord

Handsew colorful woven and twisted cords as decoration, or use cord as a drawstring to fasten storage bags. Inexpensive white piping cord is also very effective when used uncovered.

Edging lace

This lace has a straight edge to insert in a seam. Some edging laces are gathered to give a ready-made frill.

Eyelet lace

Broderie anglaise is often used for eyelet lace. Both edges of this narrow lace have a fancy finish. There is a row of eyelets along the center, which can be threaded with ribbon, either purely for decoration or as a drawstring.

Fold-over braid

This flat nylon braid is folded slightly off-center. The raw edge of the fabric is slotted inside, with the wider half of the braid underneath. The layers are then stitched together. It is available in a range of colors and can be used to neaten tablecloths and throws.

Tassel

Fringing

Most fringings have a flat edge so they can be inserted in a seam, and a zipper or piping foot is used to stitch it. If the fringe edge has a row of stay stitching, leave it in place until the item you are making is finished; otherwise stray threads will get caught in the seams.

Gimp

Used like braid, gimp has a scalloped edge rather than a straight one and is easier to fit than braid.

Insertion cord

This has a flat flange woven into it to be inserted in a seam. Apply it in the same way as piping.

Jewelry stones

Made from glass or plastic, jewelry stones are for decorative purposes only, such as on lampshades. Sew-on jewelry stones have holes drilled, or a metal back with grooves in, for sewing through. Some stones are attached with a separate metal back that goes under the fabric. The back has prongs to hold the stone in place.

Piping

Ready-made piping is available in a limited range of colors. It is easy to make by covering piping cord with bias strips of fabric. Piping gives definition and a professional finish to a seam.

Pompon edging

This retro-style edging suspends a row of small pompons, which are very effective on lampshades and drapes.

Pompons

It is very simple to make your own pompons, and they make a lively addition to cushions and throws.

Ribbon

Colorful ribbons come in all sorts of widths, materials, and finishes. They can be stitched in stripes and checks, used as ties, or as drawstrings for storage bags.

Rickrack braid

This wavy woven braid fits in well with the decor of many children's rooms.

Russia braid

This is a fine silky braid that comes in a wide range of glossy colors. Stitch it in place along its central groove.

Sequins

Strings of sequins can be sewn by hand or stitched along the center by machine. Single sequins can be sewn by hand.

Tassels

Ready-made tassels are often expensive, but they do give a satisfying finishing touch to cushions, table runners, and many other applications. It is economical to make your own tassels in exactly the color you want.

All illustrations: Plain drapes, lampshades, and cushions can be transformed into works of art by adding a decorative trimming. Some trimmings can be practical as well as decorative.

Gimp

Utility trimmings

Some of the extras needed to fasten fabrics and neaten edges are very appealing in their own right and, as well as being concealed, they can be used to make a feature in themselves. All of these trimmings are available in the soft furnishings sections of most large stores.

The style for utility furnishings has recently taken off, as designers constantly search for new fabrics and trimmings to create the newest trend. Buttons, hooks and eyes, touch-and-close tape, and different types of cord have all been called into service on the decorative front. These trimmings are also particularly useful if you are planning a nautical theme in a room. Thick cord ties and eyelets can give a vigorous air of salty tradition to a modern decorating scheme.

Binding and webbing

Choose from different widths and colors of binding for curved or straight edges.

Bias binding

This is a strip of bias-cut fabric with the edges pressed under for binding curved and straight edges. It is available by the yard/meter or in prepacks, in different colors and widths and in cotton or satin. It is easy to make your own, to match or contrast with the main fabric.

Blind cord

This strong, narrow cord is used for opening and drawing Swedish and Roman blinds, and for making drawstrings.

Drape weights

Most drapes will hang better if weights are attached inside the hems. Weights are available as button-shaped disks or as a chain. Both types come in different weights.

Eyelets

Metal eyelets have a nickel or gilt finish and come in a kit with a fixing tool. They come in a few sizes, ⅝ in./1.5 cm being the most widely available diameter. Use eyelets for hooking up shades, as a drape heading, and for assembling garden canopies. Metal eyelets of ¼-in./6-mm diameter are available in a limited range of enamel colors and are fixed with a tool rather like a pair of pliers.

Hook-and-eye tape

Metal hooks and eyes are attached to cotton tape to fasten comforter covers and cushion covers.

Piping cord

Available in different thicknesses, this inexpensive white cotton cord can be used for making your own piping.

Poppers

Like press fasteners, poppers are ball-and-socket fasteners, but are held in place with pronged rings. They are available in kits and are suitable for heavyweight fabrics.

Press fasteners

These are two-part, metal or transparent plastic, ball-and-socket fasteners, which can be used to fasten cushion covers. There are self-cover press-fastener kits available in different sizes for covering in your own fabric when you want to make a feature of them, for fastening a comforter cover for example.

Press-fastener tape

This two-part tape is sold by the yard/meter and has press fasteners along its length. It is ideal for fastening comforter covers and cushion covers.

Seam binding

This straight woven tape of cotton or nylon is used for finishing single hems where a double hem would be too bulky.

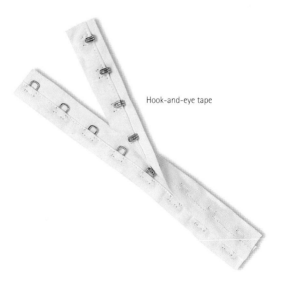

Hook-and-eye tape

Touch-and-close tape

This is a two-part tape, one tape with a looped mesh surface and the other with a hooked surface. The two layers interlock when pressed together. The tapes are available for sewing, for ironing on, or with an adhesive backing for sticking. Use them to fix loose covers and attach blinds to battens. The fastener is available in a limited number of widths and colors, and as small disks.

Twill tape

This firmly woven cotton tape is used to strengthen seams and for ties to attach bed valances, and for unobtrusive drawstrings.

Upholstery tacks

½-in./1.2-cm-long upholstery tacks are the most versatile size to use.

Piping cord is inexpensive to work with. You can add your own tassels or pompons as a lively addition to soft furnishings.

Equipment

It is vital to have the right equipment when you are contemplating beginning a new soft-furnishing project: there is nothing worse than getting part of the way through and finding that you have to go out to buy something essential! Go through what equipment you do have and add and replace as necessary from the list below.

Keep your tools together and use them only on fabrics and their trimmings, so they do not get dirty or blunted. Work on a clean, flat, and well-lit surface, and keep sharp tools beyond the reach of young children and pets.

Air-erasable pen

This pen can be used on fabric—any marks will gradually disappear; test on a scrap of fabric first.

Bias-binding maker

This small metal tool is threaded with strips of fabric, which are pulled through and pressed to form bias binding.

Carpenter's square

Use a carpenter's square for making accurate angles when drawing patterns on paper and fabric.

Dressmaking shears

Bent-handled dressmaking shears are the most comfortable and accurate to use for cutting fabric, because the angle of the lower blade lets the fabric lie flat. They are available in different lengths, so test the size before buying. A top-quality pair is expensive, but will last a lifetime and it is worth paying that extra bit in the long run.

Embroidery scissors

A small pair of sharp scissors is indispensable for snipping threads and cutting into intricate areas. Keep them in a small cloth case when not in use.

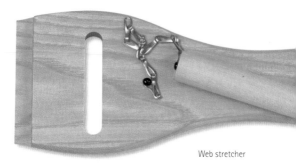

Web stretcher

Hammer

Used to hammer tacks, eyelets, and poppers in place.

Ironing board and iron

Use a sturdy ironing board, because you will find that you will be handling very large and weighty pieces of cloth and the board will need to be able to take the strain. Invest in the best iron you can afford, preferably a steam/dry iron with a reliable heat setting.

Pattern paper

This lightweight paper is faintly marked with a grid to aid the drawing of patterns. Brown wrapping paper is also suitable for this purpose. Never use newsprint—it will dirty the fabric.

Pencil

Always keep paper and a sharp pencil to hand in the planning stages to make notes and record measurements. A propelling pencil or sharp HB pencil is recommended. Use a china marker pencil on PVC fabrics.

Tailor's chalk

Pinking shears

These cut a zigzag, fray-resistant edge and are used to neaten seams and cut out fabrics that fray easily.

Pressing cloth

Use a piece of inexpensive cheesecloth or muslin about 39 in./1 m square to protect the fabric you are ironing from becoming shiny.

Screwdriver

Use this to fix screws to walls for drape rails, valances, and cleats for shades.

Seam ripper

This small implement has a sharp, inner curve for cutting seams open when mistakes have occurred, and a point for picking out threads.

Sewing gauge

This 6-in./15-cm-long rule has a slider that can be set at different levels for marking hems and seams, and as a quilting guide.

Sewing scissors

One blade is pointed and the other rounded so fabric can be trimmed without getting snagged.

Spirit level

Use this to position drape rails and cleats for shades.

Staple gun

This is a fast way of attaching fabric in upholstery, and for fixing swags and tails.

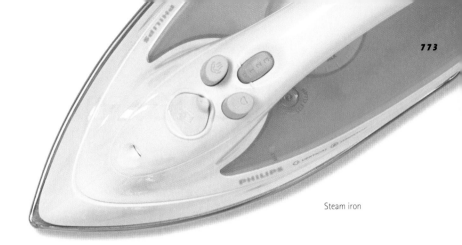

Steam iron

Steel measure

Use a retractable steel measure to measure windows and beds.

Tailor's chalk

This colored chalk, available in wedge and pencil forms, is used to mark fabric because it can be brushed off.

Tape measure

A plastic-coated or cloth tape measure is useful for measuring around curves.

Thimble

A thimble protects your finger when handsewing. Thimbles come in different sizes and are made of leather, metal, or plastic: an open-topped leather thimble is recommended. Wear a thimble on the middle finger.

Transparent rule

A 12-in./30.5-cm rule is a useful size for drawing against on paper and fabric, and for checking measurements.

Web stretcher

This is necessary only if you do a lot of upholstery. It is used to stretch webbing across the frame of a chair.

Yard/meter stick

This wood or metal measure can be used on drapes and for drawing cutting lines on fabric.

Pinking shears

Needles, pins, and threads

These items are the real nuts and bolts of the whole process of sewing and making soft furnishings. It is vital that you have the right kind of needles for the fabrics you are sewing, and you can never have too many pins. A good range of different colored threads is also a necessity.

Gather together a selection of needles, pins, and threads when you are planning your next soft-furnishings project. They are inexpensive, and having the correct ones for a project will make it easier to work on and give a better finish when making soft furnishings.

Needles

Handsewing needles

Needles for handsewing come in different sizes. The higher the number, the shorter and finer the needle.

Ballpoint needle

This needle is for knitted fabrics. The rounded point slips between the yarns instead of piercing them. The size range is 9–16 (70–100).

Betweens needle

This short-length needle should be used in quilting projects.

Bodkin

This thick, blunt needle has a large eye for threading cords, ribbon, or elastic through casings, and for turning fabric tubes right-side out. Use a safety pin if you do not have a bodkin.

T-pins

Curved needle

Curved needle

A curved needle is for sewing around curves on upholstery and lampshades, and for getting into tight corners.

Machine-sewing needles

Needles for sewing machines come in different sizes with different-shaped points. The lower the number, the finer the point. For example, size 9 (70) is the finest and should be used on fine, lightweight fabrics and size 18 (110) is the thickest. Sizes 9–14 (70–90) are the most commonly used.

Sailmaker's needle

This needle has a sharp, triangular point for inserting through strong canvas. Use it to sew heavy-duty fabrics for outdoor furnishings.

Sharp-point needle

This is the most versatile needle. Use it to stitch woven fabrics. The size range for sharp-point needles is 9–18 (70–110).

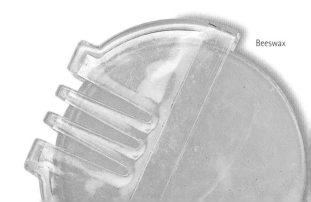

Beeswax

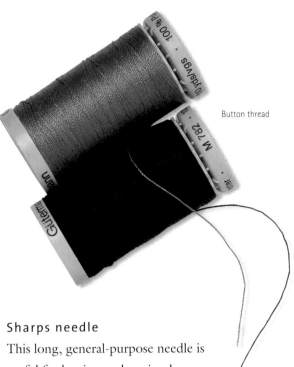

Button thread

Sharps needle
This long, general-purpose needle is useful for basting and sewing hems.

Wedge-point needle
Stitch leather and PVC with a wedge-point needle to lessen the chance of splitting and damaging the material. The size range is 11–18 (80–110).

Pins
Corkscrew pins
These small upholstery pins fix loose covers unobtrusively in place; just screw them into the upholstery.

Dressmaker's pins
There are different thicknesses of pins for different fabrics. Household pins are the most versatile. Use lace or bridal pins on silk and other delicate fabrics, because other pins will mark the surface. Colored, glass-headed pins are easy to see on a large expanse of fabric. Pins made from stainless steel are hard-wearing: nickel-plated pins may leave black marks on fabric.

T-pins
Use sturdy T-pins instead of dressmaking pins to fix fabric temporarily to upholstered items when making patterns and re-covering.

Threads
Sewing thread should be strong and durable and have some "give" in it. Choose thread to match the fabric weight and color. If an exact color match is not possible, choose a darker rather than a lighter shade.

Basting thread
Use this weak thread in a contrasting color to the fabric so it is easily seen when removing.

Beeswax
Pull thread through beeswax to strengthen it and stop it from twisting.

Button thread
This is a thick, tough thread for handsewing heavy fabrics that need to be strongly secured. It has a glazed finish to help it slip through closely woven, heavy fabrics.

Cotton-covered polyester thread
This is a strong, coarse thread for heavyweight fabrics and PVC.

General-purpose mercerized cotton thread
Use this to sew lightweight and mediumweight cotton, linen, and rayon. Smooth, silky mercerized thread is available in a large choice of colors. Do not use on stretchy fabrics, because the stitches will snap if stretched.

Sewing thread

General-purpose polyester thread
This works well on woven synthetics, knitted, and other stretchy fabrics.

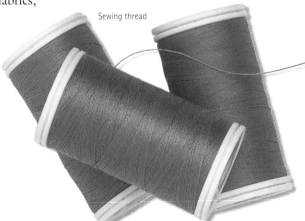

Patterns

Squares and rectangles are the shapes most often cut to make soft furnishings, and these are best marked directly onto the fabric. You will need to make a pattern for shaped items such as drape tiebacks, lampshades, and seating, especially if you need to cut out more than one piece at a time.

Making a proper pattern will ensure that you get the most economical use out of your fabric.

Patterns can be easily made from brown wrapping paper or special pattern-making paper, available from soft-furnishing suppliers. Do not use newsprint, since it will dirty the fabric. Draw the pattern piece on the paper, adding a seam allowance. Mark the grain line and any fold lines, and balance marks such as dots on the seam or notches on the seam allowance; these marks are essential if you are matching one piece of fabric to another. To make a symmetrical pattern piece, fold the paper in half and draw one half of the piece against the fold, then cut out through both layers and open the pattern out flat.

If you have made a pattern from fabric—to re-cover a chair, for example—press it flat and mark the seam lines. If you have a set of old loose covers that you wish to use as patterns, check the fit on the piece of furniture in question and make any alterations that are necessary. Carefully undo all the seams, marking balance marks as you part the pieces. Label the pieces clearly and mark the top, bottom, and side edges so you know what goes where when you put them on the furniture. Roughly repair any tears, or sew patches over large worn holes, so the pattern keeps its shape. Press the patterns flat.

Layouts

Carefully figure out how much fabric to buy and the most economical way to arrange the pattern pieces on the paper. Cut down on wastage as much as you can. Note whether the fabric has a nap—this means a pile that runs in one direction —or a design that works in one direction only, in which case the patterns need to lie in the same direction. Allow extra for matching patterned fabrics (see page 781).

Use the width of the fabric to calculate how much fabric to buy. If most of the pieces are to be cut from measurements—for example, squares or rectangles—take a sheet of paper to represent the fabric, the side edges being the selvedges. Draw the pieces on the paper, marking their dimensions and adding them up so they fit across the width. Mark on their dimensions and grain lines, and butt the edges together to lessen wastage. Check that seam allowances and hems are included. Next, add the dimensions along the side selvedge edges to the amount of fabric. Keep the layout diagram for positioning when cutting.

For shaped pattern pieces, use long rules and tape measures on a large table or the floor to mark out an area that is the width of the fabric, or half the width of the fabric if you need to cut patterns in pairs. Arrange the patterns within the space, keeping grain lines level with the marked edges that represent the selvedges or a selvedge and fold. If the fabric has a nap,

make sure all the pieces lie in the correct direction. Check that you have included all the pattern pieces, because some may need to be repeated. The length of the table or floor area taken up by the patterns is the length of fabric needed. It is a good idea to make a rough sketch of the layout so that you can refer to it when positioning for cutting.

Make patterns for shaped items such as drape tiebacks, lampshades, and seating. Use brown wrapping paper or special pattern-making paper, but not newsprint.

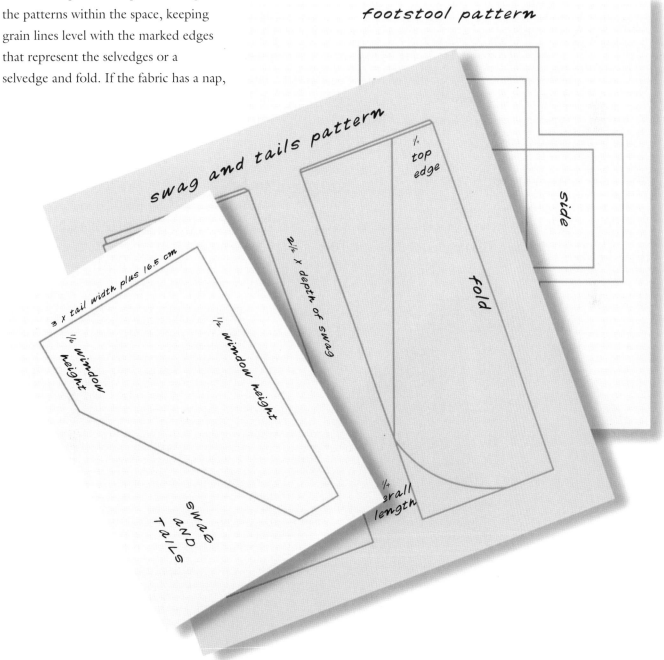

footstool pattern

swag and tails pattern

Preparing the fabric

Fabrics for larger projects, such as making drapes and covering sofas and chairs, can be very expensive, and it is worth handling the fabric properly so it doesn't spoil. Check whether a fabric will shrink or not, and always test for washability. Finding the grain line is also vital, and will save you a lot of time and frustration.

Many fabrics shrink. Ask the retailer when you buy a fabric if this is likely to happen. If it is liable to shrink, add an extra 10 percent to the fabric quantities, then wash the fabric before cutting. To test washability, dampen a corner of the fabric to see if water marks the surface; if it does, do not wash it but dry-clean when necessary.

Grain lines

Woven fabrics stretch differently if pulled in different directions, and this affects the way a fabric hangs. The lengthwise grain, called the warp, runs the length of the fabric parallel to the selvedges. The warp has less stretch, making it easier to sew in this direction without stretching or puckering the fabric. The crosswise grain is called the weft and runs from selvedge to selvedge. It has a little more stretch than the lengthwise grain.

The bias is any line that is not the lengthwise or crosswise grain. The bias will stretch and the true bias, which is at 45 degrees to the lengthwise or crosswise grains, stretches the most. Take care when stitching along the bias, because seams will stretch.

Some woven fabrics have obvious grains. In others they are harder to see.

Finding grain lines

There are two ways to find the crosswise grain. The first method is suited to lightweight and loosely woven fabrics. First, snip into the selvedge and carefully pull out a crosswise thread. Cut along the channel that is left in the weave. Alternatively, on firmly woven fabrics snip into the selvedge and tear across the fabric to the other selvedge.

If the fabric has a woven stripe or check, this will be the grain line. This method does not work on printed stripes and checks, because they are unlikely to be printed exactly on the grain.

Once the crosswise grain has been found and torn or cut across, fold the fabric in half lengthwise. The layers should lie smoothly together with the selvedges matched. If they do not match, dampen the fabric and pull it diagonally to stretch it back into shape. Leave it to dry flat with the corners and edges aligned.

Pressing and smoothing

Pressing is a vital part of sewing and should be done throughout a project and not just at the final stage. The difference between pressing and smoothing is that, in pressing, the iron is pressed down onto the fabric, then lifted up and moved onto the next section, and in smoothing, the iron glides over the surface of the fabric. Use a light pressure, letting the weight and heat of the iron do the work.

Smooth out any wrinkles and creases on the fabric before cutting out. If the fabric has a definite fold line, press it out before cutting. If a faint line is left along the fold, this must be avoided when laying out the pattern pieces.

Smooth and straighten the fabric, removing pins and basting because these will leave indentations if pressed. Press each seam after it is stitched. Do not press in any sharp creases until you are sure they are in the correct position,

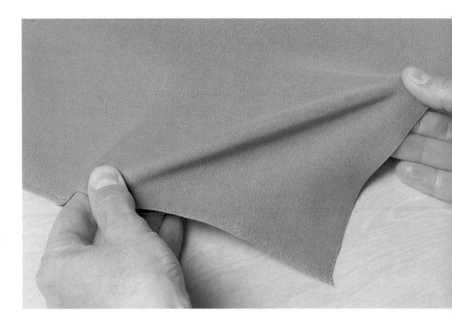

because they may be difficult to remove. In general, press from the wrong side of the fabric.

Set the iron to the correct heat setting for the fabric and test on a scrap or discreet corner of the fabric. Wool needs a warm setting and benefits from a lot of steam when pressing. Great care must be taken when pressing velvet: lay the fabric pile-side down on a towel and hold the iron over, but not touching, the fabric on a steam setting.

Always use a pressing cloth when pressing the right side of the fabric, to stop the fabric from becoming shiny. Cheesecloth or muslin are the most versatile fabrics to use, because you can see through them. Use a lightweight cotton for heavyweight fabrics. Do not use calico or a dish towel, because they hold too much water, which will produce a lot of steam and ruin some fabrics. Use a dry cloth with a steam iron and a damp cloth with a dry iron. The seam allowances on some fabrics can make an indentation, so cut a strip of brown wrapping paper and slip it under the seam allowance before pressing.

When dealing with embroidered fabrics, lay them face down on a soft fabric, such as interlining, to protect the raised surface when pressing.

Woven fabrics stretch differently if pulled in different directions, according to the crosswise and lengthwise grains. The grains affect the way a fabric hangs and stretches.

YOU WILL NEED:

CUTTING OUT:

- **FABRICS**
- **PATTERNS**
- **PINS**
- **AIR-ERASABLE PEN/TAILOR'S CHALK**
- **RULE**
- **CARPENTER'S SQUARE**
- **SCISSORS**
- **PAINTER'S TAPE**

PATTERNED FABRICS:

- **FABRICS**
- **PINS**
- **SCISSORS**
- **AIR-ERASABLE PEN/TAILOR'S CHALK**
- **NEEDLE AND THREAD/SEWING MACHINE**

PROJECT
Cutting out

Cutting out the fabric is a major part of creating soft furnishings. Do not rush this stage—making cutting mistakes can be costly, because most cannot be rectified. Although you might find it tempting to rush right in and get started, it is better to take your time to position the pattern pieces correctly and economically, which will save you time later on.

CUTTING SELVEDGES

It is often advisable to cut off selvedges (the neatened edges that run the length of the fabric), because they are woven tighter than the fabric, sometimes causing it to pucker. If you join fabric widths with the selvedges on, cut into the seam allowances at 4-in./10-cm intervals in order to release any tightness.

Lay the fabric out flat on a large table or the floor, depending upon the size of the fabric: ideally, the cutting area should be accessible from at least three sides. To cut pairs of patterns, fold the fabric in half lengthwise or widthwise if that suits your layout better; otherwise keep the fabric single.

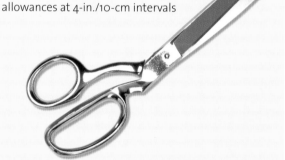

HOW TO CUT OUT

STEP 1 Pin the pattern pieces on top, matching the grain lines, or draw the dimensions of the pieces with an air-erasable pen or tailor's chalk. Use a rule and carpenter's square to draw straight lines and right angles.

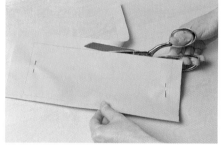

STEP 2 Cut out the pieces, cutting thick fabrics one layer at a time and patterned fabrics the same so you can match the designs accurately. Save fabric scraps for testing stitches and the heat of the iron.

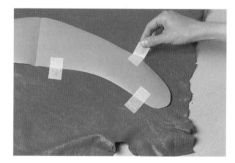

STEP 3 On PVC or leather, stick pattern pieces in place on the wrong side with painter's tape, and draw around the piece with an air-erasable pen or tailor's chalk. Remove the pattern and cut out the fabric one layer at a time.

MATCHING PATTERNED FABRICS

STEP 1 If you are making drapes, for example, you may need to match the pattern of the fabric. Use an air-erasable pen or tailor's chalk to draw a line across the fabric selvedge to selvedge. Avoid placing the line through a design motif, which will disrupt the overall effect. Cut off excess fabric above an upper seam or hem allowance. Lay the fabric out flat, right-side up, on a large table or the floor. Measure the length of the drape, including allowances, and cut off the excess fabric.

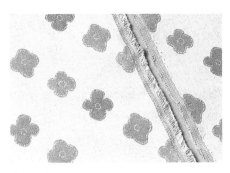

STEP 2 Lay the remaining fabric selvedge to selvedge with this first piece, matching the level of the pattern. Cut across the fabric to match the first piece. Cut any remaining pieces in the same way. Cut off the selvedges.

STEP 3 Fold under a ⅝-in./1.5-cm seam allowance along one long edge. Lay the folded edge over the adjacent edge of the other length of fabric, matching the pattern. Pin and ladder stitch the pieces together.

MATCHING PATTERN REPEATS

Extra fabric must be allowed for matching patterned fabrics. In general, add one pattern repeat for each fabric width. The pattern repeat is usually marked on the fabric label; if not, ask the retailer to measure the repeat.

Widths of fabric usually need to be joined to make drapes, but this is also sometimes necessary when making bedcovers and re-covering sofas.

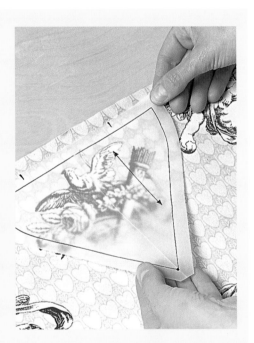

Extra fabric may also be needed for positioning an element of the fabric design to show it whole and at its best, on the center of a cushion for example. Although this means extra expense, it will give a better end result. Make a pattern from waxed or tracing paper so that you can see through it. Fold it into fourths to find the center, then open out flat and mark the fold lines and grain line. Lay the pattern over a motif on the fabric, matching the grain lines and the center of the pattern to the center of the design. Pin in place and cut out.

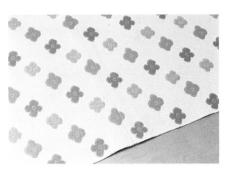

STEP 4 Now fold over the top fabric so the right sides are together. Stitch the seam, using a flat felled seam (see page 785) for unlined drapes and a flat seam for lined drapes.

The sewing machine

Although some people prefer the method of handsewing (and this always has an important place in the needleperson's skillbase), you will find that you cannot do without a sewing machine if you want to tackle larger soft-furnishing items, such as bulky drapes or a set of loose covers. It is a vital piece of equipment.

A sewing machine is the most important investment you will make. There are many considerations when choosing one; firstly, decide what you need it for. A machine that does straight stitch, zigzag stitch, and neat buttonholes is enough for most people's needs. If you have considered experimenting with machine embroidery and fancy stitches, choose a machine with push-button controls or a computerized system. An overlocking machine or serger is useful if you intend to sew a lot, because it neatens seams quickly and efficiently.

Research the market and buy from a reputable dealer. Ask for demonstrations of the machine's functions, and test-run a few machines yourself for comparisons. Look at second-hand machines too. A second-hand machine should have been well maintained and come with its original instruction manual.

When researching the best sewing machine for your requirements, check that the speed controls and bobbin-winding mechanism are easy to operate. The machine should be simple to thread. Work a buttonhole—are you pleased with the result, and was it simple to do? Can the machine be left set up in position with the lid on when not in use, or will it need to be moved each time and packed away in its case? In the latter scenario, consider the size and weight of the machine. Ask friends and family for recommendations, because every home sewer will have his or her favorite make of machine.

How it works

All sewing machines are fairly similar to operate. The presser foot holds the fabric in place; the needle, threaded with the upper thread, penetrates the fabric and goes into the bobbin area to pick up the lower thread to form a stitch. Read your sewing-machine manual carefully to familiarize yourself with the machine.

Power supply

Turn the power supply off before setting up the machine. Check that the electrical voltage of the machine is the same as your power supply. Plug in the cord socket, then insert the plug into the power supply. Switch on the power. Switch off the machine when it is not in use, and pull out the plug.

Foot control

The harder you press the foot control, the faster the machine will run. The sewing speed can be varied on most machines.

Sewing light

The sewing light is especially helpful when you are sewing dark colors. When the bulb goes, replace it immediately, following the manufacturer's directions.

Presser foot

The presser foot holds the fabric in place. Most machines have a basic foot and a few extra feet

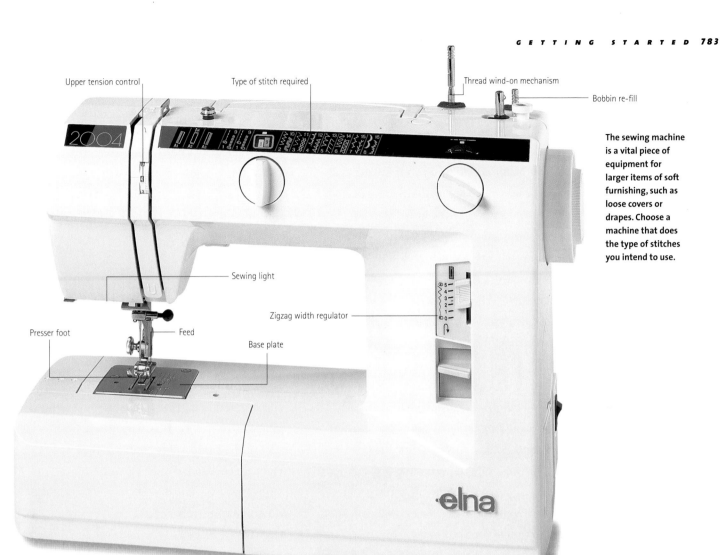

Upper tension control

Type of stitch required

Thread wind-on mechanism

Bobbin re-fill

2004

Sewing light

Zigzag width regulator

Presser foot

Feed

Base plate

elna

The sewing machine is a vital piece of equipment for larger items of soft furnishing, such as loose covers or drapes. Choose a machine that does the type of stitches you intend to use.

for special purposes, such as a zipper or piping foot, buttonhole foot, blind-stitch foot, and darning foot. Presser feet can be changed by either being snapped off and on, or unscrewed and screwed on.

Feed
The feed moves the fabric backward as you stitch. The distance the fabric is moved is controlled by the stitch-length regulator, which must be set carefully for each type of fabric.

Stitch-length regulator
The numbers on the regulator represent either the stitch length metrically in millimeters or the number of stitches per inch. The two are compatible: for example, if each stitch length is 2.5 mm, there are ten stitches per inch.

Bobbin and bobbin case
The bobbin is wound with the lower thread. The bobbin is slotted counterclockwise into the bobbin case, which then slots into the machine bed below the feed. When the bobbin runs out, it can be refilled using the main thread and wound on by the machine.

After use
Store the machine with a scrap of fabric under the foot to soak up any leaking oil. Using a stiff brush, regularly brush out any fluff from around the base plate and the feed dogs, and from the bobbin holder. Keep an eye on the belt that drives the machine, and make sure you replace it regularly.

YOU WILL NEED:

ALL SEAMS:
- **FABRICS**
- **PINS**
- **NEEDLE AND THREAD/SEWING MACHINE**
- **IRON**
- **SCISSORS**
- **PINKING SHEARS**

PROJECT
Basic techniques

Tackling a simple soft-furnishings project for the home will bring your sewing skills to light. The same basic methods are repeated throughout this part of the book, so read through this section carefully before embarking on any project. Try out new techniques on scrap fabric first rather than experimenting on the item itself. When following directions, it is important to use either the metric or the imperial measurements but not both.

Seams

Before stitching, carefully match the seam allowances and patterns. Position pins at right angles to the seam and stitch over the pins or place them along the seam line and remove them as you stitch. Experiment and see which method you prefer; it may be a combination of both, depending on the item. If you are a nervous stitcher, or are working on an awkward area, always tack the seams together first.

MAKING A FLAT SEAM

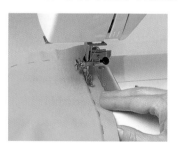

With right sides of the fabric facing, stitch the layers together along the seam line.

LAYERING SEAM ALLOWANCES

To reduce the bulk of thick fabrics in flat seams or seams of many layers, e.g., piped seams, trim each seam allowance to a different amount.

Making a flat seam

This is the simplest seam to stitch. Use a flat seam to join fabric widths for lined drapes and to join layers that will be bagged out—for example, cushion covers.

Layering seam allowances

When you have many seam allowances together, it is best to layer them to reduce their bulk. Consult the text (below left) for instructions.

Making a flat felled seam

This is a neat seam that can be used on unlined drapes and also on other items where both sides of the fabric will be visible as the raw edges are enclosed.

Making a French seam

This seam is best suited to lightweight fabrics, see-through fabrics (where you don't want a bulky seam showing through), and ones that tend to fray easily. The raw edges are enclosed within the seam, giving a neat finish and stopping loose fibers from escaping to spoil the item.

Clipping corners and curves

To reduce bulk at stitched corners, cut diagonally across the seam allowance at the corner.

Topstitching

Topstitching is worked on the right side of the fabric for both functional and decorative purposes. Topstitching is applied after the item has been stitched together.

Neatening seams

To prevent fraying, neaten flat seams with a zigzag stitch or pinking shears.

MAKING A FLAT FELLED SEAM

STEP 1 With right sides facing, stitch a flat seam, taking a ⅝-in./1.5-cm allowance. Press the seam allowances in the same direction, then trim the lower seam allowance to ⅜ in./1 cm.

STEP 2 Turn under ¼in./5 mm .on the upper seam allowance. Stitch close to the turned-under edge.

MAKING A FRENCH SEAM

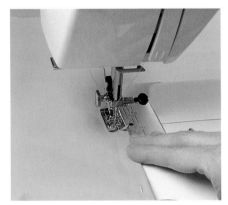

STEP 1 Stitch a flat seam with wrong sides facing, taking a ⁵⁄₁₆-in./7.5-mm seam allowance. Trim seam allowances to ¼in./5mm.

STEP 2 Turn fabric with right sides facing and stitch ⁵⁄₁₆ in./7.5 mm from the first seam.

CLIPPING CORNERS AND CURVES

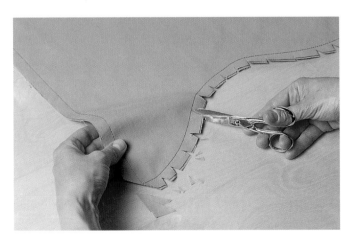

Snip into curved seam allowances. This will help the fabric lie flat on corners and more undulating shapes. Remember not to cut too close to the stitching of the seam.

TOPSTITCHING

Stitch parallel to a seam to emphasize it and to hold the seam allowance in place. Contrasting colored or thick, machine-sewing thread will accentuate the stitching.

YOU WILL NEED:

BASTING:
- FABRICS
- PINS
- CONTRASTING THREAD
- NEEDLE AND THREAD/SEWING MACHINE
- SCISSORS

SLIPSTITCHING:
- LIGHT TO MEDIUMWEIGHT FABRIC
- NEEDLE AND THREAD
- SCISSORS

CORD TIDY:
- FABRIC
- NEEDLE AND THREAD/SEWING MACHINE
- SCISSORS

HERRINGBONE STITCH:
- HEAVYWEIGHT FABRIC
- NEEDLE AND THREAD
- SCISSORS

TEMPORARY TACKING:
- TACK LIFTER/ SCREWDRIVER
- TACKS
- HAMMER

Hand stitches

Hand stitching is an essential part of any sewing process, and soft-furnishing projects are no exception. Some fabrics lend themselves to being hemmed by hand, for example, and basting is vital.

Basting

The more you stitch, the more confident you will become and therefore less reliant on basting before stitching. (However, it is often a good idea to do so.) Basting is useful for tricky areas or joining many layers of fabric. Work the basting stitches in a contrasting-colored thread so they are easy to see when you come to remove them later. Basting thread comes in a limited range of colors but any sewing thread will do.

Slipstitching

Slipstitching is used to join two folded edges or one folded edge to a flat surface, such as to close openings in seams, to secure bindings in place, or to hem light to mediumweight fabric. The stitches should be almost invisible. Working from right to left, bring the needle out through one folded edge. Pick up a few threads of the adjoining fabric and then a few threads on the folded edge. Repeat along the length.

HOW TO BASTE

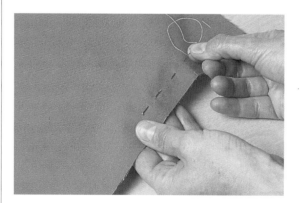

Pin the layers together, then work a long running stitch by hand. Set the machine to a long stitch-length for basting by machine.

HOW TO FINGER-PRESS

If you can't reach the seam with the iron, simply moisten your finger and run it along the seam to finger-press.

Finger-pressing

It is not always possible to get the tip of the iron into intricate corners to press the seam. *See above for more details.*

Making a cord tidy

Cords on drape tapes should not be cut off once the heading has been drawn up. Make a small bag to slip the excess cord into, to allow the heading to be opened out flat again for laundering or hanging at a different-size window.

Herringbone stitch

Herringbone stitch is used to hem heavyweight fabrics and to join the butted edges of batting together. The stitches are worked from left to right with the needle pointing to the left. Bring the needle to the right side.

Temporary tacking

This is a practical way of fixing fabric to a solid frame while working. Even if you intend to staple the fabric with a staple gun, it is often helpful to use temporary tacking first.

MAKING A CORD TIDY

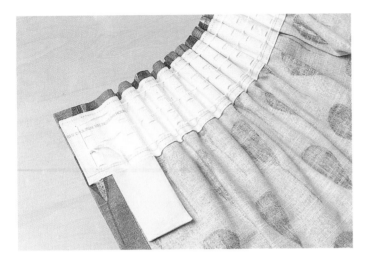

STEP 1 Cut a rectangle of fabric such as calico 4³/₄ x 4 in./12 cm x 10 cm Fold widthwise in half, with the right sides facing. Stitch the raw edges taking a ³/₈-in./1-cm seam allowance and leaving a 1¹/₈-in./3-cm gap in the short upper edge.

STEP 2 Clip the corners and turn right side out. Slip the cords into the bag and sew it to the top of the drape on the underside.

HOW TO HERRINGBONE STITCH

STEP 1 Make a small stitch through the fabric above the hem and ¹/₄ –³/₈ in./5 mm – 1 cm to the right (of a previous stitch).

STEP 2 Make the next stitch below the hem and ¹/₄ –³/₈ in./5 mm–1cm to the right. Continue to alternate stitches and space them evenly apart.

TEMPORARY TACKING

STEP 1 Lever off old tacks with a tack lifter, which is a traditional upholstery tool, or use the blade of a screwdriver. If the head snaps off a tack, hammer the shaft into the wood to prevent it from snagging the fabric.

STEP 2 Drive the tack halfway home with hammer; it is then easy to remove for repositioning. A tack hammer with a magnetic tip will hold a tack in place. Hammer the tack in straight; if it starts to lie crooked, remove it and start again or knock it upright. If it does not lie straight, the head may snag the fabric and you.

YOU WILL NEED:

BIAS BINDING:

- **TAPE MEASURE**
- **FABRIC**
- **AIR-ERASABLE PEN/TAILOR'S CHALK**
- **NEEDLE AND THREAD/SEWING MACHINE**
- **SCISSORS**
- **PINS**
- **IRON**

Bindings

Curved raw edges should be bound with bias-cut binding. The binding can be manipulated to follow the contours of the fabric, but will still lie flat. This is because the bias grain is the stretchiest part of the fabric.

Cutting bias strips

Although ready-made bias binding is inexpensive and widely available, it is very economical to make your own and it has many uses, such as binding raw edges, covering piping, and making ties. When working out what the width of the strips should be, use a tape measure to measure around the front and back of the fabric edge to be bound. Generally, cut strips for bias binding are double the finished width to allow for seam allowances and stretching. The seam allowance should match that of the item when cutting strips to make piping.

Joining bias strips

Once cut, bias strips can be easily joined and then sewn together securely with the machine.

Making bias binding

A bias-binding maker is very useful for making single bias binding and you will find the whole process very satisfying. This handy gadget is available in most soft-furnishing departments and stores.

Some fabrics are easier to handle double when applying a binding. Sheer fabric bindings should be made double. A bias-binding maker is not needed to make a double binding. Simply press the strip lengthwise in half with the right sides facing.

Attaching double bias binding

Double bias binding is useful when you are working with sheer or lightweight fabrics.

CUTTING BIAS STRIPS

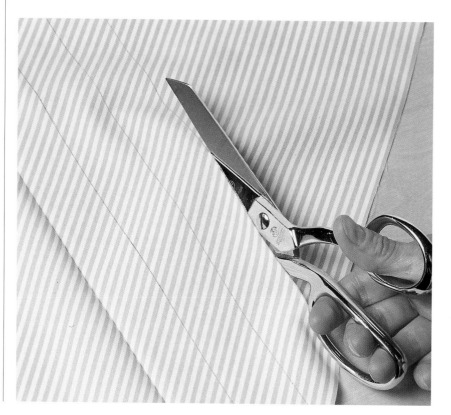

STEP 1 Measure the length of the edge that is to be bound with the bias strips, adding 4 in./10 cm for ease and turning under the ends. Extra fabric will need to be added for joining lengths.

STEP 2 Fold the fabric diagonally, at a 45° angle to the selvedge. This diagonal fold is the true bias. Press along the fold, then open out flat. With tailor's chalk or an air-erasable pen and rule, draw lines the width of the binding that are parallel with the fold line. Cut out along these lines.

ATTACHING SINGLE BIAS BINDING

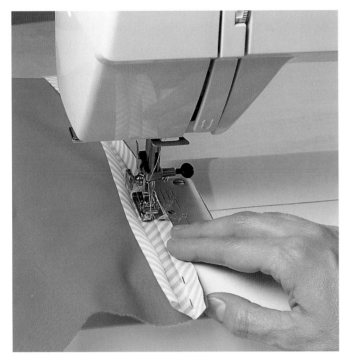

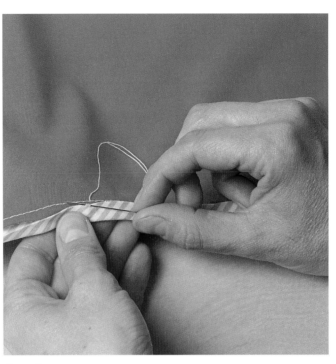

STEP 1 Open out one folded edge of the bias binding. With right sides facing and matching the raw edges, pin the binding to the fabric. Stitch along the fold line.

STEP 2 Turn the binding to the underside and slipstitch the fold along the seam line.

JOINING BIAS STRIPS

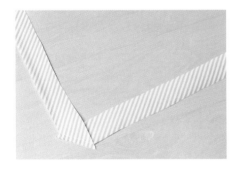

Position one end of two strips at right-angles, with the right sides facing and the raw ends matched. Stitch the bias strips together, taking a ¼-in./5-mm seam allowance. Press the seam open then cut off the corners.

MAKING BIAS BINDING

Push the strip through the wide end of the binding maker with the wrong side of the fabric face up. If the fabric is thick, a pin is useful to ease it out of the narrow end. As the strip emerges through the narrow end, the edges will be turned under. Press them in place.

DOUBLE BIAS BINDING

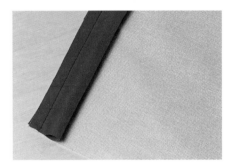

Pin double bias binding on the right side of the fabric, matching the raw edges. Stitch the bias binding in place, then turn the folded edge to the underside and slipstitch along the seam.

YOU WILL NEED:

PIPING:
- FABRIC
- CORD
- SCISSORS
- TAPE MEASURE
- PINS
- NEEDLE AND THREAD/SEWING MACHINE

BONDING WEB:
- AIR-ERASABLE PEN/TAILOR'S CHALK
- BONDING WEB
- SCISSORS
- IRON

Piping

Piping gives a nicely finished look to many handsewn items, from the edges of cushions to lampshades and throws. You can buy quite a wide range of different kinds of piping in soft-furnishing stores, but it is very easy to make your own. This is a good option if you can't find quite what you want. Then you can be sure that you will get your piping either to match or to contrast with the fabric of your finished item.

Making piping

Although piping is available readymade by the yard/meter, the color range is limited. Make your own piping by covering piping cord, which comes in various thicknesses. Wash it first to preshrink it.

Applying piping and turning corners

Piping should be basted into place and then machine-stitched. Turning corners can be daunting, but it is just a question of taking it slowly.

Joining the piping ends

Piping cord can be slightly frustrating because it can fray amazingly easily. Joining it smoothly is easier than you think, and always leaves a very pleasing (and hopefully invisible!) result.

Stitching piping

Lay the second piece of fabric on top of the basted, piped fabric with right sides facing. Baste through all the layers. With a zipper or piping foot on the sewing machine, stitch the piping in position.

Attaching cord

If cord is to be sewn along a seam, leave a 1-³/₁₆ in./3-cm gap in the seam in an unobtrusive place, such as the lower edge of a cushion, or carefully cut a gap in a stitched seam.

Mounting fabric

There are many beautiful sheer fabrics available today and it may often seem that their application is rather limited because they are

MAKING PIPING

STEP 1 Measure the cord circumference. Add a 1³/₁₆-in./3-cm seam allowance—the width of the bias strip needed to cover the cord. Cut a bias strip of fabric in this width and to the length needed. Join the bias strips if necessary. When measuring an item to see how much piping is needed, add 4 in./10 cm extra.

STEP 2 Lay the cord along the center of the strip on the wrong side. Fold the strip lengthwise in half, enclosing the cord. Pin the raw edges together. Set the sewing machine to a long-length stitch for machine-basting. Using a zipper or piping foot, stitch close to the piping.

JOINING THE PIPING ENDS

STEP 1 To join the ends of the piping neatly, allow a 1-in./2.5-cm overlap and pin the piping in place to 2 in./5 cm each side of the overlap. Unpick the piping basting for 2 in./5 cm each side of the overlap to reveal the cord. Cut off half the strands at each end of the cord to thin it.

STEP 2 Twist the ends of the cord together and bind with thread. Wrap one end of the piping fabric around the cord again. Turn under ¹/₄ in./5 mm on the other end and wrap it around the cord. Tack the cord in place ready for stitching.

quite delicate and slippery. However, this problem can be solved: sheer or unstable fabrics can be mounted onto denser fabrics, to give them some stability; then the two fabrics can be treated as one. This technique is not suitable for large areas of fabric or areas prone to lots of wear, but it is ideal for smaller cushion covers and table runners. Consider the color of the underlying fabric carefully, because it will be visible and will be affected by the color or loose weave of the fabric on top.

Bonding web

Bonding web is a fusible webbing used to apply fabric to fabric. It is ideal for appliqué work. It is simply pressed on.

APPLYING BONDING WEB

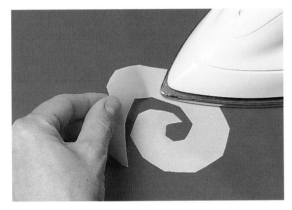

STEP 1 Draw your design on the paper-backing side of the bonding web. Be aware that a mirror image of the design should be drawn. Roughly cut out the shape and iron it onto the wrong side of the fabric.

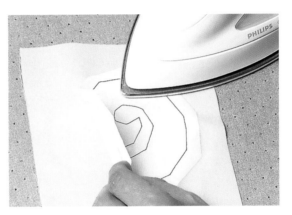

STEP 2 Cut out the design. Peel off the backing paper and position it right-side up on the background fabric. Iron the motif to fuse it in place.

PIPING AND TURNING

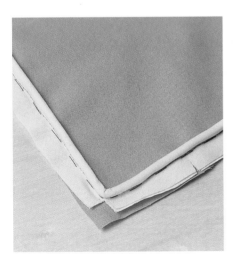

Pin the piping to the right side of the fabric. Snip the seam allowance of the piping at curves and corners. Baste in place by hand or machine using a zipper or piping foot.

HOW TO MOUNT FABRIC

Pin the sheer fabric to a background fabric, starting at the center and smoothing the layers outward. Baste the fabrics together along the outer edges.

ATTACHING CORD

Unravel one end of the cord so it is not so bulky, and poke it into the hole. Lay the cord along the seam and catch it in place with small stitches. Unravel the other end and poke it into the hole, sewing the gap closed securely.

Window treatments

Dressing windows is practical as well as decorative.

Drapes and shades offer privacy, cut out unwanted light, reduce

outside noise, and conserve heat. Because they are the source of

natural light in a room, windows are often a focal point and deserve a

treatment that will display them at their best, whether that is to

highlight their elegant shape, emphasize a glorious view, or

hide an unattractive window or outlook.

This chapter outlines a variety of superb styles to set off

your windows, ranging from using modern styles, such as tab-top

drapes, to traditional swag and tails. All the important stages are

covered, from choosing a style and measuring windows to creating

beautiful drapes and shades. Remember that drapes and shades

are not just for windows; many of the innovative ideas shown here

can be used to make bed drapes and also for

doorways and screens.

Calculating measurements

Before taking the plunge into making drapes, loose covers and bed-linen, it is vital that you take all the measurements you need. This is a part of the process that must not be rushed—you don't want to spend hours working on a pair of drapes then find that they are too short when you hang them at your window, for example.

Ideally, have the drape or shade fittings in place before measuring for fabric. If this is not possible, lightly mark their intended position on the wall or window frame. Slip a few hooks or rings onto the rail or rod. To make a window seem larger and to let in more light, extend rails or rods beyond the frame so that drapes can be pulled right back to the very edges of the frame.

Measuring the length

For gathered headings on a rail and for drapes with casings, measure the length from the top of the rail or rod. For tab-top drapes or drapes hanging from rings, measure from the bottom of the tab or ring. For case-headed drapes, measure from below the rod. For blinds, measure from the top of the cleat.

If there is furniture in front of the window, a sill-length drape may be the best option so that the drape does not interfere with it. If there is a radiator, below-sill-length drapes that finish just above the top of it will let heat from the radiator warm the room when the drapes are closed. Floor-length drapes can finish just above the floor surface or flow onto the floor.

Add an allowance to the length for the heading and lower hem. For a standard heading and pencil pleats, add 1½ in./3.8 cm to the upper edge. For drapes with a casing, add ⅜ in./1 cm for ease plus a ¾-in./2-cm seam allowance; for a frill at the top, allow twice the height of the frill.

Add a ⅝-in./1.5-cm seam allowance to the top of tab-top or tie drapes. The depth of the hem varies according to the fabric; generally, add 6 in./15 cm for unlined drapes and 4 in./10 cm for lined drapes. See individual blind instructions for hems and allowances.

Measuring the width

First measure the width of the rail or rod. For overlapping drape rails in two halves, add the length of the overlap. Multiply this measurement by 1½–3 for a gathered heading, by 2–2½ for a pencil-pleated heading, and by 2 for triple and cylindrical-pleated headings. Add a 1-in./2.5-cm hem at each side for unlined drapes, and a 1½-in./3.8-cm hem to each side for lined drapes.

Fabric widths

Divide the total width measurement by the width of your chosen fabric for the number of fabric widths required. Round up the fabric widths to the largest amount, because 1¼-in./3.2-cm seam allowances are also needed for each join. If you have an uneven number of fabric widths and there will be a pair of drapes at the window, cut one width lengthwise in half and place it at the outer edge of the drapes.

Lining

The same amount of lining is needed as for the drape fabric, but do not allow extra lining for matching patterns.

The length of a drape will depend on what lies in front of the window. Floor-length drapes are ideal for windows without furniture in front or radiators below. Sheer-fabric drapes that flow onto the floor give an elaborate effect.

Drape fabrics and rods

Drapes are a big investment if you decide to buy them ready-made, and the situation is the same even if you make them yourself. Assess your windows carefully and make sure that you select the right kind of fabric for them. Bear in mind the fact that sunlight fades textiles and that drapes need washing or dry-cleaning too.

Choosing fabrics

When choosing fabrics for windows, bear in mind how the fabric hangs and drapes, whether its color is likely to fade in sunlight, and if it is washable or will need to be dry-cleaned. Buy linings with the same washing instructions as the drape fabric, and remember to buy extra fabric if it is likely to shrink.

Consider how much privacy is needed. A bathroom with a clear glass window will need a sheer fabric to let in daylight but maintain privacy, and something denser for when the light is on in the evening; whereas other rooms may just need a drape or shade that can be closed at night. A heavyweight, lined drape is advisable in a bedroom that gets the early morning sun.

The window treatment must fit in with the other furnishings and decor in the room. Patterned wall-coverings, flooring, and upholstery need a plain area to rest the eye. Alternatively, if the walls and other furnishings are plain, boldly patterned drapes or shades can add interest to the room.

A kitchen window above a sink is prone to splashes of water or steam, so choose a hard-wearing fabric. A shade is often a better option because it can fit smoothly against the window and be rolled up when not needed. Fabrics that are specially treated to inhibit the growth of mildew and mold are ideal for well-insulated kitchens and bathrooms that have a lot of steam.

Swags require soft, pliable fabrics, whereas formal drapes and shades need a heavier weight of fabric to hang vertically. Stiff fabrics hold a pleat well and are a particularly good choice for Roman blinds.

Firm fabrics with a close weave are excellent for roller blinds. Spray-on fabric stiffener can be

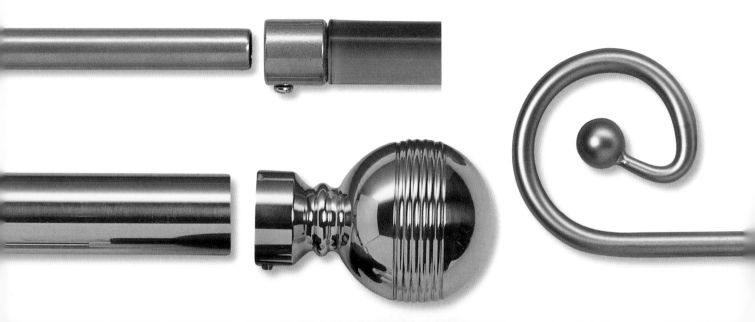

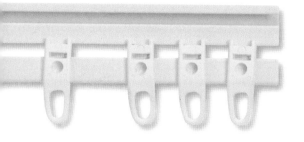

applied to many fabrics to make them suitable for making such blinds; ready-stiffened fabrics are also available.

Rails and rods

In general, a rail is discreet and hidden from view when the drapes are closed, but a rod is always visible; for this reason you need to make sure that the rod fits in with the decorative scheme of your room.

Rails

Rails can be fixed on brackets to the wall, window frame, or ceiling. Most are made of plastic, but more-expensive metal rails are available to hang large, heavy drapes that may need extra support. Rails can have a valance in front to hide them. Some rails are bendable to fit within a bay window. Rails are also available in two halves so that a pair of drapes can be overlapped. Corded tracks let the drapes be opened and closed simply by pulling a cord.

Rods

Rods are available in different thicknesses of wood and metal. Many metal rods are adjustable or can be extended, while others can be bent to fit the shape of a bay window.

Lightweight drapes, such as those made from sheer fabrics and café curtains, can be threaded onto metal or plastic rods. These are usually expandable and do not need fixings, but can be extended to fit within a window recess. Sheer fabrics can be hung from a length of sprung, plastic-covered wire that has screw eyes screwed into the ends; these are hooked onto screw hooks fixed within a recess.

Finials

Finials are the decorative ends that slot onto or into the end of rods. Most have a small screw that is tightened to secure it to the rod. There is a large range available nowadays, made from metal, wood, plastic, pottery, glass, and acrylic resin. If you don't find exactly what you want in the shops, you can even model your own finials from clay or papier-mâché and paint them to match your decor.

Rods and finials (decorative ends) are always visible so they play a significant part in the decorative scheme of a room. If you want something more discreet, choose a rail instead.

Drape headings

If you thought that tape was the only way to head a drape, then think again! There are many different finishes that can be applied to the tops of drapes, and many of these can be decorative in their own right. Assess the type of decorating scheme that you have and design your headings accordingly.

Most gathered headings are created with curtain tape, which is available by the yard/meter and has 1–3 rows of fine cord running along its length. The tape is sewn to the back of the drape and the cords are drawn up to the required width to gather or pleat the drape. There are 1–3 rows of slots on the tape to insert hooks through. Having a choice of rows of slots lets you hang the drapes at the level that is right for you and to conceal the hooks. Tapes are available in different widths and weights; lightweight mesh tapes are for use on sheer drapes. Drapes can also be attached with casings, tabs, ties, and eyelets.

Rings slot through rods and attach in different ways.

Standard heading

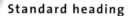

This tape produces a simple, gathered heading, which works well on small drapes, lined or unlined, in any weight of fabric.

Pencil pleats

Here, a row of neat, upright pleats is created. This heading can be used on light-to-mediumweight fabrics, either unlined or lined.

Triple pleats

Cordless tape or buckram is first sewn to the top of the drapes, then the triple pleats are made by dividing one large pleat into three smaller ones and handsewing them in place.

FAR RIGHT: **Many different finishes can be applied to the tops of drapes, from simple, gathered headings to more elaborate goblet pleats. Certain styles are suited to particular fabric weights.**

Use medium-to-heavyweight fabric for these so that they keep their shape.

Goblet or French pleats

Cordless tape or buckram is applied to the top of the drapes, then deep pleats are stitched at regular intervals. The pleats are padded out with a roll of stiff interfacing. This style is best suited to medium-to-heavyweight fabric.

Casing

This treatment works best on fine fabrics. A fine rod or wire is inserted through a channel stitched in the drape.

Hooks and runners

Hooks are made from plastic or metal. Use metal hooks on heavyweight drapes and on handsewn headings. Plastic hooks are slotted through the curtain tape and then onto runners that slot onto

the rail. Hooks are usually placed at 3-in./7.5-cm intervals. Some hooks are combined with runners as a single unit. Runners are usually supplied with a rail. The runners at the outer ends of the rail are known as end-stops because they literally stop the drape from falling off the rail.

If the curtain heading is to cover the rail, position the hooks in the lower row of slots; if the drape is to hang below a rod, place the hooks in a row of slots close to the top of the tape but not so that they show above the drape. Apply hooks to uncorded tape by slipping them behind each pleat and handsewing them securely with a strong button thread.

Rings

Wooden, plastic, or metal curtain rings slot onto rods; make sure that the ring is large enough to slide comfortably along the rod. Remove the screw eye from the bottom of the rings and then handsew the rings securely to the top of the drapes, or attach them to the drape by inserting the hook through the heading tape and onto the screw eye. Alternatively, attach a clip onto the drape then fix it to the screw eye.

Dressing drapes

To help your drapes to hang attractively, it is advisable to "dress" them for a few days, which will help to set the pleats or gathers. Hang the drapes and arrange the folds to look their best. Pin the folds in place at the bottom, then loosely tie soft tapes or ribbon around them, holding the tapes in place with pins. Remove the tapes and pins after a few days.

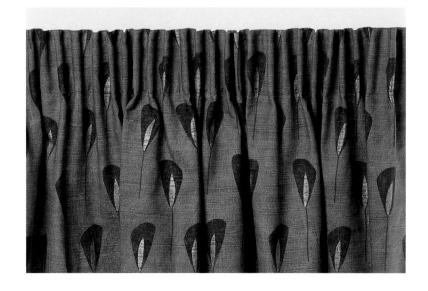

YOU WILL NEED:

DETACHABLE
LINING:

- LINING FABRIC
- NEEDLE AND
  THREAD/SEWING
  MACHINE
- SCISSORS
- LINING TAPE
- PINS
- HOOKS

UNLINED DRAPES:

- NEEDLE AND
  THREAD/SEWING
  MACHINE
- HEADING TAPE
- SCISSORS
- IRON
- PINS
- HOOKS
- CORD TIDY (SEE
  PAGE 787)

PROJECT

Making drapes

Drapes can be daunting to make—especially if you have never made them before. Start with a simple pair of unlined drapes and gradually work your way up to lined drapes as you become more confident. Make sure you have done all your measuring accurately and are using the correct type of fabric for your chosen drape.

Making a detachable lining

Less fabric is needed for a detachable lining than for the drape. Make up the drape following the directions for unlined drapes on the opposite page. Cut the lining in the same way as the unlined drape, using 1½ times the length of the rail. Detachable lining tape has two "skirts," which are applied to either side of the lining. If you are making a pair of drapes, the knotted ends of the cord should be on the meeting edges of the drapes.

Loose-lined drapes

A detachable lining is versatile, because it can be removed from the main drape for laundering. This is useful if the drape and lining have differing washing instructions. Even if they have the same washing procedure, a drape that is very bulky may not fit into a domestic washing machine with the lining, and a detachable lining can be washed separately to lighten the load.

Unlined drapes

Unlined drapes are quick and easy to make, but do not hang as well as lined drapes. They are not usually light-fast, so may not be suitable for a bedroom or bathroom. If you want the fabric to stand above the tape, add double the height of the stand to the length measurements. (See page 794 to calculate fabric quantities.) You will also need standard or pencil-pleat tape the entire width of the drape.

MAKING A DETACHABLE LINING FOR A DRAPE

STEP 1 Cut out the lining and join the widths with flat felled seams if necessary. Turn ⅜ in./1 cm of the fabric under, then ⅝ in./1.5cm on the long side edges. Machine-stitch close to the inner folds. Cut a length of lining tape the width of the lining plus 4 in./10 cm. Unthread the cords at one end and knot them together.

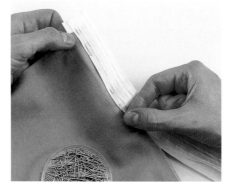

STEP 2 Cut the tape ⅜ in./1 cm from the knotted end. Part the skirts and slip the top of the lining between them, with the corded side on the right side of the lining and with the knotted end of tape extending ⅜ in./1 cm beyond the drape. Pin the layers together.

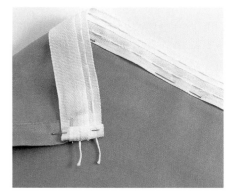

STEP 3 Unthread the cords at the other end of the tape level with the edge of the lining. Cut the tape ⅜ in./1 cm beyond the lining, but leave the ends of the cord free. Turn the tape ends to the back of the lining in a double hem and pin in place.

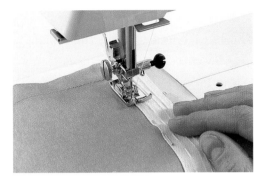

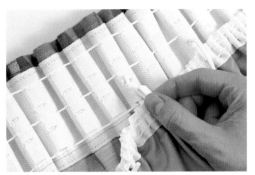

STEP 4 Stitch close to the ends and lower edge of the tape, enclosing the lining. Then pull up the cords so that the lining is the same width as the curtain heading.

STEP 5 Roll up the tape and sew to the top of the drape. Insert the hooks 3 in./7.5 cm apart through the lining tape. With wrong sides facing, slip the hooks through the tape so that both hang from the same hooks. Machine stitch a double hem so the lining is ⅝ in./1.5 cm shorter than the drape.

MAKING UNLINED DRAPES

STEP 1 Cut out the drape and join the widths with flat felled seams if necessary. Turn ⅜ in./ 1 cm under, then ⅝ in./1.5 cm on long side edges. Slipstitch or machine-stitch in place close to the inner folds.

STEP 2 Press 3 in./7.5 cm twice to the underside on the lower edge to form a double hem. Mark the corner and the point where the lower hem meets the inner edge of the side hem with a pin.

STEP 3 Unfold the hem once at the corner. Fold the corner at an angle between the pins. Refold the hem. Slipstitch the hem and miters in place.

STEP 4 Press 1½ in./3.8 cm to the underside at the upper edge, or, if you want the drape to stand above the tape, turn the fabric down that amount plus 1½ in./3.8 cm. Knot the cord ends together at one end of the heading tape. Turn under the knotted ends.

STEP 5 Pin the tape 1 in./2.5 cm below the top of the drape, covering the turned-under edge, or, if the drape is to stand above the tape, turn the fabric down that amount plus 1 in./2.5 cm. Stitch close to the long edges and ends of the tape, taking care not to catch in the cords. Stitch both long edges in the same direction.

STEP 6 Pull up the cords to gather the fabric to the required width. Knot the free ends of the cord. Adjust the gathers evenly. Slip the hooks through the slots in the tape, placing one at each end then at 3 in./7.5 cm intervals. Roll up the excess tape and sew to the top of the drape or slip the cord into a cord tidy (see page 787).

YOU WILL NEED:

LINED DRAPES:
- **TAPE MEASURE**
- **CURTAIN FABRIC**
- **LINING FABRIC**
- **NEEDLE AND THREAD/SEWING MACHINE**
- **IRON**
- **PINS**
- **SCISSORS**
- **HEADING TAPE**

INTERLINED DRAPES:
- **TAPE MEASURE**
- **CURTAINS FABRIC (E.G. CHENILLE OR FLEECE)**
- **LINING FABRIC (E.G. BRUSHED COTTON)**
- **NEEDLE AND THREAD/SEWING MACHINE**
- **IRON**
- **PINS**
- **SCISSORS**

Lined drapes

Lining drapes gives protection from dust and sunlight, and cuts down on heat loss and noise. A locked-in lining gives a professional finish.

Interlined drapes

Interlining within a drape gives body and provides insulation. With this in mind, you could line the drape in a warmer fabric, such as brightly colored, brushed cotton. This would be particularly effective if the main drape was made in a figured chenille fabric or a cozy fleece. Do not use a lining fabric that is too bulky, however; this will prevent the drapes from falling nicely when they are hanging at the windows.

MAKING LINED DRAPES

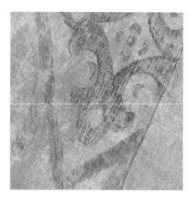

STEP 1 Measure and cut out the fabric (see page 794). Include 1½-in./3.8-cm top and side hems and a 4-in./10-cm lower hem. Cut the lining the same size, omitting the lower hem allowance. Join the drape and lining widths with flat seams. Press 1½-in./3.8-cm to the wrong side on the side edges. Secure in place with herringbone stitch (see page 786–787), finishing 6-in./15-cm above the lower edge.

STEP 2 Turn up a ¾-in./2-cm hem then a 3¼-in./8-cm deep hem on the lower edge. Make a mitered corner (see page 801, steps 2 and 3), slipstitch the miter, and then hem the lower edge with herringbone stitch. Turn up ⅝-in./1.5-cm then 1⅜-in./3.5-cm on the lower edge of the lining. Machine-stitch the lining in place.

STEP 3 Lay the drape flat, wrong-side up. Place the lining on top with wrong sides facing, lower edge 2-in./5-cm above lower edge of drape.

STEP 5 Trim side edges of the lining, level with the drape. Turn 1¼-in./3.2-cm under. Pin and then slipstitch in place, turn the corner at the lower edge, and slipstitch for 1½-in./3.8-cm. Leave the rest of the hem free. Check the length, press down the upper edge; attach heading tape (see page 801, steps 5 and 6).

STEP 4 Single-width drape: turn back one-third of the lining; align the fabric grains and top edges. Join the layers together with a double length of thread to pick up two threads of the lining fabric, then two of the drape fabric. Leave a gap of 4-in./10-cm and repeat, catching the fabric together along its length. Keep the thread loose. Fold the lining out flat. Smooth over its surface, then repeat on the opposite edge. Drapes using more than a width: start at the seam nearest the center. Lock the seams together, working outward from the seam, joining the layers at 16-in./40-cm intervals across the drape. Stitch through the seam allowance, not the surface of the drape or lining.

MAKING INTERLINED DRAPES

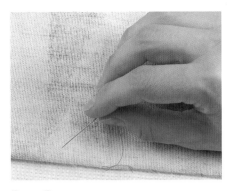

STEP 1 To join widths of interlining, overlap the edges by ½-in./1.2-cm and stitch through the layers with a zigzag stitch. If you do not have this facility on your sewing machine, butt the edges together and join them with a herringbone stitch. Take care not to stretch the interlining when joining it. Cut the interlining the same size as the drape.

STEP 2 Join the interlining, drape, and lining widths, using flat seams for the drape and lining. Lay the interlining out flat on a large table or the floor. Lay the drape smoothly on top, right-side uppermost. Fold back the drape and join the layers together with a locking stitch in the same way as locking in the lining. Work two rows of locking on each width of fabric and along the seams.

STEP 3 Gently turn the drape over so the interlining is facing upward. Turn a 1½-in./3.8-cm hem under along the side edges, and herringbone stitch in place. Turn up a 4-in./10-cm single hem, then miter the corners and herringbone stitch in place.

STEP 4 Lay the lining right-side uppermost on top, matching the lower edges. Lock the lining to the interlining. Trim the side edges level with the drape. Turn 1¼-in./3.2-cm under on the side and lower edge, and slipstitch to the drape. Check the length, then turn down the upper edge and attach the heading to the drape.

YOU WILL NEED:

CASE-HEADED
DRAPES:
• TAPE MEASURE
• LIGHTWEIGHT
  CURTAIN FABRIC
• ROD OR SPRUNG
  WIRE
• IRON
• PINS
• SCISSORS
• NEEDLE AND
  THREAD/SEWING
  MACHINE
• TIES, TABS, RINGS,
  OR EYELETS

SCALLOPED CAFÉ
CURTAINS:
• TAPE MEASURE
• CURTAIN FABRIC
• CURTAIN FACING
• ROD
• PAPER
• PAIR OF TOOL
  COMPASSES
• NEEDLE AND
  THREAD/SEWING
  MACHINE
• PINS
• SCISSORS
• TAILOR'S CHALK
• IRON

DOUBLE-LAYER
DRAPES:
• TAPE MEASURE
• CURTAIN FABRIC
• PINS
• NEEDLE AND
  THREAD/SEWING
  MACHINE

Case-headed drapes

Lightweight drapes can look very attractive with cased headings threaded onto rods or sprung wire. First, cut out the drape (see notes on calculating measurements on page 794).

For a 1-in./2.5-cm frill to stand above the rod or wire, add double the height of the frill to the length measurements, e.g. 2-in./5-cm. For the width, you should allow 1½ –3 times the width of the drape rod, depending on how much fullness you require.

Double-layer drape

You can add a valance to a simple case-headed drape. To the drape length, add an allowance for the hem, the circumference of the rod plus ¼ in./6 mm, and the depth of the valance plus ⅝ in./1.5 cm.

Flat-headed drapes

Flat-headed drapes are generally no more than 1½ times the width of the window. They can be fixed in place with ties, tabs, rings, or eyelets.

MAKING CASE-HEADED DRAPES

STEP 1 Join the fabric widths, using a French seam on sheer fabrics. Hem the sides and lower edge with double hems, either with a machine-stitch or slipstitch.

STEP 2 Press ³∕₈-in /1-cmunder at the upper edge. Next, press 1-in/2.5-cm under plus half the rod circumference plus ¼-in/6-mm for ease. Stitch ¼-in/6-mm above the lower pressed edge, then 1-in/2.5-cm below the upper pressed edge to form a channel to thread the rod through. Insert the rod through the channel and adjust the gathers.

MAKING SCALLOPED CAFÉ CURTAINS

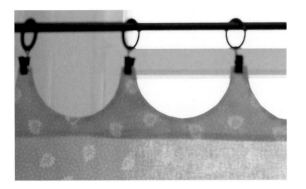

Fix the rod in position. Measure the drop of the drape from the bottom of the rod to sill length. Add a 4-in./10-cm hem and a ⅝-in/1.5-cm seam allowance. Measure the width of the rod. You will need 1½ times the width plus ⅝-in./1.5-cm for each side hem.

STEP 1 Cut out a 3⅜-in./8.5-cm-wide strip of paper, which is half the drape width less ⅝-in./1.5-cm. Label one end as the centre fold. Use a pair of compasses to describe a 4-in. /10-cm diameter semicircle on paper and cut it out as a template for the scallops. Fold the scallop in half and draw around it on the center-fold end of the strip, matching the corners.

STEP 2 Open out the scallop. Move the scallop ¾-in./2-cm along the template strip and lightly mark its position. Continue along the template to about ¾-in./2-cm from the other end. If the end scallop does not fit well, adjust the size of the gaps between the scallops. Cut out the template.

STEP 3 Cut out the drape and a 4-in./10-cm-wide strip of fabric for the facing that is the width of the drape. Join the drape widths with a flat felled seam if necessary. Stitch a ¼-in./5-mm-deep hem on the long lower edge of the facing. Pin the facing to the upper edge of the drape, right sides facing and matching the raw edges.

STEP 4 Pin the template on one half of the facing 1⅝ in./5 cm from the upper and side raw edges. Draw around the template with tailor's chalk. Flip the template to continue on the other half. Stitch along the drawn lines. Trim the scallops, leaving a ¼-in./5-mm seam allowance. Snip the curves and clip the corners. Turn right side out and press.

STEP 5 Press under ¼ in./5 mm then ⅜-in./1-cm on the side edges. Slipstitch in place. Turn a double hem on the lower edge and stitch.

MAKING DOUBLE-LAYER DRAPES

Make a double hem on the lower edge. Make a ⅝-in./1.5-cm double hem on the upper edge on the right side of the fabric. Fold the upper edge to the right side for the depth of the valance plus half the rod circumference measurement plus ¼-in./6-mm. On one edge, mark a point with a pin half the rod circumference measurement plus ¼-in./6-mm below the pressed edge. Stitch across the drape at this point to form the channel. Insert the rod.

PROJECT
Shower curtains

Shower curtains are simple to make and can be chosen to match a bathroom scheme. Make sure the curtain is long enough to tuck inside the bathtub or just above the floor of a shower tray.

There are a large range of shower curtains available on the market, but they are expensive for what they are and the colors and designs aren't always exactly what you want. There really is nothing simpler than making a shower curtain yourself, and you can choose an outer fabric curtain that will match your bathroom scheme.

In addition to preventing water from escaping when showering, a shower curtain can bring a welcome touch of color to a plain bathroom. And there is nothing nicer than being able to pick out the fabric that matches your color scheme and taste. Shower-curtain rails are expandable with a suction pad at each end, so do not need to be screwed into tiled walls. Chunky

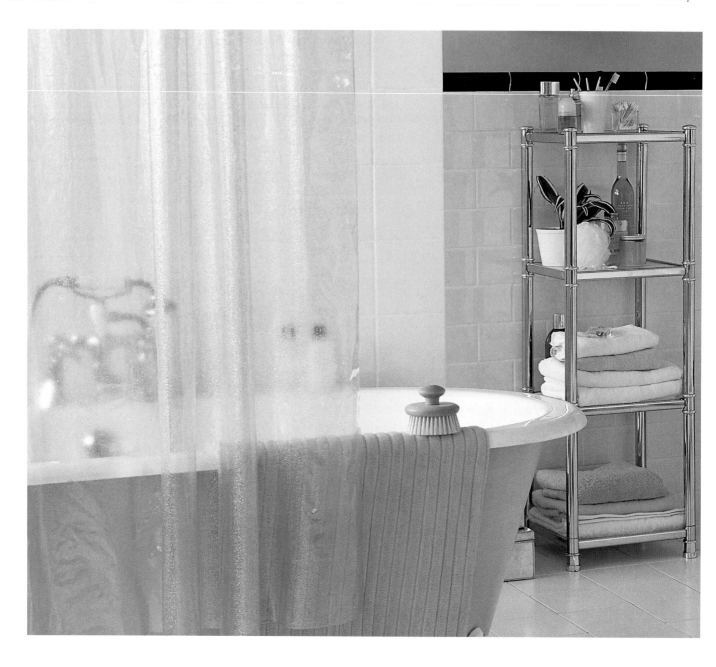

plastic rings that clip onto eyelets in the top of the curtain are then threaded onto the rail. (These are readily available at many hardware outlets and other home stores.) Eyelets are also available in a kit with a fixing; choose large eyelets that are at least ½-in./1.2-cm in diameter. If the choice of curtaining for showers seems limited, remember that an outer curtain, which does not need to be waterproof, can be added.

Choosing fabric

Obviously, a shower curtain must be waterproof. Departments and furnishing-fabric stores stock 100 percent nylon, 100 percent PVC, and 100 percent vinyl plastics in many colors and designs. In general, waterproof fabrics are available in widths of 51-in./1.3-m. This is too narrow for most showers, so the fabric widths will need to be joined. Position the join at the center of the curtain, and join the widths with a French seam. Kite shops and marine stores stock rip-stop nylon, which is a lightweight material that comes in bright colors and large widths.

Pull a wet shower curtain flat to let it dry; otherwise mildew will form in the creases. To clean waterproof fabrics, wipe down with a soft cloth and nonabrasive cleaner.

Measuring up

Standard showers are 70-in./1.8-m square, but it is important to measure your own site because circumstances vary greatly. The curtain must be long enough to tuck inside the bathtub or shower tray. Fix the shower rail in position. Measure the drop from the rail to at least 8-in./20-cm inside the bathtub or just above the floor of the shower tray. Measure the length of the fixed rail; the curtain can be made to the rail measurement or 25 percent wider—do not make the curtain any wider, because the curtains will gather, trapping moisture that cannot dry out.

MAKING A BASIC SHOWER CURTAIN

STEP 1 Cut out the shower curtains, adding 2½-in./6-cm to the width and 5-in./12.5-cm to the length for hems. Fold a ⅝-in./1.5-cm/ double hem on each side edge, and stitch close to the inner edges. Fold a 1¼-in./3-cm/ double hem on the top edge. Stitch close to the inner edges.

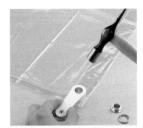

STEP 2 On the wrong side, use a china marker pencil to mark the position of the eyelets along the center of the hem on the upper edge about 6 in./15 cm apart, starting and finishing ¾ in./2 cm in from the side edges. Fix the eyelets at the marks. Fold a double hem on the lower edge and stitch close to the inner fold. When hanging the curtain, the right side faces outward.

MAKING A LINED SHOWER CURTAIN

There are two methods of making a lined shower curtain. The simplest way is to follow the basic method above to make one shower curtain from waterproof fabric and one from your chosen outer fabric. Hang both curtains from the same rings, with the waterproof curtain facing into the shower and the outer curtain facing into the room.

For a more lavish style, make the basic waterproof curtain then make an unlined curtain (see pages 800–801) using synthetic curtain tape. Pull up the tape to fit the rail and fasten the ends securely. Slip a plastic curtain ring onto each shower-rail ring. Fix the curtain tape to the rings with plastic curtain hooks. When using the shower, have the outer curtain outside the bathtub or shower stall.

YOU WILL NEED:

BORDERS:

- **BORDER FOR DRAPES**
- **LINING FOR DRAPES**
- **IRON**
- **PINS**
- **SCISSORS**
- **NEEDLE AND THREAD/SEWING MACHINE**

Adding borders can be an excellent way of recycling drapes to fit bigger windows. They can also create an attractive design, as shown by these decorative floral borders.

PROJECT
Recycled drapes

Good-quality drapes last for many years, and it is a shame to discard them because your windows are a different shape when you move house. Drapes can be adapted in many stylish ways, however—if they are too short they can be lengthened with an attractive border in a contrasting color, and if they are too long they can be hemmed.

Drapes do not suffer a lot of wear and tear, so they last a long time. You may bring drapes with you to a new home, and although they do not always fit your new windows, there are quite a few ways of adjusting them. Good-quality second-hand drapes can be found at auctions and yard sales.

It is simple to cut down drapes that are too large. Extending drapes involves a little more work. Let down a deep hem to add length, and make a false hem with seam tape if you are left with a very narrow hem allowance. Adding tabs at the top of the drape or hanging them on rings will also gain you extra length.

It is not only conventional drapes and shades that can be used at windows. You could hang a colorful tablecloth or a lightweight bedcover or throw, perhaps with an African or Asian design. Add tabs at the top for hanging, or fix to clips to hang from rings.

Drapes with borders

A border gives a smart finishing touch to drapes and is an excellent way of recycling drapes to fit bigger windows. A border can be added to all four edges or just one edge. Bagging the drape out with lining is quick to do, although it is only suitable for small drapes that use no more than one width of fabric. For best results, use fabrics of similar weight.

Swags

Beautiful fabrics do not have to be cut and sewn to create stunning window dressings. It is often the simplest treatments that work best. A swathe of fine fabric draped around a curtain rod looks very dramatic and can be used alone or with drapes or shades.

Swedish swags

Create a soft yet flamboyant effect around your windows with Swedish swags. Hardly any sewing is necessary to achieve a stunning result using only a single length of fabric. Use a lightweight or sheer fabric: a colorful sari would be ideal.

MAKING A DRAPE WITH BORDERS ON ALL EDGES

STEP 1 Unpick the drape heading and hems. Launder the drape and press it flat. Decide upon the border width and add 1¼-in./3-cm. Cut a strip of fabric this width for each edge of the drape; that is, the length of the cut drape edge plus twice the finished border width. Press under each end of the borders at right angles to create miters. The pressed line you have created will be the seam line. Now open the seams out flat.

STEP 2 Starting ⅝ in./1.5 cm from the inner edges, stitch along the seam lines with the right sides facing. Trim the seam allowance to ⅝-in./1.5-cm. Press seams open.

STEP 3 With right sides facing, stitch the inner edges of the border to the drape, pivoting the seam at the mitered border seams. Press the seam open.

STEP 4 Cut a piece of lining the same size as the bordered drape. Lay the drape flat, right-side up. Lay the lining on top with right sides facing and pin together, smoothing the layers outward from the center. Stitch the outer edges, taking a ⅝-in./1.5-cm seam allowance and leaving a gap in the upper edge to turn through. Clip the corners and turn right-side out. Press and slipstitch the opening closed. Add a heading to the top edge.

MAKING A SWEDISH SWAG

STEP 1 Fix a large cup hook into the wall at each side of the window, approximately 3-in./7.5-cm beyond the corners of the window. Lay the length of fabric across the hooks, letting it dip in the center. Cut the tails shorter if you wish, but allow 10-in. /25.5-cm at each side for the rosette. If the fabric is too bulky to drape nicely, cut it narrower.

STEP 2 Press ⅜-in./1-cm under twice on all edges to make a double hem. Stitch in place. If using a sari, hem only the ends of the fabric. Starting at each end, measure the chosen length of the tail plus 5-in./12.5-cm. Mark with a pin at the center of the strip.

STEP 3 Pick up the fabric at the pin mark and bunch it into a point with your other hand. Slip an elastic band over the bunched fabric. Repeat at the other end.

STEP 4 Insert the hooks into the bunched rosettes, with the tails hanging at each side. Adjust the swag and the tails so they drape in regular folds.

YOU WILL NEED::

SWEDISH SWAG:
- **LARGE CUP HOOK**
- **LIGHTWEIGHT FABRIC**
- **NEEDLE AND THREAD/SEWING MACHINE**
- **IRON**
- **PINS**
- **ELASTIC BAND**
- **SCISSORS**

YOU WILL NEED:

SHEER LOOSE
  WINDOW PANEL:

- **FABRIC PANEL**
- **NEEDLE AND
  THREAD/SEWING
  MACHINE**
- **IRON**
- **SCISSORS**
- **PINS**
- **CLEAT**
- **TOUCH-AND-CLOSE
  TAPE**
- **SAW AND DOWEL**
- **PAINT**

WINDOW PANEL:

- **FABRIC PANELS**
- **NEEDLE AND
  THREAD/SEWING
  MACHINE**
- **IRON**
- **SCISSORS**
- **DECORATIVE BORDER**
- **AIR-ERASABLE PEN**
- **HAMMER**
- **METAL EYELETS AND
  HOOKS**

PROJECT
Attic drapes

Angled windows, such as those in attic rooms, need careful planning. These windows are often smaller than usual, but can be emphasized by painting the frames a stronger color than the walls. A simple but effective treatment for angled windows is to have a pair of drapes with casings at the top and bottom with rods slipped through, fixed above and below the window.

Dormer windows are recessed windows within a sloping roof. The recess can make the windows appear farther away from the room than they actually are, so an attractive drape will accentuate them and make them into a real feature. It is usually best to attach the fittings to the window frame itself.

A hinged curtain rod will minimize loss of light, and can be closed across the window at night and opened against the recess during the day.

Alternatively, use a rail that bends around the recess and windows; the drapes will be in front of the recess when open, thus not obscuring the window.

Skylights

Skylights are set into roofs. They do not usually need a covering for privacy, but a covering is useful to block out light in the mornings and to create a cozy atmosphere at night. A sheer drape with a casing at the top and bottom, as suggested for an angled window, is one solution.

Window panels

A flat-hung window panel is a good idea for a window or skylight that needs a streamlined style. The panel has eyelets that fix onto hooks at each corner. If the window is wide, you will need to place more hooks and eyelets along the upper edge so the panel does not dip in the center. If lined in a contrasting fabric, the panel will look good half-open, with the lower eyelets hooked onto the top hooks or held open diagonally onto a hook on a side edge of the frame. Alternatively, the eyelets can be slotted onto dowels that are inserted into drilled holes.

Choose a firm, closely woven fabric for the best results for your window panels. Organza is really the only suitable sheer fabric to use, and will filter sunlight. If you do choose to use a lightweight fabric such as organza, it is important to test the eyelets first on a scrap of fabric to make sure that they are not too heavy for the fabric and do not tear out. A strip of lightweight interfacing applied to the top and bottom of the outer fabric will add strength and support the eyelets.

A sheer loose panel gives a sense of privacy and gives a smart, contemporary feel to the window.

SHEER LOOSE WINDOW PANEL

Instead of sheer drapes for privacy, consider a sheer loose panel for a contemporary feel. The upper edge of the panel is fixed directly to the frame, or to a cleat screwed to the frame, with touch-and-close tape so it can be removed easily for laundering.

MAKING A WINDOW PANEL

Fix a cup hook at each corner of the window, either on the frame or beyond its edges, and in a position that will let the panel lie flat. Have the upper hooks pointing upward and the lower hooks pointing downward. Measure the distance horizontally and vertically between the hooks, and then add 3¼-in./8-cm to the horizontal and vertical measurement to allow for the eyelets and seam allowances.

STEP 1 Cut two panels, either from the same fabric or from two coordinating fabrics. Stitch together with right sides facing, taking ⅝-in./1.5-cm seam allowance and leaving a gap to turn through. Clip the corners, then turn right-side out.

STEP 2 Press the panel and slipstitch the opening closed. If you wish, apply a decorative border such as ribbon or braid to the outer edges. It should be no wider than ½ in./1.2 cm so that it does not interfere with the eyelets.

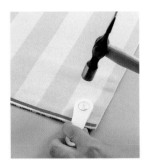

STEP 3 Mark the eyelet position ¾-in./2-cm in from each corner with an air-erasable pen. Hold the panel over the hooks and check the positions, adjusting if necessary. Following the manufacturer's directions, fix a ⅝-in./1.5-cm-diameter metal eyelet to the upper corners. Slip onto the hooks and check the lower positions. Fix the lower eyelets in place.

STEP 1 Cut a single panel the window width plus 1¼-in./3-cm by the window length plus 2½-in./6-cm. Stitch a ⅝-in./1.5-cm hem on the side edges. Press ⅜-in./1-cm under at the upper edge. Stitch a length of sew-on touch-and-close tape along the upper edge, enclosing the raw edge of the fabric.

STEP 2 Press ⅜ in./1 cm under, then 1¾-in./4-cm on the lower edge. Stitch close to both pressed edges to make a channel. Saw a length of ½-in./1.2-cm-diameter wood dowel ¼-in./6-mm shorter than the width of the panel, and paint it the same color as the panel. When dry, slip the dowel into the channel. Handsew the ends closed. Press corresponding adhesive-backed touch-and-close tape along the top of the frame or to a fixed cleat, and press the top of the panel on top.

YOU WILL NEED:
FABRIC SHUTTERS:
• "ONE BY ONE"
  WOODEN STRIPS
• WOOD GLUE
• SAW
• CLAMPS
• HAMMER
• BRADS
• FLUSH HINGES/
  SCREWS
• FABRIC
• IRON
• SCISSORS
• NEEDLE AND
  THREAD/SEWING
  MACHINE
• SCREWDRIVER
• TOUCH-AND-CLOSE
  TAPE
• HANDLE OR KNOB

SWEDISH BLIND:
• FABRIC FOR BLIND
• IRON
• SCISSORS
• NEEDLE AND
  THREAD/SEWING
  MACHINE
• ZIPPER OR PIPING
  FOOT
• WOODEN DOWEL
• TOUCH-AND-CLOSE
  TAPE
• CLEAT
• STAPLER
• LENGTHS OF
  WEBBING
• CURTAIN
  RINGS/SCREW EYES
• CORD

PROJECT
Making shutters and blinds

Stretch fabric over simple wooden frames to make a very practical pair of shutters; or vary the look with an elegant Swedish blind, which is rolled by hand from the lower edge.

However, note that a Swedish blind is not suitable for windows wider than 70 in./1.8 m because the dowel will sag and the blind will be difficult to roll up.

MAKING FABRIC SHUTTERS

STEP 1 Decide upon the finished size of the blind. To make a pair of shutters, cut four lengths of 1-in./2.5-cm "one by one" wooden strip the height of the frame, and four lengths of the same strip half the width of the frame less 2-in./5-cm. Stick the half-width strips between the top and bottom of the uprights to form the shutter frame. Ensure the corners are at right angles.

STEP 2 Clamp the joints in place while the glue dries. Hammer 1½-in./3.8-cm brads through the joints to secure. Fix a pair of 2-in./5-cm flush hinges to the shutter along the outer side edges.

STEP 3 For each cover, cut a piece of fabric the width of the shutter frame plus 1¼-in./3-cm by twice the height of the shutter frame plus 4¼-in./10.5-cm. Stitch a ⅝-in./1.5-cm hem along the side and lower edge.

STEP 4 Stitch ¾-in./2-cm wide sew-on touch-and-close tape to the right side of the lower hemmed edge. Press ⅜ in./1 cm under on the upper short end. Stitch the corresponding touch-and-close tape on top.

STEP 5 With wrong sides facing, wrap the cover around the shutter frame. Press the touch-and-close tapes together. Screw the hinges to the frame. Fix a handle or knob to the opening edges.

MAKING A SWEDISH BLIND

STEP 1 Decide upon the size of the finished blind. To make a lined version, cut two blinds the blind width plus 1¼-in./3-cm by the blind length plus 1¼-in./3-cm. Stitch the blinds together along the side and lower edges with right sides facing, taking ⅝-in./1.5-cm seam allowance. Clip the corners, then turn right-side out and press.

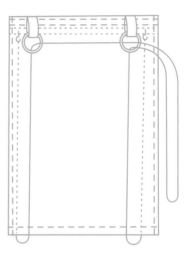

STEP 2 Saw ⅜-in./1-cm diameter wooden dowel ⅝ in./1.5 cm shorter than the width of the blind. Drop the dowel into the blind. Using a zipper or piping foot, stitch across the bottom of the blind, enclosing the dowel.

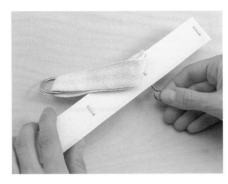

STEP 5 Slip rings onto two 10-in./25.5-cm lengths of webbing. Pin the ends together. Staple to the top of the cleat 2-in./5-cm in from the ends so the rings hang over the front. Insert a screw eye into the underside 2-in./5-cm in from the ends. Fix the cleat in place, with the touch-and-close tape facing outward.

STEP 6 Press the blind to the front of the cleat, matching the touch-and-close tapes.

STEP 7 Tie the cord to the left-hand screw eye, then bring it down under the blind and up through the left-hand ring. Tie the other end of the cord to the right-hand eye, and bring it under the blind and up through the right-hand ring, with the cord coming from the left-hand ring (see diagram above). Fix a cleat to the wall on the right-hand side. Roll up the blind, then pull up the excess cord and wind it around the cleat to hold the blind at the desired level.

STEP 3 Press ⅝ in./1.5 cm to the wrong side on the upper edge. Stitch touch-and-close tape to the upper edge, concealing the raw edge of the fabric.

STEP 4 Saw a ½-in./1.2-cm-thick, 1-in./2.5-cm wide wooden cleat ⅜-in./1-cm shorter than the width of the blind. Staple the corresponding touch-and-close tape to the front of the cleat.

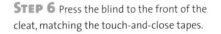

YOU WILL NEED:

• **ROLLER-BLIND KIT**
• **SPIRIT LEVEL**
• **WALL ANCHORS**
• **TAPE MEASURE/ RULE**
• **PRESTIFFENED FABRIC**
• **SNAP-BLADE KNIFE/SCISSORS**
• **PAINTER'S TAPE**
• **TACKS/STAPLE GUN/DOUBLE-SIDED TAPE**
• **NEEDLE AND THREAD/SEWING MACHINE**
• **SAW**

PROJECT
Roller blinds

Roller blinds can look cool and contemporary in a modern setting, and look neat rolled up in the day. You can use a roller-blind kit—available in various widths—or you can construct your own. You can stiffen fabric with a spray-on stiffener or you can use material produced especially for making blinds.

Roller blinds are a good choice to cover a window above a radiator or item of furniture, because they cover only the glass and suit being sill-length. If you need a different width from those available, buy the next size up and saw the roller and lower cleat to size. Measure up roughly first, then again when the brackets and roller are in position, to get an exact fit. Measure

the window; if you intend to hang the blind outside a window recess, leave 2¼-in./5.6-cm overlap. If you intend to hang the blind inside a recess, deduct 1¼-in./3.2-cm from the width to allow for the blind fittings.

Most roller-blind kits contain a wooden roller; a side control and dummy pin to fit into the ends of the roller; a wooden cleat to keep the lower edge of the fabric straight; two brackets; cord; a cord holder that is fixed to the cleat; and a cord pull.

Choosing and preparing fabric

Prestiffened fabric for roller blinds is available at furnishing-fabric stores. It has been treated to make it resistant to fraying and some fabrics are fade-resistant and spongeable. Prestiffened fabric comes in standard widths up to 78-in./2-m wide, but can be cut narrower. Most mediumweight fabrics can be stiffened with a fabric-stiffening spray specially formulated for roller blinds, which stiffens the fabric and makes it fray-resistant. Test the spray on a scrap of fabric first to make sure it is colorfast. Spray the fabric before cutting, because it may cause shrinkage.

Roller blinds can be set in a variety of positions according to the amount of light and the need for privacy. Their simple lines make them ideal for home offices or other work environments.

MAKING A ROLLER BLIND

STEP 1 Read the kit directions. Fix the brackets in place. One bracket will hold the side control and should be fixed to the side of the window where the cord will be operated. Brackets should be at least 1¼-in./3.2-cm from a recess outer edge if fixing to the outside of a recess, and at least 2-in./5-cm above the window to stop light from getting in. Brackets fixed inside a recess should be as close to the recess as possible and 1¼-in./3.2-cm below the top of the recess to leave space for the roller. Use a spirit level to check that the brackets are level. Fix the brackets to a wall with wall anchors.

STEP 2 Measure the distance between the brackets with a metal or wooden rule. If necessary, saw the roller to this length, leaving space for the side control and dummy pin. The fabric will need to be trimmed if the roller has been shortened. Lay the fabric out flat, wrong-side face up. Use a metal or wooden rule to draw a line along one side edge to narrow the fabric to match the roller. If the blind has a shaped hem, take an equal amount off each side. Cut to size with a snap-blade knife or pair of scissors.

STEP 3 Some rollers have a straight line marked along their length for positioning fabric. If yours does not, use a metal or wooden rule to draw a straight line. Lay the fabric flat and place the roller under the upper edge. Lift the fabric over the roller and match it to the straight marked line. Stick temporarily in place with painter's tape, then fix with tacks, a staple gun, or strong double-sided tape.

STEP 4 Fix the side control and dummy pin into the ends of the roller. Fix the roller onto the brackets. Measure from a bracket to below the window sill for a blind hanging outside a recess and to the sill for inside a recess. Add 10 in./25 cm to allow for the roller and cleat. If the blind needs to be shortened, cut the fabric to size. The edges must be straight and the corners at exact right angles.

STEP 5 If you have cut the blind and roller narrower, saw the cleat to ½ in./1.2 cm narrower than the blind. Turn under 1¾ in./4 cm on the lower edge to make a channel for the cleat. Check that the cleat will slot in easily; make the channel deeper if not. Stitch close to the raw edge with a zigzag stitch. Slip the cleat into the channel. Refer to the manufacturer's directions to fix the cord pull and to check the tension when lowering and raising the blind.

YOU WILL NEED:

- **SELF-ADHESIVE VALANCE FACING**
- **FABRIC**
- **TAPE MEASURE/ RULE**
- **PAPER**
- **PAINTER'S TAPE**
- **SCISSORS**
- **NEEDLE AND THREAD/SEWING MACHINE**
- **TOUCH-AND-CLOSE TAPE**
- **IRON**
- **HAMMER AND NAILS**
- **CLEATS**
- **PINS**

PROJECT
Lambrequins

A valance that extends at least halfway down each side of a window is called a lambrequin. It is usually quite shapely, creating a dramatic silhouette against the window.

A lambrequin can be used on its own in front of a small window, or can be teamed up with drapes or a shade. Avoid sheer or very lightweight fabrics.

MAKING A LAMBREQUIN WITH SELF-ADHESIVE VALANCE INTERFACING

The shape is formed from self-adhesive valance interfacing, which is then covered with fabric. Self-adhesive valance interfacing has a peel-off paper backing and is available by the yard/meter at 23¾-in./60-cm wide. If you want to make a lambrequin deeper than this, use buckram instead. Do not join self-adhesive valance interfacing because it will make a visible ridge. Buckram can be joined invisibly with carpet tape.

STEP 1 Measure the intended width and depth of the lambrequin and draw a square or rectangle to size on paper. Do not make the depth more than 23¾ in./60 cm if you intend to use self-adhesive valance interfacing. Make sure that the corners are right angles, and draw straight lines against a metal or wooden rule. Cut out and fold the paper in half, matching the side edges. Measure down the fold for the depth of the center of the lambrequin and mark its position.

STEP 2 Now draw the inner edge of the lambrequin, starting at the center. When you are happy with the shape, cut it out and open the pattern out flat. Tape the lambrequin in front of the window with painter's tape, making adjustments if necessary.

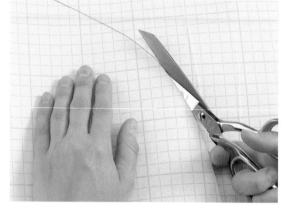

STEP 3 Tape the pattern to the paper side of the interfacing with painter's tape and draw around it. Remove the pattern and cut out the lambrequin. Use the pattern to cut one lambrequin from fabric, adding a ⅝-in./1.5-cm allowance on all edges. Cut one lambrequin from lining, adding ⅝ in./1.5 cm on the curved edges.

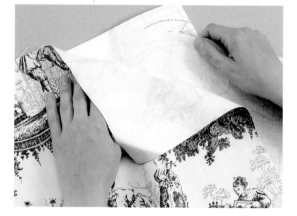

STEP 4 Ease the backing paper away from the center of the interfacing and cut it across the width. Peel back the paper a little way on each side of the cut. Carefully place the fabric, right-side up, on top. Press the fabric smoothly onto the exposed adhesive. Continue peeling back the paper and sticking down the fabric. Smooth the fabric outward to eliminate any wrinkles or air bubbles.

TOP TIP
When making a pattern for a lambrequin that is to be applied to a valance box, add the depth of the box to the side edges and apply touch-and-close tape to the top edge only.

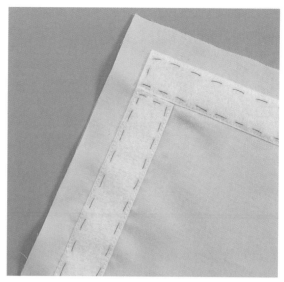

STEP 5 With the wrong side up, snip the curves and cut the corners of the fabric diagonally ¼-in./5-mm beyond the interfacing corners. Peel back the backing paper around the outer edges. Press the diagonal corner, then the straight and curved edges to the wrong side.

STEP 6 Baste and stitch a length of the soft part of ¾-in./2-cm-wide touch-and-close tape, ¾ in./2 cm below the upper edge of the lining and ¾ in./2 cm within the side edges on the right side. Stitch another length ¾ in./2 cm inside the side edges to 2 in./5 cm above the lower edge. Press under ⅜ in. /1 cm on the outer edges.

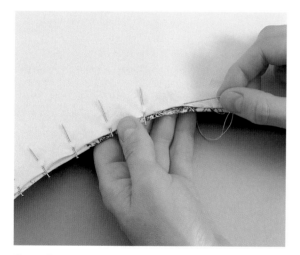

STEP 7 Ease the backing paper away from the center of the interfacing and cut it across the width as before. Peel back the paper and stick on the lining, enclosing the raw edges of the fabric. Turn under and pin the raw edges of the lining to the lambrequin about ⅛ in./3 mm inside the curved edges, snipping the curves so the lining stays flat. Slipstitch the lining to the fabric.

STEP 8 Nail corresponding lengths of touch-and-close tape to the upper and side edges of the crown molding. Press the lambrequin on top. Alternatively, attach a lambrequin to corresponding lengths of touch-and-close tape nailed to 1 in. x 1 in./2.5 cm x 2.5 cm cleats.

YOU WILL NEED:

- PAR WOOD
- SHELF
- L-SHAPED BRACKETS
- TAPE MEASURE
- PATTERN FOR SWAGS AND TAILS (SEE DIAGRAM PAGE 820)
- SCRAP FABRIC
- SWAGS AND TAILS FABRIC
- LINING FABRIC
- NEEDLE AND THREAD/SEWING MACHINE
- PAINTER'S TAPE
- THUMBTACKS
- TIN TACKS
- HAMMER
- SAW
- SCISSORS
- PINS

PROJECT
Swags and tails

Swags and tails can look softly draped or formally pleated, depending on the kind of look you are trying to achieve. They suit bigger windows better, because the pleating and large amounts of fabric need a certain amount of space in which to look their best. Don't choose fabrics that are too stiff or have a very busy pattern or you may be disappointed with the results.

Swags and tails lend an element of sophistication to a room and can enhance the appearance of a large window that might otherwise appear rather plain. Use good-quality fabric that will hold the drapery well. Fabrics with distinct patterns or designs are not suitable, because motifs will be lost among the folds and may lie at what seems an odd angle as the swag fabric is cut on the bias grain. The lining fabric will be visible on the tails, so you may wish to use a co-ordinating fabric for this.

Traditional swags and tails are constructed in three parts: the swag is fixed across the front of a shelf valance and then a tail is then fixed at each side. Try out the pattern in scrap fabric first, and then try draping it at the window to make sure you are happy with the effect that you will be achieving when you use the actual fabric.

HOW TO DO IT

STEP 1 To make a valance shelf to support the swag and tails, saw a length of PAR (planed all round) wood 6½-in./16.5-cm deep and ½-in./1.2-cm thick to 5¼-in./13-cm longer than the width of the window. Fix the shelf above the window with L-shaped brackets.

STEP 2 Measure the intended depth of the swag down from the center of the shelf. This should not be more than a sixth of the height of the window. To make a pattern (see page 820), draw a rectangle that is 8-in./20-cm wider than the shelf width by two and a half times the swag depth. Cut out and fold the rectangle in half, having the fold parallel with the depth edges. The fold will be the center of the swag.

STEP 3 Mark a point on the long edge up from the lower edge that is a fourth of the overall length. Draw a curve between the point and the lower edge of the fold line. Measure along the top-edge from the fold line and mark a point a fourth of the folded top edge measurement. Join the two points with a straight line. Draw the grain line at a 45-degree angle to the fold line. Refer to the diagram on the next page.

These softly draped swags and tails give an informal and relaxed feel to the bathroom.

STEP 4 Cut out the pattern and open it out flat to cut a swag from scrap fabric. Ideally, this should be of a similar weight and feel to the final fabric. Pin the slanted side edges into pleats 4–6 in./10–15 cm deep and facing upward.

STEP 5 To check the fit, attach the swag temporarily to the front edge of the shelf with painter's tape or thumbtacks; start by matching the centers and work outward. If necessary, re-pin the pleats or adjust the pattern. Decide how wide you want the tails to be; they will extend over the ends of the swag. Refer to the diagram on page 820 to cut a pattern, and mark the grain line parallel with the long edge. Use the pattern to cut a tail from the scrap fabric. Mark the top edge 6½ in./16.5 cm from the long edge: this mark will match the corner of the shelf, and the long edge will be the return that goes along the side of the shelf.

STEP 6 Pleat the rest of the upper edge as far as the mark, with the pleats facing outward. Stick the tail around one end of the shelf with painter's tape or thumbtacks. Check the effect and adjust if necessary. Remove the trial swag and tail, and transfer the pleat positions and any alterations to the paper pattern.

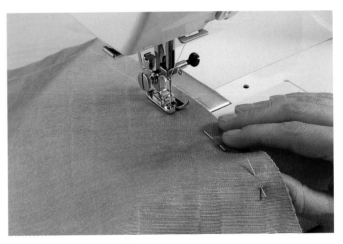

STEP 7 Use the pattern to cut a swag from fabric and lining and a pair of tails from fabric and lining, adding a ⅝-in./1.5-cm allowance to all edges. Stitch the swags together along the curved edge with right sides facing. Snip the curves and turn right-side out.

STEP 8 Baste the raw edges together. Pin the pleats in position and stitch across them. Neaten the raw edges with a zigzag stitch.

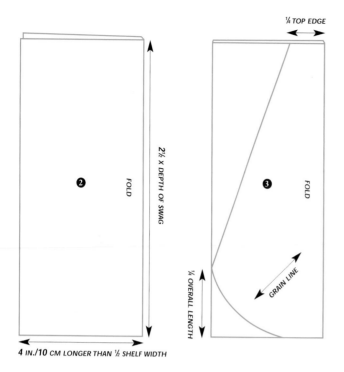

¼ TOP EDGE

2

FOLD

2½ × DEPTH OF SWAG

4 IN./10 CM LONGER THAN ½ SHELF WIDTH

3

FOLD

GRAIN LINE

¼ OVERALL LENGTH

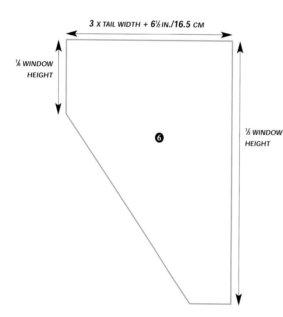

3 × TAIL WIDTH + 6½ IN./16.5 CM

⅛ WINDOW HEIGHT

6

⅓ WINDOW HEIGHT

FAR RIGHT: **This rather sophisticated, pleated look can enhance an otherwise plain window.**

STEP 10 Work outward from the center. Attach the swag to the shelf with tin tacks, with ⅝ in./1.5 cm of the upper edge going onto the top of the shelf. Adjust if needed; hammer in the tacks.

STEP 11 Pin each fabric tail to a tail lining with right sides facing. Stitch together, taking a 1.5-cm/⅝-in. seam allowance and leaving the upper edge open. Clip the corners and turn right-side out. Tack the upper edges together and pin the pleats. Stitch across the pleats, then neaten the upper edge with a zigzag stitch.

STEP 12 Temporary tack one tail to the shelf with ⅝ in./1.5 cm of the upper edge extending onto the top of the shelf. Fold the tail neatly around the corner. Hammer the tacks home. Repeat on the other side of the shelf.

YOU WILL NEED:

STRAIGHT TIEBACK:

- MEDIUMWEIGHT FABRIC
- FUSIBLE INTERFACING
- TAPE MEASURE
- 2 METAL CURTAIN RINGS PER TIEBACK
- IRON
- SCISSORS
- NEEDLE AND THREAD/SEWING MACHINE
- HOOKS

CURVED TIEBACK:

- TAPE MEASURE
- PAPER PATTERN
- VALANCE-WEIGHT FUSIBLE INTERFACING
- FABRIC
- IRON
- PINS
- 2 METAL CURTAIN RINGS PER TIEBACK
- SCISSORS
- NEEDLE AND THREAD/SEWING MACHINE
- BRAID, CORD, OR PIPING
- HOOKS

PROJECT
Tiebacks

The finishing touch to your drapes is a pair of coordinating tiebacks. As well as looking good, tiebacks help to let as much daylight as possible into the room. They are usually positioned about two-thirds of the way down the drapes. In general, a tieback is 1 ft. 6 in.–2 ft./46–61 cm long.

Straight tiebacks are best for narrow curtains, and crescent shaped, curved tiebacks for wider drapes. Choose light-to-mediumweight fabrics. Only a small amount of fabric is needed, so use

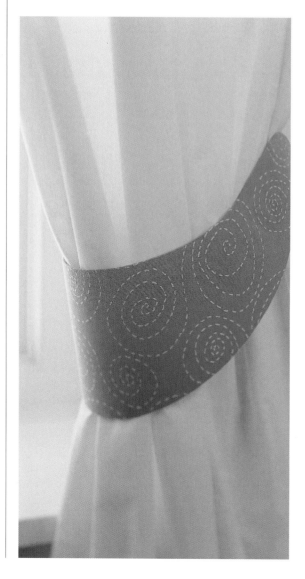

A curved tieback gives a smart, formal finishing touch to a pair of drapes. For a more informal look, you could use a chiffon scarf wrapped around each curtain.

leftover curtain fabric for a coordinating look or use a remnant of contrasting fabric. The edges can be bound or have braid or fringing added by hand when complete. If you wish to bind the edges, cut two fabric tiebacks and one of valance interfacing, and pin the interfacing between the fabric layers with the right sides facing outward, then bind the edges.

A metal ring is sewn to each end of the tieback and slips easily onto hooks attached either side of the drape. If the drapes will not be drawn closed, fancy tiebacks can be used, because they will not be handled each day. A chiffon scarf fastened around the drape in a flamboyant bow will add glamour; a string of beads will have the same effect. Specially made tasseled tieback cords are very expensive. A tasseled dressing-gown cord is an instant tieback: twist it a few times to shorten it, then wrap it once or twice around the drape and slip it over a hook.

Holdbacks

Holdbacks have the same function as tiebacks. They are rigid, often like large horizontal hooks that the drape is slipped behind. A popular style of holdback is a boss, which is a disk with a short rod behind that is fixed to the wall. To make a fabric-covered boss, either in fabric to match the drape or in a contrasting design, cut a circle of fabric 2-in./5-cm wider than the diameter of the boss; center any motifs on the fabric. Run a gathering stitch around the circumference and slightly draw up the thread. Cut out a circle of batting 1-in./2.5-cm wider than the diameter of the boss. Place the batting centrally on the wrong side of the fabric. Slip the fabric circle over the boss and pull up the thread tightly, enclosing the boss. Fasten the thread ends very securely.

MAKING A LIGHTWEIGHT STRAIGHT TIEBACK

STEP 1 Cut a strip of medium-weight fusible interfacing 18 in. x 2¹/₂ in./46 cm x 6.5 cm. Cut two strips of fabric 19¹/₄ in. x 3³/₄ in./ 49 cm x 9.5 cm. Press the interfacing centrally to one fabric tieback.

STEP 2 Stitch the tiebacks together just outside the edges of the interfacing with right sides facing, leaving an opening on the lower edge to turn through. Clip the corners and turn right-side out. Press and slipstitch the opening closed. Attach rings as described below.

MAKING A CURVED TIEBACK

STEP 1 Measure around a drawn-open drape using a tape measure, holding the tape loosely. To make a pattern, draw a rectangle on paper that is half the tieback measurement by 5 in./ 12.5 cm. One short edge will be the fold line. Draw a half-crescent shape within the rectangle.

STEP 2 Cut out the shape and hold it around the drape to check the shape and fit; pull the drape upward a little so it falls nicely over the top. Remember that if a tieback is too tight, it will crease the drape and the creases will probably be visible when the drape is drawn closed, so it is best to have a looser look. Mark the position for the hook on the wall.

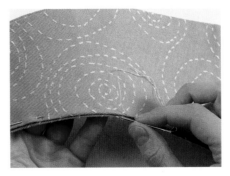

STEP 3 Cut the tieback from valance-weight fusible interfacing. Cut two tiebacks from fabric, adding a ³/₈-in/1-cm seam allowance. Press the interfacing centrally to one fabric tieback. Snip the curved edges and press them over the interfacing.

STEP 4 Pin the remaining tieback on top. Snip the curves and turn the raw edges under, then slipstitch the outer edges together.

STEP 5 Sew braid, cord, or piping to the outer edges. Handsew a curtain ring at each end on the wrong side, positioning the ring so half of it extends beyond the tieback.

PROJECT
French-pleat drape

French-pleat drapes look very stylish and suit most room styles. You can draw attention to the attractive rounded shape of the pleats by sewing a bright button under them (as here) or another trimming such as beads or pompons.

A hand-pleated heading always looks very sophisticated. Rounded French pleats are also known as goblet pleats because of their curvaceous shape. It is worthwhile investing in good-quality fabric that will hold the goblet shapes well. Here, self-cover buttons have red fabric applied and attached to each pleat, to echo the dramatic shade of the ruby-red tulips on the fabric design. When buying fabric, allow twice the width plus 1½ in./3.8 cm for each side hem. Add 12 in./30.5 cm to the length for the heading and hem. Make, line, and hem the drape as described on pages 800–801.

MAKING A FRENCH-PLEAT CURTAIN

STEP 1 Press 8 in./20 cm to the underside on the upper edge. Open out flat and cut the lining level with the fold line. Cut 4-in./10-cm wide strips of mediumweight iron-on interfacing. Place the strips on the drape, with the lower edge of the strips level with the fold line.

STEP 2 If the interfacing strips need to be joined, overlap them by ⅜ in./1 cm. Press the strips to fuse them to the drape. Fold the upper edge of the drape over the strip.

STEP 3 Fold the upper edge again to make a double hem. Press in position and baste across the lower edge. Slipstitch the ends closed. Measure the width of the drape and take 4 in./10 cm off the measurement. Divide the remainder into an odd number of sections of 4–5 in./10–12.5 cm.

STEP 4 Starting and finishing 2 in./5 cm from the ends, mark the divisions with tailor's chalk on the heading on the wrong side. Bring the chalked lines together in pairs to form rounded goblets on the right side. On the wrong side, slipstitch the edges together using a double length of thread.

STEP 5 On the right side, make a single stitch around the pleat on the basted line and pull up the thread to gather the base of the goblet. Repeat to secure in place. Open out the goblet at the upper edge and oversew to the top edge of the drape to hold the goblet open.

STEP 6 Remove the basting. Sew a button to each goblet. Check the length of the drape. Sew a metal sew-on curtain hook to the back of each pleat.

FAR RIGHT: **Invest in a good-quality fabric to make the most out of this stylish drape design.**

TOP TIP
Batting or scrunched-up tissue paper can be slipped into the goblets to hold the shape if necessary.

YOU WILL NEED:

- **VOILE CURTAIN FABRIC**
- **DUPION SILK**
- **IRON**
- **SCISSORS**
- **NEEDLE AND THREAD/SEWING MACHINE**
- **BODKIN**
- **PINS**
- **TAPE MEASURE**

PROJECT

Tab-top drapes

Drapes hung by tabs are very popular because, as well as being easy to make, they show off the wonderful choice of curtain rods available today. Most fabrics are suitable, but smooth, lightweight, or slippery fabrics are easier to draw along the rods.

HOW TO DO IT

STEP 1 To calculate fabric quantities, measure the window width and double the measurement; add 1¼ in./3 cm for both side hems. Measure the intended drop of the drape from 2½ in./6.3 cm below the rod to allow for the tabs. Add 1¾ in./4.5 cm to the drop measurement for the hem and seam allowance.

STEP 2 Now work out how many tabs will fit across the top of the finished drape. The tabs are positioned 4¾ in.–6 in./12 cm–15 cm apart and are 1¼ in./3 cm wide. Measure half the circumference of the rod with a tape measure, and add 5¾ in./14.5 cm x 2 to the measurement. The tabs will be cut 3¼ in./8 cm wide. A 2-in./5-cm-wide strip of dupion silk the width of the curtain plus 1¼ in./3 cm is needed for the upper band. Dupion silk is usually only 1 yd./90 cm wide, so it may be economical to join the band rather than cut it in a single length. Stitch a ⅜-in./1-cm seam allowance throughout.

STEP 3 Cut out the drape from voile. Press ¼ in./5 mm under then ⅜ in./1 cm on the side edges. Stitch close to the inner edges. Press ⅜ in./1 cm under then 1 in./2.5 cm on the lower edge. Stitch close to the inner edges.

STEP 4 Cut a 3¼-in./8-cm wide strip of dupion silk long enough to cut the tabs needed. Fold lengthwise in half with right sides facing. Stitch the long edges. Press the seam open. Turn right-side out with a bodkin and press, placing the seam centrally. Cut into equal lengths for the tabs.

STEP 5 Fold each tab in half with the seam inside. Pin the tabs to the upper edge on the wrong side of the drape, positioning one tab at each end and spacing the rest an equal distance apart.

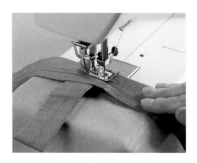

STEP 6 Use the upper band of dupion silk (see step 2). Press ⅜ in./1 cm under on one long edge. With the right side of the band facing the wrong side of the drape, stitch the band to the upper edge, with ⅜ in./1 cm extending beyond the sides of the drape.

STEP 7 Clip the corners. Turn the band to the right side, and press under the ends of the band. Tack the band to the drape and topstitch close to the band edges.

FAR RIGHT:
Lightweight fabrics are ideal for tab-top drapes; they look beautiful and glide easily along the rod.

TOP TIP
Plastic tab-top gliders are available to fit under the tabs, to help them glide along the rod.

YOU WILL NEED:
- PATTERN
- SELF-ADHESIVE
  VALANCE
  INTERFACING
- TAPE MEASURE
- NEEDLE AND
  THREAD/SEWING
  MACHINE
- VALANCE FABRIC
  AND LINING
- SCISSORS
- TOUCH-AND-CLOSE
  TAPE
- IRON
- STAPLER

PROJECT

Valance

A fabric-covered valance adds a neat border to a blind or a curtain heading. The valance is made from self-adhesive valance interfacing, which has a peel-off paper backing on one or both sides. The pelmet is attached with touch-and-close tape to a wooden valance shelf.

The valance should extend at least 2½ in./ 6.5 cm beyond each side of the window. A piece of wood about 4 in./10 cm deep and ½ in./1.2 cm thick is a versatile size for the pelmet shelf. Fix the brackets to the underside of the valance shelf about 8 in./20 cm apart, or to the top of the shelf if they would otherwise coincide with the window recess.

Closely woven mediumweight fabrics are ideal for making a valance but most fabrics are suitable. Use an inexpensive, closely woven fabric such as curtain lining to line it. This vibrant valance has a simple wavy edge. Design your own valance on scrap paper first. The top edge and the ends must be straight, but you can make the lower edge any shape you like.

FAR RIGHT: **Use your imagination when designing your valance. Create a wavy lower edge, or any other shape you fancy.**

HOW TO DO IT

STEP 1 Measure the valance shelf. To make a pattern, cut a 6-in./15-cm-wide strip of pattern paper or brown wrapping paper that is the length plus twice the depth of the valance shelf. Mark the center of the valance and the depth. Draw a wavy line along the lower edge on one half. When you are happy with the design, fold the pattern in half and cut it out.

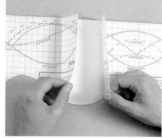

STEP 2 Use the pattern to cut one valance from self-adhesive valance interfacing. Cut one valance from fabric and lining, adding a ⅝-in./1.5-cm allowance to all edges. Ease the paper backing away from the center of the valance interfacing and cut it across the width. Peel back the paper for about 1½ in./4 cm each side of the cut, exposing the adhesive. Stick the fabric centrally on top and peel away the backing paper, smoothing the fabric outward to eliminate air bubbles.

STEP 3 Cut diagonally across the fabric ¼ in./5 mm from the corners of the valance. Snip the curves of the fabric. Peel away the valance backing paper from the edges and press the corners, then the outer edges of the fabric to the back of the valance.

STEP 4 Stitch a length of the soft part of touch-and-close tape ⅝ in./1.5 cm within the ends and upper edge of the lining on the right side. Press under ⅝ in./1.5 cm on the ends and upper edge of the lining. Peel off the paper backing from the valance interfacing and press the lining smoothly on top.

STEP 5 Snip the curves of the lining along the lower edge. Slipstitch the pressed edges of the lining to the valance then slipstitch the lower edges together, turning under the snipped edges as you work. Staple the corresponding length of touch-and-close tape to the edge of the valance shelf and press the valance in place, folding it around the corners of the shelf.

YOU WILL NEED:
- **FABRIC FOR BLIND**
- **TAPE MEASURE**
- **SCISSORS**
- **STRIP**
- **NEEDLE AND THREAD/SEWING MACHINE**
- **IRON**
- **PINS**
- **BATTEN**
- **STAPLE GUN**
- **TOUCH-AND-CLOSE TAPE**
- **SCREW EYES**
- **CLEAT**
- **DOWEL**
- **PLASTIC BLIND RING**
- **BLIND CORD**

PROJECT
Roman blind

The Roman blind is the most elegant of window treatments, particularly when a clean and neat appearance is required.

When raised, the blind lies in flat, horizontal pleats, which are kept in shape by wooden dowels threaded through narrow channels.

This Roman blind gives a neat appearance. You can cut off the excess cord once you have made your blind to make it look even neater. Thread a blind puller onto the cords and knot the cords under it, cutting off the excess.

HOW TO DO IT

STEP 1 Measure the intended width and drop of the blind. Add 2¼ in./6 cm to the width for hems and 5¾ in./15 cm to the drop for the channels and hems. Cut out the blind and a 2¾-in./7-cm-wide strip for the lower band that is the blind width plus 1¼ in./3 cm. Press under ⅜ in./1 cm then ¾ in./2 cm on the side edges. Stitch close to both pressed edges.

STEP 2 Press under ⅝ in./1.5 cm on the upper edge. Pin the soft half of a length of sew-on touch-and-close tape over the pressed edge. Stitch close to the edges of the tape. Fix a 1-in./2.5-cm-high x ½-in./1.2-cm-deep batten in position above the window. Use a staple gun to staple the corresponding length of touch-and-close tape to the front of the batten. Screw a screw eye into the underside 2 in./5 cm in from each end. Fix another screw eye ⅝ in./1.5 cm in from one end on the side of the window you want the cleat to be. Fix the batten in place.

STEP 3 Press under ⅝ in./1.5 cm on one long edge of the band. With the right side of the band facing the wrong side of the blind and with ⅝ in./1.5 cm of the band extending at each end, stitch the band to the lower edge taking a ⅝-in./1.5-cm seam allowance. Press under the ends. Press the band to the right side along the seam. Stitch close to both long edges.

STEP 4 Divide the blind drop measurement into seven equal amounts for the pleats. Working down from the upper edge, mark the following measurements on one side edge with a pin: twice the pleat measurement, plus 1½ in./4 cm, twice the pleat measurement, plus 1½ in./4 cm, twice the pleat measurement, plus 1½ in./4 cm. Repeat on the opposite edge. With right sides facing, bring the pins at one set of 1½-in./4-cm marks together on each side edge and press the fold.

STEP 5 Stitch ¾ in./2 cm from the fold, forming a channel for the dowel. Repeat on the other ¾ in./4-cm marks to form three channels. Cut four lengths of ⅜-in./1-cm diameter wooden dowel ⅜ in./1 cm shorter than the blind width. Insert the dowels into the channels and the band. Slipstitch the ends closed.

STEP 6 On the wrong side of the blind, sew a plastic blind ring to the channels 2 in./5 cm in from the side edges. Tie a length of blind cord to the lower ring on each side. Thread it up through the rings. Press the blind to the front of the cleat, matching the touch-and-close tape. Thread the cords through the screw eyes above them. Thread the cord on the opposite side of the cleat through the other screw eyes. Thread the cord on the same side as the cleat through the outer screw eye. Pull the cords to raise the blind. Knot the cords together level with the cleat.

Take a seat

Seating takes a lot of wear and tear, and a new piece of furniture is an important financial consideration. A change of address or redecoration does not mean having to discard a favorite chair because it no longer matches your home style. There are masses of ways to revitalize and update chairs that you already have, just by changing their fabric. Mismatched chairs can be harmonized by making them smart new covers. Loose covers are very practical. Once you have made the pattern, you could mark the seasons by creating simple chair covers for the chilly fall and winter months from warm, cozy fabrics, then changing to covers made of lightweight, crisp fabrics for spring and summer. Make squashy floor cushions or beanbag chairs for a relaxed, contemporary feel, or spruce up second-hand chairs with new covers or cushions. You can create stunning new seating arrangements at minimal cost.

Choosing seating and fabrics

Sofas, chairs, and footstools are another investment that it is best to get right first time. There are hundreds of different versions and styles on the market and prices vary greatly too. It is often cheaper to buy second-hand and cover older items of furniture with fabric of your own choosing.

Think carefully about the kind of style you want to achieve and stick to that. If cool and contemporary is your choice, then look for furniture that has clean lines and no fussy detailing. Your fabric choice should also match this. If you prefer a more traditional look, then there are lots of things out there that would suit, and faded chintzes can be bought cheaply.

Second-hand seating
Bargain hunters will enjoy sourcing old, forlorn chairs and stools that just need a bit of care and attention to transform them into something special. Yard sales, auctions, and junk stores offer seating at knockdown prices. Always sit on

the item, not only to see if it is comfortable but also to make sure that the arms and legs are rigid and level. A creaking chair may have had woodworm and should be considered with caution. Fine sawdust means live woodworm; if you buy it, the piece will have to be treated with a proprietary woodworm killer.

If the framework of the chair needs repairing, do so before making patterns for the soft furnishings, because some refurbishments will alter the shape of the furniture. If it will be visible, sand scruffy paintwork and treat rust on metal furniture. Fill any knocks and gouges with wood filler, then repaint the chair. Use spray paints on metal chairs. Replace flattened foam seats.

Do not just consider existing chairs and stools for re-covering. If they are well made, other pieces of furniture, such as low tables, chests, and boxes, can be made into seating. Either glue a piece of foam to the surface and make a slip-on cover for the entire item, or make a slip-on cover for the furniture and a separate, fitted box cushion

You can pick up interesting pieces of seating in junk stores or yard sales, often at bargain prices. They can be surprisingly easy to revamp, whether it's a sagging seat or a complete re-cover.

to sit on top. Similarly, adding a fitted cushion to a formal, hard chair will make it more homey and inviting to sit on.

Webbing

A sagging seat can be rectified by replacing the webbing. Purchase a web stretcher if you intend to upholster more than a couple of chairs. Remove the old webbing. Turn over 1 in./2.5 cm at the end of a length of woven webbing and hammer five tacks through the turned-under end in a "W" formation to the back of the chair frame at the center.

Pull the webbing over the front of the frame, and attach it to a web stretcher or pull it over a block of wood wedged against the front of the chair. Draw the webbing tautly downward. Hammer in three tacks in a "V" formation. Cut off the excess webbing, leaving 1 in./2.5 cm extending. Fold over the end and hammer in two tacks. Attach webbing each side of the first strip about 2 in./5 cm apart; if the chair front is wider than the back, splay the webbing apart. Attach the crosswise webbing in the same way, first weaving it in and out of the first strips.

Starting from scratch

Some styles of contemporary seating that do not need wooden structures are very easy to make, often at much less cost than their store-bought equivalents. Floor cushions and beanbag chairs are constant favorites with children and teenagers, but when made from elegant fabrics, especially the excellent fake animal hides and furs available nowadays, they become quite sophisticated. Simple cubes of high-density foam covered with fabric look splendid in loft-style homes.

Choosing fabrics

Fabric for seating should be closely woven, hardwearing, crease-resistant, and flame-retardant. Do not use knitted and other stretch fabrics, because they will not hold their shape. Avoid heavyweight fabrics, which will be tough to stitch, especially if piping is to be included. It is more economical to use plain or textured fabric, or one with a small print, rather than a fabric with a nap or large one-way design. This will enable pattern pieces to fit the fabric without too much wastage. Smart trimmings such as piping and braid will streamline soft furnishings and link the furniture to other design elements or colors within a room. Fastenings on loose covers need not only be unobtrusive zipper fastenings; make a feature of them by incorporating ties, buttons, or even buckles.

Fabric for seating should be closely woven, hardwearing, and crease-resistant.

LEFT: A favorite chair can be given new life by replacing the webbing and flattened seat before making a new loose cover. Sand the exposed woodwork and repaint or varnish it.

YOU WILL NEED:

FLOOR CUSHIONS:

- **FABRIC FOR INNER CUSHION**
- **FABRIC FOR OUTER CUSHION**
- **SCISSORS**
- **POLYSTYRENE BEADS, FEATHERS, OR KAPOK FOR FILLING**
- **IRON**
- **ZIPPER**
- **NEEDLE AND THREAD/SEWING MACHINE**
- **ZIPPER FOOT**

TASSELED CORNERS:

- **TAPE MEASURE**
- **SCISSORS**
- **CARDBOARD**
- **EMBROIDERY YARN, WOOL, OR CORD**
- **TAPESTRY NEEDLE**
- **SCISSORS**
- **NEEDLE AND THREAD**

PROJECT

Floor cushions

Floor cushions are no longer the preserve of student digs. Huge, squashy cushions made of fake fur, leather, suede, or denim are seriously cool, and add an informal air to a living room or bedroom. They are particularly good for children and teenagers, who prefer to loll about on the floor with their friends.

Large, squashy floor cushions are the simplest form of seating to make. They always lend a relaxed and informal feel to their setting and are ideal when additional seating is needed, at a party for example. The choice of fabric will determine their style, but it must be hardwearing. In general, floor cushions suit earthy, ethnic designs or bright, bold patterns rather than formal, traditional fabrics. Chunky trimmings can be added, such as fringing and bobbles, or tassels or pompons at the corners. A zipper fastening along the center of the back is most suitable for floor-cushion covers, because it makes them easy to remove for laundering.

Readymade feather-filled 36-in./90-cm square inner pads are available from department stores. If you want to make a cushion that is not a standard size, it is easy to make an inner pad and fill it with your choice of filling. Make inner pads from cotton, lining fabric, or featherproof cambric.

Choosing fillings

Polystyrene beads give firm support and are a popular choice for floor cushions. Fill the pad carefully, because spills are difficult to clear up and you will probably be finding scattered polystyrene beads for months afterward. Foam chips have a bumpy feel and deteriorate with time. Use flame-retardant foam chips only.

Feather and down is soft and resilient. Purely feather fillings are more expensive than a mixture of feather and down. Make an inner pad for a feather-and-down filling from featherproof fabric. Kapok is a traditional cushion filling made from vegetable fiber, but will become lumpy over time.

HOW TO DO IT

STEP 1 Cut two 37¼-in./95-cm squares of fabric for the inner cushion. Stitch them together with the right sides facing, leaving a gap 27½ in./70 cm long on one edge for filling. Clip the corners and turn right-side out.

STEP 2 Pour the filling into the pad, then push it into the corners (and tease out feathers and kapok to distribute them evenly). The amount of filling needed depends upon how firm you would like the cushion to be. Slipstitch the opening closed.

STEP 3 Cut one 37¼-in./95-cm square of fabric to be used for the outer cushion front, and two rectangles 37¼ in. x 19¼ in. x 95 cm x 49 cm to be used for the outer cushion backs. With the right sides facing, baste the backs together along one long edge. Stitch for 4 in./10 cm at each end of the seam, taking a ⅝-in. /1.5-cm seam allowance. Press the seam open.

STEP 4 With the back lying face down, place the zipper centrally along the seam, face down. Pin and baste the zipper in position.

STEP 5 Using a zipper foot and with the fabric right-side up, stitch in the zipper ⁵⁄₁₆ in./8 mm from the basted seam and across the ends of the zipper. Take out basting.

STEP 6 Stitch the front and back together with the right sides facing. Clip the corners and turn right-side out. Push the inner pad into the cushion cover, making sure the corners are in place. Close the zip.

MAKING TASSELED CORNERS

Add an exotic touch to a floor cushion with a tassel at each corner. Use embroidery yarn, knitting wool, or even fine cord.

STEP 1 Cut a rectangle of cardboard 6¼ in. x 4 in./15.5 cm x 10 cm. Fold in half, parallel with the short edges. Bind the yarn around the cardboard many times, depending upon the thickness of the tassel needed.

STEP 2 Fold a long length of yarn in half and thread the ends through the eye of a tapestry needle. Slip the needle behind the strands close to the fold, then insert the needle through the loop of the yarn and pull tightly.

STEP 3 Slip the tips of a pair of scissors between the cardboard layers and cut through the strands. Discard the cardboard.

STEP 4 Thread the needle with a single length of yarn. Bind it around the head of the tassel, gathering the strands together. To secure, insert the needle into the bulk of the tassel to lose the end of the yarn within the tassel. Cut the tassel ends level. Sew a tassel to each corner of a cushion, using the yarn extending at the top.

YOU WILL NEED:

- FABRIC FOR TOP AND BASE
- FABRIC FOR FRONT, BACK, AND SIDE GUSSETS (FOR THE SQUARE/ RECTANGULAR CUSHION)
- FABRIC FOR FRONT AND BACK GUSSETS (FOR THE CIRCULAR CUSHION)
- TAPE MEASURE
- ZIPPER
- IRON
- PINS
- SCISSORS
- NEEDLE AND THREAD/SEWING MACHINE
- ZIPPER FOOT
- PIPING (IF REQUIRED)

PROJECT
Box cushions

A box cushion is tailored to cover a foam block or a deep, feather-filled, gusseted inner pad, making it very comfortable to sit on. A gusset forms the sides between the top and base. The shape can be emphasized with piping or any other trimming that takes your fancy.

MAKING A SQUARE OR RECTANGULAR BOX CUSHION

STEP 1 Measure the length, width, and depth of the cushion. Cut squares or rectangles of fabric for the top and base, adding a ⅝-in./1.5-cm seam allowance to all edges. Cut a strip of fabric for the front gusset the length of the front by the cushion depth plus ⅝ in./1.5 cm on all edges. Cut two strips for the side gussets the length of the sides by the cushion depth plus ⅝ in./1.5 cm on all edges. Cut two strips for the back gusset the length of the back by half the cushion depth plus ⅝ in./1.5 cm on all edges.

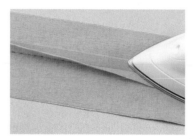

STEP 2 With right sides facing, baste the backs together along one long edge. Stitch for 1½ in./3.8 cm at each end of the seam, taking a ⅝-in./1.5-cm seam allowance. Press the seam open.

STEP 3 With the back lying face down, place the zipper centrally along the seam, face down. Pin and baste the zipper in position. Using a zipper foot on the sewing machine and with the fabric right-side up, stitch the zip in place ⁵⁄₁₆ in./8 mm from the basted seam and across the ends of the zipper. Remove the basting stitches.

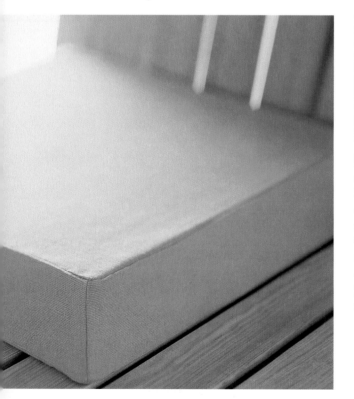

STEP 4 With right sides facing, stitch the front and back gussets between the side gussets at the short ends, taking a ⅝-in./1.5-cm seam allowance, starting and finishing ⅝ in./1.5 cm from the long edges. Press the seams open. If you wish to use piping, baste it to the long edges, joining it at the back. Snip the piping seam allowance at the corners.

STEP 5 With right sides facing and matching the seams to the corners, pin the base to the gusset. Stitch, taking a ⅝-in./1.5-cm seam allowance and pivoting the seam at the corners. Open the zipper and stitch the top to the gusset in the same way. Clip the corners. Press the seams toward the gusset. Turn right-side out and insert the cushion. Close the zipper.

MAKING A CIRCULAR BOX CUSHION

To reduce the bulk in the seams, trim the allowances to different levels. This is especially important if piping has been inserted, because it will make the seam allowance layers very thick and difficult to manage. To stop cushions from slipping, sew a 2½-in./6.3-cm length of sew-on, touch-and-close tape to the base of the cushion at the front and back, and apply a corresponding stick-on tape stuck to the seat.

STEP 1 Measure the diameter, circumference, and depth of the cushion. Cut two circles of fabric for the top and base, adding 1¼ in./3 cm to the diameter. Cut a strip of fabric for the front gusset half the circumference of the cushion depth plus ⅝ in./1.5 cm on all edges. Cut two strips of fabric for the back gusset half the circumference by half the cushion depth plus ⅝ in./1.5 cm on all the edges.

STEP 2 Follow step 3 of making a square or rectangular box cushion to insert the zipper. With right sides facing, stitch the front and back gussets together, taking a ⅝-in./1.5-cm seam allowance. Press the seams open. If you wish to insert piping, baste it to the long edges now, joining the ends at the back.

STEP 3 With right sides facing, stitch the base to the gusset, taking a ⅝-in./1.5-cm seam allowance. Open the zipper and stitch the top to the gusset in the same way. Snip the curves. Press the seams toward the gusset. Turn right-side out and insert the cushion. Close the zipper.

MAKING IRREGULAR-SHAPED CUSHIONS

Some box cushions are shaped, to fit around chair arms for example, and must have a pattern made for them. If you intend to re-cover an existing cushion, take the old cover apart and use it as a pattern; otherwise make a paper pattern.

If a box cushion is narrower at the back than the front, the zipper can be extended and the seams can be on the sides of the gusset instead of the back corners. This works well on wedge-shaped cushions. Alternatively, the base can have a seam across its widest part with a zipper inserted.

YOU WILL NEED:
- BATTING
- CALICO
- TACKS
- STAPLE GUN
- HAMMER
- BLACK FABRIC
- CHALK/
  CHINA MARKER
  PENCIL
- SCISSORS
- FABRIC
- IRON
- TACK LIFTER
- SCREWDRIVER

PROJECT
Drop-in seats

Many chairs have drop-in seats, which can get tattered if you use them a lot. These kinds of seats are very easy to lift out and cover yourself. You can also buy reasonably priced second-hand chairs to re-cover from scratch, replacing the old upholstery with fabric of your own choosing.

Here is a fast, no-sew way to bring new life to a worn chair by replacing the cover on its seat. Many dining or kitchen chairs or stools have drop-in seats that rest on a recessed ledge. Traditionally, a drop-in seat had a fabric cover over a horsehair stuffing, which was supported by tightly stretched webbing on a wooden frame. Nowadays, mass-produced foam versions are supported by a wooden base. The foam block is easy to work with, but you will find it is not as comfortable to sit on nor as long-lasting as a webbed and horsehair seat.

A calico lining under the outer cover protects the stuffing or foam and means the seat cover can be changed easily for washing or replacing without disturbing the interior of the seat. If you intend to use a thick furnishing fabric to re-cover the seat, check that there is enough clearance for the covered seat to fit the chair. Omitting the calico lining may help the fabric to fit. Use ½-in./1.2-cm-long upholstery tacks or a staple gun to fix the covers.

Tattered drop-in seat covers can be lifted out and re-covered in a favorite fabric and color—no sewing required!

HOW TO DO IT

STEP 1 Lift the seat out of the chair frame. Any backing fabric on the underside will need to be removed. Lever off any tacks or staples with a tack lifter or the blade of a screwdriver. Remove the old seat cover in the same way, but do not discard it.

STEP 2 Remove any calico lining. Discard any batting or top cover to reveal the stuffing or foam. Press the old seat cover and use it as a pattern to cut a seat cover from calico and the outer fabric. If the outer fabric is patterned, experiment by placing the fabric over the seat to judge the best position for its motifs.

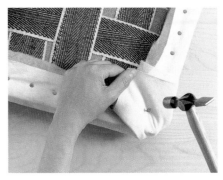

STEP 3 Cut a piece of batting 2½ in./6 cm larger all round to fit the top of the seat, and place it in position. Place the calico cover centrally on top and smooth it over the surface. Check that the grain of the fabric is straight. Turn the seat over, holding the layers in place. Pull the calico over the underside of the frame or wood base. Starting on the back edge, secure temporarily in place with a tack hammered in halfway, in the middle of each side.

STEP 4 Working outward from the middle of the back edge, tack or staple the calico to the seat, positioning the tacks or staples about 1½ in./3.8 cm apart and stopping 1½ in./3.8 cm each side of the corners. Stretch the calico toward the corners as you work.

STEP 5 Fix the front and then the side edges in the same way, removing the temporary tack first if the calico is no longer lying taut. Check that the calico is lying taut and smooth on the seat. Pull the calico over one corner and hammer a temporary tack halfway in.

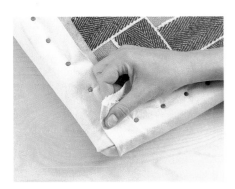

STEP 6 Fold the excess fabric under in mitered folds. Run your thumb along the folds to crease them. Open out the folds and cut away excess batting and calico underneath. Remove the temporary tack and refold the calico. Tack or staple the folds in place. Repeat on all corners. Trim the calico and wadding to just beyond the tacks or staples.

STEP 7 Fix the top cover in the same way as the calico, making sure that the second row of tacks does not connect with the first row.

STEP 8 To give a professional finish, draw around the seat on black fabric with chalk or a china marker pencil. Cut out, adding a ¼-in./6-mm allowance. Press ⅜ in./1 cm under on the edges and tack or staple to the underside of the seat, again missing the position of the previous tacks and staples. Replace the seat in the chair recess.

YOU WILL NEED:

FOR THE
FOOTSTOOLS:

• TAPE MEASURE
• PATTERN (FOR
  CIRCULAR
  FOOTSTOOL)
• SCISSORS
• FABRIC
• NEEDLE AND
  THREAD/SEWING
  MACHINE
• PINS
• IRON
• PINKING SHEARS
• TRIMMING (IF
  REQUIRED)

PROJECT
Footstools

Smart calico-covered footstools are available from furniture suppliers ready to be covered in a fabric of your choice. Alternatively, you may wish to re-cover an old, scruffy footstool. Remove any trimmings first. If the existing cover is not falling apart, leave it on and fit the new cover on top.

Slip-on footstool cover

A slip-on cover is an instant make-over for a square, circular, or rectangular footstool. The cover is made from a single piece of fabric that can be trimmed with fringing, braid, or ribbon. Because the cover extends below the base of the footstool, this style is not suitable for footstools that have legs that jut or curve outward.

A footstool of this style can be cleverly created from a low coffee table. Stick foam to the top of the table with a foam-spray adhesive to make a soft, cushioned top. Place a layer of batting over the top, then fold the fullness under at the corners and staple the batting to the underside the table. It is now ready to be covered.

MAKING A CIRCULAR SLIP-ON FOOTSTOOL COVER

STEP 1 Measure the diameter and circumference of the footstool, then measure the intended drop. Cut a circle of fabric for the top, adding 1¼ in./3 cm to the diameter. Cut a strip of fabric for the side the length of the circumference plus 1¼ in./3 cm by the drop plus 1⅝ in./4 cm. With right sides facing, stitch the ends of the sides together, taking a ⅝-in./1.5-cm seam allowance. Press the seam open. If you wish to insert piping, baste it to the upper long edge of the side of the cover now.

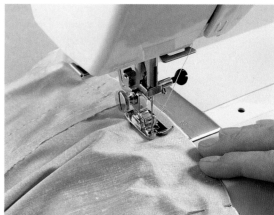

STEP 2 Fold the top, and the upper edge of the side panel into fourths and mark with pins. With right sides facing, pin the side panel to the top. Stitch, taking ⅝-in./1.5-cm seam allowance. Snip the curves. Neaten the seam with pinking shears or zigzag stitch. Press the seam toward the side panel. Press under ⅜ in./1 cm then ⅝ in./1.5 cm on the lower edge, then slipstitch or machine-stitch in place.

MAKING A SQUARE OR RECTANGULAR SLIP-ON FOOTSTOOL COVER

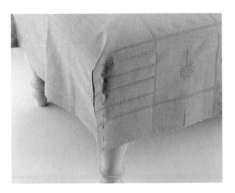

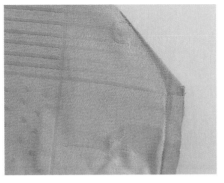

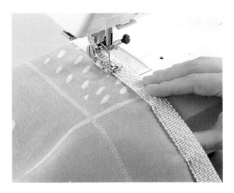

STEP 1 Measure the length and width of the top of the footstool. Measure the drop of the cover; that is, how far down the legs you would like the cover to go; it should be at least 1 in./ 2.5 cm below the base and can be floor-length.

STEP 2 To make a pattern, draw a square or rectangle on paper, the same size as the top of the footstool. Extend each side of the shape for the drop of the cover; these will be the sides of the cover. Add a ⅝-in./1.5-cm seam allowance to the side edges and a 1-in./2.5-cm hem to the lower edges.

STEP 3 To fit the cover, pin the side edges together with right sides facing, taking a ⅝-in./ 1.5-cm seam allowance. Slip the cover over the footstool and check the fit. If it is too tight, make the seams narrower. If the cover is loose, make the seams deeper. Adjust all the seams by the same amount.

STEP 4 If the corners of the footstool are quite rounded, pin the top of the seams, following the curves. Stitch the seams as pinned. Neaten the seams with a zigzag stitch. Press the seams open.

STEP 5 Press ⅜-in./1-cm under then ⅝-in./ 1.5 cm on the lower edges, and stitch in place. If you wish, sew a trimming along the lower edge.

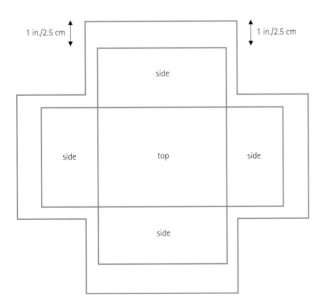

UPHOLSTERING A FOOTSTOOL

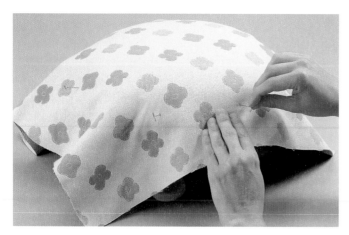

STEP 1 Lay the fabric over the footstool, centering any design motifs, and pin the fabric in place with upholstery skewers or T-pins. Smooth the fabric outward from the center and over the sides.

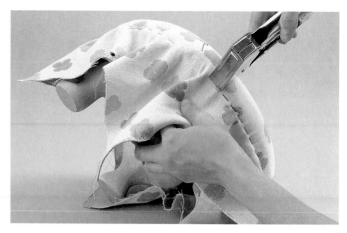

STEP 2 Check that the fabric is lying smoothly and is not wrinkled or pulling tightly. Lie the stool on its side and staple the lower edge of the fabric onto the frame with a staple gun, or hammer in tacks close to the lower edge.

STEP 3 Trim away the excess fabric, level with the base of the footstool.

STEP 4 Use fabric glue to stick braid or fringing over the lower raw edges, overlapping the ends.

YOU WILL NEED:

- FABRIC
- UPHOLSTERY SKEWERS/T-PINS
- STAPLE GUN OR HAMMER
- TACKS
- SCISSORS
- FABRIC GLUE
- BRAID/FRINGING

PROJECT
Beanbag chairs

A squidgy beanbag chair is surprisingly comfortable and supportive. The beanbag has an inner bag to contain the polystyrene beads so they are secure. Calico is a good choice for the inner bag, but any cotton or lining fabric will do as an alternative.

Animal hides and fur fabrics

Beanbag chairs made of sumptuous leather and suede and realistic fake animal hides are extremely expensive to buy, yet can be made for a fraction of their cost. Although there are special considerations to remember when stitching real and fake animal hides, these chairs are simple to assemble and should not be problematic.

Because animal skins vary in size, take a paper pattern with you to calculate how many to buy. Cut the skins separately, right-side up, so you can avoid any surface flaws or thin areas. Weight the pattern in place and draw around it with tailor's chalk, then cut out. Stitch leather and suede with polyester thread, using a wedge-point needle for both hand- and machine-stitching. Press with a warm iron on the wrong side. If the iron begins to stick, cover the skin with brown wrapping paper.

Leather can be sponged gently with warm water and a little soap or dish-washing liquid. Wipe with a damp cloth, then dry with a soft duster. Brush suede with a clothes brush; some suedes are washable.

Highly realistic imitation leather and suede fabrics are available nowadays and are very easy to work with. Make sure that the pile of imitation suede runs in the same direction on the panels when cutting out. These fabrics often have a knitted back; use a ballpoint needle to stitch with a slight zigzag stitch to let the seams stretch when the chair is sat on.

Choose fur fabrics with a short pile, otherwise the chair will lose what little definition it has. Fur fabrics usually come in 60-in./150-cm widths and are quite cheap. The pile of the fur should run down the length of the panels. Cut through the knitted backing of the fur and not the fur itself, cutting each piece singly to avoid distortion.

Stitch fur fabrics with a ballpoint needle. Trim away the fur in the seam allowances to reduce bulk and pull out any fur caught in the seams with a pin. Press the fabric lightly on the wrong side with a warm iron.

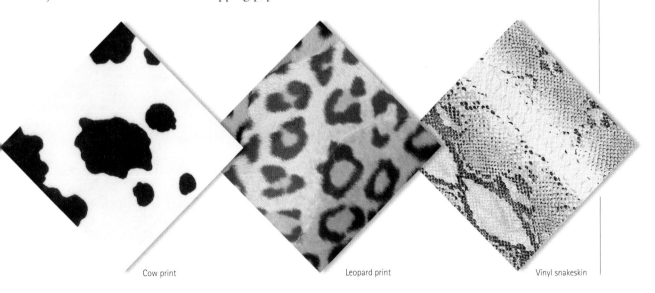

Cow print   Leopard print   Vinyl snakeskin

HOW TO DO IT

STEP 1 Refer to the diagrams below to cut patterns from paper for the panel, top, and base. Cut six panels, a top, and a base from the outer fabric and the inner bag fabric. With right sides together and taking ⅝-in./1.5-cm seam allowances, stitch the outer bag panels together, starting and finishing ⅝ in./1.5 cm from the ends of the seams. Snip the corners and press the seams open.

STEP 2 Cut a strip of fabric for the handle 9 in. x 4½ in./22.5 cm x 10.5 cm. Fold ⅝ in./1.5 cm under on the long edges and fold lengthwise in half. Stitch close to the long edges. With right sides uppermost, baste the handle centrally across the top, matching the raw edges.

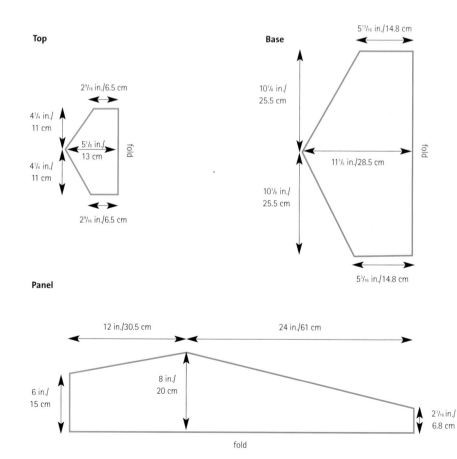

Top

2⁹⁄₁₆ in./6.5 cm

4¼ in./11 cm

5⅛ in./13 cm

fold

4¼ in./11 cm

2⁹⁄₁₆ in./6.5 cm

Base

5¹³⁄₁₆ in./14.8 cm

10⅛ in./25.5 cm

11⅛ in./28.5 cm

fold

10⅛ in./25.5 cm

5³⁄₁₆ in./14.8 cm

Panel

12 in./30.5 cm

24 in./61 cm

6 in./15 cm

8 in./20 cm

2¹⁄₁₆ in./6.8 cm

fold

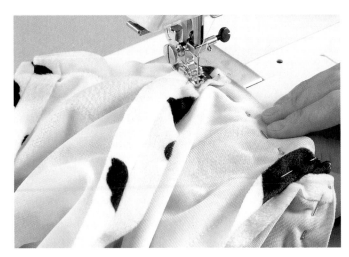

STEP 3 Pin the top to the upper edge of the panels, with right sides facing and matching the seams to the corners. Stitch, taking a ⅝-in./ 1.5-cm seam allowance and pivoting the fabric at the corners. Stitch the base to the lower edge in the same way, leaving a gap in one panel to turn through. Snip the corners.

STEP 4 Make the inner bag in the same way, omitting the handle. Turn both bags right side out. Slip the inner bag inside the outer bag. Fill the inner bag with 5 cu. ft./0.14 cu m of polystyrene beads. The best way to do this is to form a funnel from thin cardboard, overlapping the edges and taping them together. Push the narrow end of the funnel into the inner bag and carefully pour in the beads. Slipstitch the openings on both bags closed.

YOU WILL NEED:
- CANVAS OR FABRIC
- TACKS/HAMMER
- NEEDLE AND THREAD/SEWING MACHINE
- TAPE MEASURE
- PINS
- SCISSORS
- IRON
- DOWELS (FOR CHANNELS ONLY)
- TOUCH-AND-CLOSE TAPE
- FEATHER AND DOWN

PROJECT

Deckchairs

Traditional deckchair canvas is strong and hardwearing and comes in widths of 16 in.–18 in./40 cm–46 cm in plain colors and distinctive stripes. Fabrics other than the recommended canvas can be used; they will not last as long as deckchair canvas, but they will offer more choice of designs. The fabric must be tough, however, and not likely to stretch.

Preparing the deckchair

Lay the closed chair face down on a flat surface. If the old cover is attached to the top and bottom bars of the chair with tacks, ease them out with a chisel. If the top and bottom bars of the chair have been slotted through a channel of the old cover before the frame was assembled, you will have to cut the cover away. If the cover has channels at each end with a thick wooden dowel slotted through, which is trapped between a pair of wooden bars, simply pull out the dowels to release the cover. Use the old cover as a pattern to cut the new one. If the old cover no longer exists, open the frame, loop a tape measure around the top bar, and let it drop in a curve before wrapping it over the bottom bar.

Allow a ⅜-in./1-cm allowance at each end for a cover attached with tacks. For a cover with channels, add twice the depth of the channels plus 1¼ in./3 cm. If you are not using deckchair canvas, measure the width of the top bar. Cut the fabric to that width plus ¾-in./2-cm hem on each side. Cut out the cover. Sand, paint, or varnish the frame if needed.

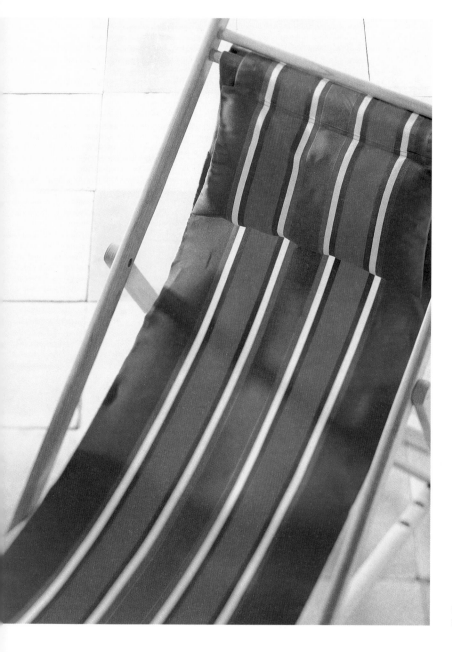

Give an old deckchair a new lease of life by re-covering it with a hardwearing fabric of your choice.

DECKCHAIR USING TACKS

STEP 1 If you are not using deckchair canvas, press ¼ in./5 mm of fabric under, then a ⅝-in./1.5-cm hem on the long edges, and stitch in place. Press ⅜ in./1 cm under at each end.

STEP 2 Lay the canvas right-side down on a flat surface and place the deckchair frame right-side down on top. Wrap the top of the canvas around the top bar so that the turned-under edge lies along the underside of the bar. Hammer a tack through the cover into the underside of the bar at the center. Hammer three tacks, evenly spaced each side of the first tack. Avoid the holes left by the previous tacks, because they will not grip the new tacks.

STEP 3 Wrap the other end of the fabric around the bottom bar, placing the turned-under edge along the underside of the bar. The bottom bar is sometimes narrower than the top bar. If the canvas is too wide for the bottom bar, turn under the edges by the same amount at each edge so the canvas lies flat. Tack in place as for the top bar.

DECKCHAIR WITH CHANNELS

STEP 1 If not using deckchair canvas, turn under ¼ in./5 mm, then ⅝ in./1.5 cm on the long edges and stitch in place.

STEP 2 Press under ⅝ in./1.5 cm, then the depth of the channel at each end. Stitch close to the inner edge, then ¼ in./5 mm from the inner edge to form a channel.

STEP 3 Lay the cover right-side down on a flat surface. Place the deckchair frame right-side down on top. Pull the ends between the top and lower bars and insert the dowels through the channels.

REMOVABLE PILLOW

A detachable pillow adds extra comfort to a deckchair. It is fixed with touch-and-close tape so that it can be removed for storage.

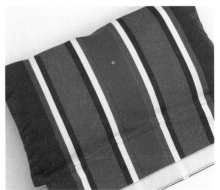

STEP 1 Cut a rectangle of canvas the width of the chair cover by 20 in./51 cm. Fold widthwise in half with right sides facing. Taking a ⅝-in./1.5-cm seam allowance, stitch the short edges and for ¾ in./2 cm at each end of the long raw edges. Clip the corners and turn the pillow right-side out. Press the opening edges to the inside. Fill the pillow with feather and down.

STEP 2 Cut a 5-in./12.5-cm-wide strip of canvas the width of the chair cover for the pillow hinge. Turn ⅜ in./1 cm under, then 1 in./2.5 cm at each end and stitch in place. Press ⅜ in./1 cm under on one long edge and stitch the sew-on half of touch-and-close tape over the raw edge.

STEP 3 Insert the long raw edge into the pillow for ⅝ in./1.5 cm. Pin in place, then stitch close to the pressed edges. Stitch again ¼ in./6 mm from the first stitching. Apply a corresponding strip of stick-on touch-and-close tape to the back of the bar on the deckchair and press the pillow hinge on top. Flop the pillow over to the front of the chair.

YOU WILL NEED:
- TAPE MEASURE
- BACK AND SEAT COVER FABRIC
- HEAVY-DUTY NEEDLE AND STRONG THREAD
- SEWING MACHINE/ ZIPPER FOOT
- IRON

Director's chairs have a minimalist style that fits many decorative schemes.

PROJECT
Director's chair

The modest director's chair fits into many room styles. Director's chairs are useful when additional seating is needed, both indoors and outdoors, and they take up little room when folded for storage. The sling-style covers are easy to make, and only a small amount of fabric is needed. You should make the chair covers from durable fabrics.

RE-COVERING A DIRECTOR'S CHAIR

The back cover of a director's chair may be fixed rigidly in place and the cover attached with tacks. Alternatively, the back may be fixed so that it can be pivoted to different angles and the wooden struts can be slipped through channels in the cover. Calculate the amount of fabric required by measuring the existing back and seat covers. Add 1 in./2.5 cm on the long edges for hems. For the seat and a back cover attached with tacks, allow enough fabric to wrap around the wooden struts plus ¾ in./2 cm. For a back cover with channels, measure the channels on the original covers. Add ⅝ in./1.5 cm to each channel. Here are directions for a chair cover that has a back cover with channels; and a seat cover with channels, with struts inside that are held in place between the wooden edges of the seat frame.

STEP 1 Cut out the new back and seat covers, including the allowances. To hem, press under ³/₄ in./1 cm, then ⁵/₈ in./1.5 cm on the long edges and stitch in place close to the pressed edges. Use strong thread and a heavy-duty needle. If using deckchair canvas, stitch a single hem, because the selvedges will not fray.

STEP 2 Press under ³/₈ in./1 cm on the short raw edges of the covers. Press the channels to the wrong side for the required depth. On the back cover, stitch close to the inner pressed edges. Place each seat strut inside a channel and use a zipper foot to stitch close to the strut.

STEP 3 Insert the back supports through the back channels and fix the seat securely in position.

For a director's chair that has the cover attached with tacks, mark the edge of the fabric on the wooden struts of the seat with a pencil. Pry off the tacks and remove the old covers. If the old covers are in a suitable condition, you could press them flat to use as patterns. Hem the long edges. Press under ⅜ in./1 cm on the ends of the seat cover. Lay the chair on its side. Wrap the seat cover around one of the wooden struts and match one pressed edge to the pencil line. Hammer a tack into the fabric at the center, close to the pressed edge. Hammer more tacks on each side of the first tack with the outer tacks close to the hemmed edges. Stretch the cover across the seat and fix the other edge. Press under ⅜ in./1 cm on the ends of the back cover. Wrap the cover around the back struts with the pressed edges along the inner edges. Working outward from the center, hammer tacks close to the pressed edges, having the outer tacks close to the hemmed edges.

MAKING A CHAIR BACK POCKET

A gusseted pocket on the back cover of a director's chair is an extremely useful addition for all sorts of situations: you can slip a book or shades into the pocket for safekeeping when the chair is used in the backyard. Attach the pocket to the back of the cover before it is attached to the chair.

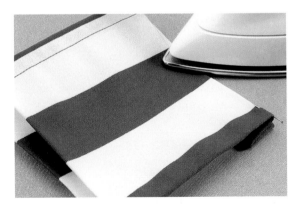

STEP 1 Cut a rectangle of fabric 10¼ in. x 6⅝ in./26 cm x 16.5 cm. Press ⅜ in./1 cm under then ⅝ in./1.5 cm for the hem on the upper long edge. Stitch in place. Press ⅝ in./1.5 cm under on the remaining edges. Mark the long edges with a pin 2 in./5 cm in from the short pressed edges. Bring the pinned marks to the short pressed edges to form pleats. Press in place.

STEP 2 Position the pocket centrally on the back cover and stitch close to the side edges; do not catch in the pleats. Stitch again ¼ in./6mm inside the first stitching. Stitch across the lower edges, securing the pleats in place.

YOU WILL NEED:

FOR POCKET:
- **FABRIC**
- **SCISSORS**
- **TAPE MEASURE**
- **PINS**
- **IRON**
- **HEAVY-DUTY NEEDLE AND STRONG THREAD**
- **SEWING MACHINE**

YOU WILL NEED:

PATTERN:

- **FABRIC FOR PATTERN: SHEET OR CALICO**
- **T-PINS**
- **TAPE MEASURE**
- **SCISSORS**
- **TAILOR'S CHALK**

LOOSE COVER:

- **FABRIC FOR COVER**
- **TAILOR'S CHALK**
- **SCISSORS**
- **NEEDLE AND THREAD**
- **SEWING MACHINE WITH PIPING OR ZIPPER FOOT**
- **PINKING SHEARS**
- **PINS**
- **IRON**
- **ZIPPERS**
- **COTTON TAPE/CORD**
- **PIPING**

PROJECT
Armchair cover

Bring new life to an old and tattered armchair with a loose cover. A removable cover is not only an economical alternative to having furniture re-upholstered—which can be an enormously expensive undertaking—but it is practical too, because it can be removed as often as you like for laundering.

Make sure that the chair is in reasonably good condition before you start. Piping will define the shape and give a professional finish, and a discreet zipper fastening at one side of the back will enable the cover to be removed easily. The cover fits snugly under the chair with a drawstring. Loose covers for sofas are made in exactly the same way as for a chair, but the fabric for the inner back will need to be joined. A center seam is unsightly, so have a seam toward the side edges on each side of the inner back and the outer back of the sofa. The zipper opening can be in one of these seams on the outer back.

MAKING THE PATTERN

The cover should fit smoothly but not be tight. The pattern must be made from fabric, because paper will not follow the chair's contours. An old sheet will do or buy a cheap remnant, such as calico, to use. Of course, if the chair already has a loose cover, simply take it apart and press flat to use as a pattern.

Look at the position of seams and grain lines on the chair, because you will match them when making the pattern. So that the pattern-making fabric is not too bulky to handle, roughly cut it into pieces about 8 in./20 cm longer and wider than the area you are working on. Use T-pins to pin the fabric to the chair, because they are easier to see on the wide expanse of a piece of furniture than dressmaking pins. Calculate the amount of fabric you will need to buy by laying out the pattern pieces (see pages 776–777).

Re-covering an armchair or sofa gives a dramatic new look. Fitting a loose cover also means it can be removed and washed easily.

STEP 1 Remove any loose cushions. Mark the exact center of the chair on the front and back with chalk; measure this accurately because the pattern will be made for only one half of the chair. Follow the grain line to cut a straight edge along the length of the fabric for the inner back. Pin the straight edge to the chalk line. Smooth the fabric outward from the pinned edge. If necessary, fold any fullness at the upper corner in neat pleats.

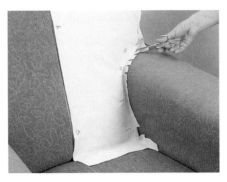

STEP 2 Cut the fabric to shape so it lies flat. Let the fabric extend 4 in. /10 cm over the seat for a tuck-in, and leave a 1-in./2.5-cm seam allowance on all other edges. Snip the seam allowance around the arm to help the fabric lie smoothly.

STEP 3 Pin the fabric to the seat, matching a straight edge to the chalk line. Extend the fabric up the back and arm, and mark a 4-in./10-cm allowance at the back edge and taper it along the arm to 1 in./2.5 cm at the front. Trim to fit, leaving a 1-in./2.5-cm seam allowance on the front edge.

STEP 4 Pin the inner arm over one arm of the chair. Extend the fabric onto the seat. Mark a 4-in./10-cm allowance at the back edge and taper along the seat to 1 in./2.5 cm at the front. Trim to fit, snipping the curves and leaving a 1-in. /2.5-cm seam allowance on the other edges.

STEP 5 Now pin the fabric to the outer arm, leaving 4 in./10 cm on the lower edge and 1 in./2.5 cm on the other edges.

STEP 6 Pin the fabric to an arm gusset and apron, matching to the chalk line. Trim, leaving 4 in./10 cm on the lower edges and 1 in./2.5 cm on the other edges.

STEP 7 Pin a straight edge to the chalk line on the back of the chair. Smooth the fabric outward and trim it so it lies flat, leaving 4 in./10 cm at the lower edge and a 1-in./2.5-cm seam allowance on other edges.

STEP 8 Pin fabric to the back gusset. Trim to fit, adding a 1-in./2.5-cm seam allowance on all edges. Snip the curves at the lower edge.

STEP 9 Make patterns for the shaped cushions. Label the pieces and mark the grain line, any pleats, and balance marks. Label the straight center edges as fold lines. Draw a line on the outer back pattern 9½ in./24 cm from the center. Cut along this line (for the zipper). Add a 1-in./2.5-cm seam allowance.

MAKING THE LOOSE COVER

Cut out the fabric pieces and label them on the wrong side with chalk. Pin the seams together on the chair. Clip the seam allowance at the curves. Unpin each section as you are about to stitch it, then try it on the chair again. Most chairs are not completely symmetrical, so it is important to keep trying the cover on and making adjustments to ensure a good fit. After stitching each seam, trim it to ¾ in./2 cm and neaten with a zigzag stitch or pinking shears.

STEP 1 Baste and press any pleats. Baste piping along seam lines on the right side. This chair has piping applied to the back gussets and arm gussets. If basting by sewing machine, use a zipper or piping foot.

STEP 2 Stitch the upper end of the zipper seams on the outer back for 8 in./20 cm, taking a 1-in./2.5-cm seam allowance. Press the seams open. Stitch the inner back to the outer back along the upper edges. Press the seam toward the inner back.

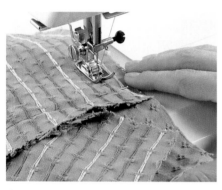

STEP 6 Pin the inner back to the back edge of the seat, matching the centers. Stitch the back edge, starting and finishing 1 in./2.5 cm from the side edges of the inner back.

STEP 7 Pin the side edges of the apron to the arm gussets. Continue pinning the side edges of the seat to the lower edge of the inner arms. Stitch in place, starting 1 in./2.5 cm from the back edges of the inner arms. Continue to the lower edge of the apron.

STEP 8 Press the arm gusset and apron seams open. Then lie the lower, unstitched edges of the inner back and inner arms flat on the seat. Pin and stitch the lower edges to the seat between the seams to form the tuck-in.

STEP 10 Slip the cover on the chair, fastening the zippers. Snip the lower edge each side of the feet to ¾ in./2 cm below the chair base. Cut away the fabric and remove the cover. Stay-stitch ¾ in./2 cm inside the cut corners, then snip to the inner corners.

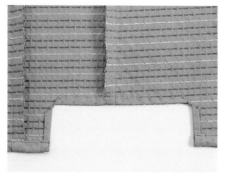

STEP 11 Turn under a ⅜-in./1-cm double hem on the stay-stitched edges. Press under ⅜ in./1 cm, then ¾ in./2 cm on the lower edges. Stitch close to the inner edges to form channels.

STEP 12 Insert a length of cotton tape or cord through the channel. Slip the cover on the chair, then pull up the cord and tie the ends in a bow. See pages 838–839 if you need to cover box cushions for the chair.

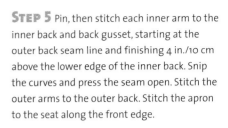

STEP 5 Pin, then stitch each inner arm to the inner back and back gusset, starting at the outer back seam line and finishing 4 in./10 cm above the lower edge of the inner back. Snip the curves and press the seam open. Stitch the outer arms to the outer back. Stitch the apron to the seat along the front edge.

STEP 3 Stitch the back gussets to the inner and outer back, starting 1 in./2.5 cm above the lower edge of the back gussets. Press the seams toward the gussets.

STEP 4 Stitch each inner arm to an outer arm. Clip the curves and press the seams open. Pin and baste, then stitch the arm gusset to the front of the arms, starting 1 in./2.5 cm above the lower edge of the back gussets. Press the seams toward the gussets.

STEP 9 Clip the corners and trim the back corners and seam allowance to ¾ in./2 cm. Turn the cover right-side out and try it on the chair. Push the tuck-ins down the sides and back of the seat. Pin under the zipper opening edges so they meet edge to edge. Remove the cover and insert the zippers, having the opening ends 4¾ in./12 cm above the lower edge.

PROJECT
Squab cushion

A tie-on cushion filled with a thin layer of foam adds some padding to a hard kitchen chair seat. Make a feature of the ties at the back of the cushion by binding them around the chair legs. You could use contrasting colored ribbons for this if you wanted.

HOW TO DO IT

STEP 1 To make a pattern, cut a piece of pattern paper or brown wrapping paper larger than the seat. Place it on the seat with a weight on top. Fold the edges of the paper over the seat to define the shape. If necessary, snip the paper around the rails so it lies flat.

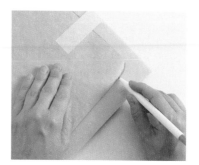

STEP 2 Remove the pattern. Add ⅝-in./1.5-cm seam allowance on all edges. Use the pattern to cut two cushion covers from fabric. Cut the seam allowance off the pattern. Tape the pattern to ½-in./1.2-cm thick foam with painter's tape. Draw around the pattern with an air-erasable pen. Remove the pattern and cut out the foam.

STEP 3 Make piping using the cover fabric (see page 790). Pin and baste it to the side and front edges on the right side of one cover, starting and finishing ⅝ in./1.5 cm from the back edges. With right sides facing, stitch the covers together, taking a ⅝-in./1.5-cm seam allowance and leaving a 11-in./27-cm opening to turn on the back edge.

STEP 4 Layer the seam to reduce the bulk. Snip the curves and corners. Lay the foam cushion on top of the cover within the seam. Reach inside the cover and pin the foam to the top cover. Turn the cover right-side out and slipstitch the opening closed. Remove the pins.

STEP 5 Cut four 1⅜-in./3.5-cm-wide bias strips 18 in./45 cm long for the ties. Fold the ties lengthwise in half with the right sides facing. Stitch, taking a ¼-in./5-mm seam allowance. Use a bodkin to turn the ties right-side out. Turn in the ends and slipstitch closed. Place the cushion on the seat and pin the ties each side of the back rails. Sew securely in place, then tie around the legs.

FAR RIGHT: **A tie-on cushion turns a kitchen chair into a comfortable seat.**

YOU WILL NEED:
- TAPE MEASURE
- PATTERN PAPER
- FABRIC/LINING
- PINKING SHEARS
- SEWING MATERIALS
- SCISSORS
- PINS
- IRON
- BUTTONS

Seat cover with skirt

You can soften the look of a hard-seated chair by making a skirted seat cover edged with a band of rich velvet. The cover is fastened to the chair with large mother-of-pearl buttons for a decorative touch. Take a ⅝-in./1.5-cm seam allowance unless stated otherwise.

HOW TO DO IT

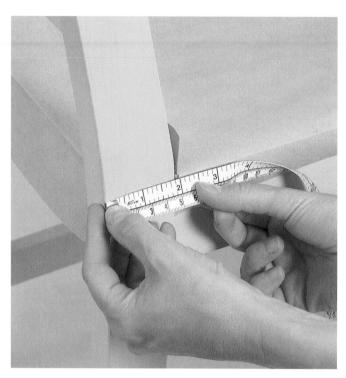

STEP 1 To make the pattern, cut a piece of pattern paper or brown wrapping paper larger than the seat. Place it on the seat with a weight on top. Fold the edges of the paper over the seat to define the shape. If necessary, snip the paper around the rails so it lies flat. Measure the side and back edge of one back rail.

STEP 2 Remove the pattern from the chair. Add a ⅝-in./1.5-cm seam allowance on all edges. Use the seat pattern to cut one seat from fabric, then use the pattern to make a 2¼-in./6-cm-deep pattern of one back corner, which will make a pattern for a corner facing. Cut two corner facings from the lining fabric.

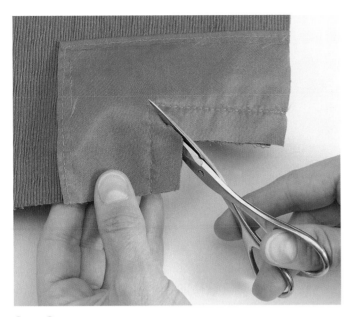

STEP 3 Stitch a ¼-in./5-mm hem on the long outer edges of the corner facings. With right sides together, stitch each facing to a back corner of the seat along the inner corner edges. Snip to the inner corners. Press the facings to the underside. Baste the raw edges of the fabric together.

STEP 4 Cut a strip of fabric for the front skirt the length of the front of the seat plus 1¼ in. x 6¼ in./3 cm x 16 cm. Cut two strips for the side skirts the length of the side of the seat plus the side of the back rail measurement plus 1¼ in./3 cm. Right sides facing, stitch the front skirt between the side skirts along the short edges. Start ⅝ in./1.5 cm below the upper long edges. Neaten seams with pinking shears or zigzag stitch; press them open.

STEP 5 Matching centers, pin and baste the front and side skirts to the front and side edges of the seat with the right sides facing, pivoting the seam at the front corners and with the ends of the side skirts extending beyond the faced corners.

STEP 6 Cut two rectangles of lining 6¼ in. x 4 in./16 cm x 10 cm for side facings and two rectangles of lining 6¼ in. x 6 in./16 cm x 15 cm for the back facings. Stitch a ¼-in./5-mm hem on one long edge of each facing. With the right sides of the facings and skirt together, pin the side facings to the ends of the side skirts, enclosing the faced corners of the seat. Stitch the ends of the side skirts, then the side and front edges of the seat. Neaten the seat seams with pinking shears or a zigzag stitch. Clip the corners, then turn right-side out and press the seat seam toward the skirt. Press the facings to the underside of the skirt.

STEP 7 Cut a strip of fabric for the back skirt that is the length of the back of the seat plus 8⅝ in. x 6¼ in./22 cm x 16 cm. Matching centers, pin and baste the back skirt to the back edge of the seat with the right sides facing, with the ends of the back skirt extending beyond the faced corners. Stitch the ends of the back skirt and along the back edge of the seat. Neaten the seat seam with pinking shears or a zigzag stitch. Clip the corners, turn right-side out, and press the seat seam toward the skirt. Press the facings to the underside. Baste the lower edges together.

STEP 8 Cut 2¼-in./5.5-cm-wide strips of velvet; join the strips if necessary to fit the lower edge of the skirts with ⅝ in./1.5 cm extending at each end. Resting the material on a towel so that the velvet is not flattened, press under ⅝ in./1 cm on one long edge of the strips. With the right side of the strips facing the wrong side of the skirts, stitch the long raw edges of the strips to the skirts, taking a ¼-in./5-mm seam allowance, with ⅝ in./1.5 cm extending beyond each end.

STEP 9 Fold the strips to the right side over the lower edge of the skirts. Turn in the raw ends and pin the long pressed edges to the skirts. Stitch close to the ends and long pressed edges. Work a pair of buttonholes ¾ in./2 cm in from the ends of the side skirts. Slip the cover on the chair and mark the position of the buttons under the buttonholes. Sew the buttons in place.

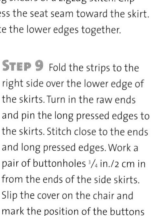

FAR RIGHT: **A skirted seat cover makes an attractive and colorful alternative to a chair cushion.**

PROJECT
Cube seat

A smart, fabric-covered foam cube is great for spare seating, and can double as a side table. Have a 18-in./46-cm square of foam cut to size professionally, and use medium-to-heavyweight fabric; avoid stretchy fabrics, since they will sag and the cover needs to be taut.

A cube seat is useful to provide additional seating for guests and will be popular with children.

HOW TO DO IT

The fabric for covering the base does not have to match the main fabric, because it will not be seen, but it should be hardwearing. A neutral-colored, textured fabric has been used here, in contrast to the straight lines of the cube. Take a ⅝-in./1.5-cm seam allowance throughout. If you want to use the cube permanently as a side table, place an 18-in./46-cm square of hardboard inside to rest on top of the foam, then slip the cover on top.

STEP 1 Cut a 19¼-in./49-cm square of fabric for the top, and four rectangles 19⅝ in./50 cm square for the side panels. With right sides facing, stitch the side panels together along the long edges, starting ⅝ in. /1.5 cm below the upper edge. Press the seams open.

STEP 2 With the right sides facing, stitch the sides to the base, matching the seams to the corners. Pivot the fabric at the corners, then clip the corners. Press the seam toward the side panels.

STEP 3 Cut a 18⅜-in./47-cm square of fabric to cover the base. Press ⅝ in./1.5 cm under on the outer edges.

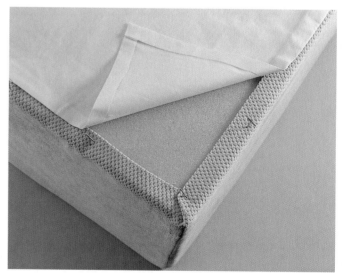

STEP 4 Slip the cover over the foam, positioning the seams at the edges. Pin the raw edges to the base of the foam with upholstery T-pins, folding under the fullness at the corners. Pin the base cover centrally on top. Slipstitch to the base with a double length of thread.

YOU WILL NEED:

- FABRIC FOR CHAIR
- FABRIC FOR TIE (SEE DIAGRAM PAGE 866)
- PINS
- SCISSORS
- TAPE MEASURE
- TAILOR'S CHALK
- IRON
- PINKING SHEARS
- NEEDLE AND THREAD/SEWING MACHINE
- PAPER

PROJECT
Tailored dining-chair cover

A set of good-quality chairs is an important furniture investment. If you want to ring the changes but avoid spending on new seating, make smart covers for a set of chairs that you have already; or a cover for a single chair that has become shabby or needs updating.

As long as your dining chair is solid, a tailored chair cover can hide a multitude of sins and give a completely new look to old furniture.

HOW TO DO IT

STEP 1 Cut a rectangle of fabric for the inner back that is the height of the inner back plus the depth of the back plus 2 in./5 cm by the width of the inner back plus twice the depth of the back plus 2 in. /5 cm. Cut a rectangle of fabric for the seat that is the seat depth plus 2 in./5 cm by the seat width plus 2 in./5 cm. Matching the centers and with the right sides facing, pin the lower edge of the inner back to the back edge of the seat, taking a 1-in./2.5-cm seam allowance.

STEP 2 With the wrong sides facing outward, place the inner back and seat on the chair. Fold the corners of the upper edge of the inner back diagonally with the right sides facing. Pin the fabric neatly along the corners of the chair.

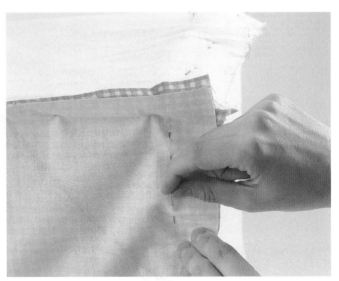

STEP 3 For the front skirt, cut a square or rectangle of fabric that is the front width plus 2 in./5 cm by the seat height plus 2¹⁄₂ in./6.3 cm. With the right sides facing, pin the front skirt to the front edge of the seat.

STEP 4 Cut two squares or rectangles of fabric for the side skirts of the cover that are the side-width measurement plus 2 in./5 cm by the seat height plus 2¹⁄₂ in./6.3 cm. With the right sides of the side skirts facing, pin the side skirts to the side edges of the seat. Snip the seam allowance on the inner back so it lies smoothly around the depth of the back, and pin the side skirts to the inner back. Pin the side edges of the side skirts and front skirt together.

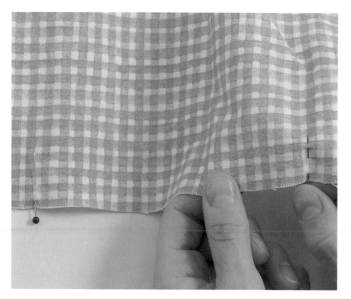

STEP 5 For the outer back, cut a rectangle of fabric that is the outer back height plus 2¹/₂ in./6.3 cm by the back width plus 14¹/₂ in. /37 cm. Mark the top and lower edge with pins at the center and 6¹/₄ in./16 cm each side of the center for the pleat.

STEP 6 With the right side facing up, bring the outer pins to the center of the fabric to form an inverted pleat. Press the pleat and baste across the upper edge.

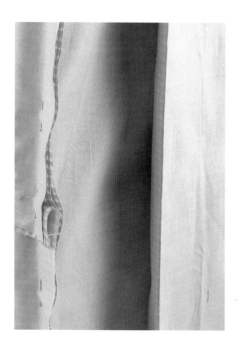

STEP 7 With the wrong side facing outward, pin the outer back to the inner back and side skirts, repinning the fit where necessary. Use tailor's chalk carefully to mark all the seam lines where they are pinned and where the seams intersect.

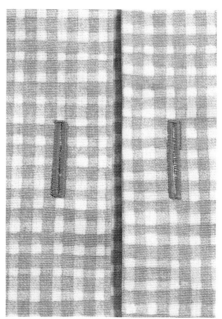

STEP 8 Mark the position on the pleat where you would like the tie fastening to be. Unpin the outer back and skirts. On the right side of the back, work a 1-in. /2.5-cm-long buttonhole ³/₄ in./2 cm in from the pressed edges of the pleat at the tie position on both edges of the pleat where they meet.

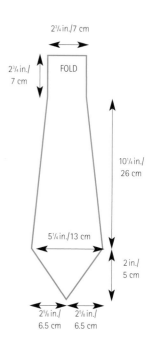

2³/₄ in./7 cm

2³/₄ in./ 7 cm

FOLD

10¹/₄ in./ 26 cm

5¹/₄ in./13 cm

2 in./ 5 cm

2⁵/₈ in./ 6.5 cm   2⁵/₈ in./ 6.5 cm

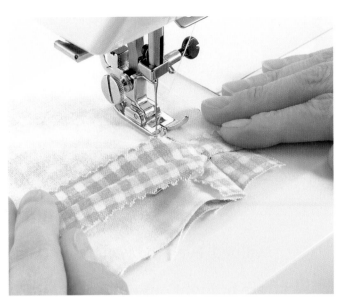

STEP 9 With the right sides facing, stitch the corner seams of the inner back as far as the outer back intersections. Again with the right sides facing, pin and stitch the inner back to the seat, starting and finishing at the side intersections. After stitching each seam, check the fit and trim the seam allowance to ⅝ in./1.5 cm with pinking shears. Press the seams open.

STEP 10 With the right sides facing, stitch the front skirt between the side skirts, starting at the seat intersections. Stitch the skirts to the inner back and seat, pivoting the seam at the front corners of the seat.

STEP 11 Pin and stitch the outer back to the inner back and side skirts, pivoting the seam at the upper corners. Slip the cover onto the chair and pin up the hem. Remove the cover and trim the hem to 1¼ in./3 cm. Press ⅜ in. /1 cm under, then ¾ in./2 cm on the lower edge, and stitch close to the inner pressed edge. Re-press the pleat at the lower edge.

STEP 12 Refer to the diagram to make a pattern from paper for the tie (see page 866). Cut the tie from fabric. Fold lengthwise in half with the right sides facing. Stitch the outer edges, taking a ⅜-in./1-cm seam allowance and leaving an opening to turn. Clip the corners and turn right-side out. Press, then slipstitch the opening closed. Insert the tie through the buttonholes and tie together.

Top tables

Historically, beautiful table linen has been highly valued. Even today, handworked pieces are considered heirlooms and are brought out only for special occasions. The style of table linen you choose will enhance the presentation of the food. Cozy, romantic dinners for two and full-blown formal dinner parties will both benefit from an ambient setting created by the table dressing. The making of tablecloths and napkins is so simple that time can be lavished upon their decoration. Alternatively, their simplicity means that, when made from easy-care fabrics, they can also be hardwearing and used daily. On a practical level, a tablecloth and table mats will help to protect the table from wear and tear and hot plates, or will hide an old, scruffy table. A table runner is a great way of accessorizing an attractive table, and also offers some protection to the table.

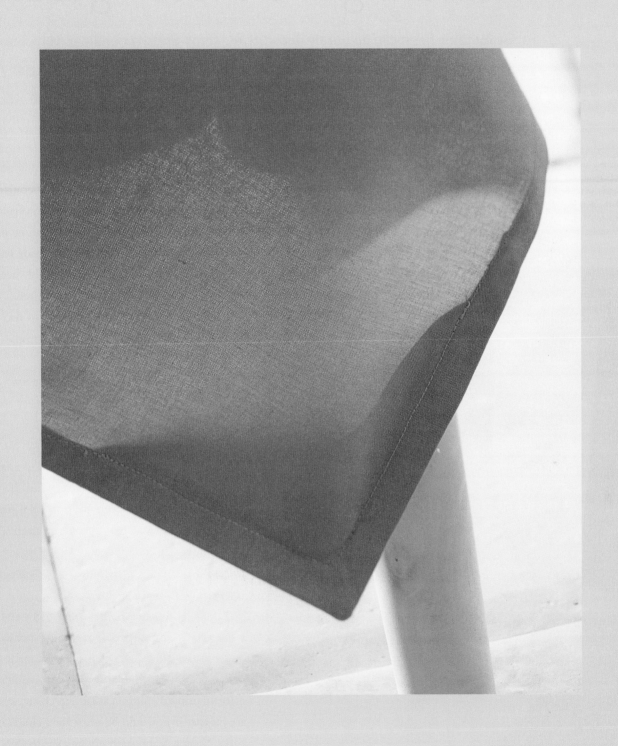

Measuring and choosing fabrics

Fabric for table linen can be purely decorative—think of rich chenille or velvet on a small side table crammed with precious ornaments—or very practical, especially if it is to be used in the kitchen or on the patio. Table linen is immensely versatile, too, and you can really let your creativity shine through.

Warm, earthy reds are said to stimulate the appetite, so they are perfect colors for a cloth to set off a kitchen table.

Choosing fabrics

Unless the cloth is to be purely decorative, fabric for tablecloths and napkins must be washable and should ideally be of a good width, although

fabric can be joined if necessary. Sheeting is a very practical choice for a large table because it is washable, inexpensive, and available in very wide widths. Special-occasion table linen can be made from furnishing fabric that comes in wide widths, but do bear in mind that it will probably need to be dry-cleaned, which may not be entirely practical. Make sure that any trimmings you choose have the same washing instructions as the fabric.

Vinyl-coated fabrics are great to use for kitchen and patio tablecloths because they are water-resistant, wipe-clean, and do not need to be hemmed because the fabric does not fray. Simply cut to size and they are ready to use. Cut a fancy scallop or zigzag edge for a touch of fun. If you want to be able to see the table but feel it needs a covering to soften its lines, make the cloth from a soft, transparent fabric such as voile. Organza is too stiff to drape over the sides of the table, but can be used to make a runner.

Patchwork works well on table linens and it is less time-consuming than creating patchwork for bedcovers and quilts. A patchwork made of handkerchiefs is very effective; one made of colorful printed children's handkerchiefs, which are inexpensive, would be great for a child's party. Neaten seams with pinking shears or a zigzag stitch, or back the patchwork with a lining. Handkerchiefs are already hemmed, so do not need neatening. Use flat seams throughout and bind the tablecloth edges.

Fabric alone will not totally protect the table from hot plates and serving dishes. Cut a piece of heat-resistant fabric, such as an old blanket or heat-resistant rubberized cotton, which is available at furnishing-fabric stores, to the size of the table top and lay it under the cloth.

Measuring up

If you already have a tablecloth the correct size, measure its length and width and add a 1-in./2.5-cm hem on square and rectangular cloths, and a ¾-in./2-cm hem on round cloths. Omit the hem allowance if the edges will be bound. If starting from scratch, measure the length and width of the table top, then the required drop. From the top of the table to the seat of a surrounding chair is a good drop for a cloth that will be sat at frequently. A decorative cloth can be floor-length or longer if it is a soft, lightweight fabric that you would like to drape onto the floor.

Decorating table linen

The large, flat expense of a tablecloth is the ideal medium for all sorts of needlework and fabric crafts such as embroidery and appliqué. There is a large range of fabric paints and pens available that are hardwearing and washable. Painting fabrics is good fun, and professional results can be achieved by stenciling and stamping onto fabric. Silk painting is popular and can be applied to runners or tablecloths for special occasions. Tie-dye takes on a modern slant when applied to silk, and lovely marbled effects can be created.

Before you embark on any embellishments, lay the cloth over the table and consider what will be placed on it. If it is to be used for meals, avoid positioning your design around the edges of the table top, where it will be hidden under plates and cutlery. Similarly, avoid the lower edges of the cloth if chairs are placed around the table and will obscure the design. A table runner

or tablecloth for show only can have delicate decoration, because it will not suffer a lot of wear and will not need to be laundered often. Fine embroidery using metallic threads, cutwork, and beading can be lavished on this sort of display. Work the design around items that will be placed on the table. Surround ornaments with an embroidered or beaded circular border on a round table top to isolate them and show them at their best. If displaying a particular collection, add a personal touch by stenciling or embroidering motifs to match the theme of the collectibles.

Floor-length tablecloths create a dramatic setting for special occasions and white sets off dining ware in a formal style.

YOU WILL NEED:
MITERED HEM:
- **TABLECLOTH**
- **IRON**
- **SCISSORS**
- **NEEDLE AND THREAD**
- **TAPE MEASURE**

PROJECT
Square and oblong tablecloths

A square or rectangular tablecloth is the easiest of soft-furnishing projects, and is a fast and simple way to coordinate a room and disguise an unsightly table: it can also be used for dining purposes. It can be made to any size you need and in any fabric and colorway.

Decide upon the finish that the tablecloth is to have. The simplest method is to hem all the edges. Ribbon, braid, or fringing can then be added to the hemmed edges. If you prefer, the cloth can be bound in a contrasting color. The binding can be narrow and subtle, or deep for a more dramatic effect. A lace edging adds a very pretty touch and is a good way of reusing an antique lace edging if its original tablecloth is very worn or stained. A small, square tablecloth looks good on top of a long circular cloth, or alone on a side table. It should hang at least 4 in./10 cm down the sides of the table. A tassel sewn to each corner is an exotic finishing touch.

Avoid a center seam if the fabric needs to be joined: it would be noticeable and could unbalance the crockery. Have the entire width of fabric across the table and a half to full width at each side. Join the widths with flat felled seams, taking a ⅝-in./1.5-cm seam allowance. Remember to allow extra fabric for matching patterns. If the fabric is just a little narrower than needed, make a feature of this by having a contrasting band of fabric at each end.

Remember that fabrics that have other purposes can also be used for tablecloths. A throw or sumptuous bedcover that no longer suits the bedroom can be cut to size to use as a tablecloth; avoid fluffy fabrics, because the fibers may get into the food. Drapes and saris can also be adapted. Create a stylish and understated tablecloth with a few remnants of coordinating dress fabrics joined edge to edge with flat felled seams.

MAKING A MITERED HEM

STEP 1 Add a 1-in./2.5-cm hem to each side of the tablecloth when cutting out. Press ³/₈ in./1 cm under, then ⁵/₈ in./1.5 cm on the edges. Open out the fabric at the corners and cut diagonally across the allowance ¼ in./6 mm from the corner.

STEP 2 Turn the diagonal edge under. Refold the hem. The diagonally folded edges should meet edge to edge.

STEP 3 Slipstitch the mitered edges together, then stitch close to the inner edges of the entire hem.

MAKING A KNOTTED FRINGED EDGE

STEP 1 Use a loosely woven fabric for this effect. Cut out the tablecloth very carefully along the grain lines. Use a long needle gently to pull away the threads along one edge, working on one thread at a time. Continue until it is at least 3 in./7.5 cm deep; repeat around the cloth.

STEP 2 Divide the strands into sections ⅝ in./1.5 cm wide and mark the divisions with pins. Knot each section together just below the cloth.

MAKING A LACE BORDER

Add a 2-in./5-cm hem to all edges if using antique lace, which is weighty and will need a deep hem for support. Otherwise, add a 1-in./2.5-cm hem on all edges.

Stitch a mitered hem as described opposite. Press the tablecloth and lay it out flat. Place the lace edging around it, overlapping the lace at the corners and, if possible, matching the lace design at the overlaps. Tack the lace edge-to-edge to the tablecloth and at the overlaps. Stitch in place with a shallow zigzag stitch or slipstitch. Cut away the excess lace where it overlaps.

MAKING ROUNDED CORNERS

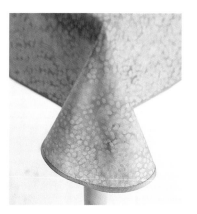

The easiest way to bind the edges of a square or rectangular tablecloth is to round the corners so that the circumference can be bound in one go, rather than mitering the binding at the corners. (See pages 188–189 for mitering binding.) Cut out the tablecloth without adding any allowances to the edges. Place a plate on one corner and draw around it at the corner with tailor's chalk or an air-erasable pen. Cut out, then bind the edges.

YOU WILL NEED:

KNOTTED FRINGE
EDGE:
- **TABLECLOTH**
- **LONG NEEDLE**
- **SCISSORS**
- **TAPE MEASURE**
- **PINS**

LACE BORDER:
- **TABLECLOTH**
- **SCISSORS**
- **PINS**
- **NEEDLE AND THREAD**
- **IRON**
- **LACE EDGING**

ROUNDED CORNERS:
- **PLATE**
- **TAILOR'S CHALK/AIR-ERASABLE PEN**
- **SCISSORS**
- **NEEDLE AND THREAD**

YOU WILL NEED:
- TAPE MEASURE
- FABRIC
- PAPER AND PENCIL
- STRING
- THUMBTACK
- SCISSORS
- BIAS BINDING
- NEEDLE AND THREAD/SEWING MACHINE
- PINS
- IRON
- BORDER FABRIC (IF REQUIRED)

PROJECT
Round tablecloths

Round and oval tablecloths are very attractive and emphasize the curved shape of a table. The best ways to finish the edges are to bind them or have a hem faced with bias binding (see page 789 for binding the edge). The cloth can have a turned-under hem, but avoid this if the tablecloth is small and of thick fabric, because it will be too bulky.

Joining widths

The fabric may need to be joined to make a large tablecloth. Cut the fabric the diameter of the tablecloth plus allowances. If using two widths of fabric, cut one width lengthwise in half. Stitch the widths together with the half widths each side of the complete width using flat felled seams, taking a ⅝-in./1.5-cm seam allowance.

Trim an equal amount from each side edge of the tablecloth to make the entire width the tablecloth diameter plus allowances. Fold into fourths and cut out the circle.

Oval tablecloths

To make a pattern for an oval tablecloth, place a large piece of paper on the table and weight it in the center. You may find that you need to join more than one piece of paper to reach the right size for a large table. Fold the paper over the edges of the table. Remove the paper and draw along the fold. Add the drop and any allowances to the circumference, then cut out to use as a pattern. The edges of an oval tablecloth can be finished using any of the methods used on a round cloth.

MAKING A FACED HEM

Open out the narrow folded edge of a length of ½-in./1.2-cm-wide bias binding. Cut the end diagonally and turn it under. With right sides facing, pin the opened-out edge to the tablecloth, matching the raw edges. Stitch along the crease line, cut the other end of the binding diagonally, and overlap the ends. Press the binding to the underside and slipstitch in place.

MAKING A PLAIN HEM

The raw edges will need to be eased so that they lie flat. Pin up the hem. Baste close to the folded edge—machine-baste rather than baste by hand (just set the machine to the longest stitch). Machine-baste ¼ in./6 mm from the raw edge, stitching through the hem only. Gently draw up the last row of stitching so the hem lies flat. Press, then turn the raw edge under along the eased basting and machine-stitch in place. Remove the first row of basting.

CUTTING OUT A ROUND TABLECLOTH

STEP 1 Measure the diameter of the table and the drop required for the cloth. Add twice the drop to the diameter plus 1½ in./3.8 cm for a hem. Add a ½-in./1.2-cm allowance on a faced hem. No allowance is needed on a bound edge. Cut a square of fabric to the cutting measurements and fold it into fourths. Cut a square of paper to the size of the folded fabric to make a pattern.

STEP 2 Tie a length of fine string to a thumbtack and fix it to one corner of the paper. Tie the other end around a pencil, holding the pencil upright on the next corner. Draw a quarter circle and cut out along the curved line.

STEP 3 Pin the pattern to the fabric, matching the corner of the pattern to the folded corner of the fabric. Cut out the tablecloth. Finish the hems according to previous directions.

MAKING A DEEP BORDER

A deep, luxurious border on a round tablecloth really shows off the curved shape and is a good way of combining contrasting fabrics, maybe to link different colors used in a room.

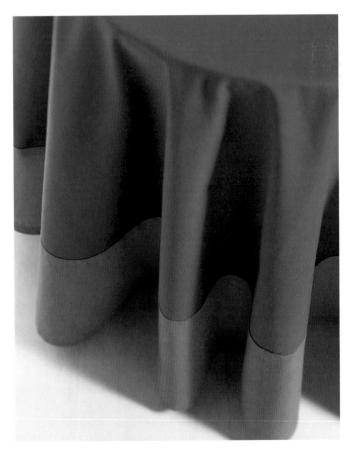

STEP 1 Measure the diameter and drop of the tablecloth. Cut a square of paper, the sides measuring the radius and drop of the cloth. Follow step 2 of cutting out a round tablecloth to draw a pattern. Decide how deep you would like the border to be and draw it with the string and pencil tool compass. Cut out the sections.

STEP 2 Using the pattern, add a ⅝-in./1.5-cm seam allowance on the curved edge of the tablecloth and inner edge of the border and ends of the border. Add a ¼-in./ 6-mm seam allowance on the outer edge of the border.

STEP 3 Cut out the pattern, fold the fabric into fourths to cut the tablecloth, and cut four borders. Join the borders with flat felled seams and press them open. Stitch to the tablecloth, then neaten seams with a zigzag stitch. Make a faced hem on the border.

YOU WILL NEED:

CORNER POCKETS:

- TABLECLOTH
- FABRIC FOR POCKETS
- SCISSORS
- NEEDLE AND THREAD/SEWING MACHINE
- IRON
- PEBBLES/WEIGHTS

PATCH POCKETS:

- TABLECLOTH
- FABRIC FOR POCKETS
- SCISSORS
- PINS
- NEEDLE AND THREAD
- TAPE MEASURE
- SEWING MACHINE WITH ZIPPER OR PIPING FOOT
- IRON
- CURTAIN CHAIN AS WEIGHT

PROJECT

Patio tablecloths

Hardwearing, easy-care fabrics are an absolute must for table linen that will frequently be used out of doors. Vinyl is the obvious practical choice for alfresco eating and a

square cut with pinking shears does not fray. A robust washable fabric will work well, too, since the tablecloth is likely to suffer food, grass, and mud stains.

Tablecloth weights

Blustery weather can spoil eating outside, because a sudden breeze can make the tablecloth start to lift off! Weighting down the cloth will anchor it in place. Ready-made clip-on weights can be attached to the corners and removed for washing, or you could add discreet pockets to the corners on the underside to conceal weights. A practical alternative is to make a tablecloth with patch pockets attached that can hold cutlery and napkins and be weighted to keep it in situ. These can be added to an existing tablecloth.

TABLECLOTH WITH CORNER POCKETS

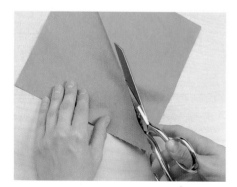

STEP 1 Cut out the tablecloth, adding a ³/₄-in./2-cm hem on all edges. Cut two 9¹/₂-in./24-cm squares of fabric. Fold the squares diagonally in half and cut along the folds to give four triangular pockets. Press ³/₈ in./ 1 cm under, then ⁵/₈ in./1.5 cm on the diagonal edges and stitch close to the inner edge. Take care not to stretch the fabric.

STEP 2 With the right sides facing and matching the raw edges and corners, stitch each triangle to a corner of the tablecloth, taking a ³/₄-in./2-cm seam allowance. Clip the corners, then turn right-side out and press.

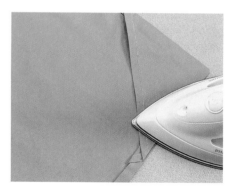

STEP 3 Press ¹/₄ in./5 mm under, then ⁵/₈ in./ 1.5 cm on the remaining edges of the tablecloth. Stitch close to the inner pressed edges, continuing the stitching along the straight edges of the pockets. Slip pebbles or curtain weights into the pockets to weight them down.

TABLECLOTH WITH PATCH POCKETS

Make a square or rectangular tablecloth (see pages 872–873). Slip the cloth onto the table and decide on the size of the patch pockets. They will be at two opposite ends of the cloth; if the table is rectangular, they should be at the short ends. Bear in mind what you are likely to put in the pockets and leave 1 in./2.5 cm at the lower edge for the weights. The pockets on this tablecloth are 8¼ in./21 cm wide and 10½ in./27 cm deep. Add ⅝ in./1.5 cm to the side and lower edges of the pocket and 1¼ in./3 cm to the upper edge and then cut out.

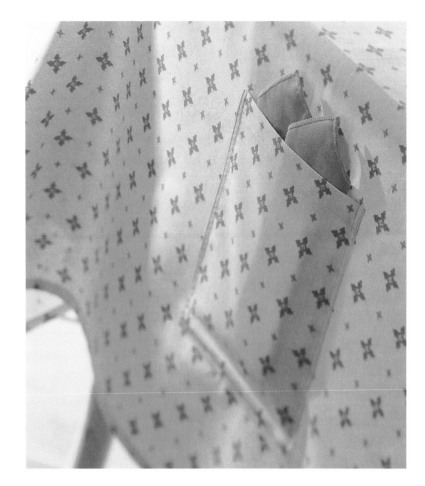

STEP 1 Press under ⅜ in./1 cm then ¾ in./2 cm on the upper edge of the pockets. Stitch close to the inner pressed edge. Press under ⅝ in./1.5 cm on the side and lower edges.

STEP 2 Pin the pockets to opposite ends of the cloth 7in./ 18 cm above the lower edge. Stitch close to the side and lower edges, then ¼ in./5 mm inside the first line of stitching.

STEP 3 Measure the distance between the inner rows of stitching on the side edges of the pocket. Cut a length of curtain chain weight three times the length of the measurement. Fold into thirds and drop to lie along the bottom of the pocket. Catch the chains in place with a few stitches at each end.

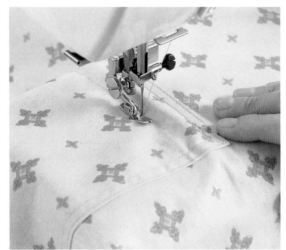

STEP 4 With a zipper or piping foot, stitch across the pockets, 1 in./2.5 cm above the lower edge, enclosing the weights.

YOU WILL NEED:

PATCH POCKETS:

- **TABLECLOTH**
- **FABRIC FOR POCKETS**
- **SCISSORS**
- **PINS**
- **NEEDLE AND THREAD**
- **TAPE MEASURE**
- **SEWING MACHINE WITH ZIPPER OR PIPING FOOT**
- **IRON**
- **CURTAIN CHAIN AS WEIGHT**

YOU WILL NEED:
- PAPER PATTERN
- TAPE MEASURE
- FABRIC FOR TOP AND SKIRT
- SCISSORS
- NEEDLE AND THREAD/SEWING MACHINE
- PINS
- IRON

PROJECT
Fitted tablecloth

Give a table a smart streamlined look with a fitted cover: this is especially effective on a small display table. Fitted cloths suit round tables particularly well. It's best to avoid heavyweight fabrics for this project because they will look bulky and inelegant. A piece of glass can be cut to fit the table top and so protect the fabric surface from dust.

Gathered skirt

A gathered skirt is cut in the same way as a pleated skirt, but just gather the upper edge instead of pleating it. If you are making a cover for a square or rectangular table, snip the skirt where it meets the corners of the cover top so it lies smoothly.

Fitted overcloth

A shallow fitted overcloth can be made to go over an ordinary tablecloth. This looks very effective, especially when made in contrasting firm fabric over a floaty fabric tablecloth. Cut out the cover top as above, then cut the skirt the circumference measurement plus 1½ in./3.8 cm by the drop plus 1⅝ in./4 cm. Taking a ⅝-in./1.5-cm seam allowance, join the ends of the skirt, then stitch the skirt to the cover top. Hem the lower edge.

If you prefer a shaped hem, cut two skirts and join the ends to form two rings. With the right sides facing, stitch together along the lower edges in scallops or zigzags. Trim the seam allowance and turn right-side out. Baste the upper edges together and stitch to the cover top.

Fitted cloths particularly suit round tables. Cover with a piece of glass cut to the table top, or a fitted overcloth in a contrasting pattern.

MAKING A ROUND FITTED TABLECLOTH

Although any shape table can have a fitted cloth, they do particularly seem to suit round or oval tables. This cover has a pleated skirt, which can be gathered if you prefer. To make a pattern for the top, turn the table upside down and draw around it on paper, adding a ⅝-in./1.5-cm seam allowance to the circumference. Cut out the pattern. Measure the drop of the table cover. This can be floor-length, or if the fabric is soft and lightweight, you may prefer it to bunch up flamboyantly on the floor—allow extra length for this, but make sure the table is not placed so the excess fabric could trip anyone.

STEP 1 Cut the top from fabric. Measure the circumference of the table top. Cut the skirt twice this measurement plus 1¼ in./3 cm by the drop plus 1⅝ in./4 cm. Join widths of fabric with flat felled seams if necessary, adding seam allowances if this is the case. With the right sides facing, stitch the ends together with a flat felled seam, taking a ⅝-in./1.5-cm seam allowance.

STEP 2 Pin the upper edge into ½-in./1.2-cm-deep pleats 1 in./2.5 cm apart, all lying in the same direction.

STEP 3 With the right sides facing, pin the skirt to the top, adjusting the pleats if needed. Stitch in place, taking a ⅝-in./1.5-cm seam allowance. Turn right-side out and slip the cover over the table. Adjust the top seam allowance toward the skirt.

STEP 4 Check the length and turn up a double hem, then remove the cover and stitch the hem. Replace the cover on the table. Although the seam allowance may lie naturally on the table surface, adjust it toward the skirt so the top of the cover sits smoothly on the top of the table. Carefully press the top of the pleats if you wish.

YOU WILL NEED:
- TAPE MEASURE
- FABRIC FOR RUNNER
- FABRIC FOR LINING
- SCISSORS
- NEEDLE AND
  THREAD/SEWING
  MACHINE
- IRON
- BEADED FRINGE

PROJECT

Runners

Because they are used mainly for decorative purposes, table runners can give free rein to your creative ideas. Only a narrow length of fabric is needed, so you may find remnants of exotic and usually expensive fabric at a discounted price that would look fantastic and really brighten up a plain table.

A runner can extend over the edges of a table, or just lie on top if you prefer. Any fabric is suitable, depending upon the effect you wish to achieve, and because runners are small items, they can be changed, perhaps to mark the seasons or a festive occasion. The dining-room table or sideboard are obvious places to display a runner, but also consider one on a table or chest in a cool, tiled bathroom, which will help to make it homey. A runner would also make a good background to a display of perfume bottles in a bedroom.

Damaged or stained antique table linen can be salvaged and the unusable areas cut off and discarded, leaving a length of finely embroidered fabric that just needs hemming or the addition of a decorative ribbon or lace edging. A long silk, velvet, or chiffon scarf is an instant glamorous table runner.

A decorative runner is a fast way to suggest a theme in a room and to pull a distinctive look together. Hem a strip of rich brocade and add a tassel at each corner to offset an antique piece of furniture; it will also help to protect the surface if ornaments are displayed on top. The same technique can be used on a strip of pale organza, providing a totally different, contemporary look.

Fray a length of rustic hessian and fasten shells to the ends with thick linen thread to give a beachcomber effect. Glue or sew chunky cabochon jewelry stones at random along the edges of a hemmed length of vibrant silk for some quirky opulence, or sew feathers to a linen runner for display on a kitchen sideboard. On a practical level, use a runner to hide a nasty stain or dent on the surface of a table. A layer of curtain interlining or a strip cut from an old blanket, applied to the underside of a runner, offers some protection if hot plates are placed on top.

Table runners add a distinctive splash of style to everyday pieces of furniture. Since they're purely decorative, they offer an ideal opportunity to be as creative as you feel.

MAKING A BEAD-FRINGED RUNNER

Runners do not have to be rectangular: pointed ends look good when suspended over the ends of a table. A densely beaded fringe makes it extra special.

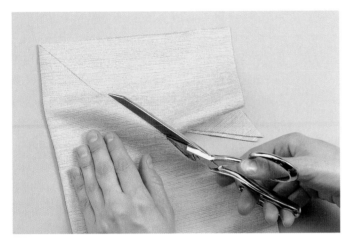

STEP 1 Decide upon the length of the runner. Cut a strip of fabric the length of the runner plus 1½ in. x 15in./4 cm x 38 cm. Fold one end lengthwise in half and cut to a point on the fold. Fold the pointed end on top of the opposite end and cut to match. Use the runner as a pattern to cut a matching runner from lightweight lining.

STEP 2 With the right sides facing, stitch the runners together, taking a ⅝-in./1.5-cm seam allowance and leaving a 6-in./15-cm gap for turning. Clip the corners and turn right-side out. Press and slipstitch the opening closed.

STEP 3 Pin the tape of a length of bead fringing under the pointed end, turning under the ends of the tape and folding neat miters at the corners. Oversew the tape to the underside of the runner. Repeat at the other end.

YOU WILL NEED:

CORDED HEM:

• TAPE MEASURE

• NAPKIN

• NEEDLE AND
  THREAD/SEWING
  MACHINE

• COLORED
  EMBROIDERY
  THREAD

• LARGE-EYED NEEDLE

• SCISSORS

• IRON

BOUND EDGE:

• TAPE MEASURE

• SCISSORS

• NAPKIN

• BIAS BINDING

• IRON

• NEEDLE AND
  THREAD/SEWING
  MACHINE

SCALLOPED EDGE:

• PAPER

• NAPKIN

• PAIR OF TOOL
  COMPASSES

• AIR-ERASABLE
  PEN/TAILOR'S CHALK

• PINS

• TAPE MEASURE

• STITCH-AND-TEAR
  INTERFACING

• NEEDLE AND
  THREAD/SEWING
  MACHINE

• SHARP SCISSORS

LACE EDGE:

• NAPKIN

• FLAT LACE EDGING

• PINS

• NEEDLE AND
  THREAD/SEWING
  MACHINE

• SCISSORS

• TAPE MEASURE

FRAYED EDGE:

• NAPKIN OF LOOSELY
  WOVEN FABRIC

• SCISSORS

• NEEDLE AND
  THREAD/SEWING
  MACHINE

PROJECT
Napkins

Napkins are the easiest items of table linen to make. Their small size is ideal for decorative finishes that would be too laborious to apply to anything larger, such as a tablecloth, so you can really let off your creative steam. Make napkins from absorbent easy-care fabrics that wash well and do not fade.

Most napkins are square and range in size from 12 in./30.5 cm for teatime napkins to 24 in./61 cm for dinner napkins: 16 in./40 cm is a size that suits both occasions. The napkin edges can be bound, hemmed, frayed, edged with lace or ribbon, or shaped with a zigzag satin stitch. Work any embroidery in one corner of the napkins before cutting out. Add ¾-in./2-cm hems for hemmed napkins. To round the corners and make binding the edges simpler, place an upturned glass on a corner and draw around it. Then cut out the curved shape and repeat on each corner.

CORDED HEM

STEP 1 Cut out the napkin including 1¼-in./3-cm hems. Press a ⅝-in./1.5-cm double hem on all edges. Set the sewing machine to a wide, open zigzag stitch. Starting halfway along one side, lay two lengths of contrast-colored stranded cotton embroidery thread ½ in./1.2 cm in from the edge. Starting about 3 in./7.5 cm from the ends of the embroidery threads, zigzag in place with the embroidery threads running along the center of the pressing foot. Pivot at the corners.

STEP 2 Before you reach the start of the stitching, use a large-eyed needle to take the embroidery threads to the underside, then continue zigzagging, overlapping the start of the stitching. Knot the embroidery thread ends together and insert the needle into the hem to lose the ends. Cut off the excess threads.

MAKING A STRAIGHT BOUND EDGE

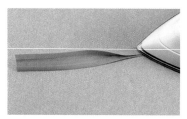

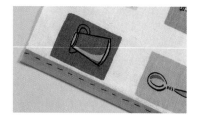

STEP 1 Cut out the napkin; no seam allowances are needed. Cut two lengths of 1-in./2.5-cm-wide bias binding the same length as the sides of the napkin and two lengths 1 in./2.5 cm longer than the sides of the napkin. Press the bindings lengthwise in half.

STEP 2 Slot one edge of the napkin into a shorter length of binding. Baste in place, sandwiching the napkin between the binding. Repeat on the opposite edge. Stitch close to the inner edges. Apply the longer bindings to the remaining edges in the same way, turning the ends under. Stitch close to the inner edges.

MAKING A SCALLOPED EDGE

STEP 1 For a 16-in./40-cm square napkin, cut a strip of paper for a template 16 in. x 1½ in./ 40 cm x 3.8 cm. Draw a line lengthwise along the center, and starting ¾ in./2 cm from one end, use a compass to describe a semicircle with a ¾-in./2-cm radius. Continue describing semicircles along the center line to form a row of eight scallops. Cut out the scallops.

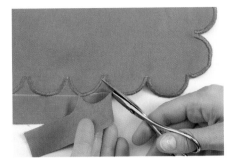

STEP 2 Cut a 18-in./45-cm square of fabric. Use an air-erasable pen or tailor's chalk to draw a 1-in./2.5-cm-deep margin around the outer edges. Butt the scalloped edge of the template up to the drawn line on one edge, and draw around the scallops with the air-erasable pen or tailor's chalk. Repeat on the other edges.

STEP 3 Cut four 18 in. x 2⅜ in./45 cm x 6 cm strips of stitch-and-tear interfacing, and pin them under the edges of the napkin to reinforce the stitching. Set the sewing machine to a wide, close zigzag stitch and thread the machine with machine embroidery thread. On the right side, work the zigzag stitch along the scalloped lines. Carefully tear away the interfacing. Use a small, sharp pair of scissors to trim away the excess fabric.

MAKING A LACE EDGE

Choose a flat lace edging about 1 in./2.5 cm wide. Neaten the raw edge of the lace with a zigzag stitch. Cut out the napkin with a ⅜-in./1-cm hem. Stitch a ¼-in./6-mm-deep double hem on all edges. Pin the straight edge of the lace under the hemmed edges, folding under the fullness at the corners in neat miters. Overlap the ends of the lace at a corner for neatness and cut off the excess lace. Stitch in place.

MAKING A FRAYED EDGE

Cut the napkin to size from a loosely woven fabric, cutting carefully along the grain lines. Machine zigzag stitch 1 in./2.5 cm in from the edges. Pull out the threads as far as the stitching on all edges. Remove the threads one at a time to prevent tangling.

YOU WILL NEED:
- **FABRIC**
- **TAPE MEASURE**
- **CURTAIN LINING**
- **TAILOR'S CHALK**
- **CURVED BASTING PINS**
- **AIR-ERASABLE PEN**
- **GLASS**
- **PINS**
- **NEEDLE AND THREAD/SEWING MACHINE**
- **SCISSORS**
- **BIAS BINDING**

PROJECT
Table mats

Fabrics for table mats need to be durable and washable, especially if they are to be used daily. Mats made from sturdy, heavyweight fabrics will help protect the table, and a layer of curtain interlining will give added protection from heat and also slightly cushion the crockery.

Because only small amounts of fabric are needed, making a set of table mats is a good way of using up leftover tablecloth fabric. A table mat should be large enough to take a complete place setting: 19 in. x 14 in./48 cm x 35.5 cm is a standard size. For just a dinner plate, which is usually 10 in./25.5 cm in diameter, a 14 in. x 12 in./35.5 cm x 30.5 cm mat would be suitable, but measure your own dinner service, because the size may be different.

The easiest method of finishing a mat that has a layer of curtain interlining is to bind the edges with bias binding; there is no need to add a seam allowance. If you prefer to bag out the mat, add ⅝-in./1.5-cm seam allowances to all edges and

carefully trim away the interlining in the seam allowances after stitching, to reduce the bulk. Add a 1-in./2.5-cm hem to single-layer mats.

To fuse practicality with a decorative touch, make a center panel for the table mat from a hardwearing fabric, then add a strip of pretty fabric to the side edges—check that all the fabrics have compatible washing instructions. Either hem the outer edges or bag out the mat with a lining. For a quick and pretty look, hem a rectangle of linen and sew a row of pearl buttons along one side edge; linen can be washed at high temperatures.

Cut shaped mats from vinyl for children's mealtimes—a chunky car or teddy is popular, and the mats just need to be wiped clean after use. Alternatively, make a mat from fabric featuring their favorite cartoon character, and fix a layer of transparent plastic on top with a popper at each corner. The plastic can be wiped clean and removed when the fabric mat needs washing.

A good sturdy mat will protect your table from heat and damage. You can make a mat more attractive by adding decorative fabric to the side edges.

MAKING A BIAS-BOUND QUILTED TABLE MAT

Ready-quilted fabric is available from fabric departments and can be used for table mats, but it is very easy to quilt fabric yourself, which means that you have a wider choice of fabrics to use. Rounded corners are simple to bind.

STEP 1 To quilt the fabric yourself, cut two rectangles of fabric and one of curtain interlining for the front and back 19¾ in. x 14¾ in./50 cm x 38 cm. Sandwich the interlining between the fabric pieces, with the right sides facing outward.

STEP 2 Draw a grid of 2-in./5-cm squares with tailor's chalk on the top fabric. Pin the layers together using curved basting pins.

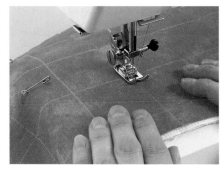

STEP 3 Starting at the center, stitch along the vertical drawn lines, stitching down one line, up the next, and so on. Turn the mat and stitch the horizontal lines in the same way. Cut the mat to 19 in. x 14 in./48 cm x 35 cm. To round the corners, place a glass upside down on one corner and draw around it with an air-erasable pen. Repeat on the other corners.

STEP 4 Open out the narrow edge of 1-in./2.5-cm-wide bias binding. Turn under one end diagonally and pin the binding to the outer mat edge with the right sides facing, taking a ¼-in./6-mm seam allowance. Overlap the binding ends, stitching along the fold line of the binding.

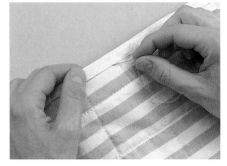

STEP 5 Clip the corners to reduce the bulk in the seam allowance. Turn the binding to the underside of the mat. Pin and slipstitch the binding in place.

Dressing table

YOU WILL NEED:

- PAPER FOR PATTERN
- FABRIC FOR TOP AND SKIRT
- LINING MATERIAL
- TAPE MEASURE
- SCISSORS
- PINS
- IRON
- NEEDLE AND THREAD/SEWING MACHINE
- CURTAIN TAPE
- CURTAIN HOOKS
- GLASS FOR TABLETOP

Most women and girls consider a dressing table to be an essential item in the bedroom. The classic kidney-shaped dressing table looks right in either a traditional or a retro-style bedroom, depending upon the fabric used.

Original dressing tables can be made over or bought plain and ready to be upholstered. They are usually made of chipboard and generally have a curtain rail under the table top. Alternatively, give a second-hand dressing table a make-over.

This kidney-shaped dressing table has a table-top cover and a skirt that is hooked onto the rail under the table top.

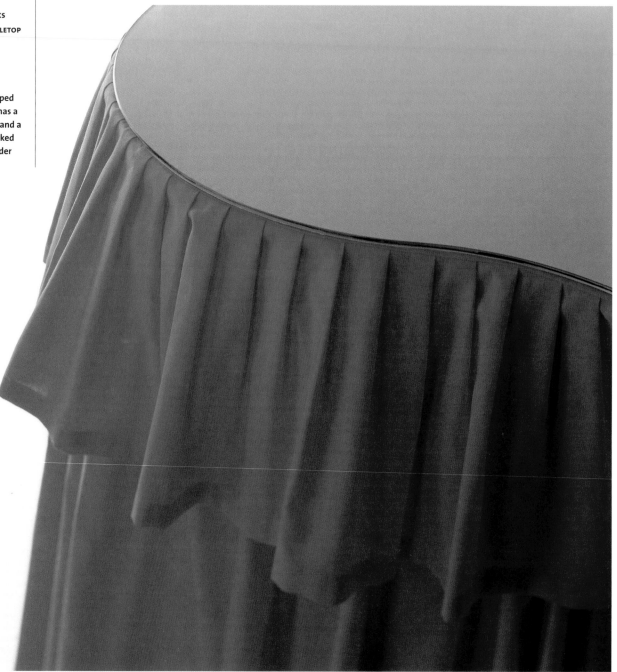

MAKING A DRESSING-TABLE COVER

Remove any original covering if you are re-covering an existing dressing table. Check the condition of the rail and replace it if necessary. This top has a deep-pleated frill over a gathered skirt, which has a front opening. Take a ⅝-in./1.5-cm seam allowance throughout.

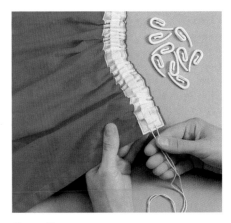

STEP 1 Make a pattern for the table top by turning it upside down and drawing around it on paper, adding the seam allowance. Use the pattern to cut the top from fabric, centering any pattern design if necessary. Cut one top from lining. (Inexpensive, lightweight cotton fabric would be suitable for the lining if you want to economize on the main fabric.)

STEP 2 Measure the circumference of the table top. Cut 10½-in./27-cm-wide strips of fabric for the top frill; the strips will be joined end to end and the finished length should be twice the top circumference. Add seam allowances for joining the strips. Join the strips end to end with flat felled seams to form a ring. Press under ⅜ in./1 cm, then ⅝ in./1.5 cm on one long edge. Stitch close to the inner pressed edge.

STEP 4 With right sides facing, pin and stitch the lining to the fabric top, sandwiching the frill: leave a 10-in./25-cm gap to turn through. Trim the seam allowance and snip the curves. Turn right-side out and slipstitch the opening closed.

STEP 5 Measure the drop of the skirt from the top of the rail to the floor. Cut widths of fabric for the skirt that are the drop of the skirt plus 2 in./5 cm. The widths will be joined to make one length of twice the top circumference plus a 1-in./2.5-cm hem at each end. Add ⅝-in./ 1.5-cm seam allowances for joining the widths. Join the widths with flat felled seams.

STEP 6 Press under ⅜ in./1 cm, then ⅝ in./ 1.5 cm on the ends and lower edge of the skirt. Slipstitch or machine-stitch close to the inner pressed edges. (See page 872 for how to make mitered corners.)

STEP 8 Pull up the cords to gather the fabric to fit around the table. Knot the free ends of the cords and adjust the gathers evenly. Slip curtain hooks through the slots in the tape, one at each end and at 3-in./7.5-cm intervals.

STEP 9 Hook the skirt onto the rail, positioning the opening edges at the front. Slip the fabric top onto the top of the table. Cut the seam allowance off the paper pattern for the top and take it to a glazier to use as a template to cut a piece of glass to fit the table top. Make sure that you have the edges beveled. Place the glass carefully on top of the dressing table.

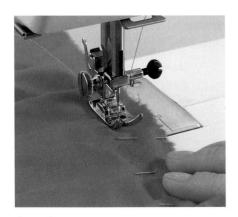

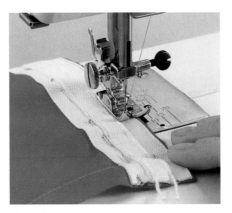

STEP 3 Pin the upper raw edge of the fabric into ½-in./1.2-cm-deep pleats 1 in./2.5 cm apart, all lying in the same direction. With the right sides facing, pin the frill to the top. Adjust the pleats if needed, and stitch in place.

STEP 7 Press the upper edge to the wrong side for 1 in./2.5 cm. Pin standard curtain tape along the upper edge, enclosing the raw edges. Turn under the ends of the tape and stitch close to the edges, without catching the cords.

YOU WILL NEED:
- FABRIC
- TAPE MEASURE
- SCISSORS
- NEEDLE AND THREAD/SEWING MACHINE
- PINS
- IRON

PROJECT
Bound-edge napkin

Make a set of napkins with crisp mitered borders to smarten the dinner table. The borders work well in a contrasting color, and could pick up the color scheme of your china or tablecloth. This napkin is 16 in./40 cm square, but you could make a larger one.

HOW TO DO IT

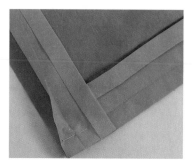

STEP 1 Cut a 16-in./40-cm square of fabric for the napkin, and two 32-in./ 80-cm-long, 3-in./7.5-cm-wide straight strips of fabric in a contrasting color for the binding. Join the lengths, taking a 1/4-in./6-mm seam allowance to make a continuous length. Press the seam open. Press the binding lengthwise in half with the wrong sides facing. Open out the binding and press the edges to meet at the center.

STEP 2 Open out the binding at one end and press 1/4 in./6 mm under. With the right sides facing and starting approximately 2 in./5 cm from one end, stitch the binding to one edge of the napkin, taking a 3/4-in./2-cm seam allowance stitching along the fold line, finishing 3/4 in./2 cm from the adjacent edge.

STEP 3 Pivot the binding to lie along the adjacent edge, folding the binding at a 45° angle from the corner. Mark the end of the previous stitching with a pin and stitch from this mark, finishing 3/4 in./2 cm from the next adjacent edge. Continue all the way around the napkin.

STEP 4 Press the binding outward from the napkin and turn it to the underside along the center fold line, then pin in place. Press along the miters with your finger. Slipstitch the pressed edges along the seams.

FAR RIGHT: **Using beautifully made napkins helps to turn a meal into a special occasion. The borders look good in a contrasting color.**

YOU WILL NEED:

- STRIP OF DUPION
  SILK FOR RUNNER
- STRIPS OF ORGANZA
  FOR BORDERS
- TAPE MEASURE
- AIR-ERASABLE PEN
- NEEDLE AND
  THREAD/SEWING
  MACHINE
- PINS
- SCISSORS
- PINKING SHEARS
- IRON

PROJECT
Tasseled table runner

Create an air of sophistication and impress your guests at a dinner party with an elegant silk table runner edged in organza.

A long silver tassel sewn to each point emphasizes the metallic threads in the organza and hangs elegantly off each end of the table.

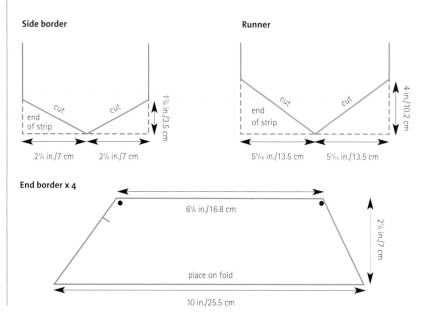

Side border

Runner

1³/₈ in./3.5 cm

4 in./10.2 cm

end of strip

cut   cut

end of strip

cut   cut

2³/₄ in./7 cm   2³/₄ in./7 cm

5⁵/₁₆ in./13.5 cm   5⁵/₁₆ in./13.5 cm

End border x 4

6⁵/₈ in./16.8 cm

2³/₄ in./7 cm

place on fold

10 in./25.5 cm

FAR RIGHT: **This table runner is made from dupion silk. The tassel adds a touch of extra elegance.**

TOP TIP
To avoid a noticeable ridge around the edge of the silk caused by pressing, first press the seam toward the runner, then run the tip of the iron around the edge of the runner under the seam allowance.

HOW TO DO IT

The runner is 3 ft. 11¼ in./1.2 m long. Take a ³/₈-in./1-cm seam allowance throughout.

STEP 1 Cut a strip of dupion silk 42½ in. x 10⅝ in./108 cm x 27 cm for the runner, and cut two strips of organza for the side borders 37³/₈ in. x 5½ in./95 cm x 14 cm. Refer to the diagrams above to cut the ends to points. Use the diagram to cut four end borders from organza.

STEP 2 Mark the dots onto the end borders with an air-erasable pen ³/₈ in./1 cm inside the corners. With right sides facing, stitch the end borders together in pairs along the notched ends between the dots. Trim the seam allowance to ¼ in./6 mm. Clip the corners and press the seams open. Finger-press the seams at points you cannot reach with the iron.

STEP 3 With the right sides facing, stitch the end borders between the side borders, inside the dots. Clip the corners and press the seams open. Trim the seam allowance to ¼ in./6 mm. Press the border in half with the wrong sides facing, matching the seams and raw edges. Baste the raw edges together.

STEP 4 With the right sides facing, pin the border to the runner, matching the seams to the corners. Stitch in place, pivoting the stitching at the dots. Neaten the seam with a zigzag stitch or pinking shears, and press the seam toward the runner. Sew a tassel to the pointed tips of the runner.

PROJECT
Fitted table cover

Put a shabby coffee table to new use by making a neat fitted cover—the deep pleats at the front make the interior accessible for storing books and other items. The top is edged with coordinating piping, either your own or ready-made. Use fabrics that hold their shape.

A fitted table is ideal for small tables that are not put to heavy day-to-day use.

HOW TO DO IT

Measure the width and depth of the table top, and measure the drop of the table. Use a flat felled seam if you need to join fabric for the skirt. Take ⅝-in./1.5-cm seam allowances throughout.

STEP 1 Cut a square or rectangle of fabric for the top that is the table width plus 1¼ in./3 cm by the depth plus 1¼ in./3 cm. Pin and baste piping to the outer edge on the right side, snipping the seam allowance of the piping at the corners. Join the piping on the back edge (see page 790).

STEP 2 For the back and sides skirt, cut a rectangle of fabric twice the table depth plus the width plus 8¼ in./21 cm by the drop plus 2⅜ in./6 cm. Cut a rectangle or square for the front skirt the table width plus 8¼ in./ 21 cm by the drop plus 2⅜ in./ 6 cm. To hem, press ¾ in./2 cm under then 1 in./2.5 cm on one long lower edge of the skirts. Stitch close to the inner pressed edges.

STEP 3 Stitch the front skirt to the back and sides skirt with French seams to form a continuous length. With the right side face up, mark both edges of the front skirt with a pin 3½ in./9 cm from one seam. Fold and press the front at the pin mark to lie flat on the side skirt. Baste across the upper edge and repeat on the other end of the front skirt.

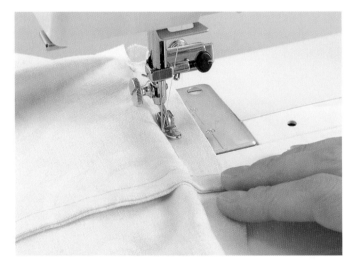

STEP 4 With the right sides facing, pin and baste the skirt to the top, matching the pleats to the front corners. Snip the skirts at the corners. Stitch in place using a zipper foot, pivoting the stitching at the corners. Clip the corners and neaten the seam with a zigzag stitch or pinking shears. Press the table cover, adjusting the top seam toward the skirt. Turn right-side out and slip the cover over the table.

YOU WILL NEED:

- FABRIC REMNANT
  FOR ROLL
- COTTON CHAMBRAY
  FOR LINING
- TAPE MEASURE
- BATTING
- GLASS (FOR CURVE)
- AIR-ERASABLE
  PEN/TAILOR'S CHALK
- IRON
- SCISSORS
- PINS
- NEEDLE AND
  THREAD/SEWING
  MACHINE
- BIAS STRIPS OF
  DENIM FOR STRAP,
  D-RING HOLDER,
  AND OUTER EDGES
- BODKIN
- D-RINGS
- BIAS-BINDING
  MAKER

PROJECT
Cutlery roll

Keep cutlery safely together in a padded cutlery roll. This simple roll is very practical and can be made to match a picnic hamper or tablecloth for use outside, or to keep in a beach bag for vacations. This is a great project for using up remnants of fabric.

This cutlery roll is made from a combination of fabrics and is very strong and practical. You will find it handy for travel, day-trips, and camping vacations.

HOW TO DO IT

A lightweight, pale-blue cotton chambray is used to line the cutlery roll, and the edges are bound with a deeper-blue denim. The front of the cutlery roll is made from a woven ikat fabric in toning colors, and the fabrics have the same laundering directions, which must be taken into consideration when combining different fabrics.

STEP 1 Cut one rectangle of fabric for the cutlery roll from the main fabric, lining, and 4 oz./113 g wadding 12 in. x 10¼ in./30 cm x 26 cm. Round off the corners by drawing around an upturned glass, and cut along the curved lines. Cut the pocket from the main fabric 12 in. x 5¼ in./30 cm x 13 cm.

STEP 2 Press ¼ in./6 mm under then ⅜ in./1 cm on one long edge of the pocket. Stitch close to the inner pressed edge. With the right sides face up, pin the pocket to the lower edge of the lining, matching the raw edges. Cut the pocket corners in a curve to match the lining.

STEP 3 To form the individual pockets, use an air-erasable pen or tailor's chalk to divide the pocket into fourths parallel with the short edges. Stitch along the divisions. Stitch back and forth a few times at the neatened edge of the pocket to reinforce. Sandwich the batting between the main fabric front and the lining, with the right sides facing outward. Now baste the outer edges together.

STEP 4 From denim, cut two 2-in./5-cm-wide bias strips, one 10 in./25.5 cm long for the strap, and one 3 in./7.5 cm long for the D-ring holder. Fold lengthwise in half with the right sides facing and stitch the long edges, taking a ¼-in./6-mm seam allowance. Press the seam open. Turn right side out with a bodkin and press. Turn in one end of the strap and slipstitch it closed. With the right sides uppermost, baste the raw end to the center of one short side of the front. Slip two ¾-in./2-cm D-rings onto the D-ring holder. Pin the raw ends together and baste on top of the strap.

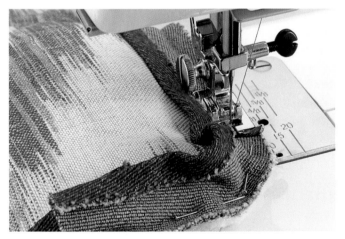

STEP 5 Cut a 1½-in./3.8-cm-wide bias strip of denim 43½ in./110 cm long, joining strips if necessary. Use a bias-binding maker to turn the raw edges under (see page 789). Open out one long edge and pin it to the outer edges of the cutlery roll, turning an end under to start and cutting off the excess. Stitch along the fold line. Turn the binding to the inside and slipstitch in place.

Storage solutions

There cannot be many people lucky enough not to have

a problem with storage. Lack of space, too many items, and a

tendency to hoard are all familiar problems. This chapter suggests

ingenious ways of making the most of neglected space around the

home, and of creating stylish containers that can store all sorts of

items and that you will be proud to display. Have a ruthless clear-out

before embarking on any of the storage projects—only then can you

see exactly what is needed and where it should be kept. Items not

constantly needed, such as spare bedding and seasonal clothing,

can be kept in fabric bags in less accessible areas, such as in

the attic or under the bed. Items that are used regularly can have

smart covers to keep off the dust, or can be kept in a

matching set of attractive bags.

PROJECT
Drawstring bag

Drawstring bags are fantastically useful, and if you make yourself a set in pretty toning colors, you'll wonder how you managed without them. They can be used in the bedroom to hold make-up and jewelry and in the bathroom for cotton absorbant balls and cotton swabs. They are essential for keeping children's rooms tidy, too!

Do not be deterred by the thought of drawstring bags! Although the concept is the same, they do not have to look like the dreary bags you used at school. They are very easy to make and can be custom-made to any size for

storing all sorts of things: a row of matching bags hung on a peg rail can be of practical use in the kitchen, a child's room, or a bathroom.

Line the bags with waterproof fabric, and they can be used as a washbag or beach bag. Jazz the bags up with trimmings such as fringing or bead edging, and they may even encourage an untidy teenager to tidy his or her belongings away. Mini-size bags made of velvet or silk can hold jewelry, and large bags made from ticking could be used to hold laundry. Choose light-to-mediumweight fabrics.

Drawstring bags keep clutter out of sight. Try making one in this pretty floral pattern for the bedroom or bathroom.

Trimming your bag

If you wish to embellish the bag, decorate the rectangles before making up. Create an understated, Swedish-style bag from gingham, using the checkered fabric as a guide for embroidering a cross-stitch heart or monogram on one rectangle.

Children can decorate their own bags. Cut the rectangles from calico, then supervise the children to create their own masterpieces on the fabric using fabric markers, which are like large felt-tip pens. Follow the manufacturer's directions to fix the drawings, then make up the bags.

To make a washbag, cut two rectangles of fabric 15½ in. x 10 in./39 cm x 25.5 cm and two of waterproof fabric 11¼ in. x 10 in./28 cm x 25.5 cm for the lining. Baste the lining to the wrong side of the fabric pieces matching the side and lower edges, then make up as described below.

HOW TO DO IT

This medium-size drawstring bag is very versatile and is a good size for storing footwear or clothing. Take a ⅝-in./1.5-cm seam allowance throughout, and simply change the dimensions of the rectangles to make a bag that will match your exact requirements.

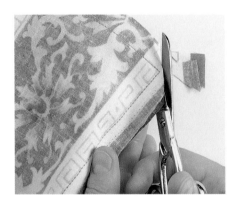

STEP 1 Cut two rectangles of fabric 24 ¾ in. x 15 in./63 cm x 38 cm. With the right sides facing, stitch the bags together along the long side edges and lower short edge, starting and finishing 5½ in./14 cm below the upper edges. Clip the corners.

STEP 2 Press the seam open, and press the side edges above the seam open. Neaten the seam with pinking shears. Press ⅝ in./1.5 cm under, then 2⅝ in./6.5 cm on the upper edges for the drawstring channels. Pin in place.

STEP 3 Stitch ¼ in./6 mm above the lower pressed edge, then 1¼ in./3 cm below the upper pressed edge to form the drawstring channels. Turn the bag right-side out.

STEP 4 Sew the end of an 31½-in./80-cm length of cord to a bodkin and thread through the channel from the left-hand side of the front channel and out of the right-hand side of the back channel. Repeat with another length of cord through the right-hand side of the front channel, emerging through the left-hand side of the back channel. Knot the cord ends together and adjust them so the knots are hidden in the channels.

YOU WILL NEED:
- TAPE MEASURE
- BASKET
- FABRIC FOR LINING BASKET
- BATTING
- SCISSORS
- BODKIN
- NEEDLE AND THREAD/SEWING MACHINE
- 8 BIAS STRIPS FOR TIE FASTENINGS
- IRON

PROJECT
Lined baskets

Baskets come in all shapes and sizes, and a complementary lining adds a nice touch, as well as giving protection to the contents. Linings can be attached to the baskets with ties threaded through the weave of the basket or tied around the handles. A lined basket is useful in lots of situations; take on picnics or on a shore vacation for towels or snacks.

A picnic basket can be lined with batting to give protection to delicate items.

LINING A SQUARE OR RECTANGULAR BASKET

Choose light-to-mediumweight fabrics, and use a straight-sided basket for the best results. This lining for a picnic basket is padded to give some protection to breakables. The tie fastenings can be in a contrasting color if you wish.

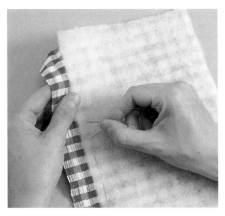

STEP 1 Measure the height of the inside of the basket, then measure the length of the sides at the top of the basket, again on the inside. Cut a strip of fabric for the side panel that is the length of the four sides plus 1¼ in./ 3 cm by the height measurement plus 2 in./ 5 cm. Cut a strip of 2-oz./56-g batting that is the length of the four sides plus 1¼ in./3 cm by the height measurement plus ⅝ in./1.5 cm. Baste the batting to the side panel 1 in./2.5 cm below the upper edge.

STEP 2 Cut one square or rectangle of fabric and 2-oz./56-g batting for the base that is the length of one side plus 1¼ in./3 cm by the length of an adjacent side plus 1¼ in./3 cm. Baste the fabric and batting base together along the outer edges.

STEP 3 With the right sides facing, stitch the short edges of the side panel together, taking a ⅝-in./1.5-cm seam allowance. Trim away the batting in the seam allowance. Press the seam open, taking care not to squash the batting flat. Press ⅜ in./1 cm under then 1 in./2.5 cm on the upper edge. Stitch close to the inner pressed edge.

STEP 6 Slip the lining into the basket and mark the position of the ties, such as one at each side of the corners. Remove the lining and match the center of each tie to the stitching line of the hem on the wrong side of the lining at the positions marked. Stitch back and forth a few times across the center of the tie to attach it securely.

STEP 4 With the right sides facing, pin the side panel to the base, taking a ⅝-in./1.5-cm seam allowance and snipping the panel at the corners so the fabric lies flat. Stitch in place, pivoting the seam at the corners. Trim away the batting in the seam allowance, and neatly clip the corners.

STEP 5 Cut eight bias strips of fabric for ties 18 in. x 1½ in./46 cm x 3.8 cm. Fold lengthwise in half with the right sides facing and stitch the long edges, taking a ¼-in./6-mm seam allowance. Turn right-side out with a bodkin. Turn in the ends and press flat. Slipstitch the ends closed.

LINING ROUND AND OVAL BASKETS

Make a paper pattern of the base by placing the paper inside the basket and tracing the base edges. Remove, and add a ⅝-in./1.5-cm seam allowance to the circumference.

Use the pattern to cut a base from fabric. On the inside, measure the circumference around the top of the basket and the height.

Cut a strip of fabric for the side panel: the circumference measurement plus 1¼ in./3 cm by the height measurement plus 2 in./5 cm. Join the ends, taking a ⅝-in./1.5-cm seam allowance. Stitch a 1½-in./3.8-cm hem at the upper edge. Gather the lower edge and stitch to the base. Attach four ties to the upper edge, either equidistant apart or at the handles.

YOU WILL NEED:

- LIGHTWEIGHT
  FABRIC FOR BOLSTER
- TAPE MEASURE
- PINS
- SCISSORS
- NEEDLE AND
  THREAD/SEWING
  MACHINE
- IRON
- PAPER
- PAIR OF TOOL
  COMPASSES
- PINKING SHEARS
- BODKIN
- CORD

PROJECT
Spare comforter bolster bag

Spare comforters often get packed away at the top of a linen closet where they can get musty. Sew a simple bolster bag to keep your spare bedding tidy and clean. It can be displayed and hung up on a rail, put away in a cupboard, or stowed neatly under the spare-room bed.

Extra bedding for overnight guests takes up a lot of space, considering that it is probably not used regularly. If you have little storage space, storing bedding in an attractive container lets it become part of the furniture, not be hidden away, thereby freeing valuable storage space for other items. A large bolster bag holds a spare comforter and can be used as a generous squashy cushion—fold the comforter in half, then roll it up and push it into the bolster. A drawstring top gives easy access.

The bolster design is very versatile, and there are endless variations to suit all occasions. Make it in luxurious fabric with a gold cord fastening to use in a living room, or in soft, faded floral print with ribbon drawstrings to match a feminine bedroom, where it could store vacation clothes or spare linens. It could alternatively be used as a laundry bag in the bathroom: make the bag from toweling, and instead of stitching a channel, fix metal eyelets to the upper edge to thread with cord. Made from a vibrant fabric, it could hold lots of toys; and made shallower, it becomes a handy beach bag for towels and lotions.

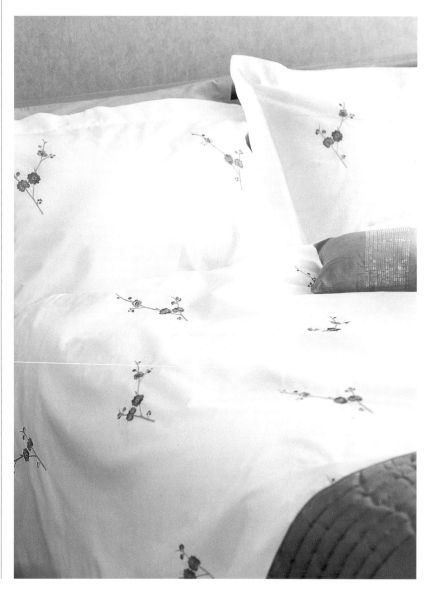

A pale-colored comforter like this one can be kept clean and dust-free in an easy-to-make bolster bag—this will make sure that it is fresh for the next visitor.

HOW TO DO IT

Make the bolster bag from light-to-mediumweight fabric, bearing in mind that lightweight fabrics are easier to draw up than thick fabrics. Take ⅝-in./1.5-cm seam allowances throughout.

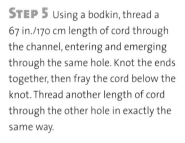

STEP 5 Using a bodkin, thread a 67 in./170 cm length of cord through the channel, entering and emerging through the same hole. Knot the ends together, then fray the cord below the knot. Thread another length of cord through the other hole in exactly the same way.

TOP TIP

If you wish to trim the bag with ribbon, stitch one bolster seam first. Stitch ribbons or braid in bands across the piece, then stitch the other seam.

STEP 1 Cut two rectangles of fabric for the bolster 50 in. x 26 in./127.5 cm x 66 cm. Pin the bolsters together along the long edges with the right sides facing, forming a tube. Stitch the side seams, leaving a 1-in./2.5-cm gap 2¼ in./5.6 cm below the upper edge for the drawstring channel.

STEP 4 With the right sides facing, pin and stitch the base to the bolster, matching the snipped notches and the notches to the seams. Neaten the seam with pinking shears or a zigzag stitch. Turn right-side out.

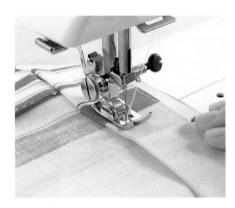

STEP 2 Press the seams open and neaten them with pinking shears or a zigzag stitch. Press ¾ in./2 cm under then 1½ in./3.8 cm on the upper edge for the drawstring channel, and pin in place. Stitch close to the upper edge, then 1 in./2.5 cm below the upper edge to form the channel.

STEP 3 To make a pattern for the base, use a pair of tool compasses to describe a 17 in./43 cm diameter circle on paper. Cut out the circle to use as a pattern to cut one base from fabric. Fold the base into fourths and snip into the circumference at the folds. Fold the lower edge of the bag in half and snip the fabric at the folds.

YOU WILL NEED:
- PAPER FOR PATTERN (SEE PAGE 906)
- FABRIC FOR COVER TO SUIT USE
- SCISSORS
- PINS
- NEEDLE AND THREAD
- SEWING MACHINE WITH ZIPPER FOOT
- CONTINUOUS LENGTH ZIPPER
- FABRIC FOR HANGING LOOP
- CLOTHES HANGER
- TAPE MEASURE
- IRON

PROJECT
Clothes covers

Clothes covers protect clothing from snagging on other items and keep them clean. Covers made in closely woven natural fabrics keep dust out but let the clothes breathe.

Plastic-coated fabrics are ideal for covers used for traveling, because they will protect against bad weather, but do not store clothes in them for very long periods.

MAKING A PLAIN CLOTHES COVER

This simple cover will hold a full-length outfit. A hanging loop at the lower edge can be slipped over the clothes hanger hook for carrying. Use a 43-in./1.1-m zipper that has been cut from a continuous length.

STEP 1 Refer to the diagram on page 906 to make a pattern for a cover on paper. Cut out the pattern and use it to cut two fronts and one back to the fold, from the fabric.

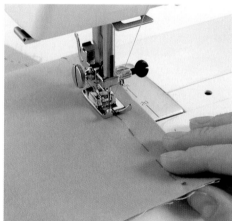

STEP 2 With right sides facing, baste the center front seam, taking a ⅝-in./1.5-cm seam allowance. Stitch the seam for ¾ in./2 cm at the upper end and 7 in./18 cm at the lower end, then press open.

TOP TIP

If you would prefer a shorter, basic-length plain cover, make the pattern to the suit-cover length and omit the hanging loop.

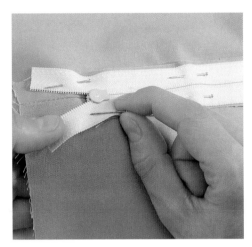

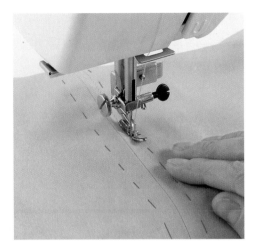

STEP 3 With the front lying face down and starting at the base of the zipper, place a 43-in./110-cm zipper face down centrally along the basted seam. Pin and baste the zipper in position. A zipper cut from a continuous length will be unfinished at the top, so open the top of the zipper a little and pin the top teeth under the seam allowances so the zipper does not slip off before stitching.

STEP 4 Using a zipper foot on the sewing machine and with the front right-side up, stitch the zipper in place ⁵⁄₁₆ in./8 mm from the basted seam and across the base end of the zipper. Continue the stitching to the upper edge of the fronts. Remove the basting stitches.

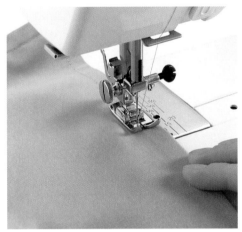

STEP 5 Cut a strip of fabric 6³⁄₄ in. x 2¹⁄₄ in./17 cm x 6 cm for the hanging loop. Press ³⁄₈ in./1 cm under along the long edges. Press the strip lengthwise in half and stitch close to both pressed edges. Pin and baste the ends 1¹⁄₄ in./3 cm each side of the center-front seam at the lower edge on the right side.

STEP 6 Open the zipper. Pin and stitch the front and back together with right sides facing, taking a ³⁄₈-in./1-cm seam allowance. Clip the corners and snip the curves, then turn right-side out and press. Topstitch ³⁄₈ in./1 cm from the outer edges.

YOU WILL NEED:

- PAPER FOR PATTERN
- FABRIC FOR COVER
  TO SUIT USE
- TAPE MEASURE
- SCISSORS
- PINS
- NEEDLE AND
  THREAD
- SEWING MACHINE
  WITH ZIPPER FOOT
- CONTINUOUS-
  LENGTH ZIP
- FABRIC FOR
  GUSSET
- PINKING SHEARS
- IRON

MAKING A GUSSETED SUIT COVER

This clothes cover has a generous gusset, making it deep enough to hold a suit or a few lightweight garments. Use a 38-in./96-cm zipper that has been cut from a continuous length.

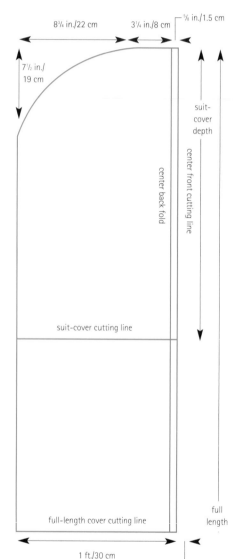

8¾ in./22 cm   3¼ in./8 cm   ⅝ in./1.5 cm

7½ in./
19 cm

suit-
cover
depth

center back fold

center front cutting line

suit-cover cutting line

full-length cover cutting line

full
length

1 ft./30 cm

⅝ in./1.5 cm

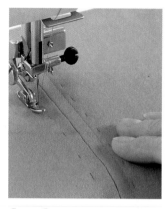

STEP 1 Refer to the diagram to make a pattern for a cover on paper. Cut out the pattern and use it to cut two fronts and one back to the fold from fabric. With the right sides facing, baste the center front seam, taking a ⅝-in./1.5-cm seam allowance. Stitch the seam for 1½ in./3.8 cm at each end and press the seam open.

STEP 2 With the front lying face down, place a 38-in./96-cm zipper centrally face down along the basted seam. Pin and baste the zipper in position, pinning the top teeth under the seam allowances so the zipper does not slip off before stitching. Using a zipper foot on the sewing machine and with the front right-side up, stitch the zipper in place ⁵⁄₁₆ in./8 mm from the basted seam and across the ends of the zipper. Remove the basting stitches.

STEP 3 Measure the outer edge of one half of the front, ⅜ in./1 cm in from the raw outer edges. Cut two 3¼-in./8-cm-wide strips of fabric for the gusset that are the front measurement plus 1 in./ 2.5 cm . With the right sides facing, stitch one end of the gussets together to make one long length, taking a ⅜-in./1-cm seam allowance. Neaten the seam with pinking shears and press open. Press ¼ in./6 mm under, then ⅜ in./1 cm on the raw ends, and stitch close to the inner pressed edges.

STEP 4 Pin and stitch the gusset to the front with the right sides facing, with the ends of the gusset meeting end-to-end at the top of the center front seam, taking a ⅜-in./1-cm seam allowance. Snip the gusset at the corners so the fabric lies smoothly. Stitch a few times over the top of the center-front seam to reinforce it.

STEP 5 Open the zipper, then pin and stitch the gusset to the back in the same way. Clip the corners and neaten the seams with a zigzag stitch or pinking shears. Turn right-side out.

PROJECT
Underbed case

The empty space under the bed is often neglected as a storage area, yet it is ideal for storing spare bed linen and out-of-season clothing. The items need to be concealed inside containers to protect them from dust: a slim fabric case with a deep gusset can hold many items. You will need two 39-in./1-m zippers.

HOW TO DO IT

STEP 1 Cut a strip of fabric for the base gusset 78 in. x 5¾ in./197 cm x 14.5 cm and a strip of fabric for the lid gusset 78 in. x 2¼ in./ 197 cm x 5.5 cm. Press ⅝ in./1.5 cm under on one long edge of both pieces, and mark the centers of the pressed edges with a pin.

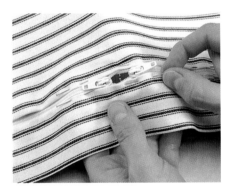

STEP 2 Pin two 39-in./1-m zippers under the pressed edges, with the top ends ⅜ in./1 cm each side of the center pins, positioning the pressed edges against the zipper teeth. Zippers cut from a continuous length will be unfinished at the top, so open the tops a little and pin the top teeth under the pressed edges so that they do not slip off before stitching. Using a zipper foot, stitch close to each side of the zipper.

STEP 3 Cut a strip of fabric for the back gusset 42¼ in. x 7 in./107 cm x 17.5 cm. With the right sides facing, stitch the ends of the zippered gussets to the ends of the back gusset, taking a ⅜-in./1-cm seam allowance, and starting and finishing the seams ⅜ in./ 1 cm from the long edges. Neaten the seams with pinking shears or a zigzag stitch. Press toward the back gusset.

STEP 4 Partly unzip the zippers to turn right-side out. Cut two rectangles of fabric 42¼ in. x 18½ in./107 cm x 47 cm for the lid and base. Open out the back seam at the top of the lid gusset. With the right sides facing, pin the back gusset to one long edge of the lid, then continue pinning the lid gusset to the lid. Snip the gusset at the front corners of the lid so the fabric lies smoothly. Stitch in place, taking a ⅜-in./1-cm seam allowance, and pivoting the seam at the corners. Stitch the base gusset to the base in the same way. Neaten the seams with pinking shears or a zigzag stitch. Turn right-side out.

YOU WILL NEED:

- CANVAS, CALICO, OR DENIM FABRIC FOR CADDY
- TAPE MEASURE
- PINS
- SCISSORS
- NEEDLE AND THREAD/SEWING MACHINE
- FABRIC FOR BINDINGS
- LENGTH OF STRIPWOOD
- IRON
- EYELETS

PROJECT
Shoe caddy

There is not always enough space to store shoes at the bottom of a closet and you might not have space for a shoe rack by the front door. A shoe caddy is a practical solution. It can be hung on a wall or the inside of the closet door. Make the caddy from a hardwearing fabric such as canvas, heavyweight calico, or mediumweight denim.

HOW TO DO IT

This caddy has pockets for twelve pairs of shoes. Metal eyelets are fixed to the upper corners so that the caddy can hang on hooks.

STEP 1 Cut three pocket strips from fabric 51 in. x 10⅝ in./1.3m x 27 cm. Press ⅜ in./1 cm, then ⅝ in./1.5 cm to the wrong side on the upper raw edges and stitch close to the inner pressed edges. Refer to the diagram (see page 992) to fold the pleats along the solid lines to meet the broken lines. Pin and baste, then press the pleats.

STEP 2 Press ⅝ in./1.5 cm to the wrong side on the lower raw edge and baste in place.

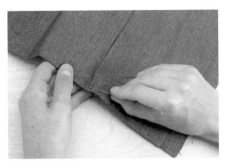

STEP 3 Cut the caddy fabric: 39 in. x 24³/₄ in./ 1 m x 58 cm. With right sides uppermost, lay the strips across the front, matching the short raw edges to the long edges of the caddy. Pin the lower strip ³/₄ in./2 cm above the lower edge. Pin the middle and top strips. Leave a 2³/₈-in./6-cm gap between the pocket strips.

STEP 4 Baste the side and lower pressed edges of all the strips. Topstitch close to the lower pressed edges of the pocket strips, then ¹/₄ in./5 mm above the first stitching.

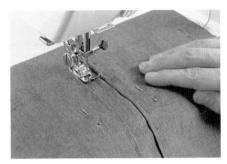

STEP 5 To form separate pockets, stitch between the broken lines of the pleats. Stitch back and forth a few times at the top of the stitching to reinforce the seam.

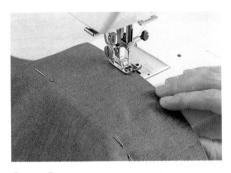

STEP 6 Cut a strip of fabric 22³/₄ in. x 4¹/₄ in./ 58 cm x 11 cm for a facing. Press under ⁵/₈ in./ 1.5 cm on the long lower edge. With right sides facing, stitch the facing to the upper edge taking a ⁵/₈-in./1.5-cm seam allowance. Press the facing to the wrong side and topstitch close to the upper edge, then ¹/₄ in./5 mm below the first stitching.

STEP 7 Stitch close to the lower edge of the facing, then 1⁵/₈ in./4 cm above the lower pressed edge to form a casing. Slip a 20-in./51-cm-long length of 1-in./2.5-cm-wide and ³/₁₆-in./4 mm-thick stripwood into the casing.

STEP 8 To bind the side and lower edge of the caddy, cut two straight 2¹/₂-in./6-cm-wide strips of fabric 39 in./1 m long for the side edges and one strip 24 in./61 cm long for the lower edge. Press under ³/₈ in./1 cm on the long edges of the bindings, then press lengthwise in half with the wrong sides facing.

STEP 9 Slip one long edge of the caddy inside a side binding with the lower edges level. Turn under the end of the binding at the upper edge and baste together through all the layers. Repeat on the other side edge. Stitch close to the inner pressed edge of the bindings.

STEP 10 Slip the lower edge of the caddy inside the lower binding (which extends at each end). Turn under the ends and baste through all the layers. Stitch close to the inner pressed edge of the binding. Remove the basting. Lay the cleat centrally in the casing. Fix an eyelet 1 in./2.5 cm inside each top corner.

TOP TIP

Use waterproof fabric for the caddy to store toiletries for the bathroom or gardening equipment for the shed. Adapt the size of the pockets to custom-make it for its contents.

YOU WILL NEED:

• FABRIC FOR
  SWEDISH BLIND
• CONTRAST LINING
• TAPE MEASURE
• WOODEN CLEAT
• TOUCH-AND-CLOSE
  TAPE
• STAPLE GUN
• NEEDLE AND
  THREAD/SEWING
  MACHINE
• IRON
• SCISSORS
• AIR-ERASABLE PEN
• EYELETS
• CUP HOOKS

PROJECT
Shelving hideaways

Most of us have a few areas in the home that would benefit from being kept hidden—an alcove of disheveled books, a bathroom shelving unit of mismatched toiletries, or a shelf of children's games that need to be concealed from view. A blind is great for hiding all sorts of clutter because you can just draw it up for access.

Swedish blinds are not just for windows. Attached to shelving, they are ideal for hiding clutter and can be made to fit the decorative scheme of a room.

HOW TO DO IT

Make this smart cover to hang in front of an open closet, alcove, or shelving unit. The cover is hung from a wooden cleat fixed to the upper edge, and a row of eyelets along the side edges is slipped onto hooks so the cover can be held open at different levels. The cover has a contrast lining, so it is reversible to ring the changes and can be hooked open to reveal the underside.

STEP 1 Fix a ½-in./1.2-cm-thick, 1-in./2.5 cm-wide wooden cleat to the upper edge of the open area. It should extend at least 1 in./2.5 cm on each side of the open area. Staple the stiff section of sew-on touch-and-close tape to the cleat. Measure the length of the cleat and the drop of the cover from the top of the cleat. For the cover, cut one rectangle or square of the main fabric and one of contrast fabric that is the length of the cleat plus 1¼ in./3 cm by the drop plus 1¼ in./3 cm.

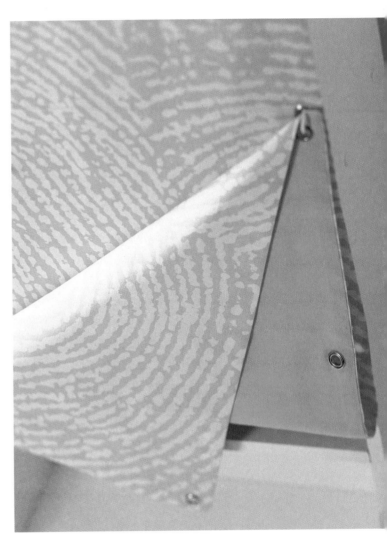

STEP 2 With the right sides facing, stitch the covers together, taking a ⅝-in./1.5-cm seam allowance and leaving a gap to turn on the upper edge. Clip the corners, then turn right-side out and press.

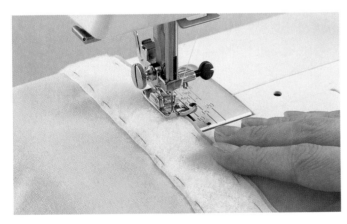

STEP 3 Baste and stitch the corresponding length of touch-and-close tape to the upper edge of the cover.

STEP 4 Following the manufacturer's directions, fix a ⅝-in./1.5-cm metal eyelet ¾ in./2 cm within the lower corners. Mark eyelet positions ¾ in./2 cm within the side edges 9 in./23 cm apart. Fix the eyelets. Press the cover onto the cleat. Fix cup hooks to the wall under each eyelet.

YOU WILL NEED:

- **PLAIN WOOD OR MDF SCREENS**
- **BATTING**
- **UPHOLSTERY SPRAY ADHESIVE**
- **SCISSORS**
- **FABRIC TO COVER PANELS**
- **T-PINS**
- **STAPLE GUN**
- **FABRIC GLUE**
- **BRAID**
- **HINGES AND SCREWS**
- **TAPE MEASURE**

PROJECT
Screens

Not surprisingly, screens are enjoying a renewed popularity. They add a regal touch to a room and can hide clutter or divide a room, concealing gym equipment or a home office. Plain wooden or MDF screens, available ready to be painted or covered in your choice of fabric, come with different-shaped tops.

Old screens can be found at second-hand stores and if they are scruffy and battered, covering them with a smart fabric will make them look brand new and disguise imperfections. Alternatively, a carpenter could make one to your specifications.

Most fabrics are suitable. Sheer fabrics need to be mounted on a plain, closely woven fabric and treated as one thickness if covering a solid screen. If you wish to use a luxurious but expensive fabric, use it on the side of the screen that faces into a room, with a cheaper coordinating fabric on the other side. Extra fabric will be needed if you want to match printed patterns across the screen.

A screen with frames instead of solid panels can have tension wires strung across and sheer fabric panels suspended between them. Alternatively, lightweight fabric panels can be attached to the top and bottom frame with the use of touch-and-close tape.

Covering a solid screen

If you are re-covering an old screen, remove any old fabric covering and trimmings. Lever out tin tacks: if any are impossible to remove, hammer them into the screen so they do not snag you or the fabric. Separate the screen panels by unscrewing the hinges.

Give careful thought to the positioning of printed fabrics. If the screen is to be stood with one panel more prominent than the others, place the main pattern on the prominent panel. Lay the screen panels side by side flat on the floor and lay the fabric on top. Tuck the edges under the panels. Try different arrangements to see what looks best: centering the design is the obvious choice, but try placing it off-center as an alternative. This screen is slightly padded with batting on one side; you can pad both sides if you prefer.

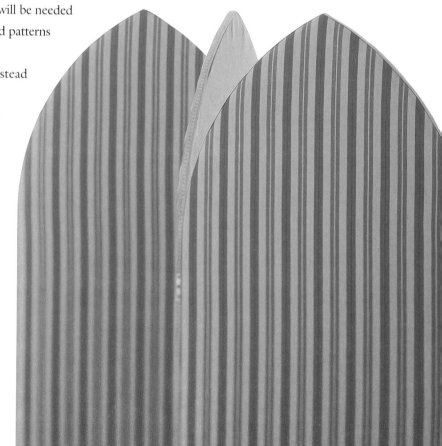

Choose a screen with the shape you prefer, and then decide on a fabric that will suit the room where it will be used.

COVERING A SOLID SCREEN

STEP 1 Cut 2-oz./56-g batting 1 in./2.5 cm larger on all edges than each screen panel. Use a spray adhesive especially recommended for upholstery to stick the batting to the screen panels. Cut away the excess batting.

STEP 2 Cut the fabric for each panel front, adding 1¼ in./3 cm to all edges. Press the fabric and lay the first piece centrally on the panel. Pin to the batting with T-pins. Fold the fabric smoothly over the side edges and use a staple gun to fix the fabric in place; work outward from the center.

STEP 3 Smooth the fabric along the length of the panel and over the upper and lower edges, folding under the fullness neatly at the corners. Staple in place, then trim away the excess fabric just inside the edges of the screen.

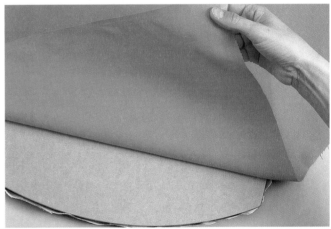

STEP 4 Turn the panel over and cover the other side in the same way, positioning the staples between the first row. Trim away the excess fabric as before. Starting on the lower edge, use fabric glue to stick braid that is the width of the panel on the edges. Cover the remaining panels. Join the panels with hinges.

YOU WILL NEED:

- FABRIC FOR COVER
  (INCLUDING STRAPS,
  PEDIMENTS,
  BORDERS, SIDES,
  DOOR, BACK, AND
  ROOF)
- TAPE MEASURE
- IRON
- PINS
- BUTTONS
- SCISSORS
- NEEDLE AND
  THREAD/SEWING
  MACHINE
- FABRIC GLUE
- TOUCH-AND-FASTEN
  DISKS

PROJECT

Tented wardrobe

Free-standing wooden units with hanging rails are very cheap and are great for storage purposes. The only drawback is that they are usually unattractive to look at and everything in them is on display. Make a streamlined fabric cover to hide the unit's contents; the cover rolls up and fastens with buttons to give easy access inside the unit.

A freestanding unit can be made much more attractive by adding a fabric cover. The cover is also good for keeping your clothes in pristine condition.

HOW TO DO IT

Take a ⅝-in./1.5-cm seam allowance throughout.

STEP 1 Measure the width, depth, and height of the unit. For the door, cut two rectangles of fabric the height of the unit minus 1½ in./4 cm, by the width of the unit. With right sides facing, stitch together along the side and lower edges. Clip the corners and turn right-side out. Press and pin the upper raw edges together.

STEP 2 Cut two strips of fabric 18 in. x 4¾ in./45 cm x 12 cm for the straps. With right sides facing, fold the straps lengthwise in half and stitch down the long edges and across one end. Clip the corners, turn right-side out, and then press.

STEP 3 Work a buttonhole to fit your buttons ⅝ in./1.5 cm from the finished ends. Pin and baste each strap to the upper raw edge of the underside of the door 2¾ in./7 cm in from the side edges.

STEP 4 Cut two strips of fabric for the pediment that are the unit width plus 1¼ in./3 cm by 4 in./10 cm. With right sides facing, pin the upper edge of the door centrally to a long edge of one pediment.

STEP 5 For the front borders, cut two 6¾-in./17-cm-wide strips of fabric that are the height of the unit minus ¾ in./2 cm. Press the borders lengthwise in half with the wrong sides facing. Pin and baste the long raw edges together.

STEP 6 Matching the raw edges, pin the short upper edges of the borders to the pediment, overlapping the edges of the door. With right sides facing, baste the remaining pediment on top, sandwiching the door, straps, and borders. Baste the upper edge. Turn the pediment right-side out and press. Tack the raw edges of the pediments together. Topstitch the pediment close to the seam and then ¼ in./5 mm from the first stitching.

STEP 7 Cut a rectangle of fabric for the sides and back, which is the height of the unit plus 2 in./5 cm, by the width plus twice the depth plus 1¼ in./3 cm. Join fabric widths if necessary with a flat felled seam. With right sides facing, stitch the front borders and ends of the pediment to the height edges, starting ⅝ in./1.5 cm below the upper edge. Press the seam open and neaten the edges with a zigzag stitch.

STEP 8 Cut a square or rectangle for the roof that measures the width plus 1¼ in./3 cm by the depth plus 1¼ in./3 cm. With right sides facing, pin the roof to the upper edge of the unit cover, matching the pediment to the width edges. Stitch, pivoting the fabric at the corners.

STEP 9 Turn right-side out and slip the cover over the unit. Pin up a double hem. Remove the cover and sew a touch-and-fasten disk to the lower edge inside the front borders. Glue corresponding disks to the lower edge of the unit. Roll up the door. Sew buttons onto the pediment.

YOU WILL NEED:

- FABRIC FOR
  ENVELOPE BACK
- TRANSPARENT
  PLASTIC FOR
  ENVELOPE FRONT
- TAPE MEASURE
- GLASS (FOR A CURVE)
- PINS
- AIR-ERASABLE
  PEN/TAILOR'S CHALK
- NEEDLE AND
  THREAD/SEWING
  MACHINE
- BIAS BINDING
- SCISSORS
- HAMMER
- POPPER FASTENING

PROJECT
Clothing envelopes

These indispensable clothing envelopes are ideal for storing summer beachwear when it is not in use in the winter, and for storing underwear all year round. You don't have to stick to the dimensions shown here—make them as big as you need them to be.

HOW TO DO IT

Plastic-fronted envelopes sealed with a popper fastening will keep contents free of dust and easy to identify and access. Choose plain or woven, striped or checked fabric, because both sides of the fabric will be seen. The edges are bound with ready-made bias binding.

STEP 1 Cut a 16¼-in./41-cm square of fabric for the back, and a 16¼ in. x 12 in./41 cm x 30.5 cm piece of transparent plastic for the front. Draw around a glass on a corner of the back to make a curve. Cut out and repeat on each corner of the back. Pin the front to the back; match the lower and side edges. Cut lower front corners to match.

STEP 3 Turn the binding to the back, enclosing the raw edges. Baste in place, then topstitch close to the pressed edges of the binding.

STEP 2 Open out one edge of 1-in./2.5-cm-wide bias binding. Turn one end under to start and pin to the outer edges, overlapping the ends. Stitch along the fold line, taking a ⅜-in./1-cm seam allowance on the envelope.

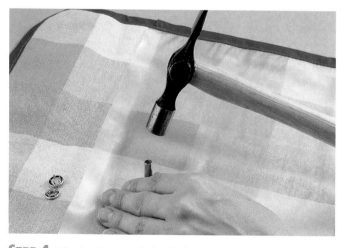

STEP 4 Following the manufacturer's directions, attach a popper centrally to the flap. Slip a few items of clothing inside to judge the position of the corresponding popper. Remove the clothes and attach the popper to the front.

FAR RIGHT: **You can make clothing envelopes in various sizes to suit your needs. They are extremely useful for carrying clothing and other items on vacation.**

YOU WILL NEED:

- PAPER FOR PATTERN
- GLASS (FOR A CURVE)
- AIR-ERASABLE PEN/TAILOR'S CHALK
- FABRIC
- LINING
- BATTING
- BIAS STRIPS
- NEEDLE AND THREAD/SEWING MACHINE
- SCISSORS
- TAPE MEASURE
- PINS

FAR RIGHT: **Covers keep toasters and other appliances clean and tidy.**

PROJECT

Toaster and food-mixer covers

Coordinate your kitchen appliances with a set of matching covers made from light-to-mediumweight fabrics. Here, linen-look fabrics in contemporary designs have a contrasting striped fabric for the lining and binding. Use the covers for items on display in the kitchen.

MAKING THE COVERS

Because toasters and food mixers vary in size, you will need to make your own paper pattern. Measure the height and depth of the machine and add 1¼ in./3 cm to the measurements. Draw a square or rectangle on paper to these measurements for the end panel. Round off the top corners by drawing around an upturned glass. Cut out the pattern and check it against the end of the toaster or mixer; it should be at least ⅜ in./1 cm larger on all sides. Draw the grain line parallel with the side edges. For the front and back panels, use a tape measure to measure around the sides and top of the end-panel pattern, from one corner of the base edge to the other corner of the base edge. Measure the length of the toaster and add 1¼ in./3 cm to this measurement.

STEP 1 Use the pattern to cut two end panels from fabric, lining, and 2-oz./56-g batting. Cut one rectangle each of fabric, lining, and batting to the front and back panel measurements. Sandwich the batting between the fabric and lining, with the right sides facing outward. Baste the layers together along the outer edges.

STEP 2 Set the sewing machine to a slightly longer stitch length than usual. Starting at the center of the upper edges, stitch along the length of the panels in random wavy lines about 2¾ in./7 cm apart. Draw guidelines with an air-erasable pen first if you prefer.

STEP 3 With the wrong sides facing, pin and baste each end piece to the long edges of the front and back panel, taking a ⅜-in./1-cm seam allowance.

STEP 4 Cut two 3¼-in./8-cm-wide bias strips of contrast fabric the length of the front and back panel, to bind the end seams. Press lengthwise in half. The binding is applied double: pin each binding to the basted seam with the right sides and front and back panel facing. Stitch, taking a ⅜-in./1-cm seam allowance. Turn the pressed edges over the raw edges and slipstitch along the seam on the end panels.

STEP 5 Cut a 3¼-in./8-cm-wide bias strip of contrast fabric the length of the lower edge plus 1 in./2.5 cm. Press the binding lengthwise in half. Turn under one edge to start, then pin the binding to the lower edge with the right sides facing. Stitch, taking a ⅜-in./1-cm seam allowance. Turn the pressed edges over the raw edges and slipstitch along the seam inside the cover.

YOU WILL NEED:

• PLAIN COTTON
  FABRIC

• LEFTOVER FABRICS
  FOR POCKETS

• TAPE MEASURE

• PINS

• COLORED RIBBONS

• SCISSORS

• NEEDLE AND
  THREAD/SEWING
  MACHINE

• IRON

• WOODEN CLEAT

PROJECT
Child's wall tidy

Encourage children to tidy up with a jolly wall tidy for storing small toys and stationery. There are four generously pleated pockets and three patch pockets for smaller items. It is stiffened with a wooden cleat at the top and hangs from hooks on colored ribbons.

Children can learn to tidy things away themselves with this wall tidy. Keep the higher pockets for storing items such as scissors that you don't want them to play with unsupervised.

HOW TO DO IT

Choose durable fabrics: a plain, dark-blue cotton fabric was used here. The pockets can be made from leftover fabrics from other furnishings in the bedroom. Only small amounts of fabric are needed for the pockets, so it may not be too costly to buy just 1 ft./30 cm of a special feature fabric. Take a ⅝-in./1.5-cm seam allowance throughout.

STEP 1 From plain fabric, cut two rectangles for the wall tidy 35 in. x 22⅝ in./88 cm x 58 cm. Cut four 1-in./2.5-cm-wide ribbons 10 in./25.5 cm long. Baste the ribbons in pairs to the short upper edge of one wall tidy on the right side, 3¼ in./8 cm in from the long side edges. With the right sides facing, stitch the wall tidies together, leaving an 8-in./20-cm gap 1 in./2.5 cm below the upper edge on one long side edge. Clip the corners, turn through, and press.

STEP 2 Cut four rectangles 13½ in. x 10¼ in./34 cm x 25.5 cm from three different fabrics for the pleated pockets. Center any design motifs. Press ⅜ in./1 cm then ¾ in./2 cm to the wrong side on the upper raw edges. Stitch close to the inner pressed edges. Press ⅝ in./1.5 cm under on the side edges.

STEP 3 Follow the diagram (see page 992) and fold the pleats along the solid lines to meet the broken lines. Pin and press the pleats. Press ⅝ in./1.5 cm to the wrong side on the lower edge.

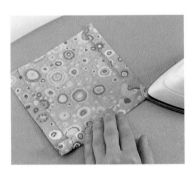

STEP 4 Cut three rectangles 7¾ in. x 6 in./19.5 cm x 15 cm from three different fabrics for the patch pockets. Center any design motifs. Press ⅜ in./1 cm then ¾ in./2 cm to the wrong side on the upper raw edges. Stitch close to the inner pressed edges. Press ⅝ in./1.5 cm under on the side and lower edges.

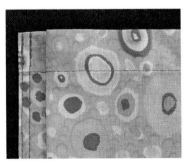

STEP 5 Arrange the pockets on the tidy, 1½ in./4 cm within the side and lower edges and 5¼ in./13 cm below the upper edge. Topstitch close to the side and lower edges, then ¼ in./6 mm inside the first stitching. Stitch back and forth a few times at the hemmed edge of the pockets as reinforcement.

STEP 6 Stitch across the wall tidy ¼ in./6 mm, then 1¾ in./4.5 cm below the upper edge to form a channel. Insert a 1¼-in./3-cm-wide wooden cleat 21¼ in./54 cm long into the channel. Slipstitch the opening closed.

YOU WILL NEED:

- CALICO, DENIM, OR CANVAS FABRIC
- TAILOR'S CHALK
- SCISSORS
- TAPE MEASURE
- IRON
- PINS
- CORRUGATED CARDBOARD
- TOUCH-AND-CLOSE TAPE
- METAL PAPER FASTENERS
- NEEDLE AND THREAD/SEWING MACHINE

PROJECT
Hanging shelves

A set of sturdy-fabric hanging shelves is great for storing T-shirts and knitwear. The shelves are applied to a closet rail with a hanging strap that fastens with touch-and-close tape. The shelves are reinforced with corrugated cardboard and are very lightweight.

Using hanging shelves can help you to make the most efficient use of your closet space.

HOW TO DO IT

Choose a hardwearing, closely woven fabric such as calico, denim, or canvas. A colorful striped canvas has been used for these hanging shelves—position the stripes centrally when cutting the fabric pieces.

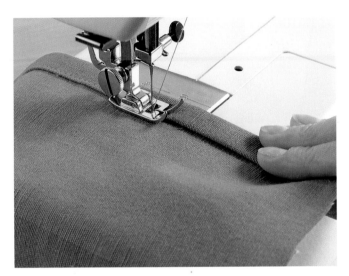

STEP 1 Refer to the diagram on page 925 to cut a rectangle of fabric for the support (the sides) 38 in. x 34³/₄ in./98 cm x 88 cm. Press ³/₈ in./1 cm under, then ⁵/₈ in./1.5 cm on the short edges. Stitch close to the inner pressed edges.

STEP 2 Cut three shelves from fabric 24¹/₂ in. x 12¹/₄ in./62 cm x 31 cm. With the wrong sides facing, press the shelves widthwise in half and topstitch ¹/₄ in./6 mm from the pressed edges; these will be the front edges. Pin the opposite raw edges together; these will be at the back of the shelves.

STEP 3 Draw the solid lines on the wrong side of the support using tailor's chalk. With the underside of the shelves facing the support, pin the back edge of the shelves along the lines, matching the centers.

STEP 4 Baste the shelves in place. Cut five 10³/₄-in./27-cm squares of corrugated cardboard. Slip one square centrally inside the middle shelf. Pin the raw edges together to enclose the card.

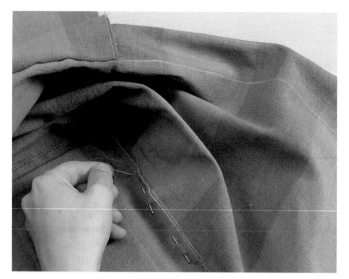

STEP 5 Fold the support around each side of the middle shelf, matching the raw edges to the drawn lines. Pin and baste the side edges of the shelves to the support. Insert a square of cardboard into the remaining shelves, and pin and baste them to the support in the same way.

STEP 6 Fold the support along the lines at the back of the shelves, enclosing the raw shelf edges. Pin and stitch the back edge taking a 1/4-in./6-mm seam allowance, and starting and finishing 1/4 in./6 mm from the side edges of the shelves. Fold the support along the lines at the sides of the shelves, enclosing the raw shelf edges. Pin and stitch the side edges, taking a 1/4-in./6-mm seam allowance, starting at the back seam and continuing to the front hemmed edges.

STEP 7 Cut a rectangle of fabric for the hanging strap 11 1/2 in. x 8 in./ 29 cm x 20 cm. Press 1/4 in./6 mm under, then 3/8 in./1 cm on the short edges. Stitch close to the inner edges. Press 3/8 in./1 cm under on one long edge. Pin and stitch one section of sew-on touch-and-close tape on top. Press 3/8 in./1 cm to the right side on the other long edge. Pin and stitch the other section of touch-and-close tape on top.

STEP 8 Cut two rectangles from fabric 25 1/4 in. x 13 in./64.2 cm x 33 cm for the roof and base. Mark widthwise across the center of the roof with pins. Pin the hanging strap centrally to one half of the roof, with the right sides facing and the long edges of the strap parallel to the center line. Stitch the strap to the roof 1/2 in./1.2 cm each side of the center of the strap. Remove the pins.

STEP 9 With the right sides facing, fold the roof and base widthwise in half. Stitch the short edges, taking a ³/₈-in./1-cm seam allowance. Clip the corners, turn right-side out; press. Topstitch ¹/₄ in./6 mm from the pressed edges; these will be the front edges. Slip a cardboard square inside. Fasten the roof layers with three metal paper fasteners along the center of the strap. With the top of the roof facing the right side of the back of the support, stitch the roof centrally to the upper edge, taking a ³/₈-in./1-cm seam allowance. Stitch the base to the lower edge in the same way. Clip the seam allowance at the end of the seam on the roof and base diagonally.

STEP 10 Press ³/₈ in./1 cm under on the raw edges of the support. Fold the roof and base over the seams. Stitch the back edge ⁵/₁₆ in./8 mm from the seam, starting and finishing ⁵/₁₆ in./8 mm inside the side edges. Pin the pressed edges and sides of the roof together. Stitch close to the outer edges. Stitch ¹/₄ in./6 mm inside the edges, starting ⁵/₁₆ in./8 mm from the back edge. Repeat for the base.

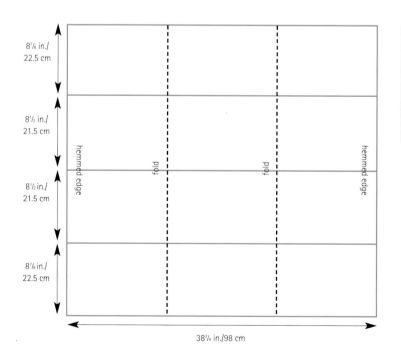

8⁷/₈ in./ 22.5 cm

8¹/₂ in./ 21.5 cm

8¹/₂ in./ 21.5 cm

8⁷/₈ in./ 22.5 cm

hemmed edge

fold

fold

hemmed edge

38³/₄ in./98 cm

TOP TIP
For strength, use double- or treble-wall corrugated cardboard at least ¹/₄-in./6-mm thick. Secure the strap with large metal fasteners and washers.

And so to bed

Although the scale is large compared to other soft furnishings, the basic techniques involved in making bedding are simple. Designer-style bedding is terribly expensive to buy, but can be created easily using fine fabrics. A handworked detail on a sheet edging or pillowcase gives an instant touch of individuality. Making your own bed-linen also means that you can use the exact choice or color of fabric to suit the bedroom—ready-made ranges may be rather limited. Flamboyant interior-design styles, such as bed canopies and coronas, look fantastic but can be intimidating to create yourself. They need only a bit of daring on your part, because they are easy to construct and can completely change the look of a room. Once you start experimenting, you will gain the confidence to try out bolder styles—in fact, you may not know when to stop!

Choosing bed fabrics

Most furnishing fabrics are not suitable for bed linen that will be against the skin because they are too coarse or textured, but they can be used for bedspreads and valances. Materials used for sheeting and pillowcases should be soft to the touch and easily washable, because they will be laundered on a regular basis.

Sheets, pillowcases, comforter covers, and cushions can all be made in a choice of fabrics to suit the decorative scheme of a room.

Pure cotton can be bought in suitable widths for bedding; some cottons have an "easy-care" finish. Percale is a closely woven cotton fabric with a fine, smooth surface that makes it a popular choice for sheets and pillowcases. Cotton polyester is hard wearing and does not crease as much as pure cotton; it is also less expensive, but does not have the softness or absorbency of pure cotton. Egyptian cotton is the best-quality cotton, being soft and hardwearing. Flannelette is a lightweight version of wool flannel, made of cotton or man-made fibers. It is soft and slightly fluffy, and is good for use in cold weather, but it is often highly inflammable. Linen is long-lasting and feels luxurious but is costly and creases badly.

Measuring up

The sizes opposite are a guide for standard sizes. It is best to measure up for bed linen yourself, because manufacturers' sizes do vary. Make up the bed with sheets, pillows, comforters, or blankets if measuring for a bedspread or coverlet. If a flexible measure does not reach the full distance to be measured, mark the place the tape ends with a pin and start again from the pin.

When measuring the bed base for a valance, a yard/meter stick can be poked between the mattress and base about 2 in./5 cm in from the edge. Measure from the outermost edges; for example, if there is piping around the edge of the base. Do not worry about any rounded corners on the base, because the valance will curve naturally around these edges. Measure pillows and comforters with a cloth tape from seam to seam.

Bedding sizes

Mattresses are usually about 7 in./17.5 cm deep.

Small single

mattress	2 ft. 6 in. x 6 ft.	75 cm x 190 cm
flat sheet	5 ft. 6 in. x 8 ft. 3 in.	165 cm x 250 cm
comforter	4 ft. x 6 ft. 5 in.	120 cm x 195 cm

Standard single

mattress	3 ft. x 6 ft. 7 in.	90 cm x 200 cm
flat sheet	5 ft. 10 in. x 8 ft. 6 in.	180 cm x 260 cm
comforter	4 ft. 5 in. x 6 ft. 7 in.	135 cm x 200 cm

Standard pillow 2 ft. 5 in. x 19 in. 74 cm x 46 cm

Standard double

mattress	4 ft. 5 in. x 6 ft. 7 in.	135 cm x 200 cm
flat sheet	7 ft. 6 in. x 8 ft. 6 in.	230 cm x 260 cm
comforter	6 ft. 7 in. x 6 ft. 7 in.	200 cm x 200 cm

King size

mattress	5 ft. x 6 ft. 10 in.	150 cm x 210 cm
flat sheet	9 ft. x 9 ft.	275 cm x 275 cm
comforter	7 ft. 3 in. x 7 ft. 3 in.	220 cm x 220 cm

Square pillow 2 ft. 2 in. x 2 ft. 2 in. 66 cm x 66 cm

The beauty of making your own bedding is that it gives you the opportunity to add a touch of individuality. You can buy prepatterned fabric or add a pattern yourself with decorative patches.

YOU WILL NEED:
FLAT SHEET:
• SHEETING FABRIC
• TAPE MEASURE
• IRON
• NEEDLE AND
  THREAD/SEWING
  MACHINE

FITTED SHEET:
• SHEETING FABRIC
• PINS
• SCISSORS
• NEEDLE AND
  THREAD/SEWING
  MACHINE
• TAPE MEASURE
• ELASTIC
• BODKIN

PROJECT
Sheets

Sheets are very simple to make and you can save a great deal of money if you do decide to make your own. Ready-made sheets are certainly expensive for what they are. You can also individualize your bed linen if you make it yourself—you can add personal touches such as blocks of embroidery or trimmings.

Bed sheets are quick and easy to make. It may seem a waste of time to make sheets yourself, because they are generally widely available, but it is easier to incorporate your own design features before construction. A fabric-painted motif or embroidered border gives a lovely finishing touch, and just a simple length of ribbon or a strip of contrast fabric applied along the top edge can tie into a bedroom's color scheme.

Choose a smooth, easy-care fabric. Sheeting fabric is recommended because it is very wide— usually 89¾ in./2.28 m—and is available in pure cotton and cotton/polyester mixes, which crease less than pure cotton. Flat sheets should be at least 29 in./73.5 cm wider than the bed and 34 in./86 cm longer, to allow for tucking in. Add 4¾ in./12 cm to the length of the sheet and 2 in./5 cm to the width for hems.

Always check that the fabric grain is straight before cutting out. Cut out the sheet with the selvedge parallel with the long side edges. Use a flat felled seam to join fabric to make a king-size sheet.

Fitted sheet

Fitted sheets are used for bottom sheets only and fit the mattress snugly. The corners are elasticated to give a tight fit so they do not get untucked and they don't wrinkle up uncomfortably if you happen to have a restless night.

A fitted sheet measures the length of the mattress plus twice the depth plus 8½ in./21 cm for tucking in and the hem, by the width of the mattress plus twice the depth plus 8½ in./21 cm for tucking in and the hem.

MAKING A FLAT SHEET

STEP 1 Press ³⁄₈ in./1 cm, then ⁵⁄₈ in./ 1.5 cm to the wrong side on the side edges. Stitch close to the inner pressed edges.

STEP 2 Press ³⁄₈ in./1 cm to the wrong side on the top and bottom edges. Open out the corners, then press under diagonally. Press 2 in./5 cm to the wrong side. Stitch close to the inner pressed edges.

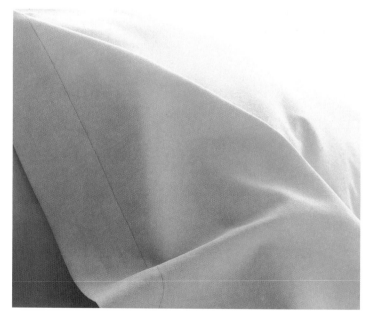

Bed sheets are very easy to make and you can incorporate your own design features.

MAKING A FITTED SHEET

STEP 1 With wrong sides facing, fold the sheet diagonally from one corner, matching the straight edges. Mark a point that is the depth plus 4 in./10 cm along the raw edges from one corner. Stitch from the mark at right angles to the diagonal fold. Trim the seam allowance to ¼ in./6 mm.

STEP 2 Turn to the wrong side and stitch again ⅜ in./1 cm from the seam. Repeat at each corner.

STEP 3 Fold under ¼ in./6 mm, then ¾ in./2 cm on the outer edges. Stitch in place close to the inner edge, leaving a ¾-in./2-cm gap 7 in./17.5 cm each side of the seam.

STEP 4 Insert a 8-in./20-cm length of ⅜-in./1-cm-wide elastic through one gap and out of the other with a bodkin. Pin, then stitch the elastic securely across the ends. Stitch the gap closed. Repeat on the other corners.

CORDED TRIM

It is simple to create the elegant rows of fine cording found on the top edge of some sheets. Press ⅜ in./1 cm, then 2 in./5 cm to the wrong side at the upper edge of the sheet. Lay a length of perle cotton embroidery yarn along the right side 1¾ in./4.5 cm from the fold. Use a cording foot to zigzag over the yarn. Repeat 1½ in./3.8 cm from the fold. You could omit the cord and use a twin needle on the sewing machine, or work two rows of close zigzag stitch using a machine embroidery thread. Turn the lower edge and side edges under, and hem.

YOU WILL NEED:
- SHEETING FABRIC
- PINS
- TAPE MEASURE
- IRON
- SCISSORS
- NEEDLE AND THREAD/SEWING MACHINE
- PINKING SHEARS
- DECORATIVE FEATURES

PROJECT
Pillowcases

Pillowcases lend themselves to many decorative features, and you can really go to town if you are skilled with your needle. Decorate the edges of pillowcases with ribbons or lace, or work a design in fine embroidery silk. You might also like to experiment with fabric paints and pens, which can be used over the whole of the pillow.

A housewife pillowcase has a flap to hold the pillow in place and supports the head during sleep. A pillow sham is a pillow cover for a decorative pillow or for back support. Pillow shams that are to be propped upright often have decorative borders: scalloped or flat, or with frills extending beyond three edges. The fourth, lower edge conceals the fastening. Pillow shams are made in the same way as cushions, but do not have zipper fastenings.

The size of a pillowcase provides an ideal opportunity for decoration. Apply the decoration to the front before it is made up. Position any motifs about 2 in./5 cm in from the flap and up from the lower edge so it does not get lost over the curve of the pillow. Avoid placing any decoration other than fabric painting on the center of the pillowcase, because it could irritate the sleeper. A little lavender oil sprinkled on the pillow will aid peaceful sleep.

Delicate decorative touches can be applied to the edges of pillows and the whole of cushions.

MAKING A HOUSEWIFE PILLOWCASE

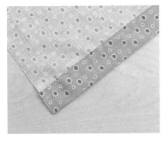

STEP 1 To make a standard-size housewife pillowcase, cut a front 38 in. x 20¼ in./96.5 cm x 51 cm and a back 31⅝ in. x 20¼ in./ 80.5 cm x 51.6 cm. Press ⅜ in./ 1 cm under then 1⅝ in./4 cm on one short edge of the front and back. Stitch close to the inner pressed edges.

STEP 2 With right sides facing, pin the front and back together along the remaining short edges. Fold the other end of the front over to form a flap, then pin the layers together.

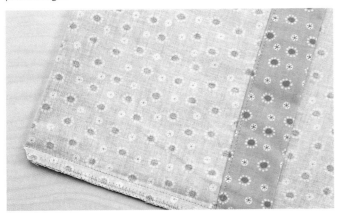

STEP 3 Stitch the raw edges together, taking a ⅝-in./1.5-cm seam allowance. Clip the corners. Neaten the seam with a zigzag stitch or pinking shears. Turn right-side out, turning the flap inside.

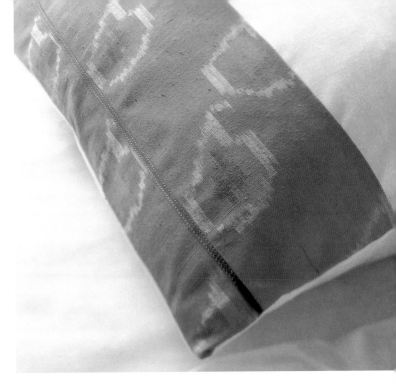

MAKING A DECORATIVE-FLAP HOUSEWIFE PILLOWCASE

This version of a housewife pillowcase has a flap that closes over the front of the pillowcase. This flap can be of a contrasting color or fabric to the pillowcase decorated with all sorts of techniques; or fastened with buttons and buttonholes. The buttonholes are worked on the flap.

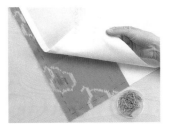

STEP 1 Cut a front and back 30¼ in. x 20¼ in./77 cm x 51 cm. Cut a flap 9 in. x 20¼ in./22.5 cm x 51 cm. Press ⅜ in./1 cm under, then ⅝ in./1.5 cm on one short edge of the front, and stitch close to the inner pressed edges. Press the flap in half with right sides facing, parallel with the long edges. If you wish to decorate the flap, open it out flat and apply the decoration to one half only.

STEP 2 With right sides facing, baste the raw edges of the flap to one end of the back.

STEP 3 With right sides facing, pin the front on top, with the hemmed edge over the flap. Stitch the outer edges, taking a ⅝ in./1.5 cm seam allowance. Clip the corners. Neaten with a zigzag stitch or pinking shears. Turn right-side out, turning the flap over the front.

YOU WILL NEED:

- **FOUR FABRICS FOR PATCHWORK**
- **IRON**
- **SCISSORS**
- **TAPE MEASURE**
- **PINS**
- **NEEDLE AND THREAD/SEWING MACHINE**
- **STRINGS OF IRIDESCENT SEQUINS**
- **FABRIC FOR CUSHION BACK**
- **CUSHION PAD**

PROJECT
Pillow shams and cushions

Pillow shams are used to lean on when you sit up in bed—cushions are generally more decorative, but can also be used for the same purpose. Don't be mean with cushions, pile them up generously, and let them spill over the bed to create an inviting atmosphere. Use luxurious fabrics for that feel-good factor.

A pile of squashy pillows and cushions on a bed looks very cozy and welcoming. Pillows and cushions are easy to make and offer lots of opportunities for trying out different needlecraft techniques. If you wish to add trimmings, such as fringing or beading, to the outer edges, apply these to three sides only—pillow shams are traditionally meant to sit upright to support the back, so any trimming on the lower edge would be squashed and hidden from view.

The traditional craft of patchwork has long been associated with making beautiful heirloom quilts for the bedroom. They are time-consuming and labor-intensive to create, but a work of art when completed. Making a patchwork pillow sham is a much simpler process, as well as being a great introduction to the technique. Patchwork is a marvelous way to use up small pieces of fabric and those that have sentimental value. Choose fabrics of similar weight: lightweight interfacing can be applied to the back of very fine or unstable fabrics to give them more body. Baste lightweight sew-on interfacing to the back of a piece of lace, worn fabric from a favorite dress you want to incorporate for sentimental reasons, or a delicate piece of an antique textile.

You can use up fabric oddments to make a patchwork cushion cover to brighten up your bed. Making patchwork is time-consuming but worthwhile; it gives a very personal touch to your home.

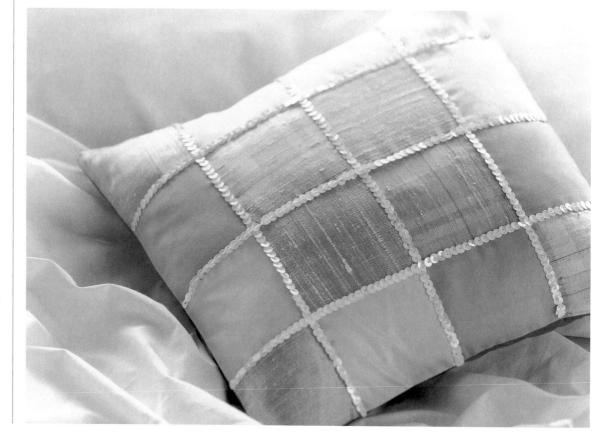

MAKING A PATCHWORK PILLOW SHAM

The finished size of the pillow sham is 12 in./30 cm square. Take ⅜-in./1-cm seam allowances throughout. The patchwork is machine-stitched using silk fabrics in coordinating colors. The seams are outlined with rows of shiny sequins.

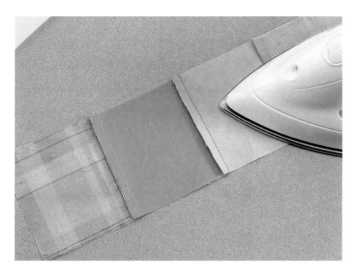

STEP 1 Cut sixteen 3¾-in./9.5-cm-squares from four coordinating fabrics. Arrange the squares in different sequences of four rows of four squares to see what looks best. With the right sides facing, stitch the four squares together in four rows. Press the seams of the first row in the same direction, the seams of the next row in the opposite direction, and so on.

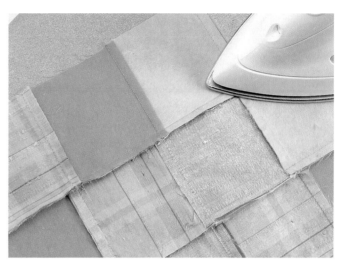

STEP 2 With the right sides facing, stitch the first two rows together, matching the seams. Join the remaining rows to form a square for the front of the sham. Press the seams downward.

STEP 3 Cut two rectangles of fabric for the back 8½ in. x 12¾ in./ 21.5 cm x 32 cm. Press a ⅜-in./1-cm-deep double hem under on one long edge of each piece, and stitch in place.

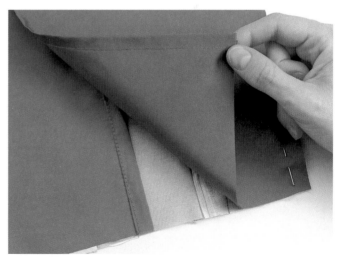

STEP 4 With the right sides facing, pin the backs to the front, matching the raw edges and overlapping the hems at the center. Stitch the outer edges. Clip the corners and turn right-side out. Handsew a string of iridescent sequins along each seam, then slip a 12-in./30-cm cushion pad inside.

YOU WILL NEED:

- FABRIC FOR
  PILLOWCASE
- IRON-ON
  INTERFACING
- TAPE MEASURE
- IRON
- PINS
- SCISSORS
- STRANDED COTTON
  EMBROIDERY
  THREAD AND
  NEEDLE

PROJECT

Fancy pillowcases

Develop your craft skills by creating some fancy decorative touches on pillowcases. A design that is painted, stamped, or stenciled with fabric paint can be machine-washed and will prove very long-lasting. Choose matching colors to your color scheme or go for a bold or subtle contrast.

Keep any hand-worked decoration to the opening or upper edges of the pillowcase, where they will be away from the face. Do not decorate the lower edge, because it will be obscured. Appliqué is very effective on bed linen. Apply simple shapes in contrasting fabrics, making sure the fabrics have the same washing instructions. Add a touch of embroidery for emphasis. You could embroider a garland on a pillow sham, for example, then pick out single flowers to

embroider on the edges of pillowcases; and then scatter them on a comforter cover or quilt.

Gingham looks particularly fresh in a bedroom —choose larger checks for a comforter cover and smaller ones for pillows and sheets, or mix and match them on the same item. A housewife pillowcase with the main case in larger check and the flap in a smaller check would look very pretty— and you could even work a set of drapes to match. Your bedroom is the most personal space in your home, so this means that you can choose to decorate it however you like—and you don't necessarily have to invite visitors in if you don't want to! Shades of blue are restful in a bedroom— and lilacs and purples—so if you have a stressful working life, go for these calming colors and you'll be guaranteed a good night's sleep.

You can use your imagination and create your own designs. Choose bright colors to look cheerful, or go for calmer shades to encourage relaxation.

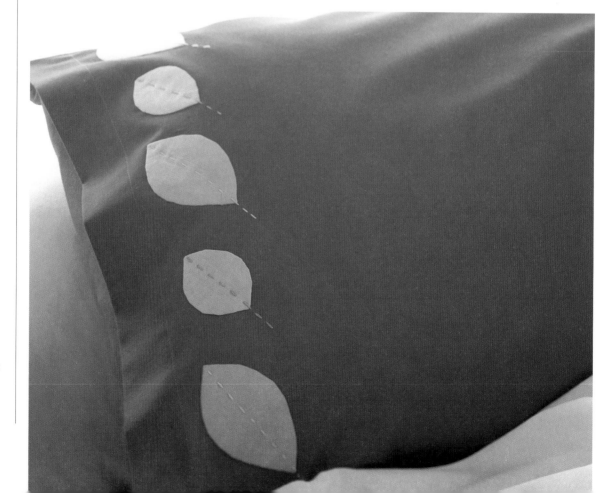

MAKE A HAND-APPLIQUÉ PILLOWCASE

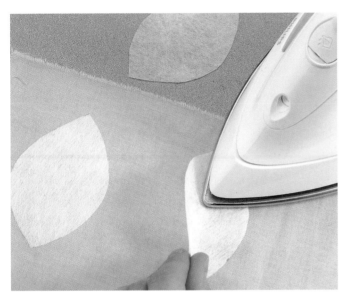

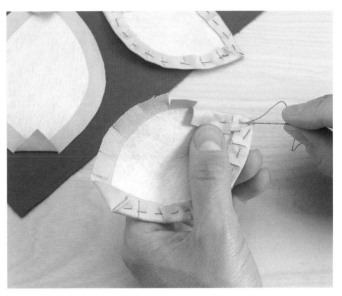

STEP 1 From deep-red fabric, cut one rectangle for the front of the pillowcase 38 in. x 20¼ in./96.5 cm x 51 cm and one rectangle for the back 31⅝ in. x 20¼ in./80.5 cm x 51 cm. Cut a selection of leaves from mediumweight iron-on interfacing. Press the leaves to the wrong side of two shades of light-brown fabric to fuse them together.

STEP 2 Trim the fabric, leaving a 5/16-in./8-mm allowance around the interfacing. Press the tips of the fabric over the leaves. Snip the curves of the fabric and turn the allowance to the back of the leaves. Baste in place.

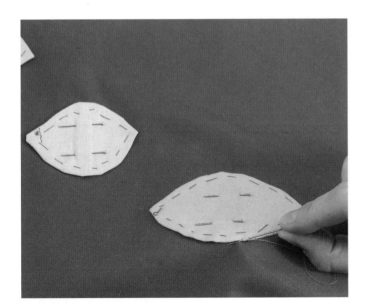

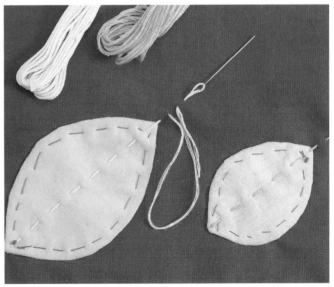

STEP 3 Arrange the leaves 4 in. /10 cm in from one short edge of the pillowcase and 1½ in./4 cm within both long edges of the front on the right side. Pin in place, then slipstitch the outer edges securely to the front.

STEP 4 Using three strands of stranded cotton embroidery thread, work a running-stitch along the center of the leaves, extending onto the front for a few stitches to suggest stems. Unpick the basting and press. Refer to the directions on page 933 to make a housewife pillowcase, positioning the appliqué at the flap end.

YOU WILL NEED:
- SHEETING FABRIC
- PINS
- TAPE MEASURE
- IRON
- SCISSORS
- NEEDLE AND THREAD
- SEWING MACHINE WITH ZIPPER FOOT
- PRESS-FASTENER TAPE

PROJECT
Comforter covers

Comforters are extremely popular—probably because they make bedmaking easy—and comforter covers are very simple to make. Sheeting fabric is recommended for making comforter covers because it comes in wide widths in easy-care fabrics, but if you want something different, any smooth, washable fabric will do.

Most comforter covers have an opening at the bottom edge and can be fastened in many ways: a press-fastener tape is the most usual and discreet method, or you could make a feature of the fastening by using buttons and buttonholes or fabric ties (see page 960).

Unless you use sheeting, the fabric will probably need to be joined to achieve the required width of a comforter cover. Avoid a center seam, and try to have a full width of fabric along the center of the length of the bed and an equal amount of fabric at each side. The central panel on the top layer could be of a contrasting fabric to those at each side and a feature can be made of the seams by adding ribbon or lace along them. If you do use more than one fabric and add trimmings, make sure that the wash-care instructions are compatible. Add ⅝-in./1.5-cm seam allowances for joining the widths, and join the fabrics with flat felled seams.

For versatility, make the front and back of the comforter cover in contrasting colors so you can ring the changes by just turning over the cover.

As long as it is soft to the touch and easily washable, fabric for comforter covers can be used to make pillowcases and drapes, to tie in with the decorative scheme of a room.

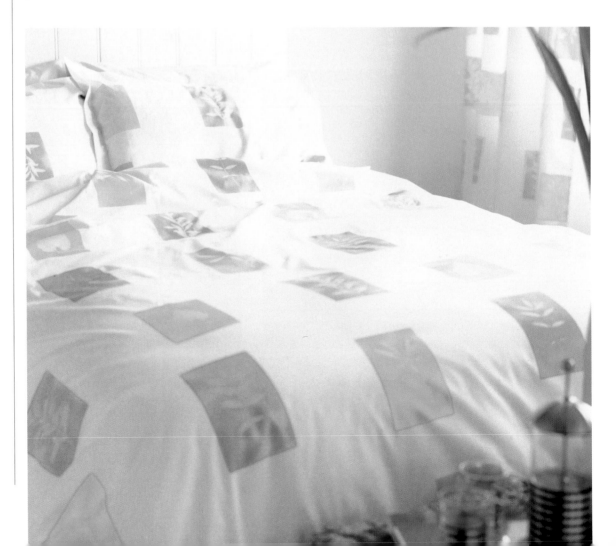

HOW TO DO IT

STEP 1 Measure the comforter, adding 1¼ in./3 cm to the width and 3 in./7.5 cm to the length. Cut out a back and front to these measurements. Press ⅜ in./1 cm, then 1 in./2.5 cm to the wrong side on the lower end of the front and back. Stitch close to the inner pressed edges.

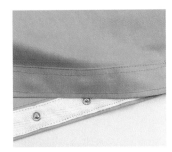

STEP 2 Cut a length of press-fastener tape 16 in./40 cm shorter than the width of the comforter, and separate the tape sections. Pin one half of the tape centrally to the right side of each hem. Check that the press fasteners correspond on both tapes and turn under the ends. Stitch close to the long edges of the tapes, using a zipper foot if the press studs are large and butting against a standard presser foot.

STEP 3 With the right sides facing, match the front and back together along the opening edges and fasten the poppers. Pin, then stitch across the ends of the tapes, then stitch to the side edges just above the hem.

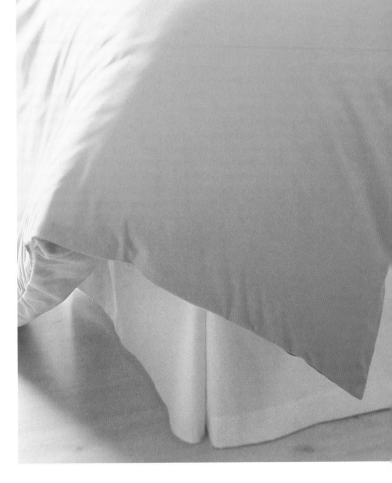

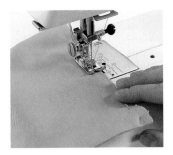

STEP 4 With the wrong sides facing, stitch the front and back together along the raw edges, taking a ¼-in./6-mm seam allowance. Snip the corners.

STEP 5 Turn the cover through to the wrong side and stitch again ⅜ in./1 cm from the seam. Snip the corners. Now turn the cover right-side out.

TOP TIP

If you wish to fasten the comforter cover with buttons and buttonholes or fabric ties instead of press-fastener tape, just omit the tape. To make a buttoned cover, work a row of buttonholes along one hemmed edge about 7 in./17.8 cm apart. Sew buttons at corresponding positions on the opposite edge. To fasten a comforter cover with ties, mark one hemmed edge with pins about 7 in./17.8 cm apart. Make two narrow ties 9 in./23 cm long for each pin mark. Neaten the ends of the ties and stitch them securely at the pinned marks.

YOU WILL NEED:

FOR ALL VALANCES:

• SHEETING FABRIC

• IRON

• SCISSORS

• TAPE MEASURE

• PINS

• NEEDLE AND
  THREAD

• SEWING MACHINE
  (WITH PIPING FOOT
  IF REQUIRED)

• SEAM TAPE

• PIPING (IF
  REQUIRED)

PROJECT
Bed valances

A bed valance hides the base of a bed. It is particularly necessary when a comforter is used and there is no bedspread to hide an unsightly base and legs. If the base is not at floor level, a valance will also obscure anything stored under the bed and give it some protection from dust.

The valance can be plain with a box pleat at each corner, gathered, or pleated all round. You can make the valance of the same fabric as the comforter, so it blends in seamlessly, or you can go for a contrast to it. A valance with pleats will benefit from a good-quality fabric that will hold the pleats well for a tailored look.

The valance has a base the same size as the bed base; this will be hidden from view, so it can be made of any inexpensive fabric—sheeting is a good choice for the valance base because it is available in wide widths and is therefore more economical. A border of the valance fabric is applied on top of the edges of the valance base for a neat appearance.

Measuring up

For the valance base, measure the length and width of the bed base, then measure from the top of the bed base to the floor for the drop of the skirt. The average drop is 12 in.–14 in./ 30.5 cm–35.5 cm. The skirt does not continue around the head of the bed. To make it more economical, cut the skirts across the width of the fabric, then add seam allowances and join with flat felled seams. This is particularly important if the fabric is too narrow to cut from a continuous length.

Another name for a valance is a dust ruffle; it helps to protect the bed from dust and dirt, as well as covering an unattractive base. The valance is made with lengths of seam tape so the valance can be tied to the headboard supports.

MAKING A PLAIN VALANCE WITH CORNER PLEATS

A plain valance needs a box pleat at the corners of the foot of the bed for ease and to provide access under the bed. The skirt is assembled from five pieces, one for each side, one for the foot end and two pleat inserts.

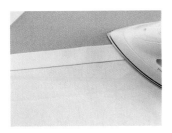

STEP 1 Cut out the valance base, adding 2⅜ in./6 cm to the length and 1¼ in./3 cm to the width for allowances. Join the fabric with a flat felled seam if necessary. To hem the base, press ¾ in./2 cm under, then 1 in./2.5 cm on one short edge. Stitch close to the inner pressed edges. This will be the head end.

STEP 2 Cut two side skirts the length of the bed base plus 5⅜ in./13.5 cm by the drop plus 2⅜ in./6 cm, and one end skirt the width of the bed base plus 7¼ in./18 cm by the drop plus 2⅜ in./6 cm. Cut two pleat inserts 7 in./18 cm by the drop plus 2⅜ in./6 cm.

STEP 3 To hem, press ¾ in./2 cm under, then 1 in./2.5 cm on one long lower edge of the skirts, the lower edge of the pleat inserts, and one end of each side skirt. Stitch close to the inner pressed edges.

STEP 6 With wrong sides facing, baste the skirt to the raw edges of the valance base. Match the side skirts to the long edges and the end skirt to the foot end. Match the center of the pleats to the corners, snipping the seam allowance so it lies smoothly. For the borders, cut two strips of fabric the length of the bed base plus 1¼ in. x 5¼ in./3 cm x 13 cm and one strip of fabric the width of the bed base less 6¾ in. x 5¼ in./17 cm x 13 cm.

STEP 4 Using flat felled seams and taking a ⅝-in./1.5-cm seam allowance, stitch a pleat insert between the side and end skirts in order to form a continuous length.

STEP 7 With the right sides together and taking a ⅝-in./1.5-cm seam allowance, stitch the ends of the short border between one long edge of the long border, starting ⅝ in./1.5 cm from the inner edges. Press the seams open.

STEP 9 Press the border to the right side of the base. Press ⅝ in./1.5 cm under on the raw edges, and stitch close to the pressed ends. Cut four 12 in./30.5 cm lengths of seam tape. Pin and sew them in pairs to the head end of the valance base.

STEP 5 With the right sides uppermost, bring the side and end skirts to meet at the center of the pleat inserts to form the box pleats. Baste across the upper edges and press the pleats.

STEP 8 With the right sides facing and taking a ⅝-in./1.5-cm seam allowance, baste the borders to the base, enclosing the skirt. Stitch through all the layers. Clip the corners and turn them right-side out.

MAKING A GATHERED VALANCE

Make a gathered valance to add a gentle, feminine touch to a bedroom. Avoid heavyweight fabrics—soft, lightweight fabrics work best for gathers. The skirt should be three times the length of the bed plus one-and-a-half times its width. Cut strips across the width of the fabric to make up the entire length of the skirt plus 3½ in./9 cm that are the drop of the skirt, plus 2⅜ in./6 cm in depth.

STEP 1 To prepare the valance base, see step 1 of making a plain valance with corner pleats on page 941. Join the skirts end to end with flat felled seams. To hem the skirt, press 2 ³/₄ in./2 cm under, then 1 in./2.5 cm on one long, lower edge and the ends. Stitch close to the inner pressed edges.

STEP 2 On such a large expanse of fabric, balance marks will be needed for placing the gathers evenly. Add both sides and the foot end of the valance base and divide the measurement into sixths, then mark the valance base with pins, dividing the raw edges into six equal sections.

STEP 3 Fold the skirt in half, matching the ends and upper raw edges. Mark the fold with a pin at the raw edge. Divide the skirt into three equal sections between the ends and fold, marking the divisions with pins on both layers of fabric.

STEP 4 To gather the raw edges of the skirt, set the sewing machine to the longest stitch length and stitch two rows ¹/₄ in./6 mm apart, ⁵/₁₆ in./7 mm from the raw edges. With the wrong sides facing, pin the skirt to the valance base, matching the pins and skirt ends to the head end of the base. Adjust the gathers evenly, but allow slightly more gathers around each corner. To complete, follow from step 6 of making a plain valance with corner pleats on page 941.

MAKING A PLEATED VALANCE WITH PIPING

A valance that is pleated all around uses more fabric than the other methods, but will give a smart, tailored finish to the bed. Choose crisp fabric that will hold the pleats well. Piping around the valance base will add definition.

Add together the width of the bed base and twice the length. The length of the valance skirt should be three times this measurement. You need to add 3½ in./8 cm onto this amount to allow for the hems. Cut strips across the width of the fabric to make up the entire length of the skirt. These strips should measure the drop of the skirt plus 2⅜ in./6 cm in depth. Add 1¼ in./3 cm to each piece cut for skirt seams.

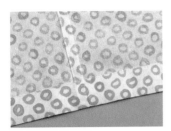 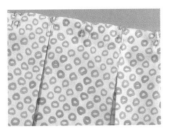  

STEP 1 To prepare the valance base, see step 1 of making a plain valance with corner pleats on page 941. Join the skirts with flat felled seams to make one long length. To hem the skirt, press ¾ in./2 cm under, then 1 in./2.5 cm on one long edge and the ends. Then stitch close to the inner pressed edges.

STEP 2 Mark the center of the skirt with a pin at the raw edge. Working outward from this point, fold and pin the skirt into even-sized box pleats, aiming to work the pleats so there will be an inverted pleat at the corners of the base. Baste the pleats in place.

STEP 3 With the wrong sides facing, pin the skirt to the valance base, matching the raw edges and the skirt ends to the head end. Check the fit. If adjustments need to be made to the size of the pleats, make the end pleats smaller or larger—they will be less noticeable at the head end of the bed. Snip the skirt seam allowance at the corners so the fabric lies smoothly. Baste the skirt in position.

STEP 4 See the technique on page 790 to make a length of piping from the valance fabric, or use ready-made piping twice the length of the bed base plus its width and 2 in./5 cm. With the right sides facing, pin and baste the piping to the raw edges of the skirt, taking a ⅝-in./1.5-cm seam allowance.

STEP 5 Snip the seam allowance of the piping at the corners so it lies flat. To make the border, follow steps 7–8 of making a plain valance with corner pleats on page 941.

STEP 6 With the right sides facing and taking a ⅝-in./1.5-cm seam allowance, baste the borders. Working on the right side of the base, stitch through all the layers, using a piping foot. Clip the corners and turn right-side out. To finish, follow step 9 on page 941.

YOU WILL NEED:
- FABRIC FOR QUILT
- TAPE MEASURE
- POLYESTER BATTING
- NEEDLE AND
  THREAD
- SCISSORS
- SEWING MACHINE
  WITH WALKING
  FOOT OR DUAL-FEED
  FOOT
- TAILOR'S CHALK/
  AIR- ERASABLE PEN
- RULE
- PAINTER'S TAPE
- CURVED BASTING
  PINS
- DINNER PLATE (FOR
  A CURVE)
- BIAS BINDING

PROJECT
Eiderdowns and quilts

Eiderdowns, quilts, comforters, and coverlets are all terms for sumptuous, padded bed coverings. They add warmth to a bed in addition to looking inviting. Batting is sandwiched between two layers of fabric, which can then be quilted or left unadorned, or the layers can be joined with buttons or knotted threads.

Lightweight furnishing fabrics such as glazed cottons are ideal for making eiderdowns and quilts. If you have chosen an expensive fabric, it is economical to use a cheaper fabric such as curtain lining for the lining. Quilting can be worked in straight lines in bands or a grid, at random or along the outlines of printed designs. Quilting a striped or checkered fabric is easy, because you simply follow the lines of the stripes or checks. Ready-quilted fabric is available, although in a limited choice of fabrics and colors.

Alternatively, create a family heirloom by making a patchwork for the top layer and quilt it by hand or machine.

Measuring up

Make up the bed with its blankets or comforter, but not the pillows. Measure the width and length of the bed. Decide how far you would like the cover to overhang the sides, then double the overhang measurements and add them to the width. Decide how far you would like the cover to overhang the foot of the bed—this may be the same as for the sides, or less if there is a footboard. Add the foot overhang measurement to the length. Do not add seam allowances, because the edges will be bound. If the cover is to be quilted, add 4 in./10 cm to the width and length to allow for slippage.

Joining widths

If the fabric needs to be joined to achieve the required width, have a full width of fabric along the center of the length of the bed and an equal amount of fabric at each side. Remember to allow extra fabric for matching patterns. Add ⅝-in./ 1.5-cm seam allowances for joining the widths. Join the widths with flat seams and then press the seams open.

Quilts add a sumptuous and inviting look to beds. A simple, two-colored checkered pattern is easiest to quilt, but random patterns or printed designs can also be used.

MAKING A QUILT

STEP 1 Cut two quilts from fabric and one from 2-oz./56-g polyester batting, cutting the batting and lining about 2 in. /5 cm larger on all sides than the top fabric. Join the fabric widths, if necessary, with flat seams. You will probably need to join the batting widths by butting the edges together and oversewing them with a large herringbone stitch.

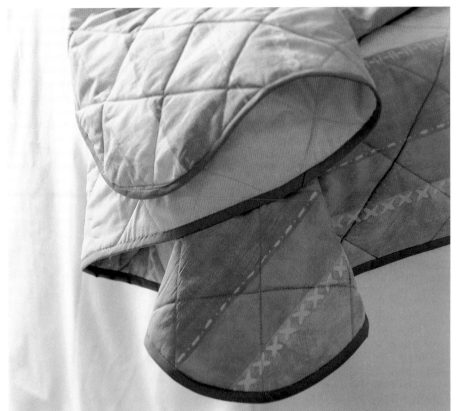

STEP 2 Lay the top fabric right-side up. Start at the center and draw quilting lines using tailor's chalk and a rule. This has a diagonal grid, and the lines are 3¼ in./8 cm apart.

STEP 3 Lay the lining wrong-side up on a flat surface and stick it in place with painter's tape. Lay the batting, then the top fabric on top, right-side up, 2 in./5 cm in from the taped edges. Use curved basting pins to pin or baste the layers together, smoothing the fabric from the center.

STEP 4 Set the sewing machine to the longest stitch length, and use a walking foot or dual-feed foot if your machine has one. Using quilting thread and working outward from the center, stitch along the drawn lines. Stitch all the diagonal rows in the same direction, then stitch those running across them. Use both hands to smooth the fabric as it passes under the sewing machine. Check the size and cut the quilt smaller if necessary, trimming an equal amount from both the opposite edges rather than just the one edge.

STEP 5 The quilt is easier to bind if it has rounded edges. Place an upturned dinner plate on one corner, then draw around it with tailor's chalk or an air-erasable pen and cut out. Use this corner as a template to trim the other corners. Bind the outer edges with 1-in. /2.5-cm-wide bias binding, following the technique on page 789 and again using a walking foot or dual-feed foot if you have one on your sewing machine.

TOP TIP

Because the quilt is large and bulky, roll up the right-hand side to let it pass comfortably under the arm of the sewing machine.

YOU WILL NEED:
- TAPE MEASURE
- FABRIC FOR
  BEDSPREAD
- IRON
- SCISSORS
- PAPER FOR PATTERN
- PAIR OF TOOL
  COMPASSES
- PATTERN FOR CIRCLE
- FOLD-OVER BRAID
- NEEDLE AND
  THREAD/SEWING
  MACHINE

PROJECT
Bedspreads

Because a bedspread covers such a large expanse, it will be a major focal point of the bedroom. Bedspreads are a great way of either creating a dramatic effect with a bright splash of color in an otherwise subtle room, or calming down a color scheme by making the bedspread in gentle, soothing tones.

From a practical point of view, a bedspread will add warmth and hide dreary blankets. It will also hide the bed base and anything stored under it, making a bed valance unnecessary.

A throw-over bedspread is very simple to make, because it is just a rectangle of fabric that is large enough to reach the floor at the sides and foot of the bed. It can be a single layer of fabric or it can be lined. A contrasting colored lining makes the bedspread reversible, which is very versatile. On a single layer bedspread, add a 1-in./2.5-cm hem to all edges or, alternatively, bind the edges, in which case no allowances are needed. Lined bedspreads can also have bound edges, or add a ⅝-in./1.5-cm seam allowance to all edges if you prefer to bag it out. Most fabrics are suitable, but avoid any that are stiff because the bedspread will not drape nicely over the bed. If lining the bedspread, make sure the fabrics have compatible wash-care instructions.

Joining widths

The large size of a bedspread means that fabric will probably need to be joined to achieve the required width. As on drapes and tablecloths, a central join will look ugly, so try to have a full width of fabric along the center of the length of the bed and an equal amount of fabric at each side. Making the central panel from a contrasting fabric to those at each side can be very effective. Add ⅝-in./ 1.5-cm seam allowances for joining the widths. Use flat felled seams on single layer bedspreads and flat seams on lined bedspreads. The corners at the foot end will need to be rounded off on a floor-length bedspread; otherwise they will bunch up on the floor and could be tripped over.

A bedspread can add a decorative touch to an otherwise plain room as well as keeping dust off comforters and pillowcases.

MAKING A THROW-OVER BEDSPREAD WITH BOUND EDGES

To measure for a throw-over bedspread, make up the bed in your usual way, complete with pillows and comforter or blankets. With a tape measure, measure the width from the floor at one side of the bed, up over the bed, and down to the floor at the other side. Measure the length from the floor at the foot of the bed, up and along the length of the bed, over the pillows to the headboard. If you require a tuck-in under the pillows, you will need to add 16 in./ 40 cm to the length. Add a 1-in./2.5-cm hem to the head end.

STEP 1 Cut out the bedspread. Join the widths if necessary, matching patterns. Press under ³/₈ in./1 cm, then ⁵/₈ in./1.5 cm on the head end. Stitch close to the inner pressed edge. Fold the bedspread lengthwise in half with the right sides facing. Measure the height of the made-up bed. On paper, use a pair of tool compasses (or improvise with string and a thumbtack) to describe a quarter circle with a radius that is the bed height measurement. Cut out the quarter-circle pattern and pin it to the foot end corners. Cut around the curves.

STEP 2 Remove the pattern and open the bedspread out flat. Open out a length of fold-over braid and turn under one end. Starting at the hemmed edge, slot the raw edge of the bedspread into the braid. Baste in place, through all the layers, enclosing the raw edges. Turn under the extending end to finish. Stitch close to the inner edges of the braid through all the layers, then carefully remove all the basting.

YOU WILL NEED:

UPHOLSTERED
 HEADBOARD:

• **FABRIC FOR
 HEADBOARD**

• **TAPE MEASURE**

• **T-PINS**

• **STAPLE GUN**

• **SCISSORS**

SLIP-OVER
 HEADBOARD
 COVER:

• **FABRIC FOR
 HEADBOARD**

• **TAPE MEASURE**

• **WIDE RIBBON
 FOR TIES**

• **SEAM TAPE**

• **PINS**

• **BATTING**

• **LINING**

• **SCISSORS**

PROJECT
Headboards

Fabric-covered headboards give a neat finishing touch to a bed, and they can be comfortable to rest against if they are padded. A wooden headboard can be transformed by having a layer of foam glued to the front, which is then covered with fabric. Ready-made headboards can be covered with your choice of fabric.

Alternatively, make a slip-over cover, which fastens around the existing headboard with ties at the sides and can be removed for laundering. A row of laced eyelets could be used instead.

Straight-sided and convex-edged headboards are easier to upholster than those with concave curves because the excess fullness of fabric that occurs at corners and convex edges can be neatly folded under. The fabric on concave edges needs to be snipped to lie smoothly, which will let the headboard show through. If the headboard is shallow in depth, braid can be glued on to cover the snipped fabric.

A deep headboard with concave edges will need a different approach, and a fitted cover can look very good. Draw around the headboard on paper. Measure the outer edges, omitting the lower edge. Add a 1-in./2.5-cm hem on the lower edge and a ⅝-in./1.5-cm seam allowance on the other edges, and cut out. Use as a pattern to cut two headboard covers. Cut a gusset from fabric the depth of the headboard plus 1¼ in./ 3 cm by the outer edge measurement plus 2 in./5 cm. Stitch a 1-in./2.5-cm hem on each end of the gusset and the lower edges of the headboard covers. Stitch the gusset between the outer raw edges of the covers. Snip the curves, then turn through and slip the cover over the headboard. Fasten the lower edges with tape ties.

UPHOLSTERING A HEADBOARD

Measure the height, width, and depth of the headboard. Cut fabric that is the height plus twice the depth plus 2¼ in./5.6 cm by the width plus twice the depth plus 2¼ in./5.6 cm.

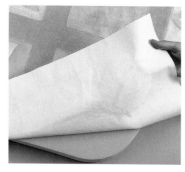

STEP 1 Lay the headboard face up and place the fabric on top, centering any design motifs. Pin the fabric in place with T-pins.

STEP 2 Turn the headboard over and fold the fabric to the underside. Working outward from the center on the upper edge and sides, use a staple gun to staple the fabric to the back of the headboard. Neatly fold under any fullness at the curves and corners and staple in place. Staple the fabric to the back of the headboard at the lower edge. If necessary, snip the fabric so that it lies smoothly around the supports.

MAKING A SLIP-OVER HEADBOARD COVER

STEP 1 Measure the height, depth, and width of the headboard. Cut one rectangle of fabric, 2-oz./56-g batting and lining that is twice the height plus the depth plus 1½ in./3.8 cm by the width plus the depth plus 1½ in. /3.8 cm. Cut eight 18-in./46-cm lengths of 1½-in./3.8-cm-wide ribbon for the side ties. Baste each ribbon to the side edges 5¼ in. /13 cm and 22 in./56.6 cm from the lower and upper edges. Cut the extending ends in chevrons.

STEP 2 Cut four 14-in./35.5-cm lengths of ½-in./1.2-cm-wide seam tape. Pin and baste to the upper and lower edges 8⅝ in./21.5 cm in from the side edges. Pin the fabric right-side up on the batting, smoothing the fabric outward from the center.

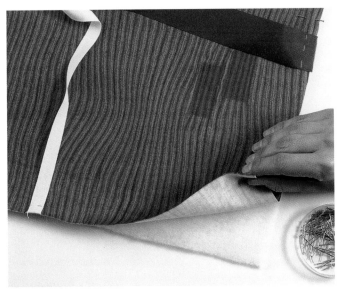

STEP 3 With the right sides facing, stitch the lining on top, taking a ⅝-in./1.5-cm seam allowance and leaving a 16-in./40.5-cm gap in the lower edge to turn through. Trim away the batting in the seam allowance and clip the corners. Turn right-side out and press. Slipstitch the opening closed.

STEP 4 Slip the cover over the headboard and tie the ribbons together. Tie the tapes together under the headboard. (The ribbons can be omitted if preferred.)

YOU WILL NEED:
- CURTAIN RODS/FINIALS
- TAPE MEASURE
- VOILE (OR LIGHTWEIGHT FABRIC) FOR CANOPY
- IRON
- PINS
- NEEDLE AND THREAD/SEWING MACHINE

PROJECT
Bed canopies

Canopies can give beds a dramatic, regal effect, the centerpiece of any bedroom. Choose thick, voluptuous fabric that hangs in deep folds or sheer muslin or voile for a more delicate look.

A canopy of fabric over the bed will give the bedroom a very individual look and set a distinctive style. The canopy can be at the head end or can stretch over the entire bed. Choose muslin or voile for a delicate touch. Even if you choose bright colors, the look will still be soft and filmy. Thicker fabric will soften the hard support edges.

To create an instant canopy to be draped either side of the bed, fix a cup hook into a ceiling joist, about 12 in./30.5 cm out from the head end of the bed. Thread two tab-headed sheer drapes onto a 24-in./61-cm-long curtain rod, alternating the tabs from the two drapes. Fix a finial onto each end and suspend from the hook with a fine chain. Let the drapes hang down each side of the bed.

The style of the canopy that you choose can instantly transform a bedroom. You can create a minimalist look, using pale-colored gingham or smart, thin stripes, with a narrow border to the fabric. An exotic, ethnic room can be instantly conjured up using rich fabrics—choose deep reds and pinks, and ultramarine and jade green as a contrast—and you can really dress it up with chunky silk tassels and deep thick fringing. Alternatively, you can opt for a more romantic "cottage" look, using faded flowered chintz and sprigged cotton, accessorized with plenty of vintage lace and large luxurious bows. The choice is yours!

MAKING A BED CANOPY FROM VOILE

This canopy, made from voile, is suspended on two curtain rods threaded through channels above the head end of the bed. A deep swathe of the canopy will hang at the head end against the wall and a narrower valance at the front of the canopy. The finials on the poles have been chosen to match the vibrant color of the fabric.

STEP 1 Use a tape measure to measure the circumference of the curtain rods. Add ¹/₂ in./ 1.2 cm to the measurement for the channel measurement. Refer to the diagram (see page 993) to cut the canopy from lightweight fabric to your chosen width, such as the width of the bed; add 1¹/₂ in./4 cm to the width for hems.

STEP 2 Press and stitch a ³/₈-in./1-cm deep double hem on all edges. Mark the position of the channels on the long edges with pins.

STEP 3 With right sides facing, bring the pins at one set of marks together on each long edge. Stitch between the marks to form the channel. Repeat with the other marks to make the other channel.

STEP 4 Insert a curtain rod through both the top channels. Check the length, allowing for finials at each end, and cut the rod shorter if necessary. Fix on the finials and hang the canopy on the wall.

YOU WILL NEED:
- PLYWOOD FOR CORONA BOARD
- SAW
- SCISSORS
- FABRIC FOR CORONA
- STAPLE GUN
- TOUCH-AND-CLOSE TAPE
- L-SHAPED BRACKET
- SCREWDRIVER
- AWL
- SCREW-EYES
- SELF-ADHESIVE VALANCE INTERFACING
- LINING
- DECORATIVE TRIM
- TAPE MEASURE
- IRON
- CURTAIN TAPE
- CURTAIN HOOKS
- CURTAIN BOSS
- HOLDBACK

PROJECT
Corona

Coronas make an attractive addition to any bedroom and they will create a cozy atmosphere around your bed. They can be simple to put up—to create a gauzy corona quickly, fix a mosquito net above the bed. Use fabric glue to stick silk flower heads or silk leaves at random to the fabric.

Bed drapes were traditionally used for functional purposes only—to maintain privacy and to keep out drafts. In the nineteenth century, heavily draped four-poster beds were thought to be unhealthy and the half-tester became the popular alternative. The half-tester is a rectangular canopy at the head end of the bed only, and will keep out drafts while adding a traditional and aristocratic feel to a bedroom. The corona has a curved board with drapes attached and these hang to either side of the bed; it has a softer look than a half-tester and it lends itself equally well to both traditional and contemporary styles.

The corona curtains are attached with hooks to screw eyes fixed to the underside of a corona board. The board can have a valance attached and drapes with a standard heading underneath; or no valance and drapes with a pencil-pleat heading. The drapes can continue behind the head end of the bed, in which case it would be worthwhile lining them, perhaps using a coordinating color of plain fabric.

As a modern adaptation of bed curtains around a four-poster, coronas add a regal, aristocratic look to any bedroom. Choose strong patterns or simple, sheer fabrics in plain colors to create your throne!

MAKING A CORONA

This corona has a matching valance with unlined drapes edged in braid.

STEP 1 Using a saw, cut a 24-in./60-cm-diameter semicircle of ⅝-in./1.5-cm-thick plywood for the corona board. Cut a 28-in./68-cm-diameter semicircle of fabric using scissors. Place the corona centrally on the wrong side of the fabric. Working outward from the center, lift the edges of the fabric over the corona board and staple in place with a staple gun, folding under the fullness at the corners.

STEP 2 Staple a length of touch-and-close tape to the curved edge with a staple gun. Screw an L-shaped bracket to the top of the corona board on the straight edge, 4 in./10 cm in from the ends.

STEP 3 On the underside of the corona board, make an even number of holes with an awl ⅜ in./1 cm in from each corner, then approximately 1½ in./4 cm apart ⅜ in./1 cm within the curved edge. Fix a screw eye into each hole, with the eyes parallel to the curved edge. Attach the corona board centrally above the bed. If the windows in the bedroom have a valance, match the height of the corona board with that of the valance shelf if possible.

STEP 4 Measure the length of the curve of the semicircle. Cut a 4-in/10-cm-wide strip of self-adhesive valance interfacing the length of the curve. Cut 2 strips of fabric (the same width) for the valance, adding a ⅝-in./1.5-cm allowance on each edge. Peel the paper backing off one side of the interfacing and stick centrally to one strip of fabric.

STEP 5 Cut diagonally across the fabric ¼ in./5 mm from the corners of the valance. Peel away the valance backing paper from the edges and turn over and press the corners, then the straight edges of the fabric to the back of the valance.

STEP 6 For the lining, pin the corresponding half of the touch-and-close tape 1 in./2.5 cm below the upper long edge of the remaining strip of fabric, ⅝ in./1.5 cm in from the short edges. Stitch in place close to the edges of the tape. Press under ⅝ in./1.5 cm on the edges of the fabric.

STEP 7 Peel off the valance backing paper completely. Press the lining smoothly on top. Slipstitch together along the outer edges. Handsew or glue a decorative trim along the lower edge of the valance. Press the valance to the corona, matching the touch-and-close tapes.

STEP 8 Use a tape measure to measure the intended drop of the drapes from the underside of the corona to the floor. Refer to the unlined curtain directions on page 801 to make a pair of drapes, each the length of the valance in width plus a gathering. Stitch a decorative trim along the inner edges if you wish. Use standard curtain tape for the curtain heading.

STEP 9 Slip curtain hooks through the tape and slot the hooks through the eyelets on the underside of the corona. Fix a curtain boss or holdback either side of the bed to keep the drapes in place.

YOU WILL NEED:
- WASHABLE FABRIC
- BATTING
- PAINTER'S TAPE
- BASTING PINS
- TAILOR'S CHALK/AIR-ERASABLE PEN
- CREWEL NEEDLE
- SINGLE TWIST THREAD
- SAUCER (FOR CURVES)
- SCISSORS
- NEEDLE AND THREAD
- SEWING MACHINE WITH ZIPPER OR PIPING FOOT
- RIBBON
- TAPE MEASURE
- PINS
- IRON

PROJECT
Crib bumpers

Creating items for a baby is always rewarding, and a cot bumper is a practical and beautiful gift. The bumper is tied to the inside of the crib, protecting the youngster from knocks, and keeping out drafts. Because babies are fascinated by bright colors and patterns, back this bumper with a muted color for reversing at nighttime.

HOW TO DO IT

Choose washable fabrics such as cotton or polyester or polyester/cotton mixes. Sheeting is ideal because its generous width means that it is economical to use. This bumper extends halfway along each side of the crib and across the head end. Measure the drop from the top rail to the base of the mattress, and measure the width and length of the crib. The bumper is spot-quilted, which is a simple technique to master and it looks fantastic when it's finished.

STEP 1 Cut one rectangle of printed fabric the length of one side plus the width of the crib by the drop measurement. Join the fabric if necessary, remembering to match patterns. Cut 6-oz. /170-g batting and plain fabric 2 in./5 cm larger on all sides. If necessary, join the batting by butting the short edges together and oversewing with a large herringbone stitch.

STEP 2 Prepare the bumper for quilting by laying the plain fabric rectangle wrong-side up on the flat surface and taping it in place with painter's tape. Lay the batting smoothly on top. Place the printed rectangle on top, 2 in./5 cm within the taped edges. Secure the layers together with curved basting pins or rows of basting.

STEP 3 Within 2 in./5 cm of the outer edges, use an air-erasable pen to mark a grid of dots on the top layer about 8 in./20 cm apart. To spot-quilt, thread a crewel needle with a double length of single twist thread. Here, a variegated coton à broder embroidery yarn was used. Make a small stitch at one dot through to the back of the lining and back through to the right side, leaving a tail of 2½ in. /6.3 cm of thread.

STEP 4 Make another stitch back through the same holes and tie the thread ends together with a double knot on top of the fabric. Trim the thread ends to ³/₄ in./2 cm.

STEP 5 Trim the the outer edges level with the top fabric. Round the upper corners by drawing around a saucer with tailor's chalk or an air-erasable pen. Cut out the curves.

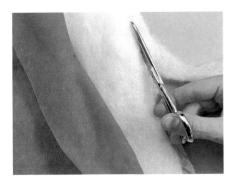

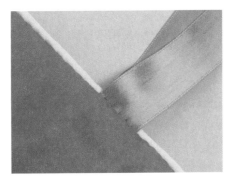

STEP 6 Tuck the lining out of the way around the upper and side edges. Pin, then use a zipper or piping foot to stitch a length of piping along the side and upper edges, taking a ⁵/₈-in./1.5-cm seam allowance and taking care not to catch in the lining. Carefully trim away the batting in the seam allowance. Snip the corners of the piping in the seam allowance so it lies flat.

STEP 7 Cut four 32-in. /81.5-cm lengths of 1-in./2.5-cm-wide ribbon. Place the bumper in position in the crib. Fold the ribbons in half and pin to the bumper at the best positions for tying to the rails. Remove the bumper. Stitch the ribbons securely to the bumper, cutting the ends in chevrons. Turn the upper and side edges of the lining under. Pin and slipstitch to the bumper.

STEP 8 Baste the lower edges together. Cut a 2-in./5-cm-wide straight strip of fabric the length of the lower edge plus 2 in./5 cm for a binding. Press ³/₈ in./1 cm under along one long edge. With the right sides facing, stitch the long raw edge of the binding to the lower edge, taking a ³/₈-in./1-cm seam allowance and with 1 in./2.5 cm extending at each end.

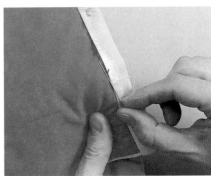

STEP 9 Turn the binding to the underside. Turn the ends under and slipstitch the ends together and the pressed edge along the seam.

YOU WILL NEED:

- WHITE SHEETING
- COLORED SHEETING
  FOR BORDER
- TAPE MEASURE
- BONDING WEB
- NEEDLE AND
  THREAD/SEWING
  MACHINE
- IRON
- PAPER TEMPLATE
- SCISSORS
- CREWEL NEEDLE
- STRANDED COTTON
  EMBROIDERY
  THREAD

PROJECT

Paisley border sheet

Appliqué applied by the sewing machine gives a very professional finish. This sheet is edged with a colorful border of paisley shapes, highlighted with simple hand embroidery. You can also apply the border to a ready-made sheet.

HOW TO DO IT

The measurements given here are for making a single sheet. To make a double sheet, cut the sheet 92 in. x 102 in./2.35 m x 2.59 m and the border 91¾ in. x 8⅛ in./2.33 m x 21 cm.

FAR RIGHT: **A colorful border can make a regular sheet into a special item of bed linen.**

STEP 1 Cut a rectangle of white sheeting 98 in. x 77 in./2.49 m x 1.7 m. Press ⅜ in./1 cm, then ⅝ in./1.5 cm to the wrong side on the long side edges. Stitch close to the inner pressed edge. Press ⅜ in./1 cm, then 2 in./5 cm to the wrong side on the short lower edge. Stitch close to the inner pressed edge.

STEP 2 Cut a strip of turquoise sheeting for the border 66¼ in. x 8⅛ in./1.68 m x 21 cm. Press the border lengthwise in half with the wrong sides facing. Open the border out flat again and press under ⅜ in./1 cm on one long edge.

STEP 3 Make a paper template of the paisley pattern; draw around it seven times on the paper backing side of the bonding web. Apply the motifs to two striped fabrics and cut them out. Working outward from the center, refer to the technique on page 791 to apply the motifs in alternate directions and colorways to the unpressed half of the border 4⅛ in./10.5 cm apart and 1 in./2.5 cm in from the long raw edge.

STEP 4 Set the sewing machine to a close zigzag stitch ⅛ in./3 mm wide. Stitch along the edges of the motifs to conceal the raw edges. Pull the end threads to the back of the border and knot them together.

STEP 5 Thread a crewel needle with six strands of stranded cotton embroidery thread. Embroider three stars on each paisley with six straight stitches radiating outward from the dots. Press the paisleys face down on a towel so the embroidery does not get flattened.

STEP 6 Fold the ends of the border along the fold line with right sides facing. Stitch the ends, taking a ⅝-in./1.5-cm seam allowance. Clip the corners and turn right-side out. With right sides facing, stitch the border to the upper edge of the sheet, matching the raw edges and taking a ⅝-in./1.5-cm seam allowance. Clip the corners. Press the seam toward the border.

STEP 7 Re-press the border in half along the center fold line. Pin the pressed edge of the back of the border along the seam, enclosing the seam allowance. On the right side, topstitch close to the seam.

YOU WILL NEED:

- TAPE MEASURE
- EASY-CARE FABRIC
- IRON
- PINS
- NEEDLE AND
  THREAD/SEWING
  MACHINE
- SCISSORS
- AIR-ERASABLE
  PEN/TAILOR'S CHALK
- RULER
- RIBBON

PROJECT
Oxford pillowcase

Shiny satin ribbon outlines this pillowcase to emphasize the generous flange edge that is characteristic of an Oxford pillowcase.

Choose a smooth, closely woven easy-care fabric to make the pillowcase and buy ribbon in a matching color.

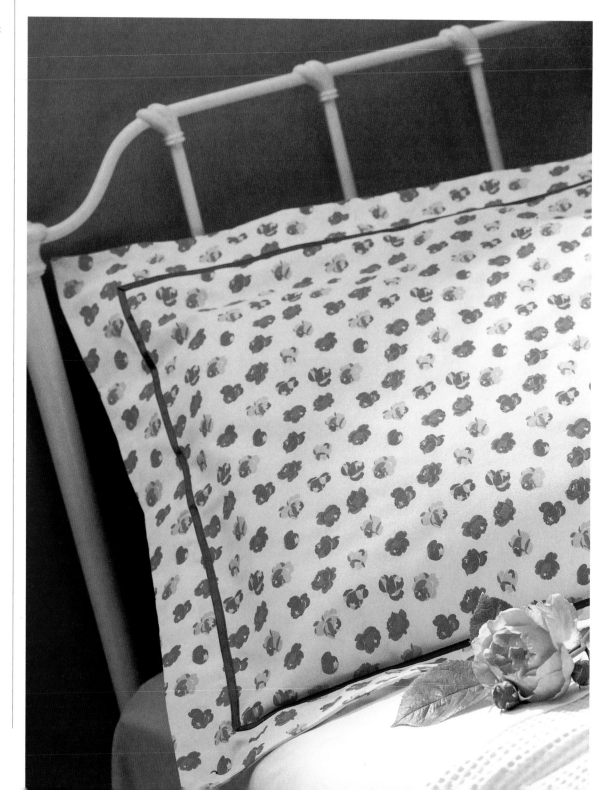

A pair of these beautiful pillowcases will brighten up any bedroom.

MAKING AN OXFORD PILLOWCASE

STEP 1 Cut one front 34¹/₂ in. x 24¹/₂ in./88 cm x 62 cm, one back 32¹/₄ in. x 24¹/₂ in./82 cm x 62 cm, and one flap 24¹/₂ in. x 14 in./ 62 cm x 35.5 cm. Press ³/₈ in./1 cm under then 1⁵/₈ in./4 cm on one short edge of the back and one long edge of the flap. Stitch close to the inner pressed edges.

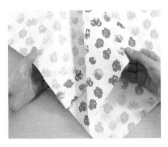

STEP 2 With the right sides facing, pin the back and flap to the front, matching the raw edges and overlapping the hemmed edge of the flap over the hemmed edge of the back. Stitch close to the outer edges, taking a ³/₈-in./1-cm seam allowance. Clip the corners, turn right-side out, and press.

STEP 3 Use an air-erasable pen or tailor's chalk and a ruler to draw a border 2¹/₂ in./6 cm inside the outer edges to form the flange. Starting ³/₈ in./1 cm beyond one drawn corner and placing the inner edge of the ribbon on the stitching line, stitch ⁵/₁₆ in./7 mm-wide satin ribbon along the drawn line to ⁵/₁₆ in./7 mm beyond the next corner. Fold the ribbon at the end of the stitching with the right sides facing.

STEP 4 Fold the ribbon diagonally at the corner and pin it along the adjacent drawn line. Then tack the miter in place at the corner.

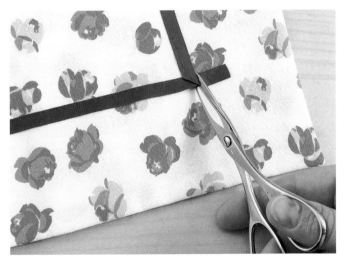

STEP 5 Fold the ribbon diagonally under at the first corner. Cut off the excess ribbon under the folded corner. Baste in place, then stitch the outer edges of the ribbon.

YOU WILL NEED:

- SHEETING FABRIC
- NEEDLE AND
  THREAD/SEWING
  MACHINE
- IRON
- GINGHAM FOR TIES
  AND FLAP
- PINS
- SCISSORS

PROJECT
Comforter cover with ties

Make a feature of the fastening on a comforter cover with a row of pretty ties across the top of the cover. A generous flap is made from classic checked gingham with matching ties. Gingham is cheap to buy, and most of the comforter cover is made from inexpensive sheeting.

Ties make a welcome change from the normal poppers or buttons on comforter covers.

MAKING A SINGLE COMFORTER COVER WITH TIES

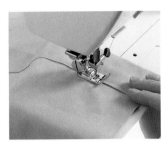

STEP 1 Cut a front 76 in. x 56¼ in./ 1.93 m x 1.43 m and a back 80 in. x 56 in./2.03 m x 1.43 m from plain sheeting fabric. Press ¾ in./1.5 cm under, then 2 in./5 cm on one short edge of the front. Stitch close to the inner pressed edge.

STEP 2 Cut ten 4⅜-in. /11-cm-wide strips of gingham for the ties 10⅝ in./27 cm long. Fold lengthwise in half with the right sides facing, and cut diagonally across one end. Stitch the outer edges, taking a ⅜-in./1-cm seam allowance, leaving a 3-in./7.5-cm gap to turn through. Clip the corners, then turn right-side out and press. Slipstitch the openings closed.

STEP 3 Cut a strip of gingham fabric 56¼ in. x 21¼ in./1.43 m x 54 cm for the flap. Press the flap lengthwise in half with the wrong sides facing. Pin the raw edges together. Mark the center with a row of pins parallel with the short edges. Pin one tie to the center line with the tie extending over the fold and the straight end 2 in./5 cm from the fold.

MAKING A DOUBLE-COMFORTER COVER WITH TIES

Cut a front 76 in. x 80 in./ 1.93 m x 2.03 m and a back 80 in. x 56¼ in./2.03 m x 1.43 m. Cut a strip of fabric 80 in. x 21¼ in./ 2.03 m x 54 cm for the flap and cut fourteen ties. Make a double-comforter cover in the same way as you made a single one.

STEP 4 Baste the remaining ties to the flap 8¼ in./20.5 cm apart. Stitch in place close to the edges and across the tie at the straight end, forming a 1½-in./3.8-cm square. Stitch a cross formation within the square.

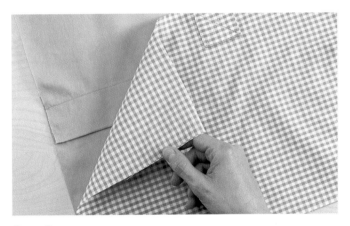

STEP 5 With the wrong sides facing, pin the front to the back, matching the short lower and long side raw edges. Pin the flap on top. The seams are stitched with a French seam. Stitch the outer edges, taking a ¼-in./6-mm seam allowance. Clip the corners. Turn wrong side out and stitch again, taking a ⅜-in./1-cm seam allowance. Turn right-side out. Pin the remaining ties to the front 4¾ in./12 cm from the lower edge of the flap.

YOU WILL NEED:

• THIN CARDBOARD
  FOR TEMPLATE
• PEN
• PLAIN FABRIC
• PRINTED FABRIC
• TAPE MEASURE
• TOOL COMPASSES
• BATTING
• NEEDLE AND
  THREAD/SEWING
  MACHINE
• CURVED BASTING
  PINS
• TAILOR'S CHALK
• SCISSORS
• IRON
• LONG RULE

PROJECT
Scalloped quilt

This pretty, scallop edged quilt is reversible, with a classic Toile de Jouy fabric on one side and a muted plain fabric on the other.

The quilt measures 76 in. x 57 in./1.92 m x 1.44 m, and it can therefore be made from 60-in./1.5-m wide fabric.

A reversible quilt gives you some flexibility when trying to match your bed linen and provides an easy way to have variety without needing two separate quilts.

HOW TO DO IT

If using a narrower-width fabric, join the widths with flat seams, with the full width along the center and an equal amount at each side. Remember to allow extra fabric to match patterns. Join the widths before drawing the scallops.

STEP 1 Cut a 4³/₄-in./12-cm diameter circle of thin cardboard for a template for the scallops. Divide the circle into quarters with a pen. Lay the plain fabric out flat, wrong side face up. With tailor's chalk, draw a 76 in. x 57 in./1.92 m x 1.44 m rectangle on the plain fabric. Draw a 2³/₈-in./6-cm deep margin inside the rectangle. Place the circle template on one corner, matching the quarter lines to the inner corner of the margin. Draw around three-quarters of the circle on the margin. Repeat on each corner. Move the template along the inner edges of the margin and draw a row of semicircles edge to edge for the scallops.

STEP 2 Cut 13 ft./4 m of 36-in./90-cm wide 2-oz./56-g batting widthwise in half. Butt the long edges together and join with a herringbone stitch. Place the printed fabric on top with the right side face up, smoothing the layers outward from the center.

STEP 5 Carefully trim away the batting in the seam allowance close to the stitching. Trim the seam allowance to ¹/₄ in./6 mm. Snip the curves and corners. Turn right-side out and gently press the edges of the scallops so the batting is not squashed flat. Turn the raw edges to the inside and slipstitch together.

STEP 3 With the right sides facing, place the plain fabric wrong-side up on the printed fabric. Smooth the layers outward from the center and baste or pin together with curved basting pins. Stitch along the scallops, leaving a 20-in./50-cm gap to turn.

STEP 6 Baste the layers together or pin with curved basting pins. Lay the quilt out flat, printed side face up. Use a long rule and tailor's chalk to draw straight lines along the length between the inner corners of the scallops. Set the sewing machine to a long stitch length. Starting on a center line, stitch along the lines.

STEP 4 On the right side of the printed fabric, mark the position of the unstitched scallops with tailor's chalk. Stitch along the drawn lines to secure the batting to the fabric, taking care not to catch in the plain fabric.

Finishing touches

It is the final decorative touches that can really make a soft furnishing project special. A touch of ribbon or braid is quick to apply and is a great way to introduce a new color or to play down an overpowering pattern. Similarly, a small handcrafted accessory, such as a photo frame or lampshade, will make a room complete and can solve the problem of hunting in stores for a certain item in an exact color that probably doesn't actually exist. A handcrafted item makes a great gift, because it will have a very special personal touch and show that thought and care has gone into the choice.

Braids and trimmings

Trimmings can really finish off a soft-furnishings project beautifully. Take your time to choose the braid or trimming that matches your fabric and the style of your room. Many trimmings are handmade and expensive in their own right, so choose with care and you won't make a costly mistake.

Many decorative braids and tapes are handmade using traditional methods. This makes them expensive, but only a small amount is needed to add that special touch.

A trimming should not overpower the item, but enhance it. Many fabric manufacturers produce a range of cords, braids, fringing, and gimp in matching colors to offset their fabrics.

Ribbons can set off a curtain rod and make a real feature of a window. Choose wire-edged ribbons to hold their shape when tied in bows.

You can add to cheap trimmings to make them fuller and more substantial. If you cannot find the exact color of a tassel, for instance, you can make your own (see page 837) or perhaps add a few yarns to hang among the top layer of threads. Make an exotic tassel from fine silk or organza ribbon. A row of beads or jewelry stones sewn around the edge of a tassel adds a touch of sparkle.

Trimming projects

A cushion can be livened up with an insertion into its seams. Cut strips of imitation suede or leather and cut a fringe along one side or trim with pinking shears. Sew ready-made ribbon roses about 2 in./5 cm apart along a length of ribbon and attach them to bedroom furnishings for a feminine touch.

Another idea is to collect fallen bird feathers, or buy them from craft suppliers, and glue them onto a lampshade. To make a feather-trimmed fastening, dab all-purpose household glue on the ends of a length of leather thonging, and poke each end into beads with large holes. Dab glue on the ends of the feathers and poke them into the other side of the beads for a Santa Fe-style curtain tieback. Colorful marabou feathers can be sewn to the curtain heading—this is a particularly effective technique when used on sheer drapes.

Surprisingly, silk flowers and leaves have many soft furnishing applications: they can be taken apart and sewn to cushion covers, drapes, tiebacks, and tablecloths. Sew a bead or sequin in the flower centers. Silk leaves trapped beneath a layer of organza on a cushion front look extremely pretty.

Using trimming effectively

Sew beads, jewelery stones, and sequins at random to a drape—they will sparkle when the light catches them. Buttons can be used decoratively in the same way: glistening mother-of-pearl buttons sewn in grid formation to the front of a cushion or along the edge of a throw provide an instant designer look. A string of tiny pearls or sequins can be used as an edging on drapes, cushions, and throws. Lampshades can be lavished with all sorts of items: attach gemstones or tiny pebbles to the shade by "sewing" them on with fine wire. A row of shells hung from drape clips adds a beachcomber theme to a bathroom.

If you have seen a beautiful trimming but can not think of a soft-furnishing use for it, consider other applications. A tassel fastened to a cabinet key gives it a sense of importance. Similarly, you can fasten a length of pretty gimp around the neck of a vase, or wind fringing around a lamp base for added effect.

Ribbons come in masses of colors, materials, and finishes. Wire-edged ribbons hold their shape well when formed into bows. Organza ribbons can be used quite lavishly without being over-powering. Lace edging instantly softens soft furnishings and gives a romantic, feminine look. To make a match for an antique-lace setting, dye white cotton lace by placing it in a cup of tea (without milk) for a few minutes, or longer for a darker shade.

Exotic ribbons can transform the look of your cushions and tablecloths.

PROJECT

Rosettes and bows

Trimmings that have been personally handcrafted always look particularly special, and you will come up with many opportunities to use them to show off a soft-furnishing feature.

Bows can be added to valances and tiebacks to create a romantic look, and rosettes attached to the corners of cushions and throws give them a sense of importance.

MAKING A ROSETTE

STEP 1 Cut a strip of fabric 18 in. x 3¹/₂ in./45 cm x 8.5 cm. Pin and baste an 18-in./45-cm length of ¹/₂-in. /1.2-cm-wide ribbon along one long edge on the wrong side, overlapping the fabric by ¹/₄ in./5 mm. Stitch close to the long inner edge of the ribbon.

STEP 2 Press the ribbon to the right side. Stitch close to the new inner edge of the ribbon. Pin a length of ribbon along the opposite long edge on the right side, overlapping the fabric by ¹/₄ in./5 mm. Stitch close to the inner edge of the ribbon. Press the ribbon to the wrong side. Stitch close to the ribbon's new inner edge.

STEP 3 Stitch the short ends together with a French seam taking a ³/₈-in./1-cm seam allowance, forming a ring. Set the sewing machine to its longest stitch length. Run a gathering stitch 1 in./2.5 cm from the outer edge of the second ribbon.

STEP 4 Pull up the gathers tightly, folding the second ribbon to the outside along the gathering. Secure with hand-stitches. Now fan open the rosette.

MAKING A BOW

STEP 1 Cut a strip of fabric 17 in. x 7 in./ 43.5 cm x 17.8 cm for the bow. Fold in half with the right sides together and stitch the long edges, taking a $^3/_8$-in./1-cm seam allowance. Press the seam open. Turn right-side out, position the seam along the center, and press. Mark the center with a row of pins on the seamed side of the bow.

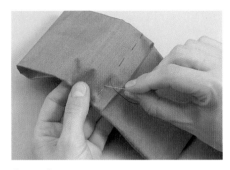

STEP 2 With the seamed side inside, lap each end over the center by $^5/_8$ in./1.5 cm. Baste across the center through all the layers.

STEP 3 Cut a strip of fabric 4$^3/_4$ in. x 2$^1/_4$ in./ 12.5 cm x 5.6 cm for the "knot." Press $^5/_8$ in./1.5 cm under on one long edge, then press the knot lengthwise in half.

STEP 4 Fold across the center of the bow in concertina pleats about $^5/_{16}$ in./8 mm deep. Bind the pleats with thread to secure them. Starting on the back of the bow, wrap the knot strip tightly around the bow center. Turn under the end and sew to the back of the bow.

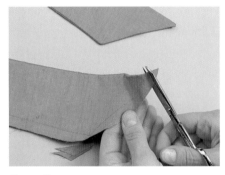

STEP 5 Refer to the diagram to cut the tails (see page 992). Press $^3/_8$ in./1 cm under at the narrow ends. Fold and pin lengthwise in half, with the right sides facing. Stitch the raw edges, taking a $^3/_8$-in./1-cm seam allowance. Clip the corners and turn right-side out.

STEP 6 Pin the upper edges of the tails into thirds to make a pleat, then oversew the edges. Pin the tails to the bow back and sew in place.

YOU WILL NEED:

• CONTRASTING WIDE RIBBONS (FOR WARP AND WEB)
• FABRIC FOR CUSHION
• IRON-ON INTERFACING
• IRON
• PINS
• SCISSORS
• CUSHION PAD
• MEASURING TAPE

PROJECT
A woven ribbon cushion

You can really go to town with decorative techniques on cushions. Ready-made cushions can be further enhanced by sewing on buttons, adding a beaded fringe or stamping, stenciling, and hand-painting the surface. Handweaving a cushion from strips of luxurious ribbon is also very effective.

Remove the cushion pad and slip a piece of plastic, such as a shopping bag, inside when stamping or painting to stop paint from seeping through to the back of the cushion. Relief-paint pens are a lot of fun to use—paint is squeezed from a tube through a nozzle leaving a fine line that stands proud of the fabric. When the paint has dried, simply follow the manufacturer's instructions to fix the paint. Relief-paint pens come in lots of bright colors, and also in exciting pearlized and glitter effects. (Children particularly love using these.) Sew ready-made embroidered or sequinned motifs to cushions for instant glamour. Ribbons can be applied to ready-made cushions too. Sew a scattering of ribbon roses to a cushion front or gather along the center of a length of ribbon and handsew it in swirling patterns.

More intricate ribbon designs will need to be worked on a cushion before it is made up. In this project, woven ribbons are applied to iron-on interfacing to form a panel or complete cushion front. They are extremely effective when a mix of printed and plain ribbons are used. Once you have mastered the basic weaving technique, experiment with other effects by mixing different textured ribbons in differing widths.

The technique of weaving ribbons has been used on this cushion cover to create an impressive effect. You could try using a variety of ribbons of different widths.

HOW TO DO IT

To make a 12-in./30-cm-square woven ribbon cushion, you will need 3½ yd./3 m of two 1½-in./3.9-cm-wide ribbons. Here, a printed ribbon is woven with a plain metallic ribbon. The cushion is made from metallic fabric to continue the effect.

STEP 1 Cut a 13-in./33-cm square of mediumweight iron-on interfacing and fabric for the front. Place the interfacing on an ironing board with the adhesive side face up. Cut eight 13-in./35-cm lengths of 1½-in./3.9-cm-wide printed ribbon for the "warp" ribbons. Working outward from the center, lay the ribbons across the interfacing, pinning them in place along the top edge only.

STEP 2 Cut eight 13¾-in./35-cm lengths of 1½-in./3.9-cm-wide plain ribbon for the "weft" ribbons. Weave the first weft ribbon in and out of the warp ribbons, passing it over one warp ribbon and under the next until you reach the opposite side.

STEP 3 Weave the second weft ribbon under the first warp ribbon, over the next and so on. Continue with the remaining ribbons, forming a checkered pattern. Adjust the ribbons so they lie evenly. Press with a hot iron to fuse the ribbons to the interfacing. Remove the pins and cut off the excess. Baste the interfacing to the fabric front with right sides uppermost. Cut two rectangles of fabric for the back 7½ in. x 13 in./ 19 cm x 33 cm. Press under a ³⁄₈-in./1-cm-deep double hem on one long edge of each piece and stitch in place.

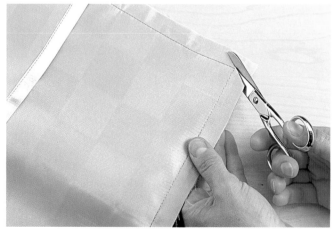

STEP 4 With right sides facing, pin the backs to the front, matching the raw edges and overlapping the hems at the center. Stitch the outer edges. Clip the corners and turn right-side out. Slip a 12-in./30-cm cushion pad inside.

PROJECT
Lampshade covers

A softly pleated lampshade can be made from a remnant of lightweight furnishing fabric that has been used elsewhere in the room, or from a remnant of silk in a dramatic color. You can trim it in a style of your choosing—perhaps using pompons if you wanted to create a retro look.

The lampshade is attached to a coolie-shape lampshade frame, or can be slipped over an existing lampshade. If using a metal lampshade frame, bind the top ring with cotton tape, overlapping the ends and sewing them together.

A stunning trimming, such as the marabou feathers used here, provides an element of fun.

Ruched lampshade

Swathes of organza caught at random on a plain lampshade give a contemporary approach to a retro style. Use silk organza because it drapes more fluidly than synthetic versions. Silk organza with metallic threads has been used here to make the most of the lamp when it is illuminated. Ideally, use a conical paper shade for this project.

MAKING A LOOSE LAMPSHADE COVER

STEP 1 Cut a strip of fabric that is twice the circumference of the top of the shade plus 1¼ in. /3 cm for seam allowances, by the height of the shade plus 3⅝ in. /9 cm. Press ⅜ in./1 cm under, then ⅝ in./1.5 cm on one long edge for the lower hem. Machine or handsew in place.

STEP 2 Press ⅜ in./1 cm under, then 1¼ in./3 cm on the upper long edge. Stitch close to the inner pressed edge.

STEP 3 Start 1¼ in./3 cm from an end: fold the upper edge in ⅝ in./1.5-cm-deep pleats 1¼ in./3 cm apart. Pin in place 1 in./2.5 cm below the upper edge. Slip the cover on the lampshade to check the fit. Overlap the short raw edges by 1¼ in./3 cm. Adjust the pleats if needed.

STEP 4 Sew the pleats in place 1 in./2.5 cm below the upper edge. With right sides facing, stitch the short edges together, taking a ⅝-in./1.5-cm seam allowance.

STEP 5 Neaten the seam with pinking shears; press open the seam. Put the cover on the lampshade. Catch to the top ring with a few stitches. Sew a decorative trim around the pleat.

MAKING A RUCHED LAMPSHADE

STEP 1 Fold a 1¼-yd./1-m square of silk organza diagonally in half and work on the fabric through both layers. Lay the fabric over the front of the lampshade with the fold ¼ in./5 mm below the lower edge; have the seam of the lampshade at the back.

STEP 2 Arrange the organza in random and irregular pleats, pinning the organza to the lampshade as you work. Pin the organza to the lampshade as far as the seam on one side and 2 in./ 5 cm from the seam on the other.

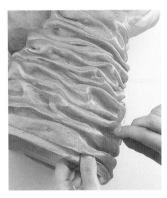

STEP 3 Catch the pleats to the shade with tiny hand-stitches. It is not necessary to sew all the pleats as the stiffness of the organza will hold the shape.

STEP 4 Trim the organza to ⅝ in./1.5 cm beyond the seam on both raw edges at the back. Fold under ⅝ in./1.5 cm on the second raw edge and fold and pin the organza in pleats along the seam. Handsew securely in place.

STEP 5 Cut off the excess fabric ¾ in./2 cm above and below the shade with pinking shears. Glue the raw edges inside the shade with all-purpose household glue.

YOU WILL NEED:

- LAMPSHADE RING
- SHOT SILK FABRIC FOR LANTERN (SEE DIAGRAM)
- NEEDLE (INCLUDING FINE NEEDLE) AND THREAD
- SEWING MACHINE
- IRON
- SCISSORS
- LARGE AND SMALL BEADS
- TAPE MEASURE

PROJECT
Moorish lantern

Lend an exotic feel to a room with a flamboyant fabric lantern. Ideally suited to Eastern-style decor, lanterns are inexpensive to create and can be embellished with beads and tassels. Instead of a lampshade frame, the lantern is supported by a utility lampshade ring, which can be bought cheaply and in various sizes from craft suppliers.

Ribbon and paper lanterns

A very simple way to use remnants of ribbons is to cut them into lengths and wrap one end over a utility lampshade ring and handsew in position, enclosing the ring. Turn under the lower raw ends, either straight across or to a point, and sew in place, then attach a large bead to each ribbon end. Embellish inexpensive Chinese paper lanterns by sewing long streamers of fine ribbons to them. This is great for decorating a garden party, because the ribbons will move in the breeze.

It is easy to change the color of a plain paper lantern by making a tube of colored organza to slip over it. Sew on a few beads or sequins at random to catch the light. Catch the organza to the top of the lantern with a few discreet stitches.

This Moorish lantern will lend an exotic air to any decorative scheme. It looks particularly effective when made in rich-colored silks.

HOW TO DO IT

If this shapely lantern is made from shot silk, it will subtly change color when viewed from different angles. Beads are sewn to the points, but attach tassels instead if you prefer. Take ⅜-in./1-cm seam allowances throughout.

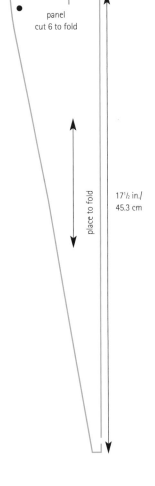

STEP 1 From fabric, cut six panels and six pediments (see diagrams right). Stitch the panels together in pairs along one long edge, ending the stitching at the lower dot.

STEP 2 Stitch all the panels together along the long edges, stitching two opposite seams between the dots for attaching to the lampshade ring. Press each seam open after stitching. Trim the seam allowance to ¼ in./ 5 mm at the lower edge and point to reduce the bulk. Turn the lantern right-side out.

STEP 3 With right sides facing, stitch the pediments together in pairs, leaving the straight upper edges open. Snip the curves; clip corners. Turn right-side out; press. Thread a fine needle with a double length of thread and knot the ends securely. Insert the needle through the point of the lantern and bring it out on the right side. Thread on four large beads, then a small bead.

STEP 4 Pull the beads along the thread so the first large bead is against the lantern point. Insert the needle up through the large beads to the inside of the lantern so the small bead rests on the last large bead. Repeat to fix securely. Sew a large and a small bead to the point of each pediment. Baste the raw edges together.

STEP 5 Slip the lantern through a 12-in./30-cm-diameter utility lampshade ring. Lift each pediment over the ring, positioning the seams with a ⅜-in./1-cm gap at the intersections of the ring.

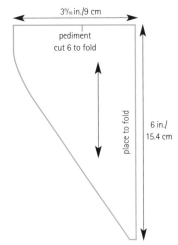

STEP 6 Slipstitch the top of the pediments together edge to edge for ⅜ in./1 cm Catch to the panel seams with a few stitches, enclosing the ring. With right side of pediments facing wrong side of lantern, stitch each pediment to a lantern panel, matching the notches. Press the seams open.

YOU WILL NEED:
- SOFT, FLEECE FABRICS FOR THROW
- NEEDLE AND THREAD/SEWING MACHINE
- IRON
- SCISSORS
- PINS
- AIR-ERASABLE PEN
- SINGLE TWIST YARN AND NEEDLE
- MOTHER-OF-PEARL BUTTONS
- TAPE MEASURE

PROJECT
Double-layer throw

An elegant throw provides a swift cover-up on shabby seating and can change the mood of a room, from summer to winter for example, as a sumptuous throw looks warm and inviting on a cold night. Velvet, chenille, or fake fur fabrics can all be used, but fleece is also a good choice because it is washable and wears well.

A throw is a very simple soft furnishing project to create. Make an instant no-sew throw by using a bedspread or tablecloth, or rug, or add finishing touches to a ready-made throw by adding fringing or tassels to the edges. Drape the throw loosely over a sofa or chair. Alternatively, tuck it in or secure it in place with corkscrew pins.

For a throw that will cover your piece of furniture completely, measure the sofa or chair from the floor at the front to the floor at the back with a tape measure, following the contours of the furniture. Next, measure from side to side in the same way. Add 12 in./30 cm to the measurements for each tuck in. For a single-layer throw, add a 1-in./2.5-cm hem on all edges. Alternatively, a small throw that drapes across part of a chair is very effective. If you need to join fabric widths, use flat felled seams on a single-layer throw or flat seams on a double-layer throw.

A double-layer throw is bagged out, or the edges are bound. Add seam allowances for bagging out. The two layers need to be caught together, either by quilting, spot-quilting, or just

catching the layers with a few strong but discreet stitches. If the throw has fabric widths joined, catch the layers together along the seams. There are many ways to decorate a throw. If you want decoration in just a few areas, put the throw in position and mark the best spots for showing off your handiwork. Large appliquéd shapes cut from felt are quick to apply with bonding web—felt does not fray, so you could highlight the design with a few bold embroidery stitches.

Satin ribbons stitched in grid formation to an entire throw give a lovely shiny contrast on a matt-textured throw. A row of eyelets or buttonholes along two opposite edges can be laced with cord for a nautical look.

Most fabrics are suitable for throws, but avoid stiff ones because they will not drape well. A double-layer throw can be made from two coordinating fabrics.

ABOVE RIGHT:
A bedspread makes a practical loose throw, which can transform a sofa and instantly alter the mood of a room.

HOW TO DO IT

This small, vibrant throw is made from soft, fleece fabric in two colorways.
It is spot-quilted with pretty mother-of-pearl buttons.

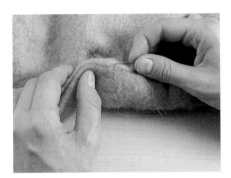

STEP 1 Cut one rectangle from two fabrics 59 in. x 49 in./1.5 m x 1.25 m. With the right sides facing, stitch the outer edges, taking a ³⁄₈-in./1-cm seam allowance and leaving a 12-in./30-cm gap to turn through. Clip the corners and turn the throw right-side out. Press and slipstitch the opening edges together.

STEP 2 Smooth the throw out flat and pin the layers together. Use an air-erasable pen or pins to mark a grid of dots about 10 in./25.5 cm apart on the top layer. Spot-quilt the layers together at each dot, using a single twist yarn, threading on a ¹⁄₂-in./1.2-cm button and knotting the yarn on top. See the spot quilting technique in steps 3–4 on pages 944–945.

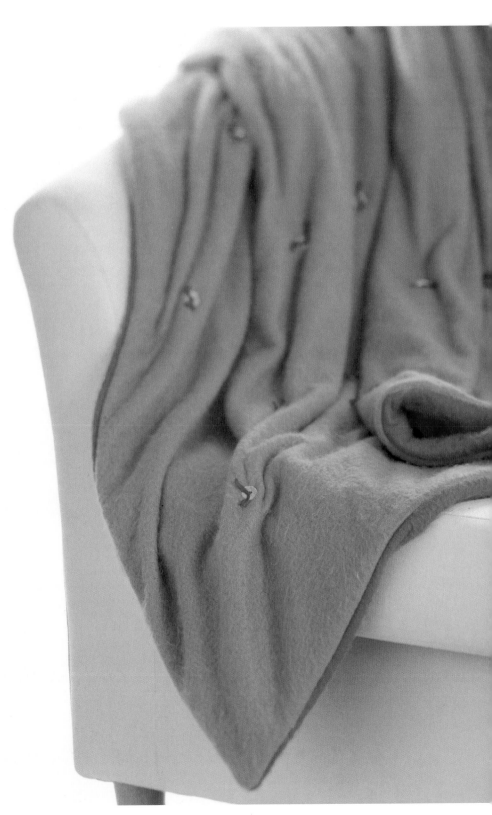

YOU WILL NEED:
- FABRIC FOR DISPLAY
- CURTAIN ROD
- DECORATIVE FINIALS OR TASSELS
- WOODEN DOWELING
- NEEDLE AND THREAD/SEWING MACHINE
- IRON
- SAW
- ROD SUPPORT AND ATTACHMENTS

PROJECT
Wall hangings

There is often that favorite piece of fabric that seems just too good to cut up and make into something. The design may mean that it looks its best only if kept in one piece, or it may be an embroidery, a handworked quilt, or painted silk scarf. Fabric can be framed, but there is an easier way to display these treasured textiles.

Hanging the piece on a wall is an ideal way to show it off. To hang an embroidery or quilt, a length of touch-and-close tape can be handsewn to the back of the hanging at the upper edge. If attaching to a quilt, sew through the backing fabric and the batting so it is supported well, but do not let the stitches show on the right side. Fix the hanging to a wooden cleat attached to the wall. A hanging sleeve can also be attached to the back of the hanging. Cut an 4½-in./11-cm-wide strip of fabric that is 2 in./5 cm shorter than the width of the quilt. Stitch a ⅝-in./1.5-cm-deep double hem at each end. Press under ⅝ in./ 1.5 cm on the long edges. Pin the sleeve centrally to the back of the hanging just below the upper edge. Handsew securely in place, taking the stitches through to the batting of the quilt. Cut a wooden cleat ¾ in./2 cm shorter than the sleeve. Insert the cleat through the sleeve.

HOW TO DO IT

The simplest way to display a length of fabric is to make a channel at the top and lower edge. A length of wood doweling slotted through the lower channel will hold the fabric taut. A curtain rod threaded through the top channel can have decorative finials or tassels attached to the ends.

STEP 1 Press under ⅜ in./1 cm, then ⅝ in./1.5 cm on the long edges. Stitch close to the inner pressed edges.

STEP 2 Press ⅜ in./1 cm, then 2¾ in./ 7 cm to the underside on the upper edge to form a channel. Stitch close to both pressed edges.

STEP 3 Press ⅜ in./1 cm, then 1 in./2.5 cm to the underside on the lower edge to form a channel. Stitch close to the inner pressed edge. Cut a length of ⅜-in./1-cm-thick wood doweling ⅜ in./ 1 cm shorter than the width of the lower edge. Insert the doweling into the lower channel. Slipstitch the ends closed.

STEP 4 Insert the curtain rod through the upper channel, then check the length (allowing for finials at each end) and cut the rod shorter if necessary. Fix on the finials. Attach the curtain rod to the wall using a rod support.

PROJECTS
Padded photo frame

A treasured photograph needs a special setting. A padded photo frame is very effective and would make a delightful gift. Adapt the technique to make frames to your personal requirements by altering the shape and size. Although velvet can be difficult to sew, only a small amount of stitching is involved in covering the frame, so don't be put off.

YOU WILL NEED:
- PHOTOGRAPH FOR DISPLAY
- THICK CARDBOARD
- BATTING
- FABRIC GLUE
- COTTON FABRIC FOR FACING
- PINS
- VELVET
- NEEDLE AND THREAD
- IRON
- SCISSORS
- SNAP-BLADE KNIFE

HOW TO DO IT

STEP 1 Cut two frames from thick cardboard and one frame from 4-oz./113-g batting (see diagram on page 993). Cutting along the solid lines, cut out the window on one cardboard frame for the front. Stick the batting to the front frame with fabric glue.

STEP 2 Cut two frames from velvet along the broken line: do not cut out the window (see diagram on page 993). Cut a facing from cotton fabric, cutting ¼ in./5 mm inside the outer solid line. Draw the window on the facing. Matching right sides, pin the facing to one velvet frame and stitch along the window outline. Cut out the window, leaving a ¼-in./5-mm seam allowance. Snip the curves. Press the facing inside.

STEP 3 Place the front frame batting-side down on the velvet frame. Adjust the seam allowance to lie on the underside of the front frame and pull the facing through to the back. Glue the facing to the underside of the frame, then pull the outer edges smoothly over the underside and stick in place.

STEP 4 Cover the remaining cardboard frame with the remaining velvet frame, gluing the raw edges onto the underside. With the wrong sides facing, slipstitch the frames securely together along the outer edges, leaving a gap at one side between the dots to insert a 5 in. x 4 in./12.5 cm x 10 cm photograph.

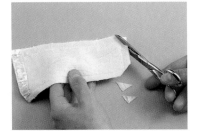

STEP 5 Cut two stands from velvet, following the broken lines. Press under ³⁄₈ in./1 cm along the lower wide ends. With right sides facing, stitch the stands along the raw edges, taking a ³⁄₈-in. /1-cm seam allowance, leaving the lower edge open. Clip the corners and turn through.

STEP 6 Cut a stand from thick cardboard, cutting along the solid lines. Score across the dotted lines with a snap-blade knife. Bend the stand outward along the scored line. Insert the cardboard stand into the velvet stand. Slipstitch the lower edge closed. Glue the upper 1½ in./4 cm of the stand to the back of the frame.

YOU WILL NEED:

- STRIPED COTTON
  FABRIC FOR CANOPY
- COTTON FABRIC FOR
  FACING
- PINS
- TAPE MEASURE
- NEEDLE AND
  THREAD/SEWING
  MACHINE
- IRON
- SCISSORS
- METAL EYELETS
- WOOD DOWELING
  POLES
- PAINT OR VARNISH
- SANDPAPER
- AWL
- HAMMER AND
  LARGE NAILS

PROJECTS

A yard canopy

Make the most of sunny days with a protective canopy in the yard. The canopy can be freestanding with a pole at each corner and cords tied to tent pegs, or it can have poles at each side of one end and be tied at the other corners to a building or to the branches of a tree.

The poles can be supported in flagstaff sockets fixed permanently into a concrete floor, or wedged in flower pots weighted with pieces of brick and gravel inside.

Although large, yard canopies are easy to make. The basic canopy as described opposite can be enhanced in many ways: add a zigzag or scalloped border at each end, or tie cascading ribbons from the eyelets for a celebration yard party, binding ribbons around the poles to continue the theme. The canopy can be made from wide bands of contrasting fabrics, or can have braid or colored tapes sewn along its length.

Avoid stretchy fabrics and those that are very heavy; mediumweight canvas is a good choice. A sheer-fabric canopy would look very pretty. A row of awnings made from deckchair canvas can be extremely smart especially if coordinated with yard seating.

Canopies can be freestanding or attached to walls or yard furniture.

HOW TO DO IT

This canopy measures 57 in. x 78 in./1.45 m x 2 m and is made from striped cotton fabric. It has metal eyelets at the corners and a smart border at each end. You can adapt the size to suit your own requirements.

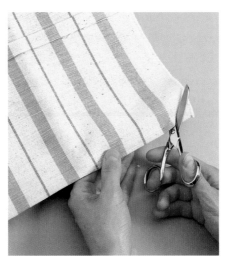

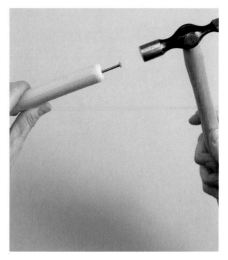

STEP 1 Cut the canopy 59 in. x 102³/₄ in./1.5 m x 2.61 m from fabric. Press ⁵/₈ in./1.5 cm under on the short edges. Fold 6³/₄ in./17 cm to the right side at the pressed ends to form a facing.

STEP 2 Stitch the side edges, taking a 1-in./2.5-cm seam allowance. Clip the corners and trim the seam allowance. Turn right-side out. Press ³/₈ in./1 cm under, then ⁵/₈ in./1.5 cm on the long edges. Stitch close to the inner pressed edges, continuing the stitching to the ends of the canopy.

STEP 3 Stitch close to the inner pressed edges of the facings, then 1¹/₂ in./3.8 cm from the first stitching.

STEP 4 Fix a ⁵/₈-in./1.5-cm metal eyelet centrally between the stitched lines of the facings ³/₄ in./2 cm inside the long edges. If the canopy is to be freestanding, fix an eyelet halfway along the long, side edges to tie cord through.

STEP 5 Apply two coats of exterior paint or varnish to 78-in./2-m-long, ³/₄-in./2-cm-diameter wood doweling poles. Sand one end of each pole to curve the edges. Make a hole in the center of the rounded ends with a awl, and then hammer in a large nail, leaving about ¹/₂ in./1.2 cm of the nail standing proud to slot through the eyelets.

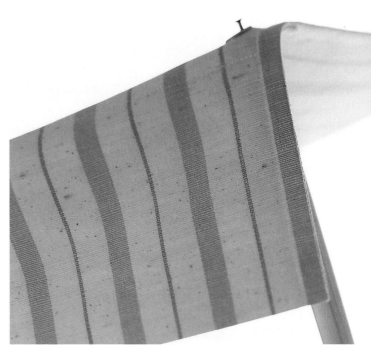

YOU WILL NEED:
- **LAMPSHADE FRAME**
- **DUPION SILK REMNANT FOR SHADE**
- **LINING FABRIC**
- **NEEDLE AND DOUBLE THREAD**
- **WHITE COTTON TAPE AND ELASTIC BAND**
- **TAILOR'S CHALK**
- **SCISSORS**
- **PINS**
- **IRON**
- **BEADED TRIM AND VELVET RIBBON**

PROJECT
Lined lampshade

Ready-made lampshades come in a limited range of fabrics. Making your own lined lampshade gives you far more freedom to create the right ambience in a room with some well-chosen lighting. Use a pale-colored dress-weight lining inside the shade to reflect the light.

The lampshade needs a trimming at least ⅜ in./1 cm wide at the upper and lower edges to conceal the edges of the lining. Metal or plastic-coated-metal lampshade frames are cheap to buy. Metal frames must be wrapped in tape. Light-to-mediumweight fabrics that drape well, such as silk, fine cotton, linen, and crêpe, are recommended to cover the shade. Make sure that you avoid stiff fabrics and fabrics that are likely to fray easily.

Making your own lampshades means you can include the lamps in the decorative scheme of a room. Choose new fabric or use remnants of fabric used elsewhere in the room.

HOW TO DO IT

A remnant of dupion silk was used to cover this 7-in./18-cm-diameter drum lampshade frame. Keep the tape reel from unraveling as you bind the frame by securing it with an elastic band. A beaded trim and velvet ribbon are beautiful finishing touches.

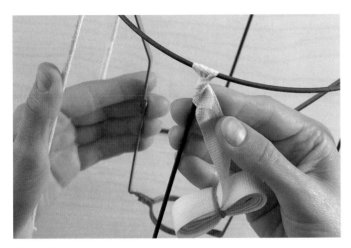

STEP 1 To tape a metal frame, start at the top of one strut by binding the end of ¹/₂-in./1.2-cm-wide white cotton tape over the top ring and around the tape end, securing it against the strut. Tightly bind the tape diagonally down the strut so each wrap of the tape slightly overlaps the previous one. At the lower ring, pull the tape through the last wrap. Cut off the excess. Repeat on all the struts except the last one. Tape the top ring starting at the last strut, then work down the last strut and around the bottom ring.

STEP 2 Fold a square of the silk fabric diagonally in half with right sides facing; it must be large enough to cover one half of the frame with at least a 1¹/₂-in. /4-cm margin all around. With the folded edge parallel to the lower ring, lay the fabric over one half of the frame. Pin to the frame at the top and lower edge of two opposite struts. Adjust and re-pin the fabric to half of the frame at regular intervals, pulling the fabric so it lies taut and smooth.

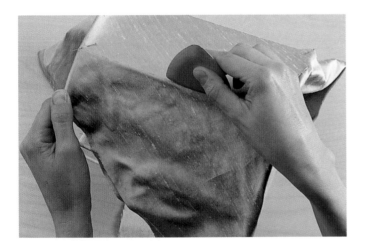

STEP 3 When the fabric is free of wrinkles and lies evenly, mark the fabric along the center of the pinned struts with tailor's chalk. Mark the position of the upper and lower rings. Remove the fabric, keeping the two layers pinned together. Cut along the fold.

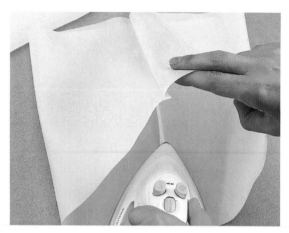

STEP 4 Stitch along the drawn lines, starting and finishing ³/₄ in./2 cm beyond the ring positions. Trim the seam allowances to ¹/₄ in./5 mm. Press the seams to one side. Cut the upper and lower edges level with the ends of the seams. Fold, fit, pin, and mark the lining fabric in the same way. Stitch ¹/₈ in./3 mm inside the drawn lines; this is because the lining should be smaller to fit inside the frame. Trim and press.

STEP 5 Slip the cover over the frame, right side outward. Adjust the seams along two opposite struts. Pin the cover to the frame rings so the fabric is taut and smooth. Using double thread, oversew the cover to the rings using very small, neat stitches. Trim away the excess fabric close to the stitching.

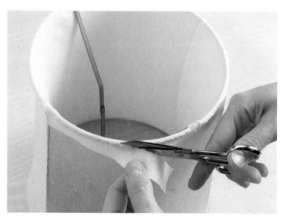

STEP 6 Slip the lining into the frame with the wrong sides facing and match the seams, pinning in place. Snip the lining at the gimbals where they join the upper ring. Wrap the lining over the frame rings and re-pin so the lining is taut. Oversew the lining to the rings, taking care not to sew through to the lining inside the lampshade. The stitches on the outside will be covered with the trimming. Trim away the excess lining close to the stitches.

STEP 7 Cut a 1-in./2.5-cm-wide strip of lining 5³/₄ in./14 cm long. Press lengthwise in half, then in half again. Cut the strip in half. Slip one strip under a gimbal and pin the ends over the outside of the lampshade. Oversew to the upper edge. Cut off the excess strip and repeat on the other side. Sew the trimming to the upper and lower edges of the lampshade. If using a beaded trim, sew it in place first, then sew a ribbon on top to cover the tape edge.

FAR RIGHT: **Lighting is an extremely important element in a room. Make sure you choose a fabric that will reflect the light just the way you want it to.**

YOU WILL NEED:
- CHENILLE FABRIC FOR THROW
- SILK FOR BORDER
- NEEDLE AND THREAD/SEWING MACHINE
- SCISSORS
- PINS
- TAPE MEASURE
- IRON

PROJECT
Bordered throw

Make a sumptuous throw from luxurious fabrics to snuggle into on cold winter evenings. A soft chenille has been used to make this warm and cozy throw. A deep border of chocolate-brown dupion silk edges the throw with neat mitered corners.

A new throw is a simple and effective way to transform a sofa or armchair.

HOW TO DO IT

STEP 1 Cut a rectangle of chenille 52³/₈ in. x 38¹/₂ in./ 1.33 m x 98 cm. For the border, cut two strips of silk 61¹/₂ in. x 9¹/₈ in./ 1.56 m x 23 cm and two strips 47⁵/₈ in. x 9¹/₈ in./1.21 m x 23 cm. Refer to the diagram below to cut the ends of the borders to points. Press ⁵/₈ in./1.5 cm under on one long edge of each border.

STEP 2 With the right sides facing and matching the pressed edges, stitch the short borders between the long borders at the mitered ends, finishing ⁵/₈ in./ 1.5 cm from the long raw edges. Now clip the corners and press the seams open.

STEP 3 With the right sides facing, stitch the long raw edges of the border to the throw, pivoting the seam at the corners. Press the seam toward the border.

STEP 4 Pin the pressed edges along the seam, then press the border in half. Slipstitch the pressed edge along the seam.

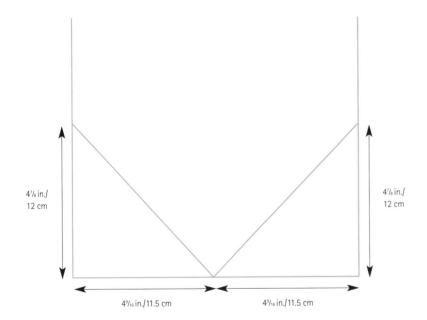

4⁷/₈ in./ 12 cm

4⁷/₈ in./ 12 cm

4⁹/₁₆ in./11.5 cm

4⁹/₁₆ in./11.5 cm

TOP TIP

Add a glamorous silk border to an inexpensive ready-made throw by cutting it to size and following the instructions above.

YOU WILL NEED:

• SHOT SILK FABRIC
  FOR ROSETTE AND
  TAILS
• TAPE MEASURE
• VALANCE
  INTERFACING
• PENCIL
• FINE BRIDAL PINS
• NEEDLE AND
  THREAD
• IRON
• SCISSORS
• CURTAIN RING

PROJECT
Choux-rosette picture hanger

Add a touch of opulence when displaying a favorite picture with a couture-style choux rosette with long tails to hang behind the picture.

Silk suits the design, especially shot silk—the hand-stitched ruching will catch the light and change color in the shadows of the rosette.

You can use a stylish rosette to draw attention to a favorite framed picture.

HOW TO DO IT

Use fine bridal pins to pin the rosette so as not to mark the silk.

STEP 1 Cut a 3½-in./9-cm-diameter circle of valance interfacing. Divide the circle into quarters with a pencil on the right side. Cut a 10½-in./27-cm square of fabric, i.e. three times the diameter of the circle.

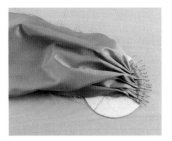

STEP 2 Fold one edge of the square into pleats and, with right sides uppermost, pin the pleats to the circumference of one quarter of the circle. The pleats do not have to be equal in size. Handsew the pleats in place. Continue pleating the sides of the square onto the circle quarters.

STEP 3 Turn the rosette over and lift the edges of the silk over the edge of the circle for about ¼ in./6 mm. Catch in place, taking care not to take the stitches through to the silk on the right side.

STEP 4 On the right side, gently scrunch the fabric to reduce its bulk. Push pins through to the back of the rosette to hold the shape. Catch in place with tiny discreet stitches, taking the thread through to the back of the rosette. Cut a 4-in./10-cm-diameter circle of silk to neaten the back. Pin to the back of the rosette and turn under the edges, then slipstitch in place.

STEP 5 Refer to the diagram to cut out the tails. Press ⅜ in./1 cm under at the narrow ends. Fold and pin lengthwise in half, with the right sides facing. Stitch the raw edges, taking a ⅜-in./1-cm seam allowance. Clip the corners, then turn right-side out and press. Sew to the back of the rosette, fanning the tails outward. Sew a curtain ring to the back for hanging up the rosette.

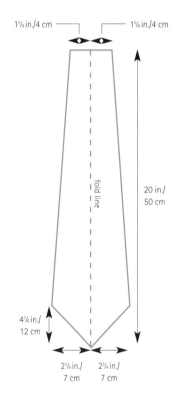

1⅝ in./4 cm   1⅝ in./4 cm

fold line

20 in./50 cm

4⅞ in./12 cm

2¾ in./7 cm   2¾ in./7 cm

YOU WILL NEED:
- CAFETIÈRE
- TAPE MEASURE
- FABRIC FOR COZY
- IRON
- BATTING
- IRON-ON-
  INTERFACING FOR
  STRAPS
- PINS
- SCISSORS
- NEEDLE AND
  THREAD/SEWING
  MACHINE
- POPPERS

PROJECT
Cafetière cozy

Keep the coffee piping hot with a neat, padded cozy that wraps around a cafetière. The cozy is custom-made for an exact fit and it incorporates a pocket on the front where you can store a small spoon. Overlapping straps fasten the cozy with poppers.

This cozy keeps the coffee hot for a second cup and it is more attractive and colorful than a plain cafetière.

HOW TO DO IT

With a tape measure, measure the height of the cafetière from the base of the pot to just below the spout. Next, measure the circumference, passing the tape through the handle. Measure the distance between the inner ends of the handle for the depth of the straps. Take ⅜-in./1-cm seam allowances throughout.

STEP 1 For the cozy, cut two rectangles of fabric and one of 4-oz./112-g batting that is the height measurement plus ³/₄ in./2 cm by the circumference measurement less ³/₈ in./1 cm. Cut two rectangles of fabric and iron-on interfacing for the straps 3¹/₈ in./ 8 cm by the depth of the strap plus ³/₄ in./2 cm. Press the interfacing to the wrong sides of the straps to fuse them together.

STEP 2 Fold and pin the straps in half along their depth with the right sides facing. Stitch the upper and lower edges. Clip the corners, then turn and press the straps. Pin a strap to each end on the right side of one cozy.

STEP 3 Cut a rectangle of fabric for the pocket 5¹/₄ in. x 2³/₄ in./ 13 cm x 7 cm. Press ³/₈ in./1 cm under, and then ³/₄ in./2 cm on the short upper edge. Stitch close to the inner pressed edge. Now press ³/₈ in./1 cm under on the remaining pressed edges.

STEP 4 Wrap the cozy around the cafetière to check the fit. The straps should slip through the handle and overlap. Pin the pocket to the front of the cozy, and baste the straps and pocket in place. Stitch the pockets in position close to the side and lower edges, stitching back and forth a few times at the upper edge to reinforce them.

STEP 5 Place the cozy with the straps and pocket right-side up on the batting, then pin the remaining cozy on top with the right sides facing. Cut the corners diagonally to angle them. Stitch the outer edges, leaving a 4-in./10-cm gap in the lower edge. Carefully trim away the batting in the seam allowance. Clip the corners and turn through.

STEP 6 Press the edges, then slipstitch the opening closed. Topstitch ¹/₄ in./6 mm from the outer edges. Attach two poppers to the straps, following the manufacturer's directions.

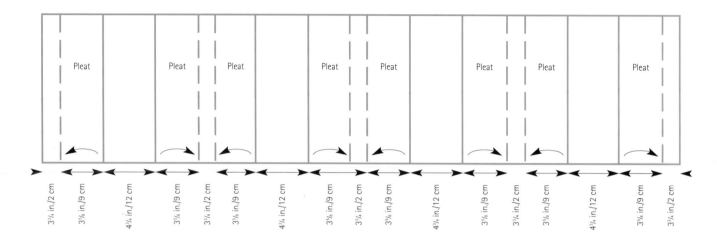

Shoe caddy—pocket strip pattern
(pages 908–909)

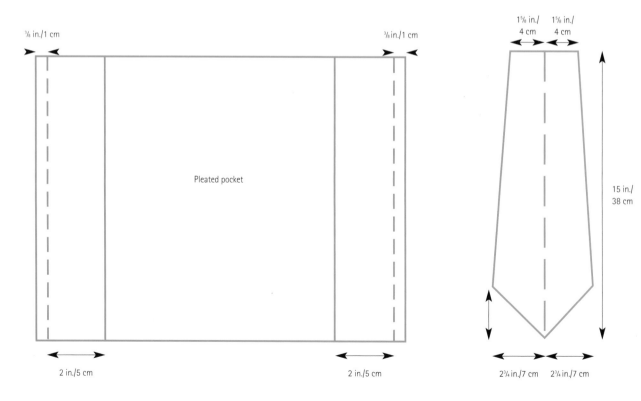

Child's wall tidy (page 920)

Bow tail pattern (page 969)

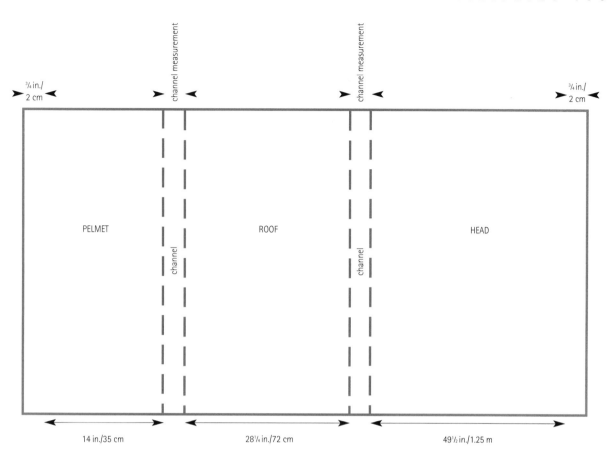

³⁄₄ in./ 2 cm

channel measurement

channel measurement

³⁄₄ in./ 2 cm

PELMET

channel

ROOF

channel

HEAD

14 in./35 cm

28¹⁄₄ in./72 cm

49¹⁄₂ in./1.25 m

Bed canopy (page 951)

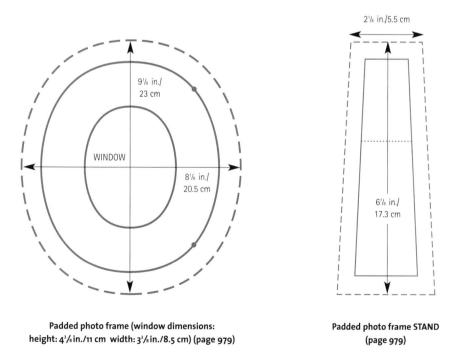

2¹⁄₈ in./5.5 cm

9¹⁄₈ in./ 23 cm

WINDOW

8¹⁄₈ in./ 20.5 cm

6⁷⁄₈ in./ 17.3 cm

**Padded photo frame (window dimensions:
height: 4³⁄₈ in./11 cm width: 3³⁄₈ in./8.5 cm) (page 979)**

**Padded photo frame STAND
(page 979)**

PLEASE NOTE: THESE PATTERNS ARE GUIDES ONLY AND ARE NOT TO SCALE

glossary

Abrasives
Sheet materials with differing grit sizes used for taking back a surface, removing a finish or a sheen. Abrasives are available in a variety of grades from coarse to very fine.

Admixtures
Additives to a mortar mix, for example liquid plasticizer, mixed in to provide a supply of minute air bubbles. This makes the mix easier to work and improves resistance to frost when set.

Anchor bolt
A fixing bolt securing a wood or metal frame to a masonry wall or solid floor. Anchor bolts are also called shield anchors, or sleeve anchors for a low-stress fix.

Appliqué
Fabric shapes applied to a background fabric by hand, or zigzagged by machine.

Aspect
The direction that a house or room faces: a southerly aspect faces directly south.

Auger bit
Large-channeled, self-starting spiral drill piece for boring through wood.

Awl
A small pointed tool for piercing holes in leather.

Backsaw
A small to medium size handsaw for accurate cross-cutting, especially wood joints. It is called a backsaw because it has a stabilizing steel or brass strip folded along the top of the blade.

Bagged out
Two pieces of fabric the same size, stitched all round and turned to the right side.

Batten
A strip of wood slotted into blinds to hold fabric taut, or attached above a window to hang blinds from.

Bias
A 45-degree angle on fabric. Bias-cut strips are used to make bindings and to cover piping.

Binding
Narrow strips of fabric bound around the raw edges of fabric to neaten them. Binding can be bought from a store or it can easily be made using a sewing-machine.

Blistered work
This is a defect, a finish in paint or varnish where small air bubbles have appeared on the surface.

Bond
In brickwork, this is a decorative system used to mortar bricks together to form a strong and cohesive wall arrangement.

Bouclé

A yarn spun with a looped finish, either knitted or woven.

Bowing

Wood lengths bent out of true by uneven shrinkage or supporting heavy weights.

Bradawl

A small tool for piercing holes in wood for screws, nails, and hooks.

Butt

As in butt joint: where items meet but do not overlap.

Canopy

A fabric panel fixed above head height, for example above a bed or a sunscreen for an outdoor chair.

Casement

Hinged, opening window frame, in metal, plastic, or wood, forming part of a larger frame.

Chair rail

Beading or paneling fixed on the lower half of a wall, well above the baseboard. It is a traditional feature that has become more popular again in recent years.

Chalk line

A taught, straight string, fixed at each end and dusted with chalk. When "snapped" against a surface, it leaves an accurate guideline.

Chamfer

A 45-degree symmetrical bevel, removing the right angle of a board.

Chuck

Lockable, adjustable jaws where a bit is inserted. A chuck is used for rotary drilling applications.

Circuit breaker

A protective device that disconnects the mains supply to a power tool in the case of fault or overload.

Cleat

A length of softwood, often used as an invisible support.

Clipping

Cutting across the corner of a seam allowance to reduce the bulk of the fabric at the seam.

Contact adhesive

A glue that is applied to two surfaces that bond instantly on meeting, without the use of cramps or support fixings.

Counterbore

To drill a straight-sided hole, to be filled later with a plug, letting a screwhead to be hidden below a wood surface.

Counterpunch

To set a nail below the wood surface, filling the entry hole with a matching colored filler.

Countersink
To drill a cone shaped recess in wood, allowing a similarly shaped screwhead to sit flush with, or slightly below, the surface.

Crown molding
Traditionally a molding for doors and windows, covering the gap between frame and wall. Often crown molding is incorrectly used as a generic term for moldings.

Distemper
Traditional water-based colored paint with a mat finish that dries to a powdery bloom. Distemper is lighter in color when it is dry than when it has been applied.

Dowel
A length of rounded wood inserted into blinds to hold the fabric taut.

Drop
The distance of a vertical descent, such as a window or a table.

Drop-in seat
An upholstered board dropped into the frame of a chair.

Dry rot
Lumber decay, caused by damp and poor ventilation, appearing as right-angled splits with a powdery appearance.

End grain
The exposed wood fibers at the ends of cut lengths, prone to splitting and very absorbent.

Epoxy grout
A two-part, epoxide-resin-based, ceramic-tile grout, with a tough, hygienic waterproof finish, which has to be mixed on site.

Fabric grain
The lengthwise direction of the fibers of a piece of fabric, parallel with the selvages.

Face
The front surface of a wall.

Facing
A panel or strip of fabric used to back a section of the main fabric.

Feather edge
Using abrasives to sand back the rough, chipped edges of a previous finish, to provide a smooth starting surface.

Finials
Ornamental ends for curtain poles.

Flat felled seam
A strong seam that encloses the raw edges.

Flat seam
A single stitched seam, the most commonly used seam.

Floating floor
A thin layer of flooring laid on top of the existing surface, designed to "float" by the use of a cushioning sub-floor between the two.

Flogger
Specialist long-haired, wide, flat brush, used dry to drag through a finish.

Flush fit
An exact and even fit of two joining surfaces.

French seam
A seam stitched on the right side then the wrong side to enclose raw edges.

Gathering stitch
A long stitch, worked by hand or machine, and is drawn up to gather fabric.

Glazing
Fitting glass cut to size into a recess in a cupboard door, room door, or window.

Grain
Wood fibers running through timber length, indicating the direction of growth. Grain is often used as a decorative feature.

Grout
A thin, coarse mortar that is used for filling up cracks (cement grout), or can be the fine plaster used for finishing ceilings or filling between tiles.

Gusset
A strip of fabric inserted to make a three-dimensional item, such as a box cushion cover for example.

Half-wall finish
Where the lower part of a wall has a different decorative scheme from the top half.

Halving joint
A simple wood joint, made by joining two halves. It can also be where rebates meet, each one half the thickness of the timber.

Hardboard
Thin, manufactured compressed fiberboard, often used as floor covering support.

Heading tape
Curtain tape that forms the heading on a curtain.

Housewife pillowcase
A traditional pillowcase with an internal flap to hold the pillow inside.

Housing
Sometimes called a mortise, this is a rectangular piece cut out of lumber, across the grain, into which a tenon or tongue is slotted.

Insulation
The use of thermal materials to slow down or eliminate heat loss or the entry of cold air.

Interfacing

A layer of stiffening material applied to the main fabric to give it more body or to stiffen it.

Invisible pinning

Where a matchboard or similar is nailed in such a position that the subsequent board will cover up the fixing.

Jamb

The sides and top of a fixed frame, such as a door.

Joist

Heavy-duty horizontal support for floors and ceilings.

Kerf

The cutting slot made when a saw blade passes through lumber.

Kettle

Small container with handle into which small amounts of paint or varnish are decanted on site.

Key

When a smooth surface is abraded, so that the roughened face will provide a grip for a paint finish.

Knot

A circular wood defect in timber lengths where branches joined the tree.

Lambrequin

A fabric-covered valance around a window.

Laminate

In flooring this is an ultra thin layer of artificial veneer with a photographic wood effect, on a base of manufactured board. Used as a cheap "floating floor."

Laths

Thin wood strips pinned to studs (walls) or joists (ceiling) to act as plaster supports.

Laying off

Final long surface strokes through a paint layer, evening out the finish and preventing runs.

Locking rail

The centre, horizontal support ("locking") timber in a paneled door.

Making good

Restoring a surface to its previous standard of finish.

Mat

A surface finish description for dull, non-reflective paints and varnishes.

Miter

To cut wood at a 45-degree angle, so that the two equal halves form a right-angled corner.

Mitering

A neat method of turning a corner by folding under the fullness of the fabric diagonally.

Monochromatic
Designer's color scheme employing shades and tints of only one color.

Molding
Small wood strips cut to a decorative surface shape by a router bit.

Mortar
Bonding mix for brick and stone, consisting of cement, soft sand, water and any additives such as plasticizer.

Muntin
Glazing bar or divider between panes of glass in a window, or the vertical rail in the center of a paneled door.

Nail set
A nail punch is a small carpenter's tool used to sink a nail or pin head below the wood surface, prior to filling.

Nippers
Pincers with powerful cutting jaws, used to press between two surfaces to remove or sever by pinching. Nippers are often used for cutting tiles.

Noggin
Short horizontal wood piece (stud) used to reinforce upright members in a stud or partition wall.

Nominal size
The sawn size at which lumber lengths are specified, not the finished size.

Notch
A snip cut into the edges of fabric to match when stitching.

Open plan
A single large area in a property with no permanent room divisions.

Out of plumb/out of true
When something is not vertical, straight, or level.

Oxford pillowcase
A housewife pillowcase with a wide, flat border.

Painter's tape
A low-tack sticky tape for sticking items temporarily in place. It masks off small areas to allow painting.

Patchwork
A technique of joining fabric squares or shapes edge to edge.

Pier
Rectangular, vertical column of bonded brickwork, used to support a beam or structure on top.

Pile
The raised surface of a fabric such as velvet. Pile fabrics must have the patterns cut in the same direction.

Pilot hole

Small drill hole used as a guide for a larger one, or for a screw thread.

Pinking

Cutting fabric with pinking shears to prevent fraying.

Piping

A fabric-covered cord used in seams as a decorative feature.

Plinth

A rectangular wood or panel construction, acting as a base for a unit.

Plugging chisel

Special tool with a slanted leading edge, for fast waste removal when chasing along brick joints.

Plumb bob and line

A weight hung on a string so the string is kept straight and vertical.

Pointing

Decorative and weatherproofing finish for mortared brick joints.

Primary colors

For general use, the primary colors are red, yellow, and blue. Mixing these primaries in a variety of proportions creates all other colors.

Primer

The preparatory first coat of paint applied to a face, acting as a sealer.

Proud

One surface sitting raised above another.

Quilting

Two layers of fabric joined together with wadding sandwiched between them.

Rafters

Support lumber forming the roof shape, meeting at the ridge and supporting the roof covering.

Ratchet

Mechanism used in screwdrivers allowing driving movement only in one direction.

Rendering

The first application of a mix (e.g. plaster) onto a brick wall.

Rip

Using a rip saw to cut wood following the direction of the grain structure.

Roller blind

A stiffened fabric blind suspended from a roller, which is sprung to allow the roller to move up and down.

Roman blind

A fabric blind, stiffened with dowels, that folds in pleats.

RSJ (Rolled steel joist)
A heavy steel support beam set onto slate, holding up a floor or replacing a lower support wall.

Sample board
Mix of material, texture, paint, flooring, and color-finish samples together on a board to help selection of matching decorative items.

Sanding
Generic term for using abrasives on surfaces, either by hand or by a sanding machine.

Sash frame
Vertically sliding frame housed in a box and operated on runners or with cords.

Satin finish
A surface finish with a semimat sheen, offering slight luster and minimal reflection.

Satin stitch
A closely worked hand or machine stitch that has the sheen of satin fabric.

Seam line
A marked or imaginary line to be stitched along.

Screed
A mix, such as a layer of mortar that is laid down to level a floor area.

Screw eye
A metal screw that has a loop at the head end.

Seam allowance
An amount of fabric added to a measurement to allow for sewing a seam.

Seasoned wood
Cut wood that has been horizontally racked and allowed to dry naturally over a long period of time, the ultimate in dimensional stability.

Selvage
A woven, finished edge of a length of fabric.

Shakes
Splits along wood grain, caused by uneven shrinkage.

Silicon carbide
An abrasive that can be used with a lubricant (water, sugar, soap) on paint finishes, or dry on bare wood.

Skew nailing
Driving nails in at different angles, for a more secure fixing.

Soft jaw
Fiber or softwood pieces used in jaws or cramps to protect the workpiece.

Squab
A cushion, tied to the seat of a chair.

Stipple
Raising or texturing a surface finish with tiny dots, using the bristle tips of a brush.

Straight-edge
A wooden batten, steel rule, or similar, having a true edge.

Sweating
Condensation of moisture droplets on a wall surface.

Template
Accurate shape or pattern cut from card or similar thin material, used as a guide for cutting or drilling.

Tenon
Projection or tongue cut into timber, intended to slot accurately into a cut housing (mortise) or groove.

Tertiary color
A color made by mixing a secondary color with an equal amount of color next to it on the color wheel.

Thread
Continuous spiral groove cut into a screw, letting it to grab the wood or plug securely.

Tongue-and-groove
Refers to a paneling joint: a tongue on one edge of a board fits into a corresponding groove on the edge of an adjoining board.

Transom
A window directly above a door, letting light into a small room or corridor.

Two-way switching
Electrical wiring that lets artificial light be controlled from two different floor levels.

Undercoat
The middle application in a paint job. It is a mat coat covering (minor) discrepancies in the surface and providing the key for the finish.

Underlay
Hard-wearing cushioning under a floor covering, carpet, or floating floor.

Valance
A wood or stiffened fabric border that conceals the top of a curtain or blind.

Veneer
Thin sheets of decorative wood, with a support core board of blocks or sheets glued at right-angles to each other.

Visible spectrum
The colors that lie between ultraviolet and infrared in the electromagnetic spectrum. These colors make up visible light, or light we can see.

Wallboard
A thin sheet of solid plaster with paper facing both sides, or one side with a damp resistant shield.

Warp
The threads that run along the length of fabric, parallel with the selvages.

Warped timber

Lengths of wood that have been twisted out of true by uneven shrinkage, or extreme changes in temperature.

Webbing

A wide, woven braid, traditionally made from hessian, used in upholstery.

Weft

The threads that run across a length of fabric, at right angles to the selvages.

Wet rot

Decay in timber as a result of water saturation and inadequate ventilation.

Whitewash

Traditional white mat paint containing slaked lime, breathable and non-washable.

Yacht varnish

Expensive, superior quality clear varnish intended for outside use, ideal for floors.

Yarn

A spun or twisted thread.

Zigzag stitch

A machine stitch used for neatening seams or for decoration.

Zonal planning

Dividing areas up according to specific requirements.

acknowledgments

HOME DECORATING

The author would like to express his grateful thanks to the many working professionals whose advice and time has willingly been given during the preparation of these pages. Special thanks are due to Martin Gowar, whose depth of knowledge in finishing was frequently an inspiration; to Cheryl Owen, a fellow author in this series for help and advice; to Russell Sadur, Theo Dorou and Steve Tanner, whose photographic studios were virtually taken over at times during shooting; to Diana Sibil, who styled the projects; and to photographer Steve Gorton. Cheerful in all weathers, Steve's commitment to the job and unfailing logistical support made a sometimes difficult task that much easier.

The photographers would like to thank the following for the use of properties:
Oak-engineered laminate flooring on pages 168/9 supplied by **EC Forest Product** Sales Ltd. Units 5 & 6 The Woodland Centre, Whitesmiths, near Lewes, East Sussex BN8 6JB.
Moran & Co Builders. ICI Paints, Farrell & Ball, **B&Q, Wickes, Brewers & Sons Ltd, Master Tiles, Covers, Travis Perkins, Paint Magic.**

Picture credits:
Anaglypta Wallpaper: p. 18, 226L.

Crown Paints: pp. 12, 34B, 40, 43, 44TL, 60, 137, 171.

Elizabeth Whiting & Associates: pp. 24, 25, 26, 27, 31, 33R, 36, 37B, 44B, 45, 46, 47, 58, 64, 66, 67, 69, 70, 71, 73, 74, 77, 78R, 99, 101, 103, 104, 105, 106L, 107TL & BR, 125, 126, 130T, 140, 141L, 144, 147, 154, 156R, 157, 158, 161, 165, 166, 167, 170, 174, 183, 184, 185, 188, 189, 193, 195, 196, 197, 103, 105, 109, 210, 211, 223, 224R, 226R, 227, 228L, 229R, 247, 252, 253T.

Houses & Interiors: pp. 23, 32BR, 37T, 41, 68, 72, 106R, 107TR, 156L, 199.

Image Bank: p.21.

Jaafar Designs/Florida squares & spirals: p. 141BC.

Laura Ashley: pp. 48T, 49B, 201, 229L, 233TL.

Morris & Co.Collection: pp. 78L, 80L, 178.

Next Directory: pp. 32L, 123B, 151R, 162, 172/3, 207B, 224L, 225, 228R, 230, 231, 232, 233TR & B, 253B.

Osborne & Little/V&A The Historic Collection: p.79T.

Painted Tile Company/Wellington Tile Co/Crazy Chicken & Tulips: p.141B.

Sanderson: p.33T.

Stock Market: p.12.

COLOUR IN YOUR HOME

Special thanks go to Nicola Liddiard for design, Alistair Hughes for photography, Lynda Marshall for picture research and Stewart Walton for styling and illustrations.

The publishers would like to thank the following for help with properties:
For Mediterranean and Chalk Collection paints (used in New Natural Room and Neutrals):

Zest Essentials, 281 King's Road, London SW3 5EW. www.zestessentials.com

For specialist paints (used in African, Moorish, Tuscan and Provençal projects):

Casa Paint Co. Ltd, 9 Bicester Road, Aylesbury, Bucks HP19 9AG.

For emulsion paints (used in English Country, Modern Country, Indian, Miami, Romany and Scandinavian projects):

Dulux Paints (all major DIY stores).

For the loan of styling properties:
Interior Illusions, 46 High Street, Old Town, Hastings, East Sussex TN34 3EN.

For the shelf used in the Urban Minimalist project:
Spur Shelving (branches of Homebase)

Picture credits:
Crown Paints: pp. 278, 297B, 309T, 332, 339B.

Elizabeth Whiting Associates: pp. 13, 260, 269, 270, 271T, 272, 275, 279B, 280, 281T, 282, 283, 284, 287, 290, 295T, 296, 297T, 298, 303T, 305, 306, 314T, 315T, 321, 326, 327, 333B, 335, 337T, 338B, 339T, 344, 345, 349T, 350, 351, 353, 355B, 357T, 363, 398, 402, 403L, 405R, 412, 413.

GettyOneStone: pp. 266, 267TL, 293, 294, 323, 324, 325T, 336, 343T, 347, 348, 349B.

Image Bank: pp. 261, 271L, 273, 295B, 311, 312, 313, 317, 318, 319, 325B, 329, 331, 343B.

Laura Ashley Ltd 2001: pp. 265, 279T, 303B, 307T, 308, 309B, 315B, 333T, 362, 403R, 404, 405B, 406, 407B.
Next: pp. 265, 307B, 399, 407CR.

Telegraph Colour Library: pp. 267TR, 337B, 341, 342, 355T.

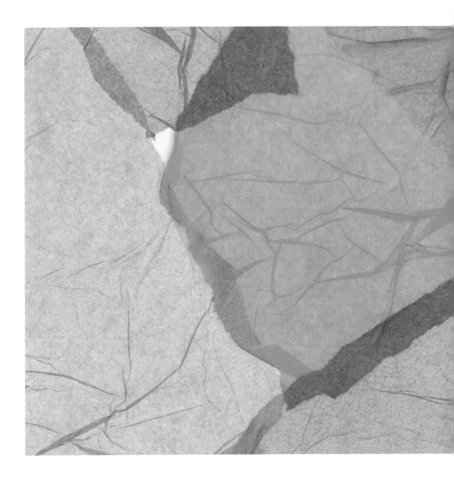

DESIGNING NEW ROOMS

The authors would like to thank Clare Shanahan, for her irrepressible good humor, patience, and expert styling of the photographs, which are by Alistair Hughes. They would also like to thank Alistair's mum Doris for her patience during the photoshoot.

The publishers would like to thank the following for loan of props:
Embrotrap (Oriental) Market, 10 Church Road, Hove, East Sussex.

Evolution: 42 Bond Street, Brighton, East Sussex.

Interior Illusions: 46 High Street, Old Town, Hastings.

Middle Farm: Firle, East Sussex.

Saffron: 21 Bond Street, Brighton, East Sussex.

The Ship Wreck Centre: Rock-an-ore, Hastings, East Sussex.

Stewart Gallery: 48 Devonshire Road, Bexhill, East Sussex.

Sussex Marble: 16 Wainwright Close, St. Leonards on Sea, East Sussex.

T.C. Carpets and Beds: Earl Street, Hastings, East Sussex.

W.H.Clarke Scaffolding: Hackney Road, London.

Wood Bros: 66 George Street, Brighton, East Sussex.

Picture credits:
Elizabeth Whiting & Associates: pp. 514, 515, 522, 523, 530, 531, 538, 539, 548, 549, 550, 558, 559, 560, 561, 563, 567, 575, 582, 583, 590, 591, 596, 597, 604, 605, 612, 613, 614, 615, 620, 621, 626, 627, 636, 637, 644, 645, 650, 651, 660, 661, 662, 663, 672, 673, 680, 681, 690, 691, 696, 697, 698, 699, 706, 707, 716, 717, 718, 730, 731, 732, 733, 734, 735, 736, 737, 738, 739, 742, 243, 746.

MAKING SOFT FURNISHINGS

The author would like to give special thanks to Steve Tanner for his superb photographs and attention to detail, Jack Britton for her beautiful styling, Karl Adamson for his excellent additional photography, and Jan Eaton, Gwen Diamond and Carol Hart for their practical advice and for making up many of the projects.

The author and publisher would also like to thank those who supplied materials and props:
The Dormy House: for blank furniture e.g. screens, dressing tables, headboards and footstools. Available by mail order.

Scumble Goosie: for blank furniture e.g. screens. Available by mail order.

3M: for spray adhesive, available at good art and craft shops.

Offray: for ribbons, available at good haberdashery shops and sewing departments.

Gütermann: for threads, beads and sequins, available at good stores and sewing departments.

DMC: for embroidery threads, available at good stores and sewing departments or by mail order.

Academy Costume Hire: for antique shoes.

Bunny London: Unit 1, 22 South Side, Oxo Tower, London SE1 UK for children's clothes.

Crystal Franken, John Harmer, Robert and Georgina McPherson for lighting and flowers.

Picture credits:
Elizabeth Whiting & Associates: pp. 754, 755, 756, 767, 276, 808, 818, 850, 870, 871, 878, 880, 928, 966, 980.

GettyOneStone: p. 834.

Laura Ashley: pp. 814, 852L, 946, 950.

Next Directory: pp. 771T, 806, 902, 929, 932, 938, 944, 967, 976, 982.

The Holding Company: p. 910.

index